# ARCHITECT OF GLOBAL JIHAD

*To my friends and colleagues at FFI's*
*Terrorism Research Group*

BRYNJAR LIA

# Architect
# *of* Global Jihad

*The Life of al-Qaida Strategist
Abu Mus'ab al-Suri*

Columbia University Press
New York

Columbia University Press
*Publishers Since 1893*
New York, Chichester, West Sussex

Library of Congress Cataloging-in-Publication Data

Lia, Brynjar.
  Architect of global jihad : the life of al-Qaida strategist Abu Mus'ab al-Suri / Brynjar
Lia.
    p. cm.
  Includes bibliographical references and index.
  ISBN 978-0-231-70030-6 (hardback : alk. paper)
  1. 'Abd al-Hakim, 'Umar. 2. Terrorists—Syria—Biography. 3. Terrorism—Religious
aspects—Islam. 4. Qaida (Organization) I. Title.

  HV6430.A23L53 2007
  363.325092—dc22
  [B]

                        2007020783

∞
Columbia University Press books are printed on permanent and durable acid-free paper.
This book is printed on paper with recycled content.
Printed in India

c 10 9 8 7 6 5 4 3 2 1

# CONTENTS

# CONTENTS

CONTENTS

# ACKNOWLEDGEMENTS

I wish to thank Abdel Bari Atwan, Mark Huband, Peter Bergen, Camille Tawil, Noman Benotman, Saad al-Faqih and Abdallah Anas for sharing with me insights and impressions from their encounters with Abu Mus'ab al-Suri. I am indebted to Andrew Higgins and Alan Cullison who shared with me the full text of al-Suri's letter to Osama bin Laden from July 1998, recovered from the famous Kabul computer. I wish to thank Camille Tawil for providing me with copies of the *Al-Ansar* magazine where al-Suri was a contributor. I have benefited from valuable comments and constructive criticism from Javiér Jordán and Jeffrey Cozzens, and am grateful to René Pita for sending me Spanish-language sources and press articles on al-Suri.

I am indebted to my research assistants Anne Stenersen and Tine Gade at FFI for collecting and translating some of the source materials used for this book. Anne has also translated the lion's share of excerpts from al-Suri's *Global Islamic Resistance Call* reprinted at the end of this volume. I would also like to thank Iman Lofti for her tireless efforts at transcribing many of al-Suri's almost inaudible audiotapes and Jane Margaret Chanaa for her very helpful copy-editing.

My colleagues and friends at FFI, Petter Nesser, Thomas Hegghammer, Laila Bokhari and Truls H. Tønnessen deserve mention for their critical feedback and friendly advice. Thomas's comments have been particularly useful and I am greatly indebted to him for sharing with me his valuable sources on the Afghan-Arabs. Finally, my boss Jan Erik Torp has greatly contributed to this book by providing me with the right mixture of encouragement, guidance, and not least, the necessary resources.

All errors and faults are of course my responsibility alone.

*Oslo, May 2007*                                                                 B. L.

# ABBREVIATIONS

EIJ     Egyptian Islamic Jihad, *jama'at al-jihad bi-misr*

FBIS    Foreign Broadcast Information Service

GIA     Groupe Islamique Armé, Armed Islamic Group, *al-jama'ah al-islamiyyah al-musallahah* (Algeria)

GICM    Groupe Islamique Combattant Marocain, Moroccan Islamic Fighting Group, *al-jama'ah al-islamiyyah al-mujahidah bi'l-maghrib*

GSPC    Groupe Salafiste pour la Prédication et le Combat, The Salafist Group for Preaching and Combat, *al-jama'ah al-salafiyyah li al-da'wah wa'l-qital* (Algeria)

JI      The Islamic Group, *al-jama'ah al-islamiyyah* (Egypt)

LIFG    Libyan Islamic Fighting Group, *al-jama'ah al-islamiyyah al-muqatila bi'libiya*

xi

# NOTE

The transcription of Arabic names and terms has been simplified by making no distinction between emphatic and non-emphatic consonants, and by only using ' and ' to indicate 'ayn and alif when these consonants occur inside a word. Since Arabic does not distinguish between small and capital letters, I have chosen to use only small letters in the transliterations. For the most part, I have translated titles of Arabic-language books, articles and website articles into English. With regards to the names of well-known jihadi websites, they have been rendered mostly in transliteration. As I refer to many names that have no agreed English transcription, I have in general transcribed names according to how they are spelt in Arabic. This being said, I have made a few exceptions with regards to names that have a relatively established spelling in the English-language media and research literature, such as Noman Benotman, Saad al-Faqih, and Abdel Bari Atwan, three of the interviewees for this book.

# 1
# INTRODUCTION

On 31 October 2005, several bearded men entered the al-Madina Utilities Store in the Goualmandi district in Quetta, Pakistan. It was seven o'clock in the evening, the sun had set and it was time for *iftar*, the evening meal taken when breaking the daily fast during Ramadan. The men felt safe here but were watchful. They kept their handguns at the ready, hidden in their baggy clothes. Unknown to them, Pakistani intelligence agents had been tailing the group for quite some time, looking for a suitable place to capture them. One of them had to be taken alive. There were many wanted men in Quetta, but only this individual had a $5 million reward from the US government offered for his capture. The police raid began. In seconds, the buzzing street life of Quetta was cut short by volleys of gunfire, the screams of wounded men and bystanders running for their lives. As the smoke drifted away, a crowd gathered. One of the men sharing the *iftar* meal was dead, the others arrested, among them a short, red-bearded man. His name was said to be Mustafa bin Abd al-Qadir Setmariam Nasar.

Nasar, better known by his *noms de plume* Abu Mus'ab al-Suri and Umar Abd al-Hakim, has been a prominent figure in radical Islamist circles since the early 1990s. Little has been written about him by Western scholars, and till recently he rarely featured in the media. Nasar first came to prominence in the West in late 2004 when Spanish investigators referred to him as a possible mastermind of the Madrid train bombings.[1] A Syrian militant with Spanish citizenship,

---

1    Ahmad Rafat, 'Al-Qa'idah chief in Europe is Spanish' (in Spanish), *El Tiempo de Hoy*, 24 Aug. 2004, via FBIS.

1

al-Suri had served as a military instructor and lecturer in the Arab-Afghan training camps from 1987-92. In the mid-1990s, he spent several years in Spain and the United Kingdom before returning to Afghanistan in 1998 where he ran a terrorist training camp and a media center. Al-Suri has been sought by the Spanish authorities since November 2001.[2] In November 2004, the US State Department announced that it was offering a $5 million reward to anyone who provided information leading to his arrest, highlighting his centrality in global terrorism, even though he was mostly known as a 'pen jihadist'.[3]

Abu Mus'ab al-Suri defies easy characterization and fits poorly with prevailing stereotypes and images of al-Qaida terrorists. Many people who met him recalled his appearance. In the overwhelmingly Arab al-Qaida, al-Suri stood out with his fair skin, ginger hair and a look such that he would easily pass for 'an Irish pub patron'.[4] Those who knew him well remember al-Suri as bookish. An avid reader, with an encyclopaedic memory, he impressed acquaintances with his knowledge of literature, classical music, history, politics and the sciences, far beyond the standard curriculum of an average jihadi. Unlike many other militants, he drew freely upon Western sources in his writings: the most important source he used when lecturing at the Afghan training camps was - after the *Holy Quran* - an Ameri-

---

2   Ministracion de Justicia, 'Juzgado Central de Instruccion no.005, Madrid, Sumario (Proc. Ordinario) 0000035 /2001 E', dated 17 Sept. 2003, [indictment against the Abu Dahdah network], available at www.FindLaw. com, accessed Feb. 2004, hereafter referred to as 'Juzgado Central de Instruccion no.005, Madrid, Sumario', 17 Sept. 2003; and Audiencia Nacional, Sala de lo Penal, Sección Tercera, 'Sentencia Núm. 36/2005', Madrid, 26 Sept. 2005, [verdict against the Abu Dahdah network], available at http://estaticos.elmundo.es/documentos/2005/09/26/sentencia. pdf, accessed July 2006, hereafter referred to as 'Sentencia Núm. 36/2005', Madrid, 26 Sept. 2005.

3   'FBI finds link between Sept 11, Madrid bombs-paper', *Reuters*, 28 Nov. 2004.

4   Katherine Shrader, 'Wanted Muslim extremist hopscotches the globe connecting terrorists', *Associated Press*, 3 Aug. 2005.

can book on guerrilla warfare. This frequent citation of non-Islamic sources earned him criticism from others within the global jihadi movement.

Abu Mus'ab al-Suri is the antithesis of the fanatical, pre-programmed suicide terrorist stereotype. He has been described as a 'born-critic'[5] and had a penchant for satire and ridicule with which he entertained his readers. A hot-tempered and fiercely independent figure, he never shied from criticizing jihadi leaders whose policies he felt were erroneous. al-Suri rebuked bin Laden's appetite for international media attention and denounced Abu Qutadah al-Filastini, the foremost jihadi cleric in London, for justifying internecine violence in Algeria and for his doctrinaire understanding of Islam. It would be a mistake, however, to think that al-Suri represents a softer, more human face of al-Qaida terrorism. On the contrary, his mercilessness towards 'the enemies of Islam' knew no limits: he explicitly advocated mass casualty terrorism in the West, including the use of weapons of mass destruction. Yet he differed from other jihadi ideologues by always insisting that the use of violence should be based on a thorough, rational long-term strategy. For him, this was the only way through which the ultimate goals of the jihadi movement could be achieved. He defined this goal as liberating the Islamic world from direct and indirect occupation, and overturning non-Islamic governments. More than any other figure in al-Qaida, Abu Mus'ab al-Suri produced withering critiques of the jihadi movement. His *modus operandi* was to reassess earlier terrorist campaigns and insurgencies in order to learn from the movement's mistakes. Sharply analytical and rational in his approach, he has written numerous pseudo-academic studies in which he castigates the jihadi movement for living in the past and misjudging the challenges of the post-Cold War and post-9/11 eras.

In short, Abu Mus'ab al-Suri was a dissident, a critic, and an intellectual in an ideological current in which one would expect to find obedience rather than dissent, conformity rather than self-criticism,

---

5 Author's interview with Noman Benotman, London, 15 Sept. 2006.

doctrinaire ideologues rather than introspective individuals. During his twenty-five year career as a global jihadi militant, al-Suri has used his training as an historian to collect, record, summarize and analyze his jihadi experiences. In doing so, he discarded traditional jihadi rhetoric about God's promised victory in favor of brutal honesty, putting hard-nosed realism before religious wish-fulfillment and pragmatic long-term strategies before utopianism. By subjecting the objects of his study to secular academic scrutiny and by integrating Western literature on guerrilla warfare, international security and power politics, al-Suri evolved fascinating doctrines about decentralized jihadi warfare in the post-9/11 security environment. He has also provided a strategic rationale for the use of weapons of mass destruction by al-Qaida against the West.

In the aftermath of 9/11, it was commonplace to assert that al-Qaida pursued no underlying strategic plan. The accepted argument was that the obsessive fanaticism of jihadi terrorists, their religious dogmas, their pursuit of martyrdom, and visceral hatred for the West made them blind, and their behaviour was not rooted in any kind of rational strategy. While this school of thought still has numerous protagonists, a growing number of studies have already begun to debunk the myth of a non-existent al-Qaida strategy.[6] As a biography of one of the foremost jihadi strategists of our time, it is hoped that *Architect of Global Jihad* will be regarded as belonging to the latter category.

The present volume is partly a contribution to the study of jihadi strategic thought. It discusses and cites at length many of al-Suri's

---

6   See, for example, Robert Pape, *Dying to Win: The Strategic Logic of Suicide Terrorism* (New York: Random House, 2005); Brynjar Lia and Thomas Hegghammer, 'Jihadi Strategic Studies: The Alleged Al Qaida Policy Study Preceding the Madrid Bombings', *Studies in Conflict and Terrorism*, 27, 5 (Sept./Oct. 2004), pp.355-75; Jarret M. Brachman and William F. McCants, 'Stealing Al-Qa'ida's Playbook', *CTC Report* , Feb. 2006, p.15, www.ctc.usma.edu/Stealing%20Al-Qai%27da%27s%20Playbook%20--%20CTC.pdf, accessed Oct. 2006; Robert Pape, 'Al Qaeda's strategy', *The New York Times*, 12 July 2005; Stephen Ulph, 'Al-Qaeda's Strategy Until 2020', *Terrorism Focus*, 2 (6) (17 March 2005), www.jamestown.org/images/pdf/tf_002_006.pdf, accessed Oct. 2006.

works, explores the various ideological debates in which he participated, and traces the development of his strategic thinking. It also
contains, as an appendix, a translation of his most important work on
jihadi strategy and training. However, the main objective behind this
book is to discover the man behind the writings and ideas for which
he is now renowned. In recent years, especially, al-Suri's output has
become a key item on the jihadi curriculum. More and more of his
early works and lectures are now being republished on the Internet
by his followers (see below). In order to contextualize and understand this body of writing, we need to explore his biography: who
is Abu Mus'ab al-Suri, what is his background, how did he become
involved in al-Qaida, what role has he played in the jihadi movement over the past decades, and how should we interpret his new
doctrine of jihadi warfare? Another important reason for researching
al-Suri's biography is that his personal trajectory sheds new light on
al-Qaida's history. Most of the literature on the Arab-Afghans and
al-Qaida today revolves around Abdallah Azzam, Osama bin Laden,
and Ayman al-Zawahiri, and examines the jihadi current from their
perspectives. By tracing al-Suri's life from his birthplace in Aleppo
in Syria, via his exile in Europe, the period in Peshawar, then back to
Madrid and London, his return to Afghanistan under the Taleban,
and the time spent in hiding in Pakistan, it allows us to read the history of the Arab-Afghans, of al-Qaida and of the jihadi movement
through new lenses.

## HOW IMPORTANT IS ABU MUS'AB AL-SURI TODAY?

al-Suri has left behind a large body of biographical material that allows us to follow the evolution of a senior jihadi, one who at an early
stage established himself as an independent intellectual. Through his
numerous books, articles and audiotaped lectures, his large global
network of contacts, his publicity efforts on behalf of the jihadi current, and his teaching at the training camps in Afghanistan, al-Suri
influenced a whole generation of jihadis in a way that has thus far

gone largely unnoticed. His life story helps us understand not only al-Suri's role, but also the fascinating complexity of the jihadi current and the role of dissidents and critics like al-Suri within it.

One of the most interesting facets of Abu Mus'ab al-Suri is that from early on he introduced concepts and ideas that were later espoused by al-Qaida's leadership. In spring 1991, al-Suri wrote his first contribution on the necessity of 'a Global Islamic Resistance', advocating a global terrorist campaign against the West that would rely on diffuse, decentralized and non-hierarchical networks. In doing so, he departed from the traditional jihadi focus on 'the near enemy', i.e. Arab regimes. This was seven years before bin Laden signed his global declaration of war.[7] In 1991, al-Suri also advocated a restructuring of jihadi groups, which till then had relied almost exclusively on secret hierarchical regional organizations, usually termed *tanzimat*. He believed that such units had proved to be largely ineffective and instead he suggested the creation of 'phantom organizations', consisting of self-sufficient cells acting independently of any central command.[8]

Al-Suri's recommendations failed to find a responsive audience at the time, so he continued reformulating and adjusting his warfighting doctrine throughout the late 1990s. He witnessed America's precision cruise missile strikes against al-Qaida's Afghan training camps in 1998, and, deeply impressed by the US's technological superiority, he again questioned al-Qaida's reliance on fixed training camps in an era of US hegemony and total air dominance. Al-Suri's response to what he termed bin Laden's 'Tora Bora mentality' was to develop theories for a decentralized jihadi struggle by autonomous

---

7   See 'The Text of the Communique by The World Islamic Front for Jihad against Jews and Crusaders', (in Arabic) *al-Quds al-Arabi*, 23 Feb. 1998, p.3.

8   For more on this, see chapter 8. His ideas at the time may be interpreted as a jihadi equivalent to the 'leaderless resistance' concept, usually attributed to an essay by Louis Beam, an American anti-government activist from 1983. See Louis Beam, 'Leaderless Resistance', *The Seditionist* (issue 12, Feb. 1992: final edn), www.louisbeam.com/leaderless.htm, accessed Nov. 2006.

cells without any fixed bases or traceable organizational ties. His new warfighting doctrine was encapsulated in the slogan *nizam la tanzim*, 'system, not organization', and was presented in a series of videotaped lectures in Afghanistan in August 2000.[9] His vision for al-Qaida was clearly broader than that of bin Laden's. As Lawrence Wright has correctly noted, al-Suri viewed al-Qaida's preeminence only as 'a stage in the development of the worldwide Islamist uprising. "Al Qaeda is not an organization, it is not a group, nor do we want it to be," he wrote. "It is a call, a reference, a methodology." Eventually, its leadership would be eliminated, he said.'[10]

Four and a half years later, in January 2005, his *magnum opus*, *The Global Islamic Resistance Call* (da'wat al-muqawamah al-islami-yyah al-alamiyyah), was published online.[11] This 1,600pp. volume is not only a formidable historical account of jihadi movements but it has also become the most significant written source in the strategic studies literature on al-Qaida. More than any other of his works, *The Global Islamic Resistance Call* has attracted widespread attention, from among jihadis themselves as well as the academic and intelligence communities. It has become a standard work to cite and to refer to in new studies on al-Qaida. This is partly explained by the fact that al-Qaida appears to have moved towards the organizational model that al-Suri prescribed, with decentralized cells linked pri-

---

9   For more on this concept, see Brynjar Lia, 'Abu Mus'ab al-Suri: Profile of a Jihadi Leader', paper presented at 'The Changing Faces of Jihadism: Profiles, Biographies, Motivations', Joint FFI/King's College Conference, London, 27-28 April 2006, see www.mil.no/multimedia/archive/00080/Abu_Musab_al-Suri-80483a.pdf, accessed Oct. 2006.

10  Cited in Lawrence Wright, 'The Master Plan: For the New Theorists of Jihad, Al Qaeda is Just the Beginning', *The New Yorker*, 11 Sept. 2006, p.50.

11  The full title of the book is Umar Abd al-Hakim (Abu Mus'ab al-Suri), *The Global Islamic Resistance Call. Part I: The Roots, History, and Experiences* (in Arabic) (Place and publisher unknown, Dec. 2004); and Umar Abd al-Hakim (Abu Mus'ab al-Suri), *The Global Islamic Resistance Call. Part II: The Call, Program and Method* (in Arabic) (Place and publisher unknown, Dec. 2004). Hereafter cited as *The Global Islamic Resistance Call*.

marily by ideology and solidarity. Reports of al-Suri's alleged role in the Madrid bombings and the US reward for his capture put him in the media spotlight and raised his profile. But most important was the launching of his own website, in January 2005, through which his many books, articles and audio- and videotaped lectures for the first time became widely available.

As of early 2007, Abu Mus'ab al-Suri is probably the world's foremost 'jihadi theoretician', a description bestowed on him, among others, by numerous participants in jihadi webforums[12] who frequently cite and refer to his works. Their evaluation should not be overlooked, however, as the Internet is the key arena for propagating the message of al-Qaida. In order to appreciate al-Suri's importance, one needs to situate him in the broader landscape of actors in violent Islamism. There are many potential roles to play in the global jihadi movement, but al-Suri has first and foremost earned great respect as a strategic thinker.

The term 'architect' is an appropriate one for al-Suri. Through his writings he has designed a comprehensive framework for future jihad. He has brilliant ideas, but his job is done when the designs, sketches and maps have been handed over. For despite his extensive field experience from Syria and Afghanistan, al-Suri has not become a cherished icon such as Emir Khattab, the leader of the Arab mujahidin in Chechnya till his death in 2002 or Abu Mus'ab al-Zarqawi, the notorious head of al-Qaida in Iraq till his death in an American missile strike in June 2006. That said, for some webforum partici-

---

12 See, for example, 'What you don't know about Abu Mus'ab al-Suri's book' (in Arabic), *muntada al-ansar al-islami*, 25 Aug. 2005, www.ansary.info/forums/showthread.php?t=1877&page=1&pp=10, accessed Aug. 2005; 'Make this a permanent link: A collection of all jihadi movies from all fronts. God is great!' (in Arabic), *muntadayat al-nusra*, 11 Feb. 2006, http://www.alnusra.net/vb/showthread.php?t=157&highlight=%C3%C8%E6+%E3%D5%DA%C8+%C7%E1%D3%E6%D1%ED, accessed Feb. 2006; and 'Al-Qaida's most important publications by al-Qaida's most brilliant theoretician' (in Arabic), *muntadayat risalat al-ummah*, 16 Jan. 2006, www.al-ommh.net/vb/showthread.php?t=2324&highlight=%E3%D5%DA%C8+%C7%E1%D3%E6%D1%ED, accessed Feb. 2007.

pants al-Suri has iconic status and in their postings they sometimes include his name alongside those of al-Qaida's top leaders.[13]

Unlike many other well-known jihadi figures, al-Suri never surrounded himself with a large crowd of followers, neither in London, nor in Afghanistan after 1998. His style was not that of a firebrand preacher like Abu Hamzah al-Masri or Omar Bakri Muhammad in London. In fact, he detested their vulgar rhetoric and abhorred their lack of operational security. Furthermore, even though al-Suri was a good classroom teacher, he did not reach out to his listeners emotionally—his speeches were almost exclusively lectures. Nor did he instigate the crowd to join the struggle or inspire them to self-sacrifice and martyrdom. Al-Suri was an intellectual, not a preacher. He applied logical reasoning, historical analysis and secular knowledge.

Al-Suri was in many ways a military man whose main preoccupation was guerrilla warfare. He lacked the aura of a religious scholar and did not aspire to be one. Despite his encyclopaedic memory and wealth of knowledge, he was never very comfortable with the finer points of religious exegesis. He had broad familiarity with Islamic law and jurisprudence but nothing more. Al-Suri was well aware of this and never tried to pose as a cleric or a scholar, preferring instead to call himself a writer. Besides, he despised the salafis for their inflexible dogmatism and narrow-mindedness. Hence, in the theological-ideological jihadi literature, he would never have the same standing as contemporary salafi-jihadi clerics such as Abu Muhammad al-Maqdisi in Jordan, Abu Qutadah al-Filastini in London, or Hamid bin Abdallah al-Ali in Kuwait. However it would be a mistake to assume that his influence is minimal; even if al-Suri has little renown in terms of offering legal Islamic justifications for terrorism, his importance in terms of providing strategic and operative frameworks for future jihadi warfare is unprecedented.

---

13 For example 'May God protect our Shaykh Abu Abdallah, Shaykh Ayman, Shaykh Abu Mus'ab al-Suri and the Emir of the Slaughters who has raised the banner of jihad in Mesopotamia, Abu Mus'ab al-Zarqawi'. Cited from a posting by 'al-Hamam' (in Arabic) on *muntada minbar suriya al-islamiyyah*, 27 Oct. 2005, www.islam-syria.com/vb/, accessed Nov. 2005.

Perhaps only a small segment of the jihadi community would have paid attention to theoreticians like al-Suri, had his popularity not been boosted by the international media attention surrounding him from late 2004 onwards. The fact that the US authorities pledged such a huge reward for his capture, even though they regarded him primarily as a 'pen jihadist',[14] did not go unnoticed. A participant at the leading jihadi webforum *al-Ansar* noted in mid-2005 that 'Abu Mus'ab al-Suri is now considered the most dangerous individual in al-Qaida to the West because he is truly a theoretician for al-Qaida'.[15] Furthermore, the Western media interest in al-Suri's alleged involvement in al-Qaida's weapons of mass destruction efforts also boosted his status, judging by postings on jihadi websites.[16]

Due to such publicity, al-Suri's writings, especially his *The Global Islamic Resistance Call*, are being discovered by a growing number of online jihadi sympathisers. The enthusiasm that his writings have aroused among some of their number is striking: 'This is among the best jihadi books. It is comprehensive, varied, and contains many ideas and information. It is in short "Your Guide to Jihad".'[17] In August 2005 another *al-Ansar* participant contributed a long posting about al-Suri's book with the following introduction:

My brothers, I have spent nearly a week reading this book ... this book is not like any other book. It explains to you, *in practical terms*, how you with

---

14  See Robert Windrem, 'U.S. hunts for "pen jihadist",' *MSNBC News*, 9 Dec. 2004, www.msnbc.msn.com/id/6685673/, accessed July 2005.

15  Cited in posting by 'salah22' in 'What you don't know about Abu Mus'ab al-Suri's book' (in Arabic), *muntada al-ansar al-islami*, 25 Aug. 2005, www.ansary.info/forums/showthread.php?t=1877&page=1&pp=10, accessed Aug. 2005.

16  See, for example, 'What you don't know about Abu Mus'ab al-Suri's book' (in Arabic), postings by 'al-batarah' (in Arabic), and 'nasir al-mujahidin' (in Arabic), *muntada al-ansar al-islami*, 25 Aug. 2005, www.ansary.info/forums/showthread.php?t=1877&page=2&pp=10, accessed Aug. 2005.

17  'The most dangerous book to the Crusaders ... new links' (in Arabic), *shabakat muhajirun al-islamiyyah*, 14 Sept. 2005, www.mohajroon.com/vb, accessed Feb. 2006.

your capabilities can become a mujahid in your own country. Nobody has any longer any excuse [not to fight].[18]

Al-Suri's ability to present operational doctrines is appreciated, as are his writings about 'individual terrorism' by loners or self-sustained independent cells.[19] His popularity also stems from the fact that many see him as a non-conventional writer whose perspectives represent a fresh approach to jihadi warfare. He is also considered a farsighted strategist whose works have anticipated future developments. Says a jihadi website contributor, who authored a study on the 9/11 attacks:

> This great terrific carnage [i.e. the September 11th events], showed that the words Abu Mus'ab al-Suri Umar Abd al-Hakim wrote years ago have come true, as if he had seen these events when he wrote his words. The clairvoyance of this extraordinary man is the clairvoyance of a true mujahid with deep perspicacity.[20]

Al-Suri has become a famous figure in online jihadism, even though his popularity is far less than that of Abu Mus'ab al-Zarqawi, Ayman al-Zawahiri, and Osama bin Laden. All of the key webforums, which have been aptly dubbed 'the town square of online jihadism',[21] have posted links to websites where his works can be ac-

---

18 'What you don't know about Abu Mus'ab al-Suri's book' (in Arabic), *muntada al-ansar al-islami* 25 Aug. 2005, www.ansary.info/forums/showthread.php?t=1877&page=1&pp=10, accessed Aug. 2005.

19 See, for example, 'How to become a [jihadi] squad on your own', *shabakat ana muslim*, 9 April 2006, www.muslm.net/vb/showthread.php?t=157322&highlight=%C3%C8%E6+%E3%D5%DA%C8+%C7%E1%D3%E6%D1%ED, accessed May 2006.

20 Cited in '96 Benefits to Islam from the Blessed Manhattan Raid Events (first published by the al-Ansar Forum)' (in Arabic), *muntadayat risalat al-ummah*, 21 Oct. 2005, www.al-ommh.net/vb/showthread.php?t=265&page=2&highlight=%E3%D5%DA%C8+%C7%E1%D3%E6%D1%EC, accessed Feb. 2007. Also republished in *muntadayat al-firdaws al-jihadiyyah*, Feb. 2007, www.alfirdaws.org/vb/showthread.php?t=26403&highlight=%E3%D5%DA%C8+%C7%E1%D3%E6%D1%ED, accessed Feb. 2007.

21 An expression borrowed from my colleague Thomas Hegghammer, cited in Frank Gardner, 'The growth of "online Jihadism"', *BBC News*, 25 Oct. 2006,

cessed. Most forums have postings where al-Suri's works are cited or referred to in one way or another, and his biography has been widely distributed. Participants at these webforums have repeatedly requested the posting of new links for downloading his works, especially *The Global Islamic Resistance Call.*[22] In some instances, they have also discussed the formation of reading groups to help one another understand and appreciate the book.[23] As early as March 2005, two months after its online posting, *The Call* was apparently so well-known that webforum participants talked about it as 'the book that needs no introduction'.[24]

Key jihadi media outlets have also advertised and disseminated al-Suri's works and lectures, sometimes converting them into sleeker and more accessible formats, for which there is obviously a certain demand. For example the compiler of a directory of jihadi websites inserted a comment over the entry for al-Suri's website stating that: 'some of the brothers have been asking for Abu Mus'ab al-Suri's works and publication'.[25] Al-Suri's websites and links for downloading his works

---

http://news.bbc.co.uk/2/hi/uk_news/6086042.stm, accessed Feb. 2007.

22  See, for example, 'God will help his servant, as long as his servant helps his brother' (in Arabic), *muntadayat al-firdaws al-jihadiyyah*, Jan. 2007, www.alfirdaws.org/vb/showthread.php?t=24712&highlight=%E3%D5%DA%C8+%C7%E1%D3%E6%D1%ED, accessed Feb. 2007; and 'Request: the book "Global Islamic Resistance" by Shaykh Abu Mus'ab al-Suri' (in Arabic), *shabakat al-ikhlas al-islamiyyah*, 14 Feb. 2007, www.alekhlaas.net/forum/showthread.php?t=46502&highlight=%E3%D5%DA%C8+%C7%E1%D3%E6%D1%ED, accessed Feb. 2007.

23  See, for example, 'My brothers, who would like to read with me the book "The Global Islamic Resistance Call",' (in Arabic), *muntadayat al-firdaws al-jihadiyyah*, 20 May 2005, www.alfirdaws.org/forums/showthread.php?t=2154&highlight=%C3%C8%E6+%E3%D5%DA%C8+%C7%E1%D3%E6%D1%ED, accessed Feb. 2006.

24  See 'Hurry up in distributing and uploading ... the films and audio-recordings from Abu Mus'ab al-Suri's library' (in Arabic), *muntadayat al-firdaws al-jihadiyyah*, 25 March 2005, www.alfirdaws.org/forums, accessed Feb. 2006.

25  'The largest collection of jihadi films and hymns', (in Arabic), *muntadayat al-firdaws al-jihadiyyah*, Jan. 2007, www.alfirdaws.org/vb/showthread.php?t=24794&highlight=%E3%D5%DA%C8+%C7%E1%D3%E6%D1%ED, accessed Feb. 2007.

have figured on many jihadi directories as well as in lists of recommended literature for jihadis.[26] Another sign of a growing interest in al-Suri is the fact that his lesser known works, including articles in his obscure jihadi journal that only appeared in two issues in Kabul in 2000-1, have been advertised and circulated on jihadi websites.[27] Furthermore, scanned pdf-files of his earliest works written in the late 1980s have also been made available online, in addition to his more recent works.[28]

The interest in al-Suri seemed to peak in late 2005, following the news of his alleged capture in Pakistan, after which *The Global Islamic Resistance Call* was heavily promoted by several of the top ten jihadi webforums. For example, by mid November 2005 the password-protected *al-Hisbah* webforum had already more than thirty postings dealing with al-Suri and his works.[29] The *al-Ikhlas* ran a very popular permanent posting about the book with the telling title: 'O Ye Blessed Jihadi Cells! Here You Have the Great Fundamental Encyclopaedia! Go Ahead and Use It!'. The posting had more than 5,800 visitors and

26  See, for example, a list posted on *muntadayat risalat al-ummah*, 29 Jan. 2007, www.al-ommh.net/vb/showthread.php?t=12375&highlight=%E3%D5%D A%C8+%C7%E1%D3%E6%D1%EC, accessed Feb. 2007.

27  See, for example, 'Download now! The Victorious in Righteousness Journal by Shaykh Abu Mus'ab al-Suri – May God release him from prison' (in Arabic), *muntadayat al-firdaws al-jihadiyyah*, Jan. 2007, www.alfirdaws. org/vb/showthread.php?t=24845&highlight=%E3%D5%DA%C8+%C7 %E1%D3%E6%D1%ED, accessed Feb. 2007. This posting also appeared on *muntadayat risalat al-ummah*, 15 Nov. 2006, www.al-ommh.net/vb/ showthread.php?t=8447&highlight=%E3%D5%DA%C8+%C7%E1%D3% E6%D1%ED, accessed Feb. 2007.

28  See posting by 'al-Lahibi' on *muntada al-tajdid*, 31 May 2006, www.tajdeed. org.uk/forums/showthread.php?s=6548b36708e3c3eff8db8327623a51e8&t hreadid=41941, accessed June 2006.

29  *Muntadayat shabakat al-hisbah* at www.al-hesbah.org/v. Documents on file with the author.

more than 220 written responses.[30] Al-Suri was also promoted by the important *al-Ansar* webforum.[31]

Al-Suri's works have not figured prominently on the numerous official websites run by al-Qaida in Iraq or other Iraqi insurgent groups. He has been promoted online, however, by other jihadi groups. Since late 2006, the Algerian *Salafi Group for Preaching and Combat* (GSPC) has posted *The Global Islamic Resistance Call* on its main website, recommending it as essential reading.[32] The GSPC's endorsement is significant, given that it has recently been accepted as a fully-fledged branch of al-Qaida, under the name *The Al-Qaida Organization in Islamic Maghrib*, and is considered a key actor in the future evolution of global jihadi terrorism. In January 2006, a media spokesman of the GSPC posted a statement criticising al-Suri for his book on Algeria (see chapter 5), suggesting that its embrace of al-Suri is not unqualified, even though his latest book is very popular among the group. Critical or dismissive remarks about al-Suri on jihadi websites are extremely rare, however. When he is singled out for condemnation, it is usually by mainstream Islamists, especially the Syrian Muslim Brotherhood, against whom al-Suri has fought a bitter ideological battle since the late 1980s.

The various jihadi online journals have not promoted al-Suri as prominently as the GSPC's website. Since many of them are associated with local or regional jihadi groups, they tend to devote less space to more independent jihadi writers like al-Suri. A few of them have nevertheless brought al-Suri to the attention of their readers. The *risalat al-mujahidin* journal, which describes itself as 'The voice

---

30  See 'O Ye Blessed Jihadi Cells, Here You Have the Great Fundamental Encyclopaedia. Go Ahead and Use It!' (in Arabic), *shabakat al-ikhlas al-islamiyyah*, www.alekhlaas.net/forum/showthread.php?t=13902, accessed Nov. 2006.

31  See, for example, 'Reading of the book The Global Islamic Resistance Call' (in Arabic), *muntada al-ansar al-islami*, 10 Nov. 2005.

32  See *al-jama'ah al-salafiyyah li al-da'wah wa'l-qital – al-jaza'ir website*, at http://moonnight1234.com/ and www.moon4321.com, accessed between March and June 2006.

of the mujahidin in the Levantine countries' has published excerpts of his books.[33] In late 2005, another Levantine-oriented online magazine, the *minbar al-sham al-islami* bulletin dedicated nearly an entire edition to republishing al-Suri's audiotaped address to the European countries, al-Suri's last known public statement.[34] Another prominent jihadi bulletin, the *sada al-jihad* magazine, published a poem in al-Suri's honour following his capture in Pakistan, praising him as 'one of the greatest symbols of jihad and one of the greatest remaining mujahidin in terms of experience and faithfulness to the Prophet's tradition'.[35]

Perhaps more important in terms of outreach is the Global Islamic Media Front (GIMF)'s coverage of al-Suri and his writings. The GIMF, which enjoys the status as the largest jihadi online media producer and distributor of recent years, has repeatedly advertised and disseminated al-Suri's works, in particular *The Global Islamic Resistance Call*.[36] The GIMF has also reformatted and popularised al-Suri's audio-taped lectures in their 'Precious Lectures-series' (*al-muhadarat al-thaminah*). More than twenty excerpts from his

---

33 See Umar Abd al-Hakim (Abu Mus'ab al-Suri), 'A Call to the Mujahidin Youth and the Jihadi Groups in the Islamic World' (in Arabic), *majallat risalat al-mujahidin* no.3, Muharram 1426 (Feb. 2005), pp.1, 18-19, posted *inter alia* on www.nnuu.org, accessed Feb. 2006.

34 See 'Text of Audio Communique by Shaykh Umar Abd al-Hakim (Abu Mus'ab al-Suri) Addressing the British and the Europeans regarding the London Explosions, and the Practices of the British Government' (in Arabic), *minbar al-sham al-islami*, bulletin no.4 (16 Dec. 2005), pp.4-23. This publication was previously called *minbar suriya al-islami* and was associated with the *minbar suria al-islami* website, previously located at www.nnuu.org and www.islam-syria.com.

35 'My Letter to the Hero Prisoner Abu Mus'ab al-Suri' (in Arabic), *sada al-jihad* Dhu al-Qa'dah 1426 (Dec. 2005), posted *inter alia* on http://albadeel.100free.com/majallat/others/others.htm, accessed Feb. 2006.

36 For one example of the GIMF's promotion of *The Global Islamic Resistance Call*, see 'The Global Islamic Resistance Call ... [Abu Mus'ab al-Suri] ... Ready for Downloading' (in Arabic), *shabakat al-ikhlas al-islamiyyah*, 10 June 2005, www.alekhlaas.net/forum/showthread.php?t=13097&highlight=%E3%D5%DA%C8+%C7%E1%D3%E6%D1%ED, accessed Feb. 2007.

most important audiotaped lecture, 'Jihad is the Solution', have been advertised and distributed in two editions of this series, each accompanied with commentaries, banners, and illustrations.[37] Furthermore, the GIMF's newest and most prestigious media outlet, The Voice of the Caliphate Channel (CVC), a jihadi web-TV, had already broadcast excerpts from al-Suri's videotaped lectures during their first and second week on air in early 2007.[38] Although the CVC started broadcasting sporadically in summer 2005, it first launched streaming video broadcasts only on 20 January 2007.[39] The promotion of al-Suri's videotaped lectures is significant. In them al-Suri explains his global Islamic resistance principles in great detail and the lectures serve as the 'film version' of *The Global Islamic Resistance Call*, so to speak. Due to the book's huge size (1,600pp.), the existence of an audio-visual shortcut has been applauded on the jihadi web.[40]

Fame in the world of online jihadism revolves around stars. Hence, the fact that several high-profile figures in the jihadi web community have endorsed and recommended al-Suri to their readers is significant. One such figure is Shaykh Atiyat Allah, a senior jihadi veteran and cleric with a long history of jihadi activism from Peshawar, Afghanistan, Algeria and elsewhere. His standing is such

---

37 See, for example, 'The Media Front Presents "Precious Lectures": "Jihad is the Solution"' ... Excerpts from Abu Mus'ab al-Suri, The Ghuraba Camp' (in Arabic), *minbar ahl al-sunna wa'l-jama'ah*, 29 Sept. 2005, www.sunna-minbar.net/forum/viewtopic.php?t=493, accessed April 2006, and 'The Media Front Presents Part Two, "Jihad is the Solution"' ... Excerpts from Abu Mus'ab al-Suri, The Ghuraba Camp' (in Arabic), *multaqa al-mujahidin* (www.mojahedon.com/vb), 5 Oct. 2005. These postings have also appeared on the very important *al-Hisbah* web forum (*muntadayat shabakat al-hisbah*, www.alhesbah.org/v/). See, for example, two postings by 'The Islamic Media' (in Arabic) in the political section on 30 Sept. 2005 and 5 Oct. 2005.

38 See Global Islamic Media Front, *Caliphate Voice Channel*, available on mms://87.118.96.168:88/firdaws, accessed Feb. 2007.

39 Hanna Rogan, 'Jihadist Online Media Strategies', *FFI Research Report* (forthcoming).

40 See, for example, posting by 'Abu Hamzah2005' (in Arabic) on 'What is your opinion about distributing this ... important CD' (in Arabic), *muntadayat shabakat al-hisbah*, 3 May 2006, www.al-hesbah.org/v, accessed May 2006.

that his opinions and fatwas are regularly consulted on top jihadi webforums. In one of these question and answer sessions on *al-Hisbah* in September 2006, he warmly recommends al-Suri and his book *The Global Islamic Resistance Call* as essential reading, 'especially for the brothers who are interested in jihadi political ideology and the brothers in leadership positions'.[41] Shaykh Atiyat Allah also says he got to know al-Suri very well in Afghanistan, especially during the Taleban period. Another prominent web-jihadi who has promoted al-Suri is Abu Marya al-Qurashi. A prolific and well-known writer on most jihadi webforums, he claims to have met with and sworn an oath of allegiance to Abu Mus'ab al-Zarqawi and says he resides in 'the occupied territories' in Baghdad.[42] To a Western audience he is perhaps best known for having propounded action plans for how jihadis should exploit the Muhammad cartoon crisis in 2006.[43] Al-Qurashi has described al-Suri as 'among the most important thinkers' in terms of 'explaining the future jihadi strategy' and referred to his book on global Islamic resistance as 'extremely important'.[44]

---

41 See The meeting with Shaykh Atiyat Allah on *muntadayat shabakat al-hisbah*'. Reproduced and distributed by Global Islamic Media Front, and posted inter alia on *The al-Qaida Organisation in Islamic Maghreb website*, http://www.qmagreb.org/, accessed May 2007.

42 See 'The diary of a traveller in Mesopotamia: Part 1: Allegiance to Abu Mus'ab al-Zarqawi' (in Arabic), *shabakat ana muslim*, 13 June 2006, www.muslm.net/vb/showthread.php?t=165658, accessed Feb. 2007.

43 See Stephen Ulph, 'and Set Course of Action Against Denmark', *Terrorism Focus*, 3 (6) (14 Feb. 2006), http://jamestown.org/terrorism/news/article.php?articleid=2369901, accessed Feb. 2007; and 'The Global Islamic Media Front Presents an Article: "What After the Denmark Happenings... A Work Plan",' *SITE Institute* website, 10 Feb. 2006, http://siteinstitute.org/bin/articles.cgi?ID=publications147206&Category=publications&Subcateg ory=0, accessed Feb. 2007. A few of Abu Marya al-Qurashi's works have been posted in the prestigious *minbar al-tawhid wa'l-jihad* library; see www.tawhed.ws/a?i=425, accessed Feb. 2007.

44 See 'A piece of advice to my brothers ... Abu Marya al-Qurashi' (in Arabic), *shabakat al-muhajirun al-islamiyyah*, 20 Feb. 2006, www.mohajroon.com/vb/showthread.php?t=6662&highlight=%E3%D5%DA%C8+%C7%E1 D3%E6%D1%ED, accessed Feb. 2006.

Significantly, in his recommended reading list for prospective jihadis al-Suri's book appears first.[45]

Another significant promoter of al-Suri is a well-known web jihadi calling himself 'Ozooo', who runs a web directory and several hosting sites for popular jihadi material, and participates frequently on jihadi webforums. From May 2006 till early 2007 'Ozooo' has hosted and promoted a website containing most of Abu Mus'ab al-Suri's works.[46] The most persistent advocate of al-Suri's output is 'Muhammad Ahmad Khalaf', the supervisor of the *madad al-suyuf* webforum (www.almedad.com/vb), of which he devoted an entire section to al-Suri's training and warfighting doctrines.[47] 'Khalaf' is also the editor and promoter of 'The Mujahidin Talk' (*al-mujahidun yatakallamun*), a popular series of articles that have circulated on most jihadi web forums in more than fifty editions. Al-Suri has featured on at least half a dozen of these articles, and his books have been extensively cited.[48]

---

45  Ibid.

46  See *ozooo.tk* and *ozooo3@hotmail.com* websites at www.ozooo.tk and http:// w1000.jeeran.com/index.html respectively. See also ozooo's posting on 'What is your opinion about distributing this ... important CD' (in Arabic), *muntadayat shabakat al-hisbah*, 3 May 2006, www.al-hesbah.org/v, accessed May 2006.

47  See 'Your guide to jihad' (in Arabic), *madad al-suyuf*, 3-14 Dec. 2006, www. almedad.com/vb, accessed Dec. 2006. See also his posting 'Urgent and Important Call to the Media Mujahidin', *minbar al-muslim*, 1 Dec. 2006, www.aaa3.net/vb/showthread.php?t=454&highlight=%C7%C8%E6+%E3 %D5%DA%C8+%C7%E1%D3%E6%D1%ED, accessed Feb. 2007.

48  See 'No.26: "The First and the Most Dangerous Enemy are the Apostates" by Abu Mus'ab al-Suri' (in Arabic), in *The Series of The Mujahidin Talk*, 3rd edition, pp.19-31, accessed via *minbar al-muslim* 5 Oct. 2007, http:// www.aaa3.net/vb/showthread.php?t=637&highlight=%C7%C8%E6+% E3%D5%DA%C8+%C7%E1%D3%E6%D1%ED; 'The mujahidin talk no.27: "God's verdict on the apostate rulers" by Abu Mus'ab al-Suri' (in Arabic), *muntadayat risalat al-ummah*, 5 July 2006, www.al-ommh.net/ vb/showthread.php?t=5296&highlight=%E3%D5%DA%C8+%C7%E1% D3%E6%D1%ED. See also 'The mujahidin talk: Words by [our] leaders and clerics about the rulers of the apostates (in Arabic), *shabakat al-ikhlas al-islamiyyah*, 4 Feb. 2007, www.alekhlaas.net/forum/showthread.php?t=4

One way of gauging the impact of al-Suri's writings in the jihadi community is the frequency with which his works are read and downloaded. A good location for checking his 'sales figures' is the *minbar al-tawhid wa'l-jihad* website (lit. 'The Pulpit of Monotheism and Jihad'), which hosts the most comprehensive online library of salafi-jihadi literature. Among the more than one hundred authors in its catalogue, al-Suri is prominently listed and introduced to the readers with a photograph and a two page biography. Not all of his written works are posted there, however. Those that are, have all been widely read and frequently downloaded, according to information provided on the website. By February 2007, more than 22,000 users were recorded to have 'visited' al-Suri's book about the Saudi opposition, while more than 11,000 people had clicked links to his books on the jihadi movement in Syria and about Yemen.[49] Compared to the bestsellers on *minbar al-tawhid wa'l-jihad*, al-Suri's sales figures were modest: Shaykh Abu Muhammad al-Maqdisi's 'The Creed of Abraham' (*millat ibrahim*) has been visited nearly 48,000 times, and

---

5425&highlight=%E3%D5%DA%C8+%C7%E1%D3%E6%D1%ED; 'The mujahidin talk no.51: The Fatwas by Shaykh al-Islam Ibn Taymiyyah on the Nusayriyyah' (in Arabic), *minbar al-muslim*, 16 Oct. 2005, http://www.aaa3. net/vb/showthread.php?t=37&highlight=%C7%C8%E6+%E3%D5%DA% C8+%C7%E1%D3%E6%D1%ED; 'The mujahidin talk no.52: The Sunnite People in the Levant seek aid from the Nusayri-Alawites' (in Arabic), *minbar al-muslim*, 19 Oct. 2006, http://www.aaa3.net/vb/showthread. php?t=74&highlight=%C7%C8%E6+%E3%D5%DA%C8+%C7%E1%D3 %E6%D1%ED; and 'The mujahidin talk, no.53: Abu Mus'ab al-Suri and the Jihad against the Nusayri Alawites' (in Arabic), *minbar al-muslim*, 25 Oct. 2006, www.aaa3.net/vb/showthread.php?t=108&highlight=%C7%C 8%E6+%E3%D5%DA%C8+%C7%E1%D3%E6%D1%ED. All websites accessed mid-Feb. 2007.

49 In Aug. 2005 the lowest download figure was too low to be recorded while the highest was 10,293. The average figure was 4,315. By mid-Feb. 2007, these numbers had increased to 714 for the lowest figure and 11,895 for the highest, while the average number of downloads was 6,137. The average number of visitors to the sites where the books were posted showed a more significant increase. The most visited book in Aug. 2005 had 6,789 hits, while in Feb. 2007 that number had risen to 22,641. The lowest figure was 2,636, and the average number of visitors in Feb. 2007 was 10,493.

Abu Qutadah's 'Signposts of the Victorious Sect' (*ma'alim al-ta'ifah al-mansurah*) had 51,356 visitors by mid-February 2007.[50] Such a comparison is invidious. The *minbar al-tawhid wa'l-jihad* is reportedly run by followers of Shaykh al-Maqdisi and focuses more on theological and religious issues than al-Suri's political-strategic genre. Besides, at the time this book went to press in early 2007, *The Global Islamic Resistance Call* has not yet been posted on the website—for reasons unknown.[51]

Since popular and influential works by jihadi scholars are increasingly translated into foreign languages, the fact that very few of al-Suri's have appeared in other languages should perhaps caution us against inflating his importance. True, sections of his book on Afghanistan have been translated by Tibyan Publications, perhaps the foremost jihadi media outlet for English language salafi-jihadi literature.[52] Media reports have also suggested that an 82pp. jihadi manual published in Bahasa (Indonesian) was based on *The Global Islamic Resistance Call*.[53] Nevertheless, al-Suri's works have still not yet begun to circulate widely in the non-Arab speaking jihadi community.

Another way to assess al-Suri's importance is the extent to which his works are cited in discussions about strategy, ideology or related

50  Figures from 16 Feb. 2007. See 'The File of Abu Muhammad al-Maqdisi' (in Arabic), *minbar al-tawhid wa'l-jihad*, undated, www.tawhed.ws/a?i=2, accessed Feb. 2007.

51  None of his two most important works, *The Global Islamic Resistance Call*, and *The Islamic Jihadi Revolution in Syria* can be found in the library. The reason for this is not known. Perhaps their formats did not fit into the library's database. Both works are very large, 13 MB and 22 MB respectively. Or they might be considered too operational for a library specialising primarily in religious literature.

52  See 'Are the Taliban from Ahl as-Sunnah?', article containing extensive quotes from al-Suri's book *Afghanistan, the Taliban, and the Battle of Islam Today* (in Arabic, 1998), posted at *At-Tibyaan Publications* website, http://tibyaan.atspace.com/tibyaan/articlef7c9.html?id=1116, accessed Feb. 2007.

53  See '2006-Sept. The New Handbook On Terrorism', *Tempo Interaktif*, no.2/VII (12-18 Sept. 2006), www.tempointeractive.com/majalah/free/cov-1.html, accessed Sept. 2006.

issues on prominent jihadi webforums. Many such examples can be found, though not on a daily or even weekly basis. One occurred following the important Abqaiq operation on 24 February 2006 when the Saudi al-Qaida wing launched an unsuccessful carbomb attack on one of Saudi Arabia's most strategic oil facilities. The operation had raised the issue of the future strategy of the al-Qaida in the Kingdom, and of the pros and cons of targeting either oil installations, the foreign presence in the country or symbols of the Saudi regime. In these discussions, al-Suri's writings on the legitimacy and importance of attacking oil targets and how such attacks should be carried out were used as an important reference work.[54]

Another example was the discussion following the car bomb attacks on the Egyptian tourist resorts of Sharm al-Shaykh (July 2005) and Taba (October 2004). One article posted on the prestigious *al-Hisbah* webforum presented an analysis in which the attackers were criticised, *inter alia*, for failing, on account of their weak media efforts, to frame the attacks in a meaningful political context. The article drew heavily upon al-Suri's works, such as his writings about the legitimacy and importance of attacking tourist targets, his global jihadi concepts of fighting 'the Crusaders' wherever they can be found, his recommendation to avoid, if at all possible, direct confrontation with local Muslim authorities, his list of recommended targets, as well as his concepts for jihadi training.[55]

Al-Suri has also been cited in discussions about the legitimacy of fighting Muslim apostate rulers, and has been repeatedly featured in 'The Mujahidin Talk'-series (see above). In the same vein, al-Suri of-

---

54 See, for example, 'Proposal to the Lions of al-Qaidah in the Arab Peninsula' (in Arabic), *muntadayat shabakat al-hisbah*, 27 Feb. 2006, posted by Abu Mujahir (in Arabic), www.al-hesbah.org/v/showthread.php?t=55464, accessed March 2006.

55 Abu Muhammad al-Hilali, 'Message to the People of the Bay of Sinai' (in Arabic), *muntadayat shabakat al-hisbah*, 22 Sept. 2005, www.alhesbah.org/v. For an English summary of the article, see 'Message to the People of the Bays of Sinai Suggests Future Strategies for Jihad in Egypt', *SITE Institute*, 10 Oct. 2005, http://siteinstitute.org/bin/articles.cgi?ID=publications104005&Category=publications&Subcategory=0, accessed Feb. 2007.

ten has been used as a reference point for jihadi activists condemning Muslim Brotherhood sympathisers and the Islamic revivalist current (*al-sahwah al-islamiyyah*), who mostly reject violence as a means of fighting Muslim rulers.[56] Similarly, al-Suri's writings about the Syrian regime and the legitimacy of fighting what he has termed the 'Nusayri occupation of Syria' have been cited in debates about the Lebanese conflict by Sunni opponents of Hizbullah and its Syrian backers.[57]

Occasionally al-Suri has also been drawn upon to comment on specifically theological themes, on which he is not the greatest authority, such as a posting explaining the meaning of the salafi terms 'the Saved Sect' (*al-ta'ifah al-mansurah*) and 'The Strangers' (*al-ghuraba*). Al-Suri used the latter term about his training camp in Afghanistan and therefore devoted space to explaining its meaning (see chapter 8).[58] The wide variety of themes on which he is cited demonstrates

---

56 See, for example, 'The Battle between Truth and Evil in Palestine' (in Arabic), *muntadayat al-firdaws al-jihadiyyah*, Jan. 2007, www.alfirdaws. org/vb/showthread.php?t=25257&highlight=%E3%D5%DA%C8+%C7% E1%D3%E6%D1%ED, accessed Feb. 2007; and 'The most wonderful thing I have read in the book of Abu Mus'ab al-Suri' (in Arabic), *muntadaws al-firdaws al-jihadiyyah*, 17 May 2005, www.alfirdaws.org/forums/showthread. php?t=2035&highlight=%C3%C8%E6+%E3%D5%DA%C8+%C7%E1 %D3%E6%D1%ED, accessed Feb. 2006. The latter posting contains an excerpt from *The Global Islamic Resistance Call*, pp.128-9.

57 See, for example, 'Urgent message from Abu Mus'ab al-Suri to the People of Lebanon and the Levant' (in Arabic), *muntadayat al-firdaws al-jihadiyyah*, Jan. 2007, www.alfirdaws.org/vb/showthread.php?t=24787&highlight=%E 3%D5%DA%C8+%C7%E1%D3%E6%D1%ED, accessed Feb. 2007; and 'Nasr al-Lat is burning Lebanon: Call to the Sunnite youth in Lebanon' (in Arabic), *muntadayat risalat al-ummah*, 23 Jan. 2007, www.al-ommh. net/vb/showthread.php?t=11987&page=2&highlight=%E3%D5%DA%C8 +%C7%E1%D3%E6%D1%ED, accessed Feb. 2007.

58 See, for example, 'The Saved Party and the Victorious Sect' (in Arabic), *muntadayat al-firdaws al-jihadiyyah*, Feb. 2007, www.alfirdaws.org/vb/ showthread.php?t=26657&highlight=%E3%D5%DA%C8+%C7%E1%D3 %E6%D1%ED, accessed Feb. 2007. This posting cites a long excerpt from al-Suri's *The Global Islamic Resistance Call* in which he explains these terms. The posting also includes a short biography of al-Suri.

not only the breadth of his authorship, but also his future potential to become a standard reference on several issues exercising the jihadi movement.

Also in terms of methodology, al-Suri's views seem to have some appeal. His structural and analytical approach has sometimes made him a reference point in jihadi webforum discussions. In April 2006 the GIMF distributed reader questionnaires to gauge their 'religious, social, cultural, and strategic levels' and 'the level of interaction on the web'. In producing them GIMF drew exclusively upon al-Suri and highlighted his writings as the best framework for such analyses.[59]

Yet another indicator of al-Suri's potential impact is the fact that his works are considered relevant not only on an ideological level but also for operational purposes. Or as one jihadi web participant noted gloatingly: 'Shaykh Abu Mus'ab al-Suri's works are factories for terrorists!!'.[60] Hence, one finds that al-Suri's works are not only posted in the jihadi webforums' politico-religious sections where most jihadi literature circulates, but they also feature in the specialised sections, dedicated to discussions of training, preparation, weapons and explosive manuals etc. The latter are known as 'forum for jihadi cells', 'military forum', 'forum for equipment and preparation', etc. The important al-Firdaws webforum has repeatedly posted al-Suri's works in its military section.[61] In February 2006, the al-safinet webforum even placed his works on its 'forum for jihadi cells' as a 'sticky posting', thereby ensuring that it remains at the top of the website for

---

59 See posting in the political section entitled 'The Media Front Presents: Useful Questionnaire in Exploring the Situation of the People of Monotheism and Jihad' (in Arabic), *muntadayat shabakat al-hisbah*, 25 April 2006, www.alhesbah.org/v, accessed April 2006.

60 Cited in posting by 'talib al-du'a' (in Arabic) on 'What is your opinion about distributing this ... important CD', (in Arabic), *muntadayat shabakat al-hisbah*, 3 May 2006, www.al-hesbah.org/v, accessed May 2006.

61 See, for example, 'The library of Shaykh Abu Mus'ab al-Suri' (in Arabic), *muntadayat al-firdaws al-jihadiyyah*, 29 June 2005, www.alfirdaws.org/vb/showthread.php?t=8946, accessed June 2005.

a long while.[62] This is clearly no coincidence. Several web postings have dubbed his collection of writings 'Shaykh Abu Mus'ab al-Suri's military library', strongly suggesting that he is seen as far more operational than many other writers.[63] Especially in the field of training and preparation, al-Suri is regarded as highly relevant. His emphasis on the power of knowledge and the obligation to prepare for jihad has often been cited.[64] Significantly, his sub-chapter on training doctrines in *The Global Islamic Resistance Call* has been reformatted and distributed as a short handy 12pp. manual with a new title: *Modern Methods in Military Training.*[65]

One may also measure al-Suri's influence in the jihadi community by examining whether his ideas have been adopted and popularised by other jihadi writers. One such example concerns Muhammad Khalil Hasan al-Hukaymah (Abu Jihad al-Masri), a spokesman of a breakaway faction of the Egyptian Islamic Group (JI), who attracted international media attention after he was interviewed by al-Sahab, al-Qaida's official media department, about his group's merger with al-Qaida in the autumn of 2006.[66] Furthermore, in

---

62 'The military library of Abu Mus'ab al-Suri' (in Arabic), *muntada al-safinet* 27 Feb. 2006, www.al-saf.net/vb/showthread.php?t=10928, accessed March 2006.

63 See, for example, 'Shaykh Abu Mus'ab al-Suri's military library' (in Arabic), *muntada al-safinet*, 18 July 2005, www.al-saf.net/vb, accessed Feb. 2006.

64 See, for example, 'The levels of resistance' (in Arabic), *muntadayat al-firdaws al-jihadiyyah*, 9 May 2005, www.alfirdaws.org/forums/showthread.php?t=1 713&highlight=%C3%C8%E6+%E3%D5%DA%C8+%C7%E1%D3%E6 %D1%ED, accessed Feb. 2006. This posting cites from *The Global Islamic Resistance Call*, pp.38-9.

65 See Abu Mus'ab al-Suri, 'Modern methods in military training' (in Arabic), *al-thabitun 'ala al-'ahd*, 13 Feb. 2007, http://altabetoun.110mb.com/news. php?action=view&id=97, accessed Feb. 2007.

66 Al-Hukaymah's reconstituted JI group has adopted the name 'al-Qaida in the Land of Canaan' (*qa'idat al-jihad fi bilad al-kananah*), and runs the website *al-thabitun 'ala al-'ahd* (lit. 'Those adhering to the covenant' located at http:// altabetoon.eur.st) where al-Hukaymah has published a number of his works. For an English translation of the al-Sahab interview with al-Hukaymah, see 'From those adhering to the covenant in the Egyptian Islamic Group',

late 2006 the publication of al-Hukaymah's extensive study of the US Central Intelligence Agency (CIA) made him even better-known, earning him titles such as 'Al-Qaida's Spymaster'.[67] In several of his recent works al-Hukaymah relies heavily on al-Suri, and in 'Towards a new strategy in resisting the occupier (targets and methods)', released on 11 September 2006, al-Hukaymah copied substantial sections from *The Global Islamic Resistance Call*, albeit without citing or mentioning al-Suri by name.[68] Some of the other works published on al-Hukaymah's website also promote ideas and concepts previously developed by al-Suri, such as the articles 'The Individual Jihad, and 'How to Fight Alone'.[69] The degree of plagiarism of al-Suri's work by al-Hukaymah is remarkable, although such unattributed borrowing is far from uncommon and is not frowned upon in the jihadi community to the same degree as it is in academia. To be fair, al-Hukaymah's website has also posted an article where al-Suri is recognised as the author.[70]

---

*Internet Archive*, http://www.archive.org/details/from-those-adhering-to-the-covenant-in-the-EGYPTION-ISLAMIC-GROUP, accessed Feb. 2007.

67 See Brian Fishman, 'Al-Qa'ida's Spymaster Analyzes the U.S. Intelligence Community', Report by Combating Terrorism Center, West Point, 6 Nov. 2006, www.ctc.usma.edu/MythofDelusion.pdf, accessed Feb. 2007.

68 Muhammad Khalil al-Hukaymah, 'Towards a new strategy in resisting the occupier (targets and methods) (in Arabic),' *al-thabitun 'ala al-'ahd*, 13 Feb. 2007, http://altabetoun.110mb.com/news.php?action=view&id=135, accessed Feb. 2007. For an English summary, see 'A New Strategic Method in the Resistance of the Occupier Prepared by Muhammad Khalil al-Hukaymah', *OSINFO* website, 30 Sept. 2006, www.opensourcesinfo. org/journal/2006/9/30/a-new-strategic-method-in-the-resistance-of-the-occupier-prepared-by-muhammad-khalil-al-hukaymah-part-i.html, accessed Feb. 2007.

69 See 'How to fight alone: proposed ideas and methods' (in Arabic), *al-thabitun 'ala al-'ahd*, 13 Feb. 2007, http://altabetoun.110mb.com/news. php?action=view&id=99, accessed Feb. 2007; and 'The individual jihad' (in Arabic), *al-thabitun 'ala al-'ahd*, 13 Feb. 2007, http://altabetoun.110mb. com/news.php?action=view&id=129, accessed Feb. 2007.

70 Abu Mus'ab al-Suri, 'Modern methods in military training' (in Arabic), *al-thabitun 'ala al-'ahd*, 13 Feb. 2007, http://altabetoun.110mb.com/news.

While al-Suri's relatively prominent status in the jihadi online community is hard to dispute, less is known about the extent to which he is read and studied by operative jihadi cells. Since al-Suri's most important works have only been available online since January 2005, it is probably too early to tell. Some of his writings have been found on computers belonging to suspected jihadi terrorists in Europe, including the Madrid cell.[71] Furthermore, audio- or video recordings of his lectures were among items discovered in jihadi cells in Syria, Jordan, Italy, Germany, the United States and elsewhere.[72] But al-Suri's works are not bestsellers, and nor are they likely to feature among the most widely read items for young jihadis. For one thing he is not, as mentioned above, considered a religious scholar of great stature, and for another his preferred genre is strategic studies in the service of jihad, which is still a marginal topic when compared to the prodigious output of works offering religious justification for violence. However, the 'jihadi strategic studies' genre appears to have become more important of late.[73] Owing to the US-led occupation of Iraq and Afghanistan, the intensifying insurgencies there, and

---

php?action=view&id=97, accessed Feb. 2007. The article is identical to the chapter on 'Theory of training' in his *The Global Islamic Resistance Call*, pp.1414-28. Al-Hukaymah also cites al-Suri as a reference source in his 42 pp. study of 'The history of the jihadi movements in Egypt 1946-2006' (in Arabic), published in Dec. 2006.

71 See 'Audiencia Nacional Madrid, Juzgado Central de Instrucción no.6, Sumario no.20/2004', (the M-11 Indictment), Madrid, 10 April 2006, available at www.fondodocumental.com/11M/documentos/Autos/auto1. doc and www.fondodocumental.com/11M/documentos/Autos/auto2.doc, accessed July 2006, pp.468, 490.

72 Interviews with intelligence analysts in several European countries. Names withheld on request.

73 See Brynjar Lia and Thomas Hegghammer, 'Jihadi Strategic Studies: The Alleged Al Qaida Policy Study Preceding the Madrid Bombings', *Studies in Conflict and Terrorism*, 27, 5 (Sept./Oct. 2004), pp.355-75; and Thomas Hegghammer, 'Strategic Studies in Jihadist Literature', Address to the Middle East Institute, Washington, DC, 17 May 2006, www.mil.no/multimedia/archive/00077/Strategic_studies_in_77872a.pdf, accessed Nov. 2006.

the highly visible human sufferings resulting from these wars, jihadi proselytisers do not have to struggle hard to convince their audiences of the need to fight 'the Crusaders'.[74] Instead, there seems to be a growing demand for strategies, concepts, roadmaps, and practical advice about how to organize disparate jihadi entities in a more efficient manner and gain maximum traction from their use of violence. Al-Suri's 'jihadi strategic studies'-genre has therefore become more relevant than ever before.

The significance of al-Suri's writings on strategic studies extends beyond how they might magnify the political impact of al-Qaida's terrorism. They most probably contribute to widening the appeal of jihadism to new audiences, especially among young, well-educated Westernised Muslims who seem to be motivated more by a mixture of leftist radicalism and militant pan-Islamic nationalism than by religiosity. Just as Marxism's alleged scientific basis appealed to young European students, so al-Suri's works—with their explicit emphasis on rationality, scientific research, self-criticism, and learning from past mistakes—might have some of the same impact on young Muslims.

While it has been suggested that several terrorist attacks over the past few years have been informed by al-Suri's thinking,[75] his long-term impact has yet to be determined, although his concepts of a decentralized jihad are taking shape on the ground, if only because circumstances have forced this upon the jihadi movements. Paul Cruickshank and Mohannad Hage Ali have noted correctly in a recent article on al-Suri that: 'The terrorist strikes in Bali, Casablanca, Istanbul, Madrid, and London were all initiated by exactly the sort

---

74 See especially Thomas Hegghammer, 'Global Jihadism After the Iraq War', *The Middle East Journal*, 60 (1) (Winter 2006), pp.11-32, www.mil. no/multimedia/archive/00076/Global_Jihadism_Afte_76427a.pdf.

75 For example, it has been suggested that the Sinai terrorist attacks in Oct. 2005 were illustrative of how al-Suri's theories are being operationalised. See Reuven Paz, 'Al-Qaeda's Search for new Fronts: Instructions for Jihadi Activity in Egypt and Sinai', *Project for Research of Islamist Movements (PRISM) Occasional Papers*, 3 (7) (Oct. 2005), www.e-prism.org/images/ PRISM_no_7_vol_3_-_The_new_front_in_Egypt_and_Sinai.pdf#search=' AlQaeda%27s%20Search%20for%20new%20Fronts', accessed Dec. 2005.

of small locally recruited cells for which Sethmariam was calling.'[76] In Iraq, his vision of decentralized jihadi warfare has also 'taken on reality'. The insurgency there now 'consists of possibly as many as a hundred groups, each with separate leaders, that often act on their own or come together for a single attack'.[77] In Europe, anti-terrorism investigators also struggle with an enemy that grows steadily more elusive. A *Washington Post* article from mid-2005 reported that investigations into recent al-Qaida operations in Europe, from London and Madrid to Casablanca and Istanbul, had captured only 'the hands', not the 'brains' behind these attacks.[78] With thousands of al-Qaida militants killed or in captivity, there seemed to be a marked shift from al-Qaida 'the group' to al-Qaida 'the movement'. A more decentralized enemy has appeared, in which hierarchical command structures and organizational affiliations are harder to identify.[79] Yet the problem is not simply that al-Qaida may be concealing its command structure in new ways. In recent years we have also witnessed the phenomenon of jihadi cells in Europe being formed exclusively through self-radicalization, self-recruitment, and self-training, relying extensively on jihadi resources accessed via the Internet.[80] There has emerged a new al-Qaida, which apparently has adopted some of the lessons that al-Suri has been teaching since the early 1990s.

## SOURCES ON AL-SURI'S LIFE

76 See Paul Cruickshank, and Mohannad Hage Ali, 'Abu Musab Al Suri: Architect of the New Al Qaeda', *Studies in Conflict and Terrorism*, 30 (1) (Jan. 2007), p.9.

77 Cited in ibid., p.10.

78 Craig Whitlock, 'Terror Probes Find 'the Hands, but Not the Brains': Attackers Often Caught As Masterminds Flee', *Washington Post*, 11 July 2005, p.A10.

79 Elaine Sciolino and Don Van Natta Jr., 'Bombings in London: Investigation; Searching for Footprints', *The New York Times*, 25 July 2005, p.A1.

80 This information was shared with me by my colleague Petter Nesser, based on his interviews with antiterrorism investigators in two EU countries.

The building blocks of this book are online jihadi sources, in particular the writings, audiotaped lectures and interviews, posted on al-Suri's own Arabic-language website, Western and Arabic media reports, judicial documents, and interviews. While previous accounts of al-Suri have drawn upon mostly secondary materials, in particular press reports based on government sources, I have used many primary sources on al-Suri's life, most of it his own words, but also by talking to people who met him at various stages of his life, the interviewees including Islamists, ex-jihadists, and Arab and Western journalists.

Al-Suri's website, *The Library of Shaykh Umar Abd al-Hakim—Abu Mus'ab al-Suri: Your Guide to the Way of Jihad* (maktabat al-shaykh umar 'abd al-hakim—abu mus'ab al-suri: dalilak ila tariq al-jihad, hereafter, *Abu Mus'ab al-Suri's Website*) has been an invaluable source of information, even though much of the same primary source material has also been circulated on jihadi online forums.[81] The website includes an official biography of al-Suri.[82] The single most extensive source of information about his life is probably a series of ten audiofiles, each of which runs to nearly forty-five minutes. These were recorded during an interview with the Kuwaiti newspaper *al-Ra'y al-'Amm* in Kabul on 18 March 1999 and subsequently posted on his website.[83] There is also much biographical information about al-Suri in his intellectual writings, in particular on his relationship and con-

---

81 For a list of websites where source material on al-Suri has been posted, see the bibliography.

82 See 'Biography of Shaykh Umar Abd al-Hakim (Abu Mus'ab al-Suri)' (in Arabic), *Abu Mus'ab al-Suri's Website*, www.deluxesuperhost.com/~morshid/tophacker/index.php?subject=4&rec=22&tit=tit&pa=0, accessed 11 April 2005; and 'The File of Abu Mus'ab al-Suri' (in Arabic), *minbar al-tawhid wa'l-jihad* website, www.tawhed.ws/a?I=78, accessed 15 July 2005.

83 Audiofile 1-10, 'Meeting with the Kuwaiti newspaper al-Ra'y al-Amm' (in Arabic), (hereafter 'Meeting with the Kuwaiti Newspaper'), originally posted on *Abu Mus'ab al-Suri's Website*, www.fsboa.com/vw/index.php?subject=4&rec=2&tit=tit&pa=0 and www.deluxesuperhost.com/~morshid/tophacker/index.php?subject=4&rec=2&tit=tit&pa=0. The audiofiles have subsequently been made available at various jihadi web forums, including *muntadayat minbar suria al-islami* 4 Nov. 2005, www.islam-syria.com/vb/showthread.php?t=1601, accessed 5 Nov. 2005.

29

tacts with various jihadi organizations, especially in his 2004 book *A Summary of My Testimony on Jihad in Algeria 1988-1996*. Biographical information has also been collected through Western and Arabic media sources, a daunting task given that media reporting on al-Suri from 2004 onwards has sometimes been very misleading. In the late 1990s, Abu Mus'ab al-Suri served as an intermediary between the Western media and bin Laden, and he was interviewed and profiled in books on militant Islam, agreeing to do so only on condition of anonymity. Other useful sources on al-Suri's life are Spanish court documents, especially with regard to his relationship with members of the Spanish al-Qaida cell headed by Imad al-Din Barakat Yarkas (Abu Dahdah). Interviews and conversations with intelligence officials and investigators from various countries have also been a helpful corrective to some of the uncorroborated open source material. Finally, al-Suri also features in several al-Qaida documents uncovered in Afghanistan following the US-led military intervention. Taken together, these sources have made it possible to write a biography of a man, who, till recently, appeared to be among the most elusive leaders in al-Qaida.

## WHO IS ABU MUS'AB AL-SURI?

Identifying Abu Mus'ab al-Suri's real name and aliases is hardly a straightforward task. As with most other jihadis with a long clandestine career, al-Suri has used many pseudonyms and *noms de plume*. Furthermore, Arabic names defy easy categorization into first names and surnames, and Western transcriptions of Arabic names vary infinitely.

In his own words, his real name is Mustafa bin Abd al-Qadir Sitt Maryam, or alternatively Mustafa bin Abd al-Qadir Sitt Maryam Nasar.[84] His official biography also provides a longer version of his

---

84 See Umar Abd al-Hakim (Abu Mus 'ab al-Suri), *The Global Islamic Resistance Call*, p.1604; al-Suri's testament 'Shaykh Abu Mus'ab al-Suri's Will to be Executed in the Case of His Capture or Martyrdom' (in Arabic), dated Dec.

name, incorporating his grandfather's, great grandfather's and great great grandfather's names: Mustafa bin Abd al-Qadir bin Mustafa bin Husayn bin al-Shaykh Ahmad al-Muzayyik al-Jakiri al-Rifa'i.[85] In Spain, where he obtained citizenship in the late 1980s, his identity papers reportedly bore the name Mustafa Setmarian Naser, which is what Spanish court documents mostly use, albeit with very many spelling variants (Mustafa, Mustafá, Setmarian, Setmariam, Sethmarian, Sethmariam, Naser, Nasar, Nasaar, etc).[86] The US government refers to him as Mustafa Setmariam Nasar.[87] He is also sometimes referred to only as Mustafa al-Rifa'i.[88]

Of his aliases and pseudonyms he is most commonly referred to as Abu Mus'ab al-Suri, his most popular pseudonym, often used in conjunction with Umar Abd al-Hakim (also spelled Omar Abdel Hakim). Other aliases include Abu al-Abd, Abu Abed el rubio [Spanish, lit. 'The Blond One'], El Pelirrojo [Spanish, lit. 'The Red-Haired']89, El Español, El Alemán90, Abu Musab, Abu Fatima,

2004 and published at *muntada al-tajdid*, 5 Oct. 2005, www.tajdeed.org.uk/forums/showthread.php?s=240e1a4cc709589d5bc8bcd7a52d0c7d&threadid=38747, accessed 20 Oct. 2005; and 'Meeting with the Kuwaiti newspaper', transcript of audiofile no.1, p.1.

85 'Biography of Shaykh Umar Abd al-Hakim (Abu Mus'ab al-Suri)' (in Arabic), p.1.

86 Antonio Rubio, 'Mustafa Setmarian Naser: Un español en la cima de Al Qaeda: Durante los diez años que vivió en España se convirtió en lugarteniente de Bin Laden', *elmundo.es*, 3 Nov. 2005, www.elmundo.es/elmundo/2005/11/03/espana/1131002447.html, accessed Dec. 2005.

87 'WANTED: Mustafa Setmariam Nasar', *Reward for Justice website*, www.rewardsforjustice.net/english/wanted_captured/index.cfm?page=Nasar, accessed July 2005.

88 'Analyst Comments: Abu Musaab al-Suri', *Terrorism Research Center* 8 July 2005, www.homelandsecurity.com/modules.php?op=modload&name=Intel&file=index&view=649, accessed Dec. 2005.

89 Antonio Rubio, 'Mustafa Setmarian Naser: Un español en la cima de Al Qaeda: Durante los diez años que vivió en España se convirtió en lugarteniente de Bin Laden', *elmundo.es*, 3 Nov. 2005, www.elmundo.es/elmundo/2005/11/03/espana/1131002447.html, accessed Dec. 2005.

90 El Español and El Alemán are Spanish for 'the Spaniard' and 'the German'

Nouradin, Khalid bin al-Abidin (a pseudonym), and Abu Abdallah (a pseudonym).[91] His many aliases reflect his belief in the need to remain anonymous, despite the fact that lecturing, proselytizing, and journalism for the jihadi cause were his main preoccupations. Consequently, al-Suri was sometimes ridiculed as 'James Bond' by fellow jihadis in London,[92] although, unlike many other jihadi ideologues, he remained relatively unknown till recently. In March 2006, CNN.com wrote that 'Abu Musab al-Suri might be the most dangerous terrorist you've never heard of'.[93]

CNN had already had dealings with him almost ten years earlier, although they did not grasp his importance at that point. In Peter Bergen's bestseller on al-Qaida, *Holy War Inc.*, al-Suri figures prominently in the opening chapter as CNN's tour guide to Afghanistan, but he is only referred to as 'Ali'.[94] In Mark Huband's well-known book *Warriors of the Prophet*, which contains one of the earliest accounts of al-Suri in the Western press, he is called 'Karim Omar'.[95]

---

respectively. The latter nickname was given to him allegedly because of his blond North-European appearance. See Luis Rendueles and Manuel Marlasca, '7-J: Los escritos del ideólogo', *Interviú*, 18 May 2005, www. interviu.es/default.asp?idpublicacio_PK=39&idioma=CAS&idnoticia_ PK=28299&idseccio_PK=547&h=050606, accessed July 2006.

91 For al-Suri's various aliases, see US Department of Justice, 'WANTED: Mustafa Setmariam Nasar', *Reward for Justice website*, www.rewardsforjustice. net/english/wanted_captured/index.cfm?page=Nasar, accessed July 2005; 'Terror suspect's profile,' *Associated Press*, 3 Aug. 2005; Ahmad Rafat, '3/11 mastermind's hideout' (in Spanish), *El Tiempo de Hoy* (Madrid), 9 Oct. 2004, via FBIS; and 'Meeting with the Kuwaiti Newspaper', transcript of audiofile no.2, p.3.

92 See Umar Abd al-Hakim, *A Summary of My Testimony on Jihad in Algeria, 1988-1996*, p.58 (hereafter *A Summary of My Testimony*).

93 Henry Schuster, 'The mastermind', *CNN.com*, 9 March 2006, www.cnn. com/2006/WORLD/meast/03/09/schuster.column/index.html, accessed Oct. 2006.

94 Peter Bergen, *Holy War Inc.: Inside the Secret World of Osama bin Laden* (London: Phoenix/Orion Books, 2002, revised edn), p.5.

95 Mark Huband, *Warriors of the Prophet: The Struggle for Islam* (Oxford and Boulder, CO: Westview Press, 1998), pp.1-4. After 9-11, Huband started to write about him as Omar Abdel Hakim. See his article 'Holy war on

To Britain's Channel 4 Television, he presented himself only as 'Oscar' when serving as their intermediary with bin Laden in late 1996.[96]

Abu Mus'ab al-Suri was born in the city of Aleppo (Halab) in North-Western Syria in October 1958.[97] His official biography, posted on his website, emphasises his prominent family background: his grandfathers were among 'the Noble Hasanides' (al-ashraf al-hasaniyun), who were the descendants of Hasan, the son of the fourth Caliph, Ali bin Abi Talib, and Fatima, who was the Prophet Muhammad's daughter.[98] Al-Suri's grandfather, Ahmad al-Rifa'i, was a master of a well-known religious Sufi brotherhood or tariqa. According to Aleppo genealogists, al-Rifa'i descended directly from Imam Qasim bin al-Imam Musa al-Kazim, and the tribe of Ali bin Abi Talib, the fourth Caliph.[99] In recent years, al-Suri's family also adopted the name 'al-Sitt Mariam' (lit. 'Lady Maryam'), after al-Suri's great great grandmother on his father's side. She was named Maryam and married a man called 'al-Muzayyik'. Her children subsequently became known as 'the children of Lady Maryam'.[100] The family also adopted the name Nasar after al-Suri's mother's father, al-Shaykh Muhammad Nasar, who originated from Egypt. His ancestors had

---

the world', *The Financial Times*, 28 Nov. 2001, http://specials.ft.com/attackonterrorism/FT3RXH0CKUC.html, accessed April 2006.

96 'Meeting with the Kuwaiti Newspaper', transcript of audiofile no.2, p.3.

97 The US Department of Justice gives the date 26 Oct. 1958 while the jihadi biography says 17 Rabi' al-Awwal 1378 which corresponds to 1 Oct. 1958. See US Department of Justice, 'WANTED: Mustafa Setmariam Nasar', *Rewards for Justice website*, www.rewardsforjustice.net/english/wanted_captured/index.cfm?page=Nasar, accessed July 2005; and 'Biography of Shaykh Umar Abd al-Hakim (Abu Mus'ab al-Suri)' (in Arabic), p.1.

98 See 'Biography of Shaykh Umar Abd al-Hakim (Abu Mus 'ab al-Suri)' (in Arabic); and 'The File of Abu Mus'ab al-Suri' (in Arabic), *minbar al-tawhid wa'l-jihad* website, www.tawhed.ws/a?I=78, accessed 15 July 2005.

99 See 'Meeting with the Kuwaiti Newspaper', transcript of audiofile no.1, p.1; and 'Biography of Shaykh Umar Abd al-Hakim (Abu Mus'ab al-Suri)' (in Arabic), p.1.

100 Ibid., p.1.

reportedly arrived in Syria during Ibrahim Pasha's famous military expedition to Syria in the mid-nineteenth century.[101]

Little is known about al-Suri's childhood and youth. He grew up in a conservative family who lived in a prominent old neighborhood of Aleppo, in a famous street, 'Aqiyo', meaning 'white hill' in Turkish.[102] Al-Suri completed most of his education in his home city, Syria's second largest.[103] He must have been a diligent and gifted pupil for in 1976, at the age of eighteen, he obtained the *al-thanawiya al-'ammah*, or graduation diploma, whereupon he enrolled at the University of Aleppo's department of mechanical engineering. The choice of engineering, rather than theology, is consistent with the fact that most Islamists have no formal training in theology and religion, despite their voluminous writings and strong opinions on religious issues. Instead, many are educated in secular sciences and qualify for prestigious middle-class professions such as lawyers, engineers, and doctors.

Al-Suri was at the University of Aleppo for four years. In 1980 he abandoned his studies two more years before completing his degree,[104] in order to join Syria's Islamist opposition. Henceforth his life was inextricably tied to the armed struggle against the Syrian regime, and subsequently, against all corrupt and oppressive Muslim rulers and their Western backers. This inaugurated his life as a jihadi.

---

101 'Biography of Shaykh Umar Abd al-Hakim (Abu Mus'ab al-Suri)' (in Arabic), p.1.

102 'Meeting with the Kuwaiti Newspaper', transcript of audiofile no.1, p.1.

103 Ibid.

104 Ibid.

# 2
# THE SYRIAN JIHAD

## TURMOIL AND UPRISING

During the 1970s, Syria was rocked by a wave of Islamist activism and political violence in which both regime and rebel elements perpetrated atrocities. The Syrian Muslim Brotherhood played a key role in this turmoil, and especially its militant offshoot, The Combatant Vanguard (*al-tali'ah al-muqatilah*).

The Muslim Brotherhood (MB) had been active in Syria since its foundation in 1944 under the leadership of Mustafa al-Sibai, but the movement was created largely through a merger of existing Islamist groups that had flourished in Syria since the early 1930s. A plethora of other Islamic groups also became active in Syria in the postwar period, such as The Islamic Liberation Party (*hizb al-tahrir*) and Muhammad's Youth (*shabab muhammad*), as well as the non-political missionary movement, The Society for Call and Preaching (*jama'at al-da'wah wa al-tabligh*), which was mostly active outside the cities. Religious activism became more widespread in mosques and a growing number of religious schools. The Syrian MB, which had fought on the Eastern front during the Arab-Israel war of 1948, prided itself in having participated in the struggle for liberation against French colonial rule. As with its Egyptian counterpart, the Syrian MB became involved in a wide range of religious, social and political activities. It entered parliamentary politics at an early stage and remained active till it was banned at the end of the 1950s. The Muslim Brotherhood then went underground, maintaining a significant presence among

35

students and in mosques. After the death of its first leader (*muraqib*), Mustafa al-Sibai, the movement was ridden by internal strife. Rival regional blocs emerged, in which the Damascus branch (headed by Isam al-Itar, who later left for Germany) competed with the Hama and Aleppo wings of the movement (headed by Sa'id Hawa and Abd al-Fattah Abu Ghiddah, respectively). The Guidance Council of the Brotherhood's international organization intervened to arbitrate, but failed to heal the rifts. Another split occurred in the 1970s when a bloc led by Muhammad Surur left the movement.[1]

During the 1970s, Syrian Islamists, first and foremost the MB and The Combatant Vanguard, launched armed campaigns against the Syrian regime.[2] Religious controversies often served to spark popular uprisings, although the underlying conflict also revolved around issues such as the distribution of power between different religious communities, the confrontation with Israel, Syria's military intervention in Lebanon, and atrocities committed by the Damascus regime. There were violent demonstrations in 1973 following attempts by the recently installed military dictator, General Hafiz al-Asad, from the minority Alawite sect, to introduce a constitution that no longer stipulated that the Syrian president should be a Muslim. When Syria intervened in the Lebanese civil war in support of the Christian Maronites in 1976, a new wave of violent protests erupted, and there were numerous assassination attempts on Syrian government officials. In mid-1979, Islamist gunmen, believed to be from The Combatant Vanguard, attacked an artillery school in Aleppo, during which more than eighty officers were killed, nearly all of them from the ruling Alawite minority. An open declaration of *jihad* on the government was proclaimed.

A series of new attacks by the Islamist rebels followed, accompanied by harsh government countermeasures, especially in the north-

---

1   See Umar Abd al-Hakim, *The Islamic Jihadi Revolution in Syria. Part I*, pp.63-4.

2   Carré and Michaud, *Les Frères musulmans: Egypte et Syrie 1928-1982* (Paris: Gallimard, 1983).

ern region, including al-Suri's home city of Aleppo. Armed groups proliferated and gained significant popular support. In early 1980, the insurrection had assumed nationwide proportions; demonstrations, general strikes, and gun battles between rebels and government forces rattled several Syrian cities, especially Aleppo, where the number of rebels may have exceeded 1,000.[3] Several hundred government officials and officers, as well as about two dozen Soviet advisers, were killed in various actions, especially car bombings and hit-and-run attacks by gunmen fleeing on motorbikes.[4] The government resorted to harsh military counterattacks, killing hundreds of protestors. Large-scale government atrocities against Islamist prisoners took place following an assassination attempt on President Asad in mid-1980.[5] Membership of the Muslim Brotherhood became a capital offence, but attacks on government and Alawite targets continued nevertheless. The insurrection culminated in February 1982, when the Muslim Brotherhood headed a rebellion in the city of Hama, nearly seizing control of the city. Syrian government forces launched an all-out counterattack, crushing the uprising and levelling the city. After nearly two weeks of fighting, between 10,000 and 30,000 people had been killed, including 1,000 government soldiers.

## JOINING THE REBELS

Al-Suri did not remain aloof from this struggle. According to his own account, he had had a traditional religious worldview till 1980, when he felt 'an internal mental pressure to return to the proper Islamic ideological norm'.[6] This religious awakening coincided with

---

3   This is al-Suri's estimate. See 'Meeting with the Kuwaiti Newspaper', transcript of audiofile no.2, p.8.

4   'Muslim Brotherhood in Syria 1965-1985', *The Armed Conflict Events Data (ACED)-project*, *OnWar.com*,16 Dec. 2000, at www.onwar.com/aced/data/sierra/syria1965.htm, accessed March 2006.

5   Carré and Michaud, *Les Frères musulmans*, pp.141-8.

6   'Meeting with the Kuwaiti Newspaper', transcript of audiofile no.1, pp.1-2.

the dramatic events taking place in Syria at the time. Al-Suri became involved with an armed jihadi group, broke off his university studies in Aleppo and eventually left the country.

The group that he joined in 1980 was The Combatant Vanguard Organization of the Muslim Brotherhood (*tanzim al-tali'ah al-muqatilah lil-ikhwan al-muslimin*), which had been founded in 1965 by Marwan Hadid.[7] The latter had become widely known in Syria after armed clashes erupted when government forces attacked the al-Sultan mosque in Hama in 1965. Hadid and several of his followers were later sentenced to death, but the intervention of leading religious personalities and the regime's fear that an already tense situation might escalate and spin out of control, led to their being released.[8]

The organization was not subordinate to the Muslim Brotherhood (MB) and differed substantially from it in ideological and tactical terms. The name was nevertheless selected because its members often considered themselves the 'real disciples' of the MB, founded by Hasan al-Banna and Sayyid Qutb, and followers of their 'true path'.[9] The Combatant Vanguard was perhaps the most prominent and active Islamist rebel group in Syria at the end of the 1970s. Through its clashes with the Syrian authorities it attempted to rally the Muslim Brotherhood in a joint campaign of violence designed to overthrow the Damascus regime. In June 1976 Hadid was captured and executed, but his group and many of his followers survived. Chief among them was Shaykh Adnan Uqlah, who became a leading figure in the

---

7   For a biography of Marwan Hadid, see 'Marwan Hadid the Martyr Star' (in Arabic), *sawt al-jihad*, no.11, pp.32-6.

8   See 'Biography of Shaykh Umar Abd al-Hakim (Abu Mus 'ab al-Suri)' (in Arabic), p.1. See also 'Meeting with the Kuwaiti Newspaper', transcript of audiofile no.2, p.7; and Umar Abd al-Hakim, *The Islamic Jihadi Revolution in Syria. Part I*, p.71.

9   Al-Suri had inquired among the organization's veterans about why The Combatant Vanguard had chosen this name, despite their differences with the MB. See 'Meeting with the Kuwaiti Newspaper', transcript of audiofile no.2, p.8.

Combatant Vanguard after Hadid's death. Around 1980, when the Syrian Muslim Brotherhood set up the umbrella group The Islamic Front in Syria, Uqlah became 'the chief co-ordinator of military organizations and the recruitment and organization of the mujahidun'.[10] At that point he was already an experienced fighter, having served many years in the Syrian army. However, Uqlah was not a member of the supreme leadership of 'The Islamic Front in Syria', and he later distanced himself from the Muslim Brotherhood in protest against the latter's willingness to ally itself with non-Islamist forces.[11]

Little is known about al-Suri's early involvement with The Combatant Vanguard. He was not involved in Marwan Hadid's group and learnt about it only later through university acquaintances. While Uqlah also lived in Aleppo, al-Suri only met him later in exile in Jordan, suggesting that al-Suri played only a minor role in the organization at this period.[12]

Al-Suri joined the The Combatant Vanguard on 27 Rajab 1400, corresponding to 11 June 1980, a date he recalled very clearly in a 1999 interview. This was the starting point of his militant career, and it must have been a dramatic experience for the 21-year-old student. After three or four months his unit began playing 'a big role' in the movement, al-Suri later recalled. They were 'providing services to the mujahidin and undertaking some minor jihadi operations'.[13] Shortly afterwards, the Syrian authorities uncovered almost the entire group to which al-Suri belonged, arresting many of its members.[14] The Combatant Vanguard was in crisis: Al-Suri and his remaining fellow jihadis were advised to leave the country and flee to Jordan[15] and he left Syria at the end of 1980.[16] Al-Suri was subsequently blacklisted

---

10  Dr Umar F. Abd-Allah, *The Islamic Struggle in Syria* , pp.127-8.

11  Ibid., pp.195-6.

12  'Meeting with the Kuwaiti Newspaper', transcript of audiofile no.1, p.2.

13  Ibid.

14  Ibid.

15  Ibid.

16  'Meeting with the Kuwaiti Newspaper', transcript of audiofile no.2, p.8.

by the Syrian government and an arrest warrant was reportedly issued against him.[17] It is not known whether he ever returned to the country of his birth.

A JIHADI IN EXILE

Al-Suri arrived in Jordan in late 1980 or early 1981 and stayed there on-and-off till mid-1983.[18] In Amman, al-Suri joined the Syrian MB proper, even though he had been a member of The Combatant Vanguard, its more radical affiliate. He later explained that this was because he and his fellow travellers were young and inexperienced—they were still only in their early twenties—and often unaware of the ideological differences and tensions inside the Syrian Muslim Brotherhood. He joined the MB 'on the premise that they were among the people of jihad'[19] and remained with it more or less till 1983. However, as will be seen, al-Suri subsequently became one of the Muslim Brothers' fiercest and most articulate critics.

The Syrian MB regrouped in Jordan and strove to rebuild the organization from among former fighters and other Syrian youths living in exile. Among them was a group of Syrian army officers who arrived in Amman and joined the Syrian MB after fleeing the crackdown on the opposition.[20] Al-Suri lived in a safe house in Amman and at the end of 1980 was appointed as 'emir of a group of brothers'.[21] Shortly afterwards, in early 1981, he was sent to Baghdad for

---

17 'Report Details Hunt for Al-Qa'ida's Abu Musab Al-Suri', (FBIS-title) *The News* (Islamabad), 24 Nov. 2004.

18 According to information in an excerpt entitled 'The Individual Jihad' (ca. 03:00-03:10) from a lecture series published as 'The Media Front Presents "Precious Lectures": "Jihad is the Solution" ... Excerpts from Abu Mus'ab al-Suri, The al-Ghuraba Camp' (in Arabic), *minbar ahl al-sunna wa'l-jama'ah*, 29 Sept. 2005, www.sunna-minbar.net/forum/viewtopic.php?t=493, accessed April 2006

19 'Meeting with the Kuwaiti Newspaper', transcript of audiofile no.1, p.2.

20 Ibid.

21 Ibid.

military training, together with many other Syrian MB youths. He remained there for several months, participating in courses run by the 'Popular Army' branch of the Iraqi army, which arranged for all military training courses for Syrian MB cadres in Iraq at that time.[22] Syrian officers who had fled Syria also assisted in training the Syrian MB.[23] Al-Suri proved a skilled trainee and was subsequently given responsibility for running a course.

This period of military training and preparation also allowed for meetings with well-known figures in other Islamist movements. Al-Suri recalled in particular his encounters with Shaykh Abd al-Aziz Ali, better known by his *nom de guerre*, Abu Usama al-Misri. He had been a member of the Egyptian Muslim Brotherhood's military wing, the so-called 'Special Apparatus' (*al-jihaz al-khass*), established around 1940 and was regarded as one of the MB's most prominent military figures. He had known and sworn an oath of allegiance to Hasan al-Banna, the founding father of the Muslim Brotherhood, and its supreme guide until his assassination in February 1949. Abu Usama had also participated in the Palestine war in 1948 and in the armed campaign against British troops in the Suez Canal zone in the early 1950s. He had been close to Sayyid Qutb, but left Egypt and offered his training services in PLO (Palestine Liberation Organisation) camps in Jordan in 1969.[24] He allegedly participated in many subsequent armed Islamist campaigns where the Muslim Brotherhood was said to have played a role, such as in Yemen and Eritrea.

In the early 1980s, Shaykh Abu Usama was heavily involved in offering assistance to the Syrian Islamists and according to al-Suri's account had brought with him twenty-eight brothers to work as mili-

---

22  Ibid. See also *The Global Islamic Resistance Call*, p.1375.

23  'Biography of Shaykh Umar Abd al-Hakim (Abu Mus 'ab al-Suri)' (in Arabic), p.1.

24  *The Global Islamic Resistance Call*, p.1375. For more details on the early history of the Egyptian Muslim Brotherhood, see Brynjar Lia, *The Society of the Muslim Brothers in Egypt, 1928-1942* (Reading: Ithaca Press, 1998).

41

tary trainers and instructors for the Syrian MB.[25] Al-Suri and another young Syrian at the Baghdad camp were picked out to become military instructors, despite their relative inexperience, and both joined Shaykh Abu Usama's team. Al-Suri and his colleagues studied with the veteran fighter for two months, focusing in particular on military explosive engineering, which subsequently became one of al-Suri's fields of expertise. Abu Usama taught al-Suri and his colleagues the jihadi doctrine of terrorism, which is partly justified by the Quranic verse 60 (Surat al-Anfal): 'Against them make ready your strength to the utmost of your power, including steeds of war, to strike terror into (the hearts of) the enemies, of Allah and your enemies.' The first words in this verse are also reproduced on the Muslim Brotherhood's banner. Al-Suri recalls that at the beginning of their first class with Abu Usama, the latter had written on the blackboard the title of the lecture: 'Terrorism is a religious duty, and assassination is a Prophetic tradition.'[26]

Shaykh Abu Usama went to Afghanistan during the late 1980s, even though by then he was sixty-five.[27] The veteran jihadi globetrotter was a great role model for the young al-Suri: 'This blessed man has left a legacy in me until this day', he later confided.[28] The example of Shaykh Abu Usama also demonstrates how the Arab-Afghan phenomenon, namely jihadi volunteers who fought in Afghanistan and later migrated from one conflict to another, was not entirely new and had deep roots in Islamist movements. As an historical phenomenon, it has obvious parallels in the dispatch of thousands of volunteer fighters to Palestine in 1948 and other anti-colonial wars in the Islamic world. Many Arab volunteers also went to fight alongside the Palestinian resistance organizations in Lebanon following

---

25 'Meeting with the Kuwaiti Newspaper', transcript of audiofile no.1, p.2.

26 *The Global Islamic Resistance Call*, p.1375.

27 Ibid.

28 Ibid. Al-Suri also mentions Shaykh Abd al-Aziz Ali and quotes him in his first book, see Umar Abd al-Hakim, *The Islamic Jihadi Revolution in Syria. Part I*, p.160.

the Israeli invasion in 1978, with strong encouragement from the Muslim Brotherhood.[29]

After completing Shaykh Abu Usama's courses, al-Suri began running training courses in military explosives engineering in Baghdad. Then he returned to Amman where he continued in his role as a military instructor at the MB's safe houses in the city. Together with one of his students, he began developing new course material in explosive engineering, combining insights from his military explosive course and his university studies in mechanical engineering. Their booklet, which became known as The Syrian Memorandum (al-mudhakkirah al-suriyyah), was later used in the Arab-Afghan camps in Afghanistan, al-Suri recalls.[30]

In 1980-2 al-Suri underwent a dramatic transformation from an ordinary university student in Aleppo to an active member of an armed Islamist organization, travelling abroad, becoming acquainted with well-known Islamist veterans, and developing the essential skills required for running clandestine violent campaigns. By 1982 he had served as a military instructor at the MB's military camps in both Jordan and Iraq. Given the role he played at this early stage, when he was known by the nom de guerre Abu al-Abd, al-Suri, also begun to develop his own network of students, disciples and contacts.[31]

In 1981, a few months before the assassination of the Egyptian President Anwar al-Sadat, the Syrian MB sent some of its cadres for military training to Egypt, according to al-Suri.[32] While it had long been known that Iraq, and, to a lesser extent, Jordan, provided such training to the Syrian opposition in the early 1980s, less has been known of Egypt's role in this regard. Al-Suri claims to have

---

29  See, for example, Document no.AFGP-2002-600087, 'Book by Mustafa Hamid', Combating Terrorism Center website (West Point), www.ctc. usma.edu/aq/AFGP-2002-600087-Trans.pdf, accessed Dec. 2006, p.3.

30  'Meeting with the Kuwaiti Newspaper', transcript of audiofile no.1, p.2.

31  'Biography of Shaykh Umar Abd al-Hakim (Abu Mus'ab al-Suri)' (in Arabic), p.1.

32  'Meeting with the Kuwaiti Newspaper', transcript of audiofile, no.1, p.2.

been an eyewitness to a clandestine security training program that Egypt organized for the Syrian Muslim Brotherhood. A prime facilitator behind this initiative was Abd al-Haqq Shahadah,[33] one of the senior officers who had fled Syria and now lived in Egypt.[34] Due to his excellent connections in the state bureaucracy, Shahadah facilitated training courses in Egypt in 'security' and 'guerrilla warfare' techniques for the Syrian MB. These differed from the organized and formal military training that the Syrian MB received in Iraq, and were therefore deemed very useful to the group. Furthermore, by seeking out training opportunities in Egypt, the Syrian Islamists hoped to lessen their dependence on their sanctuary and training bases in Baghdad. This dependency would have had catastrophic consequences had the Iraqi regime suddenly revised its policy towards the Syrian Islamist opposition.[35]

In early 1981 al-Suri was appointed second-in-command of ten Syrian MB fighters travelling to Cairo for paramilitary training, where, according to him, they stayed for nearly six weeks. The program was initially scheduled to last six months, but the length of the course was drastically reduced due to President Sadat's escalating conflict with the Egyptian Islamist opposition. The course had apparently ended well before Sadat's assassination on 6 October 1981. In an interview in 1999, al-Suri praised the quality of the course, which was conducted by Egyptian experts 'in guerrilla warfare techniques, security affairs, and external terrorist operations'.[36] It included

---

33 The exact spelling of his name is uncertain due to the poor quality of the tape recording.

34 Shahadah made frequent visits to Saudi Arabia. He was apparently responsible for 'the Eritrean file' in the Muslim Brotherhood and was a close friend of the famous Syrian MB leader Shaykh Sa'id Hawwa. Shahadah had been a political refugee in Egypt during the Nasser period and was considered a Nasserite before he became deeply religious and began 'serving with the Syrian jihadi revolution'. See 'Meeting with the Kuwaiti Newspaper', transcript of audiofile, no.1, p.2.

35 'Meeting with the Kuwaiti Newspaper', transcript of audiofile no.1, p.3.

36 Ibid., p.3. See also *The Global Islamic Resistance Call*, p.1415.

everything from basic security principles, interrogation techniques, procedures for dealing with security organizations, to how to carry out certain 'external operations'.[37] The course was not organized in a regular military camp, but was held in a residential villa. The team of instructors consisted of as many as fourteen Egyptian officers, the lowest ranking officer being lieutenant. The course supervisor was a lieutenant general, something that evidently impressed the young al-Suri.[38] Being still in his early twenties, he must have had a strong feeling that his future role as a jihadi was of immense importance, given that powerful states like Egypt were dedicating their best resources to train him. Although in hindsight he says he had certain ideological reservations about being trained by the Egyptian government, he obviously had a very strong sense of mission when he left Cairo. Al-Suri later recalled that when he and his fellow trainee comrades returned to Amman, 'we carried on our shoulders the responsibility for developing the military struggle and the training of the Muslim Brotherhood'.[39] In the late 1980s, when he started working as a trainer at the Arab-Afghan camps in Afghanistan, he took much pleasure in the notion that 'the Egyptian military had trained me, and now, I have trained for them tens, perhaps hundreds of people, who are trainees and commanders in the *Egyptian Jihad Group* (jama'at al-jihad) and the *Islamic Group* (al-jama'ah al-islamiyyah)'.[40] As is well known, these two organizations were till recently the two most deadly foes of the Egyptian regime.

The Syrian MB also trained in Jordan, which al-Suri described as being supportive of the Syrian MB's struggle. The authorities even permitted the opening of a training center, or 'an institute', located in Amman.[41] It operated relatively secretly, albeit with the knowledge and tolerance of the Jordanian government. Here, the Syrians re-

37  Ibid.
38  Ibid.
39  Ibid.
40  'Meeting with the Kuwaiti Newspaper', transcript of audiofile no.1, p.6.
41  Ibid, p.3.

ceived military, ideological and religious training in some two dozen topics, including handling of small arms, logistics, and communications. Al-Suri himself studied military engineering. Discipline was harsh, and the examinations tough to pass. Internal cohesion was also maintained through the way the Syrian MB organized its cadres. Each member was placed in a 'family' (*usrah*, pl. *usar*), consisting of five members, in which a full set of duties, rules, and guidelines were enforced. This was a well-tried model, adopted from the Egyptian mother-organization. Following the more theoretically orientated instruction imparted in Jordan, cadres were sent for a one month military training program in Iraq, where the focus was on practical skills. When he later compared the Syrian MB's program to that of the Afghan training camps in the late 1980s, al-Suri admitted that 'in terms of preparing them [i.e. the Syrian MB] and organizing them for productive work, that program was much better'.[42]

There were several reasons why the Jordanian, Iraqi, and perhaps also Egyptian regimes were willing to support the Syrian MB in its armed campaign against the Syrian regime. At the time, Syria supported Iran in its eight year-war against Iraq (1980-8), and Iraq had every reason to make Syria pay dearly for this policy. Most Arab countries also sided with Iraq. Syria strongly opposed Egypt's and Jordan's rapprochement with Israel, and provided sanctuary and support to militant groups which targeted these countries. Hence, the Syrian opposition found ample opportunity to play on these conflicts and elicit assistance from Syria's regional rivals. Jordan's support for, or at least tolerance of, activities of Syrian insurgents on its territory, resulted in counterattacks by the Syrian government. For example, in January 1981, a group of Syrian officers was arrested in Jordan for attempting to assassinate the Jordanian prime minister, Mudar Badran. The Syrian government accused him of supporting the rebels. The enmity between the two countries lasted until 1985, when several of the most contentious issues were resolved.[43]

---

42 Ibid.

43 Carré and Michaud, *Les Frères musulmans: Egypte et Syrie 1928-1982*,

## THE HAMA DEBACLE

The escalating struggle between the Damascus regime and the Islamists in the city of Hama propelled the young al-Suri into a prominent position in the Syrian MB. It is possible that the leadership's decision was in recognition of his newly-acquired military qualifications, in which he reportedly excelled. However, al-Suri later suspected that he and the other young cadres with military training had been promoted to head the offensive because the Syrian MB's political leadership did not want to get too heavily involved, in case the offensive failed.[44] The MB command in Baghdad appointed al-Suri to be a member of the Higher Military Command, headed by Shaykh Sa'id al-Hawwa,[45] and despite his young age al-Suri suddenly found himself appointed second-in-command of 'the Aleppo offensive', a campaign which was expected to advance towards Aleppo in early 1982. Al-Suri remained in Iraq and during the three critical months of 1982 he spent every day with the Syrian MB's military leadership there and became familiar with the organization from within. Fighting in Hama erupted in earnest in February 1982 when the military brought its full force to bear on the Syrian MB's strongholds in the city. Tens of thousands of people were killed. As the catastrophic outcome became clear, al-Suri grew increasingly disillusioned with the Syrian MB's political and military prowess.

As the Hama Uprising was quashed in February 1982, and the city almost destroyed by Syrian government forces, al-Suri resigned from the MB, primarily over ideological differences. He became particularly incensed by the leadership's willingness to seek political compromises with the secular Syrian nationalist and communist opposition. His condemnation also extended to the Iraqi MB's relationship with the Iraqi Ba'thist party. In al-Suri's eyes, the MB

---

pp.146-8; and 'Muslim Brotherhood in Syria 1965-1985', *The Armed Conflict Events Data (ACED)-project*, *OnWar.com*, 16 Dec. 2000, at www.onwar.com/aced/data/sierra/syria1965.htm, accessed Dec. 2005.

44  'Meeting with the Kuwaiti Newspaper', transcript of audiofile no.1, p.3.

45  Ibid.

suffered from 'corruption' and 'malfeasance'.[46] This manifested itself in its willingness to seek defeatist compromises with secularist and nationalist forces, even the Syrian regime, and to sacrifice its fighting units inside Syria to achieve short-term political gains. Al-Suri came to see the MB's leadership and its policies as the primary factors behind the failure of the Islamist uprising. It displayed hesitancy and half-heartedness in preparing for a full-scale insurrection, and it boycotted The Combatant Vanguard units in Syria which did most of the actual fighting. Worst of all, the MB began discussions with the secularist opposition, and hinted of a possible compromise with the regime: 'the result of the nationalist alliance was catastrophe and defeat. It was one of the doors to deviation on the level of Islamic activism as a whole, not only for Syria'.[47] Al-Suri also blamed the MB for 'factionalism' and for 'lying to us big time', especially with regards to The Combatant Vanguard and its leader Adnan al-Uqlah, whom the MB had accused of being a rebel who sought personal gains.[48] Al-Suri met with Adnan al-Uqlah for the first time in Amman in 1982, after the events of Hama, and found him to be a man of vision with a program for the future struggle. Al-Suri rejoined The Combatant Vanguard although the latter suffered from a lack of resources to restart the political and military campaign, and he stayed in contact with it even though he spent most of his time outside the region.

Contemporary sources describe the internal rifts within the Syrian Islamist movement in the early 1980s as a conflict revolving around the issue of alliances, both external and internal and whether a compromise with the Syrian regime was possible. The more radical and uncompromising members coalesced around Adnan al-Uqla and The Combatant Vanguard, which seceded from the Syrian MB in late 1981. The secession followed nine months of unsuccessful negotiations to achieve a unified leadership and the split was formalised in

---

46  Ibid.

47  Ibid.

48  Ibid., p.4.

April 1982, after the Hama events, though differences of opinion over these issues had been apparent since the early 1970s.[49]

On a more personal level, the destruction of Hama and the large-scale killings must have left a deep impression on the young al-Suri, even though he was not an eyewitness to the fighting and massacres. He later recalled with bitterness how other Arab states, which initially had provided assistance and training to the insurgency, had stood idly by as Syrian fighter jets and artillery bombarded the city for nearly two weeks. He claimed that nearly 40,000 people were killed and that the news agencies kept silent about the massacre for more than three years. In his view, this illustrated the extent to which there had been 'a process of conspiracy' against the Syrian people in general, and the jihadi movement in particular.[50]

### IN EXILE IN SAUDI ARABIA

In his writings al-Suri recalls his profound disillusionment with 'the military jihad' of the Syrian MB in the wake of the Hama debacle. He questioned the wisdom of launching a military campaign when the ideological and theological basis for the struggle was not, as he saw it, solid, hence he and some of his cohorts decided to 'abandon the military struggle and devote themselves to religious learning'.[51] Al-Suri and his colleagues left Baghdad for Saudi Arabia in mid-

---

49 When asked by a reporter why they seceded from 'the unified command' of the Syrian Muslim Brotherhood, The Combatant Vanguard gave the following response: 'An agreement for a unified leadership was signed to group all forces against the regime, but it went the opposite way. Our forces were frozen because the others are not trained and are not ready to fight. We made three conditions for joining the leadership: that we would not lay down our arms or give up jihad; that we would never negotiate with the regime; and that there would be no alliance with the political parties. They did not stick to their word and made a secret alliance with the political parties.' Cited in 'SYRIA: Muslim Brothers, the Question of Alliances...', *The Middle East Magazine*, May 1983.

50 'Meeting with the Kuwaiti Newspaper', transcript of audiofile no.3, p.1.

51 'Meeting with the Kuwaiti Newspaper', transcript of audiofile no.1, p.3.

1982, his intention being to study at Medina's Islamic University. He attempted to enrol at the University, but it is uncertain whether he succeeded in doing so. His recent involvement in the armed uprising in Syria, and, more importantly, his disagreements with the MB leadership and inclination to share these views with others, 'created a crisis' for him and other Syrian students in Saudi Arabia.[52] There were many Muslim Brotherhood members and sympathizers among the scholars at the University and al-Suri felt that they put obstacles in the paths of him and the other Syrian MB dissidents: their applications were denied, their monthly stipends were cut off, they were refused entrance to the university, and their rents were increased. Some of the Syrian students yielded to the pressure and renewed their allegiance (*bay'ah*) to the Muslim Brotherhood. Al-Suri felt that he could no longer endure the suffocating atmosphere and the harassment in Saudi Arabia.[53] One of his relatives offered to help him travel to France to study on the condition that al-Suri pledged to assist his fellow countrymen in attaining education after he graduated. After completing the Hajj, he left for France in 1983 to continue his studies in engineering. For the next fifteen years he would have a permanent base in Europe from which he pursued his cause.

---

52  Ibid., pp.3-4.
53  Ibid., p.4.

# 3

# EXILE IN EUROPE

## BETWEEN EXILE IN FRANCE AND THE SYRIAN JIHAD

The destruction of Hama, al-Suri's growing disagreements with the Syrian MB, and his unwillingness to conform to the MB-dominated university environment in Saudi Arabia inaugurated al-Suri's life as a jihadi activist in European exile, first in France and later in Spain and Britain. In France, he enrolled to study engineering at a university, after having taken French language courses, but it is not known which one. Al-Suri says he intended to complete his engineering degree there, but he appears to have remained heavily involved in Islamist politics. He described this period as one of uncertainty about his future course of action ('I had to choose between studies and jihadi work') and after much deliberation he postponed his engineering studies to in order devote himself more fully to 'the Syrian jihad'.[1] Hence, it is uncertain how much time he actually spent in France. According to one account, he was there for half of 1983, 1984, and early 1985.[2]

In 1983 Adnan al-Uqlah attempted to 'rebuild the jihad in Syria'.[3] In a seemingly desperate attempt to demonstrate the existence and vitality of The Combatant Vanguard, he crossed the border with seventy of his men, arriving there in small groups. However, the

---

1   Ibid.

2   'Biography of Shaykh Umar Abd al-Hakim (Abu Mus'ab al-Suri)' (in Arabic), p.2.

3   'Meeting with the Kuwaiti Newspaper', transcript of audiofile no.1, p.4.

51

Syrian intelligence services had infiltrated one of its agents in the group's Jordanian branch and al-Uqlah and his men were captured shortly after their arrival. Al-Suri was to have been among the last Combatant Vanguard group to enter Syria with al-Uqlah. When the news of the arrests came, al-Suri had already gone to Turkey where he and his comrades were awaiting orders to travel to Syria. Al-Suri then returned to France to continue his studies.

Despite the failure to get a sizeable group of fighters into Syria and the setback of al-Uqlah's capture, there were still many young Combatant Vanguard members who wished to relaunch an armed struggle. They argued that it was impermissible to settle down, get married, and begin a professional carreer when so many of their brothers had become martyrs or were languishing in Syrian jails.[4] Accordingly al-Suri participated in the second attempt to restart the military struggle around 1984.[5] He claims to have been entrusted with a leadership role and again broke off his studies in France in order to prepare for this task.[6] It appears that these endeavours revolved less around smuggling fighters into Syria, and more around identifying and contacting remaining and former Syrian Combatant Vanguard members, who, at this point, were scattered throughout the world, although most of them resided in Jordan, Iraq, Saudi Arabia and the rest of the Arabian peninsula, and in several European countries. Having taken stock of the remaining Combatant Vanguard members through visits and contacts, al-Suri claims that another attempt at reviving the Syrian jihad was launched, but he provides no further details of the campaign, other than the fact that 'it failed'.[7]

As al-Suri recounts events, this second attempt did produce one positive outcome for the Syrian jihadis. The networking among Combatant Vanguard veterans allowed for new personal relation-

---

4   Ibid.

5   The jihadi biography of al-Suri dates this attempt to 1985. See 'Biography of Shaykh Umar Abd al-Hakim (Abu Mus'ab al-Suri)' (in Arabic), p.2.

6   'Meeting with the Kuwaiti Newspaper', transcript of audiofile no.1, p.4.

7   Ibid.

ships to be established. In their search for material support and a safe haven where their fighters could gather together and train, several Jordanian MB clerics whom they still trusted advised them to travel to Afghanistan to meet Shaykh Abdallah Azzam. He was the leader of the Peshawar-based Arab-Afghan mujahidin movement, which at this point, in the early- to mid-1980s, was still in its infancy. Although born in the West Bank town of Nablus, Azzam had spent many years in Jordan and was well-known in Islamist circles there.[8] Azzam left Jordan for Afghanistan in April 1981, but came back each summer between 1982 and 1984,[9] hence it is not unlikely that al-Suri had the opportunity to meet him. In fact, he claims to have had 'a very short meeting' with Azzam in Jordan.[10] However, more important were the recommendations from Jordanian MB clerics and the military training they had received at MB camps in Iraq. These must have been important assets for al-Suri and his colleagues when they arrived in Afghanistan in 1987 in search of new avenues for their struggle.

As al-Suri had by now abandoned his studies in France, he started to look elsewhere for a place to live. In either 1984 or 1985 he enrolled at Beirut University's branch in Amman, in the Faculty of History, where he subsequently took correspondence courses. Even though he spent little time at the university, he managed to obtain the Degree of Licensiate (BA) in History in 1991.[11] By then he had

---

8    For an excellent biography of Abdallah Azzam, see Thomas Hegghammer, 'Abdallah Azzam: L'imam du jihad' in Gilles Kepel (ed.), *Al-Qaida dans le texte* (Paris: Presses Universitaires de France, 2005), pp.115-37.

9    For this information I am indebted to Thomas Hegghammer, who interviewed Abdallah Azzam's son Hudhayfa in Amman in Sept. 2006.

10   'Meeting with the Kuwaiti Newspaper', transcript of audiofile no.1.

11   The sources do not agree on the date of al-Suri's graduation. Al-Suri himself thinks it must have been in 1989 while the biographer dates it to 1991. See 'Biography of Shaykh Umar Abd al-Hakim (Abu Mus'ab al-Suri)' (in Arabic), pp.2-3; and 'Meeting with the Kuwaiti Newspaper', transcript of audiofile no.1.

already demonstrated his historiographical talents in his detailed analysis of the Syrian Islamist movement.[12]

## IN ANDALUS

Al-Suri was determined not to lose his foothold in Europe and when some of his Syrian acquaintances in Spain invited him to settle there instead, al-Suri was happy to accept their offer. In early 1985, he left France for Spain, arriving as an illegal immigrant, and made his first efforts to legalize his residency in Madrid in March 1986.[13]

It is not entirely clear how much time al-Suri spent in Spain, although he did marry and start a family there.[14] According to his own account, al-Suri stayed in Spain, on and off, for nearly ten years, till the mid-1990s, although between 1987 and 1992 he spent much of his time in Afghanistan. The US government has reported that al-Suri presumably 'travelled widely throughout the Middle East and North Africa' in this period.[15] Al-Suri seems to have lived mostly in Madrid during the mid- and late 1980s, before moving to Granada. When he returned from Afghanistan in late 1991 or early 1992, he still lived in Granada, which he termed 'his place of residence'.[16] He

---

12 He published a two volume work in Peshawar in May 1991 entitled *The Islamic Jihadi Revolution in Syria. Part I. The Experience and Lessons (Hopes and Pains)* and *The Islamic Jihadi Revolution in Syria: Part II. Ideology and Program (Studies and Basics on the Path of Armed Revolutionary Jihad)* (in Arabic).

13 José María Irujo, 'El hombre de Bin Laden en Madrid', *El País*, 2 March 2005, www.elPaís.es/comunes/2005/11m/08_comision/libro_electronico_red_islam/red_islamista_01%20doc.pdf, accessed July 2006, p.15.

14 'Biography of Shaykh Umar Abd al-Hakim (Abu Mus 'ab al-Suri)' (in Arabic), p.3.

15 'WANTED: Mustafa Setmariam Nasar', *Reward for Justice website*, www.rewardsforjustice.net/english/wanted_captured/index.cfm?page=Nasar, accessed July 2005.

16 Umar Abd al-Hakim, *A Summary of My Testimony*, p.20. See also Antonio Rubio, 'Mustafa Setmarian Naser: Un español en la cima de Al Qaeda: Durante los diez años que vivió en España se convirtió en lugarteniente de Bin Laden', *elmundo.es*, 3 Nov. 2005, www.elmundo.es/elmundo/2005/11/03/

moved back to Madrid with his family and settled in León Felipe Street before they went to London in June 1995.[17]

Southern Spain in general, and Granada in particular, has a special place in Islamic history, being known as 'Andalus', and often portrayed as a lost paradise, a Muslim land occupied by the Crusaders and Infidels during the Middle Ages. This special significance was never lost on al-Suri. He recalled that when he was based in Granada, he used to live in 'Andalus', not only in the symbolic meaning of the word, but also in a direct physical sense, since his apartment was near a road intersection in Granada called the Andalucia Crossroad.[18]

Like many other Arab refugees in Spain, al-Suri suffered the difficulties that confront immigrants in Europe. Lacking legal residency papers and a steady source of income, he lived the kind of underground life that many immigrants do. Furthermore, al-Suri probably had to be cautious about revealing too much about his own background in the Syrian Islamist movement. When explaining his inability to return to Syria, he said it was because he had evaded military service.[19] His Western appearance may have saved him from the kind of discrimination that many of his fellow Arab immigrants sometimes had to endure. A Spanish police report, probably from the early or mid-1990s, described him as 'red-haired, 1.70 meters

---

espana/1131002447.html, accessed Dec. 2005; José María Irujo, 'El hombre de Bin Laden en Madrid', *El País* 2 March 2005, www.elPaís. es/comunes/2005/11m/08_comision/libro_electronico_red_islam/red_ islamista_01%20doc.pdf, accessed July 2006, p.16; 'Un testigo identificó a Setmarian: La Audiencia Nacional reabre la causa sobre el atentado en el restaurante El Descanso en 1985', *elmundo.es*, 9 Nov. 2005, www.elmundo. es/elmundo/2005/11/09/espana/1131539640.html, accessed July 2006; and Leslie Crawford, 'A Dangerous Subject', *Financial Times Magazine*, 15-16 July 2006, p.20.

17 'Juzgado Central de Instruccion Nº 005, Madrid, Sumario, 17 Sept. 2003', pp.28-29, 296, and 466. See also 'Meeting with the Kuwaiti Newspaper', transcript of audiofile no.2, p.3.

18 'Meeting with the Kuwaiti Newspaper', transcript of audiofile no.2, p.3.

19 José María Irujo, 'El hombre de Bin Laden en Madrid', *El País*, 2 March 2005, www.elPaís.es/comunes/2005/11m/08_comision/libro_electronico_ red_islam/red_islamista_01%20doc.pdf, accessed July 2006, p.16.

tall, with green eyes, a short, trimmed beard, light complexion, and a Western appearance'.[20] During his first years in Spain, al-Suri's material situation was very difficult. He reportedly eked out a living by selling Arab and Indian items from a stall in the Rastro flea market in Madrid,[21] a period he later recalled by saying that he could not afford even to make a backup copy of his first book manuscript.[22] However, his financial circumstances gradually improved as he established a small export-import business, which gave him a steady income. He ran his business till his preoccupation with the Afghan liberation war began to consume most of his energies in the late 1980s.[23]

In late 1987 or early 1988, al-Suri married Elena Moreno Cruz, a Spanish woman, whom he had met at a language school in Madrid, where she studied English and German philology.[24] The 24-year-old Moreno Cruz also worked part-time as an odontologist assistant. Their wedding ceremony was held according to Islamic customs at a mosque in Madrid. Moreno Cruz reportedly converted to Islam, studied Arabic and the Quran, and observed Muslim dress codes by wearing a veil.[25] She also went with her husband to Miranshah on the Afghan-Pakistani border in 1988, where they

---

20  Ibid.

21  Ibid.

22  'Meeting with the Kuwaiti Newspaper', transcript of audiofile no.1, p.5.

23  Al-Suri could not recall the exact date. 'Meeting with the Kuwaiti Newspaper', transcript of audiofile no.2, pp.1-2.

24  Antonio Rubio, 'Mustafa Setmarian Naser: Un español en la cima de Al Qaeda: Durante los diez años que vivió en España se convirtió en lugarteniente de Bin Laden', *elmundo.es*, 3 Nov. 2005, www.elmundo.es/elmundo/2005/11/03/espana/1131002447.html, accessed Dec. 2005; and José María Irujo, *El Agujero: España invadida por la yihad* (Madrid: Aguilar, 2005), p.25.

25  Antonio Rubio, 'Mustafa Setmarian Naser: Un español en la cima de Al Qaeda: Durante los diez años que vivió en España se convirtió en lugarteniente de Bin Laden', *elmundo.es*, 3 Nov. 2005, www.elmundo.es/elmundo/2005/11/03/espana/1131002447.html, accessed Dec. 2005.

stayed for a considerable time. Through this marriage, al-Suri also obtained Spanish citizenship.[26]

Al-Suri's relationship with his family-in-law was reportedly difficult. Elena Moreno's mother was a housewife and her father a factory worker. They lived in a simple flat in the Madrid area of Moratalaz. When al-Suri was presented to his new future in-laws for the first time in 1987, he declined wine and he made no secret of his strong views on Islamic lifestyle. As Elena Moreno quickly began adjusting to her new life as a Muslim woman, her father had reportedly accused al-Suri of 'dragging' his daughter into Muslim religiosity, forcing her to depart from her previous worldviews as 'an agnostic and a leftist'.[27] Her parents did not attend their wedding. The relationship between her parents and al-Suri remained strained, although it did improve little by little during the 1990s. However, at the end of the decade, when the family moved to Pakistan and Kabul, the new security circumstances no longer permitted frequent and direct contact with her family.[28]

A number of jihadis in Europe have married Western women with the primary intention of obtaining citizenship. One of the suspects in the Madrid train bombings in 2004 had reportedly taken part in discussions on whether it was permissible to marry infidels in order to secure ID-papers for the jihadi cause. With regards to al-Suri, there is no doubt that he married Elena Moreno out of love and passion. Al-Suri 'parecia "ensimismado" por Elena'—'he appeared

---

26 'WANTED: Mustafa Setmariam Nasar', *Reward for Justice website*, www. rewardsforjustice.net/english/wanted_captured/index.cfm?page=Nasar, accessed July 2005; 'Terror suspect's profile,' *Associated Press*, 3 Aug. 2005; and Antonio Rubio, 'Mustafa Setmarian Naser: Un español en la cima de Al Qaeda: Durante los diez años que vivió en España se convirtió en lugarteniente de Bin Laden', *elmundo.es* 3 Nov. 2005, www.elmundo.es/ elmundo/2005/11/03/espana/1131002447.html, accessed Dec. 2005.

27 José María Irujo, *El Agujero*, p.25.

28 José María Irujo, 'El hombre de Bin Laden en Madrid', *El País*, 2 March 2005, www.elPaís.es/comunes/2005/11m/08_comision/libro_electronico_ red_islam/red_islamista_01%20doc.pdf, accessed July 2006, p.16.

to be lost in her', according to friends of the couple.[29] This being said, the Spanish passport, which he obtained through his marriage, clearly facilitated al-Suri's freedom of movement in Europe and the Middle East.

After their marriage, the couple settled in an apartment in León Felipe Street in Madrid. However, they soon left Madrid and settled in Granada in Southern Spain, where they lived in a rented flat in the nearby town of Alfacar. Al-Suri also brought his young family to Jordan in order for them to meet his parents. Back in Granada, al-Suri established a shop in Elvira Street, selling clothes, gifts and handicraft products. He procured sewing machines with the purpose of starting small-scale clothing production in the basement of their flat, a project that met with little success.[30] A reason for this was his growing preoccupation with the Afghanistan liberation war and the Arab-Afghan movement, which meant that he had little time for running a commercial business in Spain.

AL-SURI'S FIRST PUBLICATION:
'THE ISLAMIC JIHADI REVOLUTION IN SYRIA'

In Spain, al-Suri discovered for the first time his talent as an historian and writer, which he developed in tandem with his avidity for reading and learning. Despite having attended university classes in Syria, Jordan and France, al-Suri would later describe himself as an autodidact. It was his avidity for reading and learning combined with his practical experiences from the Syrian Muslim Brotherhood

---

29 Ibid. This was also confirmed by Saad al-Faqih who knew the family when they lived in London. Author's telephone interview with Saad al-Faqih, 17 Sept. 2006.

30 José María Irujo, 'El hombre de Bin Laden en Madrid', *El País*, 2 March 2005, www.elPaís.es/comunes/2005/11m/08_comision/libro_electronico_red_islam/red_islamista_01%20doc.pdf, accessed July 2006, p.16; José María Irujo, *El Agujero*, p.25, 44; and Audiencia Nacional, Sala de lo Penal, Sección Tercera, 'Sentencia Núm. 36/2005', Madrid, 26 Sept. 2005, [verdict against the Abu Dahdah network], p.303.

movement to the Afghan jihad and elsewhere that eventually made him a leading jihadi intellectual. In the interview with a Kuwaiti newspaper in 1999, he refused to name any cleric, shaykh or Muslim personality among his most prominent sources of inspiration and learning. Instead, he said that 'my main shaykh is the book and what I have gained from it directly'.[31]

During his first two years in Spain, he started writing his first study, an analysis of the jihadi movement in Syria.[32] Through his work, al-Suri deepened his knowledge of guerrilla warfare theory, with which he could compare the Syrian example in order to measure its successes and failures. It is possible that he also began writing smaller pamphlets and articles in this period. According to the US government, al-Suri began writing 'inflammatory essays' after his arrival in Spain, using the pseudonym Umar Abd al-Hakim.[33] Al-Suri has retained that pseudonym ever since.

His efforts to write a book on the Syrian jihadi movement when living in Spain met with considerable success. He had originally intended to write a small study or booklet, but by mid-October 1987, he had completed a huge handwritten manuscript of nearly 700 pages. He gave the draft to his Syrian comrades and colleagues for review and comments. Copies were made, his work became known outside his immediate circle of acquaintances, and there were suggestions that it should be published in a book format. Several hundred copies of the manuscript came into circulation after a trial print was made in early 1989.[34] This was after al-Suri had moved to Afghanistan. As al-Suri at this point was still a junior figure and a novice in the world of jihadi literature, he avidly gathered comments, criticism and

---

31 'Meeting with the Kuwaiti Newspaper', transcript of audiofile no.1, p.1.

32 See Umar Abd al-Hakim, *The Islamic Jihadi Revolution in Syria. Part I*, p.18.

33 'WANTED: Mustafa Setmariam Nasar', *Reward for Justice website*, www.rewardsforjustice.net/english/wanted_captured/index.cfm?page=Nasar, accessed July 2005.

34 Umar Abd al-Hakim, *The Islamic Jihadi Revolution in Syria. Part I*, pp.4, 21.

observations on his work, so that he could make improvements and amendments in the final official version.

The final product was a large two volume book entitled *The Islamic Jihadi Revolution in Syria* (al-thawrah al-islamiyyah al-jihadiyyah fi suria), perhaps best known as simply 'The Syrian Experience' (*al-tajrubah al-suriyah*).[35] It was published in May 1991 in Peshawar and distributed widely among the various jihadi groups present there.[36] It analyzed the Syrian jihadi experience, with a view to extract lessons for the future, but it also contained substantial amounts of primary source material on the Syrian MB and The Combatant Vanguard organizations, especially their communiqués. The book may be considered his breakthrough as a jihadi intellectual, and made his name known not only in the Arab-Afghan community in Peshawar, but also in the Syrian emigrant communities. When al-Suri later published articles in jihadi media outlets, he was often introduced as "The author of 'The Syrian Experience'".[37]

The two-volume book, which in its final version comprises more than 900 pages including appendices, also laid the foundation for al-Suri's *Global Islamic Resistance Call*. It contained some of the same elements and similar methodology, such as the emphasis on learning lessons from past jihadi experiences and synthesizing new practical theories for future jihadis.

Until recently, the work has remained relatively obscure outside Islamist circles.[38] A few Arab journalists who met with al-Suri in the

---

35 The full title is *The Islamic Jihadi Revolution in Syria. Part I. The Experience and Lessons (Hopes and Pains)* and *The Islamic Jihadi Revolution in Syria: Part II. Ideology and Program (Studies and Basics on the Path of Armed Revolutionary Jihad)* (in Arabic) (Peshawar: publisher unknown, May 1991).

36 'Meeting with the Kuwaiti Newspaper', transcript of audiofile no.1, pp.5, 7; and Umar Abd al-Hakim, *The Islamic Jihadi Revolution in Syria. Part I*, p.16.

37 See editorial introduction to Umar Abd al-Hakim, 'Between the Loyal Servants of the Merciful and the Loyal Servants of the Vatican' (in Arabic), *al-Ansar Newsletter*, no.88 (16 March 1995), p.13.

38 There are occasional references to it. See, for example, 'The Massacre of the Military Artillery School at Aleppo—Special Report', *The Syrian Human*

mid-1990s managed to obtain a copy.[39] However, for most researchers, the book has not been available. Only in May 2006 was his book published on a UK-based Islamist website, the www.tajdeed.org.uk as a scanned PDF-formatted document. At that point the news of his arrest in Pakistan attracted renewed attention to al-Suri and his writings in US and international media. This may have galvanized his followers to rediscover his old publications and post them on pro-jihadi websites.[40] The book has subsequently appeared on many Islamist websites.[41]

The subtitle of the second volume was 'Ideology and program: studies and basics on the path of armed revolutionary jihad' suggesting that al-Suri's ambitions went beyond the Syrian jihadi experience.[42] Already at this point, he aimed to develop a broad theory on how to integrate practical experiences and guerrilla warfare theory into a comprehensive jihadi war fighting theory. Furthermore, the Syrian arena soon appeared too limited and too infertile for the ideas and concepts he was developing. In the first introduction to the book, he noted that he had received the most encouragement and backing from non-Syrian Islamists, even though the book was initially meant for the Syrian community. Al-Suri was disappointed by this lack of interest from his fellow countrymen. He attributed it to the high degree of disillusionment and frustration among the remaining Syrian

---

*Rights Committee*, 16 Feb. 2002, http://www.shrc.org.uk/data/aspx/d5/315. aspx, accessed July 2006.

39 Camille Tawil of the *al-Hayat* newspaper in London was one of them. Author's interview with Camille Tawil, London, 14 Sept. 2006.

40 See posting by 'al-Lahibi' on *muntada al-tajdid*, 31 May 2006, www.tajdeed. org.uk/forums/showthread.php?s=6548b36708e3c3eff8db8327623a51e8&t hreadid=41941, and posting by 'Muhammad Ahmad Khalaf' on *muntada al-tajdid* 6 June 2006, www.tajdeed.org.uk/forums/showthread.php?s=6548 b36708e3c3eff8db8327623a51e8&threadid=42079, accessed June 2006.

41 See, for example, 'Who is Abu Mus'ab al-Suri?' (in Arabic), *muntada al-sawt* 20 June 2006, www.saowt.com/forum/showthread.php?t=16158&highlight =%E3%E4+%E5%E6+%C3%C8%E6+%E3%D5%DA%C8+%C7%E1%D 3%E6%D1%ED+%BF, accessed Sept. 2006.

42 See Umar Abd al-Hakim, *The Islamic Jihadi Revolution in Syria. Part I.*

jihadis. It had reached a point where 'they no longer want to work for their cause, they do not want to read about it, unfortunately, and they are bored even by listening to the news about it'.[43]

In his book, Al-Suri showed little mercy when characterizing his fellow Syrian Islamists. He attacked what he termed 'the school of ecclesiastical infallibility' which the Syrian MB leaders bestowed upon themselves.[44] His directness, bluntness, and severity in judging the performance of the Islamist movement became a key hallmark in most of his subsequent writings:

One of the most chronic diseases which has befallen these poor fellows [i.e. the Syrian Islamists] is the spirit of empty academic haughtiness. They imagine that they have their own experiences of this period, know everything about it, and therefore, why should they spend time reading hundreds of pages? Many of the Syrian brothers, at least in form and in name, still follow the main Islamic groups, which contributed to the jihadi cause. Their contributions have ranged from being negative to catastrophic.[45]

Unable to find a receptive audience among his own, al-Suri dedicated his book first and foremost to 'the Muslim youth working for Islam in the camps of the various Islamic groups, especially the deceived youth in the Muslim Brotherhood and similar movements'.[46] In al-Suri's view, the MB and its associated groups had abdicated their responsibility and abandoned their ideological foundations. Traditional MB slogans, which had been adopted in the 1930s when Hasan al-Banna led the movement: 'The Caliphate is our goal', 'Jihad is our way', 'Death in the way of God is our highest aspiration", were in al-Suri's view, simply empty emblems, with no real meaning. Al-Suri's work echoed a number of the same themes that Ayman al-Zawahiri raised in his work *The Bitter Harvest: The Muslim Brothers in Sixty Years* (al-hasad al-murr: al-ikhwan al-muslimun fi sittin 'aman), which was published approximately at the same time, analyzing the history of the

---

43  Ibid., p.5.
44  Ibid., p.11.
45  Ibid., p.5.
46  Ibid., p.7.

Egyptian branch of the Muslim Brotherhood. As we shall see, al-Suri got to know not only al-Zawahiri in the late 1980s, but also other leading EIJ ideologues, who read and commented on his work, and there is no doubt that al-Suri was influenced by them (see chapter 4).

Al-Suri drew the conclusion that the youth who had joined the MB and still believed in its original ideology and were raised in the spirit of obedience and commitment, should be 'the first target for the jihadi currents and groups'.[47] Al-Suri held that these youth were potentially a much more promising recruitment arena than non-observant youth who had to be trained and raised from scratch. The high motivational and ideological commitment of MB youth made them ideal cadres for the jihadi movement.

Contrary to the prevalent view that militant Islamist movements recruit highly literate cadres from the middle classes, al-Suri claimed in his book that 'most of the active jihadi fighters do not read in order to benefit from this and receive guidance for their activities. Nor do they write about their experiences so that others can benefit from this'.[48] This was not exclusively a Syrian phenomenon, but was typical in many other Islamist groups. Those Islamists who did read and write, did so at the expense of operative participation, and hence, very few, if any, fulfilled the role of being an articulate and literate jihadi. This was clearly a role model which al-Suri set for himself.

Already in this book, al-Suri articulates his ambition to develop a comprehensive body of 'operative theories' (*nazariyyat al-'amal*) and a 'program for renewal of jihadi ideology', which encompassed its political, organizational, and military aspects.[49] He devoted a whole chapter (chapter three) in the first volume to this exercise and decided to reprint the same chapter in volume two as well, in order to remind the readers of the importance of this part of his work. In order to establish an empirical foundation for his new theories of jihad, al-Suri devoted considerable space to summaries of books on guer-

---

47 Ibid., p.8.
48 Ibid., p.6.
49 Ibid., p.9.

rilla insurgencies and popular resistance movements, many of which were non-Muslim: 'these are valuable human experiences', al-Suri wrote.[50] By doing this, he demonstrated a willingness to learn from non-Islamic sources and look beyond the body of Islamic literature, integrating concepts from these sources into his own work. To be sure, the second volume focused heavily on providing the jurisprudential and theological foundations of jihad and the jihadi theories that al-Suri developed.

Al-Suri was clearly aware that publishing a book on such a sensitive topic would place him in the spotlight for criticism, expose him to harassment and even security dangers, but he felt a very strong sense of mission. Al-Suri wished passionately that the coming generation of jihadis would learn from the past and 'try to not fall into mistakes which we have paid for with pure blood'.[51]

After releasing the first version of his book, al-Suri faced criticism from Syrian Islamists as well as from members of the jihadi community, and he responded to this criticism when the final version appeared in 1991. Syrian Muslim Brotherhood members argued that his book damaged their cause because it vilified the movement's historical figures, sowed doubt about their activities and made their enemies gloat at their misfortunes. Criticism of this kind, even if it was meant as constructive criticism, should only be presented in closed meetings, not in public. Furthermore, the book revealed too many details and secrets about the Syrian MB; it was therefore more helpful to the enemy, the Syrian regime, than to their friends and sympathizers.[52] It was obvious from these reactions that al-Suri was clearly up against heavy odds when he attempted to subject the Syrian jihadi movement to an academic analysis. Self-criticism and open debates were bound to meet with heavy resistance, especially when formulated in the kind of direct and blunt language that al-Suri used.

---

50  Ibid., p.10.
51  Ibid., p.5.
52  Ibid., p.11.

His book was also greeted with scepticism from another direction. According to al-Suri's account, 'several brothers from the jihadi groups' had considered the book too lenient on the Syrian MB and accused him of adopting too much of the MB's theory and ideology.[53] Al-Suri argued that he wished to be 'neutral' and 'objective' and pointed out that the MB, especially its youth, had many sincere people in its ranks and that 'not everything the MB stood for is evil and deviation'.[54] Due to the controversies surrounding the book in the Syrian Islamist community, his first book probably had more influence outside the circle of Syrian jihadis. In fact, it became a key part of the literature of the new jihadi trend which came together in Peshawar in 1989 and in which the Egyptian jihadis, lead by Ayman al-Zawahiri were influential.

## THE BOMBING OF EL DESCANSO
## RESTAURANT IN MADRID?

In late 2005, there were speculations about al-Suri's alleged involvement in a terrorist act in Madrid during his early exile in Europe. From his own memoirs and his writings, he appears to have been focused solely on Syria. Nothing at that point indicated a desire to export the armed campaign to Europe or to shift the focus to US or Western targets. It seems clear that it was only after he arrived in Afghanistan in 1987 and became acquainted with many of the leading jihadi figures there, that al-Suri abandoned the Syrian jihad and adopted the doctrine of a global armed struggle on behalf of the Islamic Nation (*ummah*). Even then, his priority remained the fight against 'the near enemy', i.e. secular regimes in the Muslim world. In al-Suri's case, this translated into his efforts during the 1990s to support the Algerian Islamist insurgents.

Against this background, it would be surprising if it turned out that al-Suri was directly involved in Islamist terrorism in Europe in

---

53  Ibid., p.12.
54  Ibid., p.15.

the mid-1980s. True, al-Suri certainly had the training and skills to carry out terrorist bombings. Moreover, during this period, several European countries, France in particular, experienced a series of terrorist attacks by Islamic militants, often with the explicit support of Middle Eastern states.[55] Spain also suffered from such acts, although the identity of the perpetrators was not always known. On 12 April 1985 the El Descanso restaurant in Madrid was destroyed by a large bomb, in what was one of the most deadly terrorist attacks in Spain. Eighteen people were killed, all of them Spaniards, and 82 injured, 15 of them Americans. The restaurant was located close to Torrejon Airbase, one of the US military bases in Spain, and US military personnel used to visit the restaurant frequently.[56] Many organizations claimed credit for the bombings, including the leftist GRAPO organization, the Basque ETA, Islamic Jihad, and the Armed Organization of the Jewish People. According to the US State Department's annual survey for that year, 'some officials believed the bombing was the work of Middle Eastern terrorists, while others attributed it to GRAPO'.[57] A Spanish indictment suggested that an organization calling itself 'Islamic jihad' had committed the crime, but the investigation was closed in March 1987 due to lack of evidence.[58]

55  A US government report from 1986 states that 'Middle East-related attacks in Europe averaged 35 per year from 1980 to 1983, climbed to 61 in 1984, and reached 74 in 1985'. Many of these attacks were attributed to Syria, Libya, Iran and Palestinian groups. See, for example, US Department of State, *Patterns of Global Terrorism*, 1985, www.mipt.org/pdf/1986pogt.pdf, accessed Oct. 2006, pp.12-13.

56  'Un testigo identificó a Setmarian: La Audiencia Nacional reabre la causa sobre el atentado en el restaurante El Descanso en 1985', *elmundo.es*, 9 Nov. 2005, www.elmundo.es/elmundo/2005/11/09/espana/1131539640.html; and George al-Rayyis, 'Madrid connects the name Abu Mus'ab al-Suri to the restaurant explosion in 1985' (in Arabic), *al-Sharq al-Awsat*, 10 Nov. 2005, www.asharqalawsat.com/details.asp?section=4&issue=9844&article=332668, accessed Dec. 2005.

57  US Department of State, *Patterns of Global Terrorism* 1985, Spain overview, cited in MIPT Terrorism Knowledge Base, www.tkb.org/MorePatterns. jsp?countryCd=SP&year=1985, accessed Dec. 2005.

58  'Principales ideólogos o "autores intelectuales" del 11-M', *3 dias de Marzo*

In November 2005, the Spanish judge Ismael Moreno at the Spanish national court, *La Audiencia Nacional*, decided to reopen the investigation into the bombing tragedy after a witness had identified al-Suri as one of the bomb makers.[59] This happened after he was shown a picture of al-Suri, taken in the late 1980s and published in Spanish newspapers in mid-2005.[60] Apparently, al-Suri fitted witness descriptions of one of the persons who had been present at the restaurant shortly before the explosion. According to the police investigation, witnesses had identified a red-haired young man with moustache, between 25 and 30 years, who was standing close to the bar of the restaurant, with a sports bag in his hands.[61]

If these allegations turn out to be true, it is still difficult to imagine why al-Suri should have participated in the restaurant bombing in Madrid in 1985. Perhaps he was repulsed by the Lebanese conflict like many Muslim militants at the time. He may have wanted to

---

*webblog*, 18 Sept. 2005, http://3diasdemarzo.blogspot.com/2005/09/principales-idelogos-o-autores.html, accessed July 2006; and 'Un testigo identificó a Setmarian: La Audiencia Nacional reabre la causa sobre el atentado en el restaurante El Descanso en 1985', *elmundo.es*, 9 Nov. 2005, www.elmundo.es/elmundo/2005/11/09/espana/1131539640.html.

59 The reopening of the Descanso bombing investigation implies that there are now two Spanish arrest warrants against al-Suri: The first, issued by Judge Baltasar Garzón in the Abu Dahdah investigation and the second issued by Judge Ismael Moreno in the El Descanso restaurant bombing case. See Antonio Rubio, '"My husband has been abducted", says wife of Spaniard Setmariam' (in Spanish), *El Mundo*, 26 Dec. 2005, via WNC at http://search.epnet.com/login.aspx?direct=true&db=tsh&an=EUP2005122795001 9&site=isc, accessed July 2006.

60 'Un testigo identificó a Setmarian: La Audiencia Nacional reabre la causa sobre el atentado en el restaurante El Descanso en 1985', *elmundo.es*, 9 Nov. 2005, www.elmundo.es/elmundo/2005/11/09/espana/1131539640.html; and George al-Rayyis, 'Madrid connects the name Abu Mus'ab al-Suri to the restaurant explosion in 1985' (in Arabic), *al-Sharq al-Awsat* 10 Nov. 2005, www.asharqalawsat.com/details.asp?section=4&issue=9844&article=332668, accessed Dec. 2005.

61 'Un testigo identificó a Setmarian: La Audiencia Nacional reabre la causa sobre el atentado en el restaurante El Descanso en 1985', *elmundo.es*, 9 Nov. 2005, www.elmundo.es/elmundo/2005/11/09/espana/1131539640.html.

avenge the US intervention in Lebanon in 1982-1984 and, more importantly, force Western governments to exert stronger pressure on Israel to withdraw militarily from Lebanon and release Palestinian and Arab prisoners. All these motives were part of the terrorist calculus during the 1980s. Still, in the admittedly few available sources on al-Suri's life during the 1980s, there is no hint whatsoever of any such motive for attacking targets in Europe. The new arrest warrant against al-Suri appeared in the Spanish media shortly after news agencies had reported that al-Suri had been arrested in Pakistan.[62] This sequence of events lends itself to speculation that the desire to have al-Suri extradited to Spain may have played a role. It must be said that foreign and Spanish journalists who have followed the case closely have been very sceptical as to whether there exists any real basis for a new El Descanso bombing investigation.[63]

While al-Suri was not a global jihadi during the 1980s, he was soon to become one. In 1987 he departed for his first visit to Peshawar. This inaugurated a new and radically different phase in his life.

---

62 It was posted on the website of the Spanish Ministry of Justice on 9 Nov. 2005, see 'Cronología del Ministerio del Interior-Noviembre', *Ministerio del Interior website*, 9 Nov. 2005, www.mir.es/DGRIS/Cronologia/2005/noviembre.htm, accessed July 2006.

63 Email correspondence with Craig Whitlock, *Washington Post*, July 2006.

# 4
# AFGHANISTAN: LAND OF HOLY WAR

The prospects for reviving the Syrian jihad in the mid-1980s appeared slim, whilst the mujahidin resistance in Afghanistan electrified and attracted radical Islamists from most parts of the Muslim world. In 1987 al-Suri and five fellow Syrians departed for Peshawar and Afghanistan hoping to garner support for the jihad in Syria.[1] Al-Suri remained there for most of the period between 1987 and 1991, leaving the country shortly before Kabul fell in April 1992.[2]

## THE ROAD TO AFGHANISTAN

Al-Suri had been interested in the issue of Afghanistan since the early 1980s. In 1986, al-Suri and a few fellow Syrians contacted a leading Arab-Afghan commander when the latter visited Madrid, in order to gain more information about how to join the Arab re-

---

1    The sources differ slightly regarding the date of al-Suri's arrival in Afghanistan, but most of them date it to 1987. See 'Biography of Shaykh Umar Abd al-Hakim (Abu Mus'ab al-Suri)' (in Arabic), p.2; 'Communiqué from the Office of Abu Mus'ab al-Suri', 22 Dec. 2004, p.7; 'Meeting with the Kuwaiti Newspaper', transcript of audiofile no.1, p.6; and interview with al-Suri on *al-Jazeera* in 'Reports of split in Bin Ladin's group denied,' (LexisNexis Title), *'Al-Jazeera at Midday'-programme, Al-Jazeera TV*, 1 Aug. 2000 1240 GMT via LexisNexis.

2    The sources disagree on the date of al-Suri's departure from Afghanistan, specifically whether it was in 1991 or in 1992. A Libyan Islamist who knew al-Suri well said he left Afghanistan in 1991, well before the capture of Kabul and the outbreak of the Afghan civil war. See 'Meeting with the Kuwaiti Newspaper', transcript of audiofile no.1, p.6; 'Biography of Shaykh Umar Abd al-Hakim (Abu Mus'ab al-Suri)' (in Arabic), p.2; and author's interview with Noman Benotman, London, 15 Sept. 2006.

sistance in Afghanistan. The commander was Boudjemaa Bounoua, better known as Abdallah Anas or Abou Anès, an Algerian Islamist who joined General Ahmad Shah Massoud in the Afghan resistance in 1984 and became one of the most high-ranking Arab fighters in Afghanistan. Anas married the daughter of Abdallah Azzam, the head of the Arab-Afghan movement. He later joined the Algerian Islamist opposition party, Front Islamique de Salut (FIS) when it was founded in 1989. He opposed the jihadi current due to its adamant rejection of participation in party politics and democratic elections.[3]

In an interview with this author, Anas recalls the group of Syrian youth who came to him in Madrid, where he had gone on two weeks leave to meet his family. The group had heard about Anas' presence in the city, and they came to The Islamic Centre in Madrid, one of the Muslim Brotherhood's many branches in Spain. Being a Muslim Brotherhood member himself, Anas stayed at the center at the time, giving talks about the Afghan jihad. The Syrians presented themselves as Muslims and political refugees in Spain, and they wanted to learn more about how to join the Arab-Afghan resistance. Anas agreed to meet the group in a popular market district in Madrid. They sat together for an hour or so, and Anas recalls that one of the young Syrians was the same person whom he later came to know as Abu Mus'ab al-Suri. Al-Suri did not speak during the meeting.

---

3    Author's interview with Abdallah Anas, London, 16 Sept. 2006. Anas has been outspoken about his opposition to the GIA and al-Qaida's terrorist campaigns. See, for example, David Leppard and Nick Fielding, 'The Hate', *The Sunday Times*, 10 July 2005, http://entertainment.timesonline. co.uk/article/0,14929-1687681,00.html, accessed Sept. 2006. In 2003, the Algerian regime claimed that Anas was 'one of the main leaders of al-Qa'idah', and alleged that he 'was responsible for the link between GIA and al-Qa'idah's transnational networks and for incorporating Algeria's terrorist potential into al-Qa'idah'. See 'Letter dated 16 April 2003 from the Permanent Representative of Algeria to the United Nations addressed to the Chairman of the Committee', Security Council Committee established pursuant to resolution 1267 (1999), Document no.S/AC.37/2003/(1455)/14, dated 17 April 2003, www.nti.org/e_research/official_docs/inventory/pdfs/AQT_algeria20030416.pdf, accessed Sept. 2006.

Instead, one of the men who called himself Adnan appeared to be their leader and did most of the talking.[4]

According to Anas, the Syrians had asked about various mundane details pertaining to the Arab-Afghan resistance, such as salaries, housing, living conditions, etc. Anas found the conversation very discouraging. He sensed in them a lack of spirit and willingness to endure sacrifice. He claims that they had not asked about the military training, the combat experience, etc, but only about 'living conditions and salaries'. Anas does not recollect what he told them, only that he 'felt sad' after the meeting. Nothing came out of this meeting as far as Anas remembered.[5]

The contentious and hostile relationship which later developed between FIS, in which Anas was a prominent leader, and the hard-line Algerian faction, the GIA,[6] with which al-Suri was associated, might have negatively influenced Anas' recollection of the five Syrians, and of al-Suri in particular. Whatever the case, the meeting reveals that, already in 1986, al-Suri and his friends were seriously contemplating going to Afghanistan. It also shows that al-Suri had Syrian friends who shared his desire to go to Afghanistan, although it is not unlikely that their dedication to the cause and their motivations for going there varied greatly.

According to al-Suri's account, he and five other Syrians went to Peshawar in 1987. He dates the beginning of his 'field participation' inside Afghanistan to 1988.[7] In Peshawar, the Syrians met with Shaykh Abdallah Azzam, the emir of the Arab-Afghan movement, and head of *The Service Bureau* (maktab al-khidmat), the organizational precursor of al-Qaida. Their first meeting took place in July 1987, which was also the first time al-Suri visited the city.[8] When

---

4    Author's interview with Abdallah Anas, London, 16 Sept. 2006.

5    Ibid.

6    The *Armed Islamic Group* (al-jama'ah al-islamiyyah al-musallahah) better known by its French acronym, GIA.

7    *The Global Islamic Resistance Call*, p.42.

8    'Meeting with the Kuwaiti Newspaper', transcript of audiofile no.1, p.4.

71

al-Suri later recollected the event, he emphasized that the exact timing of his arrival in Peshawar was 7 o'clock on the 7 July (or 7/7) 1987; there were 'four sevens', he recalled.[9] He retold this story twice during the interview in 1999, but he mentioned it as nothing more than an amusing oddity. The fact that the London bombings in July 2005 also occurred on 7 July and al-Suri was mentioned in the press as a possible suspect must be pure coincidence.

During his first meeting with Abdallah Azzam, al-Suri discovered to his great surprise that his previous trainer and military mentor in Baghdad, Shaykh Abu Usama al-Misri, was also in Afghanistan and came to attend their meeting with Azzam. Abu Usama's presence must have facilitated al-Suri's mission greatly. One may presume that he vouched for his former student, and spoke highly of his military qualifications, and this must have made al-Suri more visible in the large crowd of young disciples surrounding Azzam. Shaykh Abu Usama al-Misri was a well-known figure in the Arab-Afghan community. He is mentioned several times in the classic works on the Arab-Afghan movement from 1991, *The Arab Helpers in Afghanistan* (al-ansar al-arab fi afghanistan).[10]

## FROM A SYRIAN TO A GLOBAL JIHAD

During the meeting with Azzam in Peshawar it soon transpired that the Arab-Afghan godfather did not share his visitors' urgency about renewing the Syrian jihad. According to al-Suri, Azzam held that the Syrian jihad had 'had its chance; people no longer believed in it and wished to support it'.[11] The Syrian MB and The Combatant Vanguard group had joined various alliances and it looked more 'like

---

9    Ibid., p.6; and Audiofile no.3, p.2.

10   See, for example, Basil Muhammad, *The Arab Helpers in Afghanistan* (in Arabic) (Riyadh, Jedda: The Islamic Benevolence Committee, Office of Studies and Documentation, 1991, second edn), pp.234-5.

11   'Meeting with the Kuwaiti Newspaper', transcript of audiofile no.1, p.4.

a political project than a jihadi cause'.[12] Azzam's response should not have come as a surprise. In his writings, Azzam was known to ridicule revolutionary jihadi strategies.[13] He represented clearly a pan-Islamist orientation within the Islamist movement, emphasizing the obligation to defend Muslim land from aggression and the willingness to seek martyrdom for that cause. Instead of encouraging any further military adventures in Syria, Azzam exhorted al-Suri and his friends to fight for the Afghan cause, flattering them about their possession of significant military skills, which, after all, were in great shortage in the Arab-Afghan movement at that point in time.

The question of abandoning the Syrian jihad and instead relocating the Islamist struggle to the mountains of Afghanistan opened up a difficult debate among the Syrian jihadis. Most of them remained in exile in various countries and there were few Syrians in Peshawar. The same issue also proved divisive for the Egyptian jihadi groups, like the Egyptian Jihad group (*jama'at al-jihad*) and the Egyptian Islamic Group (*al-jama'ah al-islamiyyah*) whose leadership was split on the question of which jihad should have priority.[14] According to his own account, al-Suri was quickly persuaded by Azzam who had not completely ruled out the possibility of a reinvigoration of the Syrian jihad, if the Syrian jihadis managed to rebuild a group of capable fighters in Afghanistan.[15] When al-Suri raised the issue of relocating to Afghanistan with his comrades in exile they were not convinced. Very few came to join his small group in Afghanistan.

Al-Suri later estimated that the number of Syrians who went to Peshawar to the training camps or fought at the frontlines in Afghanistan in the period 1985-92 was in the range of tens, but less

---

12 Ibid.

13 I am indebted to Thomas Hegghammer for this information. See his 'Abdallah Azzam: L'imam du jihad' in Gilles Kepel (ed.), *Al-Qaida dans le texte*, pp.115-37.

14 See, for example, Fawaz A. Gerges, *The Far Enemy: Why Jihad Went Global* (New York: Cambridge University Press, 2005), pp.170-5, 225-6.

15 'Meeting with the Kuwaiti Newspaper', transcript of audiofile no.1, p.5.

than one hundred. This was in sharp contrast to the much larger contingents from other Arab countries, such as Saudi Arabia, Yemen, Egypt and Algeria.[16] Abdallah Anas concurs with this estimate of the small Syrian contingent. He believes that they were no more than some twenty to thirty people. They were very few, perhaps numbering the same as the Tunisian contingency. Anas estimates that the largest contingents were the Saudis, Algerians, the Yemenis, the Egyptians and Palestinians.[17] Still, quite a significant number of Syrians are mentioned by name and their activities described in detail in the classic work, *The Arab Helpers in Afghanistan*, suggesting that even if they were numerically few, they still played an important role.[18] Three of them were even members of Azzam's first training camp in 1984.[19]

In his memoirs, al-Suri deplored the fact that the Syrian Islamists had such 'a narrow regional conception' of their struggle.[20] Although the issue was partly ideological, it was in fact the reality that had forced 'a transformation of goals'. Al-Suri later recalled that 'we left the Syrian cause because there existed no opportunity to revive it and we turned to the Afghan cause instead'.[21] The resources for restarting the Syrian jihad were simply not there; they were 'cut off', and isolated from the Syrian scene, and as time went by they were also alienated from their homeland:

---

16 *The Global Islamic Resistance Call*, pp.895-6.

17 Author's interview with Abdallah Anas, London, 16 Sept. 2006.

18 Basil Muhammad, *The Arab Helpers in Afghanistan* (in Arabic) (Riyadh, Jedda: The Islamic Benevolence Committee, Office of Studies and Documentation, 1991, second edn). See, for example, p.100 (Abu Bakr al-Suri, Abu Mu 'izz al-Suri, Abu Sutayf al-Suri), p.111 (Abu al-Hasan al-Suri), p.112 (Abu Sayf al-Suri, Abu Rida al-Suri, Abu Izz al-Suri), p.113 (Abu Bakr al-Hamawi, from Hama), p.123 (Abu Bakr al-Suri), p.226 (Abu Mahmud al-Suri), p.227 ('a Syrian brother'), and p.238 (Abu Burhan al-Suri).

19 Basil Muhammad, *The Arab Helpers in Afghanistan*, p.100.

20 'Meeting with the Kuwaiti Newspaper', transcript of audiofile no.1, p.5.

21 Ibid.

we were dissolved the way most other [jihadi] groups dissolved, by the fact that we were no longer in the field. Between us and our country were thousands of kilometers, and now, the distance in time is tens of thousands of kilometers. [...] [W]e could not do anything along that path, so we entered the framework of contributing to the international jihad.[22]

For al-Suri, this period was evidently the time when 'the global character of the duty of jihad' and the 'global nature of the Muslim causes' became apparent to him in earnest.[23]

Al-Suri and the five other Syrian jihadis who arrived with him in Afghanistan suffered losses on the various battle fronts; one of them was killed in Jalalabad and another in Khowst, while yet another left Afghanistan. The idea of reviving the Syrian jihad grew more distant every day that passed, and their struggle came to be centered on Afghanistan and other pan-Islamic causes.[24] It is probably wrong, though, to see this shift from a local to a global jihad as synonymous with al-Qaida's and bin Laden's declaration of a global war against the Crusaders in the mid- and late 1990s. For al-Suri and his fellow fighters, the priority at this point was to support other 'jihadi revolutions' in their local or regional struggles for an Islamic state, rather than to take the fight to and against the West. After all, al-Qaida declared war on US military and civilian targets around the world only in 1998.

## WITH ABDALLAH AZZAM AND OSAMA BIN LADEN

Al-Suri says that he was deeply influenced by Abdallah Azzam, and he was persuaded to join the Arab-Afghan mujahidin movement and participate, in particular, in the field of training.[25] Al-Suri repeatedly

---

22    Ibid., transcript of audiofile no.3, pp.1-2.

23    Ibid., transcript of audiofile no.1, p.5.

24    Ibid.

25    'Biography of Shaykh Umar Abd al-Hakim (Abu Mus'ab al-Suri)' (in Arabic), p.2; and 'Meeting with the Kuwaiti Newspaper', transcript of audiofile no.1, p.6.

claims that he 'accompanied' Azzam from late 1987 until the latter was assassinated with two of his sons in Peshawar on 24 November 1989, a claim other Arab-Afghan veterans have disputed.[26] Whatever the case, there is little doubt that al-Suri was deeply impressed by Abdallah Azzam, who met with most of the Arab newcomers in Peshawar and opened his house and guesthouses to Arab volunteers. Al-Suri recalls that he was particularly impressed by the fact that, unlike the MB commanders whom al-Suri had known and who used to command their troops via telephone, Azzam went to see his men personally and travelled from one frontline to the other and from one military outpost to another. This was, in al-Suri's words, 'a true leadership'.[27]

Al-Suri's relationship with bin Laden is hard to pin down in detail. Al-Suri himself says he became acquainted with Osama bin Laden in 1988, and joined al-Qaida shortly after its foundation in 1988.[28] His biographer portrays him as one of 'bin Laden's closest confidants' between 1988 and 1991.[29] Al-Suri describes himself as 'a member of the first circle around the shaykh', and claims to have been very well informed about al-Qaida's organization and activities during this period.[30] If true, al-Suri should perhaps be considered among al-Qaida's founding members. It is uncertain to what degree he worked directly for bin Laden's organization during the 1990s. According to a communiqué he issued in December 2004, al-Suri says he stopped

---

26    Ibid., pp.5-6. See also interview with al-Suri on *al-Jazeera* in 'Reports of split in Bin Ladin's group denied,' (LexisNexis Title), '*Al-Jazeera at Midday'-programme, Al-Jazeera TV*, 1 Aug. 2000 1240 GMT via LexisNexis. This claim was disputed by Abdallah Anas, Azzam's son-in-law. Author's interview with Abdallah Anas, London 16 Sept. 2006.

27    'Meeting with the Kuwaiti Newspaper', transcript of audiofile no.1, p.6.

28    'Communiqué from the Office of Abu Mus'ab al-Suri', 22 Dec. 2004, p.7; 'Biography of Shaykh Umar Abd al-Hakim (Abu Mus 'ab al-Suri)' (in Arabic), p.2; *The Global Islamic Resistance Call*, p.710; and Ministracion de Justicia, 'Juzgado Central de Instruccion no.005, Madrid, Sumario', 17 Sept. 2003, p.27.

29    'Biography of Shaykh Umar Abd al-Hakim (Abu Mus 'ab al-Suri)' (in Arabic), p.2.

30    *The Global Islamic Resistance Call*, p.711.

working for al-Qaida and Osama bin Laden in 1992.[31] It seems clear, however, that he did not severe his contacts with al-Qaida during the mid-1990s. For example, he played a central role in facilitating international media interviews for bin Laden in 1996-97. Moreover, he probably met with bin Laden and the al-Qaida leadership in Sudan in 1993-94. At the same time, it is possible that al-Suri has exaggerated his involvement with al-Qaida in the late 1980s, and that his relationship with bin Laden was perhaps not as close as depicted by himself and by his biographer.[32]

It has been difficult to verify al-Suri's claim that he worked closely with Azzam and was among bin Laden's confidants. Other Arab-Afghan veterans, such as Abdallah Anas, who fought with Ahmad Shah Massoud, married Abdallah Azzam's daughter, and knew bin Laden well, do not recall having seen al-Suri in the company of Abdallah Azzam, in the offices of the The Services Bureau (*maktab al-khidmat*,

---

31  Elsewhere, al-Suri says that their relationship was 'in practical terms interrupted' until they met again in 1996, four to five months after bin Laden's return to Afghanistan. See 'Communiqué from the Office of Abu Mus'ab al-Suri', 22 Dec. 2004, p.7; and *The Global Islamic Resistance Call*, p.711.

32  This is also supported in an account in a Spanish court document in which al-Suri is said to have been accompanied and aided by an al-Qaida courier, Muhammad Bahayah (Abu Khalid al-Suri), when he returned to Afghanistan in the late 1990s. The latter is said to have 'introduced him [al-Suri] to bin Ladin'. (The formulation is as follows: 'BAHAIAH es la persona que acompañó a MUSTAFA SETMARIAM NASAR hasta el mismo OSAMA BEN LADEN en Afganistán, a quien se lo presentó'.) If true, al-Suri cannot at this point have been a close associate of bin Laden, since he needed someone to introduce him and vouch for him. This casts some doubt upon the assertion by the biographer that al-Suri joined al-Qaida from the very beginning and was one of bin Laden's closest associates during the Afghan jihad in the late 1980s. However, the term 'introduce' is probably misleading. Elsewhere in the Spanish court document, it is reported that al-Suri had known bin Laden since 1988, that he was a 'top executive of al-Qaida' (alto dirigente de AL QAEDA), and that Muhammad al-Bahayah was in fact his 'assistant' or 'second-in-command' (segundo). See 'Biography of Shaykh Umar Abd al-Hakim (Abu Mus 'ab al-Suri)' (in Arabic), p.2; and 'Juzgado Central de Instruccion no.005, Madrid, Sumario', 17 Sept. 2003, pp.32, 293, and 686.

or MAK) in Peshawar, in the guest houses or the training camps in Khalden and Sada. Anas' recollection does not necessarily invalidate al-Suri's account, as the former spent much time at the frontlines and could not possibly keep track of everyone in the Arab-Afghan community. Furthermore, Azzam had a large following of disciples, who may have regarded themselves as being closer to the movement's father figure than they actually were.

Anas does not remember having met or even heard of al-Suri until 1989 or 1990, when he became known on account of his book on the Syrian jihad (see below). Anas' only recollection of having seen al-Suri was at the offices of the Islamic Benevolence Committee (*lajnat al-birr al-islamiyyah*), an NGO set up in 1987 by the Saudi businessman Adil al-Battarji, partly in order to provide support for the mujahidin fighting in Afghanistan.[33] They did not know each other then and nor did they greet each other, but Anas recalls having seen him there.[34]

Anas may have downplayed al-Suri's presence and role in Afghanistan, and it is also likely that al-Suri exaggerated his own proximity to Abdallah Azzam and wider influence on the Arab-Afghan resistance. Many of the volunteers did not spend years at the front in Afghanistan. Most of the Arab-Afghan veterans did little actual fighting but served instead as aid workers or in other auxiliary functions. They also treated the Afghan jihad as a part-time occupation, travelling back and forth between Peshawar and their home countries. Al-Suri also returned to Spain at irregular intervals.

What seems certain is that al-Suri was active in Peshawar and rose to prominence because of his book. His name became known both inside and outside Islamist circles at this early point. Kamal Helbawi,

---

33  Some fifteen years later, Battarji was indicted on charges of terrorist financing by the US authorities, *inter alia* for activities involving the Islamic Benevolence Committee and its successor organization, the Benevolence International Foundation (BIF). See, for example, US Department of State, 'Two Saudi Nationals Named as Terrorist Financiers', 21 Dec. 2004, http://usinfo.state.gov/ei/Archive/2004/Dec/22-862859.html, accessed Oct. 2006.

34  Author's interview with Abdallah Anas, London 16 Sept. 2006.

formerly a senior Muslim Brotherhood leader, who met with bin Laden and spent much time in Peshawar during and after the Afghan liberation war, recalls al-Suri and the impact his book had in Peshawar: 'His ideas were popular amongst the hardliners who saw him as a pioneer'.[35] The Syrian scholar, professor Najib Ghadbian, also recalls having heard about al-Suri for the first time when *The Islamic Jihadi Revolution in Syria* began circulating in 1990-1. At the same time, he also heard that this Syrian writer 'was travelling between Europe and Afghanistan'.[36] Furthermore, when Arab newspapers began writing about him in the mid-1990s, they highlighted his Afghan experience, dating his arrival to Peshawar in the mid-1980s.[37]

## TRAINING AND COMBAT

After having spent some time in Afghanistan on 'a reconnaissance visit', as he later dubbed it, making sure that he could accommodate a family there, al-Suri also brought his wife, Elena Moreno Cruz, to Pakistan. They had married in late 1987 or early 1988.[38] His wife settled in Miran-

---

35  Cited in Paul Cruickshank and Mohannad Hage Ali, 'Abu Musab Al Suri: Architect of the New Al Qaeda', *Studies in Conflict and Terrorism*, 30 (1) (Jan. 2007), p.4.

36  Author's interview with Professor Najib Ghadbian, email correspondence, 3 Oct. 2006. Interestingly, the early classic work *The Arab Helpers in Afghanistan*, from 1991, mentions several people using two of the same aliases as al-Suri did during this period, one of whom is a trainer at the al-Ghuraba Brigade (katibat al-ghuraba). This is incidentally the same name al-Suri later adopted for his own unit in Afghanistan under the Taleban. However, since *The Arab Helpers in Afghanistan* focuses mostly on the period up to 1987, it is unlikely that any of these figures is al-Suri. Basil Muhammad, *The Arab Helpers in Afghanistan* (in Arabic) (Riyadh, Jedda: The Islamic Benevolence Committee, Office of Studies and Documentation, 1991, second edn), pp.112, 233-4, 242. For more on the *katibat al-ghuraba*, see ibid., pp.173-9.

37  Jamal Khashoggi, 'Abu Mus'ab al-Suri was in the Syrian "Combatant Vanguard" and was expelled from the Muslim Brothers' (in Arabic), *al-Hayat* (London), 14 Jan. 1996, p.6.

38  The sources are contradictory with regard to the exact date for their

shah (or Miran Shah),[39] a small town located in North Waziristan, close to the Afghan-Pakistani border, which came under renewed scrutiny in 2006 due to reports of the Taleban having taking control of the town.[40] While al-Suri crossed into Afghanistan, his wife stayed behind with 'some of the sisters'.[41] She lived with the Sudanese wife of Qadi Kamal al-Sudani, a prominent figure in the Arab-Afghan community, and during her time in Miranshah she supervised Arabic classes for children.

The route via Miranshah into Afghanistan was one well trodden by many Arab volunteers.[42] Pakistan had a major forward supply base there through which it supported the training camps inside Afghanistan.[43] Al-Suri himself was located in Khowst on the Afghan side of the border, some 40 km. away. According to al-Suri's account, his wife could hear the artillery fire and see the flash of the blasts when Khowst came under Soviet bombardment. Their separation in the midst of a warzone did not put a damper on al-Suri's sense of romance: 'this

---

marriage. See José María Irujo, 'El hombre de Bin Laden en Madrid', *El País*, 2 March 2005, www.elPaís.es/comunes/2005/11m/08_comision/libro_electronico_red_islam/red_islamista_01%20doc.pdf, accessed July 2006, p.16; and 'Meeting with the Kuwaiti Newspaper', transcript of audiofile no.1, p.6.

39   On the tape it sounds like he says 'Midanshah', not Miranshah, but given the details he provides about its location, it is most likely Miranshah.

40   See, for example, 'Army regains control of Miranshah', *Dawn*, 6 March 2006; and Pazir Gul, 'Miranshah Taliban open office', *Dawn*, 28 Sept. 2006, accessed Oct. 2006.

41   'Meeting with the Kuwaiti Newspaper', transcript of audiofile no.1, p.6.

42   See, for example, Testimony of Jamal Ahmed Mohammed Al-Fadl, United States of America *v.* Osama Bin Laden, *et al.* Defendants, transcript of trial, 6 Feb. 2006, Day 2, http://cryptome.org/usa-v-ubl-dt.htm, accessed July 2006, pp.181-2; and testimony by L'Houssaine Kherchtou, United States of America *v.* Osama Bin Laden, *et al.* Defendants, transcript of trial, 21 Feb. 2006, Day 8, http://cryptome.org/usa-v-ubl-08.htm, accessed Oct. 2006, pp.1111-12.

43   Lester W. Grau and Ahmad Jalali, 'The Campaign for the Caves: The Battles for Zhawar in the Soviet-Afghan War', *Journal of Slavic Military Studies* 14 (3) (Sept. 2001), via www.globalsecurity.org/military/library/report/2001/010900-zhawar.htm, accessed Oct. 2006.

was a beautiful period; an excellent honeymoon in Afghanistan', he told his surprised interviewer in Kabul eleven years later.[44]

Al-Suri started to work as a military instructor in camps for Arab volunteer fighters near Khowst where he taught various skills, including close combat, drawing upon the black belt in judo he had acquired in France in 1984.[45] He was a strong, well-built man, as is evident from a picture of him taken in 1987 that was published in the Spanish press.[46] When he later came to London to work for various jihadi publications, journalists noted that 'he was built more like a weightlifter than a newspaper reporter'.[47]

These qualities were useful in Afghanistan, although his knowledge and training from his time with the Syrian MB were far more essential. According to his own account, he

trained some of its [al-Qaida's] first vanguards. I taught various military and organizational skills at its camps and also at the general camps for the Arab-Afghans, in particular in my fields of specialty, explosive engineering, special operations, and urban warfare. I had been highly trained in these disciplines in Egypt, Jordan and Iraq.[48]

In *The Global Islamic Resistance Call* al-Suri says he 'worked on-and-off' as a military instructor from the beginning of 1988 until 1991, in addition to lecturing on politics, strategy, and guerrilla warfare. He taught at al-Qaida camps, as well as at those of other jihadi organizations.[49] Al-Suri specifically mentions that he 'gave lectures during a cadre qualification course in the al-Qaida secret organization (*tanzim al-qa'idah*) for a selected group of young Arab mujahidin during the

---

44   'Meeting with the Kuwaiti Newspaper', transcript of audiofile no.1, p.6.

45   'Biography of Shaykh Umar Abd al-Hakim (Abu Mus'ab al-Suri)' (in Arabic), p.2.

46   Source: *El Mundo* online, at www.elmundo.es/elmundo/2005/11/03/espana/1131002447.html, accessed Dec. 2005.

47   Sean O'Neill and Daniel McGrory, *The Suicide Factory* (London: Harper Perennial, 2006), p.114.

48   'Communiqué from the Office of Abu Mus'ab al-Suri', 22 Dec. 2004, p.7.

49   *The Global Islamic Resistance Call*, p.711.

Afghan jihad in 1989, and the title was *Terrorism is a Gift* (al-irhab malakah).[50]

Al-Suri recalls that the Sada training camp was the first one he entered, but after having served as an instructor there for a while, he was relocated to the Zhawar camp.[51] The Zhawar, or Zawar Kili camp, was a large tunnel complex situated south of Khowst which had been constructed by the Pakistani military intelligence service, the ISI, in the early 1980s.[52] Al-Suri also served in more specialised camps for al-Qaida members, such as the al-Farouq training complex, but does not mention it by name.[53]

Al-Suri's training involvement in Sada and later in the specialized al-Qaida camps is significant. People who later rose to prominence in international jihadi terrorism, such as Khalid Shaykh Muhammad, Riduan Isamuddin, better known as Hanbali, and Abu Mus'ab al-Zarqawi had all been trained in Sada, although it is not known whether they actually met with al-Suri.[54] The training at Farouq was different from that of the Sada camp. The latter was located on the Pakistani side of the border, and had been established with the help of Abdallah Azzam and the Afghan warlord Abdul Rasul Sayyaf. It was only used by the nascent al-Qaida to a limited extent. In fact, at its very first meetings in August 1988, al-Qaida's Shura Council decided to send their 'limited duration'-recruits to the Sada camp

---

50   Ibid., p.1402.

51   'Meeting with the Kuwaiti Newspaper', transcript of audiofile no.1, p.6; and no.10, p.5.

52   I am indebted to my colleague Thomas Hegghammer for this information. See also Lester W. Grau and Ahmad Jalali, 'The Campaign for the Caves'.

53   Several sources claim that al-Suri had served in the Farouq camp, which was perhaps al-Qaida's main training facility at the time. Author's interview with Abdallah Anas, London 16 Sept. 2006; and author's interview with Noman Benotman, London 15 Sept. 2006.

54   See *The 9-11 Commission Report* 22 July 2004, pp.150, 164; Loretta Napoleoni, *Insurgent Iraq* (New York: Seven Stories Press, 2005), p.38; and Mary Anne Weaver, 'The Short, Violent Life of Abu Musab al-Zarqawi', *The Atlantic Monthly*, July/Aug. 2006.

for military training, while 'open-ended duration' recruits who were candidates for membership in the organization, were to go to a special 'testing camp', according to written minutes of that meeting.[55] Apparently, this 'testing camp' later became the well-known Farouq camp. A former bodyguard of bin Laden, Nasir Ahmad Nasir Abdallah al-Bahri, also known as Abu-Jandal, recalls the shift from Sada to the Farouq camp as follows:

After the arrival of many members of the Egyptian *al-jama'ah al-islamiyah* and *jama'at al-jihad* who were qualified militarily, Bin Ladin and those with whom he had a jihadist relationship established a new and more advanced training camp that was tantamount to a military college. It was called Al-Faruq Camp or the Al-Faruq Military College. The Al-Faruq Camp bypassed the 45-day period of quick training on weapons that was in force in the Sada Camp. It was established on the basis of a clear military methodology, a military college where cadets passed through a number of stages and levels until they finally graduated at the command level, as military commanders capable of leading any jihadist action anywhere. The idea of establishing that military college was a global idea. Thus, if the jihad in Afghanistan ends, graduates of the college can go anywhere in the world and capably command battles there.[56]

Al-Suri's account of his involvement in al-Qaida represents one of the many retrospective references to al-Qaida that were written after 2001. While it does not prove the existence of al-Qaida as an organization (*tanzim al-qa'idah*) in the late 1980s, it is nevertheless interesting that he reveals his own participation in the deliberate training of terrorist skills in the Afghan camps at this early point. There has been much controversy about the actual origin of al-Qaida and nature of the organization in its early phases, partly arising out

---

55   'TAREEKHOSAMA/54/TareekhOsama127⁻127a' (Documents retrieved from a computer seized at the Sarajevo offices of Benevolence International Foundation (BIF), and later entered into evidence in the Chicago trial of Enaam Arnaout, a Syrian BIF employee convicted of racketeering in 2003), cited in Peter Bergen, 'The Osama bin Laden I know: Excerpts', www.tpmcafe.com/story/2006/1/18/13810/7770, accessed Jan. 2007.

56   Cited in 'An Insider's View of Al-Qa'ida as Narrated by Abu-Jandal (Nasir al-Bahri), Bin-Ladin's Bodyguard (Part 4)', (in Arabic), *Al-Quds al-Arabi* (London), 22 March 2005, p.19. English translation from FBIS.

of the conundrum that the name al-Qaida was hardly known, at least not to outsiders, before the late 1990s. A widely held view has been that al-Qaida as an organization only came into existence much later, and that for much of the 1990s it was more of a loose network of like-minded militants, an ideological movement of some sort, rather than a structured organization.[57] Al-Suri's account here and elsewhere reinforces the view that al-Qaida was already an organization with a certain infrastructural basis, rather than simply a loose network.[58]

## FROM MILITARY INSTRUCTOR TO JIHADI INTELLECTUAL

From his arrival in 1987 until 1989, al-Suri says he concentrated almost exclusively on the practical aspects of jihad by educating young Arab volunteers in guerrilla warfare and terrorism skills.[59] In these efforts, al-Suri drew upon his experiences from various training courses in Iraq, Jordan, and, in particular, Egypt.[60] In fact, he describes his training courses in Afghanistan as 'a summary of the training course we received in Egypt and which I brought here in its entirety. We developed it further here [i.e. in Afghanistan],' adding only a course he developed himself in the field of military engineering.[61]

Al-Suri claims to have fought in several battles during the Afghan liberation war. As a rule, he used to take his trainees for a 'graduation ceremony' that included a tour to the front lines and active participation in combat inside Afghanistan.[62] He also said he took part in the combat in and around Jalalabad before the city was captured and in

---

57 See especially Jason Burke, *Al-Qaeda: Casting a Shadow of Terror* (London: I. B. Tauris, 2003).

58 For primary sources about al-Qaida's early organization and activities, see 'Harmony Document List', Combating Terrorism Center at West Point website, www.ctc.usma.edu/aq_harmonylist.asp, accessed Oct. 2006; and Peter Bergen, *The Osama bin Laden I know* (New York: Tree Press, 2006).

59 'Meeting with the Kuwaiti Newspaper', transcript of audiofile no.1, p.6.

60 Ibid., p.7.

61 Ibid.

62 Ibid.

the battles before the fall of Khowst. For a while he fought under the Afghan warlord Shaykh Jalal al-Din Haqqani.[63] There are very few details of his relationship with Haqqani, except that he attended meetings and other gatherings in Haqqani's house in Peshawar.[64]

Al-Suri did not spend his time in Peshawar and Afghanistan in 1987-92 in constant training, combat and military preparation. In fact, at least in the latter part of this period, he began to devote himself more to intellectual matters rather than to the practicalities of jihad. He studied the writings of Sayyid Qutb and Abdallah Azzam, both of whom had significant influence on his subsequent development as a jihadi theorist. Al-Suri also read other literature from which contemporary salafi-jihadism derives, such as the writings of the medieval salafi-wahhabi Ibn Taymiyyah, his disciple Ibn al-Qayyim, classical salafi-wahhabi literature, and writings of clerics associated with the contemporary revivalist movement (*al-sahwa*) in Saudi Arabia. At the training camps he urged his students to study the books of the Saudi scholars Ibn Baz and Ibn Uthaymin, albeit after cautioning his students about their 'hypocritical position', especially their acceptance of the Saudi royal family.[65]

In addition to reading and teaching salafi theology and the classics of jihad, he took correspondence courses at the Faculty of History at Beirut Arab University at its Jordanian branch in Amman.[66] This training as an historian is evident in many of his later works, which rely heavily on analysis of past historical processes and events to extract lessons learned and new strategies for the jihadi movement. His 900-page work on the Syrian jihadi revolution, which also contained a fair amount of key primary sources, was partly a by-product of his immersion in history. His inclination for intellectual work was also

---

63    'Meeting with the Kuwaiti Newspaper', transcript of audiofile no.3, p.2, and no.1, p.7.

64    *The Global Islamic Resistance Call*, p.50.

65    'Biography of Shaykh Umar Abd al-Hakim (Abu Mus'ab al-Suri)' (in Arabic), p.2.

66    Ibid., pp.2-3.

demonstrated by his efforts to develop and tailor new and more suitable training programs, for example courses in 'theories of guerrilla warfare', including command-and-control in guerrilla warfare, its military and ideological aspects, recruitment, the military and the media and so on.[67]

Over time, the training activities of the Arab-Afghans assumed larger proportions. Many graduates began giving courses themselves. They were also being reinforced by the arrival of new volunteer fighters who had served as army officers in Iraq, Egypt and other countries. The material situation also improved greatly with respect to military training.[68]

With the rapid improvement of the military training programs, al-Suri began to see deficiencies in the field of religious-theological and ideological education of the recruits. He began worrying that many of the newly arrived volunteers 'did not understand the nature of this struggle'.[69] While he noticed that at least some 'mujahidin youth' arriving from Egypt, Syria and North Africa possessed some 'ideological and political awareness', the volunteers arriving from Yemen and the Arab peninsula had only a 'superficial understanding' of the struggle; they simply wanted to 'finish the Communists, and help the Afghans win, that's it'.[70] In his writings during this period, he stresses that one cannot start a jihadi campaign with arms 'unless one has digested the principles, ideas and foundations [for jihad] [...] This is what distinguishes a knowledgeable mujahid from a warrior who may turn into a Godless brigand'.[71]

Against this background, al-Suri came to see his role evolving more towards that of an ideologue and intellectual, rather than simply a military instructor. A driving force behind this transformation

---

67    'Meeting with the Kuwaiti Newspaper', transcript of audiofile no.1, p.7.

68    Ibid.

69    Ibid.

70    'Meeting with the Kuwaiti Newspaper (al-Ra'i al-'Amm) in Kabul, 18 March 1999' (in Arabic), transcript of audiofile no.1, pp.7-8.

71    Umar Abd al-Hakim, *The Islamic Jihadi Revolution in Syria. Part I*, p.10.

was his insistence on the inadequacy of military training alone. In al-Suri's eyes, religious-theological and ideological training was far more important; the military component should preferably not exceed 20-30 % of the total training input.[72] This conviction was partly a result of his experience with the Syrian MB movement, which, in his view, had failed due to a lack of ideological awareness. Around 1990, al-Suri turned away from the specialized military training courses and devoted more time to general courses on guerrilla warfare, and from there he moved towards politico-religious topics that he termed 'legal-political Islamic jurisprudence' (*al-fiqh al-siyasi al-shar'i*) and more fundamental philosophical issues such as: 'Who are we? What do we want? Who are our enemies? What do they want? What is the nature of this struggle?'[73]

In many ways, Peshawar around 1990 seemed a fertile ground for new ideas about jihadism. At that time, it was considered 'the capital of the Islamic world', from the jihadi point of view; every ongoing discussion and debate there quickly spread to the rest of the world, through audio communiqués, books, leaflets, audiocassettes, and through couriers and visitors.[74] Hence, al-Suri had ample opportunity to find an audience for his first publication, which appeared in its final form in May 1991. In this period, he felt that he had taken 'the first steps towards becoming one of the theoreticians in the leadership [of the jihadi movement]'.[75]

Even though his work on the Syrian jihadi revolution was written mostly in the late 1980s, al-Suri's intellectual career did not start in earnest until the 1990s, when he was well into his thirties. However, he never lost contact with the real-world problems of jihadi fighters, and he approached the topic from the vantage point of a military instructor, with a keen eye for the practical aspects of jihad and with

---

72  'Meeting with the Kuwaiti Newspaper', transcript of audiofile no.1, p.7.
73  Ibid., p.8.
74  'Meeting with the Kuwaiti Newspaper', transcript of audiofile no.2, p.1.
75  Ibid.

a desire to learn from past experiences and correct the path of the jihadi movements.

## THE RISE OF THE EGYPTIAN JIHADI TREND IN PESHAWAR

Al-Suri's emphasis on the need for more ideological awareness reflected the rapid evolution of radical Islamist thinking during the late 1980s. In al-Suri's view, 'jihadi ideology had crystallised and matured' very much during that period, especially with the release of a number of important works on jihadism by important ideologues such as Shaykh Sayyid Imam al-Sharif, better known as Doctor Fadl, or Abd al-Qadir bin Abd al-Aziz, and the Jordanian cleric Issam Muhammad al-Barqawi, better known as Abu Muhammad al-Maqdisi.[76] (Al-Suri also included his own work on the Syrian jihadi revolution in this list of key readings.) Furthermore, important personalities and leaders of jihadi movements around the world gravitated to Afghanistan and contributed to developing the body of jihadi thinking, including Shaykh Umar Abd al-Rahman, the so-called 'Blind Shaykh', who was considered the spiritual authority of the Egyptian Islamic Group (JI, al-jama'ah al-islamiyyah).[77]

During this period, al-Suri befriended several prominent jihadi leaders and intellectuals, most of whom were Egyptians, such as Ayman al-Zawahiri, Umar Abd al-Rahman, and Rifa'i Taha. One of those who seemed to have influenced al-Suri the most, in addition to Abdallah Azzam, was Doctor Fadl, the supreme religious scholar of Egyptian Islamic Jihad (EIJ, jama'at al-jihad bi-misr), and perhaps also its leading theoretician.[78] Born in Bani Suweif in August 1950,

---

76   Abu Muhammad al-Maqdisi's most important works during this period included *The Creed of Abraham* (millat ibrahim) and *The Evident Proofs of the Infidelity of the Saudi State* (al-kawashif al-jaliyah fi kufr al-dawlah al-su'udiyyah). Both are available at *minbar al-tawhid wa'l-jihad*, www. tawhed.ws/t?PHPSESSID=9fd7e559c18bd59d5e23a630e0f9e4e4, accessed Oct. 2006.

77   'Meeting with the Kuwaiti Newspaper', transcript of audiofile no.1, p.7.

78   'Biography of Shaykh Umar Abd al-Hakim (Abu Mus 'ab al-Suri)' (in

he graduated in medicine, and worked at the prestigious Qasr al-Ayini Hospital in Central Cairo. In the massive security sweeps following al-Sadat's assassination, he was detained, but managed later to flee Egypt. He travelled to Peshawar where he reportedly became director of the Kuwaiti Crescent Hospital in the city.[79] Together with al-Zawahiri and a few others, he became the most influential voice in the new jihadi trend in Peshawar. Doctor Fadl was the author of several jihadi classics, including *The Pillar in the Preparation of Jihad in the Way of God* (al-'umda fi i'dad al-'uddah lil-jihad fi sabil allah) and *Compilation for Seeking Religious Knowledge* (al-jami' fi talb al-'ilm al-sharif). Both were first published around 1990 and still figure prominently in the jihadi curriculum. For example, excerpts of *The Pillar* were found in the possession of the al-Qaida cell uncovered and arrested in Spain in late 2001.[80]

Al-Suri benefited greatly from this acquaintance in terms of his own intellectual development and theological learning. Both Doctor Fadl and Abdallah Azzam volunteered to review al-Suri's early writings, including his book on the Syrian jihadi experience and a 35pp. communiqué released in 1991, an early draft of what later became *The Global Islamic Resistance Call*.[81]

The Afghan experience was a great opportunity for al-Suri to expand his contacts with and knowledge about jihadi groups from various parts of the world. As he saw it, most if not all such movements

---

Arabic), p.2.

79  Doctor Fadl later went to Sudan and Yemen, and was arrested there shortly after the 9/11 attacks. He was handed over to Egyptian authorities in Feb. 2004, where he already had been given a life sentence from 1999. See more details on his life story at 'The File of Abd al-Qadir bin Abd al-Aziz' (in Arabic), *minbar al-tawhid wa'l-jihad*, undated, www.tawhed.ws/a?i=6, accessed Oct. 2006.

80  'Juzgado Central de Instruccion, no.005, Madrid, Sumario', 17 Sept. 2003, p.172.

81  'Biography of Shaykh Umar Abd al-Hakim (Abu Mus 'ab al-Suri)' (in Arabic), p.2.

had a presence there. Peshawar and Afghanistan became a true university [...] This was a turning in Muslim history. People met, thoughts and perspectives met, and personalities met. Groups fought out their rivalries, and different thoughts and ideas competed. It was a kind of birthplace. Much of what you see today is a result of this period.[82]

Al-Suri claims to have spent most of his time in Peshawar and Afghanistan in 1987-9 in the company of Abdallah Azzam, and he says he 'got to know most of the Arab-Afghan cadres'.[83] He trained both rank-and-file members and commanders in the EIJ and the JI, the two largest Egyptian jihadi groups. He also trained Palestinians, as well as hundreds of 'brothers' from the Arabian peninsula, Yemen, and other Arab countries. Among his trainees, al-Suri mentions in particular Anwar Sha'ban, who later served as head of the infamous Islamic Centre in Milan, a hub for militant Islamists in Europe, and also a leader of the Arab mujahidin in Bosnia during the war in 1992-5.[84] While it is difficult to ascertain these claims, there were clearly several Syrian trainers in Arab-Afghan camps, although the Syrian contingent there was very small, and they also trained members of the Egyptian groups.[85]

---

82   'Meeting with the Kuwaiti Newspaper (al-Ra'i al-'Amm) in Kabul, 18 March 1999' (in Arabic), transcript of audiofile no.1, p.6.

83   Ibid.

84   'Meeting with the Kuwaiti Newspaper', transcript of audiofile no.1, pp.6-7. For a biography of Anwar Sha'ban written by his followers, see 'Biography of Shaheed Shaykh Anwar Sha'ban', (Excerpts from *Under the Shade of Swords* by Azzam Publications), *IslamicAwakening.com*, 28 April 2004, http://forums.islamicawakening.com/archive/index.php/t-13.html, accessed Oct. 2006. See also Evan Kohlman, *Al-Qaida's Jihad in Europe: The Afghan-Bosnian Network* (Oxford: Berg Publishers, 2004).

85   A significant number of Syrians are mentioned by name and their activities described in detail in Basil Muhammad's *The Arab Helpers in Afghanistan*. Furthermore, the Arabic magazine *al-Watan al-Arabi* has noted that 'the leading figures in the [Egyptian] Islamic movement benefited enormously from the war in Afghanistan, because they were able to forge a wide network with Islamic movements throughout the world. A measure of the diversity of these contacts is that Palestinians and Syrians oversaw the training of the Egyptian Islamic groups'. See Basil Muhammad, *The Arab*

In an interview with *al-Ra'y al-Amm* in March 1999, al-Suri addressed directly what lay behind the Arab participation in the Afghan jihad, as he himself had understood it from Abdallah Azzam. The aim from the very beginning was to educate and train cadres from all nationalities of the Islamic nation (*ummah*) who would then reinvigorate their respective jihadi causes upon their return home. He claims Azzam used to say that he wanted half of the 40,000 or so Arab volunteers to become martyrs for the Afghan cause and the rest to return home, 'carrying with them jihad as trained fighters': this was the 'basic goal of the presence in Afghanistan'.[86]

Al-Suri portrays Azzam as a staunch advocate of a global jihadi struggle not only against non-Muslim occupation and aggression, but also against apostate Muslim rulers and their supporters in the West. However, this reading of Azzam is misleading, as the latter was known to have ridiculed the revolutionary jihadis.[87] In essence, by the late 1980s a chasm was opening up in the Arab-Afghan community. There was a growing animosity between Doctor Fadl and several EIJ members on the one hand, and Abdallah Azzam and his Muslim Brotherhood supporters on the other. Camille Tawil, a journalist with *al-Hayat* in London and an eminent expert on the militant islamists, notes that the jihadi scene in Peshawar in the early 1990s was fluid, consisting of several competing trends. Some were

---

*Helpers in Afghanistan*, pp.100, 111-113, 123, 226-7, 238; and Mahmud Sadiq, 'Cairo Combats Islamists Overseas' (in Arabic), *al-Watan al-Arabi*, 28 May 1998, pp.4-6, cited in Anonymous, *Through Our Enemies' Eyes: Osama bin Laden, Radical Islam, and the Future of America* (Washington: Brassey's, 2002), p.108.

86  'Meeting with the Kuwaiti Newspaper (al-Ra'i al-'Amm) in Kabul, 18 March 1999' (in Arabic), transcript of audiofile no.1, p.7. This point is also mentioned in Antonio Rubio, 'Mustafa Setmarian Naser: Un español en la cima de Al Qaeda: Durante los diez años que vivió en España se convirtió en lugarteniente de Bin Laden', *elmundo.es*, 3 Nov. 2005, www.elmundo.es/elmundo/2005/11/03/espana/1131002447.html, accessed Dec. 2005, which refers to the same source.

87  I am indebted to my colleague Thomas Hegghammer for this information. See his 'Abdallah Azzam: L'imam du jihad', pp.115-37.

Muslim Brotherhood adherents, some jihadis and others were simply 'open brigades', as they were called. The latter were youths who had come to Peshawar primarily to fight and were open to various ideological influences. All the strands of jihadism competed to influence and win them over to their point of view.[88]

If al-Suri had a close relationship with Abdallah Azzam, he probably had to take sides, and he chose the jihadi camp. In fact, al-Suri was known to belong to a hard-line faction of the Arab-Afghan movement, which rose to prominence in 1989, prior to Abdallah Azzam's death, and launched vicious attacks on the mainstream Muslim Brotherhood trend that had dominated the Arab-Afghans. When *al-Hayat* wrote about al-Suri in the mid-1990s, he was said to have 'isolated himself from the Muslim Brotherhood in Peshawar. [...] There, together with some Egyptians, he formed a radical jihadi current and issued a book called "The Islamic Jihadi Revolution in Syria", in which he harshly criticised the Muslim Brothers'.[89]

The Egyptian-led jihadi current came to influence the young bin Laden towards a more uncompromising and revolutionary ideology, although he never fully adopted its program. The EIJ-faction, headed by Ayman al-Zawahiri, was reinforcing the reorientation from the classic Islamic doctrine of defending Muslim lands against foreign aggression, towards a revolutionary ideology directed against Arab governments and, increasingly, their foreign supporters.[90] This ideological strand had roots in Egyptian militant Islamism, from Sayyid Qutb's *Signposts* in the 1960s and Muhammad Abd al-Salam Faraj's 1981 epistle, *The Neglected Duty*, but al-Zawahiri gradually managed to make this revolutionary jihadism far more widespread and acceptable in the circle around bin Laden.

---

88 Author's interview with Camille Tawil, London, 14 Sept. 2006.

89 Jamal Khashoggi, 'Abu Mus'ab al-Suri was in the Syrian "Combatant Vanguard" and was expelled from the Muslim Brothers' (in Arabic), *al-Hayat* (London), 14 Jan. 1996, p.6.

90 For more on al-Zawahiri's role see, for example, Lawrence Wright, 'The Man Behind Bin Laden', *The New Yorker*, 16 Sept. 2002.

According to Abdallah Anas, Azzam's son-in-law, the hardline jihadi group in Peshawar was more akin to 'an ideological league' (*rabitah fikriyyah*) than a structured organization. They condemned the Muslim Brotherhood current, to which Abdallah Azzam belonged, and rejected any participation in political elections, party politics or compromises or coexistence with Arab governments.[91] Those associated with the new jihadi current of al-Zawahiri began saying that Abdallah Azzam was wrong, and that the armed campaign should not be limited to Afghanistan, but should move towards a revolutionary posture vis-à-vis Muslim governments.[92]

While most Arab-Afghan volunteers did not accept the new jihadi trend, a sizeable minority did, and the EIJ-faction, headed by al-Zawahiri, gradually came to dominate bin Laden's inner circle—or as Anas puts it: 'he was poisoned by the Egyptians'.[93] Al-Suri largely confirms this account, albeit in far more positive language. Osama bin Laden and many of the Saudi youths who arrived in Afghanistan, were deeply influenced by the Saudi *sahwi*, or revivalist, current, which al-Suri describes as a mix of thinking from the Muslim Brotherhood, the Muhammad Surur school, and clerics from the official salafi-wahhabi school. Against this background, it was natural for bin Laden and his Saudi contingent to accept the Saudi regime, by and large, as legitimate rulers, and to possess a deep respect for Saudi official clerics. In this regard they came from a very different perspective than did the jihadi groups from Egypt, Syria, Algeria and elsewhere. Al-Suri describes this difference as follows: 'we only shared the generalities of Islam and the common aim to achieve victory for the Afghan jihad'.[94] Al-Suri claims to have discussed these ideological differences in detail with Osama bin Laden on numerous occasions, on the basis of which he concluded, in 1990, that 'the

---

91  Author's interview with Abdallah Anas, London 16 Sept. 2006.
92  Author's interview with Camille Tawil, London, 14 Sept. 2006.
93  Author's interview with Abdallah Anas, London 16 Sept. 2006.
94  *The Global Islamic Resistance Call*, p.712.

Shaikh' was ideologically still very far from the salafi-jihadi current represented by al-Zawahiri and the EIJ.[95]

But this was to change. Al-Suri recalls that bin Laden 'gradually became convinced and digested and finally embraced the jihadi ideology and became one of its symbols'.[96] There were two main reasons for this. Perhaps the most important one was the Saudi response to the Iraqi invasion of Kuwait and the invitation extended by the Kingdom to US soldiers. Al-Suri also emphasises the fact that bin Laden's contacts with, and influence from among, the more experienced EIJ-cadres, especially al-Zawahiri in Afghanistan, made him more attuned to the hard-line Qutbist ideology.[97] Al-Suri, the EIJ and other jihadi cadres fervently advocated this ideology in the Arab-Afghan community. This went so far that 'Saudi youth received small arms training by firing shots at figures of King Fahd and senior Saudi princes', al-Suri recalls.[98]

The rise of the jihadi trend was greatly facilitated by the new geopolitical circumstances created by the end of the Cold War. These paradigmatic shifts also contributed to the propelling of al-Suri into the role of a jihadi intellectual. He recalls the year 1990 as being a turning point for himself and the Arab-Afghan movement.[99] The combined effect of the Soviet withdrawal from Afghanistan, the gradual disintegration of Communist rule in Kabul, and the onslaught of 'new crusader raids and campaigns on the Islamic world' had created a heated debate about the way ahead for the movement. By the 'new crusader raids', al-Suri and his fellow jihadis meant 'Operation Desert Shield', which involved the stationing of hundreds of thousands of US and US-allied troops on the Arab peninsula, followed by Operation Desert Storm, during which Kuwait was liberated from Iraqi occupation and Iraq was placed under perhaps the

---

95    Ibid.
96    Ibid.
97    Ibid.
98    Ibid.
99    'Meeting with the Kuwaiti Newspaper', transcript of audiofile no.2, pp.1-2.

harshest ever UN-administered sanctions regime. Within the jihadi movement controversial debates raged over the the role of Islamist clerics, especially in Saudi Arabia, and about Islamist participation in parliamentary elections, an issue which the Algerian democratic experience in the early 1990s had highlighted. Al-Suri compared the effect of these events, and especially the repercussions of the Gulf War, to that of an 'earthquake' for the Arab-Afghan movement.[100]

One witnessed what may be described as an ideological and mental earthquake, particularly for the Arab-Afghan mujahidin, when the international allied forces under the leadership of America descended on the Arab peninsula under the cover of what was called "the liberation of Kuwait". It was abundantly clear that this was only a convenient curtain for new vicious crusader campaigns, which America, Western Europe and the Jews launched towards the midst of Islam's homeland in the Levant, Iraq and the Arab peninsula. [...] There was no doubt whatsoever that the Islamic Nation, its holy places, and wealthy resources, especially its oil reserves were being targeted by a wave of direct Crusader-Jewish military occupation, an occupation which ultimately aimed at a complete liquidation of the civilizationary presence of Muslims. This earthquake was only months later, at the beginning of 1991, followed by another wave of seismic shocks with the self-proclamation of peace projects with the Jews to sell what remained of Palestine and Jerusalem.[101]

Two different factions, or 'tendencies', emerged among the training camp commanders and the jihadi leaders in Afghanistan, al-Suri recalled. The first group, supported by the considerable Saudi constituency in Afghanistan, did not want to get involved in further fighting, fearing that this would create problems with the governments at home, and that they would be accused of being *kharijites* and *takfiri*, terms which basically refer to ancient and modern day outlaws in Islam.[102] The reason for this position was that most lead-

---

100 'Meeting with the Kuwaiti Newspaper', transcript of audiofile no.1, p.8.

101 *The Global Islamic Resistance Call*, p.46.

102 The *kharijites* or the *khawarij* (literally 'Those who Go Out') refers to the Islamic sects which rejected the caliphate of Ali, the fourth Caliph. They are distinct from the two main denominations in Islam, the Sunnis and Shiites. *Takfir* is the act of declaring Muslims as infidels or *kafir*, pl.

ing Sunni clerics at the time, including the leading Islamist clerics of the Muslim Brotherhood, issued fatwas supporting the official Saudi position that the stationing of US forces in Saudi Arabia was a legitimate emergency measure by the Saudi government.

The other faction wished to respond to 'this collapse of the Islamic activism and the breakdown of the basic foundation of the Sunni officialdom', as al-Suri put it.[103] This was the jihadi trend led by al-Zawahiri, and al-Suri found himself among it. Soon, he became involved in a new initiative, entitled *The Nur Media Centre* (markaz al-nur lil-i'lam). The centre was founded and supervised by Shaykh Abu Hudhayfa, a senior EIJ member in Peshawar.[104] A group of 'thinkers, clerics, and shaykhs' was involved in setting up the centre, according to al-Suri,[105] the purpose of which was 'to give an ideological push' to the Arab-Afghan scene in Peshawar.[106] When he later wrote about the centre, he described it as follows:

A number of preachers and lecturers from the jihadi groups took upon themselves to organise a series of lectures, classes and Friday sermons at the centre. Several nascent jihadi groups would come in and listen. They held a number of ideological and educational courses there, and were able to attract the older guard in the jihadi current to teach and give lectures. Then, they began teaching their cadres on their own. In this way, the centre's idea crystallised and became productive...[107]

The Nur Centre was not entirely unknown in Islamist and jihadi circles. It was considered primarily a media centre, not really a headquarters for the new jihadi trend.[108] Al-Suri's involvement with this

---

*kuffar.*

103  'Meeting with the Kuwaiti Newspaper', transcript of audiofile no.2.

104  *The Global Islamic Resistance Call*, p.719.

105  In one part of the 1999 interview al-Suri refers to 'some Egyptian brothers who had been his students', but was unable to recall the name of the founder. 'Meeting with the Kuwaiti Newspaper', transcript of audiofile no.2, pp.1, 8.

106  *The Global Islamic Resistance Call*, p.51.

107  Ibid., p.719.

108  Author's interview with Abdallah Anas, London 16 Sept. 2006.

group was an important development in his life. It happened almost by chance, but appears to have been yet another step in his evolution as a jihadi intellectual:

The Nur Centre was created and as one of those present, I felt very strongly about the need for this. The whole thing started very randomly. In fact, until then, I knew myself as someone who had some combat skills [...] I had not really thought of myself as a thinker and intellectual, working with the great causes [concerning the Islamic Nation], but almost by coincidence I began giving lectures on guerrilla warfare, and then we moved on to the topic of politics in Islam.[109]

Al-Suri now began lecturing not only at the Nur Centre, but also at prominent guesthouses for mujahidin volunteers, such as the *bayt al-mujahidin* ('House of Islamic Warriors') in Peshawar, which had adopted al-Zawahiri's program and was known to be overseen by bin Laden.[110] At the same time, al-Suri began to record his lectures. Under the pseudonym Khalid bin al-'Abidin, he released sixteen audiocassettes, produced 'between the battle fronts and the al-Nur Center', as he put it.[111] These speeches or lectures dealt with guerrilla warfare theories and the organization of clandestine cells, and were rooted in al-Suri's reflections on the Syrian experience, and also in broader political themes such as the geopolitics of the new global political order.

In recent years, many of these audiotapes from around 1990 have been made available on jihadi websites, mostly in audiofiles. It appears that at least one of these lectures from al-Suri's 'first Afghanistan collection' was held at the Nur Media Centre in 1990, while others were reportedly given at different guesthouses in Peshawar and training camps inside Afghanistan. Available sources are slightly inconsistent with regards to the title/content, place and time they

---

109 'Meeting with the Kuwaiti Newspaper', transcript of audiofile no.2, p.1.

110 Author's interview with Abdallah Anas, London, 16 Sept. 2006.

111 'Meeting with the Kuwaiti Newspaper', transcript of audiofile no.2, p.1-2.

were given. With this in mind, it seems clear that he delivered the following series of lectures in 1989 and 1990:[112]

- 'The Bases and Components of a Secret Organization';
- 'The Political Equation of The New World Order';
- 'Overview of the History of the Islamic Movement: its Past, Present, and Future';
- 'General Rules for Addressing Muslim Clerics';
- 'On the Book "The Syrian Jihadi Experience"';
- 'Lessons in the Theories of Guerrilla Warfare';
- 'On Explaining the Global Islamic Resistance'.

In his lecture 'The Political Equation of The New World Order', al-Suri sketched the rearrangement of the frontlines in what he describes as the coming stages of war. While the confrontation with Communism had blurred the frontlines between the West and Islam, the demise of the Soviet Union, the end of the Afghan liberation war, the Gulf War, and the resultant US 'military occupation' of Saudi Arabia had radically changed the dangers emanating from the

---

112 In April 2006, for example, the *muntada al-sawt* website posted seven lecture series by al-Suri under the heading 'the first Afghanistan collection'. According to the introductions on the audiotapes at least of one these was held at the Nur Media Centre (*markaz al-nur lil-i'lam*) in Peshawar, in 1990. The other audiofiles did not have an introduction. Abu Mus'ab al-Suri's website on www.fsboa.com/vw/index.php, which used to contain the most comprehensive overview of his works, listed *nine* different audiotaped lecture series that were delivered in Peshawar and several camps in Afghanistan in 1989-1990. However, from their content it appears as if the webmaster has subdivided at least one lecture series into two lectures and added a lecture on the Algerian jihad that al-Suri probably gave much later in London. In his writings, al-Suri mentions his lectures but provides slightly different details about their titles and when they were given. See 'The Old Production of Shaykh Abu Mus'ab al-Suri, 1987-2001' (in Arabic), *Abu Mus'ab al-Suri's website*, www.fsboa.com/vw/index.php, accessed Sept. 2005; 'Who is Abu Mus'ab al-Suri?' (in Arabic), *muntada al-sawt* 20 June 2006, www.saowt.com/forum/showthread.php?t=16158 &highlight=%E3%E4+%E5%E6+%C3%C8%E6+%E3%D5%DA%C8+ %C7%E1%D3%E6%D1%ED+%BF, accessed Sept. 2006; 'Meeting with the Kuwaiti Newspaper', transcript of audiofile no.2, p.1; and *The Global Islamic Resistance Call*, pp.51-2.

Crusader enemy and its allies. In al-Suri's view, the political equation was simple: 'new world order versus the armed jihadi current'.[113] While this was not very controversial, he had nevertheless provoked his audience by including both the 'Sunni Islamic official religious hierarchy' and the 'democratic Islamic revivalist movement' on the side of the Crusader Enemy.[114]

| The New World Order | X | The Armed Jihadi Current |
| --- | --- | --- |
| The Crusaders and their leader, USA<br>The Jewry-Zionism and its leader, Israel<br>Apostate Rulers in Muslim Countries<br>Deviant Sects opposing the Sunni Islam<br>Sunni Islamic official religious hierarchy<br>Democratic Islamic Revivalist Movement | | The Armed Islamic Groups<br>which are the Vanguard<br>of the Islamic Nation |

Source: *The Global Islamic Resistance Call*, p.52; and 'The Bases and Components of a Secret Organization', audiotaped lecture, tape 1.

In another lecture that was delivered around 1990, al-Suri explored the organizational underpinnings of successful jihadi groups. It was recorded on three further audiotapes, entitled 'The Bases and Components of a Secret Organization' (*usus wa muqawwimat al-tanzim*).[115] Although he addressed the theme on a general basis, he clearly had the two Egyptian groups, the EIJ and JI, in mind and mentioned them repeatedly during the lecture, which appears to have been part of efforts to unite them. Al-Suri mentioned his own discussions with the JI leader, Umar Abd al-Rahman, about the ideological differences between JI and EIJ.

---

113  See figure and explanation in *The Global Islamic Resistance Call*, p.52.

114  Ibid.

115  'The Bases and Components of a Secret Organization'. Audiotaped lecture, delivered in Peshawar or Afghanistan in 1989 or 1990. Accessed via *muntada al-sawt*, 20 June 2006, www.saowt.com/forum/showthread. php?t=16158&highlight=%E3%E4+%E5%E6+%C3%C8%E6+%E3%D5 %DA%C8+%C7%E1%D3%E6%D1%ED+%BF, accessed Sept. 2006.

In his lecture, al-Suri identified the following factors as being key to success:

- Ideology and a program of action: This is indispensable, since all action has to be based on ideological awareness. Otherwise, the group would be reduced to a militia.

- Leadership and Shura Council: All groups need an emir, and a Shura (or Consultation) Council. Consultation with members is not obligatory. In fact, democracy, in the sense that a majority vote should decide, ought to be rejected as a principle. The Emir should instead appoint a small number of councillors and seek their advice.

- Long-term financial support: Dependence on governments and rich donors is unreliable and risky, while members are often unable to raise sufficient funds. Al-Suri offered two options. One was the possibility of 'raising funds through jihad', for example by seizing money from infidels and Muslims who do not support jihad. The second was to invest in long-term businesses, even if it reduces the group's operational activity Appointing a body responsible for the group's financial activities is mandatory.

- Planning and strategy: The group needs certain 'objectives' that do not change over time, even though the details may occasionally vary.

- Absolute obedience and allegiance among the membership: Loyalty to the group should be absolute, but the leadership cannot expect obedience if the group keeps changing its goals. If the leadership fails to uphold its ideology or pursue a clearcut plan, it cannot expect complete loyalty among it members. Similarly, if financial sources dry up, disobedience among members will set in.

Much of the above are commonsensical observations, although his two recommendations for a new financial strategy are interesting in the light of subsequent developments. As will be seen in subsequent chapters, al-Suri was to devote most of his efforts to supporting the Algerian GIA during the early 1990s, and its supporters in Europe were heavily involved in fundraising for the group through petty crime and racketeering. Furthermore, as it turned out, al-Qaida did build an independent financial empire *before* its terrorist campaign started in earnest and it also shunned any kind of financial dependence on a state sponsor.

In his lecture, al-Suri concluded that most of the so-called 'secret organizations' (*tanzimat*) did not fulfill the five requirements he had outlined. In an interview in 1999, he recalled that his lectures caused much consternation because he indirectly accused the jihadis of lacking the necessary organizational abilities needed for success, even if he professed to do so in the interest of correcting the path of jihad.[116] Al-Suri's recollection seems to have been correct, and judging by the audiotape, whose quality is poor, he said something like this:

With regards to our group, we lack preparations for action. Our strategy is not established. Our leadership does not carry out "legitimate consultation" [i.e. within the inner circle of councillors]. If the Emir asks for advice, he asks the whole group! Furthermore, our financial plans are not sufficient for our needs. Our ideology is also not developed. We also lack a thorough understanding for the need of selfcriticism and opportunities for reporting to the leadership about needs for change. This is a vital part for any group who wishes to improve its performance.[117]

Al-Suri's outspokenness was yet another indication of his desire to be a fearless critic of and intellectual in the jihadi movement. Although he saw himself as a participant and contributor to the causes of jihad, he took upon himself the duty of pointing out deficiencies, shortcomings, and errors. This quality was exactly what later earned him a reputation as a 'controversial' figure and a 'born critic', one whom it was difficult to locate in the landscape of jihadi groups, many of which were dominated by charismatic personalities.[118]

---

116 'Meeting with the Kuwaiti Newspaper', transcript of audiofile no.2, p.1.

117 'The Bases and Components of a Secret Organization'. Audiotaped lecture, held in Peshawar or Afghanistan in 1989 or 1990. Accessed via *muntada al-sawt*, 20 June 2006, www.saowt.com/forum/showthread.php?t=16158 &highlight=%E3%E4+%E5%E6+%C3%C8%E6+%E3%D5%DA%C8+ %C7%E1%D3%E6%D1%ED+%BF, accessed Sept. 2006.

118 The term 'born critic' has been used by Noman Benotman who knew al-Suri well during the 1990s. Author's interview with Noman Benotman, London 15 Sept. 2006. See also Pierre Akel, 'Abu Mus'ab al-Suri: "I deplore that there were no weapons of mass destruction in the planes that destroyed

## INTRODUCING 'A GLOBAL ISLAMIC RESISTANCE' CONCEPT

The changing geopolitical situation, the impulses from jihadi theoreticians in Peshawar, combined with his own experiences in Syria,
had convinced al-Suri about the need for a new approach to organizing jihadi groups. Some time in mid-1990, al-Suri went back to
Spain for a longer visit, returning only in early 1991. It was during
these months that he devoted himself to writing about how the jihadi
movement should be restructured successfully to face the growing
threats from the New World Order. The result was the first version of what fifteen years later became his most influential work, *The
Global Islamic Resistance Call*.[119] The study was a 35-page *bayan*, or
communiqué, with an awkwardly long and tedious title, typical of
working titles: *Communiqué to the Islamic Nation in Order to Establish
a Global Islamic Resistance*. Its cover featured a picture of the Holy
Ka'bah in Mecca, flanked with the Prophet's Mosque in Medina,
and the al-Aqsa mosque in Jerusalem, all of them behind bars.[120]
He later used this emblem on his websites and on the front page of
*The Global Islamic Resistance Call*. The choice was not coincidental.
When he later explained his rationale for embarking on his new book
project, he emphasized the transition to 'an open, overt and military
occupation by the Jews and the Christians' of the three most holy
places in Islam, Mecca, Medina, and Jerusalem, following decades of
'an indirect occupation'.[121]

---

New York and Washington on 11 Sept.",' (in Arabic), *Shafaf al-Sharq al-
Awsat/Middle East Transparent*, 22 Jan. 2005, www.metransparent.com/
texts/communique_abu_massab_al_suri_response_to_us_accusations, p.1.

119  *The Global Islamic Resistance Call*, p.55.

120  This author has not seen the original draft. When al-Suri returned to
Afghanistan in 1997, he resumed his series of lectures in Khowst, Jalalabad
and later in Kabul at his newly founded media center. A lecture series
in Aug. 2000 in Kabul, lasting nearly 15 hours, was videotaped and has
become a classic in Abu Mus'ab al-Suri's online library. In the first of these
tapes, approximately two-and-a-half minutes into the lecture, al-Suri
shows his students a copy of the 35-pp. *bayan* from 1990-1.

121  Videotaped lecture by Abu Mus'ab al-Suri, no.1, Kabul, Aug. 2000.

Another reason for writing the communiqué was his frustration with the failure of established forces and groups in Peshawar to confront the situation precipitated by the New World Order. He had probably not expected much from the official religious establishments and Muslim Brotherhood-affiliated movements, but he was profoundly disappointed by the various jihadi organizations in Peshawar whose only preoccupation was the traditional aim of the typical regional *tanzim*: to prepare for jihadi action in their home countries as a step towards toppling Arab regimes, seizing power, and establishing an Islamic state: 'I felt at the time that [these] people and their general orientations were in one valley and the unfolding events and the consequences were in another'.[122]

Al-Suri began discussing his ideas for a new concept of jihadi resistance with prominent figures in Peshawar's Arab-Afghan community. He and his colleagues called for meetings to 'assess the course and the current status of the jihadi ideology and movements' and 'appraise the Afghanistan experience' and two high level seminars were held.[123] According to al-Suri's recollection, there was a general consensus that 'a security storm was looming on the horizon'; while the media had begun referring to the mujahidin as 'rebels', 'splinter groups' and even 'terrorists'.[124] Apparently in the context of these seminars, al-Suri gave lectures presenting his ideas and his new booklet on a Global Islamic Resistance. One of these presentations, a one-and-a–half-hour long session, was tape recorded and distributed alongside his other recordings. The audiotape has been made available recently on Islamist websites, and has the title 'On Explaining the Global Islamic Resistance'.[125] The recorded lecture is very inter-

---

122  *The Global Islamic Resistance Call*, p.49.

123  Ibid., p.50.

124  Ibid.

125  See 'On Explaining the Global Islamic Resistance'. Audiotape of lecture held in Peshawar or in Afghanistan c. 1990. Accessed via *muntada al-sawt* 20 June 2006, www.saowt.com/forum/showthread.php?t=16158&highlig ht=%E3%E4+%E5%E6+%C3%C8%E6+%E3%D5%DA%C8+%C7%E1 %D3%E6%D1%ED+%BF, accessed Sept. 2006.

esting in that it seems to confirm that al-Suri's ideas about a *global* jihad, a jihad without any *tanzim*, and a new decentralised jihadi structure shorn of vulnerable organizations were propagated as early as 1991, and that they do not simply represent post-9/11 ideas.

In his lecture, al-Suri emphasises the need for creating what he labels 'a phantom organization' (*tanzim ashbah*) or 'an imaginary organization' (*tanzim wahmi*).[126] He outlines various measures for doing so, and his 'phantom organization' concept appears to be a precursor of his later 'system, not organization' slogan (*nizam la tanzim*) for which he has become famous.[127] Al-Suri also introduces the term 'individual action' (*al-'amal al-fardi*), which would become a cornerstone of his later strategic thinking. This refers to acts of violence carried out by individuals without any organizational adherence. Such acts will become increasingly important because 'they fill a large gap in Islam', he argues.[128] He cites examples from Yemen where a Palestinian stabbed ten tourists, acting completely independently.[129] This is a *modus operandi* that must be encouraged and developed into a more systematic method of warfighting. In this lecture, he has apparently not entirely dismissed the usefulness of the *tanzim*s, the secret organizations, and discusses how individual jihadi action should work in tandem with the existing *tanzim*s.[130] The lecture's underlying theme is the security difficulties of operating a traditional hierarchical structure.

At the beginning of 1991 al-Suri returned to Peshawar from Madrid with a view to publicizing his 35-page booklet. He wished to

---

126  Ibid., audiotape no.2, 20:30.

127  One of the first people to highlight and grasp the importance of this concept was Jeffrey Cozzens in his review of one of this author's papers on al-Suri. See Jeffrey Cozzens, 'Dr Brynjar Lia's "The al-Qaida Strategist Abu Mus'ab al-Suri: A Profile", *Counterterrorism Blog* 21 April 2006, http://counterterrorismblog.org/2006/04/post_1.php, accessed April 2006.

128  'On Explaining the Global Islamic Resistance', audiotape no.2, 05:03.

129  Ibid., audiotape no.2, 17:30.

130  Ibid., 18:50.

publish it 'in secrecy' because of the 'dangerous ideas in the book', he later recalls.[131] In his audiotaped lecture he did not acknowledge authorship of the communiqué, but claims instead that he has received it from one of the Islamic centres outside Peshawar several months earlier. He goes on to explain that it had recently been distributed to houses and posted on walls in Peshawar.[132] Al-Suri's ideas for the reorganization of jihadi groups met with little enthusiasm. He later accused his fellow Arab-Afghans of lacking ideological awareness: 'they were highly trained militarily, but had not received the necessary doctrinal, programmatic, ideological and political guidance'.[133] At this stage he was still a junior jihadi and did not have the authority to address the issue forcefully. His theories were still embryonic and they apparently lacked sufficient clarity to convince people. These factors probably explain why Al-Suri's ideas met with such a lukewarm reaction.

As a consequence, al-Suri found it difficult to mobilise support from among the various guesthouses and institutions in Peshawar for publishing the booklet; only 'four brothers' agreed to assist him in publishing his booklet. By June 1991 they had printed in secret and distributed some 1,000 copies, mainly in Peshawar. Since the Arab-Afghan community was on the verge of being dispersed, al-Suri hoped that his work would be circulated throughout the Islamic world if he managed to distribute it widely among the Arab-Afghan veterans in Peshawar.

### LEAVING PESHAWAR

In the early 1990s al-Suri felt increasingly that the jihadis' battlefield 'was about to close' and that he wanted to 'fulfill his mission' in Afghanistan and move on.[134] Al-Suri had also grown disillusioned with

---

131  *The Global Islamic Resistance Call*, pp.55, 1394.

132  'On Explaining the Global Islamic Resistance', audiotape no.1, c. 00:00–02:00.

133  *The Global Islamic Resistance Call*, p.53.

134  'Meeting with the Kuwaiti Newspaper', transcript of audiofile no.2, p.1.

his own role as a military instructor, given the lack of support for the revolutionary jihadi cause among the broader Islamist movement in Peshawar:

I am not prepared to train [people] in shooting practices because I think they will fire back at us justifying this by the fatwas of the Muslim Brothers and the Azhar clerics [...] People come to us with empty heads and leave us with empty heads [...] The have done nothing for Islam. This is because they have not received any ideological or doctrinal training.[135]

A more immediate reason for al-Suri's departure from Afghanistan was the infighting between warlords. Furthermore, the 'forebodings of a security storm' in Peshawar had become stronger. The Pakistani authorities had begun arresting and deporting wanted fugitives in Peshawar and elsewhere, and many Arab-Afghans were leaving. Al-Suri also departed, returning again to Granada, which he liked to call 'the last Muslim stronghold in Andalucia'.[136]

While most of the Arab-Afghan veterans from the Gulf and Jordan were able to return home, a significant number of them were still on the wanted list in their respective countries and were unable to go back, especially the Egyptian, Syrian, and Libyan jihadis, and to a lesser extent the North African veterans. Many of those who were unable to return either remained in Pakistan or migrated elsewhere; some left for a new war in Tajikistan, later Chechnya and Bosnia, and another contingent relocated to Sudan with the al-Qaida leadership.[137] Many of them eventually settled in Europe during the 1990s, especially in London. Al-Suri was among the few jihadis who held a European passport and hence was able to return to Europe from Peshawar.

The Arab-Afghan community was now being dispersed, and al-Suri later dubbed the period 1991-6 as 'the phase of diaspora and

---

135  Ibid.

136  *The Global Islamic Resistance Call*, p.55.

137  I am indebted to my colleague Thomas Hegghammer for some of this information. For more details on the Saudi contingent in the Arab-Afghan movement, see his *Violent Islamism in Saudi Arabia 1979-2006*.

temporary safe havens'.[138] The wanted fugitives among them went to several safe havens, which were still available in the early 1990s, at least till 1995-6 when the US-led anti-terrorist campaign specifically began focusing on the elimination of safe havens for the Arab-Afghan jihadis and other Islamic militants. According to al-Suri, the most important refuges for the Arab-Afghans in the early and mid-1990s were:

- Europe, especially Britain, and Scandinavia, but also Canada and Australia;

- Sudan, where the EIJ leadership, the JI leadership, the al-Qaida leadership, a large bloc of LIFG members, and also a number of other jihadi groups gathered;

- Other Muslim countries that had no security restrictions on wanted jihadi fugitives, especially Yemen, where a number of Egyptian jihadis sought refuge in the early 1990s. Turkey and Syria also served as safe havens, in particular for North African and Libyan youths. A smaller number of Arab-Afghan veterans emigrated as far as the Philippines, Indonesia, Thailand, and Latin America or to the African continent.

- Chechnya and Bosnia, both of which became new arenas for the jihadi movements, especially the latter, which attracted several thousand mujahidin fighters, including many Arab-Afghan veterans.[139]

This period was also characterized, according to al-Suri, by the dissemination of jihadi ideology, especially from Britain and the Scandinavian countries, 'where they, at least for the time being, were able to exploit the relatively relaxed security conditions and the welfare conditions'.[140] Publications, research papers and news bulletins were printed and distributed, lecture series, seminars, forums and conferences were held, audio-recorded and distributed globally. In al-Suri's opinion, the flourishing of the jihadi message in the West may even have surpassed the efforts of their counterparts in the Arab Islamic world.[141]

---

138  *The Global Islamic Resistance Call*, p.721.

139  Ibid., p.722.

140  Ibid., p.723.

141  Ibid.

The early 1990s also witnessed new emerging arenas of jihad, among which Algeria gradually came to figure very prominently, alongside Bosnia and Chechnya. Hundreds, if not thousands of Algerians returned from Afghanistan to Algeria during these years, and many of them became the backbone of the most radical factions in the Islamist opposition. 'Jihad in Algeria' also became al-Suri's main objective after he returned to Europe.[142]

---

142 For al-Suri's involvement with the Algerian jihadis see the next chapter or al-Suri's own account in Umar Abd al-Hakim, *A Summary of My Testimony.*

# 5
# BEHIND ENEMY LINES

In late 1991 or early 1992 al-Suri left Afghanistan and returned home to Spain.[1] Unlike several of his comrades-in-arms, al-Suri did not relocate with the al-Qaida leadership from Afghanistan to Sudan in 1991-2. In Spain, he resumed his export and import business specializing in crafts.[2] One account states that he imported 'leather jackets and similar stuff' from Turkey, and when this business began to thrive was bringing in 200-300 a time.[3] This period of rebuilding his business lasted till 1993 or 1994.[4] Court records show that he had registered his company with the local authorities in Granada in May 1993 and had a valid business card as a comerciante ambulante ('travelling salesman').[5] In Madrid, where he returned prior to his departure for London in 1994, he apparently also had a shop selling handicrafts, ceramics and second-hand furniture.[6]

---

1    See 'Biography of Shaykh Umar Abd al-Hakim (Abu Mus'ab al-Suri)' (in Arabic), p.3; and 'Meeting with the Kuwaiti Newspaper', transcript of audiofile no.2, pp.1-2.

2    Antonio Rubio, 'Mustafa Setmarian Naser: Un español en la cima de Al Qaeda: Durante los diez años que vivió en España se convirtió en lugarteniente de Bin Laden', elmundo.es, 3 Nov. 2005, www.elmundo. es/elmundo/2005/11/03/espana/1131002447.html, accessed Dec. 2005.

3    Author's interview with Noman Benotman, London 15 Sept. 2006.

4    'Meeting with the Kuwaiti Newspaper', transcript of audiofile no.2, p.2.

5    The card was registered for three years at Junta de Andalucía. His items of business were artesanía-complementos moda ('traditional handicraft products'), and his registered domicile was in Alfacar, Granada in Era del Cura 32. See 'Juzgado Central de Instrucción núm. 5, Audiencia Nacional, Sentencia Núm. 36/2005, En Madrid a 26 de septiembre de 2005', p.72.

6    Luis Rendueles and Manuel Marlasca, '7-J: Los escritos del ideólogo',

His life was nevertheless dominated by his connections and involvement with militant Islam. New developments on the jihadi scene, driven in particular by the events in Algeria, consumed him more than his commercial activities. He later recalled that he returned to Spain in order to 'reorganize his commercial businesses in preparation for devoting himself fully to the cause of Algerian jihad'.[7]

As a well-known Arab-Afghan veteran and jihadi author, al-Suri must have attracted attention in Spain's Islamist circles. Possessing authority and connections, al-Suri reportedly helped to establish structures that subsequently evolved into an extensive al-Qaida support network with its epicenter in Spain in the late 1990s.[8] Still, the exact nature of al-Suri's relationship with the al-Qaida leadership during this period is uncertain. He visited Sudan 'sporadically' when bin Laden stayed there between 1991 and 1996, according to Spanish investigators,[9] but Al-Suri claims that he had stopped working for bin Laden in 1992.[10] Nor does he mention any visits to Sudan in his biographical writings.

His movements in this period are shrouded in secrecy, and sources are few and often conflicting. He had a permanent residence in Spain during 1991-4 and in London from 1994-7 before he departed for Afghanistan. Moreover his family moved to London in 1995 and to Afghanistan in 1998.[11] For most of the 1990s al-Suri travelled

---

Interviú 18 May 2005, www.interviu.es/default.asp?idpublicacio_PK=3 9&idioma=CAS&idnoticia_PK=28299&idseccio_PK=547&h=050606, accessed July 2006.

7   Umar Abd al-Hakim, *A Summary of My Testimony*, p.21.

8   'How the March 11 local cell was born', (in Spanish) *El País*, 12 Sept. 2004.

9   'Juzgado Central de Instruccion no.005, Madrid, Sumario', 17 Sept. 2003, p.27.

10  See 'Communiqué from the Office of Abu Mus'ab al-Suri in Response to the US Department of State's Announcement' (in Arabic), 22 Dec. 2004.

11  A Spanish court document from 2003 claims, probably erroneously, that al-Suri remained in Afghanistan between 1991 and 1995, while 'sporadically visiting Sudan' and that he moved to Spain and Great Britain only in 1995. It dates al-Suri's final transfer to London to 26 June 1995.

extensively and met with his contacts and cadres from among the Syrian diaspora and Arab-Afghan veteran community in Europe and elsewhere. In many ways, Granada, Madrid and London were more suitable bases from which he was able to pursue his jihadi activism, rather than a permanent place of residence. Hence, al-Suri alternated between Afghanistan, Sudan, Britain, and Spain during these years, while also paying shorter visits to other countries. Most jihadis of some stature had extensive travel agendas, nurturing contacts in many countries. This also fitted al-Suri's profile, according to the US authorities, which portrayed him 'as a European intermediary for al-Qaida ...[who] travelled extensively between Europe and Afghanistan throughout the late 1990s'.[12]

## ALGERIA: HIS NEXT JIHAD

The situation in Algeria had preoccupied al-Suri since the late 1980s, when he was still in Afghanistan,[13] and he was to devote himself fully

---

Later Spanish court documents emphasize the lack of a permanent place of residence: 'between 1995 to 1998, this person lived in the United Kingdom, Afghanistan and Spain'. However, al-Suri's official jihadi biography says that he moved back to Spain around 1991 and that he stayed in London between 1994-7. This is also the version al-Suri himself has presented in his writings, lectures, and interviews. In the tape-recorded interview with *al-Ra'y al-'Amm*, al-Suri does not recall the exact date of his relocation to London, but he believes it was some time in 1994, perhaps at the end of 1994, when he, for all practical purposes, had settled in London. According to his recollection, he stayed in London for nearly three years, until mid-1997, when he moved to Afghanistan. He does not mention his visits to Sudan during the first half of the 1990s. See 'Meeting with the Kuwaiti Newspaper', transcript of audiofile no.2, p.3; Audiencia Nacional, Sala de lo Penal, Sección Tercera, 'Sentencia Núm. 36/2005', Madrid, 26 Sept. 2005, [verdict against the Abu Dahdah network], pp.30-1, 392; and 'Juzgado Central de Instruccion no.005, Madrid, Sumario', 17 Sept. 2003, pp.27, 435.

12   'WANTED: Mustafa Setmariam Nasar', *Reward for Justice website*, www. rewardsforjustice.net/english/wanted_captured/index.cfm?page=Nasar, accessed July 2005.

13   See especially Umar Abd al-Hakim, *A Summary of My Testimony*, pp.5-7,

to this cause for several years. Al-Suri later described the Algerian case as 'among the most important experience for the jihadi movement in the second half of the twentieth century'.[14]

The rise of the Algerian Islamist movement in the late 1980s, and the decision by the newly formed Islamic Salvation Front (FIS), established in 1989, to participate in the Algerian elections in 1990 and 1991, raised a host of new questions. The FIS did surprisingly well in the municipal and first round of the parliamentary polls before the military regime cancelled the elections and declared a state of emergency in Algeria. These events generated a debate in the Islamist movement in general and in the Arab-Afghan community in particular about the option of armed struggle or political activism as the preferred path to political power, and whether democracy and elections were permissible in Islam.

Al-Suri's direct involvement in the Algerian jihad appears to have started some time after he had returned to Spain in the early 1990s. In 1994, he was contacted by some 'Algerian brothers in London' whom he had already met towards the end of his stay in Afghanistan.[15]

This special relationship with the Algerian jihadis dates back to 1989 or 1990 when al-Suri became acquainted with a prominent Algerian jihadi commander by the name of Qari' Sa'id, or Qari Saïd, as he was known in the Western media[16] (his real name was reportedly Abd al-Rahim Gharzouli[17]). According to al-Suri, Saïd had founded a secret organization (*tanzim*) which came to be known as 'the Algerian Afghans'. Many of its members later joined the *Armed Islamic*

---

20-59, 70-3.

14   Ibid., p.5.

15   'Meeting with the Kuwaiti Newspaper', transcript of audiofile no.2, p.2.

16   Ibid.

17   See 'Abu Mus'ab al-Suri's Communiqué to the British and Europeans regarding the London Bombings in July 2006', *Middle East Transparent* website, 23 Dec. 2005, www.metransparent.com/texts/abu_massab_assuri_communique_calling_for_terror_in_europe.htm, accessed Oct. 2006.

*Group* (al-jama'ah al-islamiyyah al-musallahah), better known by its French acronym, GIA, the most extremist and violent of the Algerian Islamist groups during the 1990s.[18] Like many other jihadi leaders, Saïd was neither middle-aged nor old. Al-Suri described him as a 'virtuous youth, who had memorised the Quran'.[19] The two activists had lived next door to one another in a Peshawar guesthouse, where al-Suri had learnt about the Algerian Islamist scene and Saïd had told him about his ambitions to build a jihadi organization in Algeria after his involvement in Afghanistan ended.[20] Saïd urged his followers to benefit from al-Suri's presence and the latter took under his wing several Algerian youths whom Saïd left behind in Afghanistan when he returned to Algeria. He spent six months with them in a training camp near Jalalabad.[21] Al-Suri also delivered lectures and talks in the guesthouses for Algerians in Peshawar on themes such as 'jihadi ideology', 'legitimate Islamic politics', and 'the management and comparative analysis of guerrilla warfare'.[22] He maintained these contacts when he returned to Spain around 1992. Al-Suri recalls that he made a solemn pledge to Saïd, when they were both still in Afghanistan, that should Saïd and his fellow-fighters be able to 'establish the jihad in Algeria and there is a need for me there, I will go to Algeria, like I went to Afghanistan'.[23]

Qari Saïd became a well-known figure in the new jihadi trend that rose to prominence in Peshawar at the end of the 1980s. Saïd had fought with Abdallah Anas and Ahmad Shah Massoud following his arrival in Peshawar in 1986, as did several other Algerians who later became GIA leaders.[24] In Anas' view, Saïd had been a successful fighter, not only at the front, but also in terms of the religious

---

18    Umar Abd al-Hakim, *A Summary of My Testimony*, p.13.

19    Ibid.

20    Ibid.

21    'Meeting with the Kuwaiti Newspaper', transcript of audiofile no.2, p.2.

22    Umar Abd al-Hakim, *A Summary of My Testimony*, p.20.

23    'Meeting with the Kuwaiti Newspaper', transcript of audiofile no.2, p.2.

24    Author's interview with Abdallah Anas, London, 16 Sept. 2006.

learning that he had acquired when a student of Islamic law in Medina, Saudi Arabia. According to Abdallah Anas' recollection, their relationship was severed in 1989. At that time, Saïd had told him that he had heard about a group called *jama'at al-jihad* who said they would start a new organization called *al-qa'idah*. At the end of 1989, Saïd left the Panshir valley for Peshawar to join this group.[25] All contacts between them were cut, and Saïd emerged as a staunch enemy of Massoud, Abdallah Anas' commander.[26] Saïd became associated with a guesthouse in Peshawar that bin Laden supervised, and from which money was distributed to Arab-Afghan returnees who vowed to sever ties with the mainstream Muslim Brotherhood parties and launch an armed jihad against their local governments. Saïd's group benefited from this support.[27] According to Anas, bin Laden used his financial means to achieve leverage over the Algerian Islamists, by promising money, training, and military assistance, but only on the precondition that they relinquished loyalty to FIS and its related organizations.[28]

The rise of the jihadi trend in Peshawar was closely linked to the fierce debate in the Arab-Afghan community over its future course of action. Some of these discussions were even tape-recorded and distributed outside the Arab-Afghan community.[29] The internal struggle was perhaps most visible in the sizeable Algerian-Afghan contingent, since the establishment of FIS in September 1989 posed

---

25  Ibid.

26  See interview with an Arab-Afghan veteran and Saudi scholar and cleric Dr Musa al-Qarni in Qari Jamil Ziabi, 'The legal ideologue of Al Qaeda leader, Mussa al Qarni, recalls the stages of the rise and fall of the Islamic State dream in Afghanistan' (in Arabic), *Al-Hayat*, 13 March 2006, http://english.daralhayat.com/Spec/03-2006/Article-20060313-f43ae91a-c0a8-10ed-003f-58bb000ba59d/story.html, accessed Sept. 2006.

27  When Saïd met with Anas a few years later, Saïd had reportedly explained to him why he had become convinced about the jihadi program and had decided to accept money and material support from bin Laden. Author's interview with Abdallah Anas, London, 16 Sept. 2006.

28  Ibid.

29  Author's interview with Camille Tawil, London, 14 Sept. 2006.

the question of the legitimacy of political parties and democratic elections with more urgency than ever before.[30] The FIS, which in many ways represented the Muslim Brotherhood in Algeria, had a solid following, led by, among others, Abdallah Anas, who had become an important Arab-Afghan commander, and was also considered to be the leader of the Algerians fighting in Afghanistan.[31] However, a sizeable minority opposed FIS, and the revolt against Abdallah Anas was led by Qari Saïd. He was a key factor drawing Algerian-Afghan veterans away from FIS. According to Camille Tawil, an acknowledged expert on the jihadi trend, and Algerian jihadism in particular, it was Qari Saïd who brought the idea of the GIA to the fore. He had the contacts in Algeria to realize this new jihadi project in opposition to the mainstream Islamist FIS movement.

In some sources, Saïd has been described as 'an Algerian member of Ayman al-Zawahiri's group in Peshawar', where he was responsible for the organization's Algerian members.[32] In the early 1990s, Saïd and his followers emerged on the Algerian Islamist scene, sometimes described as 'Qutbists' operating under al-Zawahiri's leadership and sometimes known as 'the monotheists' among the Algerian-Afghan veterans.[33] This hard-line faction later coalesced under the banner of the Armed Islamic Group (GIA), and they became 'the decisive element at the core of the GIA'.[34] Saïd was among the most prominent

---

30  Ibid.

31  Ibid.

32  International Crisis Group (ICG), 'Islamism, Violence And Reform In Algeria: Turning the Page', *ICG Middle East Report*, no.29 (30 July 2004), www.crisisgroup.org/library/documents/middle_east___north_africa/ egypt_north_africa/29_islamism__violence_and_reform_in_algeria.pdf, accessed Dec. 2005, p.12.

33  Ibid; and Luis Martinez, 'Le cheminement singulier de la violence islamiste en Algérie', *Critique internationale*, no.20, juillet 2003, www.ceri-sciencespo. com/publica/critique/article/ci20p164-177.pdf#search='Qari%20Said%20 GIA', accessed Dec. 2005, pp.168-9.

34  International Crisis Group (ICG), 'Islamism, Violence and Reform in Algeria: Turning the Page', *ICG Middle East Report*, no.29 (30 July 2004), www.crisisgroup.org/library/documents/middle_east_north_africa/egypt_

GIA leaders. He had reportedly participated in several daring raids at the beginning of the Algerian conflict and had also led a famous prison escape. Al-Suri came to consider him, for all practical purposes, 'the founder' of the GIA.[35] Al-Suri found himself ideologically close to Qari Saïd. Through his writings and his lectures, al-Suri contributed to Saïd's and al-Zawahiri's vicious attack on the Muslim Brotherhood trend. Al-Zawahiri's book, *The Bitter Harvest: The Muslim Brothers in Sixty Years* (al-hasad al-murr: al-ikhwan al-muslimun fi sittin 'aman), a 150pp. work with nearly 400 footnotes and references, was released in Peshawar around 1991. It became an important component in the intellectual foundation for the jihadis' attack on the Muslim Brotherhood and reinforced the message conveyed in al-Suri's *The Jihadi Revolution in Syria: Hopes and Pains*, which also purported to document the 'corrupt' and failed strategies of the Muslim Brotherhood. Both works gave the jihadis intellectual ammunition to condemn the reformist and accommodationist position of the Muslim Brotherhood. These works and the accompanying proselytization efforts contributed significantly to radicalising the community. Many blamed al-Suri and Saïd for attracting Algerians away from Anas and the FIS and over to al-Zawahiri's revolutionary jihadi trend.[36]

Several years later al-Suri was reminded of his pledge to Saïd. By this time, the GIA had already been active for at least two years, and Saïd had been captured and imprisoned by the Algerian authorities. The Algerian civil war had become one of the major issues in international and Arab news, and it preoccupied the jihadi movements more than any other issue at the time, except perhaps for the Bosnian civil war. Initially, al-Suri was contacted by one of Qari Saïd's senior aides and invited to a meeting with GIA supporters in London.[37] He de-

---

north_africa/29_islamism_violence_and_reform_in_algeria.pdf, accessed Dec. 2005, p.12.

35   'Meeting with the Kuwaiti Newspaper', transcript of audiofile no.2, p.2.

36   Author's interview with Camille Tawil, London, 14 Sept. 2006.

37   Umar Abd al-Hakim, *A Summary of My Testimony*, p.20; and 'Meeting

cided to go there and abandoned his import-export business in Spain once again, after only two years of business. The news that Qari Saïd had managed to escape from prison also reached him. During his stay in London, al-Suri spoke with his friend Qari Saïd. According to al-Suri's account, Saïd had called him from Algeria to remind him of his promise to return there to fight. Saïd also urged him to assist the GIA's media cell in London until the preparations for his travel to Algeria were finalized.[38] Other leading GIA commanders also contacted al-Suri to persuade him to join their cause. As a result, al-Suri made several visits to London in late 1993 or early 1994 in order to prepare for an eventual relocation to Algeria.[39]

These visits appear to have become a starting point for al-Suri's direct involvement in the Algerian conflict and a closer relationship between himself and the Algerian jihadi community in Europe. They were also an important part of al-Suri's efforts at building a network of contacts throughout Europe from among the Algerian-Afghan veterans whom al-Suri had come to know back in Afghanistan:

I arrived in London and got to know some brothers, and discovered that several of the brothers who supported the jihad in Algeria, and who had been with us in Afghanistan, were now present in a number of European countries. I went to see them on many visits in a number of regions.[40]

Al-Suri provides few details of his European-wide network of contacts. His intimate knowledge of this community probably contributed to elevating him to a position of prominence in the European-based jihadi groups in general and among GIA supporters in particular. It is likely that al-Suri kept in close contact with leading GIA supporters in Europe, such as Abd al-Karim Deneche in Sweden and Said Mansour in Denmark, both of whom were distributors

---

with the Kuwaiti Newspaper', transcript of audiofile no.2, p.2.

38  Umar Abd al-Hakim, *A Summary of My Testimony*, p.20.

39  Al-Suri was not entirely certain about the time of these visits, but thought they had taken place in early 1994. See 'Meeting with the Kuwaiti Newspaper', transcript of audiofile no.2, p.2.

40  Ibid.

of the GIA's newsletter *Nashrat al-Ansar* (lit. 'The Bulletin of the Prophet's Partisans', hereafter the *al-Ansar Newsletter*), for which al-Suri was an editor, and the Ahmed Zaoui network in Belgium,[41] as well as many others.[42]

The prominent newspaper editor, Abdel Bari Atwan, who met with al-Suri repeatedly, recalls that the latter travelled extensively in Europe and beyond when he stayed in London between 1994 and 1997.[43] Having a Spanish passport and a Western appearance, he faced fewer hurdles than many of his Syrian countrymen when crossing international borders. Al-Suri frequently went back and forth to Spain, where his family lived until mid-1995 and which also hosted one of the most important al-Qaida networks in Europe at the time (that of Abu Dahdah, see below). He also went to France, Germany, Turkey, the Netherlands, and Belgium several times, in

---

41   This network also included Tariq al-Ma'rufi (Tarek ben Habib Maaroufi) in Belgium, a prominent figure in jihadi circles, who was imprisoned in 1995-6 for illegal arms trafficking. Maaroufi came into the spotlight after 9/11 due to his alleged involvement in providing falsified Belgian passports to two men who later went to the Panshir valley in Afghanistan, posing as journalists, and assassinated Ahmed Shah Massoud, the leader of Afghanistan's Northern Alliance, on 9 Sept. 2001. In Dec. 2001, Maaroufi was arrested in Belgium and later convicted. See 'Maaroufi, Tarek Ben Habib', *MIPT Database*, www.tkb.org/KeyLeader.jsp?memID=5891, accessed Oct. 2006.

42   A study from Oct. 1995 claims that al-Suri 'travel[ed] regularly between Sweden and London'. It also found that the *al-Ansar Newsletter* had a Swedish mailing address. Abdelkrim Deneche was later arrested in Sweden on suspicion of involvement in the Paris train bombings in 1995. See Muriel Mirak-Weissbach, 'The case of the GIA: Afghans out of theater', *Executive Intelligence Review*, 13 Oct. 1995, www.larouchepub. com/other/1995/2241_gia.html, accessed Jan. 2006. See also "Swedish police seek to deport Algerian," *Reuters*, 23 Aug. 1995; and 'The European Bases of the Armed Islamic Group Shaken by the Belgian Link: The Presumed GIA Terrorists Arrested in Belgium Had Contacts in Italy and Scandinavia' (in French), *La Libre Belgique*, 7-8 March 1998, p.1, via FBIS; and 'Brussels: Europe's Hub of Terror', *The Flemish Republic website*, undated, www.flemishrepublic.org/extra.php?id=1&jaargang=1&nr=1, accessed Aug. 2006.

43   Author's interview with Abdel Bari Atwan, London, 28 April 2006.

particular Brussels, where he reportedly met with GIA supporters and others. In the Netherlands, he met with Usama Rushdi, then an active member and spokesman for the Egyptian Islamic Group (JI, *al-jama'ah al-islamiyyah*) apparently in order to persuade him to drop his and JI's criticism of the GIA.[44] Al-Suri also paid visits to one or several Scandinavian countries.[45] It is not known for certain with whom he met, but he recalls that during this period, he had ideological discussions with Abu Talal in the JI, most probably referring to Tal'at Fu'ad Qasim, who resided in Denmark in the first half of the 1990s.[46] Denmark, Norway and Sweden all hosted jihadi militants at that time, including many GIA activists. In fact, for several years, the *al-Ansar Newsletter*'s official address was reportedly a postbox address in Haninge in Sweden. In the mid-1990s, al-Suri had even recommended to *al-Ansar Newsletter* staff in London that they transfer all their activities to one of the Scandinavian countries.[47]

It is possible that al-Suri went to Italy and the Balkans to visit mujahidin veterans, and he himself claims to have trained Anwar Sha'ban, one of the most important Arab mujahidin commanders during the Bosnian war.[48] Sha'ban served as head of the Islamic Cultural Institute in Milan, Italy, a centre which US authorities later described as 'the main Al Qaeda station house in Europe'—until 1995 when he escaped an Italian police investigation. He was later killed at

---

44    Author's interview, Nov. 2006. Name and place withheld on request.

45    Ibid. See also Umar Abd al-Hakim, *A Summary of My Testimony*, pp.21-2.

46    'Meeting with the Kuwaiti Newspaper', transcript of audiofile no.9, p.6.

47    Umar Abd al-Hakim, *A Summary of My Testimony*, p.32. A prominent Syrian Muslim Brotherhood veteran, whom Spanish authorities subsequently linked to al-Suri, lived in the Danish city of Aarhus. Umar Abd al-Rahman, the so-called 'blind shaykh', who was the JI's spiritual leader, and perhaps the most prominent jihadi cleric at the time, also visited Copenhagen and held conferences there in the early 1990s.

48    'Meeting with the Kuwaiti Newspaper', transcript of audiofile no.1, pp.6-7.

a Croatian road bloc in murky circumstances in Bosnia in 1996.[49] The Abu Dahdah network in Spain, within which al-Suri was an integral and leading member from the very beginning, was initially heavily involved with the mujahidin movement in Bosnia (see below). Furthermore, the GIA had a number of supporters and members in the Arab mujahidin community in Bosnia, and it is possible that al-Suri followed up these contacts.

In *The Global Islamic Resistance Call* al-Suri mentions his busy travel schedules during these years. He recalls how he benefited from 'the numerous travels' he undertook in the 1992-6 period 'to many Arab, Islamic and European countries' and how this enabled him to examine different segments of the Islamic revivalist movement (*al-sahwah*) in general and 'get to know most of the movements, secret organizations and the leaders of the contemporary jihadi current in particular'.[50]

In his audiotaped memoirs, al-Suri may have overemphasised the GIA's invitation for him to go to Algeria, and his own willingness to travel there. Military participation in the bloody and chaotic insurgency campaign in Algeria was probably not al-Suri's first choice. He had already begun to make a name for himself as a jihadi intellectual and writer and clearly felt a much stronger attraction to London and its vibrant environment of Islamists and exiled jihadis, than to the GIA's self-declared 'Caliphate' and its vulnerable 'liberated zones' south of Algiers.[51]

---

49    Tom Hundley, 'Mosque denies link as terror incubator', *Chicago Tribune*, 22 Oct. 2001, www.chicagotribune.com/news/nationworld/chi-0110220252 oct22,1,5726868.story, accessed Oct. 2006. For more on Islamic militancy in Italy, see Guido Olimpio, 'Italy and Islamic Militancy: From Logistics Base to Potential Target', *Terrorism Monitor*, 3 (18) (21 Sept. 2005). http://jamestown.org/terrorism/news/article.php?articleid=2369789, accessed Oct. 2006.

50    *The Global Islamic Resistance Call*, p.43.

51    For more on the 'emirates', see Luis Martinez, *The Algerian Civil War 1990-1998* (London: Hurst , 2000), pp.94-118. See also 'Armed Islamic Group', *Wikipedia.org* at http://en.wikipedia.org/wiki/Algerian_Armed_Islamic_Group, accessed Oct. 2006.

Compared to Spain, which al-Suri described as 'closed' in terms of possibilities of 'Islamic activity', London was a totally different place:

It has 75 daily newspapers, weekly and monthly magazines, that are published in Arabic; it has huge libraries. As an imperialist state, it has lived together with the Islamic world. Political opposition movements of all shades and colours are there. All literary schools, in poetry and prose, are present in London. [...] Among the Islamists, you will find everyone from Shaykh Muhammad Surur to the jihadis, and lately it has become a refuge for everyone. [...] I found that being in London during that period would place you at the centre of the events.[52]

Al-Suri was greatly attracted to everything that the United Kingdom, and London in particular, had to offer a jihadi intellectual, especially its large Muslim diaspora and the significant presence of jihadi organizations, including groups and individuals whom he already knew from Afghanistan, such as the Libyan Islamic Fighting Group (LIFG), the Egyptian Islamic Jihad Group (EIJ), the Egyptian Islamic Group (JI), the Algerian GIA, Moroccan jihadis, Osama bin Laden's supporters, etc.[53] The extent of their activities in the United Kingdom was so conspicuous that al-Suri thought that:

London must have acted according to a well-studied and well-known international plan and opened its doors to the Islamists and the jihadis; not only the UK, but also other European states, like the Scandinavian countries. Consequently, there was a concentration [of jihadis] there, and I found that there was an opportunity to resume my contribution [to jihad], and my participation in writing, by staying in London.[54]

Al-Suri began to consider seriously moving permanently to London.[55] He nurtured the idea of transferring his business there or alternatively continuing his academic studies in the city. He had previously

---

52   'Meeting with the Kuwaiti Newspaper', transcript of audiofile no.2, p.2.
53   Ibid., pp.2-3.
54   Ibid., p.3.
55   Ibid., p.2.

obtained a degree in history and now wished to study for an MA or PhD in political science at one of London's many universities.

Before deciding finally on bringing his family to London, the invitation to come to Algeria had to be dealt with. According to his own account, al-Suri decided to postpone the plan to move to London, and started making travel arrangements for Algeria, in coordination with the GIA leadership. This happened at a time when Shaykh Abu Abdallah Ahmad (Sherif Ghousmi, Sharif al-Qawasmah), also an Afghan war veteran, was the GIA's top commander, from February 1994 till his death in September of that year.[56]

During his emirate, there was much optimism among the Algerian jihadi supporters in London and Madrid, and the relationship with the GIA leadership was very close. Al-Suri later recalled that:

The coordination and contacts between us at the time became so good that they sent us Algerian sweets which they had taken as war booty from army storehouses in Algeria. We were blessed to receive them and distributed them to the supporters in Britain and Spain.[57]

A major reason for the optimism was that the GIA was gaining ground and other Islamist insurgents decided, at least temporarily, to join the GIA in Algeria. This included the Makhloufi group, segments of Chebouti's group, and parts of the FIS network in central Algeria led by two prominent clerics-cum-jihadis, Muhammad Saïd and Abd al-Razzaq Rajam.[58] Al-Suri himself was very excited about

---

56 See, for example, 'Key leader profile: Ahmed, Abu Abdallah', *MIPT Terrorism Knowledge Base*, www.tkb.org/KeyLeader.jsp?memID=20, accessed Jan. 2006.

57 'Letter to the British and the Europeans – Its People and Governments – Regarding the London Explosions, July 2005' (in Arabic), p.22.

58 The Makhloufi group was also called 'Movement for an Islamic State' (*Mouvement pour un État Islamique*), and was led by Saïd Makhloufi, a former FIS leader. The Chebouti-group was also called 'Armed Islamic Movement' (*Mouvement Islamique Armé*) and consisted of veterans of Mustapha Bouyali's movement in the 1980s, in addition to Arab-Afghan veterans. The organization disintegrated in late 1993, following the death of its leader. See survey of armed groups in Algeria in International Crisis Group (ICG), 'Islamism, Violence and Reform in Algeria: Turning the

this 'great unity', which he characterised as 'a very important event in Algerian history. [...] I then thought that finally, the events have taken their proper course, and I considered that the GIA has truly been born in unity'.[59] Indeed, when looking back, al-Suri argued that 'the situation under Abu Abdallah Ahmad and before him had been excellent'; it was only with Jamal Zaytuni's emirate that the massacres began, mujahidin leaders were executed and the whole Algerian jihad deviated.[60]

In this atmosphere of optimism in 1994, al-Suri flew once again to London and made arrangements with his contacts there. The trip was scheduled in detail, and plans to move his family to London, where they would be accommodated and cared for, were set in motion. Al-Suri was in principle going to stay in Algeria for six to twelve months, depending on the situation there, accompanied by one of his most trusted fellow jihadis, someone who had been with him since the 1980s and during his entire Afghanistan period. He is not mentioned by name, but it can be inferred that this person was his long-time associate and assistant Muhammad Bahayah (Abu Khalid al-Suri). In addition 'a few other noble brothers' would also accompany al-Suri to Algeria.[61]

Al-Suri and his fellow jihadis discovered that their contacts, who had taken it upon themselves to arrange their journey to the GIA's strongholds in Algeria, had been expelled from Europe so their travel plans were again put on hold.[62] In his memoirs al-Suri describes the support cell in Belgium, which also offered insights into his thinking about the organization of jihadi groups:

---

Page', *ICG Middle East Report*, no.29 (30 July 2004), www.crisisgroup. org/library/documents/middle_east_north_africa/egypt_north_africa/29_ islamism_violence_and_reform_in_algeria.pdf, accessed Dec. 2005, pp.10-17.

59    'Meeting with the Kuwaiti Newspaper', transcript of audiofile no.2, p.3.
60    'Meeting with the Kuwaiti Newspaper', transcript of audiofile no.3, p.5.
61    'Meeting with the Kuwaiti Newspaper', transcript of audiofile no.2, p.3.
62    Ibid.

The issue of my travel to Algeria was supposed to be arranged through another Algerian cell, in Belgium. I actually went to Belgium and met with the cell there, who were involved in providing rear support services to the jihad in Algeria from among the North African emigrant community. Their security situation was better than the London cell, but they committed fatal errors due to their desire to expand from logistical support activities into the realm of media and propaganda activities and the collection of donations for the cause.

In Belgium my travel to Algeria was set up. I was going there by sea. I returned to London to await departure, but shortly afterwards, news came that the Algerian cell [in Belgium] had been discovered. It was exactly what I had expected and warned them about: the kind of secret organizational work which they practiced over a year and a half was disrupted because of the expansion of their activities into the field of media and propaganda. Regrettably, because this group had many excellent cadres.[63]

Shortly afterwards, the GIA emir, Abu Abdallah Ahmad, whom al-Suri had intended to meet, was killed.[64] Al-Suri and his group then made direct contact with the new GIA leadership, headed by Jamal Zaytuni (Abu Abd al-Rahman Amin), who led the GIA from September 1994 to July 1996. The GIA responded that they were unable to send another envoy to bring al-Suri and his group safely to Algeria so he was asked to stay behind in London and 'help the brothers there'.[65] Much later, al-Suri learned that Zaytuni had cancelled the plan to return al-Suri's team to Algeria, as he had vetoed the participation in the struggle of all non-Algerian jihadis.[66]

Al-Suri appeared relieved by this outcome. It was not the first time he had arrived too late to participate in risky jihadi campaigns: in 1985 he had also missed The Combatant Vanguard's ill-fated infiltration of Syria. Years later, al-Suri later thanked God that he 'did not travel and ended up in the catastrophe which later took place in

---

63    Cited in Umar Abd al-Hakim, *A Summary of My Testimony*, pp.21-2.

64    Ibid., p.22.

65    Meeting with the Kuwaiti Newspaper', transcript of audiofile no.2, p.3.

66    Umar Abd al-Hakim, *A Summary of My Testimony*, p.22.

Algeria'.[67] Henceforward, al-Suri's support for the GIA was limited to what he could achieve as a jihadi in European exile, and more specifically his contributions in the realms of propaganda, lobbying and jihadi journalism.

## THE GIA AND AL-QAIDA IN SUDAN

Al-Suri's activism on behalf of the GIA in the early and mid-1990s was not limited to London or his unsuccessful attempt to rejoin the Algerian battlefield. Several sources suggest that al-Suri travelled repeatedly to Sudan to consult with the al-Qaida leadership on various issues, in particular on how best to assist the nascent jihad in Algeria. After 1992, the epicenter of the global jihadi movement shifted away from Peshawar, following the eruption of the Afghan civil war, Pakistan's clampdown against the Arab-Afghan community, and the relocation of bin Laden to Khartoum. A host of Islamist and jihadi groups also found refuge and established training camps in Sudan. Dr Hasan al-Turabi, a Sorbonne graduate and the leading ideologue in the new military regime in Sudan after the 1989 *coup d'état*, had already invited bin Laden to Sudan in late 1989. It was during his time in Sudan, from 1991-6, that bin Laden's organization evolved into a fully-fledged global network. The 9/11 Report describes this period as follows:

Bin Ladin now had a vision of himself as head of an international jihad confederation. In Sudan, he established an 'Islamic Army Shura' that was to serve as the coordinating body for the consortium of terrorist groups with which he was forging alliances. It was composed of his own al Qaeda Shura together with leaders or representatives of terrorist organizations that were still independent. In building this Islamic army, he enlisted groups from Saudi Arabia, Egypt, Jordan, Lebanon, Iraq, Oman, Algeria, Libya, Tunisia, Morocco, Somalia, and Eritrea. Al Qaeda also established cooperative

---

67    Meeting with the Kuwaiti Newspaper', transcript of audiofile no.2, p.3. See also Umar Abd al-Hakim, *A Summary of My Testimony*, p.21.

but less formal relationships with other extremist groups [...] The ground-work for a true global terrorist network was being laid.[68]

'The Islamic Army Shura' or 'Al-Qaida'—both terms were used in the early 1990s[69]—provided support in terms of equipment, training and/or financial aid to a host of different entities, according to US authorities. These included groups from the Philippines, Indonesia, Pakistan, Tajikistan, the Balkans and several Middle Eastern countries. Although it is possible that al-Qaida was already a sprawling terrorist business empire at this early stage, it was not directly in-volved in terrorist operations, with the possible exception of a few anti-American attacks in Yemen and Somalia in 1992-3. Al-Suri ob-served that al-Qaida did not have any ongoing 'field activities' outside Afghanistan around 1990. The only exception was Southern Yemen, where bin Laden had 'his special jihadi project' against the Commu-nist regime,[70] and where he sought to build a jihadi movement from 1989 onwards. Al-Suri was not involved in these activities, but he claims to have been among those who egged on the Saudi leader to implement his plans. Bin Laden was hesitant, however, and did not want to move before he had secured support from the mainstream Islamist current, including the Muslim Brotherhood and the lead-ing Yemeni cleric Shaykh Abd al-Majid al-Zindani. This support was not forthcoming, and 'a golden opportunity was lost', al-Suri lamented.[71]

The Algerian GIA was one of many groups who benefited from bin Laden's support. As alluded to above, bin Laden had report-edly agreed to provide financial support to Qari Saïd and his faction,

---

68  Cited in Chapter 2.3, 'The Rise of Bin Ladin and Al Qaeda (1988-1992)', *The 9/11 Commission Report*, www.9-11commission.gov/report/911Report_Ch2.htm, accessed Oct. 2006.

69  See Testimony of Jamal Ahmed Mohammed Al-Fadl, United States of America *v.* Osama Bin Laden *et al.* Defendants, transcript of trial, 6 Feb. 2001, www.ict.org.il/documents/documentdet.cfm?docid=43, accessed Oct. 2006, p.212.

70  Ibid.

71  Ibid., p.775.

which vehemently opposed the FIS. He also promised to offer money and military assistance to another Algerian rebel faction headed by Mansur al-Miliyani on the precondition that al-Miliyani disavowed his loyalty to his friend and ally Abd al-Qadir Shabuti, head of the Mouvement Islamique Arme (MIA) in Algeria, which was close to the FIS.[72] Al-Miliyani agreed and severed his ties with Shabuti, laying the groundwork for the first active GIA units in Algeria in 1991 or 1992.[73]

When al-Suri wrote his memoirs about Algeria, in 2004, he emphasised how a whole range of jihadi groups, many of them based in Sudan, began involving themselves with the Algerian cause, in the hope that that they would be able to recreate the spirit of Peshawar. Al-Qaida was heavily involved in these efforts up to the mid-1990s:

From the beginning of 1994 the hopes of all jihadis were linked to the Algerian cause and that it would be the second step for the Arab-Afghans towards the Arab world after the Afghanistan period. Osama bin Laden sent some of his assistants to reconnoitre the situation, and he attempted to offer assistance in terms of money and weapons. Doctor Ayman al-Zawahiri, Emir of the Egyptian Jihad Group, corresponded with 'Amin', the

---

72  Author's interview with Abdallah Anas, London, 16 Sept. 2006.

73  The origin and early history of the GIA is admittedly obscure. According to an interview with a GIA spokesman in 1994, it was founded in 1989 and carried out its first armed operation in 1991. The group traced its roots back to the so-called Bouyali Group (1982-7), which was one of the first Islamist armed underground organizations in Algeria after independence. Its combat preparations had started in 1989 and were reinforced by the release from prison of Bouyali's main comrade-in-arms, al-Miliyani, which facilitated the formation of the movement. The GIA spokesman described the GIA's early history as follows: 'Many youth joined Shaykh al-Miliyani. They set up cells in villages and towns, and played a large part in the launching of the armed holy struggle. In addition, young holy fighters (*mujahidin*) who fought in Afghanistan, joined the group. Out of these groups, the GIA was formed, and a communiqué of unity (*bayan al-wahdah*) was issued in which it explained some main points about the group's work. After two years, on 18 Nov. 1991, the GIA launched its first operation.' Cited in 'In the first press meeting since its foundation two years ago: The Armed Islamic Group in Algeria reveals to 'al-Wasat' its plans and goals' (in Arabic), *al-Wasat*, 30 Jan. 1994.

emir of the GIA. This was before his [i.e. Amin's] deviation was discovered. Al-Zawahiri supported the jihad and reminded 'Amin' of the importance of unifying the efforts of the jihadis there. The Libyan [Islamic] Fighting Group sent tens of its best mujahidin to participate in the field in the Algerian jihad. Many of the Moroccan jihadis worked in rear logistical services, transporting weapons and fighters to Algeria. Similarly, some of the Tunisians contributed with jihadi efforts. Hence, this cause constituted the main axis of interest for the jihadis in that period.[74]

Hence, in al-Suri's eyes, it appeared as if the destiny of the Algerian jihad depended, in part, on the backing it could mobilize from its external supporters, including the Arab-Afghan diaspora in Sudan.

Other sources also confirm the role of bin Laden and his Arab-Afghan followers in assisting the GIA with funds, fighters, and weapons. The GIA had representatives in Sudan, and even a small base there, just outside Khartoum, and GIA fighters infiltrated Algeria via Sudanese territory. Bin Laden had concrete plans for establishing training camps inside Algeria for his fighters, although the details of that story vary. There were negotiations between the GIA and the al-Qaida leadership in Khartoum about this and other issues, mostly over the ultimate control over external aid and the planned camps. In 1995, under the new emirate of Jamal Zaytuni, the GIA no longer tolerated any external assistance if it were channelled beyond its control. There were also ideological differences due to Zaytuni's extreme ideological orientation, in which all other jihadi trends were considered heretical. According to al-Suri, Zaytuni had sent a letter to Ayman al-Zawahiri in which he flatly rejected the latter's strategic recommendations.[75] During a famous meeting at bin Laden's house in Khartoum, the GIA envoy had addressed him, threatening 'to kill you and those who arrive' if bin Laden sent money and fighters other than via the GIA's channels. To illustrate the seriousness of the threat, the envoy had drawn his finger across his neck. This dramatic episode put an end to the relationship between al-Qaida

---

74    Umar Abd al-Hakim, *A Summary of My Testimony*, p.21.
75    Ibid., p.22.

and the GIA, although tensions had been welling up for some time, not least because of the GIA's execution of leading Algerian Islamist commanders as well as foreign fighters. These events made the Algerians jihadis almost outcasts in the wider jihadi movement for many years.[76]

Al-Suri was party to these discussions, albeit he was not among the inner decision-making circle. As far as is known, nor was he present at the famous Khartoum meeting. Still, he did travel to Sudan to meet with bin Laden in the early 1990s, according to US sources.[77] People who knew him in London also heard about his visits to Sudan in the early and mid-1990s, where he had been present at meetings with bin Laden.[78] There are conflicting reports on how much time al-Suri spent in Sudan in the mid-1990s but Spanish court documents assert, probably inaccurately, that he continued in his role as a training instructor there in the 1990s.[79]

Noman Benotman, a former Shura Council member of the Libyan Islamic Fighting Group, who had been in Peshawar and Afghanistan since 1989 and arrived in Khartoum in 1994, says that al-Suri attended meetings with al-Qaida in Sudan only once, in 1993.[80] Other Arab-Afghan veterans who were in Sudan at the time, such as Abdallah Anas, also recalled seeing al-Suri there. In Anas' opinion,

---

76    Author's interview with Noman Benotman, London, 15 Sept. 2006; and author's interview with Camille Tawil, London, 14 Sept. 2006. See also Craig Whitlock, 'Al-Qaeda's Far-Reaching New Partner: Salafist Group Finds Limited Appeal in Its Native Algeria', *Washington Post*, 5 Oct. 2006, p.A01.

77    Robert Windrem, 'U.S. hunts for "pen jihadi",' *MSNBC News*, 9 Dec. 2004, www.msnbc.msn.com/id/6685673/, accessed July 2005.

78    Author's interview with Abdel Bari Atwan at *al-Quds al-Arabi* offices, London, 28 April 2006; author's interview with Camille Tawil, London, 14 Sept. 2006; author's interview with Noman Benotman, London, 15 Sept. 2006; and author's interview with Abdallah Anas, London, 16 Sept. 2006.

79    'Juzgado Central de Instruccion no.005, Madrid, Sumario', 17 Sept. 2003, p.27.

80    Author's interview with Noman Benotman, London, 15 Sept. 2006.

al-Suri went often to Sudan. On one occasion, around 1994, al-Suri came to see him in Khartoum, asking for a meeting with the FIS. By then, al-Suri had made a name for himself as a jihadi theoretician and GIA supporter; he was also known as a distributor of recordings of speeches by jihadi clerics, including his own lectures, which circulated throughout Europe at the time. Many of these attacked the FIS.[81]

In Khartoum, Abdallah Anas and several other FIS members had a three hour meeting with al-Suri. Anas recalls that al-Suri did most of the talking, attempting to demonstrate the 'deviancy' of the FIS program and the futility of its strategies. According to Anas, al-Suri also insisted that participation in elections and acceptance of democracy constituted 'unbelief', irrespective of whether they were fraudulent or not, saying that: 'Democracy is forbidden in our religion'.[82] For Anas, armed jihad had been launched in Algeria 'in order to defend the legitimate rights of which the Algerian people had been deprived', while for the GIA the armed jihad had the purpose of 'repentance from the deviancy of politics'.[83]

Not much came of the meeting: Anas and his FIS members remained unconvinced by al-Suri's arguments. However, the meeting shows, as did similar discussions that al-Suri held with leading Islamists in London,[84] that he actively promoted the GIA cause in the wider Islamist landscape. The meeting with Anas and FIS leaders

---

81   Author's interview with Abdallah Anas, London, 16 Sept. 2006. Al-Suri also mentions his lectures in support of the GIA; see Camille Tawil, 'The Egyptian "al-Jihad", the Libyan "Combatant Group", "Abu Qutadah" and "Abu Mus'ab" retract their support from the Algerian "Group",' (in Arabic), *al-Hayat* (London), 10 June 1996, p.6. See also Jamal Khashoggi, 'The "Salvation" accuses the "Group" of attempting to impose their influence on them by force' (in Arabic), *al-Hayat* (London), 24 May 1994, p.1.

82   Author's interview with Abdallah Anas, London, 16 Sept. 2006.

83   Ibid.

84   For example, he asked for a meeting with Saad al-Faqih and his CDRL organization in London in 1995 in order to persuade them to not criticize the GIA. Author's telephone interview with Saad al-Faqih, 17 Sept. 2006.

in Sudan around 1994 probably came in response to the unification efforts in Algeria at the time, when several important rebel factions and commanders associated with the FIS decided to join the GIA. Al-Suri's meeting was probably meant to further these efforts by attempting to convince the FIS leaders to fight under the GIA's banner or, at the very least, not to obstruct and fight the GIA. The power struggle between the GIA and the FIS intensified in 1994 and the FIS leaders were actively involved in lobbying efforts in attempting to undercut 'foreign support' for the GIA, presumably from Sudan and elsewhere.[85] In a blunt attempt to undermine the GIA in Sudan, the FIS reported statements attributed to Abu Mus'ab al-Suri in which he allegedly had issued 'religious rulings permitting the killing of Hasan al-Turabi'.[86] *Al-Hayat*, which published these attributed statements, was later forced to pay al-Suri an indemnity for this and similar articles (see chapter 6).

## A NEW SYRIAN JIHAD GROUP?

Apart from making the case for the GIA, al-Suri himself was, according to several sources, apparently also one of the numerous beneficiaries of bin Laden's spending bonanza on more or less promising jihadi projects during the 1990s. There were money transfers to his account from individuals who later figured on US and UN lists of al-Qaida suspects.[87] Furthermore, in the early 1990s al-Suri had reportedly received financial backing from bin Laden in order to enable him to relaunch a Syrian jihadi group.[88] It is uncertain to what kind

---

85   See interview with FIS leader in Jamal Khashoggi, 'The "Salvation" accuses the "Group" of attempting to impose their influence on them by force' (in Arabic), *al-Hayat* (London), 24 May 1994, p.1.

86   Cited in Jamal Khashoggi, 'Abu Mus'ab al-Suri was in the Syrian "Combatant Vanguard" and was expelled from the Muslim Brothers' (in Arabic), *al-Hayat* (London) 14 Jan. 1996, p.6.

87   'Juzgado Central de Instruccion no.005, Madrid, Sumario', 17 Sept. 2003, p.54.

88   Author's interview with an Arab press source. Name withheld on request.

of project or organization this referred. For all practical purposes, The
Combatant Vanguard, in which al-Suri had formerly been a leading
member, was inactive in the 1990s, although it was mentioned in
Spanish court documents in 2003.[89] However, former group members kept in touch and several Syrians with a history of involvement
in The Combatant Vanguard or the Syrian Muslim Brotherhood
gravitated towards the al-Qaida support networks in Europe headed
by Imad al-Din Barakat Yarkas, also known as Abu Dahdah (see
below), who was based in Spain from October 1995 onwards. One
of them was a Syrian called Riyad al-Uqla (Abu Nabil), whom the
Spanish authorities considered to be the top representative of the
Jordan-based branch of The Combatant Vanguard. Through telephone intercepts and surveillance they found that al-Uqla was Abu
Dahdah's primary contact in Jordan. Al-Uqla travelled repeatedly to
Spain and Germany to hold meetings with Abu Dahdah and his
network. Abu Dahdah also visited al-Uqla in Jordan on several occasions.[90] As a leading member in Abu Dahdah's network, al-Suri also
stayed in frequent contact with al-Uqla, according to one study.[91]

It is possible that al-Suri's initial aim was to build a new Syrian
organization, allied with al-Qaida, perhaps along the lines of al-Zawahiri's group, with which he had been very close since the late 1980s.
During the trial against the East African Embassy bombers in 2001,
Jamal al-Fadl, the prosecution's star witness, who worked for al-Qaida
in Sudan until 1995, recalled having met al-Suri in Sudan. He also
described him as a leader of a Syrian jihadi group. The trial transcripts
of the cross examination of al-Fadl on this issue are cited below:

Q. Were there any groups within al Qaeda from the country of Syria?
A. Yes, Jamaat e Jihal al Suri.
Q. Do you know who the leader of Jamaat e Jihal al Suri was?

---

89   See 'Juzgado Central de Instruccion no.005, Madrid, Sumario', 17 Sept.
     2003.

90   'Juzgado Central de Instruccion no.005, Madrid, Sumario', 17 Sept. 2003,
     pp.51, 58.

91   Jean-Charles Brisard with Damien Martinez, *Zarqawi: The New Face of
     al-Qaeda* (Cambridge, UK: Polity Press, 2005), p.186.

A. Abu Musab al Suri.

Q. Do you recall what color hair Abu Musab al Suri had?

A. He got yellow hair.

Q. Was that unusual within the group?

A. No, but he is from Syria, and he looked like Germany people.

Q. He looked like what kind of people?

A. Germany people.

Q. Did he have any special training, Abu Musab al Suri?

A. Yes.

Q. What was his specialty?

A. He got training how to fight from close without weapons, like with knife or hands or like that.[92]

In light of al-Suri's characteristically blond appearance and his judo skills, this witness statement seems quite credible. The statement suggests that al-Suri was indeed considered a member of al-Qaida at the time, or at least an associate of bin Laden's 'Islamic Army Shura', and that he had been present in Sudan or at least that he was well-known among people like al-Fadl.

Al-Fadl's reference to the *Jamaat e Jihal al Suri* (sic!) seems to confirm that al-Suri had ambitions for reviving a jihadi organization in his homeland, as many other Arab-Afghans had when they left Peshawar in the early 1990s. Several sources have suggested that bin Laden 'had entrusted him' a jihadi project in Syria during the 1990s, but that the attempt had failed.[93] Al-Suri's own account of this period also shows that he took practical steps to prepare for a new Syrian jihadi organization.[94] He recalls that upon leaving Peshawar, he and several of his Syrian friends were searching for a new organizational platform:

---

92  Cited in Testimony of Jamal Ahmed Mohammed Al-Fadl, United States of America *v.* Osama Bin Laden, et. al. Defendants', transcript of trial, 6 Feb. 2006, Day 2, http://cryptome.org/usa-v-ubl-dt.htm, accessed July 2006, p.299.

93  'Abu Mus'ab al-Suri's Communiqué to the British and Europeans regarding the London Bombings in July 2006', *Middle East Transparent* website, 23 Dec. 2005, www.metransparent.com/texts/abu_massab_assuri_communique_calling_for_terror_in_europe.htm, accessed Oct. 2006; and author's interview. Name and place withheld on request.

94  Meeting with the Kuwaiti Newspaper', transcript of audiofile No.9, p.4.

While we were in Afghanistan, and after the Afghanistan period, we were not in any organization (*tanzim*) and I felt that we were in a vacuum: we had training, we had capabilities, but we were still in a void. We had to join an organized group and present our capabilities as cadres.[95]

This quote from 1999 seems to contradict what al-Suri later said about his association with al-Qaida and bin Laden between 1988-92. However, it should be recalled that al-Qaida was not meant to be a traditional jihadi *tanzim*, but rather a framework for training, financing, and supporting local jihadi insurgencies around the Islamic world. Hence, when leaving Peshawar, trained al-Qaida associates like al-Suri were expected to organize their own new units that would in turn instigate jihadi uprisings in their own countries or support ongoing insurgencies elsewhere in the Islamic world.

But al-Suri and his friends had no effective organizational infrastructure established in Syria. In their search for a new base, they contacted a well-known Syrian scholar, Muhammad Surur bin Nayif Zayn al-Abidin, better known as Shaykh Muhammad Surur. Al-Suri knew his background well. Surur had been a leading figure in the Syrian Muslim Brotherhood, but in the 1970s he had split from the organization and formed his own group, which later came to be known as 'the Sururi Group' or 'the Sururi Trend'.[96] He left for Saudi Arabia, where he taught at a religious institute in Burayda (in the northern province of Qasim). A number of prominent militant ideologues had graduated under him, including Salman al-Awdah.[97] Surur later settled in Birmingham, in the United Kingdom, where he founded an Islamic research center from where the journal, *majallat al-sunnah* ('The Sunna Journal')), was published. Shaykh Surur reportedly had a significant following in many countries, including Syria and Jordan, and al-Suri had known many Sururi adherents in

---

95    Ibid.

96    Umar Abd al-Hakim, *The Islamic Jihadi Revolution in Syria. Part I*, p.65.

97    See Mashari al-Dhaydi, 'What is the Story of the Sururi Current?' (in Arabic), *al-Sharq al-Awsat*, 28 Oct. 2004. I am indebted to Stephane Lacroix for identifying this source on Shaykh Surur.

Peshawar. Surur's school of Islamist thought, which differed significantly from that of the Muslim Brotherhood, appealed to al-Suri:[98]

I liked his personality and his ideas. [...] I had the opportunity to meet with Shaykh Surur and explain this to him. This was in Germany. I went there with the intention to join this group.[99]

Even though Surur propagated a hardline and partly Qutbist-inspired ideology, he was unwilling to offer advice or any organizational assistance to al-Suri and his comrades. Their nightlong meeting with the Shaykh in Germany had started very well, with long discussions on ideological issues, but when Surur realised that al-Suri was serious about actually *preparing militarily* for a violent revolutionary struggle, he refused to offer him any further help. Surur opposed the use of violence as a means of toppling Muslim regimes *before* an alternative state-like structure existed that could replace the government. Surur and his like spoke of building 'a solid base' (*qa'idah sulbah*), ideologically and organizationally, but rejected any military preparation since such steps would in their view only jeopardize the movement.[100] Shaykh Surur had apparently told al-Suri that youths were too impatient for change, and they should therefore not be part of his group.[101]

Al-Suri was very frustrated by this outcome. Without backing from senior clerics like Surur, the prospects for reviving a jihadi campaign in Syria looked bleak. His preoccupation with Shaykh Surur is evident in his audiotaped lectures from this period.[102] When al-Suri

---

98  Surur's thinking was reportedly characterized by an attempt to merge Muslim Brotherhood activism, including some of the revolutionary thinking of Qutb, with the theological dogmas of salafi-wahabi orthodoxy. The trend was sometimes dubbed 'salafiyyah-ikhwaniyyah'. See ibid. and Su'ud al-Qahtani, 'The Saudi Islamic Revivalism' (in Arabic), *Gulf Issues website*, www.gulfissues.net/mpage/gulfarticles/article53-1.htm, accessed Jan. 2007.

99  Meeting with the Kuwaiti Newspaper', transcript of audiofile no.9, p.4.

100  Ibid., no.9, p.1.

101  'The Bases and Components of a Secret Organization'. Audiotaped lecture, held in Peshawar or Afghanistan in 1989 or 1990.

102  Ibid.

returned to Peshawar, he upset many Sururi followers there with his derogatory remarks about Shaykh Surur. He also created a scene when he later went to see Shaykh Surur at a conference in Holland, ostensibly to mend fences with him, but the meeting ended in a fierce verbal confrontation.[103]

Al-Suri recalls that when Surur had visited Peshawar, the EIJ leaders Ayman al-Zawahiri and Doctor Fadl had encouraged him to meet with Umar Abd al-Rahman, the infamous 'Blind Shaykh' who was later convicted for his role in the first World Trade Center bombings in 1993. At the time, he was the JI emir and regarded as 'the mujahidin's shaykh'. Surur had rejected the invitation, however, saying that Umar's 'hands were sullied with blood'.[104]

Surur's criticism of the jihadi trend remained a constant irritant to al-Suri, especially when he later became heavily involved in supporting the media efforts of the Algerian jihadis (see chapter 6). During the 1990s, Surur's rejection of the jihadis grew more intense: He blasted the Egyptian JI and EIJ as '*kharijites*' (outlaws) and later also called bin Laden a 'madman', al-Suri later lamented.[105] Surur's continuous attacks on the jihadi current were a source of considerable concern for al-Suri. He tried in vain to obtain another meeting with Shaykh Surur, and sent him numerous letters, which were usually returned unopened.[106]

It is not known whether anything concrete came of al-Suri's strategy for a revived jihad in Syria. Whatever his plan may have been, they left very few traces. By contrast, the Syrian-dominated Abu Dahdah-network, in which al-Suri played a prominent role, has left indelible marks in the history of European jihadism, by paving the way for the Madrid bombings of March 2004, one of the most deadly acts of terrorism in post-war European history.

---

103  Ibid.

104  Meeting with the Kuwaiti Newspaper', transcript of audiofile no.4, p.6.

105  Meeting with the Kuwaiti Newspaper', transcript of audiofile no.9, pp.4, 5.

106  Meeting with the Kuwaiti Newspaper', transcript of audiofile no.4, p.9.

## THE RISE OF AN AL-QAIDA CELL IN SPAIN

When interviewed in 1999, al-Suri made no mention of Spain as an arena for jihadi activism, dismissing it as a country which was virtually 'closed' for this type of activity.[107] Al-Suri obviously wished to avoid drawing attention to what was among the most important al-Qaida cells in Europe at the time.

In the early and mid-1990s, Spain became an important European center for jihadis associated with al-Qaida.[108] In 1994-5 an Islamist extremist group emerged in Spain under the name 'Soldiers of Allah' (*jund allah*), or the 'Mujahedeen Movement'.[109] It was based on 'the doctrines of Osama bin Laden', and was 'formed in the worldview of its principal members, Abu Dahdah, Abu Qatadah, Abu Zubaydah, and al-Suri', as the Spanish indictment stated somewhat cryptically.[110] What is important here is that its leading members were former Arab-Afghan veterans, and were well-connected to the upper echelons of al-Qaida. Furthermore, the network initially consisted of mostly Syrian or Syrian-born Islamists, although Moroccans and other nationalities gradually became more prominent in its ranks. Al-Suri was considered among its leading figures.

The Spanish investigation into the Soldiers of Allah/the Mujahedeen Movement began in earnest in the mid-1990s, if not before, following reports of links to Algerian terrorists, who were then at the top of the terrorist threat list in several European countries. The Spanish intelligence service, *La Comisaría General de Información*,

---

107 Meeting with the Kuwaiti Newspaper', transcript of audiofile no.2, p.2.

108 For more details on the Spanish al-Qaida cell, see Rohan Gunaratna, 'Spain: An Al Qaeda Hub?', *UNISCI Discussion Papers / IDSS*, Singapore, May 2004, www.ucm.es/info/unisci/Rohan2.pdf#search='Rohan%20AN D%20UNISCI', accessed Jan. 2006.

109 See statements by the Spanish Interior Minister in Nov. 2001 in 'Spanish Police Arrest 11 Accused of Working for bin Laden', *The New York Times*, 14 Nov. 2001.

110 'Juzgado Central de Instruccion no.005, Madrid, Sumario', 17 Sept. 2003, p.338. See also 'Spain Arrests 3 Suspects; Tapes of U.S. Sites Seized', *The New York Times*, 17 July 2002.

had begun surveillance of the principal jihadis in Spain, including al-Suri, as early as 1993.[111]

The Spanish al-Qaida cell emerged from this network under the leadership of a Syrian militant, Imad al-Din Barakat Yarkas, often referred to by his *nom de guerre* Abu Dahdah. He became head of the group in October 1995 after its former leader, the Palestinian Anwar Adnan Muhammad Salih, or Shaykh Salah, left Madrid for Peshawar, where he worked as an al-Qaida recruiter in cooperation with Abu Zubaydah (whose real name is Zayn al-Abidin Muhammad Hussayn) at the Khalden training camp in Afghanistan. Together with al-Suri, Shaykh Salah was believed to have coordinated the arrival and training of recruits in the Afghan training camps. Salih was reportedly arrested by Pakistani authorities in Peshawar in 2000.[112]

Some sources have elevated al-Suri to the position of 'the founder of the al-Qaida cell in Spain'.[113] Press sources have claimed that he established the cell in the early 1990s shortly after his return to Spain, and left the leadership to Shaykh Salah when he later moved to London.[114] Others dispute this, saying that Shaykh Salah, and later Abu Dahdah, played the critical role in forming the cell, although al-Suri clearly contributed to these efforts.[115] After he moved

---

111 According to the Spanish parliamentary commission on the M-11 attacks, see 'Proyecto de Dictamen de La Comisión de Investigación sobre el 11-M de 2004', 22 June 2005, via www.elPaís.es/elPaísmedia/ultimahora/media/200506/22/espana/20050622elpepunac_1_P_DOC.doc, accessed July 2006, p.53.

112 José María Irujo, 'El hombre de Bin Laden en Madrid', *El País*, 2 March 2005, www.elPaís.es/comunes/2005/11m/08_comision/libro_electronico_red_islam/red_islamista_01%20doc.pdf, accessed July 2006, p.18.

113 George al-Rayyis, 'Madrid connects the name Abu Mus'ab al-Suri to the restaurant explosion in 1985' (in Arabic), *al-Sharq al-Awsat*, 10 Nov. 2005, www.asharqalawsat.com/details.asp?section=4&issue=9844&article=332668, accessed Dec. 2005.

114 'How the March 11 local cell was born', (in Spanish) *El País*, 12 Sept. 2004.

115 Email correspondence with Professor Javiér Jordán, University of Granada, 15 July 2006.

to London, he clearly continued to operate as a key member of the network. According to the Spanish verdict against the Abu Dahdah cell, al-Suri maintained links with the overwhelming majority of those prosecuted in the case, 'as well as with those convicted, as with those acquitted'.[116]

Abu Dahdah had a background similar to that of al-Suri. He had fled Syria following the crackdown on the Syrian Muslim Brotherhood movement in the early 1980s.[117] Abu Dahdah came to Spain from Jordan in 1986, only a year after al-Suri had arrived there. He established himself in Madrid as a small-time importer and wholesaler and also married a Spanish woman, a former 'mujer progresista' who had a role in one of Pedro Almodóvar's movies.[118] Through this marriage, Abu Dahdah gained Spanish citizenship.[119]

Al-Suri's relations with Abu Dahdah have been described by Spanish court documents as 'close'.[120] They maintained that relationship even after al-Suri moved to London in 1994, although it reportedly soured due to an internal conflict in the GIA media cell in London, where Abu Dahdah sided with al-Suri's rivals.[121] Abu Dahdah also maintained close links with al-Suri when the latter moved from London to Afghanistan in 1997-8.[122] In fact, al-Suri was de-

116 Cited in Audiencia Nacional, Sala de lo Penal, Sección Tercera, 'Sentencia Núm. 36/2005', Madrid, 26 Sept. 2005, [verdict against the Abu Dahdah network], p.315.

117 'Juzgado Central de Instruccion no.005, Madrid, Sumario', 17 Sept. 2003, p.26.

118 Antonio Rubio, 'Mustafa Setmarian Naser: Un español en la cima de Al Qaeda: Durante los diez años que vivió en España se convirtió en lugarteniente de Bin Laden', elmundo.es, 3 Nov. 2005, www.elmundo. es/elmundo/2005/11/03/espana/1131002447.html, accessed Dec. 2005.

119 John Crewdson, 'Spain query links Syrians to 9/11 attacks in U.S.', Chicago Tribune, 19 Oct. 2003, http://deseretnews.com/dn/view/0,1249,515039793,00.html, accessed Nov. 2005.

120 'Juzgado Central de Instruccion no.005, Madrid, Sumario', 17 Sept. 2003, p.93.

121 Author's interview with Camille Tawil, London, 14 Sept. 2006.

122 According to Spanish investigators, Abu Dahdah had travelled seventeen

scribed as one of Abu Dahdah's 'main contacts in Afghanistan'.[123] During his trial, Abu Dahdah admitted that he knew al-Suri. He said their children attended the same school at the Abu Bakr mosque in Madrid: 'we would see each other and chat'. He also claimed, most probably falsely, that he lost track of al-Suri when the latter moved to Britain.[124]

Located in Anastasio Herrero Street in the downtown area of Tetúan, the Abu Bakr mosque was one of the meeting points for former Syrian Muslim Brotherhood members in Spain. Al-Suri frequented the mosque and distributed jihadi material there, including his book on the Syrian jihadi movement.[125] The mosque's Imam, Riay Tatari, also a Syrian, recalls meeting with al-Suri who attracted attention because of his militant viewpoints.[126]

The scope of al-Suri's involvement in the proselytization efforts of Abu Dahdah's network remains unknown. He continued to lecture and teach after he returned to Spain from Afghanistan and, according to a Spanish journalist who studied al-Suri's life in some detail, he 'gave classes in political sharia (Islamic law) among Muslims and instructed them on "who we are and who are our enemies"'.[127] When

times to London between 1995 and 2000 and cooperated closely with Shaykh Umar Mahmud Uthman (Abu Qutadah), widely considered to be among the top spiritual jihadi guides in Europe since the 1990s. See 'Juzgado Central de Instruccion no.005, Madrid, Sumario', 17 Sept. 2003, p.26.

123   'Spanish Police Arrest 11 Accused of Working for bin Laden', *The New York Times*, 14 Nov. 2001.

124   Cited in 'Spanish al-Qaida suspect denies helping to plot', *Inland Valley Daily Bulletin* (Ontario, CA), 26 April 2005.

125   Antonio Rubio, 'Mustafa Setmarian Naser: Un español en la cima de Al Qaeda: Durante los diez años que vivió en España se convirtió en lugarteniente de Bin Laden', *elmundo.es*, 3 Nov. 2005, www.elmundo. es/elmundo/2005/11/03/espana/1131002447.html, accessed Dec. 2005.

126   José María Irujo, 'El hombre de Bin Laden en Madrid', *El País*, 2 March 2005, www.elPaís.es/comunes/2005/11m/08_comision/libro_electronico_ red_islam/red_islamista_01%20doc.pdf, accessed July 2006, p.15.

127   Antonio Rubio, 'Mustafa Setmarian Naser: Un español en la cima de Al Qaeda: Durante los diez años que vivió en España se convirtió en

*al-Hayat* wrote about al-Suri in the mid-1990s, the newspaper also reported that he recorded the lectures he delivered in his home and in the homes of his supporters in Spain and London.[128] However, al-Suri's official website, which has an extensive list of these and other lectures, refers to two of his lecture series from Britain in 1993 and 1995 but none from Spain.[129]

Lectures mostly at closed meetings were a consistent element of his life since he became involved with the al-Nur Media Center in Peshawar around 1990. Such teaching activities also provided ample opportunities to seek out potential recruits and motivate youths to join the jihadi movement. Indeed, according to a Spanish verdict from September 2005, both al-Suri and Abu Dahdah were heavily involved in the recruitment of jihadi volunteers: 'Already in 1995 [they] committed themselves to picking up young Muslims living in Spain in order to send them to training camps in Bosnia'.[130] They were both dominant personalities, according to other cell members. One of them, Abdallah Khayata Kattan, described them as follows: 'Both displayed their leadership positions, and, by their dominant personalities and insistent character, imposed themselves on others, inciting them to go for training'.[131] Al-Suri's background as an Afghanistan war veteran and his effectiveness were duly noted too: 'He had been in Afghanistan, he was a great fighter; he came as a sudden

---

lugarteniente de Bin Laden', *elmundo.es*, 3 Nov. 2005, www.elmundo. es/elmundo/2005/11/03/espana/1131002447.html, accessed Dec. 2005.

128 Jamal Khashoggi, 'Abu Mus'ab al-Suri was in the Syrian "Combatant Vanguard" and was expelled from the Muslim Brothers' (in Arabic), *al-Hayat* (London), 14 Jan. 1996, p.6.

129 According to the website, the two lectures are placed under the subheading 'audiotape collection Britain'. See 'The Old Production of Shaykh Abu Mus'ab al-Suri, 1987-2001' (in Arabic), *Abu Mus'ab al-Suri's website*, www.fsboa.com/vw/index.php, accessed Sept. 2005.

130 Audiencia Nacional, Sala de lo Penal, Sección Tercera, 'Sentencia Núm. 36/2005', Madrid, 26 Sept. 2005, [verdict against the Abu Dahdah network], p.31.

131 Ibid., p.172.

impulse to Spain. He was swift and powerful with the boys of Abu Dahdah and all the others.'[132]

While al-Suri moved to London and later to Afghanistan, Abu Dahdah remained in Spain. In the wake of 9/11, he was arrested by the Spanish anti-terrorism police in Operación Dátil (Operation 'Date Palm') and charged with heading a terrorist organization and providing support for the 9/11 conspiracy. At the same time, Spanish authorities also issued an international arrest warrant for al-Suri, which is still in force.[133] Abu Dahdah was convicted by a Spanish court in September 2005 and sentenced to 27 years imprisonment for having played a leading role in a terrorist group and for helping to organize the 9-11 conspiracy.[134] He was later acquitted of the latter charge.

Until its partial dismantlement in late 2001, the Abu Dahdah network was involved in a wide range of support activities. It worked systematically in the field of proselytism and propaganda, and financed jihadi networks through the use of commercial front companies (construction and estate businesses, music and video stores, etc.), credit card fraud, money laundering, and Islamic tax collection (*zakat*). Propaganda activities were conducted around the Abu Bakr mosque in Madrid, especially the distribution of journals and news bulletins published on behalf of militant Islamist organizations in Libya, Algeria and Egypt. Ten or more copies of the GIA-affiliated *al-Ansar Newsletter* were distributed by cell members every week in and around the mosque, according to the Spanish authorities.[135] Among the network's priorities were recruitment for jihadi

---

132  Ibid.

133  Carlos Fonseca, 'Setmariam Lived in Madrid for Three Years', *El Tiempo* (Madrid), 3 Sept. 2004, pp.14-15, via FBIS.

134  Jennifer Green, 'Sept. 11 Figure Is Convicted in Spain', *The Washington Post*, 27 Sept. 2005, p.A16, www.washingtonpost.com/wp-dyn/content/article/2005/09/26/AR2005092601612.html?nav=rss_world, accessed Jan. 2006.

135  Mar Roman, 'Alleged al-Qaida financier denies giving money for jihad', *Associated Press*, 11 May 2005, via LexisNexis. See also Luis Rendueles and

units fighting in Bosnia, Chechnya, Afghanistan, and Indonesia, supplying them with funds, weapons, and false travel documents, and financing medical treatment and otherwise caring for returning jihadi veterans.[136] The network also searched for new areas in which to operate or to base new training camps.[137]

The list of Abu Dahdah's contacts has been likened to a *Who's Who* of the jihadi movement, encompassing more than a dozen countries, including, *inter alia*, Germany, Great Britain, Denmark, France, Belgium, Afghanistan, Pakistan, Indonesia, Saudi Arabia, Syria, Morocco and Lebanon.[138] Nor was the network peripheral to al-Qaida: Abu Dahdah allegedly met with Osama bin Laden at least twice in Afghanistan in order to 'receive precise instructions' according to police sources quoted by the international media.[139] He took orders directly from Muhammad 'Atif (Abu Hafs al-Masri), al-Qaida's military commander, till his death in November 2001.[140]

While the Bosnian jihad preoccupied the group in the mid-1990s, and several cell members fought in the Balkan wars, the focus later shifted to other fronts, including Afghanistan, Chechnya and even

Manuel Marlasca, '7-J: Los escritos del ideólogo', *Interviú*, 18 May 2005, www.interviu.es/default.asp?idpublicacio_PK=39&idioma=CAS&idnotic ia_PK=28299&idseccio_PK=547&h=050606, accessed July 2006.

136 'Juzgado Central de Instruccion no.005, Madrid, Sumario', 17 Sept. 2003, p.338. See also 'Spanish Court Lists Evidence Against Al-Qa'idah Suspects, Arab Journalist', (BBC-title)," *ABC* (Spanish newspaper, Madrid), 18 Nov. 2004 via BBC Monitoring; and Darko Trifunovic, 'Pattern of Bosnian and Other Links to Madrid Bombings Becoming Increasingly Clear' (LexisNexis-title), *Defense & Foreign Affairs/International Strategic Studies Association*, 21 June 2005 via LexisNexis.

137 Emma Daly, 'A Nation Challenged: Madrid', *The New York Times*, 14 Nov. 2001.

138 'Juzgado Central de Instruccion no.005, Madrid, Sumario', 17 Sept. 2003, p.338.

139 'Spanish Police Arrest 11 Accused of Working for bin Laden', *The New York Times*, 14 Nov. 2001.

140 According to intelligence sources interviewed in Daniel McGrory, 'Spanish suspects "plotted attacks across Europe",' *The Times* (London), 19 Nov. 2001.

countries as far away as Indonesia. One member of the network was an Indonesian student in Spain who returned to Indonesia in October 2000 to run an al-Qaida-affiliated training camp. Other cell members, including its only Spanish cadre, Luis José Galán Gonzalez, known as Yusuf Galan, and Abu Dahdah himself, visited the camp in mid-2001.[141] Galan was believed to have received training there in July 2001.[142] The group's main financier is believed to have sent money to Islamic militants in many other countries, including the United States, Belgium, Saudi Arabia, Syria, China, Jordan and the Occupied Territories.[143]

Abu Dahdah also maintained close contacts with the large circle of Islamists in London, especially Abu Qutadah al-Filastini, his collaborators Abu Walid al-Filastini and Abu Mus'ab al-Suri, both of whom later relocated to Afghanistan, and Khalid Fawwaz (see below).

In Belgium, Abu Dahdah's contacts included Tarek ben Habib Maaroufi, also known as Abu Ismail, a Belgian citizen of Tunisian origin. Belgian authorities believe that he was recruited by the 'Office of Afghan Mujahideen' in the mosques around Brussels and received training in Afghanistan. He was later suspected of having co-founded and headed the Tunisian Combatant Group, often considered to be one of al-Qaida's regional branches. Consequently, he was described by the Belgian press as 'one of the most prominent al-Qa'eda agents in Europe'.[144] Between March 1995 and December 1996 Maaroufi

---

141 'Proyecto de Dictamen de La Comisión de Investigación sobre el 11-M de 2004', 22 June 2005, via www.elPaís.es/elPaísmedia/ultimahora/media/200506/22/espana/20050622elpepunac_1_P_DOC.doc, accessed July 2006, pp.53-4.

142 See Daniel McGrory, 'Spanish suspects "plotted attacks across Europe",' *The Times* (London), 19 Nov. 2001.

143 According to interview with police intelligence officials, see Tim Golden, 'Traces of Terror: The Terror Network', *The New York Times* 17 July 2002. See also 'Detenido en Madrid un segundo responsable de la red financiera de Al Qaeda', *terra.es* 24 April 2002, www.terra.es/actualidad/articulo/html/act40672.htm, accessed July 2006.

144 'Brussels: Europe's Hub of Terror', *The Flemish Republic website*, undated,

was jailed in Belgium for involvement in weapons trafficking. According to Belgian sources, Maaroufi was distributing GIA publications which incited violence and contained 'calls for crime'.[145] After 9/11 he was rearrested and convicted for his role in supplying fake identity papers to the two Tunisians who assassinated Ahmad Shah Massoud, the head of the Northern Alliance in Afghanistan, on 9 September 2001.[146]

In addition, there were extensive contacts between the predominantly Syrian network and the Algerian militants from the GIA and later its offshoot *The Salafist Group for Preaching and Combat* (GSPC), and these relationships continued up to 2001.[147] For example, in early April 1997, the Spanish police operation 'Appreciate' dismantled a GIA cell in Valencia and Torrent, Alicante, which had links to the Abu Dahdah group, some of whose members were later indicted for involvement in the Madrid train bombings.[148] The Abu Dahdah cell was also suspected of having close links to Nabil Nanakli Kosaibati,

---

www.flemishrepublic.org/extra.php?id=1&jaargang=1&nr=1,   accessed Aug. 2006.

145   See Sénat de Belgique, Annales des réunions publiques de commission, Commission de la Justice, 'Demande d'Explications de Mme Lizin au Ministre de la Justice Sur « La Filière des Intégristes Tunisiens, Installés dans Notre Pays et mis en Cause par le Procureur Général de Tunis', dated 26 Nov. 1996, www.senate.be/www/?MIval=/publications/viewPubDoc& COLL=C&LEG=1&NR=63&PUID=16777477&TID=16780282&LA NG=fr, accessed Oct. 2006.

146   See 'Juzgado Central de Instruccion no.005, Madrid, Sumario', 17 Sept. 2003, pp.58, 91-92; and 'Al Qadea's New Front: Belgium', *Public Broadcasting Service website*, 25 Jan. 2005, www.pbs.org/wgbh/pages/ frontline/shows/front/map/be.html, accessed Aug. 2006.

147   GSPC is the French acronym. The Arabic name is *al-jama'ah al-salafiyyah li al-da'wah wa'l-qital*. See Daniel McGrory, 'Spanish suspects "plotted attacks across Europe",' *The Times* (London), 19 Nov. 2001 via LexisNexis.

148   See 'Proyecto de Dictamen de La Comisión de Investigación sobre el 11-M de 2004', 22 June 2005, via www.elPaís.es/elPaísmedia/ultimahora/ media/200506/22/espana/20050622elpepunac_1_P_DOC.doc, accessed July 2006, p.54.

also called Abu Salah, a Spanish national of Yemeni origin, who had shot an Italian tourist in Sanaa in 1997 and was later convicted for having plotted to assassinate the Yemeni vice-president. Kosaibati had allegedly received funds from Abu Dahdah's financiers.[149]

The Spanish secret services had apparently just launched their surveillance of Abu Dahdah and al-Suri when the latter left the country in 1994. According to court documents, they monitored al-Suri's home and family in Madrid in March 1995, and discovered that Abu Dahdah allowed al-Suri's family to use one of his cars, a Mercedes 280. They also reported how Abu Dahdah himself accompanied al-Suri's wife, Elena Moreno, and their two sons, Abdulkader and Omar, when they moved to London.[150] Out of sight and out of mind, al-Suri was now less interesting for Spanish investigators, and they consequently paid him less attention. Hence the Spanish court records about him are relatively sparse and far less comprehensive than those on Abu Dahdah.

Abu Mus'ab al-Suri's exact role in the Spanish al-Qaida cell remains unclear. Was he ever a co-founder and a co-director of the cell, or was he merely one of Abu Dahdah's numerous senior

---

149  Spanish investigators have described Kosaibati as Abu Dahdah's 'right hand'. See 'Proyecto de Dictamen de La Comisión de Investigación sobre el 11-M de 2004', 22 June 2005, via www.elPaís.es/elPaísmedia/ultimahora/ media/200506/22/espana/20050622elpepunac_1_P_DOC.doc, accessed July 2006, p.95. See also 'Juzgado Central de Instruccion no.005, Madrid, Sumario', 17 Sept. 2003, pp.44-5; Joshua Levitt and Jimmy Burns, 'Spain claims success in drive against terror', *Financial Times*, 2 May 2002, http://specials.ft.com/attackonterrorism/FT3SZHDQF0D.html, accessed July 2002; 'Written Testimony of Jean-Charles Brisard, International Expert on Terrorism Financing, Lead Investigator, 911 Lawsuit, CEO, JCB Consulting International, Before The Committee On Banking, Housing And Urban Affairs, United States Senate', 22 Oct. 2003, http://banking.senate.gov/_files/brisard.pdf, accessed July 2006; and 'Detenido en Madrid un segundo responsable de la red financiera de Al Qaeda', *terra.es* 24 April 2002, www.terra.es/actualidad/articulo/html/act40672.htm, accessed July 2006.

150  'Juzgado Central de Instruccion no.005, Madrid, Sumario', 17 Sept. 2003, p.28.

contacts in al-Qaida and Europe's wider jihadi community? Or was he simply a senior and knowledgeable figure whom cell members looked up to? Whatever the answer, previous association with al-Suri became a tremendous liability after 2001 for many of Abu Dahdah's acquaintances. The fact that al-Suri was considered a senior al-Qaida member with responsibility for 'an al-Qaida training camp' in Afghanistan (which was not entirely accurate), made any connection to him, beyond the most superficial contact, tantamount to a criminal offence.

# 6

# A MEDIA JIHADI IN
# LONDONISTAN 1994-97

In 1994, al-Suri moved to London, joining the large exiled community of jihadis living there at that time. He brought his family over
in mid-1995, settling in a house in Neasden.[1] Al-Suri's wife, Elena
Moreno, had reportedly told her parents that al-Suri was assuming
responsibility for a news magazine in London.[2] This was not entirely
untrue since he had been asked to join the editors of the *al-Ansar
Newsletter*, the GIA's main mouthpiece in Europe at that time.[3] The
magazine was one of the main projects of a GIA 'media cell supporting the jihad in Algeria', of which al-Suri was about to become a
leading member.[4] It has been alleged that al-Suri had been tipped off
about the growing interest on the part of the Spanish secret service
in him and his contacts in Spain, and therefore decided to leave the

1   Nick Fielding and Gareth Walsh, 'Mastermind of Madrid is key figure',
    *The Sunday Times*, 10 July 2005, www.timesonline.co.uk/article/0,2087-
    1688244,00.html, accessed July 2005; David Williams, 'Wanted: The red-
    haired man of terror with links to Madrid', *Daily Mail*, London 11 July
    2005, p.4; and José María Irujo, 'El hombre de Bin Laden en Madrid',
    *El País*, 2 March 2005, www.elPaís.es/comunes/2005/11m/08_comision/
    libro_electronico_red_islam/red_islamista_01%20doc.pdf, accessed July
    2006, p.17.
2   José María Irujo, 'El hombre de Bin Laden en Madrid', *El País*, 2 March
    2005, www.elPaís.es/comunes/2005/11m/08_comision/libro_electronico_
    red_islam/red_islamista_01%20doc.pdf, accessed July 2006, p.17.
3   'Biography of Shaykh Umar Abd al-Hakim (Abu Mus'ab al-Suri)' (in
    Arabic), p.3.
4   Ibid.

country, but this is uncertain.[5] After all, he had personal motives for moving to London. He planned to continue his academic studies,[6] but the simple fact was that by the mid-1990s, London had emerged as the major jihadi hub in Europe, where many leading clerics resided, and it had more to offer al-Suri than Madrid. By 1993 London was already his ideological headquarters, which he visited many times.[7]

Al-Suri had seemingly few problems adjusting to his new environment though it is not known how he earned a living. He established a media office in 1996-7, but it is uncertain whether that was ever profitable. It has been suggested that he lived on social welfare benefits, which was quite usual for many jihadis at that time. One of al-Suri's acquaintances in London noted that: 'He did not have expensive habits, like going to night clubs or drinking, so it was perfectly possible to survive on welfare, and even put aside money'.[8] Visitors noticed that he lived in a small and modest house, with hardly any furniture. They were obviously quite poor, one reporter noted.[9] Apparently lacking a steady income, al-Suri incurred debts and his extensive travelling must also have eaten into the household budget, even though he is known to have received financial support from other Syrian Islamists.[10]

---

5    Jean-Charles Brisard with Damien Martinez, *Zarqawi: The New Face of al-Qaeda* (Cambridge: Polity Press, 2005), p.186.

6    'Biography of Shaykh Umar Abd al-Hakim (Abu Mus 'ab al-Suri)' (in Arabic), p.3.

7    Elaine Sciolino and Don Van Natta Jr., 'For a Decade, London Thrived As a Busy Crossroads of Terror', *The New York Times*, 10 July 2005.

8    Author's telephone interview with Saad al-Faqih, 17 Sept. 2006.

9    Author's interview with Peter Bergen, 1 Feb. 2007.

10    According to the Spanish authorities, Mamoun Darkazanli, a Syrian businessman based in the Hamburg district of Uhlenhorst, allegedly transferred *c.* 4,600 DM in two instalments from his and his wife's bank accounts in Germany to accounts in al-Suri's name in Granada and London in Nov. 1993 and in Feb. 1996. Darkazanli was later indicted by Spain and the United States for allegedly being a key al-Qaida financier, and of assisting the Hamburg cell. However the German courts investigated Darkanzali and acquitted him on all counts. See 'Juzgado Central de

Al-Suri possessed a valid Spanish passport, and soon he also obtained British and other ID documents which he used when traveling. Press reports have described his skill at changing his appearance and some journalists dubbed him 'The Chameleon', claiming that al-Suri was 'an expert forger' and provided many al-Qaida recruits with false identity papers.[11]

After his plans to enter Algeria to fight with the GIA had been postponed indefinitely, al-Suri resumed his writing, primarily for three jihadi newsletters that were published in London (see below). He now considered himself 'one of the jihadi current's thinkers' and a promoter of 'the Islamic world's causes', especially through his journalism. He wished to guide the jihadi movement, 'correct' many of its mistakes and errors and reassess 'the directions and courses which we as jihadis have taken', he later recalled.[12]

In a 1999 interview, al-Suri reflected upon the possibilities to broaden the jihadi presence in London by exploring the possibility of cooperation with other Islamic currents, including the Muslim Brothers. His lists of potential partners even included non-Muslims who might sympathize with the jihadi cause out of a concern for human rights, a desire for peaceful coexistence with the Islamic world, etc. It is unlikely that he was very serious about this, or that he established long lasting relationships with moderate Islamists and non-Muslim sympathizers.

What really preoccupied al-Suri was improving the quality and impact of the jihadi groups' use of the media, which he then considered 'one of the very greatest gaps in jihadi activity'.[13] As usual, al-Suri was not slow to offer scathing criticism of the status quo:

---

Instruccion no.005, Madrid, Sumario', 17 Sept. 2003, p.54.

11　David Paul and Mike Parker, 'Hunt For Terror Boss', *Sunday Express*, 10 July 2005, p.11; Mentz Tor Amundsen, 'The Chameleon' (in Norwegian), *Dagbladet* (Oslo), 5 Aug. 2005; and Katherine Shrader, 'Wanted Muslim extremist hopscotches the globe connecting terrorists', *Associated Press*, 3 Aug. 2005.

12　'Meeting with the Kuwaiti Newspaper', transcript of audiofile no.2, p.4.

13　Ibid., p.3.

We in the jihadi movements present ourselves to the Islamic Nation, to the world, to our friends, enemies, and supporters in a very erroneous manner. The jihadi media is extremely limited, narrow and to a large degree it is badly articulated. Its core message is, from many different angles, obfuscated and clouded, and the way to reach out is wrong.[14]

Al-Suri took it upon himself to rectify these flaws and made plans to establish a media centre in London, perhaps drawing inspiration from the al-Nur Media Centre in Afghanistan, where he had lectured in the early 1990s.

## IN THE SERVICE OF THE ALGERIAN GIA

In the meantime, al-Suri began contributing to a variety of jihadi publications in London. Apart from his work for the GIA's *al-Ansar Newsletter*, he also assisted the production of the Libyan bulletin *Majallat al-Fajr*, which was associated with the Libyan Islamic Fighting Group (LIFG), and the Egyptian magazine *al-Mujahidun*, the mouthpiece of the Egyptian Islamic Jihad (EIJ).[15] In both *al-Mujahidun* and *Majallat al-Fajr*, al-Suri published under his usual pseudonym Umar Abd al-Hakim. In *Majallat al-Fajr* he also used other pseudonyms, including Abu Abdallah. The best known of these pieces was a series of essays entitled 'Perspectives on politics and jurisprudence for the real world' (*afaq fi al-siyasa wa fiqh al-waqi*), which reportedly appeared regularly in the eighteenth to the thirtieth editions of *Majallat al-Fajr*. The title was indicative of al-Suri's approach to religious learning, namely his ambition to integrate it into politics and the practicalities of jihad.[16]

---

14    Ibid.

15    'Biography of Shaykh Umar Abd al-Hakim (Abu Mus 'ab al-Suri)' (in Arabic), p.3. According to the French authorities, al-Suri was 'one of the principal editors of the extremist newspaper *al-Fajr*'. Cited in Jean-Charles Brisard with Damien Martinez, *Zarqawi*, p.186.

16    The sources differ slightly on the title of these articles and the names which al-Suri published this article under. See 'Meeting with the Kuwaiti Newspaper', transcript of audiofile no.2, p.3; and 'About this website' (in

As for the GIA media cell in London, he defined the following role for himself:

My position was that I should assist the GIA as best as I could, especially in the field of external media, provide advice and consultation to its leadership inside Algeria, gather supporters around it, and attempt to reach the inside to participate in the field.[17]

His main preoccupation in 1994-6 was the *al-Ansar Newsletter*, which was considered a GIA mouthpiece at the time. Some sources claim he was the editor and even the founder of the magazine.[18] Although he wrote numerous articles, he was not with the magazine from its inception. Al-Suri said he had followed the bulletin very closely from the outset and had read nearly every edition, but he only became actively involved in writing and editing the bulletin when its eighty-second edition came out, i.e. a year and a half after the magazine was launched. In a 1999 interview, he claimed that for all practical purposes he had stopped working for the *al-Ansar Newsletter* after no.122, published in late 1995.[19] This seems to be roughly correct. Most of al-Suri's articles under the pseudonym Umar Abd al-Hakim appeared in *al-Ansar* between March and December 1995.[20] They

---

Arabic) *Abu Mus'ab al-Suri Website*, www.fsboa.com/vw/index.php?subjec t=4&rec=23&tit=tit&pa=0, accessed Feb. 2006.

17   Umar Abd al-Hakim, *A Summary of My Testimony*, p.26.

18   Amanda Figueras, 'Abu Dahdah dice que su relación con líderes islamistas era "de tomar té, lo normal entre musulmanes", ' *elmundo.es*, 25 April 2005, http://www.elmundo.es/elmundo/2005/04/25/espana/1114426155.html, accessed Oct. 2005.

19   Meeting with the Kuwaiti Newspaper', transcript of audiofile no.3, p.3.

20   The author's collection of *al-Ansar* editions was generously provided to this author by Camille Tawil of *al-Hayat*. Although it is not 100 per cent complete, it is sufficiently comprehensive to give a rough impression of when al-Suri was most active. The first article under his pseudonym, Umar Abd al-Hakim, appears in issue 88 from 16 March 1995, and the last in 128, from 21 Dec. 1995. However, it is apparent from the editorial introduction to his article in 88 that al-Suri had written articles in earlier editions too, but that he had been absent from the newspaper for a period of time. See Umar Abd al-Hakim, 'Between the Loyal Servants of the Merciful and the Loyal Servants of the Vatican' (in Arabic) *Al-Ansar Newsletter*, no.88, 16

deal almost exclusively with political issues, with a particular focus on the conflict with the Islamic Salvation Front (FIS), the futility of dialogue with the Algerian regime and the undermining effect of FIS' political reconciliation initiatives.[21]

The offices of the *al-Ansar Newsletter* were raided by the British security services because of the suspected involvement in the Paris bombings of 1995 of some figures associated with the magazine, and publication was halted for a while. When it was later resumed, al-Suri was persuaded to continue contributing a few more articles.[22] The magazine was discontinued after more than 164 editions, an impressive record compared to most other jihadi publications.[23]

In the 1999 interview, al-Suri considered the *al-Ansar Newsletter* to be an important 'jihadi bulletin', albeit with 'some superficial material', and some which needs to be corrected and improved.[24] In his memoirs, released in 2004, he went much further in criticizing the *al-Ansar Newsletter* and GIA's media cell for their lack of professionalism and operational security:

From the day of my arrival in London and involvement in the Algerian London cell I immediately discovered a number of shocking facts. Their work was characterised by chaos and complete absence of security awareness. I also noticed the organizational overlap and interference between this cell (which was supposed to be a media unit) and other jihadi cells in Britain and Europe, which were involved in efforts beyond the field of media activities. Their administration of affairs was surrounded by a lot of nonsense and fruitless work. [...] Most of the work of this small group of Algerian Afghan

---

March 1995, p.13.

21  See in particular his series of articles entitled 'Study in the Ideology and Program and Positions of the Islamic Salvation Front' (in Arabic), *Al-Ansar newsletter*, nos 96 to 114 and 'Dialogue in Algeria: Promise from Someone Who has None to Someone Who Does Not Deserve One' (in Arabic), *Al-Ansar Newsletter*, nos 116 to 128.

22  Umar Abd al-Hakim, *A Summary of My Testimony*, pp.31-2.

23  Al-Suri says that some 152 editions were published, but this author has copies of more recent issues, including 164. See "Meeting with the Kuwaiti Newspaper', transcript of audiofile no.2, p.3; and audiofile no.3, p.3.

24  Ibid.

veterans was concentrated in the hands of a number of young Algerian supporters, who had sought political asylum in Britain as well as older members
of the Algerian diaspora in Britain. Most of them were novices in terms of
religious adherence. They did not know anything about how to organize
movements of this kind, nor about its roots and its ultimate goals. Most of
them had scant knowledge of various religious and worldly affairs. I really
thought of abandoning all of them and returning to where I came from.[25]

Al-Suri nevertheless joined the GIA media cell, partly because the
head of the administration at *al-Ansar Newsletter* was one of Qari
Saïd's disciples and an old friend from Peshawar, and partly because
he strongly believed in the GIA's cause and wished to defend it
against the 'conspiracies and attacks' from FIS-supporters and activists from the democratic Islamist currents.[26]

Al-Suri's description of the GIA media cell was heavily coloured
by his frustrating experiences with its chief editor Abu Qutadah, as
will be seen in the next chapter. Furthermore, the high expectations
which al-Suri and his fellow jihadis had attached to the Algerian jihad (see above), were thoroughly quashed by the spiralling barbarism
of the GIA's violence under the emirate of Jamal Zaytuni (1994-6)
and his successor Antar al-Zouabri (1996-2002), which also consumed many leading jihadi clerics and fighters.

Under Zaytuni's leadership, the GIA extended its attacks on civilians to France. Air France Flight 8969 was hijacked at the end of
December 1994, in an attempt to crash it into the Eiffel Tower, an
event which must be considered an important precursor to the 9/11
attack. The GIA continued its campaign with a series of bombings
inside France in the latter part of 1995. This strategy of international-
ising the conflict was not condemned by al-Suri, rather the opposite.
He later bragged about his role in drawing the famous picture on the
*al-Ansar Newsletter's* front page featuring the Eiffel Tower exploding. Furthermore, he claims to have recommended to al-Zaytuni's
predecessor, the GIA commander Abu Abdallah Ahmad (Sherif

---

25    Cited in Umar Abd al-Hakim, *A Summary of My Testimony*, p.21.
26    Ibid., p.30.

Ghousmi), during their correspondence in 1993, that the GIA take the war to France:

> I recommended to the GIA emir at that time, Abu Abdallah Ahmad and his leadership, may God have mercy on them, that they strike deeply in France in order to deter and punish her for her war against the GIA and for the French support for the dictatorial military regime. I told them that it would be beneficial to draw France into an openly declared support for the Algerian regime, a support which existed, but only in secrecy. This will unify the Islamic Nation around the jihad in Algeria as it unified the Islamic Nation in Afghanistan against the Soviets. To strike against France is our right. We are at war, and we do not play games, and our enemies should know that.[27]

The idea to focus on the far enemy, instead of only on the local enemy regime, and expose the hidden hand of the West with a view to unifying the jihadi camp is a striking element in al-Suri's more recent thinking. It has its parallel in his insistence on 'dragging the enemy' into becoming occupiers or into other unfavorable battlefields and thereby expose their presence in the Islamic world, which was a theme he focused on in lectures he gave throughout the late 1990s. A jihadi internet site summarised his main points in one of these audiotapes:

> [He explains] the strategy of dragging the enemy to the battlefield and thereby demonstrating the Western-Jewish military presence in the lands of the Muslims. He deals with why this strategy is among the most important goals of the mujahidin. This is because it resolves the mental complex in the Islamic Nation with regards to defining the enemy.[28]

As for his role in the GIA, he insists that he remained a media jihadi only and was not directly involved in any of the GIA's opera-

---

27    Cited in 'Text of Audio Communiqué by Shaykh Umar Abd al-Hakim (Abu Mus'ab al-Suri) Addressing the British and the Europeans regarding the London Explosions, and the Practices of the British Government' (in Arabic), Aug. 2005, p.5.

28    See posting by the Global Islamic Media Front: 'It is necessary to drag the enemy' (in Arabic), *muntadayat shabakat al-hisbah*, 30 Sept. 2005, www.alhesbah.org/v/. [Exact url not available]. The audiofile was part of Abu Mus'ab al-Suri's lecture series 'Jihad is the Solution' and has been downloaded from http://1.blurg.com/dl/481224/012855600M6.mp3.

tions in Europe. He was asked by the GIA leadership in Algeria to offer technical advice to its operatives in bomb-making, but he says he refused: 'I wished to maintain the wonderful media and proselyting activities which we ran from London in support of numerous Islamic causes'.[29] He insisted on this even after he became a fugitive with a $5 million reward for his capture: 'I, like all the other jihadis in London, pursued only ideological, literal, and journalistic activities which was known even among the security agencies'.[30] Even though this was not entirely accurate, it highlighted the fact that most jihadis in London at that time considered themselves first and foremost in a support role, not as active jihadi cells. His assertion is also consistent with his strategic thinking that in the jihadi movement, the media and proselytising cells should always be strictly separated from the operational units.

As for the Algerian jihad, al-Suri distanced himself gradually from the GIA's violent excesses inside Algeria, but he broke with the group long after its barbarity had disgusted Islamists of nearly every stripe. He later admitted that they had waited too long: 'we decided to stay firm, fight back and bridge the gap, but the deviations of the GIA broke the alliance of the jihadis'.[31] The GIA steadily increased its indiscriminate attacks, including car bombs, assassinations of musicians, athletes and unveiled women. The lack of a discernible strategy behind the attacks led to speculation, encouraged by the GIA's opponents that the group had been infiltrated by Algerian secret services, a claim that subsequently received corroboration from a variety of sources.[32] A turning point for al-Suri and his like-minded associates was the execution of several prominent GIA

---

29  Cited in 'Text of Audio Communiqué by Shaykh Umar Abd al-Hakim (Abu Mus'ab al-Suri) Addressing the British and the Europeans regarding the London Explosions, and the Practices of the British Government' (in Arabic), Aug. 2005, p.5.

30  Ibid.

31  Umar Abd al-Hakim, *A Summary of My Testimony*, p.30.

32  See Habib Souaïdia, *La sale guerre* (Paris: Le Découverte, 2001).

leaders from the *al-Jaz'arah* faction, and the fact that the GIA failed
to provide 'court records' from their 'trial' that allegedly proved that
the *al-Jaz'arah* faction had betrayed it.[33] Al-Suri publicly expressed
his reservations about the GIA in mid-January 1996,[34] having previously distanced himself from the *al-Ansar Newsletter* after the British
police raid, mentioned above.[35] His ideological differences with Abu
Qutadah had also prompted him to lessen his involvement to writing
for the magazine 'from afar', using new pseudonyms, in addition to
'giving advice as best as I could and sending my advice to the inside
through their channels'.[36] In June 1996, together with several other
jihadi groups in London, al-Suri declared his disavowal of the GIA
and retracted his support from it.[37] Al-Suri also stopped working for
the GIA media cell in London.[38]

From 1996 onwards, he 'pursued independent literary and journalistic work'.[39] The Spanish indictment from 2003 claimed that
al-Suri 'has continued to operate as an GIA associate [...] until
today,' which seems inaccurate given that the GIA lost the support of al-Qaida and most European based jihadi networks, which
switched their support to the GIA splinter group, the GSPC, in the
late 1990s.[40] If al-Suri maintained contact with the Algerian jihadis
after 1996, it was probably with independent individuals, or GSPC
supporters. It was the GIA's style and methods of warfare that he
questioned, not the legitimacy of an armed uprising in Algeria. In

---

33   Umar Abd al-Hakim, *A Summary of My Testimony*, pp.33-4.

34   Ibid.

35   Ibid., pp.31-2.

36   Ibid., p.31.

37   See Camille Tawil, 'The Egyptian "al-Jihad", the Libyan "Combatant
     Group", "Abu Qutadah" and "Abu Mus'ab" retract their support from the
     Algerian "Group",' (in Arabic), *al-Hayat*, 10 June 2006, p.6.

38   'Biography of Shaykh Umar Abd al-Hakim (Abu Mus'ab al-Suri)' (in
     Arabic), p.3.

39   Ibid.

40   'Juzgado Central de Instruccion no.005, Madrid, Sumario', 17 Sept. 2003,
     p.27.

a 2005 communiqué, al-Suri professed that he still 'supports jihad against the traitor apostate government' in Algeria as long as 'the jihad' is in accordance with Islamic law.[41]

Due to his participation in the GIA media cell in London, his long 'history of jihad', and his voluminous writings, al-Suri is still being read in Algerian Islamist circles, and is held in high esteem as a jihadi thinker and strategist. In 2006-7, *The Global Islamic Resistance Call* was featured prominently on the GSPC's website and was recommended as essential reading.[42] Al-Suri is nevertheless regarded as a controversial figure by some GSPC factions. In January 2005, the group's media department issued a special communiqué, warning their followers against al-Suri's memoirs, namely where he writes extensively about Algeria, the GIA and its media cell in London.[43] The GSPC interpreted his book as 'a glorification of the role of the FIS and a detraction of that of the Salafis' in the Algerian insurgency.[44] However, this attack on al-Suri's memoirs does not appear to reflect the official GSPC position.[45] With the GSPC's new alliance with

---

41 Cited in Umar Abd al-Hakim (Abu Musʻab al-Suri), 'Letter to the British and the Europeans – Its People and Governments – regarding the London Explosions, July 2005' (in Arabic), dated Aug. 2005.

42 See the GSPC's website at http://moonnight1234.com/ and www.moon4321.com, accessed between March and June 2006. See also the website of its successor, al-Qaida in Islamic Maghreb.

43 'The "Salafi Group" criticizes Abu Musʻab al-Suri's book' (in Arabic), *al-Hayat*, 23 Jan. 2005, www.daralhayat.com/arab_news/nafrica_news/01-2005/20050122-23p01-08.txt/story.html, accessed Jan. 2006.

44 A communiqué reportedly signed by a member of the GSPC's information department, Mouloud Kettouf, a.k.a Abou Yasser Sayaf, characterized al-Suri's statements as 'abusive discourse *vis-à-vis* the Salafis and complaisance with regards to the impostors of the Group of Salvation [i.e. the Islamic Front of Salvation, FIS].' Cited in 'Le GSPC essuie un nouveau revers: un prédicateur syrien désavoue l'action salafiste', *Algérie Confidentiel*, 24 Jan. 2005, www.algerieconfidentiel.com/frmArticle.aspx?ArticleId=390, accessed July 2006.

45 In early 2005 this was interpreted as a reflection of a power struggle within the GSPC triggered in part by policy differences over the reconciliation and amnesty initiatives offered by the Algerian government at the time.

al-Qaida and the group's more pronounced global jihad orientation, they continue to embrace al-Suri's latest book on a global Islamic resistance strategy.[46]

## BIN LADEN'S MEDIA AGENT

In the mid-1990s, al-Suri maintained contact with al-Qaida's leadership in Sudan; he was close to bin Laden's primary spokesmen in the United Kingdom, and he also spoke repeatedly on the phone with the EIJ leader Ayman al-Zawahiri, who gradually came to assume the role of al-Qaida's second in command. When bin Laden returned to Afghanistan in May 1996, al-Suri went there four or five months later to meet him.[47]

Al-Suri saw himself as being most useful to al-Qaida in the field of 'jihadi journalism'. In London, he began contacting the media beyond the immediate community of militant Islamists, striving to broaden the appeal of bin Laden's message.

In 1996, al-Suri founded a media and studies centre in London, registered as the *Islamic Conflict Studies Bureau Ltd*, also termed *Bureau for the Studies of Islamic Conflicts*.[48] It was located in al-Suri's

The incumbent GSPC leader Abu Musab Abd al-Wudud had reportedly issued a fatwa on the GSPC website against the GSPC founder and former leader Hassan Hattab, accusing him of treason. The latter responded by suggesting that former GIA elements had infiltrated the GSPC leadership, and by accusing Abd al-Wudud, the GSPC leader, of 'attacking civilian targets, like some common Djamel Zitouni or uncouth Antar Zouabri', both of whom were former GIA leaders. The Algerian daily, *al-Khabar*, 17 Feb. 2006, cited in Stephen Ulph, 'Schism and collapse of morale in Algeria's GSPC', *Terrorism Focus*, 2 (7) (March 31, 2005), http://jamestown.org/terrorism/news/article.php?articleid=2369528, accessed July 2006.

46   For GSPC's new orientation towards al-Qaida and global jihad, see Craig Whitlock, 'Al-Qaeda's Far-Reaching New Partner', *Washington Post*, 5 Oct. 2006, p.A01.

47   'Meeting with the Kuwaiti Newspaper', transcript of audiofile no.2, p.4; and *The Global Islamic Resistance Call*, p.713.

48   'Meeting with the Kuwaiti Newspaper' transcript of audiofile no.2, p.3;

home in London, not far from the media offices of Egyptian Islamic Jihad (EIJ), led by Adil Abd al-Bari, and *The Advice and Reform Committee* (ARC), run by Khalid al-Fawwaz, from which bin Laden's statements in the mid-1990s were publicized.[49] Al-Suri's media centre also appears to have been a front organization, serving as a media facilitator for al-Qaida. It was run by al-Suri and his associate Muhammad Bahayah (Abu Khalid al-Suri). Spanish investigators identified a company account in a London-based bank established in March 1997 in the name of al-Suri's media bureau, to which both al-Suri and Bahayah had authorization. The latter was named as al-Suri's 'co-director'.[50] The fact that the account was opened in March 1997, precisely at the time of al-Suri's involvement with the CNN, suggests that he wished to funnel back to the company the fees he presumably charged for his media liaison services to CNN (see below). Al-Suri recalls that he officially registered the media centre, obtained a license for it, and began preparing to launch a website. They strived to establish it on 'the level of contemporary media'.[51]

Al-Suri planned to produce online newsletters with the intention of developing a paid online service for other news agencies in order to generate income.[52] He also intended to mobilise his excellent contacts in the world of militant Islam to offer exclusive news items to the international media and therefore tried to convince other jihadi groups to channel their communiqués and media statements through

---

and 'Juzgado Central de Instruccion no.005, Madrid, Sumario', 17 Sept. 2003, p.55.

49   Spanish investigators located the centre in '4 Paddock Road, Cricklewood, London, NW2 7DL. This was al-Suri's home address. People who knew him in London also recall that the media centre operated from his home. See 'Juzgado Central de Instruccion no.005, Madrid, Sumario', 17 Sept. 2003, p.55; author's telephone interview with Saad al-Faqih, 17 Sept. 2006; and author's interview with Camille Tawil, London, 14 Sept. 2006.

50   See 'Juzgado Central de Instruccion no.005, Madrid, Sumario', 17 Sept. 2003, p.55.

51   'Meeting with the Kuwaiti Newspaper' transcript of audiofile no.2, p.3.

52   Ibid., p.4.

his centre. However most militant groups jealously guarded their media activities, which were a key element of their struggle, and were unlikely to outsource them.[53] One statement by bin Laden, on the occasion of the Saudi Prince Sultan's visit to the United States, appears to have been relayed through al-Suri's media center in early March 1997 but otherwise the *Islamic Conflict Studies Bureau Ltd* has left few traces. People who knew al-Suri in London have described it as 'a short-lived affair', lasting only a year or so. Lacking both practical experience and funds to invest in a media operation, al-Suri was unsuccessful in realizing those ambitions in London.[54]

Having said that, through his experience with the media centre al-Suri built relations with several news agencies in London, including Reuters and AFP, and several of the largest Arabic language newspapers interviewed him, especially on matters related to the GIA.

As an experienced traveller in Afghanistan who had a European passport, al-Suri was ideally placed to be an intermediary for al-Qaida's efforts to obtain media coverage for bin Laden's message to the United States and the world. Khalid al-Fawwaz, who ran the ARC in London (Advice and Reform Committee) in conjunction with bin Laden, could not fulfill that role since he lacked travel documents because of his political refugee status.[55] Hence, it was al-Suri who took it upon himself to serve as intermediary for Channel 4 and CNN when they went to Afghanistan to interview bin Laden in 1996 and early 1997.[56] But his role was bigger than that of a tour guide, for in the 1990s he served in many ways as bin Laden's media adviser. These events were not peripheral to al-Qaida. The CNN interview in

---

53 Author's interview with Noman Benotman, London, 15 Sept. 2006.

54 Author's telephone interview with Saad al-Faqih, 17 Sept. 2006; and author's interview with Camille Tawil, London, 14 Sept. 2006.

55 Author's telephone interview with Saad al-Faqih, 17 Sept. 2006.

56 'Meeting with the Kuwaiti Newspaper', transcript of audiofile no.2, p.3; and 'Biography of Shaykh Umar Abd al-Hakim (Abu Mus'ab al-Suri)' (in Arabic), p.3.

particular was one of bin Laden's most important steps on his ascent to global notoriety.

## AL-SURI'S FILM ON CHANNEL 4

In 1996 al-Suri contacted Channel 4, the British television channel and suggested that they make a film about the Arab-Afghan movement. Using the cover name 'Oscar' he approached a reporter, Gwynne Roberts, who eventually went to Afghanistan in late 1996 and obtained an exclusive interview with the Saudi celebrity, one of the first Western journalists to meet bin Laden in Afghanistan.[57]

Al-Suri (or 'Oscar') acted as Channel 4's intermediary and travelled with its reporters into Afghanistan in late 1996.[58] The film crew was told to go to Jalalabad and wait for him at a hotel. There, Roberts ran into Abdel-Bari Atwan, the editor-in-chief of the London-based Arab newspaper *al-Quds al-Arabi*, who also was on his way to interview bin Laden, but neither would reveal to the other the real purpose of their visit.[59] Al-Suri imposed strict security precautions on the foreign media team, as he also did when he assisted the CNN team a few months later. On the way to bin Laden's lair, he also added to the tense atmosphere by spelling out what would happen to journalists who assisted foreign intelligence services in locating bin

---

57 Ibid. In a telephone interview with the author, Gwynne Roberts initially provided details about his meetings with al-Suri. However, he subsequently requested that they not be divulged since he intended to include them in his memoirs. Hence, the information below is based primarily on other sources. Author's telephone interview with Gwynne Roberts, Sept. 2006.

58 In the 1999 interview al-Suri did not quite recollect the exact time of the interview, but says it took place before the CNN interview and before he settled in Afghanistan permanently. Elsewhere, al-Suri says he met with bin Laden four or five months after the latter returned to Afghanistan (which was in May 1996). See Meeting with the Kuwaiti Newspaper', transcript of audiofile no.2, p.4; and *The Global Islamic Resistance Call*, p.713.

59 Abdel Bari Atwan, *The Secret History of al-Qa'ida* (London: Saqi Books, 2006), p.17.

Laden. When the programme aired in February 1997, it contained footage of Gwynne Roberts in Afghanistan, from where he tells his viewers that:

I have been told not to watch out and tell nobody my plans. I wait for days and begin to think the intermediary will never show up, but, at last, he arrives. He says he has contacted Bin Ladin by radio at a base 5 miles away and is trying to fix a meeting. Bin Ladin is not prepared for me to interview him on film, however, and it is a great disappointment. Instead I prepare questions and show my intermediary how to use my camera. I want him to do the interview. Several nights later he returns, the meeting is arranged and we are to leave immediately. As we walk from my hotel, he tells me that the Americans supplied a small tracking device to Terry Waite before he left for negotiations in Beirut. I ask him what would happen if I had such a device hidden in my clothes. It is made clear–I would not return alive.[60]

In the programme, Gwynne Roberts was filmed together with bin Laden but he was not allowed to interview him directly. Instead, it was 'Oscar' who shot the video-clips, to ensure that only a carefully edited version reached the media:

Days later my video cassettes are returned apparently showing the camp used by Bin Ladin. [Video shows Bin Ladin, cutting to show a stone building, protected by look-out posts, cutting to show a tank on an embankment] My intermediary has indeed filmed Bin Ladin, but although some of my questions are touched upon, this is not my interview. The cassette is clearly intended for Bin Ladin's own followers in the Middle East.[61]

'Oscar' felt justified in claiming, in an interview three years later, that he 'made a film about bin Laden for Channel 4 in cooperation with some of bin Laden's supporters'.[62] Al-Suri considered the film

---

60  'Correspondent Meets With Opposition Leader Bin Ladin', *Channel 4 Television Network* (London), 2100 GMT, 20 Feb. 1997. [Report by correspondent Gwynne Roberts on meeting with Osama Bin Laden, Saudi opposition leader, near Jalalabad, date not given, including recorded remarks by Bin Ladin; from the *Dispatches* program], http://binladenquotes. blogspot.com/2004/02/fbis-document-10-years-of-osama-bin.html, accessed Sept. 2006.

61  Ibid.

62  'Meeting with the Kuwaiti Newspaper', transcript of audiofile no.2, p.3.

'to a certain degree a success,' despite having had serious reservations about it. The producers had allegedly inserted an extra segment in the film that 'benefited the Saudi Shiites' without al-Suri and his associates' knowledge.[63] On the other hand, the film brought bin Laden's cause to worldwide attention, and the experience of the Western media not necessarily producing exactly what you want them to also proved 'a useful experience' for al-Suri and his team.[64]

## FACILITATING CNN'S BIN LADEN INTERVIEW

Al-Suri recalls that he accompanied another film crew to Afghanistan in early 1997.[65] This was the CNN team, consisting of Peter Arnett, who had been awarded the Pulitzer Prize for his reporting on Vietnam, Peter Bergen, whose books on al-Qaida are highly regarded, and veteran cameraman Peter Jouvenal.[66] The interview was finally held on 20 March 1997 and broadcast on CNN on 10 May 1997.[67] The interview was bin Laden's first television interview on a global TV network and one of his first interviews in the Western media.

Al-Suri avoided mentioning any details about whom Channel 4 and CNN cooperated with in London and Afghanistan to set up their interviews, but Peter Bergen subsequently detailed how the interview came about and al-Suri's role in facilitating it.[68] Bergen

---

63    Ibid., p.4.

64    Ibid.

65    Again, al-Suri did not recall the exact time. He variously estimates that it was in Dec. 1996 and in Feb. 1997. See 'Meeting with the Kuwaiti Newspaper', transcript of audiofile no.2, pp.3-4.

66    Peter Bergen, *Holy War Inc.*, p.6.

67    See 'Prosecution uses bin Laden interview in embassy bombings trial', *CNN.com*, 21 Feb. 2001, at http://edn.cnn.com/2001/LAW/02/21/embassy.bombing/, accessed July 2006.

68    For details on the interview, see Peter Bergen, *Holy War Inc.*; and Muhammad al-Shafi'i, 'American terrorism expert: al-Qaida has lost its headquarters in Afghanistan, but it has occupied the Internet space' (in Arabic), *al-Sharq al-Awsat*, 27 June 2005, www.asharqalawsat.com/details.asp?section=4&issue=9708&article=308296, accessed 22 Nov. 2005.

describes Khalid al-Fawwaz, whom US authorities have dubbed bin Laden's 'representative' in London[69] as their main contact point to secure the interview. Al-Suri's precise role is not clear. Al-Fawwaz clearly had superiors, with whom he had to consult before he could agree to the CNN request, and after their first contact al-Fawwaz suggested to Bergen that he meet with several other people in London, including the Saudi dissident Saad al-Faqih, who would give Bergen 'more background on bin Laden'.[70] Fawwaz also introduced Bergen to al-Suri who would be the person guiding the CNN team to Afghanistan if bin Laden agreed to an interview. When he wrote about the bin Laden interview in *Holy War Inc.*, in 2001, Bergen simply referred to al-Suri as 'an Arab I will call Ali'.[71] Al-Suri had presented himself as Omar Hakim. Since Bergen thought this was his real name, he chose to call him 'Ali' in his book.[72]

After his meetings with Faqih and 'Ali', Bergen met again with al-Fawwaz, who told him that he had 'received a call from bin Laden's media adviser' on how to proceed.[73] It is quite possible that this person was al-Suri. The media adviser considered the BBC, CBS's *60 Minutes*, as well as CNN for bin Laden's first television interview but the fact that CNN had the widest coverage of the three may have been decisive. Bergen left London for Washington and after a month or so he received the green light from al-Fawwaz to begin the trip to Afghanistan.

---

69    United States of America *v.* Usama Bin Laden, *et al.* Defendants (Kenyan Embassy Bombing), United States District Court, Southern District of New York, Indictment S(9) 98 Cr. 1023 (LBS), www.terrorismcentral. com/Library/Incidents/USEmbassyKenyaBombing/Indictment/ Introduction.html   and   www.terrorismcentral.com/Library/Incidents/ USEmbassyKenyaBombing/Indictment/Count1.html,   accessed   July 2006.

70    Peter Bergen, *Holy War Inc.*, p.4.

71    Ibid., p.5.

72    Author's interview with Peter Bergen, Washington, 1 Feb. 2007.

73    Peter Bergen, *Holy War Inc.*, p.6.

When the media started to pay more attention to al-Suri in 2004 and 2005, Bergen recognized him as his facilitator and gave interviews about his impression of al-Suri.[74] In an interview with the present author, he recalls that they met on and off in London for some two weeks. Al-Suri presented himself as a journalist and an historian and hardly made any overtly anti-American statements. Furthermore, they never spoke of religious issues. Al-Suri invited Bergen to his modest home in London that was also the base of his newly established *Islamic Conflicts Bureau Ltd*. He told Bergen that the Bureau had branch offices in Kabul and Tajikistan.[75]

As for his personal impression of al-Suri, Bergen describes him as 'a smart man, a cool-nerved guy, who knew what was going on around him'.[76] Al-Suri had said he spoke no English, forcing them 'to communicate in rudimentary French'.[77] Despite the language barrier, al-Suri seems to have made an impression on Bergen, who described him as a tough, battle-hardened Islamist with 'somewhat gruff manners' who he nevertheless warmed to after a while:

[Ali] had served with bin Laden's guerrillas as a medic for three years during the Afghan war against the communists. [...] Ali had spent more than a decade in Europe and had written extensively on Islamist struggles in the Middle East and Asia. A compact, muscular man, not given to smiling from behind his bushy red beard, Ali projected an intense seriousness of purpose. One had the sense that he would be very calm under fire.[78]

After their initial meetings in London, they flew together to Peshawar.[79] There, al-Suri switched from Western clothing to the traditional *shalwar kameez*, widely worn in Pakistan. Together with one of his associates, a Syrian man, he spent several days making contacts and arranging the details for the trip over the border to Afghanistan.

---

74 Muhammad al-Shafi'i, 'American terrorism expert'.

75 Author's interview with Peter Bergen, Washington, 1 Feb. 2007.

76 Muhammad al-Shafi'i, 'American terrorism expert'.

77 Peter Bergen, *Holy War Inc.*, p.5.

78 Ibid.

79 Author's interview with Peter Bergen, Washington, 1 Feb. 2007.

From there, they took the CNN team on a rough journey to Jalalabad and then to the Tora Bora mountains.[80]

As the CNN team's guide on the demanding trip across the Khyber Pass into Afghanistan, al-Suri had ample opportunity to talk about the Arab participation in the Afghan war of liberation and his own role in it. He showed them graveyards of Arabs who had fallen during the war, where green flags fluttered in the wind, and where he himself had fought against the Soviet Army.[81]

From the outset, al-Suri was very circumspect and thorough with regards to security precautions. As opposed to many other Islamist activists in London, he had insisted that his name should not be revealed to Western journalists. When traveling with the CNN team to Afghanistan, he instructed them to speak in code on the phone and never to mention bin Laden by name. The visit was to be referred to 'as a trip to "meet the man in Kuwait"'.[82] From Jalalabad al-Suri took the CNN team on an arduous journey to a secret meeting with bin Laden which was held in a rough mud hut.[83]

Fearing electronic tracking devices, bin Laden's media advisers forbad the CNN team from using their camera and sound equipment and even their watches had to be left behind. Instead, the journalists were given a hand-held digital camera to shoot the interview.[84] Anxious not to jeopardize his security, bin Laden had agreed to hold only an hour-long interview. All questions had been screened beforehand and inquiries relating to his personal life, family, and finances had been deleted from the list. Al-Suri later described bin Laden as 'tense' during the CNN visit[85] and he departed the location as soon as the interview was completed. According to Atwan, who spoke repeatedly with al-Suri during this period, bin Laden had arranged for

---

80    See also Peter Bergen, *Holy War Inc.*, pp.8-9.

81    Ibid.

82    Ibid., p.6.

83    Ibid., p.13.

84    Ibid., p.17.

85    Author's interview with Abdel Bari Atwan, London, 28 April 2006.

a temporary camp to be set up specifically for the interview in order to make it harder to trace his location, should the US intelligence services, or any other spying agency, attempt to exploit the CNN visit for that purpose.[86]

After the interview ended a dispute erupted over whether the CNN team should be allowed to use the entire tape recording or only excerpts from the interview.[87] One of bin Laden's media advisers started to delete those parts he considered unflattering, and even threatened to withhold the tapes altogether. Al-Suri then intervened and, after a long argument, handed the two tapes to the CNN reporters. After having rescued CNN's interview, al-Suri ('Ali') spoke to Bergen outside the hut where the filming had taken place, inquiring whether the news organization would broadcast bin Laden's vitriolic attack on the United States, including his diatribe against President Bill Clinton. 'Of course', Bergen had replied reassuringly.[88] The interview was broadcast on 12 May 1997 and shown in 100 countries. When reflecting on the event two years later, al-Suri said he considered the interview 'a very, very successful experience' for bin Laden; in fact, the CNN program quickly featured in al-Qaida's 'media glory' (*al-majd al-i'lami*)', apparently a collection of al-Qaida's top media feats at that time.[89] Initially, al-Suri had feared that CNN would distort the image of bin Laden and had even considered demanding a contract from CNN so that they could be sued if they 'defamed' bin Laden in the program. In 1997, he had recently won a libel case against the *al-Hayat* newspaper (see below) and this had given him confidence in his ability to draw on the Western legal system to advance the jihadi cause. Al-Suri primarily wanted the film to be neither positive, nor negative, only 'objective'. When it was broadcast, the jihadi community reportedly greeted it as a 'very positive' portrayal of bin

---

86    Ibid.

87    Peter Bergen, *Holy War Inc.*, p.23.

88    Ibid., p.23.

89    'Meeting with the Kuwaiti Newspaper', transcript of audiofile no.2, p.4.

Laden, which conveyed 'very nicely' his cause to the world.[90] The extremely wide coverage it received around the world, including in the Arab Peninsula and the Middle East, was hailed as a great success by al-Suri and his associates.

## WITH AL-QUDS AL-ARABI IN TORA BORA

In late 1996 Abdel Bari Atwan went to Afghanistan and spent three days with bin Laden. When Atwan arrived at bin Laden's cave complex in Tora Bora, he was warmly received by al-Suri. They knew each other well from London and had met often at *al-Quds al-Arabi*'s offices in King Street. In his book, *The Secret History of al-Qa'ida*, Atwan recalled his arrival at Tora Bora:

Seeing nothing else in the dark, I hurried towards the lit cave and entered it alone. A man was there to meet me; I was absolutely astonished to recognize him as a Syrian writer I knew quite well from London, Omar Abdel Hakim, also known as Abu Mus'ab al-Suri, a specialist on *jihad* and Islam. We spoke for a few moments and I learned that he had left Spain, where he had both citizenship and a wife, to join al-Qa'ida. Later, he was to join the Taleban, and became Mullah Omar's media advisor. 'Come', he said, leading the way into another cave. 'The Sheikh is waiting for you'.[91]

In an interview with this author, Atwan said that al-Suri was present at all of his meetings with bin Laden and it was he who took the well-known photo of Atwan together with al-Qaida's leader. Atwan recalls that al-Suri played quite an active role during his conversation with bin Laden and in fact his constant interjections were an irritating nuisance to Atwan who wished bin Laden to speak freely in a relaxed atmosphere. Al-Suri interrupted whenever he disagreed with the way the interview was conducted. He also vetoed the use of a tape recorder or other audio-recording equipment, justifying his decision by saying that bin Laden's opponents might exploit grammatical errors he might make, or inaccuracies in his citation of Quranic verses and Prophetic

---

90   Ibid.
91   Cited in Abdel Bari Atwan, *The Secret History*, p.27.

Traditions, in order to discredit him to Muslim audiences. Atwan perceived al-Suri's role as that of 'the *de facto* media adviser' for the al-Qaida leader.[92] Bin Laden already had a media adviser called Abu Walid, but in meetings with the international media al-Suri appeared to have supplanted his role for the time being.[93]

## MEETING THE *FINANCIAL TIMES*

Al-Suri also gave interviews to Western newspapers in the late 1990s. Among those he met was the *Financial Times'* security correspondent Mark Huband, an experienced reporter who had previously covered militant Islam in Algeria, Morocco, Sudan, Somalia and elsewhere. They met twice in Khalid al-Fawwaz's London home in January 1997, through whom al-Suri was introduced to Huband.[94]

Huband noted at the time that 'nobody really knew what kind of structure was developing out of the Arab-Afghan veterans and in which direction these seemingly disparate groups were heading after Afghanistan'.[95] In the mid-1990s, there was a feeling that 'something extraordinary was taking place' and that this period was an important turning point. Huband had reported from Sudan and Somalia in the early 1990s and had noted the 'military capabilities' that the Arab-Afghan fighters brought into play in Somalia. Although details of the foreign jihadi involvement in Somalia remained disputed, the role of Arab-Afghan veterans was very much a live issue in the Algerian civil war that he covered after moving to Morocco in 1995. Their involvement was thought highly significant by American, British, French and other security officials whom he met during that period. The war in Bosnia had also brought the Arab-Afghan movement into focus, and analysts had started talking more specifically about bin Laden. The respected journalist Robert Fisk had identified him as a

---

92    Author's interview with Abdel Bari Atwan, London, 28 April 2006.
93    Ibid.
94    Author's interview with Mark Huband, London, 29 April 2006.
95    Ibid.

key figure as early as 1993 and had begun interviewing bin Laden. From 1996 onwards a number of the world's most influential media outlets took steps to meet with bin Laden. Mark Huband too felt that 'I must meet this man' and in seeking out opportunities for an interview he encountered al-Fawwaz many times in 1996 and 1997. During their conversations al-Fawwaz was vague about his own role in bin Laden's organization and stressed that there were many things about bin Laden that he did not like and that he disagreed with him on many points. Al-Fawwaz was very curious about why Huband was interested in the Arab-Afghans and wished to meet with bin Laden. Satisfied that Huband's interest in the topic was genuine, al-Fawwaz told him that 'there is someone you should meet'.[96] This was al-Suri, and the three of them met twice, on 15 and 16 January 1997.

Al-Suri presented himself only as 'Omar' and again insisted in speaking in French. They agreed that he be referred to only as 'Karim Omar', an alias he had rarely used before.[97] The reasons for his great caution were obvious. By early 1997, al-Suri felt that he was being intimidated by the British authorities and the Arab press and confided that he feared expulsion by the British government 'if he talked about his politics'.[98] Later the same year he did indeed relocate to Afghanistan.

To Huband, 'Omar' appeared highly intelligent and far-sighted. It was clear from the very beginning that Fawwaz deferred to 'Omar' and considered him his superior. 'Omar' had a much deeper and more nuanced perspective on the Arab-Afghan movement than had al-Fawwaz. Moreover his vision and depiction of the history of the jihadi movements were new to Huband. 'Omar' specifically emphasized the role of bin Laden: 'Osama is important for the past and for the future. He has passed through many stages. He represents the

---

96   Ibid.

97   See interview with Karim Omar in Mark Huband, *Warriors of the Prophet: The Struggle for Islam* (Oxford and Boulder, CO: Westview Press, 1998), pp.1-4.

98   Ibid., p.1.

method.'[99] 'Omar' seemed to portray bin Laden as the new leader who would draw things together, and more than most other Islamist militants of the period, he had a very clear vision about the need to form an organized structure.

In their two conversations, al-Suri struck Huband as someone who was very keen to explain his ideas and who acted in a public relations capacity for the Arab-Afghan movement. Like a teacher or a lecturer, he provided a wealth of information, interspersed with his own assessments. When Huband later wrote his bestselling book, *Warriors of the Prophet*, he devoted ample space to his meeting with al-Suri, or 'Karim Omar', and quoted him extensively.[100]

Al-Suri was not a jovial, backslapping and convivial figure in his meetings with journalists in London. Like most of those who met him in the mid-1990s, Huband does not recall him smiling. He had a sharp tongue, and there was a satirical tone in his descriptions of fellow jihadis, especially of the Saudis. When elaborating on his experience with the Arab volunteer fighters in Afghanistan in the late 1980s, he observed that the Saudis spent time in Bangkok's red light district and they 'would come to fight the jihad to purify [themselves]'.[101]

Although he clearly was a prominent figure in London's Islamist community, he was not an imposing or intimidating personality. Huband recalls that he was relatively small in stature, relatively soft-spoken, quiet, and careful in how he expressed himself. Initially, Huband wondered why al-Fawwaz thought that al-Suri was such an important man to meet. After all, al-Fawwaz went by the nickname 'bin Laden's ambassador to Britain' among Arab journalists in London.[102] It was obvious that he greatly respected and looked up to al-Suri and

---

99   Ibid., p.3.

100  Ibid., pp.1-4, 13, 14, 15, 58-9, 61, and 164.

101  Ibid., p.3. See also his 'Holy war on the world', *The Financial Times*, 28 Nov. 2001, http://specials.ft.com/attackonterrorism/FT3RXH0CKUC. html, accessed April 2006.

102  Abdel Bari Atwan, *The Secret History*, p.16.

considered him to be far senior in the Arab-Afghan hierarchy than himself. And al-Fawwaz clearly wanted Huband to meet this important figure and to show him that there were bright and accomplished intellectuals like al-Suri in the Arab-Afghan movement.[103]

## SUING THE ARAB WORLD'S LARGEST NEWSPAPER

Al-Suri's important role in facilitating bin Laden's successful appearance on CNN and couching the al-Qaida leader in his dealings with the international media was matched by his own success in confronting the Arab world's most prestigious newspaper, the London-based, Saudi-owned *al-Hayat* daily. It ran investigative journalism in a range of fields, and in the mid-1990s the Islamist opposition in Algeria received broad coverage in the paper's special section on that country.

In mid-1994, if not earlier, *al-Hayat* began reporting on al-Suri, devoting considerable attention to the FIS's verbal attacks on the GIA and its non-Algerian ideologues. In May 1994, *al-Hayat* mentioned al-Suri's name in a quote from a FIS source:

He is one of the [Armed Islamic] Group's ideologues and calls himself Abu Mus'ab al-Suri. He previously worked in Afghanistan, and lives currently in Spain. He records audio-cassettes in which he attacks the [Islamic Salvation] Front and its program for political change. He also accuses Shaykh Abbas al-Madani and Ali Bilhajj for misguidance by their acceptance of democracy and interaction with the people.[104]

*Al-Hayat's* reporting of the FIS's criticism of the GIA and its supporters in London continued in 1995 and reached a climax at the end of the year.

In December 1995 and January 1996, *al-Hayat* ran four pieces where al-Suri was specifically singled out for criticism. These articles

---

103  Author's interview with Mark Huband, London, 29 April 2006.

104  Jamal Khashoggi, 'The "Salvation" accuses the "Group" of attempting to impose their influence on them by force' (in Arabic), *al-Hayat* (London), 24 May 1994, p.1.

cited communiqués and statements made by FIS sources and other GIA opponents in Algeria and elsewhere. One such statement came in the aftermath of the disappearance of a number of leading FIS-associated commanders who had joined the GIA during the unification efforts in mid-1994. These were Muhammad Sa'id and Abd al-Razaq Rajam of the so-called Algerianist trend in the FIS. The GIA leadership in Algeria had subsequently assumed responsibility for executing them on treason charges. Al-Suri claims to have issued communiqués clarifying his position on the executions, and they were later published in the *al-Hayat*, but only after a series of articles was published accusing him of incitement to murder.[105] In a communiqué cited in *al-Hayat* on 1 January 1996 and signed by 'The Group who escaped the massacre conspiracy', a group of Algerians claimed to possess 'clear evidence' that the notorious GIA emir Jamal Zaytuni, was not the real ruler, but 'only a vehicle in the hands of the Algerian intelligence service as well as Abu Qutadah al-Filastini and Abu Mus'ab al-Suri'.[106] Furthermore, the communiqué alleged that the execution of the two Algerian mujahidin leaders had been carried out 'in accordance with rulings' from these two shaykhs. *Al-Hayat* wrote: 'the communiqué states: "they issue religious rulings that Muhammad Sa'id and his group, which is known as the Algerianist, do not differ from the Muslim Brotherhood and they are more dangerous than the regime".'[107]

A second article, published on 12 January 1996, also relied on FIS sources and detailed a meeting in Khartoum at which al-Suri allegedly was present and in which he allegedly called for the liquida-

---

105 Al-Suri stated that the GIA had not provided any legal justifications for the execution, and if they did not have such proof, they had shed innocent blood. See 'Meeting with the Kuwaiti Newspaper', transcript of audiofile no.5, p.1; and Camille Tawil, 'Umar Abd al-Hakim: "I am not responsible for the "[Armed] Islamic Group",' (in Arabic), *al-Hayat* (London), 17 Jan. 1996, p.6.

106 Camille Tawil, 'An Algerian group relinquishes their allegiance to the "Group" [GIA],' (in Arabic) *al-Hayat* (London), 1 Jan. 1996, p.6.

107 Ibid.

tion of the head of the FIS executive committee, Rabah Kabir, who then resided in Germany. (Elsewhere he was also accused of being behind the group that killed Abd al-Baqi al-Sahrawi, a FIS leader, who was assassinated in Paris.[108]) The Khartoum meeting had allegedly been held two years earlier, and during its course al-Suri 'had started as usual to defame the Islamic Salvation Front and its leaders ... and until he said: "I believe that Rabah Kabir should be physically liquidated"'.[109] The other attendees at the meeting had protested and asked for his legal justifications, which he could not produce. He had allegedly responded: 'I believe in political assassinations'.[110] The article also listed al-Suri's pseudonyms and his full name, although it was misspelled as 'Safwan Sitt Maryam'.

A third attack on al-Suri in *al-Hayat* came two days later, containing the hitherto most detailed account of him in Arab media. In what appeared to be a determined attempt by the FIS to intimidate al-Suri, the article relayed the FIS's plans for instigating legal action against al-Suri, suing him for his 'incitement' against their leaders and his alleged 'religious rulings permitting the killing of Hassan al-Turabi'.[111] This last statement was evidently an attempt to undermine the GIA's position in Sudan, and the support provided to the group by bin Laden and the Arab-Afghans in Khartoum was cut off for a while in the mid-1990s. The FIS stated that in their efforts to prepare a legal case against al-Suri, they had been aided by several Syrians in Spain who were angry with al-Suri for 'his extremist activities and deviant views which distorted the image of Islam'.[112]

---

108 'Apology to Mr Umar Abd al-Hakim "Abu Mus'ab al-Suri"' (in Arabic), *al-Hayat* (London), 20 April 1997, p.6.

109 Camille Tawil, 'The Algerian "Salvation" accuses a Syrian shaykh of calling for the elimination of Rabah Kabir' (in Arabic), *al-Hayat* (London) 12 Jan. 1996, p.6.

110 Ibid.

111 Cited in Jamal Khashoggi, 'Abu Mus'ab al-Suri was in the Syrian "Combatant Vanguard" and was expelled from the Muslim Brothers' (in Arabic), *al-Hayat* (London), 14 Jan. 1996, p.6.

112 Ibid.

For the first time, *al-Hayat* also revealed his real name (almost) correctly, Mustafa Abd al-Qadir Sitt Maryam. It also detailed his background in The Combatant Vanguard, his role in Afghanistan, and his ideological beliefs as expressed through his articles in the *al-Ansar Newsletter*, again stressing his extremism. The newspaper also attributed statements about Hasan al-Turabi to al-Suri: he was 'an heretic of the Islamic movement', who deserved to be executed. And it alleged that one of his audiotaped lectures was entitled 'the execution of a heretic',[113] of which it claimed to have a copy. The latter reportedly contained several threatening statements about al-Turabi, and its voiceover was interspersed with gunfire, explosions, and zealous songs, emphasizing its inciting character.

According to al-Suri, the press campaign against him in *al-Hayat* was followed up by a number of other Arab as well as French newspapers. He felt he had to defend himself against the accusations, many of which he thought were unfair and incorrect, aiming at tarnishing his name and distorting the truth about the Algerian struggle. He issued a communiqué denying that he was part of the GIA's leadership or that he had provided religious justifications for or incited the killing of FIS leaders.[114] The gravity of the allegations against him made him feel insecure, especially when he was said to have ordered the killing of the two FIS commanders Sa'id and Rajam: 'The escalation continued and they attributed to me communiqués from inside and outside, and the situation became unbearable. My situation became very much a security case. I was summoned to interviews with the anti-terrorism intelligence agencies about my role in this.'[115]

The fact that *al-Hayat* had mentioned his real name had clearly irritated al-Suri immensely, not least because it had imperilled his own

---

113   Ibid.

114   Camille Tawil, 'Umar Abd al-Hakim: "I am not responsible for the "[Armed] Islamic Group"', (in Arabic), *al-Hayat* (London), 17 Jan. 1996, p.6.

115   'Meeting with the Kuwaiti Newspaper' transcript of audiofile no.2, p.4; no.3, p.5.

carefully guarded security. However, what disturbed him most was the claim that he was the GIA's religious reference point and mufti: 'I have never ever claimed for myself the ability to be a mufti, neither in excommunicating people, nor in declaring someone's blood permissible to shed.'[116] As opposed to Abu Qutadah and other clerics, al-Suri never saw himself in that role. In his lectures and writings, he drew heavily upon other scholars when outlining the religious basis for his military strategy.

Al-Suri was assisted by some of his 'sincere brothers' in launching a legal case against *al-Hayat* in the British courts. He had initially considered such a process entirely unrealistic, given the potentially high expenditures involved, but some friends funded his litigation after lawyers recommended that the chances of winning were good since it involved 'tarnishing someone's reputation and exposing his life to danger'.[117] Al-Suri's lawyer started preparing a case, and after four or five months the *al-Hayat* newspaper agreed to settle out of court by paying him an indemnity and publishing an apology.[118]

The newspaper initially attempted to back up its allegations by means of the audiotapes themselves and a witness statement from Sudan. Abdallah Anas, a prominent FIS leader who lived in Sudan in the early 1990s, was one of their sources. He had not been present at the meeting himself, but had been contacted shortly afterwards by someone who had, Abu Ibrahim al-Iraqi.[119] He came to warn Anas that al-Suri and other jihadis 'would not step back from assassina-

---

116 Cited in Camille Tawil, 'Umar Abd al-Hakim: "I am not responsible for the "[Armed] Islamic Group",' (in Arabic), *al-Hayat* (London), 17 Jan. 1996, p.6. See also Umar Abd al-Hakim, *A Summary of My Testimony*, p.56.

117 Umar Abd al-Hakim, *A Summary of My Testimony*, p.56.

118 'Meeting with the Kuwaiti Newspaper', transcript of audiofile no.3, p.6; and 'Apology to Mr Umar Abd al-Hakim "Abu Mus 'ab al-Suri" (in Arabic), *al-Hayat* (London), 20 April 1997, p.6.

119 Abu Ibrahim al-Iraqi was reportedly related by marriage to Abu Hajir al-Iraqi (Mamdouh Mahmoud Salim), a co-founder of al-Qaida and an important leader until his arrest in Germany in 1998. Author's interview with Abdallah Anas, London 16 Sept. 2006.

ing Muslims, including FIS leaders' and that 'this might begin any time'.[120] Al-Suri and others had convened at bin Laden's house in Khartoum to discuss strategies for assisting the GIA in Algeria. They had talked of the necessity of 'physical liquidation' (*tasfiyyat jasadi-yyah*) and al-Suri himself had spoken about the need to establish 'the principle of assassination' (*mabda' al-ightiyalat*) against the FIS leaders who did not recant. According to Anas' recollection, bin Laden was present when this was said and had reacted very negatively to these proposals. And it was Anas who had taken the story to *al-Hayat*. When al-Suri filed his libel suit, Abu Ibrahim al-Iraqi had reportedly signed a sworn statement and had it signed and approved by the Sudanese foreign ministry who verified that it was written by the correct person.[121]

It is hard to verify this account, but what is known is that *al-Hayat*'s lawyers failed to produce the tapes during the pre-trial hearings. It is also possible that they may never have existed. None of al-Suri's other recordings contain anything as exciting as explosions, gunfire and music, only dry academic lectures.

Al-Suri was delighted with the outcome of his litigation and later recalled that the detailed apology had appeared in *al-Hayat* on the second day of the Feast of Sacrifice holiday. The newspaper had also been forced to pay his legal costs as well as the indemnity.[122] It is not known how much the latter amounted to though al-Suri explained that it was enough to pay off his accumulated debts and cover the cost of the *hijrah*, or 'emigration', with his family to Afghanistan in order to make a new start there.[123]

The *al-Hayat* story is illustrative of al-Suri's 'struggle to reconcile his beliefs with his surroundings', as the *Washington Post* once acutely observed.[124] Al-Suri rejected on principle the authority of non-Is-

---

120  Author's interview with Abdallah Anas, London 16 Sept. 2006.
121  Ibid.
122  'Meeting with the Kuwaiti Newspaper' transcript of audiofile no.3, p.6.
123  Umar Abd al-Hakim, *A Summary of My Testimony*, p.56.
124  Craig Whitlock, 'Architect of New War on the West', *Washington Post*, 23

lamic courts and thus went to great lengths in his 1999 interview explaining his decision to sue *al-Hayat* in London, justifying it with references to religious authorities and the practices of the spiritual godfather of the Arab-Afghans, Abdallah Azzam.

Al-Suri reacted strongly when his sense of personal security was at stake, and this was perhaps not surprising since he was a father and husband. However, being a jihadi of some standing whose ideology stressed the omnipresence of enemies and the need for sacrifice and martyrdom, these allegiances were hard to reconcile. He had lectured on themes such as 'terrorism is a gift' in the Arab-Afghan camps around 1990, but in London he strongly rejected, and even ridiculed, any suggestion that he was involved in international terrorism. Al-Suri was extremely satisfied that *al-Hayat* had issued a legal document in English denying its allegations against him, which he then was able to show to the British security services whenever they questioned him about what the Arabic language media were saying about him.[125]

According to the worldview he later preached, it was only to be expected that jihadis such as him should be vilified and persecuted by the enemy's press; after all, 'these were all the Tyrant's newspapers and the enemies of Islam', he later stated.[126] In al-Suri's lectures and writings, he incorporated everyone, from the infidels to the democratic Islamists, into the same enemy camp. Still, he was anxious that his opponents recognized the ideological nuances and differences between the various strands within the jihadi school. He accused the democratic Islamists, and Muhammad Surur of the Syrian MB in particular, of using the excesses of one group to vilify all the others.[127] He paid little attention to the double standards which this clearly represented, and his strong ideological convictions only accentuated his self-righteousness.

---

May 2006, p.A01.

125  'Meeting with the Kuwaiti Newspaper', transcript of audiofile no.3, p.6.

126  Ibid., no.4, p.6.

127  Ibid., no.4, pp.5-6.

# 7

# COMPANIONS, RIVALS, ACQUAINTANCES

Al-Suri's book on the Syrian jihadi revolution and his active role in the *al-Ansar Newsletter* made him a well-known figure in 'Londonistan', so-called because of the plethora of radical Islamist groups that had coalesced in and around the capital since the early 1990s. His network of contacts was extensive. Beyond the circles of Algerian GIA supporters, he had befriended Moroccan militants, as he had done previously in France, Spain, Afghanistan, and Peshawar. 'I got to know many outstanding cadres among them,' he later recalled.[1] Al-Suri also maintained ties with Combatant Vanguard veterans, some of whom were still based in Jordan, and with the EIJ, especially the head of its media office in London, Adil Abd al-Bari (see below). He was in telephone contact with the EIJ leader Ayman al-Zawahiri on several occasions,[2] had many friends and acquaintances in the growing diaspora of Libyan jihadis from the early 1990s and also befriended key members of the Saudi opposition in London, especially Saad al-Faqih and Khalid al-Fawwaz (see below).

These contacts with Algerian, Egyptian, and Libyan extremists in the mid-1990s demonstrated that his involvement in the global jihadi movement went beyond Abu Dahdah's cell in Spain, consisting of mainly Syrian and Moroccan Islamists. Al-Suri's network of contacts may have allowed him to facilitate support for jihadi movements as new fronts in the 'Crusader war' opened up over the course of time.[3]

---

1    *The Global Islamic Resistance Call*, p.782.
2    Umar Abd al-Hakim, *Summary of My Testimony*, p.53.
3    In 2004, for example, it was alleged in the press that one of al-Suri's

What concerns us here is al-Suri's network of contacts in London in the 1990s. His companions, rivals and acquaintances reveal how the different Islamist struggles and arenas of conflict were interwoven and interlinked. They also help us to situate al-Suri in the broader landscape of salafi-jihadi activism and terrorism during this period. The examples below illustrate the diversity of the network which he, as a relatively independent jihadi intellectual, sought to build, what kind of relationships he had with other jihadis, and in some cases, how he was perceived by those he met and knew in Islamist and jihadi circles.

## ABU QUTADAH AL-FILASTINI:
### A LOVE-HATE RELATIONSHIP

From 1994 until mid-1996 al-Suri worked closely with a well-known Palestinian cleric residing in London, Shaykh Umar Mahmud Uthman Abu Umar, better known as Abu Qutadah al-Filastini.[4] Born in Bethlehem in 1960, and a Jordanian national, he arrived in London in September 1993 and was granted refugee status a year later.[5] He quickly emerged as the key salafi-jihadi cleric and spiritual leader 'at

---

London-based funding networks, established back in the mid-1990s, had played a role in channelling aid to the Zarqawi-led organization in Iraq. These came under closer scrutiny following the beheading of a British engineer, Kenneth Bigley, in Iraq by Zarqawi's men in mid-2005. See Sharon Churcher, 'Revealed: American internet link to Ken Bigley torture videos: London connection to hostage killer', *Mail on Sunday* (London), 17 Oct. 2004, p.25.

4   He was also known under other aliases such as Abu Ismail, Abu Omar Abu Umar, Abu Umr Takfiri, Abu Umar Umar, Al-Samman Uthman, Umar Uthman. See 'Commission Regulation (EC) No 2062/2001 of 19 Oct. 2001', *Official Journal of the European Communities*, 20.10.2001, www.eurunion.org/partner/EUUSTerror/AfghanReg2062_2001.pdf, accessed Sept. 2005; and 'Juzgado Central de Instruccion no.005, Madrid, Sumario', 17 Sept. 2003, p.25.

5   'Profile: Abu Qatada', *BBC News*, 9 May 2006, http://news.bbc.co.uk/2/hi/uk_news/4141594.stm, accessed Oct. 2006.

the European level'.[6] The Jordanian government have long sought his extradition, after having found him guilty on terrorism charges, and he was repeatedly taken into custody by the British authorities, who have called him 'the most significant extremist Islamic preacher' in the country.[7] In October 2001, the UN Al Qaeda and Taliban Sanctions Committee listed him as an 'individual belonging to or associated with the Al-Qaida organization'.[8]

In the mid-1990s, Abu Qutadah became chief editor of the *al-Ansar Newsletter*, which explains al-Suri's close relationship with him. In his interviews and writings the latter makes no secret of his contacts with Abu Qutadah, but describes their relationship as increasingly strained due to differences over how to relate to the GIA's 'deviations' in the mid-1990s.[9] Other sources also confirm that al-Suri 'had bitter ideological disputes with Abu Qutadah, but the two men remained in contact, these differences notwithstanding. According to al-Suri's parents-in-law, who visited his family at their house in London in January 1997, Abu Qutadah came to their house several times. They described him as 'a corpulent bearded guy', and his appearance did little to calm the elderly couple's anxiety about their daughter.[10]

Abu Qutadah and al-Suri's relationship was characterized by many ups-and-downs. A former Libyan Islamic Fighting Group member in London describes it as 'a love-hate relationship' that was

---

6    'Juzgado Central de Instruccion no.005, Madrid, Sumario', 17 Sept. 2003, p.27.

7    Citing former Home Secretary David Blunkett, see 'Profile: Abu Qatada', *BBC News*, 9 May 2006, http://news.bbc.co.uk/2/hi/uk_news/4141594. stm, accessed Oct. 2006.

8    See United Nations Al Qaeda and Taliban Sanctions Committee, 'The list of individuals belonging to or associated with Al-Qaida organization/Last updated on 25 July 2006', www.un.org/Docs/sc/committees/1267/pdflist. pdf, accessed July 2006, p.28.

9    'Meeting with the Kuwaiti Newspaper', transcript of audiofiles nos 3-5.

10   José María Irujo, 'El hombre de Bin Laden en Madrid', *El País*, 2 March 2005, www.elPaís.es/comunes/2005/11m/08_comision/libro_electronico_ red_islam/red_islamista_01%20doc.pdf, accessed July 2006, p.17.

'a headache for everyone'. Sometimes they were on good terms, while on other occasions they hardly talked to each other: 'One never knew what to expect' is how Benotman characterises the dynamic between the two men.[11] During the latter part of al-Suri's stay in London, the relationship soured. His involvement with the *al-Ansar Newsletter* and the GIA media cell seems to have been his most difficult experience as a jihadi in the 1990s. Abu Qutadah was a key source of Abu Mus'ab al-Suri's frustration, coupled with the stress he suffered over the Arab media campaign against him and the failure of the jihadi campaign in Algeria. According to acquaintances, he spent 'his saddest days' in London.[12]

There was not only an ideological dimension to his conflict with Abu Qutadah, who had a much stricter and rigid salafi orientation than the hard-line, but pragmatic, militarily oriented jihadism of al-Suri (see below). The sociable, highly articulate and charismatic Abu Qutadah had overshadowed al-Suri and won over to his camp many of his former followers. Al-Suri had simply failed to establish himself as a leader or to gather round him a large crowd of disciples, even though he was respected for his knowledge and expertise.[13]

When he abandoned London in 1997, one of the first objectives he set for himself was to write his memoirs of his involvement in the GIA media cell in order to expose Abu Qutadah and reveal his 'catastrophic influence' on the jihadi current in Algeria, a project many of his fellow Arab-Afghans strongly discouraged him from fulfilling.[14]

Abu Qutadah arrived in London after al-Suri's first visit to the GIA media cell in 1994. He had also been in Peshawar since 1990, but went to Afghanistan only in 1992, after Kabul had been recaptured.[15] In Peshawar, he had attracted many followers. After they fell

---

11 Author's interview with Noman Benotman, London, 15 Sept. 2006.

12 Ibid.

13 Author's interview with Camille Tawil, London, 14 Sept. 2006; and author's telephone interview with Saad al-Faqih, 17 Sept. 2006.

14 Cited in Umar Abd al-Hakim, *Summary of My Testimony*, p.27.

15 'Q&A with Muslim cleric Abu Qatada', *CNN.com*, 29 Nov. 2001, http://

out, al-Suri reminded his readers that Abu Qutadah only came on the Afghanistan scene 'after the Afghan jihad had ended' and was not a proper jihadi with field experience.[16]

Abu Qutadah started to preach in a prayer hall in London and adopted the Algerian jihad as his core objective. This is how al-Suri explains his rise to prominence:

His prayer hall became a place where bulletins were distributed, donations were collected, and a place where jihadis and zealots gathered. It also became a spot where the British security service and other secret services monitored the Islamists. With his simplicity and easy manners, Abu Qutadah became the religious reference point for these Algerian youth, Arab-Afghans and others in London who joined his school. After a period of time, he became the reference point for many others in European capitals. [...] This happened in spite of the fact that Abu Qutadah himself was not a jihadi and had no history in that field. However, his salafi background, his oratory zeal, and his adoption of the jihadis' ideas together with the thirst in jihadi circles for any scholar or student of knowledge, who would support their program and cover their needs, made him into a shaykh and a jihadi reference point for this circle'.[17]

Al-Suri was initially very close to Abu Qutadah. He stayed at his house in London for roughly a month while looking for a residence for himself and his family. Al-Suri later described him as 'hospitable, generous, and sociable, and I found him to be well educated, and committed to his family and children'.[18] Al-Suri recalls how Abu Qutadah attracted a crowd in a way he found disconcerting due to his own constant awareness about security:

He had been a supporter of the Tabligh group[19] before he converted to the salafi ideology. He inherited these oratory qualities, the open, unsnobbish

---

archives.cnn.com/2001/WORLD/europe/11/27/gen.qatada.transcript. cnna/, accessed Oct. 2006.

16  Umar Abd al-Hakim, *Summary of My Testimony*, p.29.

17  Ibid., p.21.

18  'Meeting with the Kuwaiti Newspaper', transcript of audiofile no.4, p.1.

19  The Tablighi Jamaat (lit. 'Proselytizing Group'), has roots dating back to the late 1920s. The movement was founded in India, has spread across

and sociable manners. He loved extensive meetings. He opened his house and subsequently his mosque to every visitor, where every issue was discussed with each and everyone in a spontaneous and unsnobbish manner. Secret houses were opened, where dinner parties were held for the group. In spite of what this style [of activism] brought in terms of a warm atmosphere and many followers, its security complications were an inescapable issue, especially in the climate of London and among the supporters of jihad in Algeria.[20]

When the headquarters of the *al-Ansar Newsletter* was raided by the British police in 1995, al-Suri called upon Abu Qutadah and his followers to see this as a wake-up call. After all, they were behind enemy lines and should start applying guerrilla warfare tactics to their media work:

I made them understand that we were in a hit and run war. I presented to them a plan for how to continue: work on the publication of a new journal, change the place of issuing it to one of the Scandinavian countries, and spread the activities to more than one place. I warned them that "the security storm" was coming, and that we were forced to deal with it in the manner of a guerrilla war of hit and run, even in the field of our media activities'.[21]

Their ideological differences soon became evident. Al-Suri's socio-revolutionary and 'leftist' brand of jihadism clashed with Abu Qutadah's strict purist salafi orientation:

Abu Qutada was extreme in his support of salafism and the Ahl al-Sunna school and the ideas of the Wahhabite Call. He was strongly opposed to other schools within the broader circle of Ahl al-Sunna. He vehemently fought sectarianism (*madhhabiyyah*); he was aggressive in his discussions, stern in his expressions, issued bold fatwas and rulings, had excessive confidence in himself, and was not tolerant of other opinions. [...] He had a list of heresies, (lit. 'innovativism', *al-mubtadi'ah*) in Islam. He dubbed it 'the school of straying from the right path and heretic tendencies' (*ahl al-dalal*

---

150 countries and its active following is estimated at 70-80 million. It is one of the largest missionary movements in the world, and remains largely apolitical. See 'Tablighi Jamaat', *Wikipedia*.org, http://en.wikipedia.org/wiki/Tablighi_Jamaat, accessed Oct. 2006.

20    Umar Abd al-Hakim, *Summary of My Testimony*, p.28.

21    Ibid., p.32.

*wa'l-ahwa'*), and it included most of the Islamic doctrinal, legal and missionary, reformist and political schools, even a number of the jihadi schools, new as old, their programs and their men.[22]

Their ideological differences went so far that Abu Qutadah's followers reportedly accused al-Suri of being an heretic. Al-Suri claims he attempted to dissuade Abu Qutadah from adopting hard-line positions on doctrinal issues since they distracted from or even worked against the broader struggle, but Abu Qutadah and his followers did not heed him:

In their eyes, we were only activists (*harakiyyun*), who theorized in politics. We were not clean of the Muslim Brotherhood virus, despite the fact that we were among the jihadis. We did not understand the issues of Islamic doctrine! [...] It did not last long before his followers, especially Abu Walid al-Filastini, began issuing fatwas saying that I was an heretic (lit. 'innovator', *min al-mubtadi'ah*).[23]

These ideological and religious differences notwithstanding, the real conflict appears to have erupted when al-Suri saw many of his former disciples from Peshawar joining Abu Qutadah's circle and looking up to Qutadah instead of to him. His feeling of being overshadowed by someone he considered an inferior jihadi in terms of organizational experience is evident in his memoirs:

With these ideological characteristics, these personality traits, the absence of organizational experience from secret groups and a lack of security awareness, Shaykh Abu Qutadah al-Filastini burst into the arena of the Algerian cause, which was the most complicated and interwoven of all jihadi experiences and the most difficult one security-wise and organization-wise. This was the background for the way he dealt with and handled the Algerian jihad. [...] This also had consequences for the 'salafi-jihadi excessiveness' school (*minhaj 'ghulat al-salafiyyah al-jihadiyyah'*), which gradually became more prominent in the shadow of this cause. Abu Qutadah should be considered-in my view-among the most prominent theoreticians of this school. Together with a few others, Abu Qutadah threw himself into its chairmanship role in the period that followed. He seduced them to his side and they

---

22  Ibid., p.28.
23  Ibid., p.31.

issued fatwas on whatever the extremist listeners in Algeria and followers in London and elsewhere in Europe requested from them.[24]

Not being a recognized religious cleric or shaykh, it was perhaps inevitable that al-Suri would lose out to Abu Qutadah, even though he had trained and fought together with many of those who later joined Abu Qutadah's circle: 'they were salafis who were inclined to extremism like him [Abu Qutadah]. The youth adhere faithfully to their shaykhs, and attach a holiness and infallibility to them'.[25]

For a while Abu Qutadah and al-Suri effectively boycotted each other, and during the crisis following the GIA's execution of two leading mujahidin leaders from the Algerianist current, violent quarrels occurred between them.[26] The *al-Ansar Newsletter* was completely taken over by Abu Qutadah's followers, and al-Suri says he had to buy his copy from a vendor at the entrance to Qutadah's prayer hall, where he was treated like 'a stranger'.[27] He was especially incensed by the fact that his name remained so closely associated with Abu Qutadah's writings in the *al-Ansar Newsletter* where the latter bestowed legitimacy on the killings in Algeria after the jihad had 'deviated' under Zaytuni's emirate. Al-Suri portrayed Abu Qutadah as someone who had whitewashed the GIA, but not as the GIA's primary religious reference point:

The GIA leadership in Algeria was a group of deviants already and the Algerian intelligence completed their deviance and employed them, but Abu Qutadah's role was that of a mufti who bestowed legitimacy on the deviancy after it had occurred for the audiences in exile. He had no role internally in Algeria as far as I know. [...] Abu Qutadah and Abu Walid played for Abd al-Rahman Amin [Zaytuni], and his group of criminals and supporters in exile the same role as Ibn Baz and Ibn Uthaymin play for the ruling Saudi family. This was their crime.[28]

---

24    Ibid., p.29.

25    Ibid.

26    Ibid., p.36.

27    'Meeting with the Kuwaiti Newspaper', transcipt of audiofile no.4, p.3; and Umar Abd al-Hakim, *Summary of My Testimony* , p.35.

28    Umar Abd al-Hakim, *Summary of My Testimony*, p.37.

On arriving in Afghanistan, al-Suri became obsessed by writing his memoirs in order to recount what he saw as the true story about Abu Qutadah, and he appears to have told this to all and sundry and on every possible occasion. In a letter uncovered in Afghanistan after the fall of the Taleban, which appears to have been written by al-Suri,[29] he lashes out again against Abu Qutadah: 'I know this man well and want to expose him to everybody. At the time when everyone was fighting, he was the advisor to the devil. He came to Peshawar after everything was over and started to make fatwas in return for a few dollars from the Saudi Islamic Relief Center'.[30]

The story of al-Suri's conflict with Abu Qutadah illustrates not only al-Suri's conflict with the doctrinaire salafis within the jihadi network; it also reveals his leadership ambitions and his frustration that religious oratory and zeal were being more highly valued than jihadi field experience. Perhaps above all, it highlights how personality clashes and rivalries play an important role in jihadi organizations, despite the ideological commitment to sacrifice personal ambition for the sake of jihad.

## MUHAMMAD BAHAYAH: LIFE-LONG
### FRIEND AND COMPANION

Muhammad Bahayah (also spelled Mohamed Bahaiah), best known by his *nom de guerre* Abu Khalid,[31] or Abu Khalid al-Suri, was considered one of al-Suri's closest allies. In the introduction to *The Global Islamic Resistance Call*, al-Suri refers to him as 'my brother and friend, my companion throughout my life'.[32] In Western assessments, Bahayah has been described as a 'mid-level' activist, a 'courier'

---

29　For a discussion of the authorship of the letter, see bibliography.

30　Cited in Document no.AFGP-2002-601693, 'Status of Jihad'. Combating Terrorism Center website (West Point), www.ctc.usma.edu/aq/AFGP-2002-601693-Trans.pdf and www.ctc.usma.edu/aq/AFGP-2002-601693-Orig.pdf, accessed April 2006.

31　Also referred to as 'Abu Khaleb' in the Spanish indictment of 2003, which is probably a spelling error.

32　*The Global Islamic Resistance Call*, p.10.

and a 'member of Osama bin Laden's structures in Europe'.[33] His brother-in-law, Mohamed Galeb Kalaje Zouaydi, who was convicted in 2005 of membership of a terrorist organization, described Bahayah as having been a 'mujahedeen' fighter whose 'mission had been to establish contacts at the international level'.[34] The Spanish indictment against the Abu Dahdah network dealt extensively with Bahayah, referring to him as an important member of al-Qaida and implicating those who knew him for alleged links to al-Qaida. However, apart from documenting his friendship with al-Suri and Abu Dahdah, it provided few clues about the exact nature of his relationship to the al-Qaida leadership in Afghanistan. According to media reports, Bahayah 'worked for a charitable organization in Afghanistan'.[35] He had lived in Granada and in the Canary Islands, but during the 1990s Bahayah mostly operated out of Turkey.[36] After Turkish police began searching for him in June 1999, he fled to Iran and Afghanistan.[37]

Muhammad Bahayah was believed to have been involved in financial operations on behalf of the Spanish Abu Dahdah cell.[38] He was close to Abu Dahdah, who visited Bahayah in Turkey on several occasions,[39] while a Spanish book on the M-11 attacks includes an undated picture of him with Abu Dahdah and his wife, enjoying a

---

33  See, for example, 'Juzgado Central de Instruccion no.005, Madrid, Sumario', 17 Sept. 2003, p.28.

34  Audiencia Nacional, Sala de lo Penal, Sección Tercera, 'Sentencia Núm. 36/2005', Madrid, 26 Sept. 2005, [verdict against the Abu Dahdah network], p.201.

35  Leslie Crawford, 'A Dangerous Subject', *Financial Times Magazine*, 15-16 July 2006, p.18 (hereafter 'A Dangerous Subject').

36  José María Irujo, *El Agujero*, p.50.

37  'Juzgado Central de Instruccion no.005, Madrid, Sumario', 17 Sept. 2003, pp.411-12.

38  Tim Golden and Judith Miller, 'Al Qaeda Money Trail Runs From Saudi Arabia to Spain', *The New York Times*, 21 Sept. 2002; and 'Juzgado Central de Instruccion no.005, Madrid, Sumario', 17 Sept. 2003, p.434.

39  'Juzgado Central de Instruccion no.005, Madrid, Sumario', 17 Sept. 2003, p.58.

meal at a restaurant.[40] Telephone intercepts made by the Spanish security services revealed that in 1997 Bahayah kept in contact with Khalid al-Fawwaz, head of the Advice and Reform Committee in London, from which bin Laden's statements were published.[41] They also showed that Bahayah brought money from Abu Dahdah in Spain to Shaykh Abu Qutadah in London. When one cell member asked for financial assistance during a stay in Turkey, Abu Dahdah referred him to Bahayah, but told him to keep the telephone number secret because this was 'a very special person'.[42] When Bahayah narrowly evaded Turkish police and slipped into Iran in late June 1999, only to escape a siege by Iranian security forces a few weeks later, he reported back on each occasion to Abu Dahdah in Spain.[43]

Bahayah reportedly visited Madrid four times between 1995 and 1998, and he also spent a lot of time in London, mostly with al-Suri, but also with Abu Qutadah. Spanish investigators found that he moved regularly between the training camps in Afghanistan and several European countries. Their surveillance revealed that Abu Dahdah himself came to the airport to greet Bahayah when the latter arrived in Spain in January 1998. And when visiting Madrid, Bahayah always stayed at Abu Dahdah's house. He also used to travel to Granada, where he had lived during the late 1980s. There he stayed in contact with al-Suri and Taysir Allouni who both also lived in Granada for a while.[44] Allouni, who had given Bahayah a helping

---

40   See Casimiro García-Abadillo, *11-M: La Venganza* (Madrid: Esfera Libros, 2004), collection of photos inserted between pp.128-9.

41   'U.S. Treasury Designates Two Individuals with Ties to al Qaida; UBL Former BIF Leader and al-Qaida Associate Named Under E.O. 13224', *The Office of Public Affairs*, 21 Dec. 2004, JS-2164, www.treas.gov/press/releases/js2164.htm, accessed July 2005.

42   Cited in 'Juzgado Central de Instruccion N° 005, Madrid, Sumario', 17 Sept. 2003, p.410. See also ibid., pp.410-12.

43   'Juzgado Central de Instruccion N° 005, Madrid, Sumario', 17 Sept. 2003, pp.411-12.

44   D. Martinez and P. Munoz, 'Syrian in custody in London for 11 March was "political chief" of Abu Dahdah's cell' (in Spanish), *ABC Newspaper* (Madrid, internet version), 24 March 2005, via FBIS; José María Irujo,

hand when the latter arrived in Granada, gave the following description of him:

He seemed like a good person and his wife too. He came to my house as he was looking for a flat. He spent the night, a couple of nights, in my house and then he arranged himself in Granada. He rented a flat and later he worked with Setmarian [al-Suri], in a handicraft shop on Liria Street.[45]

Like several other members of Abu Dahdah's group, Bahayah also married a Spanish woman and obtained Spanish citizenship.[46] Later, he married the sister of Mohamed Galeb Kalaje Zouaydi, a Syrian businessman, previously based in Jeddah, Saudi Arabia. Zouaydi was considered to be among Abu Dahdah's main financiers, and was convicted in Spain on charges of 'belonging to a terrorist organization as a member'. [47]

Bahayah's role in Afghanistan was intimately linked to al-Suri's. The former *al-Jazeera* journalist in Kabul, Taysir Allouni, who knew both of them, recalls that while in Afghanistan he always saw Bahayah in the company of al-Suri: they were 'hand in glove'.[48] They frequently came to see him in his office, where they used to 'exchange

---

*El Agujero* p.50; Audiencia Nacional, Sala de lo Penal, Sección Tercera, 'Sentencia Núm. 36/2005', Madrid, 26 Sept. 2005, [verdict against the Abu Dahdah network], p.66; 'Juzgado Central de Instruccion no.005, Madrid, Sumario', 17 Sept. 2003, pp.410-12; and 'Un testigo identificó a Setmarian: La Audiencia Nacional reabre la causa sobre el atentado en el restaurante El Descanso en 1985', *elmundo.es* 9 Nov. 2005, www.elmundo. es/elmundo/2005/11/09/espana/1131539640.html.

45 Audiencia Nacional, Sala de lo Penal, Sección Tercera, 'Sentencia Núm. 36/2005', Madrid, 26 Sept. 2005, [verdict against the Abu Dahdah network], p.303.

46 Ibid., pp.66, 199.

47 Jean-Charles Brisard with Damien Martinez, *Zarqawi: The New Face of al-Qaeda*, p.110; Tim Golden and Judith Miller, 'Al Qaeda Money Trail Runs From Saudi Arabia to Spain'; and Audiencia Nacional, Sala de lo Penal, Sección Tercera, 'Sentencia Núm. 36/2005', Madrid, 26 Sept. 2005, [verdict against the Abu Dahdah network], p.99.

48 Audiencia Nacional, Sala de lo Penal, Sección Tercera, 'Sentencia Núm. 36/2005', Madrid, 26 Sept. 2005, [verdict against the Abu Dahdah network], p.304.

observations of current events'.[49] Bahayah was present with al-Suri during the latter's meetings with bin Laden, Taleban ministers, and government officials. He was also a co-signatory with al-Suri of a strongly worded letter of advice to bin Laden sent in July 1998 (see chapter 8). In Afghanistan, Bahayah was reportedly involved in delivering al-Qaida videotapes to foreign news media.[50] This is consistent with his role as an assistant to al-Suri who had acted as media adviser for both al-Qaida and the Taleban. Bahayah's current whereabouts are unknown.

### TAYSIR ALLOUNI: A POINT OF CONTACT IN AL-JAZEERA

Taysir Allouni, the famous *al-Jazeera* journalist who was arrested by Spanish authorities in September 2004 on charges that he collaborated with al-Qaida, figured among al-Suri's numerous contacts.[51] In fact, it was largely based on his contacts with Abu Dahdah, al-Suri and Bahayah that Spanish authorities decided to prosecute him. On 26 September 2005, Allouni was sentenced to seven years in prison on charges that he committed 'the crime of cooperation with a terrorist organization'.[52] He is serving his term in a high security jail in Alcalá-Meco in the Castile region.

---

49  Ibid., p.200.

50  Nick Fielding and Gareth Walsh, 'Mastermind of Madrid is key figure', *The Sunday Times*, 10 July 2005, www.timesonline.co.uk/article/0,2087-1688244,00.html, accessed July 2005.

51  'Juzgado Central de Instruccion no.005, Madrid, Sumario', 17 Sept. 2003, pp.28-9, 296; and Audiencia Nacional, Sala de lo Penal, Sección Tercera, 'Sentencia Núm. 36/2005', Madrid, 26 Sept. 2005, [verdict against the Abu Dahdah network].

52  Allouni, the verdict stated, 'did not belong to the group headed by Barakat [Abu Dahdah]. Possibly, he felt very much above him. But he collaborated with this group assisting Zaher Asade and especially, he helped in a determinant way Mustafa [al-Suri] and Mohamed [Bahaiah].' Only four of the 20 convicted defendants, including Allouni, were convicted of 'the crime of belonging to a terrorist organization'. One of these was later acquitted. Most of the convicted defendants (11 out of 20) in the Abu

Allouni arrived in Spain in 1985 as an International Relations student at the University of Granada. He became head of an Islamic centre, taught Arabic classes, and worked in the handicraft trade. In the mid-1990s he started working as a translator for the Spanish news agency *Efe*, and later as an editing assistant for *Efe TV*. In 2000, he moved to Kabul after having been appointed correspondent for the pan-Arab satellite TV channel *al-Jazeera*.[53]

According to Spanish authorities, Allouni nurtured close contacts with Abu Dahdah and several other members of the latter's network while living in Granada. Abu Dahdah travelled frequently to Granada, where he spent the night at Allouni's home. He kept the latter updated on issues, such as 'the favourable situation for the mujahideen in Chechnya', or on 'the mujahideen in Bosnia' and provided Allouni with videotapes featuring foreign jihadi fighters in Bosnia.[54]

Allouni and al-Suri also knew each other well. Both of them had been members of the Syrian Muslim Brotherhood organization, and they had been in contact since the late 1980s when they both lived

---

Dahdah case were convicted of 'belonging to a terrorist organization as a member'. Two of these were later acquitted. Abu Dahdah and two others were convicted of 'belonging to or integration in a terrorist organization as a leader or as a promoter'. One was convicted of conspiring to commit a terrorist homicide, and one was sentenced for 'illegal possession of arms'. See Audiencia Nacional, Sala de lo Penal, Sección Tercera, 'Sentencia Núm. 36/2005', Madrid, 26 Sept. 2005, [verdict against the Abu Dahdah network], pp.98-100, 308-9.

53  During the trial in 2005, Spanish prosecutors claimed that Allouni did not have 'merits as a journalist' before his famous interview with al-Qaida's leader in Oct. 2001, suggesting that it was Allouni's collaboration with the terrorist organization, not his professionalism, that helped him achieve this journalistic scoop. However, Allouni had reportedly freelanced for Arabic newspapers and done occasional work for *al-Jazeera* before the network hired him for the correspondent position in Kabul. See Audiencia Nacional, Sala de lo Penal, Sección Tercera, 'Sentencia Núm. 36/2005', Madrid, 26 Sept. 2005, [verdict against the Abu Dahdah network], pp.67, 299-300; and Leslie Crawford, 'A Dangerous Subject', p.18.

54  Audiencia Nacional, Sala de lo Penal, Sección Tercera, 'Sentencia Núm. 36/2005', Madrid, 26 Sept. 2005, [verdict against the Abu Dahdah network], pp.67, 70, 189, 308.

in Granada. In fact, when al-Suri first moved to Granada, Allouni assisted him by accommodating him in his own house. According to Spanish investigators, Allouni 'maintained a close friendship' with al-Suri, and the latter stayed at Allouni's house in Granada on several occasions.[55] They had met coincidentally at 'dinners, at invitations, and religious feasts', and Allouni explained their friendship in the context of their mutual experience as Arabs and Syrians in Spain:

> We exchanged opinions. We are from the same community. I hope that you understand the peculiarity of relations within the Arab community. Thus, it is normal that an Arab and his family, who wishes to spend the night in my house, ask me. [...] So I invited him—it is not possible to deny that—and hence, relations developed.[56]

Allouni kept in close contact with al-Suri after the latter moved to London. During this period, they made 'frequent phone contacts' and Allouni also invited al-Suri to his home.[57] Furthermore, after al-Suri moved to Afghanistan, Allouni, on one occasion travelled to Afghanistan in order to interview al-Suri about rumours published in the *The Times* of an alleged schism in al-Qaida in late July 2000.[58] Al-Suri felt compelled to deny the story because the newspaper had mentioned his name and reported that he was heading a splinter group within al-Qaida.[59]

---

55  Cited in Comisaría General de Información/Dirección General de la Policía/Unidad Central de Inteligencia, *Operaciones de la C. G. I. contra el terrorismo integrista islámico entre 1996/2004* (Police report, Madrid, April 2004), p.65. The report is reprinted in its entirety in Casimiro García-Abadillo, *11-M: La Venganza* (Madrid: Esfera Libros, 2004), pp.237-313. See also Audiencia Nacional, Sala de lo Penal, Sección Tercera, 'Sentencia Núm. 36/2005', Madrid, 26 Sept. 2005, [verdict against the Abu Dahdah network], pp.67, 301.

56  Cited in Audiencia Nacional, Sala de lo Penal, Sección Tercera, 'Sentencia Núm. 36/2005', Madrid, 26 Sept. 2005, [verdict against the Abu Dahdah network], p.301.

57  Ibid., p.301.

58  Ibid., p.302.

59  For transcripts of the TV interview, see 'Reports of split in Bin Laden's group denied,' (LexisNexis Title), *'Al-Jazeera at Midday'-programme, Al-*

Beyond his close contacts with several members of Abu Dahdah's network, Allouni also allegedly assisted them in various matters. He helped al-Suri's assistant, Muhammad Bahayah, to obtain Spanish residency papers by saying that Bahayah was living at his Granada home, when he in fact stayed in Turkey. Allouni was also charged with having delivered $4,000 from Abu Dahdah to Bahayah in Kabul in March 2000. According to Spanish authorities, these money transfers were given in return for keeping Allouni informed. Allouni himself argued that it would have been rude of him to refuse to do such a favour.[60] After all, it was not unusual to be asked to bring cash to people in Afghanistan, given the absence of a banking system there.[61]

When Allouni moved to Kabul in 2000 to set up an office for *al-Jazeera*, al-Suri reportedly offered his assistance, saying that 'if you wish to come here, I can facilitate things for you and present you to some of the Taleban figures'.[62] According to the Spanish investigation, al-Suri had used his connections with the Taleban government to help Allouni open a media office in Kabul at a time when nearly all foreign press agencies were unable to operate in the country. Al-Suri, who acted as the Taleban's unofficial media adviser at the time, allegedly facilitated Allouni's movements and helped him set up interviews.

---

*Jazeera TV*, 1 Aug. 2000 1240 GMT via LexisNexis.

60   Audiencia Nacional, Sala de lo Penal, Sección Tercera, 'Sentencia Núm. 36/2005', Madrid, 26 Sept. 2005, [verdict against the Abu Dahdah network], pp.200, 301-306; Giles Tremlett, 'When a reporter got too close to the story?' *The Guardian*, 3 Oct. 2005, http://media.guardian. co.uk/mediaguardian/story/0,1583222,00.html, accessed Jan. 2006; 'Spanish Court Lists Evidence Against Al-Qa'idah Suspects, Arab Journalist' (BBC-title), *ABC* (Spanish newspaper, Madrid) 18 Nov. 2004 via BBC Monitoring; and John Crewdson, 'Spain query links Syrians to 9/11 attacks in U.S.', *Chicago Tribune*, 19 Oct. 2003, http://deseretnews. com/dn/view/0,1249,515039793,00.html, accessed Nov. 2005.

61   Leslie Crawford, 'A Dangerous Subject', p.20.

62   Cited in Audiencia Nacional, Sala de lo Penal, Sección Tercera, 'Sentencia Núm. 36/2005', Madrid, 26 Sept. 2005, [verdict against the Abu Dahdah network], p.200. See also ibid., pp.67-8, 302.

Spanish prosecutors suggested that Allouni's relationship with al-Suri may have facilitated the interview with bin Laden. Al-Suri allegedly accompanied Allouni when the latter met with Taleban officials to seek permission for the interview.[63] However, it is not clear whether al-Suri's assistance was of much help in this regard.[64] In fact, it was only after 9/11 that Allouni was granted an interview with bin Laden, and this was at the initiative of the al-Qaida leader himself. [65]

During the trial in mid-2005, Allouni admitted meeting both al-Suri and his assistant Bahayah (Abu Khalid) in Kabul. He described al-Suri as a 'source of information about al-Qaida's activities, its followers, and the world of radical Islam', in addition to being an intermediary with the Taleban government.[66] Allouni met regularly with al-Suri and his assistant in Kabul, insisting later that his only aim was to gain information: 'I took advantage of the situation to extract information from them on what the Taliban were, on what al-Qaida was and on other organizations'.[67]

During questioning in 2003, Allouni stated that he was sure al-Suri and Bahayah were not al-Qaida members, and he believed that both of them worked only for the Taleban regime.[68] Allouni had described

63   Audiencia Nacional, Sala de lo Penal, Sección Tercera, 'Sentencia Núm. 36/2005', Madrid, 26 Sept. 2005, [verdict against the Abu Dahdah network], pp.199, 201, 302-303.

64   Leslie Crawford, 'A Dangerous Subject', p.16.

65   Ibid., pp.18, 20.

66   Audiencia Nacional, Sala de lo Penal, Sección Tercera, 'Sentencia Núm. 36/2005', Madrid, 26 Sept. 2005, [verdict against the Abu Dahdah network], p.299.

67   Cited in Giles Tremlett, 'When a reporter got too close to the story?' *The Guardian*, 3 Oct. 2005, http://media.guardian.co.uk/mediaguardian/story/0,1583222,00.html, accessed Jan. 2006.

68   José María Irujo, 'El hombre de Bin Laden en Madrid', *El País*, 2 March 2005, www.elPaís.es/comunes/2005/11m/08_comision/libro_electronico_red_islam/red_islamista_01%20doc.pdf, accessed July 2006, p.18; Pierre Akel, 'Abu Mus'ab al-Suri: "I deplore that there were no weapons of mass destructions in the planes that destroyed New York and Washington on 11 Sept.".,' (in Arabic), *Shafaf al-Sharq al-Awsat/Middle East Transparent*, 22 Jan. 2005, www.metransparent.com/texts/communique_abu_massab_al_

al-Suri as merely 'an opponent of the Syrian regime', arguing that the latter's involvement with bin Laden had ended in 1992.[69] Allouni was familiar with some of al-Suri's writings, including a publication in which the latter admitted that he had worked for bin Laden's organization between 1988 and 1992. Allouni emphasised al-Suri's disagreements with bin Laden, which obviously had been a theme in their many conversations. According to Allouni, al-Suri was 'no longer' a member, because 'he blame[d] al-Qaida for having destroyed the jihadi movement'.[70]

Although the Spanish court did not believe this, Allouni's claim was not entirely unfounded. Al-Suri himself had repeatedly denied being part of the al-Qaida organization, and he had quarrelled with bin Laden in the late 1990s. Furthermore, al-Suri had told *al-Jazeera* during the interview with Allouni that he was not a member of al-Qaida although he sympathized with the group and had attended bin Laden's wedding party.[71] Furthermore, as Allouni's defence lawyers pointed out, when Allouni had a relationship with al-Suri and Bahayah, they were still legal residents of Spain and not terrorist fugitives wanted by Spanish authorities.

The conviction of Allouni remains extremely controversial. When his case was retried in the Spanish Supreme Court, one of the five judges dissented, arguing that 'the presumption of innocence was violated' and that Allouni should have been acquitted.[72] Allouni's case

---

suri_response_to_us_accusations, p.1; 'Terror Accused Tells of Bin Laden Interview,' *The Guardian*, 17 May 2005, www.guardian.co.uk/alqaida/ story/0,12469,1485488,00.html, accessed Oct. 2005; and Sebastian Rotella and Cristina Mateo-Yanguas, 'Al Jazeera Reporter Charged', *Los Angeles Times*, 12 Sept. 2003, p.A11 via LexisNexis.

69   Audiencia Nacional, Sala de lo Penal, Sección Tercera, 'Sentencia Núm. 36/2005', Madrid, 26 Sept. 2005, [verdict against the Abu Dahdah network], p.301.

70   Cited in ibid., p.303.

71   'Reports of split in Bin Laden's group denied,' (LexisNexis Title), *'Al-Jazeera at Midday'-programme, Al-Jazeera TV*, 1 Aug. 2000 1240 GMT via LexisNexis.

72   Leslie Crawford, 'A Dangerous Subject', p.21.

illustrated perhaps the difficult balance that any investigative journalist has to strike, especially in the post-9/11 and post-M-11 atmosphere, between getting access to terrorist leaders while at the same time avoiding building the kind of relations that might be deemed to be too close.

Al-Suri later took great pride in his contacts both with *al-Jazeera* and other international media outlets, emphasizing the impact these media events had on the jihadi struggle:

[There were] enormous responses from the American news media [to bin Laden in the late 1990s], and these confrontations entered the American and Arab international satellite TV-channels, especially the *Al-Jazeera* TV Channel in Qatar, which played a pivotal role in bringing this media conflict to millions of Muslim viewers throughout the world. This in turned helped the jihadi current taking a further step towards the phase of internationalization.[73]

Al-Suri also noted that the presence of bin Laden 'as a symbol and star in Arab and international media', served as an important factor in radicalizing the Islamist movement.[74]

## AMIR AZIZI: A MOROCCAN AIDE AND TRAINING ASSOCIATE?

Amir Azizi (Amer Aziz), also known by his *nom de guerre* Uthman al-Andalusi (Osman Al Andalusi, Othman El Analuci), a Moroccan with Spanish citizenship, was reportedly among al-Suri's companions from the Madrid period. He had been 'detected' by the Spanish police in early 1999, if not before,[75] and featured in Judge Garzón's indictments against Abu Dahdah's network. He was then charged with belonging to a terrorist organization by Spanish authorities. Later, he faced charges of helping to plan the 9/11 conspiracy. The

---

73   *Global Islamic Resistance Call*, p.726.

74   Ibid., p.727.

75   Grupo Parlamentario de Izquierda Verde (IU-ICV), 'Propuesta de Conclusiones y Recomendaciones Finales de la Comisión de Investigación del 11-M' (Madrid, 8 June 2005), via http://estaticos.elmundo.es/ documentos/2005/06/08/iu_icv.pdf, accessed July 2006, p.17.

Spanish government also declared him a suspect in the M-11 investigation,[76] and he thus became the first person allegedly to be linked to both attacks.[77] In a new indictment, dated April 2004, against the Abu Dahdah network Garzón portrayed Azizi as someone with 'a direct connection with al-Qaida leaders in Afghanistan who were responsible for the attacks'.[78]

Press sources have described Azizi as a 'deputy' or 'envoy' for al-Suri, sometimes claiming that he was 'one of al-Suri's closest aides' and someone whom al-Suri 'is believed to oversee'.[79] According to one study, he had been one of al-Suri's 'protégés' at the al-Ghuraba training camp in Afghanistan (see chapter 8).[80] In late 2004, Spanish investigators reportedly stated that Azizi had served as an instructor in the Abu Khabab camp in the Derunta complex, together with

---

76  The Spanish ministry of interior called him a suspect in the M-11 bombings, but the judge leading the M-11 investigation has not issued an arrest warrant against him. See Maria Jesus Prades, 'Spain Indicts Fugitive on 9/11 Charges', *Associated Press*, 28 April 2004, via http://groups.yahoo. com/group/unitedstatesaction/message/6229, accessed July 2006; and 'Madrid fugitive charged over 9/11', *The Scotsman*, 28 April 2004, http://thescotsman.scotsman.com/international.cfm?id=482642004, accessed July 2006.

77  Maria Jesus Prades, 'Spain Indicts Fugitive on 9/11 Charges', *Associated Press*, 28 April 2004, via http://groups.yahoo.com/group/unitedstatesaction/message/6229, accessed July 2006.

78  Cited in Maria Jesus Prades, 'Spain Indicts Fugitive on 9/11 Charges', *Associated Press*, 28 April 2004, via http://groups.yahoo.com/group/unitedstatesaction/message/6229, accessed July 2006.

79  Cited in Robert Windrem, 'U.S. hunts for "pen jihadi"', *MSNBC News*, 9 Dec. 2004, www.msnbc.msn.com/id/6685673/, accessed July 2005; and 'Fugitive seen as link between 9/11, Madrid', (Agencies) *China Daily*, 23 Jan. 2005, http://www2.chinadaily.com.cn/english/doc/2005-01/23/content_411467.htm, accessed Aug. 2005. See also 'Mustafa Setmariam Nasar', *Wikipedia.org*, http://en.wikipedia.org/wiki/Mustafa_Setmariam_Nasar, accessed Oct. 2006.

80  Paul Cruickshank and Mohannad Hage Ali, 'Abu Musab Al Suri: Architect of the New Al Qaeda', *Studies in Conflict and Terrorism*, 30 (1) (Jan. 2007), p.9.

al-Suri.[81] However, their exact relationship is difficult to pinpoint. Spanish court documents do not list Azizi among al-Suri's primary contacts;[82] instead, he is usually described as being Abu Dahdah's right-hand man.[83] Like al-Suri and Abu Dahdah, Azizi was also married to a Spanish woman and had Spanish citizenship. An Afghan war veteran, he had trained in a mujahidin base in Bosnia during the 1990s, notably at the camp in Zenica, where he reportedly 'spent much time'.[84] After returning to Spain he allegedly recruited young Muslims to fight in Chechnya, Afghanistan, and other jihadi campaigns.[85] Azizi was indicted on charges that involved close cooperation with Abu Dahdah in dispatching recruits 'as "mujahideen" to military terrorist-type training camps in Afghanistan'.[86] Two documents retrieved by British

---

81 The source for this information was allegedly Superintendent Rafael Gomez, who testified for the M-11 commission. See Menor Jorge A. Rodriguez, 'Islamist terrorism superintendent considers Abu Dahdah 3/11 mastermind' (in Spanish), *El País*, 26 Oct. 2004, via FBIS. Spanish press sources have also linked him to other al-Qaida camps where he allegedly met with well-known militants like the Moroccan Karim Mejjati, one of the very few foreign jihadis involved in the terrorist campaign in Saudi Arabia after 2003. See 'Principales ideólogos o "autores intelectuales" del 11-M', *3 dias de Marzo webblog*, 18 Sept. 2005, http://3diasdemarzo. blogspot.com/2005/09/principales-idelogos-o-autores.html, accessed July 2006.

82 See 'Juzgado Central de Instruccion no.005, Madrid, Sumario', 17 Sept. 2003; and Audiencia Nacional, Sala de lo Penal, Sección Tercera, 'Sentencia Núm. 36/2005', Madrid, 26 Sept. 2005, [verdict against the Abu Dahdah network].

83 'Madrid fugitive charged over 9/11', *The Scotsman*, 28 April 2004, http:// thescotsman.scotsman.com/international.cfm?id=482642004, accessed July 2006.

84 Audiencia Nacional, Sala de lo Penal, Sección Tercera, 'Sentencia Núm. 36/2005', Madrid, 26 Sept. 2005, [verdict against the Abu Dahdah network], pp.178-9.

85 Casimiro García-Abadillo, *11-M: La Venganza* (Madrid: Esfera Libros, 2004), p.110; and Ahmad Rafat, '3/11 mastermind's hideout' (in Spanish), *El Tiempo de Hoy* (Madrid), 9 Oct. 2004, via FBIS.

86 Cited in 'Juzgado Central de Instruccion no.005, Madrid, Sumario',

forces in the Afghan training camps after the fall of Taleban regime contained interviews with newly arrived recruits, and were signed by the 'public relation office' of the 'Islamic Combatant Group'.[87] This presumably referred to the *Moroccan Islamic Combatant Group* (GICM), which is considered to be the main organizational structure behind the M-11 attacks.[88] According to the documents, the interviewees say that Osman al-Andalusi, Azizi's *nom de guerre*, was the one who persuaded them to join the GICM.[89]

Azizi has been portrayed as a senior member of al-Qaida and even 'the leader of the Moroccan Islamic Combat Group', which was responsible for five bombings in Casablanca in May, 2003.[90] At the same time, according to those who frequented the M-30 mosque in Madrid, which Azizi and many of his co-conspirators visited on a regular basis, Azizi was considered a drug addict.[91] Proficient in Arabic, English, Spanish and French, he worked as a translator at the Islamic Center in Madrid.[92] Azizi called attention to himself at

---

17 Sept. 2003, p.23. See also ibid., pp.267-9; and José María Irujo, 'El hombre de Bin Laden en Madrid', *El País*, 2 March 2005, www.elPaís. es/comunes/2005/11m/08_comision/libro_electronico_red_islam/red_ islamista_01%20doc.pdf, accessed July 2006.

87   Audiencia Nacional, Sala de lo Penal, Sección Tercera, 'Sentencia Núm. 36/2005', Madrid, 26 Sept. 2005, [verdict against the Abu Dahdah network], pp.52-5.

88   There were basically two well-known 'Islamic Combatant/Fighting Groups' in Afghanistan, (LIFG and GICM), according to a former Shura Council member of the LIFG, Amer Azizi had never been a member of their group. Author's interview with Noman Benotman, London 15 Sept. 2006.

89   Audiencia Nacional, Sala de lo Penal, Sección Tercera, 'Sentencia Núm. 36/2005', Madrid, 26 Sept. 2005, [verdict against the Abu Dahdah network], pp.52-5.

90   Lawrence Wright, 'The Terror Web', *The New Yorker*, 3 Aug. 2004.

91   Ibid.

92   Audiencia Nacional, Juzgado Central de Instrucción no.6, 'Sumario no.20/2004', [Indictment against the M-11 bombers], Madrid, 10 April 2006, available at www.fondodocumental.com/11M/documentos/Autos/ auto2.doc, accessed July 2006, p.525.

the center during a visit by Arab ambassadors on the occasion of the death of Syrian president Hafiz al-Asad, when he vociferously protested against the mourning being held for the late president.[93] He fled Spain when the first arrests were made in the Abu Dahdah investigation in November 2001.[94]

Initially, Azizi's name was among the many possible candidates for the mastermind role in the M-11 conspiracy. One reason for this was that he knew several of the prime suspects in the Casablanca and M-11 bombings. A police report on the M-11 bombers reportedly said this of him:

100 per cent operational, linked with the recruitment of mujahedin for Afghanistan, having taken part on this front in support of the jihad. Knows Spain very well, is married to a Spanish woman and had close relations with the religious radicals of the Lavapies quarter [where several of the M-11 bombers were arrested].[95]

Azizi's cell phone number was also found in the house of Jamal Zougam, the first to be arrested in connection with the M-11 at-

---

93  Grupo Parlamentario de Izquierda Verde (IU-ICV), 'Propuesta de Conclusiones y Recomendaciones Finales de la Comisión de Investigación del 11-M' (Madrid, 8 June 2005), via http://estaticos.elmundo.es/documentos/2005/06/08/iu_icv.pdf, accessed July 2006, p.18.

94  Audiencia Nacional, Sala de lo Penal, Sección Tercera, 'Sentencia Núm. 36/2005', Madrid, 26 Sept. 2005, [verdict against the Abu Dahdah network], p.93; 'Propuesta de Conclusiones y Recomendaciones Finales de la Comisión de Investigación del 11-M' (Madrid, 8 June 2005), via http://estaticos.elmundo.es/documentos/2005/06/08/iu_icv.pdf, accessed July 2006, p.22; and 'Spanish police fear "revenge" attack by fugitives for Madrid suicides' (FBIS-title), *El País*, 3 Oct. 2004 via FBIS.

95  Cited in Jorge A. Rodriguez, 'Protected witness says that "a certain Amer", trained in Afghanistan, organized 3/11' (in Spanish), *El País*, 22 Nov. 2004, via FBIS. On the Lavapies district in Madrid, see Lizette Alvarez, 'Deep Unease Over the Future Gnaws at Moroccans in Spain', *The New York Times*, 15 March 2004.

tacks.[96] Azizi was also believed to be 'directly linked with Jamal Ahmidan ('El Chino'), according to the Spanish press.[97]

In October 2000, Azizi was arrested in Istanbul, together with several others, including Salaheddin Benyaich, a mujahidin veteran of the war in Bosnia and Daghestan, who was later convicted for the Casablanca attacks; Lahcen Ikassrien (also known as Muhammad Haddad), a Moroccan who was later captured in Afghanistan, sent to Guantánamo and extradited to Spain in June 2005;[98] and Said Berraj, also nicknamed 'Said el Mensajero' ('Said the Messenger'), who was later indicted in the M-11 trial. The men had arrived in the city around two weeks earlier and were detained apparently for failing to produce identity papers or because Turkish police suspected them of being Islamist militants. The Turkish authorities subsequently released them due to lack of evidence and they were deported.[99] Abu Dahdah had reportedly gone to Turkey in November 2000 to assist in their release.[100] At the time, Turkey was considered a com-

---

96  Jorge A. Rodriguez, 'Protected witness says that "a certain Amer", trained in Afghanistan, organized 3/11', *El País*, 22 Nov. 2004 via FBIS; 'Spanish judge links Madrid attacks with 9/11 Al-Qa'idah cell', (FBIS-title), *El Mundo*, 29 April 2004 via FBIS; and Grupo Parlamentario de Izquierda Verde (IU-ICV), 'Propuesta de Conclusiones y Recomendaciones Finales de la Comisión de Investigación del 11-M' (Madrid, 8 June 2005), via http://estaticos.elmundo.es/documentos/2005/06/08/iu_icv.pdf, accessed July 2006, p.18.

97  Fernando Lazaro, 'At least 15 individuals investigated over 3/11 are linked to Abu Dahdah's cell' (in Spanish), *El Mundo*, 27 Oct. 2004 via FBIS.

98  Josh White, '3 Guantanamo Detainees Freed', *Washington Post*, 21 July 2005, p.A02, www.washingtonpost.com/wp-dyn/content/article/2005/07/20/AR2005072002473_pf.html, accessed July 2006.

99  'How the March 11 local cell was born' (in Spanish), *El País*, 12 Sept. 2004; Dale Fuchs, 'More Al Qaeda links seen in Madrid blasts', *The New York Times*, 30 April 2004; 'Spanish judge links Madrid attacks with 9/11 Al-Qa'idah cell' (FBIS-title), *El Mundo*, 29 April 2004 via FBIS; and Dale Fuchs, 'Madrid Suspect Once Arrested In Turkey', *The New York Times*, 29 April 2004.

100 Grupo Parlamentario de Izquierda Verde (IU-ICV), 'Propuesta de Conclusiones y Recomendaciones Finales de la Comisión de Investigación del 11-M' (Madrid, 8 June 2005), via http://estaticos.elmundo.es/

mon transit destinations for militants heading to or returning from Afghanistan.[101] According to a Spanish parliamentary investigation into the M-11 attacks, Azizi's meeting in Istanbul dealt with how to facilitate the transportation of recruits to Afghanistan.[102]

At another meeting in Istanbul, which took place after 9/11, Azizi is believed to have met with Sarhane Ben Abdelmajid Fakhet ('El Tunecino'), the main organizer of the Madrid train bombings.[103] The meeting between Fakhet and Azizi was only one of several similar gatherings in Istanbul, which was considered 'an easy place to go' for terrorists, according to a European counterterrorism official interviewed by the *Financial Times*.[104] He was quoted as saying that 'there have been other meetings there, at which the bombings in Riyadh, Casablanca, Istanbul and Madrid were discussed'.[105] Spanish media sources claim that a meeting was held in Istanbul in February 2002, whose participants included Azizi and leading members of Libyan, Moroccan and Tunisian jihadi groups. This summit, which

documentos/2005/06/08/iu_icv.pdf, accessed July 2006, p.18.

101  'Principales ideólogos o "autores intelectuales" del 11-M', *3 dias de Marzo webblog*, 18 Sept. 2005, http://3diasdemarzo.blogspot.com/2005/09/principales-idelogos-o-autores.html, accessed July 2006.

102  Grupo Parlamentario de Izquierda Verde (IU-ICV), 'Propuesta de Conclusiones y Recomendaciones Finales de la Comisión de Investigación del 11-M' (Madrid, 8 June 2005), via http://estaticos.elmundo.es/documentos/2005/06/08/iu_icv.pdf, accessed July 2006, p.127. See also Jose Maria Irujo, 'On the trail of The Afghan' (in Spanish), *El País*, 10 Oct. 2004, via FBIS.

103  'Spanish judge links Madrid attacks with 9/11 Al-Qa'idah cell' (FBIS-title), *El Mundo*, 29 April 2004 via FBIS. See also J. A. Rodriguez, 'Police put European Al-Qa'idah chief at pinnacle of 11 March network' (in Spanish), *El País*, 4 March 2005 via FBIS; and Maria Jesus Prades, 'Spain Indicts Fugitive on 9/11 Charges', *Associated Press*, 28 April 2004, via http://groups.yahoo.com/group/unitedstatesaction/message/6229, accessed July 2006.

104  'Madrid Bombers Met in Turkey to Plan Attack', *Financial Times*, 10 April 2004, via www.novinite.com/view_news.php?id=33265, accessed July 2006.

105  Ibid.

reportedly was coordinated with al-Zarqawi, agreed that the 'jihad should be accomplished in the places they resided', and emphasised 'Morocco and Spain as targets'.[106] It is uncertain whether Fakhet attended this particular meeting.

Azizi and Fakhet knew each other from Spain where they reportedly had gone to the same Quran recital classes.[107] According to police sources cited by *El Mundo*, Fakhet and Azizi met in Istanbul at the end of 2002 or in early 2003. There, Fakhet had asked Azizi whether he could provide him with manpower from his Moroccan network, the GICM, in order to carry out strikes in Spain. Azizi turned down the request, saying that his men were already on watch lists or detained at Guantanámo. Azizi nevertheless approved of Fakhet's plans, and recommended that he contact Jamal Zougam, who subsequently became the first person to be arrested in the M-11 investigation. Azizi also gave his assurances that Fakhet acted with al-Qaida's support.[108] In this way, it appeared as if Azizi gave the M-11 conspirators 'permission to act in the name of Al Qaeda'.[109] Spanish investigators initially suspected that the Istanbul meeting was of critical importance because it ostensibly linked the attacks directly to the al-Qaida leadership.[110] In 2004, Spanish counter-ter-

---

106  Cited in 'Principales ideólogos o "autores intelectuales" del 11-M', *3 dias de Marzo webblog*, 18 Sept. 2005, http://3diasdemarzo.blogspot. com/2005/09/principales-idelogos-o-autores.html, accessed July 2006.

107  'Islamist sect linked to bombings said to be on the rise in Spain', *El País*, 20 Dec. 2005 via FBIS.

108  'Spanish judge links Madrid attacks with 9/11 Al-Qa'idah cell' (FBIS-title), *El Mundo*, 29 April 2004 via FBIS. See also J. A. Rodriguez, 'Police put European Al-Qa'idah chief at pinnacle of 11 March network' (in Spanish), *El País*, 4 March 2005 via FBIS; Maria Jesus Prades, 'Spain Indicts Fugitive on 9/11 Charges', *Associated Press*, 28 April 2004, via http://groups.yahoo. com/group/unitedstatesaction/message/6229, accessed July 2006; and 'Madrid Bombers Met in Turkey to Plan Attack', *Financial Times*, 10 April 2004, via www.novinite.com/view_news.php?id=33265, accessed July 2006.

109  Lawrence Wright, 'The Terror Web', *The New Yorker*, 3 Aug. 2004.

110  Keith B. Richburg, 'Madrid Attacks May Have Targeted Election', *Washington Post*, 17 Oct. 2004, p.A16.

rorism investigators also hypothesized that Azizi 'served as a middle-man or a facilitator between the local cell of mainly North African immigrants in Spain and bin Laden's network'.[111]

Communication intercepts in 2003 reportedly detected Azizi in Iran where many al-Qaida figures were in hiding. However, in April 2004, several witness reports suggested that he had visited Spain shortly after the M-11 attacks. The *Los Angeles Times* cited a senior Spanish investigator who claimed that 'reliable witness accounts' had seen Azizi in 'significant places connected to the plot', adding that '[t]he idea of Azizi as a leader has become more solid'.[112]

However, by 2006, Spanish authorities appeared to have abandoned the hypothesis of Azizi playing the mastermind role in the M-11 attacks. His name is mentioned in several places in the M-11 indictment, but does not figure on the list of the main perpetrators. The document described him as 'presumably an integrated member [of] the al-Qaida network in Spain', and as someone who called for jihad during prayer meetings. He recruited openly and claimed to worshippers at the mosque in Lavapiés, a mosque attended by many of the M-11 bombers, that he had fought with al-Qaida in Afghanistan.[113] Upon his return from Afghanistan in 2001, he organized meetings where Abu Dahdah and several of the M-11 inductees were present, including Fakhet and Zougam. He was evidently admired for his jihadi background.[114]

---

111 'Fugitive seen as link between 9/11, Madrid' (Agencies), *China Daily*, 23 Jan. 2005, http://www2.chinadaily.com.cn/english/doc/2005-01/23/content_411467.htm, accessed Aug. 2005.

112 Cited in Sebastian Rotella, 'Al Qaeda fugitive sought in bombings', *Los Angeles Times*, 14 April 2004, via www.spokesmanreview.com/pf.asp?date=041404&ID=s1509366, accessed July 2006.

113 Audiencia Nacional, Juzgado Central de Instrucción no.6, 'Sumario no.20/2004', [Indictment against the M-11 bombers], Madrid, 10 April 2006, available at www.fondodocumental.com/11M/documentos/Autos/auto2.doc, accessed July 2006, pp.525, 1246, 1345, 1370.

114 Ibid., pp.1218-19, 1370, 1360-61.

There have been suggestions that Azizi played a role in the 9/11 attacks. He reportedly knew Zacarias Moussaoui, who has been convicted in the United States on charges related to the September 11 attacks. Moussaoui reportedly had Azizi's telephone number in his diary.[115] It has also been rumoured that Azizi set up the meeting with Muhammad Atta and Ramzi bin al-Shibh in Tarragona, Spain, only two months before the 9/11 attacks.[116] A new indictment by the Spanish judge Baltasar Garzón made public in late April 2004, charged Azizi with helping to plan the September 11 attacks, saying that Azizi provided lodging for the Tarragona meeting and acted as a 'courier' for the 9/11 plotters. According to Garzón, the new indictment was based on information from British, Turkish and US authorities.[117]

However, these allegations have not been proved in court. According to the 9/11 Commission Report, Ramzi bin al-Shibh has claimed during interrogations that he and Muhammad Atta met nobody else during their stay in Salou in Tarragona.[118]

At the time of writing, Azizi is still on the run, and his whereabouts are unknown.

---

115  Jorge A. Rodriguez, 'Protected witness says that "a certain Amer" trained in Afghanistan, organized 3/11', *El País*, 22 Nov. 2004 via FBIS; and Grupo Parlamentario de Izquierda Verde (IU-ICV), 'Propuesta de Conclusiones y Recomendaciones Finales de la Comisión de Investigación del 11-M' (Madrid, 8 June 2005), via http://estaticos.elmundo.es/documentos/2005/06/08/iu_icv.pdf, accessed July 2006, p.22.

116  Robert Windrem, 'U.S. hunts for "pen jihadi",' *MSNBC News*, 9 Dec. 2004, www.msnbc.msn.com/id/6685673/, accessed July 2005; Dale Fuchs, 'More Al Qaeda links seen in Madrid blasts', *The New York Times*, 30 April 2004; and Lawrence Wright, 'The Terror Web', *The New Yorker*, 3 Aug. 2004.

117  'Madrid fugitive charged over 9/11', *The Scotsman*, 28 April 2004, http://thescotsman.scotsman.com/international.cfm?id=482642004, accessed July 2006.

118  *The 9/11 Commission Report*, www.9-11commission.gov/report/911Report.pdf, accessed Oct. 2006, p.261.

## ADIL ABD AL-BARI: A FELLOW JIHADI JOURNALIST

On several occasions al-Suri mentioned his contacts with Egyptian Islamic Jihad (EIJ) members and sympathizers in London. Al-Suri had been close to the EIJ, the main force behind the new jihadi current which emerged in Peshawar in the late 1980s, and during the 1990s al-Suri portrayed his relationship with the EIJ as being closer than to any other jihadi group.[119] He maintained close links with the EIJ in order to coordinate a common jihadi position on the GIA and the Algerian conflict during this period. Furthermore, his first study on the Taleban regime was undertaken in cooperation with the EIJ's media office in London, following a research trip to Afghanistan in late 1996.[120] His report was subsequently published in the EIJ mouthpiece, the *al-Mujahidun Newsletter*.[121]

In his writings and interviews, al-Suri does refer to Adil Abd al-Majid (also known as Adil Abd al-Bari) from the EIJ. He divulges very few details about their relationship, other than mentioning that he offered his advice on media strategies to Abd al-Bari and Khalid al-Fawwaz (see below), who had started a newsletter called *al-Dalil* (lit. 'The Sign'). Al-Suri says that there had been rumours that 'I was behind this newspaper', and he does not emphatically deny this.[122] Those who knew al-Suri in London say that he cooperated closely with Abd al-Bari, who played a large role in the EIJ media office in London.[123]

---

119 'Meeting with the Kuwaiti Newspaper', transcript of audiofile no.3, p.2; and Umar Abd al-Hakim, *A Summary of My Testimony*, p.31.

120 Umar Abd al-Hakim, *Afghanistan, the Taleban and the Battle of Islam Today* (in Arabic), p.2; and 'Meeting with the Kuwaiti Newspaper', transcript of audiofile no.2, pp.4-5, and no.3, p.2.

121 Author's interview with Camille Tawil, London, 14 Sept. 2006.

122 See 'Meeting with the Kuwaiti Newspaper', transcript of audiofile no.4, pp.7-8.

123 Author's interview with Abdel Bari Atwan at *al-Quds al-Arabi* offices, London, 28 April 2006; and author's interview with Camille Tawil, London, 14 Sept. 2006.

Abd al-Bari's full name is Adel Mohammed Abdul Almagid Abdel Bary and he is also known as 'Abbas' or 'Abu Dia'.[124] A lawyer by training, he had defended numerous Islamists in the Egyptian courts, including the JI's spiritual leader Umar Abd al-Rahman. In 1993, he was granted political asylum in Britain where he reportedly established the 'International Office for the Defence of the Egyptian People' (IODEP). In 1998, he was sentenced to death *in absentia* in Egypt on charges that he was involved in a terrorist plot to bomb the Khan al-Khalili bazaar, a major tourist attraction in Cairo. And in April 1999 he was also convicted by an Egyptian military court in the so-called 'Albanian returnees' case.[125]

Adil Abd al-Bari was later indicted by the United States for his alleged involvement in the East Africa Embassy bombings in 1998 and detained by the British authorities in mid-July 1999.[126] In December 2001 he was ordered to be extradited to the US by

---

124 'United States of America *v.* Usama Bin Laden, *et al.* Defendants (Kenyan Embassy Bombing), United States District Court, Southern District of New York, Indictment S(9) 98 Cr. 1023 (LBS), www.terrorismcentral. com/Library/Incidents/USEmbassyKenyaBombing/Indictment/Count1. html, accessed July 2006.

125 See Jailan Halawi, 'London militants', *Al-Ahram Weekly*, no.438 (15-21 July 1999), http://weekly.ahram.org.eg/1999/438/eg4.htm, accessed July 2006.

126 United States of America *v.* Usama Bin Laden, *et al.* Defendants (Kenyan Embassy Bombing), United States District Court, Southern District of New York, Indictment S(9) 98 Cr. 1023 (LBS), www.terrorismcentral. com/Library/Incidents/USEmbassyKenyaBombing/Indictment/Count1. html, accessed July 2006; U.S. Department of State, 'U.S. Indicts Suspects in East Africa Embassy Bombings', 9 May 2000, retrieved from www.fas. org/irp/news/2000/05/000509-terror-usia1.htm, accessed July 2006; and United States of America *v.* Usama Bin Laden, *et al.* Defendants (Kenyan Embassy Bombing), United States District Court, Southern District of New York, S(7) 98 Cr. 1023, transcript of Day 59 of the trial, 5 June 2001, http://cryptome.sabotage.org/usa-v-ubl-59.htm, accessed July 2006, p.7137.

a British court but at the time of writing the verdict had not yet been carried out.[127]

US prosecutors have alleged that Abd al-Bari, together with his associate, Ibrahim Eidarous, who arrived in London in late 1997, were in close contact with Khalid al-Fawwaz, and that they were in fact his associates.[128] They further alleged that Eidarous and Abdel Bari 'at different times led the London cell of the Egyptian Islamic Jihad (EIJ) organization'.[129] Under al-Zawahiri's leadership, the EIJ, or what was left of the organization, had gradually begun to join forces with bin Laden's organization from the mid-1990s onwards. The formal announcement of the merger came only in June 2001. Eidarous and Abd al-Bari had allegedly been found in possession of al-Qaida and EIJ statements threatening attacks against US interests. At the time of the embassy attacks on 7 August 1998, Abd al-Bari maintained an office in London, where the claims of responsibility for the bombings allegedly had been found. The US authorities believed that the statements of responsibility had been sent to London during the early hours of the day of the embassy bombings, and were then resent from London to media organizations in France, Qatar and the United Arab Emirates. US authorities charged that the fingerprints of the two men were allegedly found on these statements.[130]

Abd al-Bari's associate, Ibrahim Eidarous, or Ibrahim Hussein Abdel Hadi Eidarous, was also known by different names and

---

127 Patricia Hurtado, 'Wanted, But Kept Out of Reach; Nine Men Suspected of Terror Crimes and Links to al-Qaida are Being Held in Britain, Where Extradition Laws Keep Them From U.S.', *Newsday* (New York), 24 April 2005, p.A4, posted on www.defenddemocracy.org/in_the_media/in_the_media_show.htm?doc_id=274667, accessed July 2006.

128 Mark Tran, 'Two Egyptians face extradition over US embassy bombings', *The Guardian*, 12 July 1999, www.guardian.co.uk/wtccrash/story/0,550246,00.html, accessed July 2006.

129 U.S. Department of State, 'U.S. Indicts Suspects in East Africa Embassy Bombings', 9 May 2000, retrieved from www.fas.org/irp/news/2000/05/000509-terror-usia1.htm, accessed July 2006.

130 Ibid.

aliases, such as Ibrahim Hussein, Daoud, Abu Abdullah, and Abdelhadi.[131] He was a well-known figure in the Arab press coverage of Islamist militancy during the 1990s.[132] A former Egyptian army officer, he had reportedly led the EIJ cell in Baku, Azerbaijan, before he moved to London in September 1997. There, he was believed to have assumed the role as cell leader, while allegedly serving as a member of EIJ's Founding Council, and maintaining close relations with the EIJ leader, Ayman al-Zawahiri in Afghanistan. Until Eidarous' arrival, Adil Abd al-Bari had been the EIJ cell leader in London, according to US authorities. They were accused of providing logistical support to EIJ members, such as facilitating the delivery of forged ID papers to EIJ members in Holland and Albania. Eidarous also served as a conduit for messages to and from the EIJ leadership in Afghanistan, according to the US charges.[133]

### SAAD AL-FAQIH AND KHALID AL-FAWWAZ: ACQUAINTANCES INSIDE THE SAUDI CAMP

Another politically active Islamist in London who came to know al-Suri was Dr Sa'd Rashid Muhammad al-Faqih (Saad al-Faqih), who heads the best known Saudi dissident movement in exile, the London-based *Movement for Islamic Reform in Arabia* (MIRA).[134]

---

131  United States of America *v.* Usama Bin Laden, *et al.* Defendants (Kenyan Embassy Bombing), United States District Court, Southern District of New York, Indictment S(9) 98 Cr. 1023 (LBS), www.terrorismcentral. com/Library/Incidents/USEmbassyKenyaBombing/Indictment/Count1. html, accessed July 2006.

132  See Jailan Halawi, 'London militants', *Al-Ahram Weekly* no.438 (15-21 July 1999), http://weekly.ahram.org.eg/1999/438/eg4.htm, accessed July 2006.

133  U.S. Department of State, 'U.S. Indicts Suspects in East Africa Embassy Bombings', 9 May 2000, retrieved from www.fas.org/irp/ news/2000/05/000509-terror-usia1.htm, accessed July 2006.

134  For more details on al-Faqih and Saudi dissident politics during the 1990s, see Mamoun Fandy, *Saudi Arabia and the Politics of Dissent* (New York:

Al-Faqih has headed MIRA since its formation in 1996, after he split from the Committee for the Defense of Legitimate Rights (CDLR), another London-based Saudi dissident group. Al-Faqih was a professor of surgery at King Saud University until he left the country in 1994 and had been jailed for his opposition activism. During the late 1980s, al-Faqih had volunteered as a surgeon to treat wounded rebel fighters in the Afghan liberation war.[135] This experience gave al-Faqih intimate knowledge of the Arab-Afghan movement, although he distanced himself from violent jihadism and remains an advocate of non-violent reformism.

In an interview with this author, Saad al-Faqih says he heard about al-Suri for the first time in the early 1990s, probably around 1993 or 1994, when the latter visited London for the first time.[136] By then, al-Suri had already won a name for himself as a jihadi writer and was quite well known in Islamist circles. According to Saad al-Faqih's recollection, they met for the first time in 1995. Al-Faqih believes the meeting took place just after the bombings in Riyadh in November 1995, but it might have been earlier, and the purpose of the meeting was unconnected to events in Saudi Arabia. Al-Faqih recalls that

Al-Suri came to see us at the CDLR office, because he was not happy about the way CDLR had written about the Algerian conflict. He thought that the CDLR undermined the jihad in Algeria.[137]

This was before al-Suri himself distanced himself from the GIA and its campaign of violence. Although they disagreed on the legitimacy of the GIA's jihad, Saad al-Faqih noted that only a year or so later, al-Suri had concluded that the GIA's struggle in Algeria did

---

Palgrave, 1999), pp.149-75.

135  Tim Weiner, 'U.S. Case Against bin Laden in Embassy Blasts Seems to Rest on Ideas (Part II)', *The New York Times*, 13 April 1999.

136  Author's telephone interview with Saad al-Faqih, 17 Sept. 2006.

137  Ibid.

not constitute a legitimate jihad, and had reportedly conceded to al-Faqih that he had been right in criticising the GIA.[138]

Al-Faqih met with al-Suri on later occasions, but underlines that they never developed a close cooperative relationship. He describes his and the CDLR's relationship with al-Suri as 'careful', 'distant' and 'respectful'.[139] Although al-Faqih had criticised the GIA, he says 'we were careful not to provoke al-Suri and his supporters'.[140]

Saad al-Faqih also met with al-Suri outside the framework of Islamist activism in London, since they were almost neighbours in the same suburb of North-West London and their sons attended the same school. Al-Faqih says he found al-Suri a formidable verbal opponent: 'Abu Mus'ab al-Suri was very powerful in his arguments. He is very difficult to corner in a discussion'.[141] Al-Suri also struck him as being 'highly educated', and a 'very very intelligent man'.[142] Despite their differences on many issues, al-Faqih considered al-Suri a very interesting discussant: 'You will enjoy talking with him, even if you disagree with him'.[143] Al-Faqih found him very well informed, with an almost 'encyclopaedic' knowledge of many subjects, from physics to literature and music, someone who reads novels in French, Spanish and Arabic, as well as being well-versed in European culture. As they met in more personal and family-related circumstances, al-Faqih also discovered that al-Suri was 'a very good family man', who cared deeply about his Spanish wife and his children.[144] A *Washington Post* article on al-Suri noted that 'Unlike many of his acquaintances who favored arranged marriages, the unsmiling Nasar [i.e. al-Suri]

---

138  Ibid.
139  Ibid.
140  Ibid.
141  Ibid.
142  Ibid.
143  Ibid.
144  Ibid.

possessed a romantic streak and surprised friends by doting on his Spanish-born spouse'.[145]

Al-Suri's sharp mind and intellectual gifts also gave him a sense of pride, which sometimes bordered on 'arrogance', al-Faqih recalls. He was not a jovial, relaxed fellow. He rarely smiled and was often regarded as being 'a difficult man' who never would compromise on his principles.[146] For example, when al-Suri won his libel against *al-Hayat*, his lawyer wanted to take him and his colleagues to a top restaurant in London to celebrate. When they arrived, it transpired that a suit and tie were obligatory. Al-Suri refused to put on a jacket and tie, offered by the restaurant staff, saying a tie was a remnant of the days of colonial and Crusader rule.

A sharp and uncompromising intellectual with a deeply serious appearance, al-Suri tended to provoke hostility among potential followers. His sharp tongue spared nobody, and in al-Faqih's view, he 'was bad in presenting himself'.[147] As opposed to several other jihadi veterans arriving in London from Peshawar, such as Abu Hamza al-Masri and Abu Qutadah al-Filastini, al-Suri was unsuccessful in gathering a following of some significance in London.

Al-Faqih saw him for the last time in 1997, prior to al-Suri's departure from London for Afghanistan, and has not spoken to him since. Even though al-Faqih found al-Suri very impressive as a person, he does not consider him a leader or an influential jihadi theoretician. It is possible that al-Suri's writings 'may have an audience among the elites, but not on the wider jihadi current', al-Faqih explains.[148] Al-Faqih's assessment is not unusual among Islamists in London. Many of them had a strained relationship with al-Suri and refuse to acknowledge the importance of his extensive writings.

---

145 Craig Whitlock, 'Architect of New War on the West: Writings Lay Out Post-9/11 Strategy of Isolated Cells Joined in Jihad', *Washington Post*, 23 May 2006, p.A01.

146 Author's telephone interview with Saad al-Faqih, 17 Sept. 2006.

147 Ibid.

148 Ibid.

In his audiotaped memoirs, al-Suri spoke of his relationship with the Saudi opposition in London. There were apparently contacts between MIRA and al-Suri's media office, the 'Bureau for the Study of Islamic Conflicts' and at least one communiqué by the Bureau about bin Laden was published in MIRA's online bulletin in March 1997.[149] On an intellectual level, al-Suri was clearly quite interested in the Saudi opposition, both in London and in Afghanistan, although he at times spoke disparagingly about the Saudis. Among al-Suri's many audio-recorded speeches, there is a series of cassettes called 'Session with youth from the Arab Peninsula' (*jalsah ma'shabab al-jazirah*), recorded in Kabul, Afghanistan in 1421 (corresponding to April 2000–March 2001). In January 2001, from his media centre in Kabul, he also released an 82-page booklet reprinting and analysing selected statements and communiqués by both bin Laden and Saad al-Faqih addressing the leading Saudi clerics, Shaykh bin Baz and Shaykh bin Uthaymin.[150] It also appears as if al-Suri considered that the two trips he made to Afghanistan with Channel 4 and CNN to facilitate interviews with bin Laden were part of, or at least in coordination with, the efforts of the Saudi opposition in London. Saad al-Faqih recalls al-Suri's involvement with Channel 4 and CNN, but he insists that the initiative came from the media outlets themselves, not from people like Khalid al-Fawwaz. Al-Suri was able to undertake these trips because he had a Spanish passport and intimate knowledge of Afghanistan, not because he was so close

---

149  See 'Bin Laden Cited on Prince Sultan's US Visit', *al-Islah bulletin*, no.48 (London, in Arabic), 3 March 1997, p.1, [issued by the Islamic Reform Movement of Saudi Arabia, IRM; received by fax: 'New Offer for bin Laden'], via FBIS, http://binladenquotes.blogspot.com/2004/02/fbis-document-10-years-of-osama-bin.html, accessed Sept. 2006.

150  Umar Abd al-Hakim (Abu Mus'ab al-Suri), *The Testimony of the Leaders of the Mujahidun and the Reform [Current] about the Sultan's Clerics in the Land of the Two Holy Places, Called Saudi Arabia: A Reading and Commentary of the Letters and Communiques by Shaykh Osama bin Laden and Doctor Saad al-Faqih to Shaykh bin Baz, Shaykh bin 'Uthaymin and the Clerics of the Land of the Two Holy Places* (in Arabic) (Kabul: The al-Ghuraba Center for Islamic Studies and Media, 31 January 2001).

to bin Laden, al-Faqih explains. Furthermore, al-Suri operated his own media office and when travelling with Channel 4 and CNN was 'part of their crew'.[151]

While al-Faqih has professed a commitment to non-violent opposition since he arrived in London, the fact that he knew al-Fawwaz and al-Suri landed him in hot water after 9/11. Al-Faqih is now wanted by US authorities and stands accused of 'providing material support to al-Qaida'.[152] The US allegations against Saad al-Faqih include that he 'has had contact with' bin Laden and 'his de facto representative in the U.K.', Khalid al-Fawwaz.[153] Furthermore, it is alleged that he shared an office with al-Fawwaz in the late 1990s; a satellite phone procured with Faqih's credit card was given to bin Laden, and websites controlled by MIRA have allegedly been used for posting al-Qaida related statements and images.[154] A press release from the US Department of Treasury accuses al-Faqih of being 'associated with al Qaida member and fugitive Abu Musab al-Suri, a.k.a. Mustafa Nasar'.[155] Following the US Government's listing of al-Faqih as 'a terrorist', Saad al-Faqih was designated by the UN Al Qaeda and Taliban Sanctions Committee in December 2004 as being among 'individuals belonging to or associated with Al-Qaida organization'.[156] In July 2005, his organization, MIRA, was also

---

151 Author's telephone interview with Saad al-Faqih, 17 Sept. 2006.

152 The U.S. Department of Treasury, 'Treasury Designates MIRA for Support to Al Qaida', 14 July 2005, www.ustreas.gov/press/releases/js2632.htm, accessed Sept. 2006.

153 See 'U.S. Treasury Designates Two Individuals with Ties to al Qaida; UBL Former BIF Leader and al-Qaida Associate Named Under E.O. 13224', *The Office of Public Affairs*, 21 Dec. 2004, JS-2164, www.treas.gov/press/releases/js2164.htm, accessed July 2005.

154 Ibid.

155 Ibid.

156 United Nations Al Qaeda and Taliban Sanctions Committee, 'The list of individuals belonging to or associated with Al-Qaida organization/Last updated on 25 July 2006', www.un.org/Docs/sc/committees/1267/pdflist.pdf, accessed July 2006, p.16.

designated.[157] At the time of writing, they are still listed. However, his case is not unique. At least two other London-based Egyptian Islamists, Yasir al-Sirri and Hani al-Siba'i, have been indicted by the US government or listed by the UN Al Qaeda and Taliban Sanctions Committee, although British authorities have not authorised their arrest or extradition.[158]

As already alluded to above, Khalid Fawwaz, another prominent figure in the Saudi opposition in London, was among al-Suri's closest acquaintances. Al-Fawwaz is wanted by the United States for his alleged complicity in the East African terrorist attacks in August 1998. He was also designated by the UN Al Qaeda and Taliban Sanctions Committee in April 2002 as being among 'individuals belonging to or associated with Al-Qaida organization' and at the time of writing he remains on the list.[159] He was arrested in Britain shortly after the East African bombings. At the time of writing, Fawwaz is still in custody, awaiting the outcome of the US extradition request.

Al-Suri and al-Fawwaz cooperated closely in their efforts to bring bin Laden's cause to the world's attention in 1996-7, as discussed in the preceding chapter. The US authorities have described al-Fawwaz as Osama bin Laden's 'de facto representative to the UK'.[160] He was director of The Advice and Reform Committee (ARC), a media office established in July 1994 and based in Dollis Hill in north London.[161] The ARC published statements and epistles written by

---

157  Ibid., p.40.

158  See ibid., p.19; and United States of America *v.* Ahmed Abdel Sattar *et al.*, (02 Cr. 395 (JGK)), 22 July 2003, http://fl1.findlaw.com/news.findlaw. com/hdocs/docs/terrorism/ussattar72203opn.pdf, accessed Oct. 2006.

159  United Nations Al Qaeda and Taliban Sanctions Committee, 'The list of individuals belonging to or associated with Al-Qaida organization/Last updated on 25 July 2006', www.un.org/Docs/sc/committees/1267/pdflist. pdf, accessed July 2006, p.16.

160  'U.S. Treasury Designates Two Individuals with Ties to al Qaida; UBL Former BIF Leader and al-Qaida Associate Named Under E.O. 13224', *The Office of Public Affairs*, 21 Dec. 2004, JS-2164, www.treas.gov/press/ releases/js2164.htm, accessed July 2005.

161  Peter Bergen, *Holy War Inc*, pp.91-2.

bin Laden in the mid-1990s. According to a US indictment, the ARC was set up by bin Laden in July 1994 as 'the London office of al Qaeda', and al-Fawwaz was put in charge of the bureau.[162] It was allegedly 'designed both to publicize the statements of Osama bin Laden and to provide a cover for activity in support of al Qaeda's "military" activities'.[163] In an interview with CNN in March 1997, bin Laden himself seemed to refer to this office when he stated that: 'I collaborated with some brothers and established a committee for offering advice and we started to publish some declarations'.[164] The establishment of ARC coincided with al-Suri's arrival in London, and the two were in close contact, according to journalists and US and Spanish investigators.[165] They lived almost next door, and Faw-waz introduced foreign journalists to al-Suri on several occasions.[166]

---

162  United States of America *v.* Usama Bin Laden, *et al.* Defendants (Kenyan Embassy Bombing), United States District Court, Southern District of New York, Indictment S(9) 98 Cr. 1023 (LBS), www.terrorismcentral. com/Library/Incidents/USEmbassyKenyaBombing/Indictment/ Introduction.html and www.terrorismcentral.com/Library/Incidents/ USEmbassyKenyaBombing/Indictment/Count1.html, accessed July 2006.

163  These 'military' activities allegedly included 'the recruitment of military trainees, the disbursement of funds and the procurement of necessary equipment (including satellite telephones) and necessary services. In addition, the London office served as a conduit for messages, including reports on military and security matters from various al Qaeda cells, including the Kenyan cell, to al Qaeda's headquarters.' See 'United States of America *v.* Usama Bin Laden, *et al.* Defendants (Kenyan Embassy Bombing), United States District Court, Southern District of New York, Indictment S(9) 98 Cr. 1023 (LBS), www.terrorismcentral.com/Library/ Incidents/USEmbassyKenyaBombing/Indictment/Introduction.html accessed July 2006.

164  'CNN March 1997 interview with Osama bin Laden', *FindLaw.com*, http:// fl1.findlaw.com/news.findlaw.com/cnn/docs/binladen/binladenintvw-cnn.pdf, accessed Oct. 2006.

165  Author's interview with Abdel Bari Atwan at *al-Quds al-Arabi* offices, London, 28 April 2006; author's interview with Camille Tawil, London, 14 Sept. 2006; and 'Juzgado Central de Instruccion no.005, Madrid, Sumario', 17 Sept. 2003.

166  Author's interview with Mark Huband, London, 29 April 2006; and

Their friendship is also evident from the way al-Suri spoke about al-Fawwaz in his 1999 interview with the Kuwaiti newspaper *al-Ra'y al-Amm*.[167]

According to statements given by L'Houssaine Kherchtou at the US trial following the East African Embassy bombings, al-Fawwaz had been the 'emir' of the Abu Baker Sadiq camp in Afghanistan in the early 1990s, before he moved to East Africa and later to London. Al-Fawwaz had allegedly facilitated the purchase of a satellite phone for bin Laden and its shipment to Afghanistan.[168] From this phone numerous calls were allegedly made to Britain by bin Laden himself and by his closest lieutenants. Among the alleged recipients of these calls was Khalid al-Fawwaz, according to US authorities.[169] These claims are hard to verify from public sources. Al-Fawwaz told journalists that he opposed the use of violence and stressed that he disagreed with bin Laden on many issues.[170] However, there is little doubt that Khalid al-Fawwaz was an important point of contact for those who wished to meet with bin Laden.

## NOMAN BENOTMAN AND THE LIBYAN
## ISLAMIC FIGHTING GROUP

Another of al-Suri's acquaintances in London was Nu'man bin Uthman, better known to the Western media as Noman Benotman. Born in Libya in 1967, he went to Peshawar and Afghanistan in late 1989 to fight with the Arab-Afghan resistance against the

author's interview with Peter Bergen, Washington, 1 Feb. 2007.

167   See, for example, 'Meeting with the Kuwaiti Newspaper', transcript of audiofile no.4, p.9.

168   Sean O'Neill, 'Worldwide trail of bloodshed that leads to suburban London', *The Daily Telegraph*, 19 Sept. 2001. and United States of America *vs* Osama Bin Laden, et al. Defendants (Kenya Embassy Bombing), transcript of trial, 21 February 2001, Day 8.

169   Nick Fielding, 'Al-Qaeda's Satellite Phone Records Revealed', *The Sunday Times*, 24 May 2002.

170   See Peter Bergen, *Holy War Inc.*, pp.209-10.

Communist regime in Kabul. Later, in 1994, he moved to Sudan, where he participated in the training of the newly established 'Libyan Islamic Fighting Group' (*al-jama'ah al-islamiyyah al-muqatilah bi-libya*, LIFG). LIFG was a jihadi movement established in the early 1990s, but which declared its existence only in October 1995. It was composed mostly of former Libyan veterans from Afghanistan, and aimed to overthrow President Mu'ammar al-Qaddafi's regime. Benotman rose to become a Shura Committee member and one of the LIFG's leaders. He left Sudan for London in October 1995, but visited Afghanistan when the LIFG founded camps there during the Taleban era.[171] Later, he resigned from the LIFG and turned to political activism, notably through founding the *Libya Human and Political Development Forum* in London. An ex-jihadi, he has become a frequently cited expert commentator in British media on issues related to al-Qaida.[172]

Benotman met repeatedly with al-Suri during the 1990s, mostly in London, and probably also in Afghanistan. He was one of al-Suri's acquaintances among the numerous top-level LIFG veterans who gathered in London from the mid-1990s onwards. Due to its hostility to the Libyan regime, the British government allegedly 'allowed LIFG to develop a base of logistical support and fundraising on its soil'.[173]

---

171 See interview with Benotman in Camille al-Tawil, 'Former Leading Figure in the Libyan Fighting Group Reveals New Information about the Qandahar Meetings and the Dispute about the Jihadis Exceeding their Rights *vis-à-vis* the Taleban' (in Arabic), *al-Hayat* (London), 1 Nov. 2006.

172 See interview with Benotman in Mahan Abedin, 'From Mujahid to Activist: An Interview with a Libyan Veteran of the Afghan Jihad', *Spotlight on Terror*, 3 (2) (22 March 2005), www.jamestown.org/terrorism/news/article.php?search=1&articleid=2369457, accessed Oct. 2006.

173 Cited in Gary Gambill, 'The Libyan Islamic Fighting Group (LIFG)', *Terrorism Monitor*, 3 (6) (24 March 2005), www.jamestown.org/publications_details.php?volume_id=411&issue_id=3275&article_id=2369477, accessed Oct. 2006.

Benotman recalls that al-Suri had managed to make a name for himself in the jihadi community with his book on the Syrian jihadi revolution, but unlike other jihadi figures who rose to prominence as leaders and clerics during the 1990s, al-Suri 'had no group, no organization, no specific place' to further his leadership ambitions; 'he commanded nobody, except himself'.[174] Benotman, himself a former member of a tight-knit, hierarchical *tanzim*-type group, viewed al-Suri's lack of organizational affiliation as his major weakness. This lessened his influence among the multitude of jihadi groups in Peshawar and Afghanistan where most still had a local or national orientation. Also, during al-Suri's second period in Afghanistan, after 1997 (see below), he was largely unsuccessful in establishing a sizeable base of followers.

Al-Suri's inclination for critical analysis and theoretical studies did not serve him well when he attempted to gather a following and attract a wider audience. According to Benotman, al-Suri was 'a born critic',[175] and invariably went too far in criticizing everyone. He subjected different groups and projects to such critical scrutiny that many were offended. Others thought that his lectures were too theoretical. His theories 'were not very practical and useful. They did not match the realities. He can't practice. He cannot walk the talk', Benotman recalls.[176]

Arriving in Afghanistan only in late 1989, Benotman recalls al-Suri mostly as a lecturer, not a military trainer. Al-Suri elaborated on the justifications for jihad; but he was most known for his vicious attacks on the Muslim Brotherhood clerics: 'he slandered them'.[177]

After Afghanistan, al-Suri returned to Spain; he visited al-Qaida and other jihadis in Sudan, where Benotman was also based in 1994-5. Both of them were in London from 1995 onwards. There, al-Suri established relations with a number of Islamists and jihadis, includ-

---

174  Author's interview with Noman Benotman, London, 15 Sept. 2006.

175  Ibid.

176  Ibid.

177  Ibid.

ing the LIFG leaders. He seems to have maintained his relationship with LIFG long after 9/11. In fact, he pays homage to Abu Layth al-Libi in *The Global Islamic Resistance Call*, published in December 2004.[178] At that time, al-Libi was the most senior LIFG Shura Council member still alive and still in Afghanistan.[179]

As the situation in Algeria deteriorated, al-Suri was anxious to coordinate a common jihadi position *vis-à-vis* the GIA leadership, especially with LIFG leaders and the EIJ. This was important, not least because the Algerian jihad, in its early phases, was considered a project that concerned many jihadi groups. According to Benotman, the LIFG had a small group of fighters inside Algeria, fighting with the GIA for a period of time, but under the emirate of Jamal Zaytuni (Abu Abd al-Rahman Amin) most of them were killed by the GIA.[180] LIFG was also part of the coordinated publication of declarations of renunciation against the GIA in 1996, when Abu Mus'ab al-Suri himself issued a communiqué.[181]

Al-Suri attributed great importance to his columns and articles in *al-Fajr*, the LIFG mouthpiece that was issued from London. Together with other jihadi bulletins, it helped cement a unity of purpose among the wider jihadi current: 'There was a lot of common ground between us' al-Suri recalls, with regards to 'the essence of jihadi thought and the fundamentals of the salafi-jihadi current'.[182] Benotman recalls al-Suri's articles in *al-Fajr*.[183] He mostly wrote 'theoreti-

---

178  *The Global Islamic Resistance Call*, p.10.

179  Author's interview with Noman Benotman, London, 15 Sept. 2006.

180  Ibid. See also Umar Abd al-Hakim, *A Summary of My Testimony*, p.22; and interview with Benotman in Mahan Abedin, 'From Mujahid to Activist: An Interview with a Libyan Veteran of the Afghan Jihad', *Spotlight on Terror* 3 (2) (22 March 2005), www.jamestown.org/terrorism/news/article. php?search=1&articleid=2369457, accessed Oct. 2006.

181  See Camille Tawil, 'The Egyptian "al-Jihad", the Libyan "Combatant Group", "Abu Qutadah" and "Abu Mus'ab" retract their support from the Algerian "Group",' (in Arabic), *al-Hayat* (London) 10 June 1996, p.6.

182  Umar Abd al-Hakim, *A Summary of My Testimony*, p.31.

183  Many of the latest issues are still available online via webarchive.org. See,

cal stuff', on long-term strategic issues, using one of his aliases, not Abu Mus'ab al-Suri.[184]

The fact that al-Suri always resorted to new nicknames and aliases was a reflection of his heightened security awareness, something that Benotman also recalls. Although he lectured in closed sessions from time to time, he reportedly avoided speaking in mosques. He once said that 'we are like mice [in London], we cannot act like heroes here'.[185] However, al-Suri wrote regularly in the relatively high-profile *al-Ansar Newsletter* and participated in the distribution of the magazine and other jihadi propaganda materials. According to al-Suri's official website, which contained an extensive list of his audiotaped lectures, al-Suri had given at least two lectures in Britain in the mid-1990s. The first, 'The Righteous Call for Jihad in Algeria', took place in 1993 and consisted of three audio cassettes; the second was held in Manchester in 1995, with the title 'The Jihadi Trend at a Historical Turning Point: The Revival (*sahwah*) from Descent to Ascent'.[186] Judging by the website, the lecture seems to have been held at a meeting organized by the LIFG.[187]

---

for example, searches for www.al-fajr.net.

184  Author's interview with Noman Benotman, London, 15 Sept. 2006.

185  Ibid.

186  According to the website, the two lectures are placed under the subheading 'audiotape collection Britain'. The place for the first audiotape is not given. See 'The Old Production of Shaykh Abu Mus'ab al-Suri, 1987-2001' (in Arabic), *Abu Mus'ab al-Suri's website*, www.fsboa.com/vw/index.php, accessed Sept. 2005; and Gary Gambill, 'The Libyan Islamic Fighting Group (LIFG)', *Terrorism Monitor*, 3 (6) (March 24, 2005), http://jamestown.org/publications_details.php?volume_id=411&issue_id=3275&article_id=2369477, accessed Oct. 2006.

187  According to the website, 'the *al-muqatilah* lost the audio-cassette'. LIFG was known to have a sizeable presence in Manchester in addition to London. See 'The Old Production of Shaykh Abu Mus'ab al-Suri, 1987-2001' (in Arabic), *Abu Mus'ab al-Suri's website*, www.fsboa.com/vw/index.php, accessed Sept. 2005; and Gary Gambill, 'The Libyan Islamic Fighting Group (LIFG)', *Terrorism Monitor* 3 (6) (March 24, 2005), http://jamestown.org/publications_details.php?volume_id=411&issue_id=3275&article_id=2369477, accessed Oct. 2006.

Among the jihadi community, many thought it was ridiculous to observe tight security precautions while at the same time giving lectures and distributing cassettes. 'This was why some people said he was acting as if he was James Bond', Benotman recalled.[188] On at least one occasion, he was profiled with his full real name in *al-Hayat*, the largest Arab newspaper in London, an episode which incensed him.[189] Al-Suri feared the revelation of his real name would expose his relatives in Syria to harassment and intimidation from the authorities.[190]

Another reason why it proved difficult for al-Suri to attract many followers later in Afghanistan was the fact that he was not an observant salafi. Unlike Abu Qutadah and many others, he had gruff manners; he would swear and denounce improperly dressed women as 'whores' and 'prostitutes'; in short, he did not adhere to the code of conduct for a true salafi.[191] The dislike was mutual. Benotman recalls that al-Suri could not operate with the salafis; he considered them as being too narrow-minded, too restricted in their thinking: 'They cannot think outside the box'.[192]

Being a military strategist, more than an ideological-religious cleric, al-Suri also faced criticism for citing Western, and even leftist, sources in his lectures on guerrilla warfare theory.[193] In fact, the most important item on his guerrilla warfare curriculum appears to have

---

188   Author's interview with Noman Benotman, London, 15 Sept. 2006. See also Umar Abd al-Hakim, *A Summary of My Testimony*, p.58.

189   See, for example, 'Algeria: The FIS accuses the GIA of trying to impose its influence on them with force (in Arabic), *al-Hayat* 24 May 1994; and Jamal Khashoggi, 'Abu Mus'ab al-Suri was in the Syrian Combatant Vanguard and was expelled from the Muslim Brotherhood' (in Arabic) *al-Hayat* 14 Jan. 1996.

190   Author's interview with Camille Tawil, London, 3 Jan. 2007.

191   Author's interview, Sept. 2006. Name and place withheld on request.

192   Author's interview with Noman Benotman, London, 15 Sept. 2006.

193   See 'The Management and Organization of Guerrilla Warfare by Shaykh Umar Abd al-Hakim' (in Arabic), transcript of lectures given in Khowst, Afghanistan, 1998, p.4.

been an Arabic translation of Robert Taber's *The War of The Flea. A Study of Guerrilla Warfare Theory and Practice* (1965). During his second stay in Afghanistan, from 1998 onwards, he gave many lectures based solely on this book.[194]

In Benotman's eyes, al-Suri was a man in search of a role for himself. He offered his services as bin Laden's media adviser, but critics claim that he simply imposed himself. In the mid-1990s, bin Laden already had a media adviser named Abu Walid, a professional journalist, who had lived in Kabul since 1977.[195] Benotman dismisses reports in the press that al-Suri supervised several training camps in Afghanistan, or that he took part personally in the screening and interrogation of newly arrived recruits. Al-Qaida was not alone in Taleban-ruled Afghanistan. In fact, dozens of jihadi groups had a presence, and every one had its own structures in place to cover every conceivable topic, including media, training, security, counter-intelligence and so on. It would be 'ridiculous' for them to invite an outsider like al-Suri to take care of such sensitive matters: 'Every group had their own tradition, methods, etc. They did not refer to nobody! It was a matter of sovereignty,' Benotman recalls.[196] Precisely for this reason, al-Suri was also unsuccessful in his media project, the 'Bureau for the Study of Islamic Conflicts' in London: it depended on the willingness of other jihadi groups to share their news items with him first and thereby relinquish an important part of their media strategy to al-Suri's media bureau.

In Benotman's view, al-Suri's writings are unlikely to have had great impact on Muslim youths. Recruitment to jihadi groups 'always begins with the spiritual stuff', not with the strategic works à la *The Global Islamic Resistance Call*. What inspires youth to join jihadi groups are 'big events' which enrage Muslim opinion, and 'religious

---

194 The Arabic translation was entitled 'War of the Oppressed'. See Abu Mus'ab al-Suri, 'Explanation of the Book "War of the Oppressed"' (in Arabic), Transcript of lectures given in Khowst, Afghanistan, 1998.

195 Author's interview with Noman Benotman, London, 15 Sept. 2006.

196 Ibid.

teaching'. After this phase, it is 'the tactics of the specific group' that counts, not literature by a non-aligned writer.[197]

Benotman is also sceptical of the viability of al-Suri's theories regarding autonomous cells and 'the jihad of individual terrorism' outside the framework of a *tanzim*, a secret organization (see final chapter).[198] Such a struggle cannot be militarily effective, he argues. At its height in the early and mid-1990s, the LIFG used to be on the look out for small 'local groups' (*jama'at mahalliyyah*) who had formed on their own inside Libya in order to recruit them into the organization. However, they had to watch out for intemperate, autodidact type individuals who wished to start operating at once with little or no preparation. They were 'a security hazard', Benotman recalls.[199]

The criticism of al-Suri's strategies and thinking by someone of Benotman's standing is striking, given the ideological affinity which al-Suri obviously felt with LIFG during the 1990s. However, al-Suri drew his own lessons from the slow demise of LIFG. By the end of 2004, when his *opus magnum* was completed, the LIFG-led uprising in Libya had long been crushed. Numerous leading LIFG members had been rounded up, jailed or deported to Libya, including its top two leaders, Abdallah Sadiq and Abu Mundhir al-Sa'adi. A number of LIFG members left the organization to join al-Qaida, and LIFG became a banned terrorist entity in most countries, despite its condemnation of 9/11 and its profession that its jihad was limited to Libya. The nationally-confined and guerrilla warfare-oriented approach adopted by the LIFG had failed. The total failure of one of the most classic *jihadi tanzim*s in the Arab world, despite its many

---

197 Ibid.

198 For more on these concepts, see the excerpts included in this book or consult my previous study, 'Abu Mus'ab al-Suri: Profile of a Jihadi Leader', paper presented at 'The Changing Faces of Jihadism: Profiles, Biographies, Motivations', Joint FFI/King's College Conference, London, 27-8 April 2006, www.mil.no/multimedia/archive/00080/Abu_Musab_al-Suri_-_80483a.pdf.

199 Author's interview with Noman Benotman, London, 15 Sept. 2006.

foreign sanctuaries, well-trained cadres and an erratic and inept enemy, must only have reinforced al-Suri in his belief in the need for a completely new war fighting doctrine.

# 8

# IN THE SERVICE OF THE TALEBAN

## LEAVING LONDONISTAN

Al-Suri's involvement with the GIA and bin Laden attracted increased attention from the British security services, especially in the wake of the GIA bombing campaign in France in the mid-1990s, and bin Laden's rise to prominence in global terrorism in 1996. French authorities had long pushed for tougher British measures against GIA's supporters in London. In 1996, the US State Department characterized bin Laden as 'the most significant financial sponsor of Islamic extremist activities in the world today'.[1] The British authorities began to exert a 'certain pressure' on al-Suri, and he noticed that he was under surveillance.[2] In late 1995, following the publication of a thinly disguised call in the *al-Ansar Newsletter* to attack the Eiffel Tower, al-Suri was briefly detained and questioned by the British authorities.[3] Al-Suri later recalled how his house had been 'violently raided and searched' by the British police shortly after dawn.[4]

---

1     Cited in Peter Bergen, *Holy War Inc.*, p.2.

2     'Juzgado Central de Instruccion no.005, Madrid, Sumario', 17 Sept. 2003, pp.28, 435.

3     'Timeline of Mustafa Setmarian Nasar's activities', *Associated Press*, 3 Aug. 2005; and Katherine Shrader, 'Wanted Muslim extremist hopscotches the globe connecting terrorists', *Associated Press*, 3 Aug. 2005.

4     Umar Abd al-Hakim (Abu Mus'ab al-Suri), 'Message to the British and the Europeans – Its People and Governments – regarding the London Explosions, July 2005' (in Arabic), Aug. 2005, p.15.

In 1999, al-Suri recalled 'the media campaign' against him and his supporters by the Arab press,[5] which he believed was continued subsequently in the French media. Al-Suri felt threatened; he interpreted the Arab press campaign as a call for 'revenge', blaming him personally for the atrocities in Algeria.[6] He was also exposed to 'much hardship'. The British anti-terrorism police sought him out regularly-'every week or every ten days'-showing him Arab press articles about him and asking him to explain himself.[7] Even though he had won his libel case against *al-Hayat*, he concluded that his time in London was coming to an end.

Given the new security situation, al-Suri felt that he and his colleagues would not be able to achieve much more through his media office. If they continued to write about and for the jihadi movement, al-Suri realised that their office would either be closed or that they might be arrested, and for all practical purposes, 'we would be silenced, and we would only be permitted to write useless publications, like the writings of the Muslim Brothers'.[8] Fearing permanent imprisonment in Britain, al-Suri closed his media office and relocated to Afghanistan in July-August 1997, following the Taleban's seizure of Kabul and the return of the al-Qaida leadership to Afghanistan in May 1996.[9]

When he later looked back upon his time in London, al-Suri saw the late 1990s as a turning point for European Muslims in general

---

5    Ibid.

6    'Meeting with the Kuwaiti Newspaper', transcript of audiofile no.2, p.4.

7    Ibid. and no.5, p.2. This is partly confirmed by a former CIA official who noted that al-Suri spoke with the British Intelligence. Interview with Michael Scheuer, Washington, 14 March 2007.

8    Ibid., no.2, p.4.

9    'Biography of Shaykh Umar Abd al-Hakim (Abu Mus'ab al-Suri)' (in Arabic), p.3; 'Meeting with the Kuwaiti Newspaper', transcript of audiofile, no.2, p.4; Umar Abd al-Hakim, *Afghanistan, the Taliban, and the Battle of Islam Today*, (in Arabic), p.2; Umar Abd al-Hakim, *A Summary of My Testimony*, p.20; and 'Juzgado Central de Instruccion no.005, Madrid, Sumario', 17 Sept. 2003, p.27.

and the jihadi movement in Europe in particular. He claims to have sensed 'the beginning of a crisis', and that the repression of the Islamists and the jihadis was only the beginning of a process in which the entire Muslim diaspora in Europe would come under much harsher oppression.[10] The period of 'temporary safe havens' in the West was coming to an end: US-led international anti-terrorism coordination efforts were intensifying, Arab regimes were stepping up their efforts to have their wanted fugitives handed over, and Britain was moving closer to the US position on terrorism. In his usual satirical style, al-Suri noted that Britain of the late 1990s was losing 'its democratic virginity' following its marriage to 'the American cowboy'.[11] Al-Suri called upon other Muslims to follow his example and leave Europe,[12] but his appeal fell on deaf ears. In his later writings, he deplored the fact that so few Muslims had opted for making *hijrah* or 'emigration' to Afghanistan.

When al-Suri relocated to Afghanistan in 1997, he was well-prepared, having visited the country on several occasions in previous years. According to his own words, he had carried out 'a fact-finding mission' to the Taleban government some time in mid 1996. Based on this tour, he wrote a 35-page report, entitled *The Taleban*, in cooperation with the media office of the EIJ in London. Al-Suri returned for another 'fact-finding visit' in late 1996 or early 1997 after which he decided to emigrate and settle there permanently.[13] It is possible that some of these fact-finding trips were the same occasions as the tours during which he accompanied Channel 4 and CNN reporters.

---

10   'Meeting with the Kuwaiti Newspaper', transcript of audiofile no.2, p.4.

11   *The Global Islamic Resistance Call*, p.56.

12   'Meeting with the Kuwaiti Newspaper', transcript of audiofile no.2, p.4.

13   The exact dates for these fact-finding tours are not known. Al-Suri believed that they took place in April and Dec. 1996, but he is inconsistent when discussing precisely when these tours took place. See 'Umar 'Abd al-Hakim, *Afghanistan, Taliban and the Battle for Islam Today*, p.2; and 'Meeting with the Kuwaiti Newspaper', transcript of audiofile no.2, pp.4-5.

When he later explained his reasons for leaving the comfort of London for the Islamic Emirate of Afghanistan, he emphasized bin Laden's own move there and his declarations of war on the Americans in August 1996 and February 1998. According to al-Suri, bin Laden had pointed to the right enemy when he called upon the entire Islamic nation to confront the United States. Al-Suri later wrote that these ideas:

were very close to the ideas that had matured gradually in my mind since the Gulf War in 1990. This became clear to me after a series of conversations with him and with people close to him during my visit to them in 1996. I saw in this [...] a real opportunity to redirect the confrontation in the right direction. Shaykh Osama bin Laden had the position and the history, [...] the resources and personal abilities as a symbol to realize this confrontation, as I understood it at that time. And I wished to contribute by being present in this confrontation which would be launched from Afghanistan.[14]

People who knew al-Suri in London also believe that the 1998 declaration by the 'World Islamic Front' also played a role in persuading him to settle permanently in Afghanistan. The declaration seemed like 'a new effort at unifying the jihadi groups', which appealed to al-Suri.[15] At the same time, however, al-Suri had serious reservations about the way bin Laden had announced this new alliance (see below).

It is possible that al-Suri also had a hint about the upcoming East African Embassy bombings in August 1998 and that he wished to avoid further security risks by staying in London. At the time, Ayman al-Zawahiri had issued several calls to the jihadis to move to Afghanistan.[16] It is likely that this influenced al-Suri's decision. He was very close to those who ran the EIJ's media office in London. Finally, the compensation al-Suri received after settling his libel case

---

14   *The Global Islamic Resistance Call*, p.57.

15   Author's interview with Noman Benotman, London, 15 Sept. 2006.

16   Author's interview with Camille Tawil, London, 2 Jan. 2007.

against *al-Hayat* made it possible for him to finance his relocation to Afghanistan and establish a new media center there.[17]

In August 1997, al-Suri arrived in Qandahar, Afghanistan, later making Kabul his headquarters, and reportedly brought his family over later that year or in 1998.[18] His wife, Elena Moreno, told her parents that they were moving to Pakistan, where al-Suri would work as the editor of a news magazine. She declined to give them her address or telephone number, telling them that it was for their own safety.[19] During this period, al-Suri's family grew, and the couple now had four children. The newcomers were born at a clinic in Islamabad, Pakistan. One of them was a son named Osama.[20]

Life in Kabul was hard for the family, especially for his Spanish-born wife. Al-Suri himself hints about this in his writings, although one gets a sense that he has added extra drama and pathos to his biographical account: 'Their house was located only 12 km away from the frontline. His wife could hear the bombs and artillery shells exploding, and she used to cry every morning when she brought their four children to him so that he could kiss them farewell when he

---

17  Umar Abd al-Hakim, *A Summary of My Testimony*, p.56.

18  The sources are contradictory on the exact date for the family's transfer to Pakistan/Afghanistan. See, for example, José María Irujo, 'El hombre de Bin Laden en Madrid', *El País*, 2 March 2005, www.elPaís.es/comunes/ 2005/11m/08_comision/libro_electronico_red_islam/red_islamista_ 01%20doc.pdf, accessed July 2006, p.17; and 'WANTED: Mustafa Setmariam Nasar', *Reward for Justice website*, www.rewardsforjustice. net/english/wanted_captured/index.cfm?page=Nasar, accessed July 2005.

19  José María Irujo, 'El hombre de Bin Laden en Madrid', *El País*, 2 March 2005, www.elPaís.es/comunes/2005/11m/08_comision/libro_electronico_ red_islam/red_islamista_01%20doc.pdf, accessed July 2006, p.17.

20  *The Global Islamic Resistance Call*, p.833; Antonio Rubio, 'Mustafa Setmarian Naser: Un español en la cima de Al Qaeda: Durante los diez años que vivió en España se convirtió en lugarteniente de Bin Laden', *elmundo.es*, 3 Nov. 2005, www.elmundo.es/elmundo/2005/11/03/espana/1131002447.html, accessed Dec. 2005; and José María Irujo, 'El fundador de Al Qaeda en España está preso en una cárcel secreta de la CIA', *El País*, 15 Oct. 2006, p.1, 18-19.

left for the frontline.'[21] Due to the hardships of Kabul, it appears that al-Suri moved his family away from the city and in interviews his wife says she stayed mostly on the Pakistani side of the border.[22] Her parents last heard from their son-in-law after Baltasar Garzón issued an indictment against him and the Abu Dahdah cell in 2003. Al-Suri had then sworn that he had been falsely accused and vowed to write to Garzón to clear his name 'and explain everything'.[23] Al-Suri remained in Afghanistan till the fall of the Taleban regime in late 2001.

## TALEBAN: THE TRUE ISLAMIC EMIRATE

Al-Suri described his return to Afghanistan as 'a voluntary exile' and a *hijrah* or 'emigration', using the same term that is used to describe the Prophet's relocation to Medina in 622, following his and his followers' increased harassment and persecution in Mecca.[24] Al-Suri clearly considered the Taleban rule to be truly 'an Islamic state', to which *hijrah* was legitimate. He also described the Taleban as 'the best example of an Islamic state on earth today'.[25]

Al-Suri wrote extensively about the Taleban in the late 1990s. After he had completed the first report in cooperation with the EIJ media office in 1996, he published a second study in October 1998. It was a 131-page book entitled *Afghanistan, the Taleban, and the Battle of Islam Today*, an assessment of the Taleban's rule, from a

---

21 *The Global Islamic Resistance Call*, pp.833-4.

22 See, for example, José Maria Irujo, 'Setmarian, en el limbo judicial', *El País* 18 Nov. 2005, p.20.

23 Cited in José María Irujo, 'El hombre de Bin Laden en Madrid', *El País* 2 March 2005, www.elPaís.es/comunes/2005/11m/08_comision/libro_electronico_red_islam/red_islamista_01%20doc.pdf, accessed July 2006, p.19.

24 'Meeting with the Kuwaiti Newspaper', transcript of audiofile no.2, p.4.

25 Ibid., p.5.

jihadi perspective. Excerpts from the work have later been published by al-Qaida's key media outlets.[26]

In his assessment al-Suri judged that the Taleban must be considered 'a legitimate Islamic Emirate in Afghanistan', despite some shortcomings in their implementation of Islamic law (*shari'ah*).[27] His criticism of the group focused on their policy of tolerating, at least to some extent, the popular practices of praying at tombs of saints (*pirs*), holy men, and other venerated personalities, a religious practice frowned upon by the Arab salafis in al-Qaida.[28] These shortcomings were either caused by ignorance in certain religious matters, or by urgent necessity, al-Suri argued, and they were not sufficient to invalidate the status of the Taleban as a legitimate Emirate. Second, al-Suri observed many estimable qualities in the Taleban leadership in terms of religious observance, piety, and knowledge. He had met many senior Taleban officials, and he was particularly struck with their modesty and aversion to modern luxury. For example, all Taleban officials had reportedly committed themselves not to use the chairs in the government buildings they had taken over in Kabul, but preferred to sit on the floor. This was because 'they did not want to sit on the former infidels and apostates' chairs. They let the luxurious offices be vacant.'[29] Al-Suri also knew the Afghan situation and its guerrilla commanders very well from his first period in Afghanistan in the late 1980s and early 1990s. In his opinion, the Taleban commanders were far better leaders than the previous mujahidin commanders and warlords. They were also much better

---

26  See for example 'Abu Mus'ab al-Suri's description of the Afghanistan Reality', in Yusuf bin Salih al-Ayri, *The Taliban Movement in the Balance* (in Arabic) dated Nov. 2001 and published by *markaz al-dirasat wa'l-buhuth al-islamiyyah* ('Center for Islamic Studies and Research'), accessed at *jihad online al-ikhbariyya*, www.jehad.net, 3 May 2002.

27  'Meeting with the Kuwaiti Newspaper', transcript of audiofile no.2, p.5.

28  See 'Abu Musab al-Suri's description of the Afghanistan Reality'.

29  Umar Abd al-Hakim, *Afghanistan, the Taleban and the Battle of Islam Today* (in Arabic), p.26.

'neighbours' to the Arab-Afghan community than their predecessors had ever been.[30]

Al-Suri's assessment of the Taleban was clearly coloured by the Arab-Afghan experiences with the new Afghan government after the fall of Kabul in 1992. Rivalries between Afghan warlords had escalated into fratricidal infighting and civil war during the first half of the 1990s. Furthermore, the new authorities in Kabul reportedly signed agreements with Egypt 'to hand over terrorists' present on Afghan territory, even though these were people who had fought for the Afghan mujahidin.[31] In al-Suri's view, former warlords were only interested in the Arabs' money, weaponry and material support, and had little ideological or religious sympathy for the wider cause. On the contrary, they had in reality become a vehicle for 'The Crusaders'.[32] The Taleban, on the other hand, had not benefited from the Arab-Afghan war effort, since they emerged on the scene only around 1994. They had, nevertheless, extended much help to the Arab-Afghan community. When the Taleban came to power, the Arab-Afghans were merely refugees and immigrants, and only a tiny shadow of the 40,000 or so strong Arab contingent (al-Suri's estimate), that went to Afghanistan during the Afghan liberation war.

In his praise of the Taleban, there was also a warning to the Afghan-Arab presence. Although al-Suri did not explicitly criticize bin Laden and other Arab-Afghan leaders in his interview with the Kuwaiti newspaper in early 1999, he took the opportunity to 'advise his brothers' about making better use of this 'second round' in Afghanistan, especially in view of their 'bitter experiences' from the first Afghan war, when they 'only benefited very little'.[33] In al-Suri's view, the issue was larger than that of simply having a sanctuary where the jihadi movement could build bases, train and educate its members, etc. For the first time in modern history,

---

30   'Meeting with the Kuwaiti Newspaper', transcript of audiofile no.2, p.5.

31   Ibid., p.6.

32   Ibid.

33   Ibid.

a state has been established based upon Islamic law. It may be qualified to be a true place for emigration for Muslims. People have to deal with this in a manner that goes beyond the issue of refuge, training or what have you. The real issue is that there is a state which will be established now.[34]

In al-Suri's view, a geopolitical alliance had formed itself against the Taleban, consisting of Russia, Iran, the United States and its 'colony states' in Central Asia. They came together in order to restore the balance of power which had been disrupted by the rise of the Taleban in Kabul: 'the presence of the Taleban threatens to explode the region and cause the repetition of many Afghan Taleban entities throughout Central Asia', al-Suri argued.[35]

In a booklet he published roughly at the same time, entitled *The Muslims in Central Asia and the Coming Battle of Islam*, he further elaborated on the Taleban's role in the future struggle. According to al-Suri's thinking the Islamic Emirate in Afghanistan should be consolidated as one of three main bases from which jihadi efforts should be directed with a view to creating similar emirates in other Arab and Islamic countries:

We have mentioned that this wave of resistance must have areas on which to rely and the most important areas to strengthen and reinforce will be a) Central Asia, b) Yemen and c) North Africa. A strong Afghanistan, Central Asia, and the spread of jihad there is the first and most important of these bases. This is neither a military nor a security secret. Our enemy knows it. For this reason, the enemy seeks to strike at it and expel us from it and we have to strive to consolidate our position and defend it and establish similar emirates in Yemen and Northern Africa and Morocco. Now, the opportunities for this are present, and we have to unify the jihad and avoid errors which will prevent us from achieving this.[36]

---

34  Ibid.

35  Ibid.

36  Cited in Umar Abd al-Hakim (Abu Mus'ab al-Suri), *The Muslims in Central Asia and the Coming Battle of Islam* (in Arabic) (Kabul: The al-Ghuraba Center for Islamic Studies, 5 Nov. 1999, The Series Issues for the Triumphant in Righteousness no.3), p.20.

Such a proliferation of emirates would not merely be a catastrophe for Russia, al-Suri predicted, but also for the United States. The 'World Order' would never accept a state ruled by Islamic law, he argued, since such a state had its own civilization and its own ideology, independent of the World Order. For this reason, it was imperative for the US and the neighboring countries to isolate the Taleban government as much as possible. These factors were, in al-Suri's view, a more likely explanation of the animosity which the US and the West displayed towards the Taleban than the latter's hospitality towards the Arab-Afghan mujahidin community. Even without the Afghan-Arabs' presence, Taleban rule would have been unacceptable to the international community.[37]

In his 1999 interview, al-Suri downplayed the international pressure on the Taleban to expel suspected terrorists who were being sheltered by the Arab-Afghan community. This pressure was 'not very strong', and he did not expect it to lead anywhere. The mujahidin were not numerous; and al-Suri correctly anticipated that the Taleban would only grow more intransigent in response to increased international pressure.[38] The situation deteriorated from late 1999 onwards, after international sanctions were imposed. In mid-2000, after much arm-twisting by the United States and Pakistan, a number of the foreign camps were temporarily closed. In the mounting conflict between the geopolitical realities facing the Taleban and bin Laden's ambition to wage a global jihad from Afghanistan through high profile media appearances and spectacular acts of violence, al-Suri came to side with the host rather than the guest. One should give highest priority to preserving the Islamic Emirate and avoid rash and erratic actions that would endanger the survival of the Taleban regime, he claimed. His outspokenness on this issue and other issues brought him into conflict with al-Qaida's leadership. Another contentious issue in the Arab-Afghan community, in which al-Suri was actively involved on bin Laden's side, revolved around whether or not

---

37  'Meeting with the Kuwaiti Newspaper', transcript of audiofile no.2, p.6.
38  Ibid.

the Taleban regime was a legitimate Islamic state and whether it was right for the Arab-Afghans to fight 'under its banner', which in practical terms meant participating in the Taleban's war efforts against the Northern Alliance. Letters and other documents retrieved from Arab-Afghan training camps, guesthouses, and computers illustrate that many Arab volunteers strongly disapproved of the Taleban, viewed them as backward and ignorant, and were reluctant to fight for their cause. In one letter, an Arab-Afghan fighter noted condescendingly that 'the Taliban's mentality is based on fabrications, wrongdoing, beating around the bush and running away from reality'.[39] Another letter described the Taleban as being 'created and controlled by Pakistan' and accused them of being 'extremists of the Sufi sect and straying from the right path'.[40] In both letters the authors inveighed against the Taleban's requests to join the United Nations (only Saudi Arabia, the UAE and Pakistan recognized the Taleban as the government of Afghanistan), a request which represented 'infidelity' because it revealed a willingness to make agreements with infidels. Al-Suri himself described the views among his fellow Arab jihadis in Afghanistan towards the Taleban as varying from 'total rejection, especially among the so-called salafis, to support'.[41]

While doctrinal and political reasons clearly played a role, 'the widespread contempt' for the Taleban in the Arab-Afghan community stemmed from the fact that they 'found Afghanistan such an inhospitable place: primitive, backward, dirty and chaotic', according to Andrew Higgins, a *Wall Street Journal* reporter, who reviewed hundreds of documents retrieved from a computer in Kabul used

39 See Document no.AFGP-2002-602181, 'Political Speculation', *Combating Terrorism Center website* (West Point), www.ctc.usma.edu/aq/AFGP-2002-602181-Trans.pdf and www.ctc.usma.edu/aq/AFGP-2002-602181-Original.pdf, accessed April 2006.

40 Document no.AFGP-2002-601693, 'Status of Jihad'. *Combating Terrorism Center website* (West Point), www.ctc.usma.edu/aq/AFGP-2002-601693-Trans.pdf and www.ctc.usma.edu/aq/AFGP-2002-601693-Orig.pdf, accessed April 2006.

41 *The Global Islamic Resistance Call*, p.59.

by several al-Qaida leaders.[42] Still, the ideological dispute over the Taleban's Islamic credentials must be treated with due seriousness, because it made many jihadis consider the Islamic Emirate as simply another temporary safe haven, not a kernel or a starting point for the coming Islamic Caliphate. This opened up a serious cleavage in the Arab-Afghan diaspora regarding the way forward.

Al-Suri was convinced that the Taleban regime was worth fighting for and offered his services. Abdel Bari Atwan, the Arab news editor who met with him several times in the mid- and late 1990s, recalls that al-Suri had telephoned him in late 1997 or 1998, saying that he had stopped working for al-Qaida, and that instead he now served as a media adviser for the Taleban.[43] Due to his differences with the al-Qaida leadership, he could obviously not afford also to be on bad terms with the Afghan government, but there was clearly a strong ideological component behind his decision. Al-Suri became the spokesman for a current of thinking that advocated paying allegiance to Mullah Omar, the Taleban's supreme leader and working directly with the Taleban authorities.[44] Already in 1998, he was travelling from one training camp to the other, giving speeches and inciting the mujahidin emigrant community to fight with the Taleban and defend Kabul when it came under attack.[45] However, his relationship with the Taleban expanded gradually, and it was only in early 2000 that he met with Mullah Omar and swore an oath of allegiance to

---

42    Email correspondence with Andrew Higgins, a *Wall Street Journal* reporter who was able to access a computer used by al-Zawahiri and other al-Qaida members in Kabul. See also list of 'al-Qaida Documents Reportedly Uncovered in Afghanistan' in the bibliography.

43    Author's interview with Abdel Bari Atwan, London, 28 April 2006.

44    'Abu Mus'ab al-Suri's Communiqué to the British and Europeans regarding the London Bombings in July 2006', *Middle East Transparent* website, 23 Dec. 2005, www.metransparent.com/texts/abu_massab_ assuri_communique_calling_for_terror_in_europe.htm, accessed Oct. 2006.

45    Umar Abd al-Hakim, *Afghanistan, the Taleban and the Battle of Islam Today* (in Arabic), no.1, p.42.

him.[46] From then on, he 'maintained extensive relations with Mullah Omar', according to Spanish court documents.[47] According to one source, al-Suri used to spend many hours sitting with the Taleban leader at the latter's office in Qandahar.[48]

As for the controversy over the Taleban's Islamic credentials, al-Suri vigorously defended the Emirate. Seeing himself as a jihadi strategist, theoretician, and thinker, rather than an ideologue and a cleric, al-Suri had always displayed pragmatism and leniency vis-à-vis non-adherence to the strict salafi code of conduct as long as the zeal and determination to fight a jihad were beyond doubt. It was these qualities that he found among the Taleban. He too had been accused of 'innovation' by the hard-line salafis in the GIA's London cell, while al-Suri's quarrel with Abu Qutadah partly reflected this clash between salafis and jihadis (see chapter 7).

In the debate about the Islamic legitimacy of the Taleban, al-Suri was clearly an active participant, judging by letters and documents uncovered in Afghanistan after the US-led invasion. In one letter discussing the 'Taleban's infidelity' he was accused of having written a long research paper stating that 'it is permissible to fight under the banner of infidelity', supporting his opinion with quotes from here and there.[49] In other correspondence, his name arose when the Tale-

---

46  At the time of interview by the Kuwaiti newspaper *al-Ra'y al-'Amm* in April 1999, he had not yet met with Mullah Omar. See 'Meeting with the Kuwaiti Newspaper', transcript of audiofile no.2, p.5; and 'Communiqué from the Office of Abu Mus'ab al-Suri' (in Arabic), 22 Dec. 2004, p.7.

47  'Juzgado Central de Instruccion no.005, Madrid, Sumario', 17 Sept. 2003, p.28.

48  José María Irujo, 'El hombre de Bin Laden en Madrid', *El País*, 2 March 2005, www.elPaís.es/comunes/2005/11m/08_comision/libro_electronico_red_islam/red_islamista_01%20doc.pdf, accessed July 2006, p.18. See also Paul Cruickshank and Mohannad Hage Ali, 'Abu Musab Al Suri: Architect of the New Al Qaeda', p.5.

49  Document no.AFGP-2002-601693, 'Status of Jihad'. *Combating Terrorism Center website* (West Point), www.ctc.usma.edu/aq/AFGP-2002-601693-Trans.pdf and www.ctc.usma.edu/aq/AFGP-2002-601693-Orig.pdf, accessed April 2006.

ban's request for UN membership was condemned.[50] Al-Suri's book on the Taleban regime was also referred to by al-Qaida trainees.[51]

One place where this ideological conflict apparently raged was during training at Khalden camp where Ibn Shaykh al-Libi was the commander (see below). During the mid and late 1990s, it was regarded as an entry-level camp where a large number of militants of various nationalities received military and ideological training, before some of them moved on to more specialised camps. At the time of the rise of the Taleban in 1995-96, there had been very tense relations between the Arab base commanders and the Afghans in general and the Taleban in particular, according to one eye witness account.[52] The camp commanders feared that the Taleban would close the camps and disarm them. Furthermore, the revulsion over Afghan religious practices was particularly strong, and Arab trainees were forbidden to speak to the Afghans.

Another Arab-Afghan veteran who attended Khalden camp from 1996 onwards also recalls the strong anti-Taleban sentiments there, especially at the *Institute for the Faith Brigades* (ma'had kata'ib al-iman), located next to the camp.[53] This aversion also translated into

---

50  The letter stated: 'We saw, through the story of the Syrian brother Abi-Mos'ab and others, how they were making insignificant excuses in order to continue requesting a seat at the United Nations. Once they declare, "We only need the seat to prompt the countries of the world to acknowledge us," they consider that as a license to have rights. Meanwhile, they say "This is a rotten organization; let's send a bad man." Where can we find people who are able to challenge the world [to recognize that] destroying the idols that were left behind is not as great a sin as joining the United Nations?' Cited in Document no.AFGP-2002-602181, 'Political Speculation', *Combating Terrorism Center website* (West Point), www.ctc.usma.edu/aq/AFGP-2002-602181-Trans.pdf and www.ctc.usma.edu/aq/AFGP-2002-602181-Original.pdf, accessed April 2006.

51  See Document no.AFGP-2002-801138, 'Various Admin Documents and Questions', www.ctc.usma.edu/aq/AFGP-2002-801138-Trans.pdf, p.45, and www.ctc.usma.edu/aq/AFGP-2002-801138-Orig.pdf, accessed April 2006, p.50 (translation).

52  Omar Nasiri, *Inside the Global Jihad* (London: Hurst, 2006), p.xii.

53  I am indebted to my colleague Truls Hallberg Tønnessen for this

an anti-bin Laden attitude when the latter's alliance with the Taleban was consolidated. The students at the Institute, who were mostly North African jihadis, began publicizing bin Laden's 'misguided errors', especially the fact that he fought with the Taleban, many of whom were 'immersed in the greatest of sins'.[54] This agitation against the Taleban and al-Qaida led to heavy pressure being placed on the Khalden camp administration to discipline the radicals. While some of the radicals chose to leave the camp, others began changing their views about the Taleban. This shift came partly as a result of al-Suri's efforts in propagating the case for the Taleban. Together with other leading jihadis, such as Abu Layth al-Libi, a leading LIFG member, he was instrumental in persuading them to accept al-Qaida's policy of fighting for the Taleban.[55]

Al-Suri's advocacy of the Taleban cause took many forms. He seems to have worked actively to reduce tensions which arose among the Arab-Afghan community over the Taleban's policies, especially with regards to the latter's imposition of greater control over the training camps.[56] He also attempted to calm anti-Taleban sentiments by interviewing bin Laden about al-Qaida's relationship with the Taleban. The interview was held some time in 1998 or 1999, and was probably undertaken as part of al-Suri's work for the Taleban's

---

information and for locating these memoirs on the web (see reference below).

54    Their criticism of bin Laden also included his relationship with Sudan and leading politicians in Pakistan. They also accused a leading figure in al-Qaida's juridical committee, Abu Hafs al-Mawritani of being a follower of *mu'tazilah*, an unorthodox school in early Sunni Islam, best known for denying that the Quran was eternal and insisting upon free will. See 'The Truth of Abu Abdallah Muhajir who led al-Zarqawi astray and enabled the latter to shed blood' (in Arabic), *muntadayat al-mahdi* 14 July 2005, www.almahdy.name/vb/showthread.php?t=3354, accessed Aug. 2006.

55    Ibid.

56    See, for example, the videotaped presentation listed on Abu Mus'ab al-Suri's website, entitled 'Clarifications regarding the Decisions by the Leader of the Faithful on Organising the Emigrants' Jihad', dated June 2001.

Arabic-language radio (see below). Judging by the interview's title, 'The Reality and Truth about the Taleban Movement', one may presume that it aimed to refute misconceptions about the Taleban and inculcate obedience to the Taleban's orders.[57]

Notwithstanding al-Suri's efforts, anti-Taleban sentiments remained an important undercurrent in the Arab-Afghan movement, not only in Afghanistan, but also, and perhaps more so, among exiled jihadis in the West. Al-Suri's 1998 study on the Taleban was clearly written with a view to refute fatwas issued by salafi clerics in London, who had argued that the conditions for the *Abode of Islam* (dar al-islam), to which true Muslim believers should emigrate, were not yet present in Afghanistan. Thus, the Taleban government was not a legitimate government, and their war against the Northern Alliance was not a jihad ('in this war both the killer and the killed will go to hell').[58] This criticism has also been referred to on later occasions on jihadi web forum discussions about the Taleban.[59]

Judging by his writings after his arrival in Taleban-ruled Afghanistan, al-Suri appears to have grown increasingly disillusioned by the inability of the jihadi organizations to rally the Islamic Nation (*ummah*) in defense of the Taleban. When he reflected on the Afghan experience of 2004, he lamented the fact that so few had decided to

---

57    The interview has subsequently circulated on jihadi websites. It took place in 1419h (corresponding to April 1998 - April 1999), according to the web posting. It was listed among ten lectures and speeches which bin Laden gave during the 1990s. See 'Old Lectures by Shaykh and Mujahid Osama bin Laden' (in Arabic), *muntada al-saqifah*, 27 Nov. 2001, www.alsakifah. org/vb/showthread.php?t=11595, accessed Oct. 2006; and 'The Biography of Shaykh Osama bin Laden' (in Arabic), *ozooo3@hotmail.com* website, undated http://alwazzan86.jeeran.com/osama.html, accessed May 2006.

58    'Umar Abd al-Hakim, *Afghanistan, the Taleban, and the Battle of Islam Today* (in Arabic), pp.2-3.

59    See 'An Interpretation of Imam Mullah Umar, May God Protect him' (in Arabic), *muntada al-safinet* 10 Nov. 2005, www.al-saf.net/vb/showthread. php?t=18448&highlight=%E3%D5%DA%C8+%C7%E1%D3%E6%D1 %ED, accessed Nov. 2005.

emigrate to the Islamic Emirate. He also refuted Western assessments about the size of the foreign jihadi diaspora in the country:

It was yet more regrettable that the *Abode of Islam* (dar al-islam) was established in Afghanistan during that era of the Taleban. For six years, the door was wide open to establish camps and frontlines. An opportunity for jihad was provided under the banners of Islamic law, but the number of those who made the emigration (*hijrah*) to the country and joined jihad did not exceed 1,500 mujahidin, and among these 300 came with their families. Hence, the ratio was one in a million of the Islamic Nation's population!! Only a very limited number of mujahidin were blessed by God and benefited from the opportunity to prepare and train, and attend the field of jihad. Worse yet was that none of the Muslim scholars, particularly renowned clerics, and none of the symbols of *da'wah* who deafened the world with empty slogans about jihad, emigrated there.

We will find that the ratio remains 1:1 million if we include the number of those who mobilized for jihad to help their brothers in Afghanistan—who fell under the oppression of the former blatant occupation of the Russians— Bosnia, Chechnya, Palestine, or other Islamic countries that came under occupation recently. This was actually the percentage, despite the pounding drums of the media, which did not stop over-playing armed jihad or the so-called "terrorism" to justify aggressive objectives. Do not believe the imaginary numbers that US intelligence published in the media about the size of al-Qaida in order to achieve its goals. I reconfirm the numbers I mentioned, since I witnessed this period in the field myself, God be praised.[60]

Al-Suri and those Arab-Afghans who wished to make the Taleban a pillar of their jihadi project failed, not only because they fought an uphill battle against the Taleban's external enemies, but perhaps even more so because of the sizeable anti-Taleban opposition *within* the jihadi currents themselves, let alone the general condescending Arab attitude towards the Islamic Emirate.

---

60  *The Global Islamic Resistance Call*, p.40. See slightly different figures on p.725. This excerpt can also be found in 'Thirteenth Part of Serialized Book on Al-Zarqawi and Al-Qa'ida Published Part 13 of serialized book: "Al-Zarqawi... The Second Generation of Al-Qa'ida"' by Fu'ad Husayn, Jordanian writer and journalist', *Al-Quds Al-Arabi* (London) 11 July 2005, via FBIS.

## THE AFGHAN TRAINING CAMPS

After having settled down in Afghanistan, al-Suri soon established his own media centre and training camp near Kabul. It was not part of bin Laden's training complexes but rather belonged to a group of fourteen camps or camp complexes, registered and acknowledged by the Taleban government.

The popular image of the Afghan camps is that of a collection of al-Qaida-run bases for terrorist training purposes only. However, al-Qaida, defined here as bin Laden's organization, was only one actor among many foreign militant Islamist entities in Afghanistan. The existence of this diversity has long been acknowledged in the research literature. Rohan Gunaranta has noted that with the influx of Islamist militants and fighters from around the world during the late 1990s, Afghanistan became 'a "terrorist Disneyland" with about 40 Islamist groups receiving both guerrilla and terrorist training'.[61] However, little has been known about the actual composition of the camp structures. Frequently, most descriptions of the training facilities focus heavily on their links or associations with al-Qaida, inflating the importance of bin Laden.

Al-Suri saw himself as a player, an observer, and an eye witness in Afghanistan. In his book, *The Global Islamic Resistance Call*, he intermittently assumes the role of an historian, recounting the rise of the Arab-Afghans under the Taleban. Al-Suri recalls that by the year 2000, the Arab training camps and guest houses had spread to most of the largest Afghan cities, especially in Kabul, in the Taleban capital of Qandahar, as well as in the eastern cities of Khowst and Jalalabad.[62] His description of the overall camp structure by 2000 is helpful in locating his own base, the *al-Ghuraba* camp, in the wider geography of militant Islam in Afghanistan at the time. Further-

---

61    See, for example, Rohan Gunaratna, 'The Rise and Decline of Al Qaeda', Statement to the National Commission on Terrorist Attacks Upon the United States, 9 July 2003, www.9-11commission.gov/hearings/hearing3/witness_gunaratna.htm, accessed Dec. 2003.

62    *The Global Islamic Resistance Call*, pp.724-5.

more, given the rarity of unclassified, and not forcibly extracted, accounts by top al-Qaida figures about the camp structures, it merits attention:

By 2000, the number of jihadi groups, training camps, or formations and projects had reached fourteen formations, organizations or camps, which enjoyed formal recognition by the Taleban. They were linked to the ministry of defense, the ministry of interior and the intelligence branch through a programme of discipline, coordination and cooperation, partly with a view to coordinating their support and jihad alongside that of the Taleban, but also to facilitate their own programmes. In addition there were the Pakistani groups that were also organized through a special programme, and they were numerous.

These formations, which were completely independent of each other, were as follows:

The non-Arab groups:

1  The Uzbek mujahidin were a relatively large group, compared to the other entities. Their programme aimed to take the jihadi campaign back to Uzbekistan and overthrow the American-Communist Karimov regime! This would take place after the situation in Afghanistan had stabilized for the Taleban, and through the complete programme they had planned. Their programme at that time consisted of recruitment, preparation and training, and they had links to the Taleban. Their Emir, Muhammad Tahir Khan, had sworn allegiance to Mullah Muhammad Omar, acknowledging him as the general *imam*, and his deputy, the famous military commander Jum'ah Bey [Namangani], God's mercy upon him, had sworn allegiance as well. The group had a very ambitious programme for recruiting and propagating [the jihadi cause] among the Afghani Uzbeks, a community of more than five million people. Many of them were descendents of emigrants who left Uzbekistan in the period starting with the Tsarist occupation of the country, and followed by the massacres carried out by Stalin and Lenin... The group was well organized, highly qualified and possessed large resources, enjoying support from the various Uzbek diasporic communities in many countries.

2  The mujahidin from Chinese-occupied Eastern Turkmenistan were a small group. Most of them had fled secretly from the Chinese regime. They had a comprehensive long-term educational programme, due to

247

the difficult circumstances under which the Muslims in Eastern Turkmenistan lived, after the successive Chinese governments had adopted a policy of Chinese immigration to their country, and succeeded in altering the country's demographical map, lowering the ratio of Turkmen Muslims from an overwhelming majority to about half of the population. They called it 'Xinjang', meaning 'the new soil', to say nothing of the harsh regulations [that had been in place] since the Communist regime of Mao Tse-Tung. A part of the group's programme was to send members back to their country with a view to attracting more emigrants [to Afghanistan] and train them [there], in preparation for the military campaign which they intended [to carry out] against China. Their Emir was the martyred Shaykh Abu Muhammad al-Turkistani, an extraordinary man and activist, and among the most magnificent examples for mujahidin who were fugitives of their religion. [...] He was killed by the Pakistani Army in Waziristan in November 2003, may God fight them, and show him great mercy. The group had also sworn allegiance to Mullah Muhammad Omar by a general pledge. The latter had requested them to halt their programme of [military] action against China, and confine their activities to the training of those joining them only, due to the fact that the Taleban were in need of developing good relations with China to counterbalance the American pressure, and [the mujahidin] committed themselves to this.

3   The Turkish mujahidin consisted of a small and very secretive group of Turks and Kurds. They had an educational programme, but I do not know whether they also had a programme of activity in their home countries at that time.

The Arab groups:

4   The 'al-Qaida' organization was headed by shaykh Osama bin Laden – may God the Almighty protect him – and their programme is well-known. Shaykh Osama swore allegiance to the Emir of the Faithful acknowledging him as imam as previously stated.

5   The Libyan Islamic Fighting Group. Its Emir was Abu Abdallah al-Sadiq – may God release him from prison – and their main programme was to prepare for jihad against the Qaddafi regime in Libya, and also to participate in supporting the jihadi causes in general and assisting the Taleban regime. They served a good role in this regard.

6   The Islamic Fighting Group in Morocco (Marakesh). Their programme was to prepare and train their cadres, but most of them gave up their lives or left. Their aim was to fight jihad against the regime in Morocco. Their Emir was called Abu Abdallah al-Sharif.

7   The Egyptian Islamic Jihad group had shrunk considerably [by 2000]. Their aim was to rebuild their organization, even if it had been dispersed. Their goal was well-known, namely to fight jihad against the Egyptian regime. Their Emir was the shaykh and doctor Ayman al-Zawahiri, may God the Almighty protect him.

8   The Egyptian Islamic Group was a very small group whose presence had decreased due to emigration. It had no important activities since it adopted the ceasefire initiative with the Egyptian regime, known as the 'initiative to stop violence'. Most of its important symbolic figures resided in Iran, as is well-known, while some of them moved to Afghanistan during the last days of the Taleban.

9   The Algerian jihadi formation, whose goal was to restore to good condition as many of their brothers as possible, in order to rearrange the jihad in Algeria after the tragedies to which it had befallen.

10  The Tunisian jihadi formation aimed to prepare and train [their members], and recruit Tunisian youth for jihad inside Tunisia. Their camp contributed to the training, and some of their cadres had previously fought jihad in Bosnia.

11  The formation of mujahidin from Jordan and Palestine. Their programme consisted of training and preparing [their fighters] for fighting jihad in Jordan and Palestine. Their Emir was Abu Mus'ab al-Zarqawi.

12  The Khalden camp (a general training camp) which was among the oldest Arab training camps. It was established at the time of the Service Bureau and Shaykh Abdallah Azzam. Its Emir was the famous mujahidin Shaykh Ibn Shaykh Salih al-Libi, may God release him from prison, assisted by his brother Abu Zubaydah, may God release him. The goal of this camp was purely to offer training for jihadis in every place. It had a decent production. Over the years, since its foundation in 1989, the number of trainees exceeded perhaps 20,000.

13 The Shaykh Abu Khabab al-Masri training camp (a general training camp) was a specialized training camp devoted to providing instruction in the production and use of explosives and chemicals.

14 The group of the *al-Ghuraba* camp (which was our group).[63]

By providing this survey, al-Suri evidently wished to point out that bin Laden, despite his increasingly important role, was only one actor in a much wider spectrum of players. The failure to communicate this diversity and win international recognition for a more nuanced description of the training camps became very costly to the jihadi movement in the post-September 11 world. Al-Suri noted that the United States pursued a strategy of:

subsuming, under the term 'al-Qaida', all jihadi currents, their structures, and everyone else it wished to eliminate from among the Islamic revivalist movement, irrespective of their different schools, and thereby making all of them a legitimate target for war under the slogan of 'combating terrorism'.[64]

The US success in reducing, in the eyes of world opinion, the entire jihadi movement to al-Qaida, was an outcome many jihadis had not foreseen. If they had known, many would probably have been far more hesitant about creating camps in Afghanistan, as al-Suri himself had done only a year and a half before 9/11.

### THE AL-GHURABA TRAINING CAMP

Al-Suri's training camp, the *mu'askar al-ghuraba* (lit. 'The Strangers' Camp') was founded in the spring of 2000. The choice of name was not unusual among salafi-jihadis fighting in foreign countries. The term *al-ghuraba*, or 'strangers', was illustrative of the Arab-Afghan community in Afghanistan, many of whom were fugitives and estranged from their homelands.[65] The term is borrowed from

---

63 Cited in ibid., pp.727-9.

64 Ibid., p.730.

65 For example, the training camp for Arab mujahidin in the Ansar al-Islam controlled enclave in Iraqi Kurdistan in 2002-3 went by the name *al-*

a Prophetic Tradition saying that: 'It is narrated on the authority of Abu Huraira that the Messenger of Allah (may peace be upon him) said: Islam initiated as something strange, and it would revert to its (old position) of being strange. So good tidings for the stranger'.[66] The religious connotation of the term is that of being chosen. In

---

*Ghuraba Centre* (markaz al-ghuraba). Abu Mus'ab al-Zarqawi was known to use the term as his *nom de guerre* (*al-gharib* in singular). The term *al-Ghuraba Brigade* (katibat al-ghuraba) was also the name of the first Arab-Afghan combat unit which had been formed in Afghanistan in the early 1980s and which fought together as a group. According to one account, the unit was hurriedly created in response to the Soviet capture of the Zhawar camp, which was a key rebel base, commanded by the Afghan mujahidin commander Jalal al-Din Haqqani and his Hizb e-Islami. A group of Arab-Afghans led by bin Laden then bought weapons and received extra equipment from Haqqani, and at the offices of Hizb e-Islami they swore an oath of loyalty to Abdallah Azzam to fight. This small group of fighters was initially called *katibat al-ghuraba*. According to the diary of Abu Hajir, then Emir at the 'Service Bureau' (*maktab al-khidmat*), Abdallah Azzam had told them that 'we called you by this name because you are the 'Strangers' (*ghuraba*)'. The unit was apparently dissolved after its first operation inside Afghanistan. Several militant groups in Europe have also used the term *ghuraba* about themselves. In 1997 a GIA splinter faction issued a bulletin from Europe entitled *Al-Ghuraba*, claiming to represent the true GIA and accusing the GIA Emir Antar Zouabri of acting under the influence of the Algerian security services. The name *al-ghuraba* has also been adopted by one of the many successor groups of the Muslim extremist group *al-Muhajiroun* in Britain. See 'Yasin al-Bahr martyrdom history. The Martyrs of Iraqi Kurdistan: The Emir of the Arab Mujahidin in the Ansar al-Islam Group in Iraqi Kurdistan, (in Arabic) *Ansar al-Islam website*, undated www.yaesean.8m.com, accessed 12 Aug. 2003; Hamd al-Qatari, 'Abu Shahid al-Sharqi', *qisas shuhada' al-'arab website*, undated, www.saaid.net/Doat/hamad/59.htm, accessed 19 April 2005; Basil Muhammad, *The Arab Helpers in Afghanistan*, pp.173-9, 233; and Quintan Wiktorowicz, 'The Centrifugal Tendencies in the Algerian Civil War', *Arab Studies Quarterly*, 23 (3) (Summer 2001), p.76. For al-Zarqawi's aliases, see 'Interpol-United Nations Security Council Special Notice, Subject To UN Sanctions: Al Khalayleh, Ahmad (alias Abu Musab Al-Zarqawi)', *Interpol website*, www.interpol.int/Public/NoticesUN/Search/2.asp, accessed Oct. 2006.

66 According to the translation of Sahih Muslim (Book #001, Hadith #0270), see *SearchTruth.com*, www.searchtruth.com/searchHadith.php?keyword=stranger&translator=2&search=1&book=&start=0&records_display=10&search_word=all, accessed Oct. 2006.

salafi theology, it is often used synonymously with other terms such as 'the Saved Sect' (*al-firqah al-najiyah*), and 'The Victorious Sect' (*al-ta'ifah al-mansurah*). The phrases refer to the one group that will be saved on the Day of Judgment, chosen from the 73 sects of the Islamic Nation.[67]

Al-Suri offers the following explanation for the establishment of his camp:

The group of the *al-Ghuraba* camp (which was our group) had bonds with the Taleban. It had a general training camp and a centre for studies, research, and lectures. I founded it myself in 2000, to create a training school for comprehensive ideological, programmatic, political, religious and military educational preparation. In my judgment, this was what the arena of the Afghan-Arabs lacked to an equal degree in both of its two phases [i.e. in the 1980s and the late 1990s]. The other reason for founding it was in order to launch *The Global Islamic Resistance Call* [...], in addition to becoming a part of the Islamic Emirate, and to assist in building and defending it, and operating in Afghanistan through direct coordination with the Emir of the Faithful.[68]

The camp was, formally speaking, a Taleban facility, located at the Kargha military base outside Kabul. Al-Suri founded it only after he had pledged an oath of obedience (*bay'ah*) 'hand to hand with the Emir of the Faithful Mullah Omar' in April 2000.[69] (However, he had operated a media and research centre there since 1999. His first lecture series at the *al-Ghuraba* centre was a class called 'Jihad is the Solution', which is cited at length later in this chapter.[70]). In spring

---

67   See, for example, Abuz-Zubair, 'Al-Ghurabaa'—The Strangers', *IslamicAwakening.com* undated, www.islamicawakening.com/viewarticle. php?articleID=688&. accessed Oct. 2006.

68   Cited in *The Global Islamic Resistance Call*, p.729.

69   'Communiqué from the Office of Abu Mus'ab al-Suri' (in Arabic), 22 Dec. 2004, p.7; Audiencia Nacional, Sala de lo Penal, Sección Tercera, 'Sentencia Núm. 36/2005', Madrid, 26 Sept. 2005, [verdict against the Abu Dahdah network], pp.200, 302; and 'Biography of Shaykh Umar Abd al-Hakim (Abu Mus'ab al-Suri)' (in Arabic), p.3.

70   Transcript of 'Jihad is the Solution'-audiofile no.1, tape no.1, 01:00 – 2:00, *muntada al-sawt* www.saowt.com/forum/showthread.php?t=16158,

2000, he started to work with the Taleban government's Ministry of Defence.[71] The Kargha base had reportedly been the headquarters of the Taleban's 8th Division, and was later one of the bases used for training Pakistani volunteers.[72] It is possible that the al-Ghuraba Camp was co-located with other units, but al-Suri stresses that the camp and the group he headed in Afghanistan 'operated independently'.[73] Al-Suri's official biography refers to the al-Ghuraba Camp as a 'mujahidin unit' which fought side-by-side with the Taleban forces under al-Suri's command.[74]

According to Benotman, who met with al-Suri in 1998, the 'al-Ghuraba Brigade', as he dubbed it, was a small group located north of Kabul, a training camp and fighting unit located near the Northern frontline in Kargha. Due to its strategic location near the capital, it helped to 'defend Kabul', hence the Taleban were more tolerant of it than they were of other Arab-Afghan training camps at the time. International pressure meant that camps sometimes were closed or placed under various forms of restrictions. The al-Ghuraba Brigade was small, numbering only some 20-30 people, although its numbers were not fixed. It was a new unit, funded by the Taleban, not by bin Laden, with whom al-Suri had fallen out with in 1998.[75] Al-Suri probably hoped to attract highly qualified jihadi cadres to his camp, given the ambitious theoretical training program he had envisaged.

---

accessed Oct. 2006.

71   A similar account, albeit with a different year, is presented in his writings. When he was interviewed in Feb. 1999, he stated that he had not yet met Mullah Omar. See 'Communiqué from the Office of Abu Mus'ab al-Suri' (in Arabic), 22 Dec. 2004, p.7; *The Global Islamic Resistance Call*, p.729; and 'Meeting with the Kuwaiti Newspaper', transcript of audiofile no.2, p.5.

72   'Afghanistan—Militia Facilities', *GlobalSecurity.org* undated, www.globalsecurity.org/military/world/afghanistan/militia-fac.htm, accessed July 2006.

73   *The Global Islamic Resistance Call*, p.59.

74   'Biography of Shaykh Umar Abd al-Hakim (Abu Mus'ab al-Suri)' (in Arabic), p.3.

75   Author's interview with Noman Benotman, London, 15 Sept. 2006.

It is uncertain whether he was successful in this, but according to Bakr Atyani, Al-Arabiyya's bureau chief in Islamabad, al-Suri had managed to recruit a number of al-Qaida members to his base.[76]

The Western media has published many contradictory stories about al-Suri's role *vis-à-vis* the Arab-Afghan training camps. Several accounts allege that his base was financed by bin Laden, even though they also highlight the conflicts between the two.[77] Given the topsy-turvy relationship between al-Suri and bin Laden during this period (see below), this funding cannot have been very reliable, and al-Suri probably relied on independent sources of funding. It seems clear that he operated only a small-scale camp, where he could keep expenditures low.

Official US sources have reported that al-Suri taught at Derunta, a large al-Qaida training complex near Jalalabad, in addition to his al-Ghuraba camp in Kabul.[78] The London-based daily, *al-Quds al-Arabi*, whose editor has met with bin Laden, claimed in 2000 that al-Suri commanded two training camps in Afghanistan, but located them instead in the Khowst region, near the Pakistani border.[79] Press reports have also claimed that al-Suri was at some point the 'overall commander' of al-Qaida's camps and 'headed its worldwide propaganda operation'.[80] This is most probably incorrect.

---

76 Paul Cruickshank and Mohammad Hage Ali, 'Abu Musab Al Suri: Architect of the New Al Qaeda', p.7.

77 See, for example, Katherine Shrader, 'Wanted Muslim extremist hopscotches the globe connecting terrorists', *Associated Press*, 3 Aug. 2005.

78 US Department of State, 'Press Statement (Revised): Secretary of State Colin L. Powell Authorizes Reward', Nov. 18, 2004, www.state.gov/r/pa/prs/ps/2004/38377.htm, accessed Oct. 2006; and 'WANTED: Mustafa Setmariam Nasar', *Reward for Justice website*, www.rewardsforjustice.net/english/wanted_captured/index.cfm?page=Nasar, accessed July 2005.

79 'Saudi prince earmarks £275,000 for assassinating bin Laden' (in Arabic), *Al-Quds al-Arabi* (London), 31 July 2000, www.alhramain.com/text/alraseed/974/tqareer/6.htm, accessed Sept. 2005.

80 David Paul and Mike Parker, 'Hunt For Terror Boss', *Sunday Express*, 10 July 2005, p.11.

Al-Suri has also been portrayed as someone who initially operated under Muhammad Atif's (Abu Hafs al-Masri) command, al-Qaida's top military commander from 1996 until November 2001, and allegedly was sent to Pakistan to oversee al-Qaida's 'Service Office' there, allowing him to meet in person with all new al-Qaida recruits, including the 9/11 Hamburg cell.[81] Perhaps in view of his GIA involvement, it has been suggested that al-Suri served as a kind of 'liaison officer' between the al-Qaida leadership and local jihadi groups, which were considered as its 'branches' throughout the world.[82]

While one cannot dismiss the possibility that he at various times was involved in different kinds of organizational activity on behalf of al-Qaida, these reports appear to misrepresent al-Suri's main role. What seems certain is that he visited many other training camps other than his own, giving lectures on his favourite theme, namely *The Global Islamic Resistance Call*, and teaching topics within his field of expertise, such as guerrilla warfare theories, especially in the camps at Khowst and Jalalabad. But as an independent writer and theoretician, al-Suri was unlikely to engross himself in the daily practicalities and administrative duties of a training camp coordinator. Hence, his tiny al-Ghuraba camp and his media center were probably enough for him to administer. Or, as a US intelligence official once noted: 'He is a lover of books more than bombs and his organizational skills leave a lot to be desired'.[83]

This does not mean the he was a mere theoretician. He always emphasized that his theories were based on practical field experience and prided himself on his terrorist skills, such as explosive engineering. Furthermore, he had overseen security issues related to foreign

---

81 Cited in Ahmad Rafat, '3/11 mastermind's hideout' (in Spanish), *El Tiempo de Hoy* (Madrid), 9 Oct. 2004, via FBIS.

82 Abbas al-Badri, '*Al-Sharq al-Awsat* Obtains Document that Reveals: Bin Laden Blessed the Establishment of the Kurdish 'Jund al-Islam' and Sent it a 'Gift' in Dollars' (in Arabic), *Al-Sharq al-Awsat* (London), 28 Sept. 2001, p.5, via FBIS.

83 Cited in Robert Windrem, 'U.S. hunts for "pen jihadist",' *MSNBC News*, 9 Dec. 2004, www.msnbc.msn.com/id/6685673/, accessed July 2005.

media interviews in 1997, and in his writings deals at length with ways of minimizing security risks to jihadi cells. Hence, it is perhaps not surprising that al-Suri personally participated in the process of vetting newly arrived recruits to his camps in order to weed out infiltrators. This was a job he took so seriously that he had earned a reputation for being very tough. Says Rafael Gómez Jr., a former Spanish intelligence chief:

It reminds me of how persons I interrogated remembered Mustafa Setmarian Nasar with horror, with terror. He was [like] terror in Afghanistan because he was at the head of a training camp pertaining to Osama bin Laden and he was the person carrying out the interrogations of individuals suspected by al-Qaida to be spies sent by the United States. They spoke of him with terror.[84]

This account is corroborated by a document uncovered in Afghanistan after the Taleban's fall, listing him as member of an Arab-Taleban liaison committee responsible for screening 'Arab emigrants' heading for the Islamic Emirate.[85]

Even though his camp, officially speaking, was part of the Taleban's Ministry of Defence, al-Suri nevertheless trained his recruits for a global violent struggle against the 'Crusaders' far beyond Afghanistan's borders. His teaching was specifically oriented towards terrorist operations in other regions. In 2004 and 2005, he bragged about the violent exploits of his trainees upon their return to their home countries.[86] It seems he regarded his training camp as a plat-

---

84  Cited in Cortes Generales, 'Miutes of the Congress of Representatives (in Spanish), Comisiones de Investigación Sobre el 11 de Marzo de 2004, Sesión núm. 28, celebrada el lunes, 25 de octubre de 2004, http://www.congreso.es/public_oficiales/L8/CONG/DS/CI/CI_015.PDF, accessed Aug. 2006, p.30.

85  Document no.AFGP-2002-000100, 'Synopsis: This document contains a flyer addressed to all Arab immigrants. The flyer lists the Islamic Emirate officials' names that would assist the Arab immigrants in entering the Emirate', *The Army's Foreign Military Studies Office (FMSO) website*, http://fmso.leavenworth.army.mil/documents-docex/Iraq/AFGP-2002-000100.pdf, accessed 17 March 2006.

86  'Communiqué from the Office of Abu Mus'ab al-Suri' (in Arabic), 22 Dec.

form from which to implement his ideas for a global jihadi movement of autonomous cells de-linked from any identifiable organizational structure, and whose main method of operation should be 'individual terrorism'.[87] By August 2000, he had his resistance theories ready 'in their final form', and then 'began the attempt to build its first nucleus on the soil of Afghanistan'.[88]

There is much uncertainty as to who constituted his main following in Afghanistan. As is apparent from the camp structure described above, the jihadi groups in Afghanistan were still, to a significant degree, organized along the lines of nationality. In the absence of a strong Syrian jihadi movement and in the shadow of the towering and wealthy bin Laden, al-Suri was unlikely to rise to a top leadership position. Still, he clearly had a certain following, or at least people who would listen to his advice and attend his lectures.

It is uncertain whether jihadis of Syrian origin were still his key followers by 2000. Already in the early 1990s, al-Suri had been recognized by an al-Qaida defector as a leader of a Syrian jihadi group operating under al-Qaida's banner and as a member of al-Qaida's Shura Council.[89] Probably for this reason al-Suri has sometimes been described as the 'Syrian representative' on al-Qaida's Shura Coun-

---

2004, p.8; and 'Text of Audio Communiqué by Shaykh Umar Abd al-Hakim (Abu Mus'ab al-Suri) Addressing the British and the Europeans regarding the London Explosions, and the Practices of the British Government' (in Arabic), Aug. 2005.

87 For a brief analysis of al-Suri's doctrine, see Brynjar Lia, 'Abu Mus'ab al-Suri: Profile of a Jihadi Leader', www.mil.no/multimedia/archive/00080/Abu_Musab_al-Suri-80483a.pdf, accessed Oct. 2006.

88 *The Global Islamic Resistance Call*, pp. 1355, 1406.

89 Testimony of Jamal Ahmed Mohammed Al-Fadl, United States of America *v.* Osama Bin Laden *et al.* Defendants, transcript of trial, 13 Feb. 2001, Day 4, http://cryptome.org/usa-v-ubl-04.htm, accessed March 2006, p.452; and Testimony of Jamal Ahmed Mohammed Al-Fadl, United States of America *v.* Osama Bin Laden, *et al.* Defendants', transcript of trial, 6 Feb. 2006, Day 2, http://cryptome.org/usa-v-ubl-dt.htm, accessed July 2006, p.299.

cil.[90] Spanish court documents from 2003 also portray him as the 'Emir of the Syrians' associated with al-Qaida.[91] There is little doubt that he knew many Syrian jihadis in Europe. His staff members at the Ghuraba media centre who edited their short-lived journal and compiled his bibliography were mostly Syrians, as was the spokesman who wrote an introduction to his communiqués and updated his website, judging by their *noms de guerre*. Still, al-Suri had not only Syrian lieutenants, associates and trainees in Afghanistan; two of his colleagues at Ghuraba were reportedly a Palestinian and a Tunisian.[92] Also, people who met with al-Suri at the time recall that his camp consisted of many nationalities, not only Syrians.[93]

One recent study has compared his position among the Syrian jihadis to that of Zarqawi in the Jordanian jihadi movement.[94] However, this comparison is somewhat misplaced. Al-Zarqawi was a fierce field commander who chose to decapitate a foreign hostage and (mis-)fire a machine gun in the Iraqi desert on his audio-visual

---

90 'Timeline of Mustafa Setmarian Nasar's activities', *Associated Press*, 3 Aug. 2005; and Testimony of Jamal Ahmed Mohammed Al-Fadl, United States of America *v.* Osama Bin Laden *et al.* Defendants, transcript of trial, 13 Feb. 2001, Day 4, http://cryptome.org/usa-v-ubl-04.htm, accessed March 2006, p.452.

91 'Juzgado Central de Instruccion no.005, Madrid, Sumario', 17 Sept. 2003, p.27. See also Carlos Fonseca, 'Setmariam Lived in Madrid for Three Years' (in Spanish), *El Tiempo* (Madrid), 3 Sept. 2004, pp.14-15, via FBIS.

92 They were nicknamed Abu Walid and Faysal bin Nasim. The latter was probably a Tunisian militant, who was well-known among jihadi sympathizers in Italy. He ran a reception and redistribution center for militants, known as the 'House of Tunisians', presumably in Afghanistan or on the Pakistani side of the border. The reports of al-Suri's contacts in the Italian-based jihadi community are somewhat corroborated by the Spanish indictment of 2003. See Guido Olimpio, 'A Syrian Ideologue for the Suicide Terrorist Network' (in Italian), *Corriere della Sera* (Milan), 28 Feb. 2004, via FBIS; and 'Juzgado Central de Instruccion no.005, Madrid, Sumario', 17 Sept. 2003, p.27.

93 Author's interview with Noman Benotman, London, 15 Sept. 2006.

94 Jean-Charles Brisard with Damien Martinez, *Zarqawi: The New Face of al-Qaeda*, p.186.

appearances on the jihadi web. By contrast, available online footage of al-Suri reveals him as a dispassionate and professorial lecturer, who speaks dryly and writes on a whiteboard.

### TEACHING JIHADI TERRORISM

Having arrived in Afghanistan, al-Suri quickly resumed his most important activity in the service of jihad, namely lecturing. While he had not entirely ceased giving lectures in Europe, opportunities to find an attentive audience were much greater in Afghanistan. He was also less restrained by security considerations in his new safe haven. As mentioned earlier in this book, his lectures were audio-recorded and even videotaped and have since been made available online via his website or on jihadi web forums.[95] Radio Kabul also broadcast internationally a programme containing recordings from the lectures which al-Suri gave at his camp.

With regards to his trainees and audiences in Afghanistan, they appeared to vary greatly. Al-Suri clearly possessed an expertise that many training camp commanders wished to pass on to their recruits, and hence he was allowed to lecture at many different bases, addressing nationals from all over the world. However, much of his effort went into propagating his own project, *The Global Islamic Resistance Call*, at least during the latter part of his Taleban period. Al-Suri recalls organizing tens of meetings in his own house and at other locations with a view to spreading and developing it further. Arab mujahidin formed the majority of his audience, but a few from Central Asia were also present.[96]

Al-Suri's camp reportedly received a number of recruits from Europe, where he had a substantial network of contacts. In his lectures,

---

95   For his videotaped lectures, see 'File of audiovisual publications' (in Arabic) (undated, but zipped 21, 22, 24 Jan. 2004 and 8 Feb. 2004; 28 separate wmv-files; total size: 683 Megabyte), *Abu Mus'ab al-Suri's Website* (see bibliography for weblinks).

96   *The Global Islamic Resistance Call*, p.60.

he also specifically addressed the question of 'terrorism in Europe', in which Britain, France, and the NATO member countries were singled out as priority targets.[97] According to press reports, young Muslims from Spain were sent to him between 1998 and 2001, having been recruited by Abu Dahdah or other trusted associates in Europe.[98] A Spanish indictment also states that he began receiving 'European "mujahideen" converts from France, Spain, and Italy, who were being trained to be reincorporated into their respective countries as "sleepers" awaiting orders from their organization'.[99] In 2005, al-Suri bragged that he had:

personally trained and overseen the training of both Arab and non-Arab Muslims in my camp, the al-Ghuraba Camp, a program which included ideological, military, and physical training. Among them were Arab, non-Arab and foreign Muslims. Some were British who were either born, raised or are currently living in Britain. Some were of other Western nationalities, even American Muslims.[100]

One of the first lectures al-Suri gave in Afghanistan was a long series of sessions (*jalasat*) with 'the youth of Algeria'.[101] They took place in 1998, before his media center was founded, at a camp in Khowst. Following his close involvement with the GIA and the Algerian jihadi community in London, al-Suri seized any opportunity he could to discuss this experience and to vent his frustrations about

---

97   Transcript of 'Jihad is the Solution'-audiofile no.37, tape no.10b, 06:28 – 16:00, *muntada al-sawt* www.saowt.com/forum/showthread.php?t=16158, accessed Oct. 2006.

98   Ahmad Rafat, 'Al-Qa'idah chief in Europe is Spanish' (in Spanish), *El Tiempo de Hoy*, 24 Aug. 2004, via FBIS.

99   'Juzgado Central de Instruccion no.005, Madrid, Sumario', 17 Sept. 2003, p.27.

100  Cited in Umar Abd al-Hakim (Abu Mus'ab al-Suri), 'Message to the British and the Europeans – Its People and Governments – regarding the London Explosions, July 2005' (in Arabic), Aug. 2005, p.29.

101  'List of Collection of Production and Publications by Shaykh Umar Abd al-Hakim' (in Arabic), *Abu Mus'ab al-Suri Website*, 20 Nov. 2004, www.fsboa.com/vw/index.php?subject=4&rec=1&tit=tit&pa=0, accessed Sept. 2005.

Abu Qutadah (see previous chapter). The fact that this particular lecture series has not been published online may suggest that it was not among his most successful appearances.

Al-Suri also lectured to Gulf Arabs. Among his extensive written, audio-taped, or audio-visual output are two long audio-recorded sessions with 'the youth from Yemen' in 1998 and 'the youth from the Arab Peninsula' in 2000.[102] He later prided himself that the 'infidels and apostates' in Saudi Arabia 'have tasted the strength and fortitude of some of those whom I trained'.[103]

It appears that al-Suri also played a role in training the jihadi movement in Iraq. He was well-informed about the participation of Iraqi Kurds in the Afghan liberation war during the 1980s.[104] According to his website, he held a series of audio-taped lectures for 'the youth of Iraqi Kurdistan' in Kabul some time in 1422h/2001.[105] It is possible that these youth later joined the new militant group, *Jund al-Islam* (Soldiers of Islam) in Iraqi Kurdistan, established there in September 2001. The group had many trainees with field

---

102 These audio-taped sessions have apparently been reformatted into DVDs for further distribution. Pictures of the DVDs feature many websites containing al-Suri's works. They have also been advertised on jihadi Internet sites, and many of these lectures are available for downloading via al-Suri's website or websites maintained by the pro al-Qaida *Global Islamic Media Front*, currently perhaps the largest online media company in the jihadi movement. See 'The Media Front Presents Part II of Excerpts from Abu Mus'ab al-Suri, The al-Ghuraba Camp' (in Arabic), *muntadayat shabakat al-hisbah*, 5 Oct. 2005, www.al-hesbah.org/v/showthread.php?t=34722&highlight=%C3%C8%E6+%E3%D5%DA%C8+%C7%E1%D3%E6%D1%ED, accessed Nov. 2005.

103 'Communiqué from the Office of Abu Mus'ab al-Suri' (in Arabic), 22 Dec. 2004, p.8.

104 In an interview with *Financial Times*, he noted that 'several hundred came from Iraq, in particular from Iraqi Kurdistan' to fight in the Afghan liberation war during the 1980s. See Mark Huband, *Warriors of the Prophet*, p.2.

105 These lectures were reportedly audio-taped, but have not yet been released. See 'List of the Shaykh's production: from 1407h/1987 to 1425h/2004', (in Arabic), *Abu Mus'ab al-Suri's Website*, www.fsboa.com/vw/print.php?id=1&ty=pr&img=no, accessed 7 Nov. 2005.

experience from Afghanistan, as well as some foreign fighters in its ranks. According to the Arab daily *al-Sharq al-Awsat*, al-Suri had been instrumental in channelling financial aid from al-Qaida to *Jund al-Islam*. (His involvement in this has not been confirmed from other sources.) These funds were allegedly meant as a start-up gift and a tangible measurement of al-Qaida's blessing for the unification of three radical Islamist groups in Northern Iraq into one organization.[106] In December 2001, it evolved into the well-known *Ansar al-Islam* ('Partisans of Islam') organization, which hosted a number of jihadis fleeing from Afghanistan as well as Arab volunteer fighters arriving in Iraq in anticipation of the US invasion.[107]

Another audience which al-Suri addressed was the Central Asian and especially Uzbek mujahidin. He considered this region to be a key future base for the jihadi movement and involved himself directly in lecturing and training mujahidin from this region. Later he mentioned the region as being among those countries whose 'apos-

---

106 According to the Arab daily *al-Sharq al-Awsat*, al-Suri had assisted in the transfer of a sum equivalent to $300,000 to the Jund al-Islam group. The newspaper also reported that a number of Kurdish militants had been sent to train in al-Qaida's camps in mid-July 2001. Furthermore, an estimated 60 Arab-Afghan veterans joined the Jund al-Islam after its establishment. See Abbas al-Badri, 'Al-Sharq al-Awsat Obtains Document that Reveals: Bin Laden Blessed the Establishment of the Kurdish 'Jund al-Islam' and Sent it a 'Gift' in Dollars' (in Arabic), *Al-Sharq al-Awsat* (London), 28 Sept. 2001, p.5, via FBIS.

107 The Jund al-Islam's constituent meeting reportedly took place in the village of Tawila, near Halabja in Northern Iraq, and was attended by three Arab Afghans. The new organization was led by Abu Abdallah al-Shafi'i (Warba Holiri al-Kurdi), a Kurdish militant who reportedly had travelled to Afghanistan in 1993 and had also fought with the Chechen rebels. See Abbas al-Badri, 'Al-Sharq al-Awsat Obtains Document that Reveals: Bin Laden Blessed the Establishment of the Kurdish 'Jund al-Islam' and Sent it a 'Gift' in Dollars' (in Arabic), *Al-Sharq al-Awsat* (London) 28 Sept. 2001, p.5, via FBIS; and Husni Mahalli, 'Another 'al-Qa'ida' and New Mullahs in Iraqi Kurdistan; Will Kurdistan Become [Another] Tora Bora?' (in Arabic), *al-Majallah*, 10 Feb. 2002, via FBIS. See also Brynjar Lia, 'The Ansar al-Islam Group Revisited', *Studies in Conflict and Terrorism* (forthcoming).

tate and infidel' rulers had 'tasted the strength and fortitude' of his trainees.[108]

Evidently, al-Suri had a multitude of audiences in Afghanistan and the topics of his lectures varied greatly, although politics and strategy, not religious doctrines, remained his focus. The following list of his audio-taped lecture series gives an idea of his teaching practices as well as of his audiences:

## Al-Suri's audio-taped lectures, 1998-2001

1. Explaining the Book "War of the Oppressed". (Lectures in thirty-two audiotapes). Khowst, 1419h/1998.

2. Session with the Youth of Algeria (Collection of fourteen audiotapes). Khowst, 1419h/1998 (not released!).

3. Session with the Youth of Yemen. (Lecture in four audiotapes). Khowst, 1419h/1998.

4. Managing the Organization of Guerrilla Warfare (Collection of six audiotapes). Khowst, 1419h/1998.

5. The Reality of Muslims: The Crisis and the Solution. (Lectures in seven audiotapes). Kabul, 1420h/1999.

6. Meeting with the Kuwaiti newspaper al-Ra'y al-Amm (Lectures in five audiotapes). Kabul, 1420h/1999.

7. Lessons in the Guerrilla Warfare Theory, (Collection of four audiotapes). Jalalabad, 1999.

8. Jihad is the Solution. (Lectures in twenty-one audiotapes). Kabul, 1421h/2000 or September 1999.

9. The Global Islamic Resistance (Lecture in ten audiotapes). Undated. Probably 1999 or 2000.

10. Session with the Youth of the Arab Peninsula. (Collection of six audiotapes). Kabul, 1421h/2000.

---

108 'Communiqué from the Office of Abu Mus'ab al-Suri' (in Arabic), 22 Dec. 2004, p.8.

11. Session with the Youth of Iraqi Kurdistan. (Collection of five audio-tapes). Kabul, 1422h/2001 (Not released!).

12. Reading from the Prophet's Biography. (Organizational Study of the al-Rahiq al-Makhtub, Kabul, 1422h/2001 (not released!).

Source: Abu Mus'ab al-Suri website, 20 November 2004; The Global Islamic Resistance Call, p.60.

## Al-Suri's videotaped lectures

1. The Global Islamic Resistance Call Units – Call, Program and Method. Lecture course given for a group of Arab mujahidin in Kabul. Six three hour long videotapes. 20 August 2000.

2. Clarifications regarding the Decisions by the Leader of the Faithful on Organizing the Emigrants' Jihad. Lecture together with Abu Walid al-Filastini and Abu Hamam al-Filastini. One videotape. 3/1422h or June 2001.

3. The Reference Point and Its Necessity for Jihadi Action. Lecture held for students from among the Uzbekistan mujahidin. One videotape. Undated.

4. The Reality of Muslims after the Downfall of the Caliphate until the Rise of the Emirate and Our Duty towards the New Reality. Lecture given for students from among the Uzbekistan mujahidin. Four videotapes (one copy in Arabic and one copy translated into Uzbek). Undated.

5. Lectures on Morality and the Origins of Soldiery and Leadership in Jihad. Several videotapes. Lecture given for students from among the Uzbekistan mujahidin, and a selected group of Arab-Afghan mujahidin. Undated.

Source: Abu Mus'ab al-Suri website, 20 November 2004; The Global Islamic Resistance Call, p.60.

## MOROCCAN JIHADIS, ABU LAYTH AL-LIBI
## AND ABU MUS'AB AL-ZARQAWI

Even though the list of lectures above hints at which constituency al-Suri mostly addressed in his lectures, available sources do not permit us to establish his network of contacts in Afghanistan with any degree of accuracy. Furthermore, it is important to stress that the nature of the Arab-Afghan community in Afghanistan was such that 'everyone knew everyone', without necessarily having any organizational links.[109] In fact al-Suri had some contact with the Moroccan jihadis, the Libyans and Abu Mus'ab al-Zarqawi, all of whom were important in the context of Afghanistan at that time.

Al-Suri is believed to have had close relations with several Moroccan militants. He specifically mentions the youths from a nascent Moroccan jihadi group called 'The Struggling Group in Morocco' *(al-jama'ah al-mujahidah fi'l-maghrib)*, who were 'exemplary truthful youths filled with zeal and desire for productive activities and sacrifice'.[110] He recalls that he had great hopes for this group, but the events of September 11 unfortunately 'swallowed many of their cadres'.[111] Still, he credits 'some of the Moroccan mujahidin' with 'the heroic operation' that resulted in the Spanish forces' withdrawal from Iraq, referring to the Madrid train bombings in March 2004, carried out by the *Moroccan Islamic Fighting Group* (GICM).[112] Recent reports suggest that al-Suri had meetings with leading GICM members in the summer of 2000 in Kabul. It has also been alleged that al-Suri directed a terrorist camp for Moroccans in Jalalabad in Afghanistan, where some of the M-11 suspects had been trained in the use of cell phone to activate bombs.[113]

---

109  Author's interview with Noman Benotman, London, 15 Sept. 2006.

110  *The Global Islamic Resistance Call*, p.783.

111  Ibid.

112  He claims, though, that he is not able to determine to which group these belonged. See *The Global Islamic Resistance Call*, p.783.

113  José María Irujo, *El Agujero* p.51, citing unnamed 'police reports'; 'How

The Libyan jihadi movement also appears to have been in touch with al-Suri in Afghanistan. He had been close to their leaders in London and in the introduction to *The Global Islamic Resistance Call* pays tribute to Abu Layth al-Libi.[114] It is likely that the two men knew each other well. Various assessments have placed them together, and it is known that Al-Libi was close to and cooperated with the Taleban.[115] Other sources state that both of them sought to persuade young North African radicals to accept the Taleban regime and fight under its banner.[116] After the fall of the Taleban, al-Libi emerged as an al-Qaida spokesman on several occasions. He liaised between al-Zarqawi in Iraq and bin Laden, and was instrumental in facilitating al-Zarqawi's oath of allegiance to the al-Qaida leader. In 2006, he was considered a very senior al-Qaida figure and a key point of contact between al-Qaida in Afghanistan and al-Zarqawi's organization and other jihadi elements in Iraq.[117] He is the most prominent LIFG leader still on the run.[118]

---

did Sa'd al-Hasayni form the basis for the GICM in Afghanistan', (in Arabic), *al-Alam* 25 April 2007; and 'Secret report reveals Madrid bombers' training camps', *EFE* 27 Sept. 2006.

114  *The Global Islamic Resistance Call*, p.10.

115  Author's interview with a European security official, Feb. 2006. Name and place withheld on request.

116  See 'The Truth of Abu Abdallah Muhajir who led al-Zarqawi astray and enabled the latter to shed blood' (in Arabic), *muntadayat al-mahdi*, 14 July 2005, www.almahdy.name/vb/showthread.php?t=3354, accessed Aug. 2006.

117  Author's interview with a European security official, Feb. 2006. Name and place withheld on request.

118  Al-Libi became famous when he, alongside other Libyan jihadis, was detained in the infamous al-Ruwais prison in Jedda, Saudi Arabia in the mid-1990s, but managed to escape together with two other LIFG fighters in 1995. He hailed from Tripoli in Libya, had 'emigrated to Afghanistan, joined the mujahidin and became one of the LIFG leaders'. He had been known as an al-Qaida spokesman in Afghanistan before 9/11, according to CNN, but he was primarily referred to as 'field commander' on jihadi websites. He was interviewed during and after the Shahi Kot-battle/ Operation Anaconda in March 2002, and he also figured prominently in an al-Qaida combat video distributed to the *al-Jazeera* satellite TV

Al-Suri's relationship with Abu Mus'ab al-Zarqawi (Ahmad Fadil Nazzal al-Khalayilah), perhaps the foremost and most infamous icon of international jihadism between 2004 and 2006, has been a recurrent if obscure item in biographies of al-Suri. During the Taleban period, before al-Zarqawi's rise to world prominence, they both had their semi-independent camps in Afghanistan beyond al-Qaida's direct control: al-Suri in Kabul and al-Zarqawi in Herat, on the Afghan border with Iran.[119] Al-Zarqawi and his men only came to

---

network in June 2002, which included night-time images of mujahidin attacking Afghan government forces and of the corpses of those apparently killed in that attack. He was reportedly the commanding officer during 'the Shenkay Operation' in the southern Afghan province of Zabul in Aug. 2004, which was videotaped and widely distributed among the jihadi community. Speeches by al-Libi in Afghanistan have been published on jihadi media outlets. In early 2006, an interview with him received wide coverage on key jihadi websites, suggesting that he had risen to a position of prominence in the top echelons of al-Qaida. See 'Audio-meeting with Shaykh Abu Layth al-Libi, May God Protect Him, in Afghanistan' (in Arabic), *muntadayat shabakat al-hisbah*, 21 Feb. 2006, www.al-hesbah. org/v/showthread.php?t=54340, accessed Feb. 2006; 'Interview with Al Qa'ida's Abu Laith al-Libbi'. Translated for *Mario's Spy News OSINT Newsletter* on http://mprofaca.cro.net/abu-laith.html, accessed Sept. 2005; 'Bin Laden alive, well and ready to strike', *Reuters*, 10 July 2002; 'Al-Jazeera man says he got alleged Al-Qaeda video from Pakistani journalist', *AFP*, 16 June 2002; 'Amaliyat Shenkay', video downloaded from the jihadi website *Al-Firdaws*, firdaws.virtue.nu, 24 Sept. 2004; 'Taleban claims 12 Afghan soldiers killed in Zabul' (DPA), *Khaleej Times Online*, 30 Sept. 2004, www.khaleejtimes.com/DisplayArticle.asp?xfile=data/subcontinent/2004/ Sept./subcontinent_Sept.984.xml&section=subcontinent, accessed March 2006; 'The history of Abu Layth al-Libi's escape from al-Ruwais prison' (in Arabic), *muntadayat shabakat al-hisbah*, 21 Feb. 2006, www.al-hesbah.org/ v/showthread.php?t=54348, accessed Feb. 2006; 'An audiovisual speech by Shaykh Abu Layth al-Libi' (in Arabic), *muntada al-tajdid* 2 July 2005, posting by Abu Hajir al-Libi (in Arabic), www.tajdeed.org.uk/forums/ showthread.php?s=27f4290c5cf2cb1debbe5c7df6307c73&threadid=3634 3, accessed March 2006; 'New al Qaeda threats', *CNN.com*, July 10, 2002, http://archives.cnn.com/2002/US/07/09/alqaeda.statement/index.html; and 'A Telephone Conversation with Abu Layth al-Libi' (in Arabic), *shabakat al-jihad onlayn al-ikhbariyyah* undated, www.jehad.net/audio-video.htm, accessed March 2006 via www.archive.org.

119 For a good biographical account of al-Zarqawi during his Afghanistan

Afghanistan in late 1999, long after al-Suri's arrival, but they quickly managed to establish a camp for themselves, receiving logistical support from al-Qaida. Al-Zarqawi also attracted Syrians to his base and one of his senior lieutenants, who already lived in Afghanistan, was Syrian. With this influx of volunteers arriving at his camp in Herat, several nationalities were represented in al-Zarqawi's network, including Syrians from al-Suri's hometown, Aleppo, although Palestinians and Jordanians remained his key constituents.

His relationship with al-Suri may have started in earnest when al-Zarqawi began focusing beyond his own camp, building relationships with other camps and attempting to reach out to other nationalities and ethnicities in Afghanistan, both Arab and non-Arab. Al-Zarqawi reportedly left one of his closest lieutenants, Abd al-Hadi Daghlas, in charge of the Herat camp and began traveling widely in Afghanistan, meeting many different jihadi groups and keeping updated on the latest news from their regions.[120] Sulayman Darwish Abu al-Ghadiyah, a Syrian jihad veteran, accompanied him on these trips. He managed to build relationships with several jihadi groups, in particular with Ansar al-Islam in Iraqi Kurdistan, with whom al-Suri was also in contact.[121]

According to various assessments, al-Zarqawi and al-Suri became well acquainted with each other, despite the fact that they were very different people. They both shared a mutual dislike of bin Laden's dominance of the Arab-Afghans, and insisted on having their own separate training camps, which the al-Qaida leader tried to resist.[122]

---

period, see 'The Jihadi Life Story of Commander 'the Slaughter' Abu Mus'ab al-Zarqawi: Sayf al-Adl (the security official in the Global Army of Qa'idat al-Islam) writes down the history of Abu Mus'ab al-Zarqawi' (in Arabic), *muntadayat al-hikmah*, 25 May 2005, http://www.hkmah. net/showthread.php?t=8118, accessed May 2005.

120  'The Jihadi Life Story of Commander 'the Slaughter' Abu Mus'ab al-Zarqawi', p.5.

121  Ibid.

122  Author's interview with a European security official, Feb. 2006; name and place withheld on request.

According to one source, bin Laden at one point managed to persuade the Taleban leader to order all Arab camps to be organized under al-Qaida's command although this never was put into practice.[123] Unlike al-Suri, al-Zarqawi was highly critical of the Taleban regime. A copy of a letter uncovered in Afghanistan after the Taleban's fall summarizes a meeting with al-Zarqawi and it was written by al-Suri himself or someone sharing his views.[124] The writer says that al-Zarqawi had requested a meeting with him. After the preliminaries were over al-Zarqawi began complaining about the repeated accusations of *takfir* against him, i.e. that he excommunicated fellow Muslims as infidels (*kuffar*). As with many other salafi radicals, al-Zarqawi had a hard time accepting the Afghan reality and fighting for the Taleban regime. In fact, al-Zarqawi had accused the Taleban governor in Jalalabad, among several others, of 'infidelity'.[125] Eventually, al-Zarqawi reached an understanding with the Taleban and al-Qaida leadership to coordinate his activities with their representatives.[126] However, the relationship remained turbulent. It is possible that al-Suri played a role in making him accept the reality of the situation. At the very least, al-Suri's letter appears to have been addressed to Abu Muhammad al-Maqdisi (Issam al-Barqawi), a very influential Jordanian cleric who was al-Zarqawi's foremost spiritual mentor, and

---

123 'Bin Laden Ordered the Registration of Names of Volunteers for Suicide Operations among the Arabs in Eastern Afghanistan: The Number Reached 122' (in Arabic), *arabiyyat.com*, 21 Nov. 2003, www.arabiyat. com/forums/showthread.php?s=&threadid=77762, accessed Oct. 2006.

124 See Document no.AFGP-2002-601693, 'Status of Jihad', *Combating Terrorism Center website* (West Point), www.ctc.usma.edu/aq/AFGP-2002-601693-Trans.pdf and www.ctc.usma.edu/aq/AFGP-2002-601693-Orig.pdf, accessed April 2006. For a discussion of the authorship of the document, see bibliography.

125 Document no.AFGP-2002-601693, 'Status of Jihad', *Combating Terrorism Center website* (West Point), www.ctc.usma.edu/aq/AFGP-2002-601693-Trans.pdf and www.ctc.usma.edu/aq/AFGP-2002-601693-Orig.pdf, accessed April 2006.

126 'The Jihadi Life Story of Commander 'the Slaughter' Abu Mus'ab al-Zarqawi', p.4.

perhaps the only person who could persuade him to adopt a more pragmatic attitude on ideological issues.

In the end, both al-Suri and al-Zarqawi had their camps registered among the fourteen official training complexes in Afghanistan. Being official training base commanders, both of them were appointed by the Taleban as members of an Arab-Taleban liaison committee, according to a document uncovered by US forces in Afghanistan.[127] The undated document must have been issued in 2000 or 2001. It reveals that the Islamic Emirate wished to impose better control over the influx of volunteer jihadis. It requested that 'all Arab immigrants' contact one of the liaison committee members in order to receive a written confirmation of their identity and requirements, which in turn should be used as an application for entering the Islamic Emirate. The document was signed 'The Arab Liaison Committee with the Islamic Emirate' and listed the names of its members.[128] In addition to al-Zarqawi and al-Suri the other four committee members were Abd al-Hadi al-Ansari, Ali Abu Zar'ah, Ibn Shaykh, and Muhammad Salah.[129] The document shows that al-Suri's relations with al-Zarqawi were not confined to a few meetings, but also had a certain organizational character. Furthermore, it also shows that al-Zarqawi had come a long way ideologically in agreeing to operate under the Taleban's umbrella, although we do not know for certain what role al-Suri played in persuading him to do so. According to one assessment al-Suri and al-Zarqawi never developed any extensive collaborative relationship, but they remained in contact after the

---

127  Document no.AFGP-2002-000100, 'Synopsis: This document contains a flyer addressed to all Arab immigrants. The flyer lists the Islamic Emirate officials' names that would assist the Arab immigrants in entering the Emirate', *The Army's Foreign Military Studies Office (FMSO) website*, http:// fmso.leavenworth.army.mil/documents-docex/Iraq/AFGP-2002-000100. pdf, accessed 17 March 2006.

128  Ibid.

129  The latter names probably referred to Ibn Shaykh al-Libi and Anwar Adnan Muhammad Salih (Shaykh Salah), both of whom worked with Abu Zubaydah at the Khalden training camp.

fall of the Taleban and during al-Zarqawi's rise to prominence in Iraq.[130]

Despite his extensive network of contacts, al-Suri was in many ways a loner in the jihadi community in Afghanistan. His sharp tongue and hot-headed character may have alienated potential supporters while his craving for solitude in order to write and develop his visions for a new war fighting strategy may have been difficult for others to accept. He seems to have chosen to keep a lower profile following the 1998 bombings of the Afghan camps, when the future of the Arab-Afghan safe havens was thrown into question. When he was interviewed in March 1999, the journalist noted that 'Shaykh Abu Mus'ab al-Suri has isolated himself recently' from the jihadi groups, and wished to know why.[131] Al-Suri then admitted to the journalist that over the two years prior to the interview, one might have gained such an impression, at least compared to his previous profile. Al-Suri nevertheless stressed that:

There are contacts, and my relationships with them are as they used to be in the past ten years. I am not isolated at all... my friendship with the brothers, the leaderships in the groups, with their members. I am present with them now openly. People are coming and going. So in a practical sense I am not isolated from them. I am with them, following their affairs. There is a situation of contact, consultation and consensus on many matters. But the situation now is one of standstill and holding the breath due to the conditions surrounding the jihadi groups. So when you are holding your breath, there should not be any over movement.[132] [sic]

## WRITER AND JOURNALIST

In addition to lecturing on strategy and global guerrilla warfare tactics, al-Suri's main preoccupations in Afghanistan were writing

---

130 Author's interview with a European security official, Feb. 2006. Name and place withheld on request.

131 'Meeting with the Kuwaiti Newspaper', transcript of audiofile, no.7, p.4.

132 Ibid.

and media work. He was quick to offer his services in these fields to the Taleban regime,[133] and thereafter worked with the Ministry of Information in publishing the newspaper *al-Shari'ah*, which was an official mouthpiece of the Islamic Emirate of Afghanistan. He also participated in preparing Arabic-language programs for Radio Kabul. Apparently, as part of his participation in the Kabul Arabic-language radio programs, al-Suri conducted an interview with Osama bin Laden at the end of the 1990s.[134]

In 1999 he founded a media and publication center called al-Ghuraba Center for Islamic Studies and Media, or al-Ghuraba Media Center, with himself as the director. Its goal was to 'spread the jihadi ideology and call for a global resistance'.[135] It featured a website which appears to have been active at least since December 2000 and throughout most of 2001.[136] The site only contained links to full-text versions of four of al-Suri's works, as well as four links to prominent salafi-jihadi websites. Still, The al-Ghuraba Media Center was sufficiently well-known to be listed on directories to Islamic websites.[137]

---

133 'Biography of Shaykh Umar Abd al-Hakim (Abu Mus'ab al-Suri)' (in Arabic), p.3.

134 The interview was entitled 'The Reality and Truth about the Taleban Movement', and it took place in 1419h (corresponding to April 1998 - April 1999), according to the web posting. It was listed among ten lectures and speeches which bin Laden gave during the 1990s. See 'Old Lectures by Shaykh and Mujahid Osama bin Laden' (in Arabic), *muntada al-saqifah*, 27 Nov. 2001, www.alsakifah.org/vb/showthread.php?t=11595, accessed Oct. 2006; and 'The Biography of Shaykh Osama bin Laden' (in Arabic), *ozooo3@hotmail.com*, website, undated http://alwazzan86.jeeran.com/osama.html, accessed May 2006.

135 'Communiqué from the Office of Abu Mus'ab al-Suri' (in Arabic), 22 Dec. 2004, p.8.

136 The website and email addresses were www.markaz123.8k.com or www.geocities.com/markaz123/ and markaz123@yahoo.com. According to the Internet archive at http://web.archive.org, the website was active at least since 5 Dec. 2000 and throughout most of 2001. At the time of writing its front page still existed on the original url, www.markaz123.8k.com. The site and its email account were administered by 'Abu Abdallah al-Shami'.

137 The site included links to *minbar al-tawhid wa'l-jihad* at www.maqdese.

Al-Suri's writings did not attract muh attention from Western intelligence sources at the time. Michael Scheuer, who headed the CIA's bin Laden unit in 1996-9 recalls that he only saw al-Suri's writings after the Taleban's fall when his books and epistles were discovered on hard-drives recovered from Afghanistan.[138]

The al-Ghuraba Media Center also published a journal entitled *Issues for the Triumphant in Righteousness* (qadaya al-zahirin 'ala al-haqq), of which al-Suri was chief editor and author of many of its articles.[139] Only two issues are available in the various online compilations of al-Suri's media library. The first is dated December 2000 and the last March 2001.[140] During this period al-Suri had some of his articles published in other Islamic media outlets. For example, his eyewitness report from Afghanistan appeared on the prominent *mufakkirat al-islam* website (www.islammemo.cc) on 15 March 2001.[141]

---

com, as well as to the Arabic language version of The Islamic Assembly of North America website (www.islamway.com). It figured in several directories to Islamic websites. See, for example, *shabakat rijal al-islam* website, www.islammen.net/team/showthread.php?s=&threadid=1299, accessed 22 Nov. 2005; and at *muntadayat nuss wu nuss*, www.n9wn9.com/vb/showpost.php?p=898&postcount=3, accessed Nov. 2005.

138 Interview with Micahel Scheuer, Washington, 14 March 2007.

139 The other editors listed in the journals were Hudhayfa al-Madani, Abu Nasr al-Halabi, and Abu Abdallah al-Shami. A person called Abu Abdallah al-Shami is also depicted in a famous jihadi film, entitled *Amaliyat Shenkay2*, ('The Shenkay Operation' Part II), accessed via the jihadi website Firdaws, www.firdaws.virtue.nu, downloaded 24 Sept. 2004. Abu Abdallah al-Shami is shown during live firearms training in a mountainous area, probably in Afghanistan, approximately 47 minutes into the 54.30 minute movie. See also 'Biography of Shaykh Umar Abd al-Hakim (Abu Mus'ab al-Suri)' (in Arabic), p.3.

140 See, for example, *Abu Mus'ab al-Suri's Website*, www.deluxesuperhost.com/~morshid/tophacker/index.php?subject=4&rec=22&tit=tit&pa=0; or http://abumusab.cjb.net/.

141 Abu Mus'ab al-Suri, 'A Testimony about the Reality', posted in the press section about Afghanistan on *mufakkirat al-islam* website, 15 March 2001, www.islammemo.cc/xfile/index.asp?CatNo=1&IDCategory=5, accessed Nov. 2005.

One of al-Suri's major preoccupations at the al-Ghuraba Media Center was developing and marketing his ideas on a general jihadi war fighting doctrine, which he had presented for the first time in 1991 (see chapter 4). By the summer 2000 he felt that the 'military theory' of his doctrine had reached a level and maturity whereby he felt comfortable in teaching it to selected audiences of mujahidin. Hence, he held a series of lectures in August 2000 which were video-taped and distributed.[142] They appeared online in January 2005 and al-Suri came to consider them to be his most important series of lectures.

Al-Suri also wrote several books, 'research studies', and articles in this period. He penned a lengthy study on Syria that was published shortly after the Syrian President Hafiz al-Asad's death in June 2000 in which he addresses 'a new generation of young men who are determined to join jihad', calling upon them to prepare for an armed uprising against the 'Nusayri occupation' of Syria.[143] The book is saturated with satirical descriptions of the Syrian regime, starting with his 'congratulations to every Muslim man and women on the perdition of Syria's Nusayri Pharaoh Hafiz al-Asad'.[144] It also contains religious justifications for combating the Nusayris, whom he describes at one point as being 'more infidel than the Jews and the Christians, and the most murderous to the people of Islam'.[145] The book details the Nusayris' crimes over the years, and concludes

---

142  *The Global Islamic Resistance Call*, p.1367.

143  Umar Abd al-Hakim (Abu Mus'ab al-Suri), *The Sunni People in the Levant Confronting the Nusayris, the Crusaders and the Jews* (in Arabic) (Kabul: The al-Ghuraba Center for Islamic Studies, 22 June 2000, The Series Issues for the Triumphant in Righteousness no.4), p.5. A slightly different version of this book is translated and has been published as 'Call to Jihad Against the Syrian Regime'. Document no.AFGP-2002-600966, *Combating Terrorism Center website* (West Point), www.ctc.usma.edu/aq/AFGP-2002-600966-trans1.pdf (1-6), and www.ctc.usma.edu/aq/AFGP-2002-600966-Original.pdf, accessed April 2006.

144  Umar Abd al-Hakim (Abu Mus'ab al-Suri), *The Sunni People in the Levant Confronting the Nusayris, the Crusaders and the Jews*, p.5.

145  Ibid., p.47.

with a number of recommendations for the mujahidin in their future confrontation with 'the ruling Nusayri-Alawitte sect in Syria and Lebanon'.[146]

In two studies completed in late 1999, al-Suri addressed the prospects for jihad in Yemen and Central Asia, areas which he considered highly promising and strategically very important for the future course of the jihadi movement.[147] In another work published in January 2001, al-Suri compiled statements and communiqués by bin Laden and Saad al-Faqih, in which they addressed Saudi clerics, in particular Shaykh Ibn Uthaymin and Ibn Baz, during the 1990s. He also added his own comments and analysis.[148] Al-Suri gained a reputation for being very harsh on those he termed 'the Sultan's clerics', who bestowed legitimacy on corrupt rulers.[149] This study was clearly one of those works. When interviewed in 1999, al-Suri lamented that the jihadi current had hardly any capable clerics who could speak freely and provide a strong religious basis for their struggle in defiance of the massive stream of Islamist literature condemning the jihadis.[150]

---

146  For the recommendations, see ibid., pp.57-61.

147  Umar Abd al-Hakim (Abu Mus'ab al-Suri), *The Responsibility of the People of Yemen towards the Holy Places of Muslims and their Wealth* (in Arabic) (Kabul: The al-Ghuraba Center for Islamic Studies, Oct. 1999, The Series Issues for the Triumphant in Righteousness no.2); and Umar Abd al-Hakim (Abu Mus'ab al-Suri), *The Muslims in Central Asia and the Coming Battle of Islam* (in Arabic) (Kabul: The Ghuraba Center for Islamic Studies, 5 Nov. 1999, The Series Issues for the Triumphant in Righteousness no.3).

148  Umar Abd al-Hakim (Abu Mus'ab al-Suri), *The Testimony of the Leaders of the Mujahidin and the Reform [Current] about the Sultan's Clerics in the Land of the Two Holy Places, Called Saudi Arabia: A Reading and Commentary of the Letters and Communiqués by Shaykh Osama bin Laden and Doctor Saad al-Faqih to Shaykh bin Baz, Shaykh bin Uthaymin and the Clerics of the Land of the Two Holy Places* (in Arabic) (Kabul: The al-Ghuraba Center for Islamic Studies and Media, 31 Jan. 2001, Issues for the Triumphant in Righteousness no.5).

149  'Meeting with the Kuwaiti Newspaper', transcript of audiofile no.6, p.7.

150  Audiofile no.7, p.2 in ibid.

The Algerian jihad had preoccupied him intensely before his departure from London in mid-1997. He recalls that he brought with him large files of press clippings, communiqués and documents on the Algerian experience, although due to the difficult security conditions, he had to leave 'many important things behind'.[151] His mind was set on one thing only: writing 'his testimony' on the Algerian jihadi experience, and publishing it as soon as possible. He was convinced about the usefulness of his experiences and lessons for the jihadi current. Through his testimony, he also wished to clear his name, since his role had been distorted. He had been accused of acts, events and possessing viewpoints for which others carried responsibility, in particular Abu Qutadah al-Filastini and his disciples. The 75-page booklet which al-Suri eventually published on the Algerian issue was in many ways an attack on Abu Qutadah.

Upon his arrival in Qandahar in August 1997, al-Suri locked himself away for nearly three weeks in a desert guest house. During this period, based on his recall of events and the numerous documents he had brought with him, he wrote a 130-page study, in addition to appendices consisting of 65 pages of press documents and official communiqués.[152] He had it reviewed by some of 'the brothers' and after more revisions and editing, the book manuscript was ready by the beginning of 1998. Al-Suri was clearly very eager to publish it, and in an audio-taped interview from March 1999 he shows the completed manuscript to his interviewer, informing him that it will be published the following month.[153]

This did not happen. Al-Suri met with strong disapproval from 'many senior jihadi figures and old brothers of different nationalities', especially from those who had connections with the Algerian issue.[154] The former LIFG Shura Council member, Noman Benotman recalls that he was among one of those who opposed the publication of

---

151  Umar Abd al-Hakim, *A Summary of My Testimony*, p.5.
152  Ibid.
153  'Meeting with the Kuwaiti Newspaper', transcript of audiofile no.3, p.6.
154  Umar Abd al-Hakim, *A Summary of My Testimony*, p.5.

al-Suri's study.[155] Nearly everyone al-Suri consulted discouraged him from publicizing the manuscript at that point because they feared that it would sow confusion on the Arab-Afghan scene. The Algerian issue was a very divisive one, and there were a multitude of views among the different jihadi groups: 'why stir up disagreements on a new arena due to an old cause?'[156] Second, in 1998 many felt that it was still too early to assess the Algerian experience. One needed to wait for more details, especially from Algerian mujahidin veterans who were expected to leave the Algerian scene and who might be able to provide more information about the events inside Algeria.[157]

Al-Suri had to postpone publication, but kept updating his manuscript, relying on press sources and his own interviews and conversations with returnees from Algeria. After September 11 and the US-led invasion of Afghanistan, al-Suri and the rest of the Arab-Afghan community fled Kabul. Al-Suri attempted to rescue as much as he could of his archive of books, documents and unpublished writings. Although he had to leave much behind, his manuscript on Algeria was dear to him, and he carried it along with the few things he was able to bring. When the security situation deteriorated further, and they were forced to cross the border into Pakistan in January 2002, they had to leave everything behind apart from their clothes. Al-Suri's manuscript on Algeria as well as his documents and drafts were entrusted with one of the groups who decided to stay behind in Afghanistan. He was later informed that they had burnt all his papers and fled, leaving as few traces behind as possible. Al-Suri's manuscript was lost forever. When the news reached him, he deeply regretted that he had not gone ahead and published it earlier, despite the objections he had encountered.[158] Al-Suri eventually wrote a new manuscript based on his memory only, and it was published online in early 2005 under the title *A Summary of My Testimony on Jihad in*

155  Author's interview with Noman Benotman, London, 15 Sept. 2006.
156  Umar Abd al-Hakim, *A Summary of My Testimony*, p.6.
157  Ibid.
158  Ibid.

*Algeria, 1988-96*. It remains the most personal and biographical of all his studies.

## AL-SURI AND THE AL-QAIDA LEADERSHIP

The relationship between al-Suri and bin Laden was turbulent, especially in the late 1990s, and most biographical accounts of the former refer to this conflict. In 2004 Spanish investigators told reporters that al-Suri had 'emerged as a prominent figure in a faction that has distanced itself from Bin Laden'.[159] US authorities also held that al-Suri 'attempted to form his own extremist group prior to September 11, 2001'.[160] Pierre Akel[161] of *Middle East Transparent*, noted about al-Suri that, 'One day he is with bin Laden and the next day he is strongly against him. [...] They are both allies and adversaries' at one and the same time.[162]

The details of al-Suri's conflict with bin Laden are little known, as is al-Suri's relationship with Ayman al-Zawahiri, who became the key strategic adviser to bin Laden during the Taleban period and has remained the undisputed deputy leader of al-Qaida ever since. Al-Suri saw himself as part of the revolutionary jihadi current which al-

159 Sebastian Rotella, 'Terrorism Suspects Traced to Iran', *The New York Times*, 1 Aug. 2004.

160 'WANTED: Mustafa Setmariam Nasar', *Reward for Justice website*, www. rewardsforjustice.net/english/wanted_captured/index.cfm?page=Nasar, accessed July 2005.

161 A professed Arab liberal, and owner of the trilingual *Middle East Transparent* website, Pierre Akel says that after 9/11, he stayed in frequent contact with 'the Londonistan leaders', read their literature and explored jihadi websites. See Michael Young, 'No Red Lines: A Reason Magazine interview with Middle East Transparent's Pierre Akel', *Middle East Transparent*, 9 Feb. 2006, www.metransparent.com/texts/michael_young_ interview_with_metransparent_pierre_akel.htm, accessed March 2006.

162 Pierre Akel, 'Abu Mus'ab al-Suri: "I deplore that there were no weapons of mass destructions in the planes that destroyed New York and Washington on 11 Sept.",' (in Arabic), *Shafaf al-Sharq al-Awsat/Middle East Transparent*, 22 Jan. 2005, www.metransparent.com/texts/communique_ abu_massab_al_suri_response_to_us_accusations, p.1.

Zawahiri and other EIJ leaders had promoted in Peshawar from the late 1980s. During his European exile in the 1990s, al-Suri was close to the EIJ, and especially its media office in London, even though he quarrelled with and alienated several figures associated with the EIJ in Britain.[163] He wrote articles and reports with the EIJ, he consulted them closely on the GIA crisis, and he spoke repeatedly with al-Zawahiri on the telephone, even during the latter's secret travels in the mid-1990s after he and other senior EIJ members had been expelled from Sudan and Yemen.[164] When returning to Afghanistan, al-Suri appears to have retained a close relationship with al-Zawahiri. In declassified documents which appear to be al-Suri's correspondence, he defended al-Zawahiri from criticism and seemed very well informed about developments inside the EIJ.[165] Significantly, he did not lash out against al-Zawahiri the way he did against bin Laden.

Al-Suri's troubled relationship with bin Laden was coloured by his mistrust for Saudi jihadis. He suspected them of being Muslim Brothers in disguise or dogmatic salafis who blindly obeyed their clerics and shaykhs. Based on his own extensive experience from the Afghan training camps, he also considered them weak fighters, who lacked the necessary political and ideological consciousness. Above all, al-Suri knew that the Saudi jihadis had a standing offer from the Saudi authorities to repent and return safely home to their families, a courtesy which Syrian, Egyptian or Algerian jihadis were not extended by their regimes. For the Saudis, the jihadi camps in Afghanistan were a kind of adventure seeking experience, al-Suri held, or simply

---

163  Ibid.; and author's telephone interview with Saad al-Faqih, 17 Sept. 2006.

164  Umar Abd al-Hakim, *A Summary of My Testimony*, p.53.

165  See Document no.AFGP-2002-601693, 'Status of Jihad', *Combating Terrorism Center website* (West Point), www.ctc.usma.edu/aq/AFGP-2002-601693-Trans.pdf and www.ctc.usma.edu/aq/AFGP-2002-601693-Orig.pdf, accessed April 2006, pp.4–5. For a discussion of the authorship of the document, see bibliography.

a way of purifying themselves after having 'spent time with a whore in Bangkok', as he indelicately put it.[166]

Al-Suri's attitude to Ayman al-Zawahiri and the EIJ group was different. There was never any doubt in his mind about the EIJ's commitment to fight the tyrannical regimes of the Arab Muslim world. The organization had fought the Egyptian regime from its inception and al-Zawahiri's slogan, at least till the mid-1990s, had been that 'the road to Jerusalem passes through Cairo'.[167] (By this he meant that Palestine could only be liberated after the Mubarak regime had been toppled and replaced by an Islamic one.) Yet al-Suri was never completely convinced about bin Laden's willingness to take the fight into the heart of the Middle East. In al-Suri's mind, the Saudis' unwillingness to fight their own corrupt rulers weakened the grand strategy of the struggle against 'the Crusaders'. In his lectures, al-Suri put enormous emphasis on the strategic impact of striking Jewish, American, and Western interests in the heart of the Arab world: the Arab Peninsula and the Levant. In his mind the 'new Crusader imperialism' aimed to take control of the oil resources and the holy places, both of which were strategically located precisely in that region. Any attack here would damage the Crusaders many times more than attacks elsewhere. (I have quoted one of these lectures extensively below.)[168] Hence, when bin Laden chose to strike against the US embassies in Dar es-Salaam and Nairobi instead, probably

---

166 See interview with al-Suri (or Omar Karim) in Mark Huband, *Warriors of the Prophet*, p.3. See also Mark Huband, 'Holy war on the world', *The Financial Times*, 28 Nov. 2001, http://specials.ft.com/attackonterrorism/FT3RXH0CKUC.html, accessed April 2006; *The Global Islamic Resistance Call*, pp.712, 1421; and 'Meeting with the Kuwaiti Newspaper', transcript of audiofile no.2, p.1.

167 See Ayman al-Zawahiri, 'The Road to Jerusalem Passes through Cairo' (in Arabic), *al-Mujahidun*, accessed via *minbar al-tawhid wa'l-jihad*, www.tawhed.ws/r?i=1102, accessed Oct. 2006.

168 Transcript of 'Jihad is the Solution'-audiofile no.37, tape no.10b, 06:28 – 16:00, *muntada al-sawt* www.saowt.com/forum/showthread.php?t=16158, accessed Oct. 2006.

because he had very few assets inside Saudi Arabia[169], al-Suri was quick to criticize.[170] It is possible that al-Suri faulted bin Laden for building an over-centralized, overt, and immobile organizational structure in Afghanistan, which was extremely vulnerable to US air strikes. In his later writing, al-Suri claimed that he warned of this after the 1998 cruise missile attacks:

I noticed the precise targeting, and the intensity of the shooting, when 75 cruise missiles hit the targets during a few minutes, when America was able to put one missile in every room in the camps... I talked to many of our brothers at that time, saying that after this event, the era of fixed camps had ended, and that we had to rely on the methods of training in houses and 'camps of nomadic mujahidin' as I called them... fake houses, two cars, a number of individuals, a camp in the desert and the wasteland. The training programme is implemented and they leave... Another group arrives at another place, and so on... However, the Arab circles were relying on the methods of propaganda, mobilization and calling upon the Islamic Nation to go to the camps, not paying any attention to the era of satellites and long-range targeting.[171]

While differences over al-Qaida's centralised structure and targeting strategies played a role, by far the most important issue in al-Suri's conflict with bin Laden was the relationship with the Taleban regime. Al-Suri harshly criticised the al-Qaida leader for not respecting the rules of conduct set by the Taleban. In doing so, bin Laden endangered the Arab presence in Afghanistan as a whole, al-Suri argued.

In his assessment of the Taleban movement, published in October 1998, al-Suri had highlighted the Taleban's willingness to host and protect bin Laden and Arab mujahidin who were fugitives in their own countries as their most positive characteristic.[172] Al-Suri says he

---

169  I am indebted to Thomas Hegghammer for the assessment of bin Laden's organization inside Saudi Arabia. See his *Violent Islamism in Saudi Arabia 1979-2006*, forthcoming.

170  Author's telephone interview with Saad al-Faqih, 17 Sept. 2006.

171  *The Global Islamic Resistance Call*, pp.1425-6.

172  Umar Abd al-Hakim (Abu Mus'ab al-Suri), *Afghanistan, the Taleban, and*

had been 'a visiting guest' with Osama bin Laden in Jalalabad when the Taleban entered the town in 1996. He had been present at a number of meetings between Taleban officials and bin Laden, and he was deeply moved by the warmth with which the Taleban had greeted them.[173]

When bin Laden began taking advantage of the Taleban's hospitality and trust, or so he thought, al-Suri raised his voice in protest. Things apparently came to a head during a meeting in spring 1998 in Jihad Wal, one of the older training camps near Khowst, Afghanistan, when a fierce quarrel erupted between the two. Al-Suri had been particularly incensed by the fact that bin Laden had acted as if he were Afghanistan's ruler, treating him and his life-long comrade-in-arms, Abu Khalid al-Suri, as 'guests', not as 'brothers and supporters'.[174] Bin Laden had reportedly told al-Suri that:

You are guests. Just like you are entitled to hospitality, the host also is entitled to accommodate his guests where he pleases. We don't necessarily have to accommodate you here. Give us the freedom to choose how to host you![175]

Al-Suri had been in slanging matches with Abu Qutadah in London, and in Afghanistan he did not hold back, not even in front of a dignitary such as bin Laden. Like most Saudis, bin Laden strongly disliked hot-headed, vociferous quarrels; he nurtured an image of himself as 'a man of politeness, humbleness and bashfulness'.[176] The altercation reportedly ended with bin Laden saying: 'Let us keep away from one another to keep our mutual respect as Muslims. Stay

---

*The Battle of Islam Today* (in Arabic), p.25.

173 Ibid., pp.25-6.

174 Emailed Letter from Abu Mus'ab al-Suri and Abu Khalid al-Suri to Osama bin Laden, Kabul, Afghanistan, dated 19 July 1998, p.4.

175 Ibid.

176 See, for example, document no.AFGP-2002-801138, 'Various Admin Documents and Questions', www.ctc.usma.edu/aq/AFGP-2002-801138-Trans.pdf, accessed April 2006, p.30.

away so we can keep this mutual respect'.[177] Their fallout was never absolute, and to the outside world al-Suri usually denied that any such differences existed (see below). The main consequence was that al-Suri would no longer be considered a member of bin Laden's inner circle[178] and hence was unable to take part directly in bin Laden's future strategic planning.

Noman Benotman, who met with al-Suri in this period, recalls that he had expressed his deep frustration with bin Laden, using very harsh words about the al-Qaida leader, calling him 'a Pharaoh' and 'things that later he would not even use about Bush and Rumsfeld'.[179] His contempt for bin Laden was such that he reportedly portrayed him as a child to his contacts in the Taleban government: 'he does not know what he is doing. You have to take his hand and prevent him from doing what he is doing'.[180]

Al-Suri and bin Laden did not exchange words for a very long time.[181] When he was interviewed by the Kuwaiti newspaper *al-Ra'y al-Amm* in 1999, al-Suri let it be known that he and bin Laden had different views and opinions: 'It is my conviction that our brother bin Laden is a man with a mission, a man with a cause, irrespective of my opinion, or the opinions of the enemies and adversaries on this cause'.[182] While he was careful to emphasise that his relationship with bin Laden was based on mutual sympathy (*ta'atuf*), he rejected

---

177  Author's telephone interview with Saad al-Faqih, 17 Sept. 2006.

178  Ibid.

179  Author's interview with Noman Benotman, London, 15 Sept. 2006.

180  'Bin Laden Ordered the Registration of Names of Volunteers for Suicide Operations among the Arabs in Eastern Afghanistan: The Number Reached 122' (in Arabic), *arabiyyat.com*, 21 Nov. 2003, http://www.arabiyat.com/forums/showthread.php?s=&threadid=77762, accessed Oct. 2006.

181  Author's interview with Noman Benotman, London, 15 Sept. 2006.

182  Cited in 'Meeting with the Kuwaiti Newspaper', transcript of audiofile no.2, pp.3-4.

emphatically that bin Laden was his leader: 'I do not have any organizational relationship with Shaykh bin Laden'.[183]

Al-Suri's honest opinion of bin Laden is revealed in an email he and his aide, Abu Khalid al-Suri, sent to bin Laden on 19 July 1998 (not 1999 as reported elsewhere).[184] Their forceful vocabulary is striking, although it must be noted that there was a frankness and outspokenness in the Arab-Afghan community that was unheard of in the states where most of the Arab jihadis hailed from. Al-Suri's letter was among thousands of stored al-Qaida documents and email correspondence on a computer purchased by a *Wall Street Journal* reporter in Afghanistan in late 2001. The computer had been stolen from al-Qaida's headquarters only days before the Taleban fled Kabul in late 2001, and had been used primarily by Ayman al-Zawahiri.[185] In this email correspondence, al-Suri and his companion Abu Khalid al-Suri addressed the ongoing crisis in Arab-Taleban relations, strongly admonishing bin Laden for his hunger for publicity and arrogance towards the Taleban government. The following quote, published in *The Atlantic Monthly* in September 2004, is revealing:

Noble brother Abu Abdullah, Peace upon you, and God's mercy and blessings. This message [concerns] the problem between you and the Leader of the Faithful …

The results of this crisis can be felt even here in Kabul and other places. Talk about closing down the camps has spread. Discontent with the Arabs has become clear. Whispers between the Taliban with some of our non-Arab brothers has become customary. In short, our brother Abu Abdullah's latest troublemaking with the Taliban and the Leader of the Faithful jeopardizes the Arabs, and the Arab presence, today in all of Afghanistan, for no good reason. It provides a ripe opportunity for all adversaries, including America, the West, the Jews, Saudi Arabia, Pakistan, the Mas'ud-Dostum alliance, etc., to serve the Arabs a blow that could end up causing their most faithful

---

183  Ibid., p.4.

184  Emailed Letter from Abu Mus'ab al-Suri and Abu Khalid al-Suri to Osama bin Laden, Kabul, Afghanistan, dated 19 July 1998.

185  Alan Cullison, 'Inside Al-Qaeda's Hard Drive', *The Atlantic Monthly*, Sept. 2004, www.theatlantic.com/doc/200409/cullison, accessed Sept. 2005.

allies to kick them out ... Our brother [bin Laden] will help our enemies reach their goal free of charge! ...

The strangest thing I have heard so far is Abu Abdullah's saying that he wouldn't listen to the Leader of the Faithful when he asked him to stop giving interviews ... I think our brother [bin Laden] has caught the disease of screens, flashes, fans, and applause ...

The only solution out of this dilemma is what a number of knowledgeable and experienced people have agreed upon ...

Abu Abdullah should go to the Leader of the Faithful with some of his brothers and tell them that ... the Leader of the Faithful was right when he asked you to refrain from interviews, announcements, and media encounters, and that you will help the Taliban as much as you can in their battle, until they achieve control over Afghanistan. ... You should apologize for any inconvenience or pressure you have caused ... and commit to the wishes and orders of the Leader of the Faithful on matters that concern his circumstances here ...

The Leader of the Faithful, who should be obeyed where he reigns, is Muhammad Omar, not Osama bin Laden. Osama bin Laden and his companions are only guests seeking refuge and have to adhere to the terms laid out by the person who provided it for them. This is legitimate and logical.[186]

This excerpt has become a much quoted source on al-Suri's conflict with bin Laden, but it is only a small part of the letter in question. Due to the generous courtesy of Andrew Higgins and Alan Cullison, who came across the famous Kabul computer, this author has studied the seven page letter in its entirety, the most salient features of which will be explored in some detail.

Al-Suri's emailed letter was obviously part of something bigger. True to his penchant for prolix correspondence, al-Suri described it as merely 'a summary' of his main points in a forthcoming 'comprehensive advice message' to bin Laden, which he had not yet been able to complete due to 'emergency travel circumstances'.[187]

---

186 Ibid.
187 Emailed Letter from Abu Mus'ab al-Suri and Abu Khalid al-Suri to

It is clear from al-Suri's letter in July 1998 that his relationship with bin Laden had been chilly for quite some time. He was already past the point where he thought his advice would benefit the al-Qaida leader; instead, he remarked that 'I have observed the futility of this. I felt that my advice to our brother have become more irritating than useful'.[188] The purpose of the letter was simply to exercise 'our Islamic legal right in preventing harm to ourselves and to Muslims'. Together with his forthcoming 'comprehensive advice message', the emailed letter would be 'our last advice to you to absolve ourselves before God and so that you don't later say you weren't warned'.[189]

The key event which prompted al-Suri to write such a harshly worded letter was the conference organized by bin Laden in May 1998 to announce the establishment of 'The World Islamic Front for Jihad against Jews and Crusaders'.[190] Al-Suri objected neither to the declaration as such, nor to the new alliance of jihadi groups. On the contrary, he reportedly regarded it as a great step forward.[191] But he was dismayed that bin Laden had acted unilaterally, without the Taleban's permission, and that his media event had proved highly embarrassing to the Taleban regime. Bin Laden's conference had been held in 'camps, the existence of which was constantly denied by the Taleban', al-Suri wrote.[192] Such 'whims' by bin Laden had a very

---

Osama bin Laden, Kabul, Afghanistan, dated 19 July 1998, p.2.

188  Ibid.

189  Ibid.

190  See 'The Text of the Communique by The World Islamic Front for Jihad against Jews and Crusaders', (in Arabic) *al-Quds al-'Arabi*, 23 Feb. 1998, p.3; and Alan Cullison and Andrew Higgins, 'A Once-Stormy Terror Alliance Was Solidified by Cruise Missiles', *The Wall Street Journal*, 2 Aug. 2002;

191  Author's interview with Camille Tawil, London, 14 Sept. 2006.

192  Emailed Letter from Abu Mus'ab al-Suri and Abu Khalid al-Suri to Osama bin Laden, Kabul, Afghanistan, dated 19 July 1998, p.5. According to the Pakistani journalist Rahimullah Yusufzai, Mullah Omar had learned of the press event from a BBC report. Yusufzai had himself received a phone call from Mullah Omar who vented his anger over bin Laden's media publicity campaign: '"How can he [bin Laden] hold a press conference without my

strong negative impact on the Arab-Afghan community, al-Suri argued, referring to the fact that the Taleban had responded by closing the important Khalden camp as well as the Pakistani camps.[193]

Al-Suri was clearly concerned that anti-Arab factions within the Taleban regime might gain more influence due to bin Laden's 'troublemaking'. He pointed out to bin Laden that the Taleban consisted of a 'mixture' of different trends, some of which included corrupt individuals. Furthermore, the Arab presence in Afghanistan had benefited the Taleban very little in practical terms. Bin Laden's promises to the Taleban had ranged from 'urbanisation projects, road-building, economic projects, introducing 300 mujahidin to defend Kabul etc', but all these pledges came to nothing: 'the wind blew [them] away', al-Suri noted sarcastically.[194] Instead, bin Laden's policies had increased international and regional pressure against the Taleban. Worse still, they had 'humiliated [Mullah Omar] and made him look like a man who is not aware of even what takes place in his land'.[195]

It is clear from the correspondence that in mid-1998 al-Suri had already attended several meetings between bin Laden and representatives of the Taleban regime. According to al-Suri, the Taleban had told bin Laden in no uncertain terms that: 'if you wish to fight America and your adversaries then do so without much talk and shouting from our lands as our condition is critical'.[196] In al-Suri's eyes, bin Laden had failed to grasp the new geopolitical reality. While al-Suri himself had been heavily involved in bringing bin Laden and his cause to the attention of the global media in 1996-97, by mid-1998

---

permission? There is only one ruler. Is it me or Osama?'" Yusufzai says bin Laden later apologized to Mullah Omar and promised not to hold any more news conferences without permission. Citation from Alan Cullison and Andrew Higgins, 'A Once-Stormy Terror Alliance Was Solidified by Cruise Missiles', *The Wall Street Journal*, 2 Aug. 2002.

193 Emailed Letter from Abu Mus'ab al-Suri and Abu Khalid al-Suri to Osama bin Laden, Kabul, Afghanistan, dated 19 July 1998, p.5.

194 Ibid.

195 Ibid.

196 Ibid., p.3.

he clearly judged that bin Laden's continued 'media war' had lost its purpose: it 'now serves the infidels rather than the believers'.[197]

Al-Suri also addressed the reasons for Laden's disobedience *vis-à-vis* the Taleban. He contended that it was largely a result of bin Laden's experience in Sudan, where he had obeyed the regime's restrictions from the start. As a result, the powers that be in Khartoum had become emboldened and steadily extracted more concessions and money from bin Laden. This did not prevent the Sudanese government from evicting him and his followers from the country. Thereafter, bin Laden had sworn: 'we don't want the Taleban to deal with us with the same insolence that the Sudanese dealt with us when we were lenient on them. They silenced us, then restricted us, then kicked us out'.[198]

Al-Suri did not object to bin Laden's description of the Sudanese government's policy towards him. In fact, he depicted the al-Qaida leader as someone who had been more than willing to stumble 'from one humiliation to another'.[199] Al-Suri only touched on this theme in his letter, vowing to discuss it in detail in his forthcoming comprehensive advice, but his main criticism of bin Laden's policy in Sudan is clear: Bin Laden had proved himself submissive to a corrupt regime to the extent that he betrayed his brothers:

You testified falsely that they apply Sharia and support Islam. You offered them everything. They asked you to keep silent and you accepted. You even accepted when they asked you to kick out some of your brothers and the Libyans. Then they kicked you out and held even the women of our brothers and the elderly at gunpoint. Nevertheless, you again offered to fight with them under a flag that enjoys no shred of legitimacy when their false god al-Zubayr [referring to a Sudanese minister] delivered our Libyan brothers to their death and the violation of their honour.[200]

---

197  Ibid., p.7.

198  Ibid., p.5.

199  Ibid.

200  Ibid. See also Umar Abd al-Hakim (Abu Mus'ab al-Suri), *Afghanistan, the Taleban, and the Battle of Islam Today* (in Arabic) p.39.

In al-Suri's view, bin Laden drew the wrong lessons from the Sudanese experience. By adopting a much tougher line towards the Taleban government, which in al-Suri's eyes was a far more legitimate, helpful, and worthy regime than the Sudanese, bin Laden proved to be an ungrateful guest. The Taleban had imposed no restrictions other than an end to bin Laden's media interviews. This was a small price to pay for the sanctuary and freedom of operation they enjoyed in Afghanistan, al-Suri argued. He went so far as to taunt bin Laden for his dishonorable behaviour:

Where, then, is manhood when you oppress those helpless people when they only promised you protection and permitted you to fight only on the condition of silence? Wouldn't they be right if they tell you: 'A lion against me and an ostrich at war'. Or as poor people say: 'My father only has power over my mother'.[201]

Al-Suri's criticism of bin Laden was not confined to the specific issues mentioned above, but went to the very heart of the Sheikh's style of leadership and management. He used words such as 'obstinacy, egotism and pursuit of internal battles' to describe bin Laden's leadership.[202] Furthermore, he claimed that since the foundation of al-Qaida, bin Laden had failed properly to practice 'shura', or consultation, with his experienced cohorts:

Due to our brother Abu Abdallah's behaviour concerning opinion and decisions, as he accustomed us for over 10 years, it is my conviction that most of the advice he receives from us and other people with experience has not benefited him.[203]

Al-Suri claimed, furthermore, that key members of the al-Qaida's leadership shared his views on bin Laden's management style:

---

201  Emailed Letter from Abu Mus'ab al-Suri and Abu Khalid al-Suri to Osama bin Laden, Kabul, Afghanistan, dated 19 July 1998, p.5.

202  Ibid., p.3. See also Alan Cullison and Andrew Higgins, 'A Once-Stormy Terror Alliance Was Solidified by Cruise Missiles', *The Wall Street Journal*, 2 Aug. 2002.

203  Emailed Letter from Abu Mus'ab al-Suri and Abu Khalid al-Suri to Osama bin Laden, Kabul, Afghanistan, dated 19 July 1998, p.2.

Opinions we received from those around him [i.e. bin Laden], including Abu Hafs [i.e. Muhammad Atif, al-Qaida's top military commander], the Doctor [i.e. Ayman al-Zawahiri], most of the brothers and the many people who advise him indicate they disagree with this attitude on his part and think it's wrong.[204]

Interestingly, al-Suri specifically highlighted that al-Zawahiri had been promoting *shura* (consultation) and 'listening to people with experience [...] as a path that Abu Abdallah has pledged to follow'.[205] In other words, it was bin Laden and only him al-Suri criticised, not the al-Qaida leadership as a whole.

The fierceness of al-Suri's frontal attack on the al-Qaida leader appears to stem, at least in part, from al-Suri's general mistrust of the Saudi jihadis. In his letter, he set out his suspicions that bin Laden was secretly considering a bargain with the Saudi ruling family to allow for his safe return back to Saudi Arabia: 'Abu Abdallah and the imprisoned clerics [from the *sahwi* or revivalist trend] may surprise us tomorrow with a compromise with prince Abdullah al-Su'ud. Abu Abdallah may even return to Sudan to monitor the farm'.[206] By souring the Arab-Afghan community's relations with the Taleban regime, bin Laden had put the entire Arab community in Afghanistan at risk, al-Suri argued.[207] While bin Laden had several options, many Arab-Afghans did not. They had made Afghanistan their home and had nowhere to go. From al-Suri's letter, the fear of losing the Afghanistan sanctuary seems to have been very real:

We are in a ship that you are burning on false and mistaken grounds of good deeds. We left our land to defend our religion in response to the call to fight the Jews and the Christians. [...] Then, you acted the way you did, leaving us only this final hole. What right have you to destroy our and others' homes! [...] You admit that if the Taleban and the Afghans dare break the highest ranking Arab then those below him have no hope. All the brothers

---

204  Ibid., p.6.
205  Ibid.
206  Ibid.
207  Ibid.

will then be vulnerable and we won't have anywhere to go except Iran, or God forbid, seeking asylum with Islam's enemies [...][208].

Al-Suri concluded his letter by warning bin Laden that he might soon find himself isolated, bereft of any leadership position, if he did not mend his ways:

Do you want the Arabs here [...] to have no other alternative than to tell the Taliban and the leader of the believers of the reality? Do you want them to tell them that Abu Abdallah only represents himself and his groups of guards but not the Arabs? And that we don't agree with his wrong attitude and his position towards the Taleban? This also involves the obvious harm of hanging our dirty laundry for others to see.[209]

Al-Suri's letter to bin Laden in July 1998 provides a rare insight into the tense rivalries and disagreements both inside al-Qaida and between al-Qaida and the Taleban regime at a point when little of this was known to the outside world. Alan Cullison and Andrew Higgins who reviewed many other internal al-Qaida documents from that period confirm that the relations between al-Qaida and the Taleban were indeed very stormy. In mid-1998 there had been a near rupture in relations, and it appeared as if the Taleban were on the verge of agreeing to US requests to evict bin Laden and his entourage.[210]

What appears to have radically shifted the temperature of the chilly relationship was the US missile strikes against six suspected terrorist training camps in Afghanistan on 21 August 1998, in retaliation for the terrorist bombing of the US embassies in Nairobi and Dar al-Salaam.[211] The attacks 'shut off Taliban discussion of

---

208  Ibid.

209  Ibid.

210  Alan Cullison and Andrew Higgins, 'A Once-Stormy Terror Alliance Was Solidified by Cruise Missiles', *The Wall Street Journal*, 2 Aug. 2002; and Alan Cullison and Andrew Higgins, 'Computer in Kabul holds chilling memos: PC apparently used by al-Qaida leaders reveals details of four years of terrorism', *The Wall Street Journal*, 31 Dec. 2001.

211  'U.S. missiles pound targets in Afghanistan, Sudan', *CNN.com*, 21 Aug. 1998, www.cnn.com/US/9808/20/us.strikes.02, accessed Feb. 2007.

expelling the militants.'[212] This outcome was not evident at the time. Al-Suri recalls that the Taleban had convened a three day meeting to decide what their response would be:

All of us expected that they would request Abu Abdallah and the Arabs to freeze their activity and close their camps. I hurried to get the latest news from some of the Taleban ministers about the result of the meeting. To my surprise, I learned from one of them that: 'The Emir of the Faithful only reprimanded some of us who had been struck with fear and hesitation. He gave us a lesson in putting your trust in God (*tawakkul 'ala Allah*) and not fearing America'.[213]

Osama bin Laden also mended his relationship with Mullah Omar. By flattering the Taleban chief with lofty titles such as Islam's new caliph, and predicting that he would become the head of an expanding Islamic state encompassing most of Central Asia, bin Laden managed to win over Mullah Omar and gain his full support.[214] Bin Laden also issued an apology to Mullah Omar, pledging not to organize news conferences without the Taleban's explicit permission and recognizing Omar as the sovereign leader of Afghanistan.[215] This was exactly what al-Suri had demanded in his letter to bin Laden. Hence, it is possible that al-Suri's criticism helped to propel bin Laden towards rebuilding al-Qaida's relationship with the Taleban, but al-Suri's acid tongue and outspokenness clearly chilled the *personal* relationship between the two.

---

212  Cited in Alan Cullison and Andrew Higgins, 'A Once-Stormy Terror Alliance Was Solidified by Cruise Missiles', *The Wall Street Journal*, 2 Aug. 2002.

213  Cited in Umar Abd al-Hakim (Abu Mus'ab al-Suri), *Afghanistan, the Taleban and the Battle of Islam Today* (in Arabic) p.27.

214  Alan Cullison, 'Inside Al-Qaeda's Hard Drive', *The Atlantic Monthly*, Sept. 2004, www.theatlantic.com/doc/200409/cullison, accessed Sept. 2005.

215  Alan Cullison and Andrew Higgins, 'A Once-Stormy Terror Alliance Was Solidified by Cruise Missiles', *The Wall Street Journal*, 2 Aug. 2002.

## A SECESSIONIST LEADER?

In mid-2000 the Arab, Asian and Western media reported that al-Suri had emerged as leader of a dissident faction within al-Qaida. This came amid reports of the Taleban government asserting stricter control over al-Qaida and its training camps.[216] The new policy by the Taleban government came in response to increased US and international pressure to extradite bin Laden and al-Qaida leaders. In June 2000 Pakistan announced a new policy of curbing militant Islamist networks in both Pakistan and neighboring Afghanistan. In May that year, responding to Pakistani pressure, the Taleban had closed well-known training camps including the Rishkor complex outside Kabul. The Pakistani government, upon which the Taleban regime depended heavily for fuel, weapons and other strategic goods, also aired the possibility that it would demand the shutting-down of eighteeen training camps, the extradition of Pakistani and Arab fugitives, and improved border controls.[217]

The internal disputes and alleged 'secession' in al-Qaida's ranks was reportedly the result of a new Taleban decree ordering all foreign training camps to be subordinated to the Taleban Ministry of Defence. Six al-Qaida camps were placed directly under the Afghan Ministry of Defence and subsequently amalgamated into three camps. The Taleban also decreed in July 2000 that it was temporarily shutting down all the training bases. The Taleban's irritation over bin Laden's media profile and their fears that he might be tracked and

---

216 See, for example, 'Laden's party splits' (DPA) *The Tribune* (India), 31 July 2000, http://www.tribuneindia.com/2000/20000801/world.htm#4, accessed April 2006; "Saudi prince' earmarks £275,000 for assassinating bin Laden' (in Arabic), *Al-Quds al-Arabi* (London), 31 July 2000, www.alhramain.com/text/alraseed/974/tqareer/6.htm, accessed Sept. 2005; and 'Bin Laden reportedly changes headquarters, guards, wife,' (LexisNexis Title), *Al-Jazeera TV*, 1 Aug. 2000 0530 GMT via LexisNexis citing the London-based *Sunday Telegraph*.

217 Judith Miller, 'Pakistan Outlines Plans To Curb Militant Networks', *The New York Times*, 10 June 2000.

assassinated led also to the confiscation of some of his communication equipment.[218]

Many al-Qaida members vehemently opposed this new policy and bin Laden himself was said to have resisted the new Taleban orders. However, not all of them agreed with bin Laden's disobedient stance *vis-à-vis* the Taleban, and al-Qaida was said to be divided on this issue. Media reports had it that a group of some fifty to sixty bin Laden followers, who were Afghan-Arab veterans from Algeria, Jordan, Saudi Arabia, Egypt and Syria, had 'split off to form a pro-Taleban faction' under al-Suri's leadership. Al-Suri was described as 'one of his oldest associates'.[219] He had reportedly voiced the demand that all Arab-Afghan fighters in Afghanistan be united and placed under Taleban command.[220]

Al-Suri was at this point relatively unknown outside jihadi circles. His pseudonym was even misspelled by the well-informed *al-Quds al-Arabi* daily in London.[221] Given his devotion to writing, teaching, and training, he did not seem a likely candidate for a renegade faction

---

218 See *Washington Times*, 30 July 2000, p.C7, available via 'Weekly Intelligence Notes', no.31-00, 4 Aug. 2000, *Association of Former Intelligence Officers website*, www.afio.com/sections/wins/2000/2000-31.html, accessed April 2006; and 'Afghan Taleban Ask US to Stop Repeating "False" Claims Over UBL' (WNC-title), *AFP* (Hong Kong), 16 Aug. 2000, via WNC-Dialogue.

219 See article in *Washington Times*, 30 July 2000, p.C7, available via 'Weekly Intelligence Notes', no.31-00, 4 Aug. 2000, *Association of Former Intelligence Officers website*, www.afio.com/sections/wins/2000/2000-31.html, accessed April 2006; and "Saudi prince' earmarks £275,000 for assassinating bin Laden' (in Arabic), *Al-Quds al-Arabi* (London) 31 July 2000, www.alhramain.com/text/alraseed/974/tqareer/6.htm, accessed Sept. 2005.

220 'Laden's party splits' (DPA) *The Tribune* (India), 31 July 2000, http://www.tribuneindia.com/2000/20000801/world.htm#4, accessed April 2006; and Mahendra Ved, 'Wedding could open Yemeni door for Osama', *The Times of India*, 5 Aug. 2000, http://timesofindia.indiatimes.com/articleshow/858910034.cms, accessed April 2006.

221 "Saudi prince' earmarks £275,000 for assassinating bin Laden' (in Arabic), *Al-Quds al-Arabi* (London), 31 July 2000, www.alhramain.com/text/alraseed/974/tqareer/6.htm, accessed Sept. 2005.

commander. Furthermore, as was noted by a contemporary source: 'Osama has become a hero. Who knows Suri?'[222] The CIA and other Western intelligence agencies noted the rumours of a split, but found no confirmation of an al-Qaida dissident group. Al-Suri was judged to be 'talker, not doer.' Hence, his statements were thought to be of little significance.[223]

In mid-2000, press accounts of tensions between the Taleban and al-Qaida portrayed al-Suri as 'less of an extremist' than bin Laden and a person that 'holds moderate views on the Islamists' differences with the West'.[224] There was conflicting information as to what influence the secessionists under al-Suri's leadership had on the Taleban. Some sources say they were allowed to operate and communicate freely on Afghan territory and were promised that their training camps would be reopened. Other press accounts, also citing Afghan sources, claimed that the Taleban had banned all training camp activities in July 2000. The ban also included a three month closure of al-Suri's offices and camps. In fact, the closure of al-Suri's camps came 'at the request of Osama'.[225]

The closure of the al-Qaida camps did not last long. Less than two weeks after the initial reports of the secession, Pakistani newspapers reported that the Taleban government had reopened the training camps. The reason for this swift turnabout stemmed from the fact that in their war against the Northern Alliance, the Taleban depended to a certain extent on recruits, trainers, and military expertise emanating from the camps of al-Qaida and other foreign jihadi groups.[226]

---

222  'Split in Bin Laden's Al Qaida outfit', *India News Online*, 7 Aug. 2000, http://news.indiamart.com/news-analysis/split-in-bin-laden-s-8054. html, accessed April 2006.

223  Interview with Michael Scheuer, Washington, 14 March 2007.

224  Cited in 'Laden's party splits' (DPA) *The Tribune* (India), 31 July 2000, http://www.tribuneindia.com/2000/20000801/world.htm#4, accessed April 2006.

225  'Laden's party splits' (DPA) *The Tribune* (India), 31 July 2000, http://www. tribuneindia.com/2000/20000801/world.htm#4, accessed April 2006.

226  'Taleban Reopen Military Training Camps (WNC-title)', *Pakistan*

One of the reasons why leading Arab-Afghan veterans such as al-Suri might have been conceived of as a challenge to bin Laden was the nature of the jihadi community in Afghanistan. As already alluded to above, many of the 1,500 or so foreign mujahidin veterans in Afghanistan in 2000 were either 'freelancers' or were affiliated first and foremost to a local or regional jihadi group.[227] Even if they respected and collaborated with al-Qaida, only a minority had sworn the oath of allegiance or *bay'ah* to bin Laden. Outspoken and eloquent critics such as al-Suri could easily stir up unrest in al-Qaida's support base.

Another reason was the mounting US and international pressure on the Taleban regime to hand over bin Laden. Although the US cruise missile strike on the Afghan training camps in 1998, following the East African Embassy bombings, reportedly had the adverse effect of solidifying the al-Qaida-Taleban alliance, the issue remained an open one.[228] In the Asian press, it was rumored that Pakistani authorities were looking for new ways to remove bin Laden from Afghanistan in order to avert military action near its borders. Security experts, interviewed by an Indian newspaper, envisioned a scenario in which Pakistan and the Taleban would hand over bin Laden clandestinely to the Americans, and publicly blame the CIA for the incident. In this context, the al-Suri-led secession was reportedly seen as an opportunity: 'All those who broke away from the Saudi Arabian billionaire are being tapped for this operation', the

---

(Islamabad, in Urdu), 10 Aug. 2000, p.5, via WNC-Dialogue.

227  For an estimate of the number of foreign fighters in Afghanistan, see 'Welcome no longer warm in Taleban "terrorist" camp', *Reuters*, 14 June 2000. These numbers were Western intelligence estimates and included also Arabs, Chechens and Uzbeks. According to the Pakistani daily *The News*, there were some 1,000-1,100 Arab militants in Afghanistan; see 'Laden's party splits' (DPA), *The Tribune* (India), 31 July 2000, http://www.tribuneindia.com/2000/20000801/world.htm#4, accessed April 2006, citing *The News*, 31 July 2000.

228  Alan Cullison and Andrew Higgins, 'A Once-Stormy Terror Alliance Was Solidified by Cruise Missiles', *Wall Street Journal*, 2 Aug. 2002.

newspaper reported.[229] Another scenario was that bin Laden would move on to either Chechnya or Yemen. His marriage to a Yemenite woman in July 2000 gave rise to speculation that Yemen was highest on his list of alternative destinations.[230]

There may also be a financial explanation for the ups-and-downs of the al-Qaida-Taleban relationship. With the freezing of bin Laden's assets worldwide, he was less able to provide financial support to the cash-strapped Taleban government, which was also suffering from a UN sanction regime imposed in 1999.[231] Money had clearly become an issue in al-Qaida-Taleban relations that could not be ignored. This gave weight to al-Suri's call for unity under the Taleban's banner and for a less confrontational policy in order to secure the future existence of the Islamic Emirate.

As news of the al-Qaida secessionists was reported in Western and Arab media at the end of July 2000, al-Suri promptly gave an interview to *al-Jazeera* TV in which he strenuously denied the reports and criticized the TV channel for broadcasting 'unfounded and totally baseless allegations'.[232] The interview is interesting in light of the role which al-Suri then claimed for himself in the jihadi movement. He said

---

229 O. P. Verma, 'Pak, Taliban may get rid of Laden', *Deccan Herald* (Bangalore), 14 Sept. 200o, http://web.archive.org/web/20010918222829/http://www.deccanherald.com/deccanherald/sep15/iladen.htm, accessed April 2006.

230 Mahendra Ved, 'Wedding could open Yemeni door for Osama', *The Times of India*, 5 Aug. 2000, http://timesofindia.indiatimes.com/articleshow/858910034.cms, accessed April 2006.

231 'Split in Bin Laden's Al Qaida outfit', *India News Online*, 7 Aug. 2000, http://news.indiamart.com/news-analysis/split-in-bin-laden-s-8054.html, accessed April 2006, citing the Pakistani daily *The News*. See also O P Verma, 'Pak, Taliban may get rid of Laden', *Deccan Herald* (Bangalore), 14 Sept. 2001, http://web.archive.org/web/20010918222829/http://www.deccanherald.com/deccanherald/sep15/iladen.htm, accessed April 2006.

232 'Reports of split in Bin Laden's group denied,' (LexisNexis Title), 'Al-Jazeera at Midday'-programme, *Al-Jazeera TV*, 1 Aug. 2000 1240 GMT via LexisNexis.

[O]ver the past few years, I have been present in the jihad or Islamic movement as a writer, researcher, thinker, and theorizer or ideologist so to speak. I do not enjoy any party or organizational capacity. I belong neither to the Al-Qaʻida organization nor to any other organizations. I back their ideas and call upon this nation to stand against all its enemies. However, from an organizational point of view, I am not a member of the Al-Qaʻida group.[233]

However, he did describe himself as being 'very close to the circles here', and he took pride in being 'at the top of the list of invitees to Shaykh Osama's wedding' in mid-2000.[234] He describes his relationship with them as 'that of fraternity, friendship, and participation in good and sad occasions. We are one family. I mean those who you termed as the Arab-Afghans. We were, and are still, one family.'[235] For Abu Musʻab al-Suri, Osama bin Laden was the foremost role model and 'at the top of the list of those who are awaiting martyrdom. [...] We support him, his call (daʻwah), and position'.[236] To al-Jazeera TV, al-Suri claimed that bin Laden and the Afghan-Arabs' relationship with the Taleban was 'as good as it used to be, and nothing other than that'.[237]

These statements were clearly meant to maintain a façade of unity to the outside world, although it is possible that the relationship had improved slightly since their fallout in 1998. After the 9/11 attacks and the US-led invasion of Afghanistan, al-Suri mended his relationship with bin Laden and abjured from his overt criticism of al-Qaida's leader. In *The Global Islamic Resistance Call*, al-Suri hails bin Laden in a way, which, barred from its religious undertones, would have made Soviet speechwriters of the Stalinist era nod approvingly: '[you are] the symbol of our struggle, the sun of our Islamic Nation, [...] delighted is the Islamic Nation by you being safe and healthy'.[238]

---

233  Cited in ibid.
234  Ibid.
235  Ibid.
236  Ibid.
237  Ibid.
238  *The Global Islamic Resistance Call*, p.9.

In a statement issued in August 2005, al-Suri refers to himself again as a member of 'the family of mujahidin, or al-Qaida as we are usually named today'.[239]

## WEAPONS OF MASS DESTRUCTION

The issue of al-Suri's writings on, and alleged involvement in, al-Qaida's alleged pursuit of Weapons of Mass Destruction (WMD) capabilities is perhaps the most popular theme in discussions about him, rivalled only by reports of his alleged, but unproven, involvement in the Casablanca, Madrid, and London bombings.[240]

According to the US Government, al-Suri was 'an expert in the use of poison' and taught these skills at terrorist training camps when he returned to Afghanistan in the late 1990s.[241] While in Afghanistan, al-Suri allegedly worked closely with Midhat Mursi al-Sayyid Umar (b. 1953), better known as Abu Khabab al-Masri (Abu Hasan, Abu Rabbab), a top-level EIJ operative and well-known al-Qaida expert in the field of non-conventional weapons.[242] Together, they reportedly 'trained extremists in poisons and chemicals'.[243] Their relationship had started in the aftermath of the November 1995 bombing of the Egyptian Embassy in Islamabad, a twin car bomb operation that killed 17 people. Abu Khabab had organized the attack in response to Pakistan's tougher stance against the EIJ members seeking refuge on its territory.

---

239 Umar Abd al-Hakim (Abu Mus'ab al-Suri), 'Message to the British and the Europeans—it's People and Governments—regarding the London explosions, July 2005 (in Arabic), August 2005.

240 See, for example, Paul Cruickshank and Mohammad Hage Ali, 'Jihadist of Mass Destruction', *Washington Post*, 11 June 2006, p.B02.

241 See, for example, 'Nasar, Mustafa Setmariam', *MIPT Terrorism Knowledge Database*, www.tkb.org/KeyLeader.jsp?memID=6065, accessed July 2005.

242 'WANTED: Mustafa Setmariam Nasar', *Reward for Justice website*, www.rewardsforjustice.net/english/wanted_captured/index.cfm?page=Nasar, accessed July 2005.

243 Ibid.

Abu Khabab operated his own facility at the Derunta training complex in Afghanistan, one of the largest al-Qaida bases in Afghanistan, occupying a quarter of a square mile and located near Derunta Lake close to the eastern city of Jalalabad.[244] The camp at Derunta became widely known in Western media after CNN released video footage of dogs being subjected to experiments with poison and chemicals there.[245] According to files retrived from a computer used by Ayman al-Zawahiri in Kabul, al-Qaida reportedly earmarked $2,000-4,000 in start-up costs to a biological and chemical weapons program, code-named *zabadi* (curdled milk) from 1999 onwards. Abu Khabab seems to have played an important role in this program by developing new weapons formulas, conducting crude experiments, and reporting these results directly to Ayman al-Zawahiri.[246] Other materials recovered after the toppling of the Taleban regime suggested that conventional explosives training was also an important activity at the Abu Khabab camp.[247]

The American press has referred to Abu Khabab's explosives training manual as 'the bible for al Qaeda terrorists around the world'.[248] His training facility was reportedly an 'elite terrorist graduate school' inside the Derunta complex, from which terrorist operatives were

---

244 See Rohan Gunaratna and Arabinda Acharya, 'The Terrorist Training Camps of al Qaeda' in James J.F. Forest (ed.) *The Making of a Terrorist: Training* (Westport, CT: Praeger Security International, 2005), pp.180-1.

245 See Nic Robertson, 'Disturbing scenes of death show capability with chemical gas', *CNN.com*, 19 Aug. 2002, http://edn.cnn.com/2002/US/08/19/terror.tape.chemical/, accessed March 2006.

246 Alan Cullison and Andrew Higgins, 'Computer in Kabul holds chilling memos: PC apparently used by al-Qaida leaders reveals details of four years of terrorism', *The Wall Street Journal*, 31 Dec. 2001.

247 Rohan Gunaratna and Arabinda Acharya, 'The Terrorist Training Camps of al Qaeda' in James J.F. Forest (ed.) *The Making of a Terrorist: Training* (Westport, CT: Praeger Security International, 2005), pp.180-1.

248 Habibullah Khan and Brian Ross, 'U.S. Strike Killed Al Qaeda Bomb Maker : Terror Big Also Trained "Shoe Bomber," Moussaoui', *ABCNews*, 18 Jan. 2006, http://abcnews.go.com/WNT/Investigation/story?id=1517986, accessed March 2006.

despatched to Western countries.[249] One of them was Ahmed Ressam, an Algerian al-Qaida member who was detained in late 1999 when he attempted to cross the US-Canadian border with explosives in the boot of his car. Ressam became an important source of information about the camps. In October 1998, he reportedly received specialized terrorist training at Derunta in manufacturing explosives, crude chemical weapons and poisons.[250]

Abu Khabab was deemed sufficiently important for the US authorities to pledge a $5 million reward for his capture. Since 1999 he had 'reportedly proliferated training manuals that contain recipes for crude chemical and biological weapons'.[251] At the time of writing, Abu Khabab is rumoured to have been killed during a US missile attack on the village of Damadola in Eastern Pakistan in January 2006, together with several other high-ranking al-Qaida commanders.[252]

---

249  Evan Kohlmann, 'Abu Khabab al-Masri: A Master of Terror', *CounterterrorismBlog*, 18 Jan. 2006, http://counterterrorismblog. org/2006/01/abu_khabab_almasri_a_master_of.php, accessed Oct. 2006.

250  See in particular Testimony of Ahmed Ressam, United States of America v. Mokhtar Houari Defendant, transcript of trial, 5 July 2001, pp.620-6, http://news.findlaw.com/cnn/docs/haouari/ushaouari070501rassamtt.pdf, accessed Jan. 2007.

251  In Sept. 2005, he was also listed on the UN Al Qaeda and Taliban Sanctions Committee as being among 'individuals belonging to or associated with Al-Qaida organisation'. 'WANTED: Midhat Mursi al-Sayid 'Umar', www. rewardsforjustice.net/english/wanted_captured/index.cfm?page=Midhat_ Mursi/, accessed July 2005; and United Nations Al Qaeda and Taliban Sanctions Committee, 'The list of individuals belonging to or associated with Al-Qaida organisation/Last updated on 25 July 2006', www.un.org/ Docs/sc/committees/1267/pdflist.pdf, accessed July 2006, p.33.

252  Habibullah Khan and Brian Ross, 'U.S. Strike Killed Al Qaeda Bomb Maker: Terror Big Also Trained "Shoe Bomber," Moussaoui', *ABCNews*, 18 Jan. 2006, http://abcnews.go.com/WNT/Investigation/ story?id=1517986, accessed March 2006; and Evan Kohlmann, 'Abu Khabab al-Masri: A Master of Terror', *Counterterrorism Blog*, 18 Jan. 2006, http://counterterrorismblog.org/2006/01/abu_khabab_almasri_a_ master_of.php, accessed Oct. 2006.

Al-Suri's cooperation with Abu Khabab cannot be independently verified.[253] Al-Suri was very close to the EIJ, Abu Khabab's organization, and it is not entirely unlikely that al-Suri would have worked with EIJ veterans such as Abu Khabab, at least initially, till he managed to establish his own training base and media center in Kargha, outside Kabul.

There is oft-quoted source about al-Suri's involvement in al-Qaida's WMD program that should be dismissed. A number of studies have referred to the East Africa Embassy bombings trial in 2001 as proof of al-Suri's involvement in al-Qaida's procurement and development efforts of non-conventional weapons. One study, citing the testimony of the al-Qaida defector, Jamal al-Fadl, claims that bin Laden put al-Suri in charge of 'collecting all the information available on enriched uranium and obtaining samples of it'.[254] Other reports apparently rely on the same source when they repeat the assertion that al-Suri was put 'in charge of al-Qaeda's efforts to obtain uranium from Africa'.[255] However, this claim rests on a misreading of the trial transcripts. Abu Mus'ab al-Suri's name was mentioned very rarely during the Embassy trial. A close reading of the witness statements on 7, 13 and 20 February when Jamal al-Fadl is cross-examined about al-Qaida's uranium procurement efforts, shows clearly that the witness confuses him with another Syrian, Abu Rida al-Suri (Muhammad Bayazid), who, together with Mamdouh Mahmud

---

253  A former CIA official, Michael Scheuer recalls Abu Khabab as someone who headed al-Qaida's chemical weapons training, but cannot confirm whether al-Suri played any role. Interview with Michael Scheuer, Washington, 14 March 2007.

254  Cited in Jean-Charles Brisard with Damien Martinez, *Zarqawi: The New Face of al-Qaeda*, p.109, citing Testimony of Jamal Ahmed Mohammed Al-Fadl, United States of America *v.* Osama Bin Laden *et al.* Defendants, transcript of trial, 13 Feb. 2001.

255  'Analyst Comments: Abu Musaab al-Suri', *Terrorism Research Center*, 8 July 2005, www.homelandsecurity.com/modules.php?op=modload&name=Intel&file=index&view=649, accessed October 2006.

Salim (Abu Hajir al-Iraqi),[256] was indeed a significant player in the procurement efforts.[257]

---

256 Mamduh Mahmud Salim also known as Abu Hajir al-Iraqi, an al-Qaida Shura Council member, was arrested in Germany in 1998 and extradited to the United States. Abu Rida al-Suri was a Syrian-American businessman, who lived in Kansas City until 1994, and whom US prosecutors have accused of being a manager for bin Laden's Taba Investments in Khartoum, Sudan. For more on Abu Rida al-Suri, see David E. Kaplan, 'Made in the U.S.A.: Hundreds of Americans have followed the path to jihad. Here's how and why,' *U.S. News and World Report*, 10 June 2002, www.usnews. com/usnews/news/articles/020610/archive_021602_9.htm, accessed July 2006; and Laurie Cohen and Kim Barker, 'Al Qaeda operative tied to local Islamic charity', *Chicago Tribune*, 30 Jan. 2003, via http://siteinstitute.org/bin/articles.cgi?ID=inthenews1903&Category=inthenews&Subcategory=0, accessed July 2006. See also Kimberly McCloud and Matthew Osborne, 'WMD Terrorism and Osama Bin Laden', *Center for Nonproliferation Studies website*, 20 Nov. 2001, http://cns.miis.edu/pubs/reports/binladen. htm, accessed July 2006.

257 Abu Rida al-Suri and Salim are among the most important figures mentioned on day three of the trial on 7 Feb. 2001, when Jamal at-Fadl was cross-examined by the prosecutor about the uranium procurement efforts. On day four, 13 Feb. 2001, when the witness was questioned by defence lawyer David Stern, the uranium issue was only briefly touched upon at the very end of the day. In this context, Jamal al-Fadl twice corrected Stern when the latter attributes various acts to 'Salim' by saying 'no', it was 'Abu Musab al-Suri'. The witness obviously meant 'Abu Rida al-Suri'. If not, he would have contradicted the very detailed explanation he had given to the court a few days earlier on the very same issue. Compare two excerpts from day three and four where the witness is questioned about how they will test the quality of the uranium they are considering purchasing: Day 3: 'Q: Did Abu Rida al Suri tell you where the machine to test the uranium was coming from? A: He told me going to come from Kenya.' Day 4: 'Q: And according to you, he [i.e. Salim] told you or you were told that he was going to get some kind of machine to test this uranium, right? A: 'Not Salim, Abu Musab Suri told me machine going to come from Kenya'. Cited in Testimony of Jamal Ahmed Mohammed Al-Fadl, United States of America *v.* Osama Bin Laden et. al. Defendants, transcript of trial, 13 Feb. 2001, Day 4, http://cryptome.org/usa-v-ubl-04.htm, accessed Oct. 2006, p.529; and Testimony of Jamal Ahmed Mohammed Al-Fadl, United States of America *v.* Osama Bin Laden *et al.* Defendants, transcript of trial, 7 Feb. 2001, Day 3, http://cryptome.org/usa-v-ubl-03.htm, accessed Oct. 2006, p.364.

Another report, which appears to link al-Suri to al-Qaida's WMD programme, was a 15-page Arabic document entitled 'Biological weapons', which was found on a jihadi website in June 2005 by Rebecca Givner-Forbes, an Arabic specialist at the Terrorism Research Center (TRC) in Arlington, USA.[258] She recalls that during her regular monitoring of jihadi websites, she came across a link entitled 'the Military Bureau of Abu Musab al-Suri'. Entering that site, she found the 'Biological weapons' document.[259] Her finding was reported in a *Washington Post* article in August 2005. In the document, the author reportedly describes 'how the pneumonic plague could be made into a biological weapon'.[260] The handbook drew upon experiences from the US and Japanese biological warfare programs of the Second World War, and gave guidelines about 'how to inject carrier animals, like rats, with the virus and how to extract microbes from infected blood ... and how to dry them so that they can be used with an aerosol delivery system'.[261] While frightening reading for the general public, CBW experts consulted by the author deny that the manual actually contains any workable formulas, only very general and unpractical ideas for BW warfare.

It is known that al-Suri produced handbooks for guerrilla warfare tactics in the 1980s. A highly intelligent and productive author, he may well have also produced similar handbooks for non-conventional warfare, especially in light of his emphasis on WMD in his strategic thinking. Still, none of al-Suri's websites, which this author has reviewed over the past two years, have contained similar handbooks bearing his name. Nor has the author seen this alleged 'Biological Weapons' document among his numerous publications. The document located by TRC appears to be identical to a crude BW manual

---

258  Steve Coll and Susan B. Glasser, 'Terrorists Turn to the Web as Base of Operations', *Washington Post*, 7 Aug. 2005, p.A01.

259  Email correspondence with Rebecca Givner-Forbes, 26 July 2006.

260  Cited in Steve Coll and Susan B. Glasser, 'Terrorists Turn to the Web as Base of Operations', *Washington Post*, 7 Aug. 2005, p.A01.

261  Ibid.

contained in al-Qaida's *Encyclopaedia of Jihad* (mawsu'at al-i'dad lil-jihad), a huge collection of weapon manuals and tactical handbooks which has circulated online in various updated versions at least since 2003. However, this does not rule out the fact that al-Suri may have had a role in its production.

There are indeed several references in his writings on the strategic imperative for the jihadi movement of acquiring weapons of mass destruction, but very rarely are there specific weapons manuals. The only exception is a two-page article in his short-lived journal, *Issues for the Triumphant in Righteousness*, published by his media center in Kabul in 2000-1. It appeared in a column in the journal dedicated to the topic of 'terrorist culture' (*thaqafah irhabiyyah*). Following an introduction about the general training and preparations for a jihadi, it featured discussion of specific weapons. The first was simply a Molotov cocktail. The second was entitled 'Poison from Rotten Meat', which purportedly demonstrated how to extract *Clostridium botulinum*. The article highlighted the fact that this toxin was an extremely lethal agent, more deadly than the nerve gas that had been used in the Tokyo subway. It contained very brief and crude instructions for its production. The final guidelines for usage focused on mixing the poison with any kind of ointment or 'hand cream and smearing it on door knobs, steering wheels, etc'. It also proposed mixing it with water in order to 'drizzle it on the victim'.[262] The article was not signed and this recipe, too, seems remarkably similar to those found in al-Qaida's *The Encyclopaedia of Jihad*.

References to non-conventional weapons in al-Suri's writings are numerous, but they do not constitute the key part of his strategic theory. In fact, the most elaborate statement on the issue seems to be the quotation cited below from his lecture series 'Jihad is the Solution'. Elsewhere, he mostly presents variants of the same argument that these weapons are necessary to achieve strategic parity with, to deter and possibly to destroy the enemy. In *The Global Islamic Resistance*

---

262 'Poison from Rotten Meat' (in Arabic), *Journal of Issues for the Triumphant in Righteousness* (dhu'l-hujja 1421 / March 2001), no.2, pp.58-9.

*Call*, for example, he urges the establishment of four different types of military units (*al-saraya*) by the international jihadi movement, and elaborates on their respective operative capabilities. The fourth and top-level category of units is the 'Units for Strategic Operations', whose capabilities should consist of, *inter alia*, 'the knowledge and operative capability of acquiring and using weapons of mass destruction in cases when it becomes necessary to respond in kind or to reach a strategic decisive outcome in the struggle with America'.[263]

In his communiqué to the US Administration, published in December 2004, al-Suri refers to the use of WMD as the only way of defeating the United States under the current circumstances. He calls upon the North Korean Government not to abandon its nuclear program, and Iran to stop co-operating with the International Atomic Energy Agency (IAEA). He also writes that if he had been involved in planning the 9/11 attacks, he would have recommended that the airplanes be filled with weapons of mass destruction. However, in his subsequent discussion, he advocates the use of 'dirty bombs' (which by no means are WMD although the media tends to confuse the public on this issue) in order to 'pollute the American people with radiation'.[264] The reason for employing these weapons, according to al-Suri, is that during their war in Afghanistan and Iraq the US Administration and its soldiers have revealed their 'dirtiness', and their people 'have voted for killing, destruction and pillaging', hence, the principle of reciprocity should apply: 'a dirty bomb for a dirty people', he writes with his usual sarcasm.[265]

In his booklet *The Muslims in Central Asia and the Coming Battle of Islam*, al-Suri also refers to weapons of mass destruction, focusing on the problem of disparity as well as on Central Asia's importance in possible procurement efforts.[266]

---

263 *The Global Islamic Resistance Call*, p.1400.

264 'Communiqué from the Office of Abu Mus'ab al-Suri' (in Arabic), 22 Dec. 2004, p.6.

265 Ibid.

266 Umar Abd al-Hakim (Abu Mus'ab al-Suri), *The Muslims in Central Asia*

The difference in armament and number between Muslims and their enemies, between the oppressed and the strong, has never been larger in the history of Muslims and mankind. The military logic shows us that it is almost absurd to launch a classical confrontational war to restore the balance of power—but only God knows. This is unless one multiplies the spread of the awareness and application of the general resistance among the people of Islam. Secondly, the renascent Islamic forces in the consolidated region such as Central Asia and the like, must attempt to acquire weapons of mass destruction (nuclear, biological, bacteriological) in exactly the same way as the aggressive oppressive world represented by the Jews and the West possesses these weapons. One has to threaten with them [these weapons] and deter the enemy exactly like they [the enemy] have been doing and which has become a military tradition. The Central Asian region has developed factories, and they have raw material for these weapons, which has made a base and a hope for Muslims to acquire these weapons. [...] This is a strategic goal which is within reach, but only God knows.[267]

He refers to WMD in his last letter addressing the British and the Europeans in August 2005.[268] The reference simply repeats his often-made remark that the Islamic world has the right to respond in kind, using WMD against the West:

You have acquired all kinds of destructive conventional and strategic weapons, such as nuclear, chemical and biological, legal weapons as well as weapons that are internationally banned, and you have used all this in your wars against us and against others without any deterrent or any law. Hence, we are serious about acquiring all possible weapons and means and will deal with you the same way, in accordance with our true religion.[269]

In a well-known lecture series, 'Jihad is the solution' held in September 1999 and audio-recorded on 21 tapes, al-Suri deals with various aspects of the jihadi struggle, including the issue of prioritization:

---

*and the Coming Battle of Islam* (in Arabic) (Kabul: The Ghuraba Center for Islamic Studies, 5 Nov. 1999, The Series Issues for the Triumphant in Righteousness no.3), p.20.

267  Ibid.

268  'Message to the British and the Europeans – Its People and Governments – Regarding the London Explosions, July 2005' (in Arabic), Aug. 2005

269  Ibid, p.54.

where and against whom terrorist operations should be carried out, and the role of WMD in overall jihadi strategy. Al-Suri considered this series to be the most important of his audio-recorded lectures, rivalled only by his videotaped lectures on 'Global Islamic Resistance' from August 2000. Excerpts from 'Jihad is the solution' lectures have repeatedly been reproduced and recommended by key jihadi media outlets such as the Global Islamic Media Front (GIMF). The following excerpts give both a more comprehensive strategic overview of al-Suri's WMD logic and provide interesting insights into al-Suri as a teacher and lecturer:[270]:

06:26: 'Now, let's return to the issue of terrorism in Europe. How should it be practised? We have said that it should be practised against all forms of presence in our countries. In reality, I do not care much about [our presence] in their countries, because it is smaller. Let's talk about this. I say that the circles of terrorism, as I said with regard to the [open] fronts, also have conditions and places. I say circles of terrorism. First of all, and this is the most important thing. Because those who practice terrorism should not involve themselves in the [open] fronts. First of all... First of all: The holy places and oil. Here, [*he draws on a blackboard*] we have the interests of the people of the Cross and the Jews. So, the first place where we should practise terrorism. Where is that? Where is that? [*he is asking his audience*]. This is the Arab Peninsula and the Levant. The Arab Peninsula and the Levant. And the neighboring countries, which means the rectangular of Iraq, Egypt, the Levant, and Yemen. This rectangular is the number one circle in terrorism. The best terrorist operations in terms of influencing our enemy are undertaken here. That is here. The basic imperialist interests are here. Here from the Levant to al-Quds [Jerusalem], Mecca, and Medina. The oil of the Levant. They have gone after the oil of Iraq now. The oil in the Arab Peninsula. The natural resources of Yemen. And their presence and interests in it. That is from Euphrates to the Nile and from Anatolia to Yemen. This rectangle is the first arena and the first place you should go when you will reach him with terrorism. If you hit the Americans here, or the French, the Englishmen or the Jews here, you hurt them two hundred times more than if you strike them in the Philippines or Nairobi. Here, you will hurt them two hundred times more! It is like you hit a man on his hand or hit him on

---

270 Transcript of 'Jihad is the Solution'-audiofile no.37, tape no.10b, 06:28 – 16:00, *muntada al-sawt*, www.saowt.com/forum/showthread.php?t=16158, accessed Oct. 2006.

the neck. It hurts more here than when you hit the arm. You may strike his arm twenty times, but he will not be affected as he would in the lethal zone. Understand?

So, the first region, here the front line [consists of] oil and the holy places, that is, in the Arab Peninsula, the Levant, and Egypt. This is region number one. Secondly, the Arab world. Thirdly, the Islamic world, especially the strategic areas. And among the most important strategic areas for the Crusaders and the Jews' interests are the neighboring regions of the Arab world, and the frontline [consisting of] oil and the holy places. Among the most important ones are, for example, countries such as Turkey, the presence of Jews basically. And the presence of causes ... You know. Understand?

The [enemy] presence in other regions such as Pakistan, India etc. In these regions, there are important interests [for the Crusaders and Jews]. We are not talking in general terms here, but if you look at the damage which will ensue from acting here and not acting here, this is obvious to you, militarily and strategically. Understand?

Now, you have gone to the frontlines and entered Afghanistan from other countries. You don't go to those frontlines. You decide for yourselves to which frontline to go. Understand?

But when this situation has ended and you are on your way to the frontline you have chosen, and you hit there, then the important thing is that the West must have strategic interests there.

The fourth region: these are the Jewish and Western interests, that is, the "World Order" [*he uses the term synonymously with the West*] in the Third World. Why did I say in the Third World? That means strike in Africa or Asia. Now, in the Third World, these regions have weak security. You can move freely. If you strike in Africa, you don't deal with African security [police]. There is corruption. It is easy to move across borders. No constraints on movement.

The fifth circle is in their countries. In their countries. The comments we have made [so far] are with regards to the enemy's interests in the four first circles: the frontline [consisting of] the holy places, the Arab Peninsula, Levant, Egypt. Secondly, the Arab world, the Islamic world, the interests of the Jews and the West. In these four regions, in these four regions there are tactics for striking the enemy's interests there.

As for their countries, the matter is different. In these regions [*presumably referring to the previous four regions*] people are Muslims. So you have to be careful when you strike so that Muslims are not affected, except in special cases. In these regions [*referring to the West*], the people are basically those you wish to hurt in war. So in this case, the situation is different. Here you strike without any restrictions. Understand? Without any restrictions. So you should only avoid women, elderly, and children if they are in separate places. And if they are not separated [from the target], you can put a bomb in a car rigged with explosives and bring a building down with 2,000 people. You may, if you wish to go and strike a soldier at a police station, and you place a device which takes away 700 or 800. Understand?

You have to be aware that there is a difference in terrorist action and its rulings *here* and terrorist action and its rulings *there*. The most important observation I tell you now is [*he speaks slower and very audible*] that guerrilla warfare in their countries should be based upon the infliction of large human losses. This is very very important! To cause large human losses! Secondly, in their countries, we have to start thinking about the use of weapons of mass destruction in terrorism. [*He makes a four second pause*] You understand? In their countries, we have to use weapons of mass destruction in terrorism. You add one kilogram of uranium to some explosives and you go and pollute some 50 countries altogether. Understand?

Why? Because between us and these people there has to be a strategic balance. They are coming with their cruise [missile] weapons, they strike against civilians, they allow themselves to use anything. They are going to use biological and chemical weapons against the terrorist bases in Afghanistan and elsewhere. This cannot be stopped without an equivalent deterrent operation. As was the case with the nuclear balance between Russia and America. I have nuclear arms and you have nuclear arms, so we keep the fight within the category of conventional arms. If you take away weapons of mass destruction, there is no parity.

Weapons of mass destruction are nuclear, plutonium/uranium very very very enriched. [...] We still remain with the last war, and we lost it. We lost the war of the twentieth century. We have to win the war of the twenty-first century. So we need a regime for warfare for the twenty-first century, and weapons on the level of the twenty-first century, and tactics on the level of the twenty-first century.

Warfare ... warfare is not based on mercy basically, except for in Islam. In a war where there is an aggressor, his aggression must be repelled. [*He asks the students for a Quranic verse related to this, and they recite the verse together*]. The issue here is not what is permitted and what is not permitted, or that this is barbaric and this is not barbaric. The first ones to put down laws of barbaric warfare in the modern world are the "World Order" [i.e. the West]. [This happened] between themselves before [it happened] between us and them. London and Berlin adopted the bombings of civilians by dropping explosives on the cities and killing 42 million in the course of four years. Then, they ended [the war] by Hiroshima and Nagasaki. 220,000 killed.

So it is they who established their laws of [barbaric] warfare. We have laws for warfare about what is permitted and what is not. And in these laws, it says that "When you are aggressed against, act back with aggression in the same manner". So, a man cannot stop his aggression unless by striking back within what is permitted. We apply this because it is permissible.

They are raping women. We cannot strike back by raping women. Understand? They kill civilians indiscriminately. For our part ... to repel this aggression, you have to kill civilians indiscriminately. But we have mercy on our part. They kill women even when they are separate from others. We do not kill women when they are separate from others. They violate the honor. We do not. Understand?

As for the matter of proficiency in killing human beings, this matter is present on their part and on our part, and we apply it from the perspective of paying back with the same coin. Therefore, I tell you that terrorism in their countries has to rely on human losses. These human losses must be caused by weapons of mass destruction. Don't come and tell me that you have placed a half-kilogram bomb on the metro at the end of the night and killed two persons for me. Understand?

The matter is that you will use weapons of mass destruction. Weapons of mass destruction are nuclear. They are quick and easy and can be obtained from most mafias in the world. This is a strategic weapon. Nuclear weapons have become mafia merchandise. They are sold. They are sold in Uzbekistan and in Pakistan. It is a beautiful and fantastic thing that the uranium sources in the world are located in the region in which we are now moving. Understand? The reservoirs of uranium in the world are in Central Asia. [16:00]

Notwithstanding these ominous-sounding quotations, al-Suri also reveals a lack of technical expertise about these weapons and glosses over the enormous difficulties of obtaining, storing and deploying them. Seeing himself primarily as a theoretician, he probably confined his role to explaining their strategic importance and conveniently left the practicalities of procuring and deploying them to others. Given his impressive productivity in terms of books, articles, and lectures in the field of jihadi strategies and political analysis from 1998 onwards, it seems unlikely that he would devote himself to the intricacies of bio-weaponry research. He had no reservations with regards to detailing his explosive manufacturing skills, so why has he not mentioned his CBRN-warfare exploits in his biographical writings, if indeed he was an adept in them?

What al-Suri did do was to provide a clear strategic rationale for the use of weapons of mass destruction by the jihadi movement. Hence, al-Suri's advocacy of the use of WMD complements other al-Qaida related statements on the issue, in particular that of the Saudi cleric Nasir bin Hamd al-Fahd's fatwa of May 2003 which provided an elaborate religious justification for the use of WMD against 'the Crusaders'.[271] Not being an acknowledged religious scholar, al-Suri's contribution was not intended to add more religious weight to these considerations, but instead to demonstrate its logical rationale and its military imperative in the face of a militarily superior enemy.

---

271  Al-Fahd wrote: 'The attack against it [the United States] by WMD is accepted, since Allah said: "If you are attacked you should attack your aggressor by identical force." Whoever looks at the American aggression against the Muslims and their lands in recent decades concludes that it is permissible... Some brothers have totaled the number of Muslims killed directly or indirectly by their weapons and come up with a figure of nearly 10 million.' See translation of excerpts of the fatwa in Reuven Paz, 'YES to WMD: The first Islamist Fatwah on the use of Weapons of Mass Destruction', *PRISM Series of Special Dispatches on Global Jihad*, no.1, www.e-prism.org/images/PRISM%20Special%20dispatch%20no%201. doc, accessed Oct. 2004.

Western media reports have overemphasized the WMD terrorist threat and ignored the plain fact that there have been no WMD terrorist attacks by al-Qaida, nor even any serious attempts to do so. Despite his frequent comments on WMD, al-Suri does not seem overly preoccupied with the issue in his writings.[272] An astute observer of Western media and politics, al-Suri knew how to play on Western fears. His comments here are typical examples of his biting, satirical style with which he entertains his audience ('I apologize for the radioactive fallout', 'dirty bomb for a dirty nation', etc). In his writings, al-Suri displays a remarkable honesty and tough realism when it comes to the actual capabilities of the remaining jihadi networks. He strenuously warns against any kind of hierarchical centralized jihadi organization because of its vulnerability in the new post-9/11 security environment. Even though he did not admit it openly, he obviously knew that such a structure would be antithetical to any realistic attempt to form and develop an effective WMD capability on the part of al-Qaida.

## THE SEPTEMBER 11 ATTACKS

Al-Suri appears to have been quite ambivalent in his views on the September 11 attacks.[273] Observers and sources close to jihadi circles in London have repeatedly stressed that he belonged to a sizeable constituency among jihadi militants that either opposed, or had strong reservations about, the attacks.[274] In his own writings, al-Suri

---

272  On this point I disagree with Reuven Paz in his otherwise excellent analysis in 'Global Jihad and WMD: Between Martyrdom and Mass Destruction' in Hillel Fradkin *et al.* (eds), *Current Trends in Islamist Ideology* (Washington: The Hudson Institute, 2005, vol. 2), www.futureofmuslimworld.com/docLib/20060130_Current_Trends_v2.pdf, accessed Oct. 2006, pp.74-86.

273  Al-Suri's view of the 9/11 attacks has also been discussed in Paul Cruickshank and Mohannad Hage Ali, 'Abu Musab Al Suri: Architect of the New Al Qaeda', *Studies in Conflict and Terrorism*, 30 (1) (Jan. 2007), p.6.

274  Author's interviews with Abdel Bari Atwan, 29 April 2006; and interview

is cautious not to overdo his criticism of bin Laden and the 9/11 strikes against the United States. He does mention that 'some members of the jihadi current' questioned the wisdom of the attacks, and 'viewed this glorious deed with unease', in light of the sufferings and losses it brought on Muslims in general and the jihadis in particular.[275] Several jihadis argued that they had not been prepared to fight the United States; furthermore, the 9/11 attacks had provided the justifications for 'invading and occupying the Islamic world and inflicting heavy losses on Muslims'.[276] Al-Suri's observation is telling:

> The outcome [of the 9/11 attacks] as I see it, was to put a catastrophic end to the jihadi current, and end to the period which started back in the beginning of the 1960s of the past century and has lasted up until September 11th. The jihadis entered the tribulations of the current maelstrom which swallowed most of its cadres over the subsequent three years.[277]

Looking back, in 2004 al-Suri nevertheless believed that this outcome was unavoidable; the confrontation with the United States had been intensifying since the early 1990s and al-Suri devotes considerable space to proving that the 9/11 attacks were exploited and instrumental to the United States' destruction of the jihadi movement and reoccupation of Muslim land.

Notwithstanding his reservations, al-Suri credits bin Laden for having 'placed the battle on its right course, by imposing a confrontation between us and our real enemy, who supports from behind the curtain all our enemies at whichever battlefront we confront them'.[278] The 9/11 attacks also had a strong mobilizing affect which al-Suri greatly appreciated:

---

with Yasir al-Sirri in 'Connection between the Madrid and London attacks and Suspicion against a Syrian Islamist who Differed with bin Laden' (in Arabic), *al-Hayat*, 10 July 2005, www.daralhayat.com/world_news/europe/07-2005/Item-20050709-fcd8eac1-c0a8-10ed-00f8-0297c980c2e8/story.html, accessed Oct. 2006.

275   *The Global Islamic Resistance Call*, p.730.

276   Ibid.

277   Ibid, p.729.

278   Ibid, p.63.

The purpose was to awaken the Islamic Nation, which has been drugged, put to sleep and been absent from the confrontation, in order to put her face to face with her duty of jihad.[279]

Henceforward, the primary aim must be to 'transform the confrontation into the Islamic Nation's battle after it has been ignited by the elite', al-Suri argued.[280] Al-Suri's experiences as a wanted al-Qaida fugitive after the fall of the Taleban made a deep impression on him and convinced him even more than before that any open confrontation with the US was doomed to fail:

My analysis after having had field experiences in Afghanistan following the September 2001 attacks and after having thoroughly and continuously examined subsequent events, has reinforced my conviction [...]: First, it is impossible to confront America or any other of its allies militarily in an open manner as long as they have complete control over the air with their overwhelming technological capacities, especially where they have local collaborating forces on the ground, which put the jihadi entity under siege and participate in the attack on this entity. Secondly, the secret organizations (*tanzimat*) cannot confront the local security organizations of governments which collaborate with the enemy after the establishment of security coordination on regional and international levels in light of what is now known as 'the global war on terrorism', administered and supervised by the United States. This is even more so if one continues to follow the old classical styles of the regional *tanzim*s consisting of hierarchical networked structures. Thirdly, since there is no other way and no escape from resistance, the only way to confront the enemy today in light of this reality, is the method of secret guerrilla war consisting of unconnected cells, numerous and different types of cells.[281]

In his post-9/11 analysis, there was a warning to bin Laden not to attempt to rebuild the old al-Qaida organization:

If we did not take a warning from these, we can blame nobody but ourselves when 80% of our forces were eliminated in the repercussions of September 11th during two years only! In order for us to realize that the period of 'Tora Bora-mentality' has to end. The times have changed, and we must design a

---

279 Ibid, p.67.
280 Ibid.
281 Ibid, p.66.

method of confrontation, which is in accordance with the standards of the present time.[282]

The time had come for a new decentralized warfare model where the Islamic Nation should not be asked to travel to a distant land of jihad, but where the masses should practise the duty of fighting for Islam in their own alleys, street corners and villages. Al-Suri's grand vision was to mobilise the masses around the banner of jihad, to ignite Falluja-type insurrections in every Crusader country, a global Intifada whose fighters should train, equip, and fight on their own, united by nothing more than a common ideology. The prospects of forging such unity were immensely improved by 9/11 and even more so when Afghanistan and later Iraq came under US occupation, and many mainstream Muslims began doubting the rhetoric that the war on terror was not a war on Islam. This, more than anything else, became the source of al-Suri's optimism after his life as a wanted al-Qaida fugitive started in earnest in late 2001.

---

282   Ibid, p.1361.

# 9

# A $5 MILLION AL-QAIDA FUGITIVE

In October 2001, shortly after the 9/11 attacks, the US air force bombed and destroyed the al-Ghuraba training camp outside Kabul, alongside numerous other al-Qaida and Taleban facilities throughout Afghanistan.[1] Al-Suri was now a terrorist fugitive without a secure sanctuary.

The official biography of al-Suri after the fall of the Taleban is largely silent on his actions and whereabouts. The only information it provides is that he 'isolated himself' and 'devoted his time' to writing, in particular to completing *The Global Islamic Resistance Call*.[2] Elsewhere, al-Suri has described the period after the fall of the Taleban as 'three meagre years which we spent as fugitives, fleeing from the Americans and their apostate collaborators, moving between safe houses and hideouts....'[3] He was 'on the move between numerous areas', and was heavily affected by 'the complicated security situation'.[4]

In one of his books he describes how they 'moved with their women and children from mountain to mountain, from one sanctuary to another' until they finally managed to bring their families, children, and elders to safety.[5] Al-Suri was still inside Afghanistan at that point, and initially he had taken part in 'the battles for defend-

---

1    'Biography of Shaykh Umar Abd al-Hakim (Abu Mus'ab al-Suri)' (in Arabic), p.3.

2    Ibid.

3    *The Global Islamic Resistance Call*, p.6

4    'Communiqué from the Office of Abu Mus'ab al-Suri' (in Arabic), 22 Dec. 2004, p.2; and *The Global Islamic Resistance Call*, p.8.

5    Umar Abd al-Hakim, *A Summary of My Testimony*, p.6.

ing the Islamic Emirate'.[6] However, at the beginning of 2002, the security situation deteriorated further and he and others were forced to cross over to Pakistan. The border areas were heavily patrolled by American forces and criss-crossed with Pakistani checkpoints and 'ambushes'. On the Pakistani side of the border, al-Suri and others moved between safe houses 'under extremely bad and dangerous conditions'.[7] This account was written in June 2003 and his life as a fugitive in Pakistan had then lasted for 'a year and a half'.[8]

## NEW BOOKS, A REWARD, AND GLOBAL FAME

From the beginning of 2002 onwards, al-Suri says he did nothing other than study and write in order to complete his research.[9] He describes his condition as one of 'house arrest and limited movement'.[10] Despite his uncomfortable circumstances as a wanted fugitive, al-Suri was nevertheless able to continue writing. At times, he was even able to draw inspiration and joy from his surroundings: '...in this phase of exile, homelessness and in hiding, I am now putting the final touches to the book in our beautiful mountainous hideout.'[11] The period in hiding was a productive one: he produced two new books after the fall of the Taleban. The first was his memoir and analysis of the Algerian jihad, which has already been cited above. It was completed by June 2004 and remains the most autobiographical of all his works.[12] He subsequently produced a 160-page study of Pakistan after 9/11, *Musharraf's Pakistan: The Problem and the Solution! And the Necessary*

---

6    'Communiqué from the Office of Abu Mus'ab al-Suri' (in Arabic), 22 Dec. 2004, p.8.

7    Umar Abd al-Hakim, *A Summary of My Testimony*, p.6.

8    Ibid.

9    'Communiqué from the Office of Abu Mus'ab al-Suri' (in Arabic), 22 Dec. 2004, p.2; and *The Global Islamic Resistance Call*, p.8.

10   *The Global Islamic Resistance Call*, p.8.

11   Ibid., p.60.

12   Umar Abd al-Hakim, *A Summary of My Testimony*.

*Obligation*, dated October 2004. This was a call for revolt against the Musharraf regime, which in many ways echoed statements later made by Ayman al-Zawahiri in his videotaped speeches. Al-Suri's book addressed Pakistani Muslims, especially its Islamic clerics, leaders, and fighters, describing the 'catastrophe' which he claimed had befallen Pakistan and Afghanistan, and calling upon them to pledge support to the Arab mujahidin fleeing from Afghanistan and to 'stand firm with us'.[13]

*Musharraf's Pakistan* presents a strategy of resistance, focusing on maintaining unity among the Islamic forces in the region and preventing the United States and the Musharraf regime from purging the army of Islamist elements or from attenuating Islamist dominance over schools and educational institutions. Furthermore, he calls for the preservation of 'the jihadi alliance of mujahid Islamic forces' in the tribal areas bordering Afghanistan, referring to the Taleban forces under Mullah Omar's leadership, al-Qaida's Arab mujahidin, and mujahidin forces from Kashmir and Central Asia.[14] Only a unified front would pave the way for the ultimate goal of overturning the Musharraf and Karzai regimes in Pakistan and Afghanistan and the expulsion of the US presence from the region.

At that time al-Suri also expressed a strong desire to produce a book on the Arab-Afghan jihadi experience during the Taleban regime along the lines of the voluminous work he had written on the Syrian jihad fifteen years earlier. He solemnly vowed to begin writing it 'immediately' after he had completed *The Global Islamic Resistance Call*:

I feel an historical responsibility to do this [...] being one of the few remaining eye witnesses alive who can still write this living testimony about this

---

13    Al-Shaykh Abu Mus'ab al-Suri Umar Abd al-Hakim, *Musharraf's Pakistan: The Problem and the Solution ..! A Necessary Obligation* (in Arabic) (place and publisher unknown, Oct. 2004), p.6. For a brief analysis of al-Suri's book, see Stephen Ulph, 'Al-Suri's Treatise on Musharraf's Pakistan', *Terrorism Focus* (Jamestown), 3 (18) (May 9, 2006), www.jamestown.org/terrorism/ news/article.php?articleid=2369990, accessed Feb. 2007.

14    Cited in Stephen Ulph, 'Al-Suri's Treatise on Musharraf's Pakistan'.

great experience and the persons involved, and transmit this insight to the coming generations.[15]

It is not known whether he ever completed a manuscript, but given his immense productivity as a writer, it is possible that he would have had a draft version ready by the time of his capture in late 2005. In light of his role in Afghanistan and the insights that his previous historical studies have offered, his reflections and memoir of the Arab-Afghans during the Taleban period would be of considerable interest.

Al-Suri also planned to write a handbook on jihadi guerrilla warfare based on his lectures at Khowst, Jalalabad and Kabul. He had already decided on a title: *The Fundamentals for Jihadi Guerrilla Warfare in Light of the Conditions of the Contemporary American Campaigns*.[16] Al-Suri acknowledged that he might not have time to complete the work, so he urged his followers to transcribe his audio-taped lectures. However, he cautioned them that 'he who undertakes this task must be extremely accurate in order to preserve their content without any additions or attachments...'.[17] This wish was subsequently fulfilled. In late 2006, three of al-Suri's audio-taped lectures on guerrilla warfare appeared on jihadi websites in transcribed versions, in which even his occasional use of colloquial Arabic was left unamended.[18]

---

15   *The Global Islamic Resistance Call*, p.724.

16   The Arabic title was *usul harb al-'asabat al-jihadiyyah fi daw' dhuruf al-hamalat al-amrikiyyah al-mu'asirah*. See *The Global Islamic Resistance Call*, p.1424.

17   Ibid.

18   'The Management and Organization of Guerrilla Warfare by Shaykh Umar Abd al-Hakim' (in Arabic), Transcript of lectures given in Khowst, Afghanistan, 1998; 'Explanation of the Book "War of the Oppressed"' (in Arabic), Transcript of lectures given in Khowst, Afghanistan, 1998; and 'Lessons in Guerrilla Warfare Theories' (in Arabic), Transcript of lectures given in Jalalabad, Afghanistan, 1999. Posted on *muntadayat al-firdaws al-jihadiyyah* 21 Sept. 2006, www.alfirdaws.org/vb/showthread.php?t=1 6892&highlight=%E3%D5%DA%C8+%C7%E1%D3%E6%D1%ED, accessed Oct. 2006.

By late 2004 al-Suri had completed a huge 1,600-page draft of *The Global Islamic Resistance Call*. It incorporated a fully developed version of his ideas on a new global guerrilla warfare strategy that he had formulated in Peshawar around 1990, while part of the Arab-Afghan resistance. He considered it 'the book of my life time'.[19] It was also the first publication that appeared bearing his real name, Mustafa bin Abd al-Qadir Sitt Maryam Nasar, highlighting the fact that he was now a public figure.[20] In its introduction, al-Suri specifically mentions four people whom he would have liked to have reviewed his manuscript before publication: bin Laden, al-Zawahiri, Abu Layth al-Libi, and his long-time associate and brother-in-arms, Abu Khalid al-Suri (Muhammad al-Bahayah).[21] Hinting at his isolation and the considerable disruption inflicted upon his network of contacts and collaborators after 9/11, he writes that, 'apart from a very few I no longer know anyone like these men'.[22]

Al-Suri feared that something might happen to prevent him from publishing this latest manuscript, and his apprehension was confirmed on 18 November 2004 when the US Administration announced a $5 million reward for information leading to his arrest.[23] He then decided to speed up the publication of his book before the final reviews and corrections had been made, promising his readers an updated and corrected version in 2005.[24] It is not known whether he managed to update his final draft.

In response to the US Department of State's announcement, al-Suri issued a communiqué via the Internet, declaring an end to his official silence:

---

19   *The Global Islamic Resistance Call*, p.8.

20   Ibid., pp.1602, 1604.

21   Ibid., p.9.

22   Ibid., p.10.

23   US Department of State, 'Press Statement (Revised): Secretary of State Colin L. Powell Authorizes Reward', Nov. 18, 2004 www.state.gov/r/pa/prs/ps/2004/38377.htm, accessed Oct. 2006.

24   *The Global Islamic Resistance Call*, p.8.

After the 9/11 events and the fall of the Islamic Emirate in Afghanistan in December 2001, I took the decision to enter into total isolation, cut my relationship with the outer world, and abstain from following and studying the events in the mass media, and devote myself to reading and writing. [...] As a result of the US Government's declaration about me, the lies it contained and the new security requirements it forced upon us, I have taken the decision to end my period of isolation, and to publish what I have written until now. I will also resume my ideological, media-related and operational activities. I wish by God that America will regret bitterly that they provoked me and others to combat her with pen and sword.[25]

The communiqué was followed shortly afterwards by the launching of a website containing most of al-Suri's written material as well as audio-recorded and videotaped lectures. It is uncertain exactly when it appeared for the first time, but the website is dated 20 November 2004, which suggests that it was hurriedly put together immediately after the US announcement.[26] The first webforum postings about al-Suri are from late January 2005, however.

His original website disappeared some time in 2006, after having been hosted on hacked website directories of a US real estate company in Ohio, as well as a small Massachusetts company that specializes in 'abrasive glass etching and custom designs'.[27] His website were also hosted by several webhosting companies.[28] Later, most of his

---

25  Cited in 'Communiqué from the Office of Abu Mus'ab al-Suri' (in Arabic), 22 Dec. 2004, p.2. See also 'Biography of Shaykh Umar Abd al-Hakim (Abu Mus'ab al-Suri)' (in Arabic), p.3.

26  Al-Suri's website was maintained by a number of people presenting themselves by their nicknames: Abd al-Tawam al-Shami was 'director of al-Suri's library'; the website manager was Abd al-Salam al-Qayrawani; and technical support was provided by Engineer Isa al-Makki. Their chosen nicknames suggested that they hailed from Syria, Tunisia and Saudi Arabia. See 'About this website' (in Arabic), *Abu Musab al-Suri Website*, www.fsboa.com/vw/index.php?subject=4&rec=23, accessed Feb. 2006; and 'List of the Shaykh's production ... from 1987-2004' (in Arabic), *Abu Musab al-Suri Website*, www.fsboa.com/vw/index.php?subject=4& tit=tit&pa=0, accessed Sept. 2005.

27  See http://carriagehouseglass.com and www.fsboa.com.

28  http://abumusab.cjb.net  and  www.deluxesuperhost.com/~morshid/tophacker.

library was also uploaded on a hacked directory of yet another private American website.[29] The repeated use of US websites as hosts may have been incidental but one should not overlook the possibility that al-Suri and his aides were piqued by the irony that US websites were helping to spread their virulently anti-American ideology. Since May 2006, al-Suri's website has appeared in a new form and is currently hosted by the infamous jihadi website 'ozooo'.[30]

Al-Suri's writings were quickly disseminated to and by many other Internet sites and have appeared recurrently as popular material on the jihadi web. The announcement of the $5 million reward helped immensely in drawing attention to this formerly relatively obscure writer, who was well-known to veteran jihadis but not to the tens of thousands of young newcomers in the sprawling online community of militant Islam. The message was that this author must be a big fish given that the Americans were willing to pay so much for his capture.

Al-Suri's decision to go public marked a major shift in his *modus operandi*. As has been noted, he was very security conscious, using different aliases and pseudonyms, and preferred to distribute his speeches on cassettes, not via the web. Hence, despite his prodigious written and audio-recorded output, al-Suri had not been a very high profile figure in the burgeoning online jihadi community. The al-Ghuraba Center for Islamic Studies and Media had a short-lived and simple website before 9/11, while a 20-page excerpt from his book on the Syrian jihadi revolution, entitled 'Observations on the Jihadi Experience in Syria', also circulated on many websites, albeit often without naming him as the author. Still, to the online audience, he remained an anonymous figure whose books and articles were little known. Judging by the responses on jihadi websites, his influence as

---

29    The website called itself 'Meat's Joke of the Day'. It presented itself as 'the most prestigious joke of the day club in the world', claiming some 110 members in different countries. See www.mjotd.com.

30    www.so86a.jeeran.com.

a jihadi theoretician has increased enormously since his writings and lectures have been made available.

## HIS ACTIVITIES AND WHEREABOUTS

It is hard to verify al-Suri's claim that he had 'entered total isolation' from after the fall of the Taleban till late 2004. The production of two new books and the completion of his *magnum opus*, *The Global Islamic Resistance Call*, must have taken much of his time, especially given his fugitive circumstances. The US authorities reportedly depicted him as 'a pen jihadi' whose operative role was peripheral and whose links to the top echelons in al-Qaida were weak.[31] European intelligence officials have pointed out that the sources on al-Suri's operative importance are contradictory, but they cite at least one source who linked him directly to the top echelon of al-Qaida in Waziristan.[32] Compared to many other senior al-Qaida figures, al-Suri kept a much lower profile in Pakistan, refraining as he did from operational activities. Nevertheless, one assessment suggested that in addition to writing he continued to lecture occasionally behind closed doors.[33] Other assessments also suggest that al-Suri was involved in counselling and giving advice to al-Qaida operatives either from the

---

31  In early 2006, Jarret M. Brachman and William F. McCants, who are based at West Point's Combating Terrorism Center, two prominent US experts on al-Suri and other jihadi theoreticians, noted: 'In one massive chart of links between jihadi leaders and operatives that the authors saw this past year, Suri was depicted as a person of little consequence, possessing a single link with another al-Qa'ida operative.' See Jarret M. Brachman and William F. McCants, 'Stealing Al-Qa'ida's Playbook', CTC Report, Feb. 2006, p.15, www.ctc.usma.edu/Stealing%20Al-Qai% 27da%27s%20Playbook%20--%20CTC.pdf, accessed Oct. 2006. See also 'Nasar, Mustafa Setmariam', *MIPT Terrorism Knowledge Database*, www. tkb.org/KeyLeader.jsp?memID=6065, accessed July 2005; and Robert Windrem, 'U.S. hunts for "pen jihadi"', *MSNBC News*, 9 Dec. 2004 www. msnbc.msn.com/id/6685673/, accessed July 2005.

32  Interview with European counterterrorism analysts, names and place withheld on request.

33  Ibid.

Pakistani-Afghan border areas or from Iran. After the destruction of its Afghan training camps in 2001, al-Qaida retained a capacity to train jihadis in small bases in Pakistan. Several European-based jihadis are known to have received training at facilities there.[34]

Al-Suri's relationship with bin Laden may have changed after 9/11. Having fiercely criticised bin Laden on several occasions in the late 1990s in letters and in conversations with acquaintances and like-minded jihadis, al-Suri seems to have patched up his relationship with al-Qaida's leader. Still, he had many reservations about the 9/11 attacks, which had been carried out without seeking advance permission from Mullah Omar (see chapter 8). According to the US authorities, al-Suri 'pledged loyalty to Osama Bin Laden as a member of al-Qaida' after September 11.[35] However, he does not go so far in his writings, stressing instead his continued allegiance to the Taleban leader Mullah Omar. He says he met Osama bin Laden 'for the last time in November 2001 during the battles for defending the Islamic Emirate'.[36] Then, 'we reminded each other of the oath of obedience to the Emir of the Faithful [i.e. Mullah Omar] and pledged to him a commitment to fight all our enemies. [...] Shaykh

---

34  For example, several Dutch militants allegedly trained at such camps in Pakistan and Afghanistan before participating in the planning of the assassination of Theo Van Gogh, an Amsterdam filmmaker killed in Nov. 2004. See Sebastian Rotella, 'Britain Sees More Links to Al Qaeda: One bombing suspect knew alleged extremists arrested last year in a foiled plot, officials say', *Los Angeles Times*, 14 July 2005; and Petter Nesser, 'The slaying of the Dutch filmmaker: Religiously motivated violence or Islamist terrorism in the name of global jihad?', *FFI Research Report*, no.2005/00376, http://rapporter.ffi.no/rapporter/2005/00376.pdf, accessed July 2006, p.14. See also Emerson Vermaat, *De Hofstadgroep.Portret van een radicaal-islamitsich netwerk* (Soesterberg: Aspekt Publishers, Oct. 2005), pp.91, 92.

35  'WANTED: Mustafa Setmariam Nasar', *Reward for Justice website*, www.rewardsforjustice.net/english/wanted_captured/index.cfm?page=Nasar, accessed July 2005.

36  'Communiqué from the Office of Abu Mus'ab al-Suri' (in Arabic), 22 Dec. 2004, p.8.

Osama bin Laden is today the symbol of our jihad and a symbol for the entire Islamic Nation.'[37]

Media reports and assessments by European anti-terrorism analysts and officials differ from al-Suri's own description of his complete isolation and cessation of activities other than writing. When the US military intervention in Afghanistan began on 7 October 2001, al-Suri is believed to have taken part in the initial combat phase. When Kabul fell in late 2001, al-Suri fled with a group of some 50-60 al-Qaida members, including several top commanders, towards Khowst, close to the Afghan border with Pakistan.[38] After crossing into Pakistan, al-Suri later relocated for a period of time to Iran, where a number of al-Qaida leaders had sought refuge, including Sayf al-Adil, Saad bin Laden, Abu Mus'ab al-Zarqawi and others.[39] The idea of fleeing to Iran was not new. Back in 1998, al-Suri had described Iran as the only possible sanctuary for him and his fellow jihadis should the Taleban regime expel the Arab-Afghans.[40] Reports of al-Qaida leaders finding a safe haven in Iran have featured in various media outlets since 2002. The exact extent of this presence remains unknown.[41] Some press reports claim that al-Suri and other

---

37  Ibid.

38  Author's interview with a European security official, Feb. 2006. Name and place withheld on request; and José María Irujo, 'El hombre de Bin Laden en Madrid', *El País*, 2 March 2005, www.elPaís.es/comunes/2005/11m/08_comision/libro_electronico_red_islam/red_islamista_01%20doc.pdf, accessed July 2006, p.18, citing interview with 'a confidential police source'.

39  Sebastian Rotella, 'Terrorism Suspects Traced to Iran', *The New York Times*, 1 Aug. 2004, citing information from former US intelligence officials, European investigators, and court documents. See also 'Timeline of Mustafa Setmarian Nasar's activities', *Associated Press*, 3 Aug. 2005; and Katherine Shrader, 'Wanted Muslim extremist hopscotches the globe connecting terrorists', *Associated Press*, 3 Aug. 2005.

40  Emailed Letter from Abu Mus'ab al-Suri and Abu Khalid al-Suri to Osama bin Laden, Kabul, Afghanistan, dated 19 July 1998. Courtesy: Andrew Higgins and Alan Cullison, pp.5-6.

41  See 'Al-Qaeda Operatives in Iran', *MSNBC news*, 26 June 2005, www.msnbc.msn.com/id/8336988/, accessed Aug. 2005; Robert Windrem, 'Al-

al-Qaida leaders were arrested by the Iranian authorities and taken into some kind of custody, but after the US Administration declared Iran to be part of the 'Axis of Evil', Iranian authorities, more specifically the Iranian Revolutionary Guard Corps (IRGC), reportedly allowed al-Qaida leaders to enter and leave Iran. Many rank-and-file members have been deported to their home countries or been forced to flee but an estimated 20 al-Qaida leaders, including al-Suri and Osama bin Laden's son Saad bin Laden, allegedly 'obtained authorization to live in Iran'.[42]

Al-Suri apparently stayed in contact with other al-Qaida leaders and participated in strategy and forward planning meetings. For example, in November 2002 he is believed to have attended 'a strategic summit' in northern Iran, where many of al-Qaida's Shura Council members were present, though not bin Laden himself.[43] According to the Spanish counter-terrorism judge Baltasar Garzón, al-Suri had told the Council that 'al-Qaida could no longer exist as a hierarchy, an organization, but instead would have to become a network and move its operations out over the entire world. [...] He pointed to the

---

Qaida finds safe haven in Iran: But former leaders reportedly under house arrest', *MSNBC news*, 24 June 2005, www.msnbc.msn.com/id/8330976/, accessed Aug. 2005; Josh Meyer, 'Some U.S. Officials Fear Iran Is Helping Al Qaeda', *Los Angeles Times*, 21 March 2006; 'Iran's Link to Al-Qaeda: The 9-11 Commission's Evidence', *Middle East Quarterly*, 11 (4) Fall 2004, www.meforum.org/article/670; Paul Hughes, 'Iran vows to expel any al-Qa'ida fighters', *The Independent*, 22 May 2003; and Julian Borger, 'Al-Qaida "sheltered in Shah's lodge",' *The Guardian*, 29 May 2003.

42   Ahmad Rafat, 'Al-Qa'idah chief in Europe is Spanish' (in Spanish), *El Tiempo de Hoy*, 24 Aug. 2004, via FBIS. See also Dana Priest and Douglas Farah, 'Iranian Force Has Long Ties to Al Qaeda, Terrorism Support Group Operates Independently of Iran's Elected Leaders', *Washington Post*, 14 Oct. 2003, p.A.17; and 'Iranian Intelligence Official Who Has Fled Abroad: Some of Our Organs Are Cooperating With Iraq To Smuggle Oil. Hamid Zakeri Talks About Some Revolutionary Guards Elements' Links With al-Qa'ida', (in Arabic), *Al-Sharq al-Awsat* (London), 18 Feb. 2003, via FBIS.

43   'Al-Qaeda Operatives in Iran', *MSNBC.com* 26 June 2005, www.msnbc. msn.com/id/8336988/, accessed Aug. 2005.

Feb. 23, 1998, fatwa for inspiration'.[44] This position is also clearly reflected in his writings at the time.

It is uncertain how much time al-Suri spent in Iran and where he was located. One account suggests that in 2004, al-Suri and some of his followers sought refuge in an area close to the Iranian town of Marivan.[45] This was also one of the most important refuges of the Ansar al-Islam fighters when they retreated in March 2003, following the US-led attacks on their stronghold in Northern Iraq, according to German court documents.[46] In August 2005, former US intelligence officials told press reporters that al-Suri had indeed entered Iran, but said that he 'was eventually asked to leave'.[47]

## AL-SURI, AL-ZARQAWI, AND THE IRAQI FRONT

Iran's hospitality towards al-Qaida fighters has varied, apparently fluctuating with the temperature of Iran's relations with the United States. Sayf al-Adl, a leading member of al-Qaida's military committee, recalls in his biographical writings that Abu Mus'ab al-Zarqawi and a number of his fighters were allowed to travel to Iran, entering the country in early 2002. However, after the US began raising the issue with Iranian authorities, many of them were rounded up by the Iranian security services. Al-Zarqawi lost nearly 80 per cent of his personnel in that campaign before escaping into Ansar al-Islam's enclave in Northern Iraq.[48] In 2002 and early 2003, the upcoming US

---

44    Cited in Robert Windrem, 'The frightening evolution of al-Qaida: Decentralization has led to deadly staying power', *MSNBC News* 24 June 2005, www.msnbc.msn.com/id/8307333/page/3/, accessed Jan. 2007.

45    Ahmad Rafat, '3/11 mastermind's hideout' (in Spanish), *El Tiempo de Hoy* (Madrid), 9 Oct. 2004, via FBIS.

46    See Oberlandesgericht München, 'Urteil [...] in dem Strafverfahren gegen Lokman Amin Hama Karim', Aktenzeichen: 6 St 001/05, dated 12 Jan. 2006, pp.80, 99, 103, 121,

47    Katherine Shrader, 'Wanted Muslim extremist hopscotches the globe connecting terrorists', *Associated Press*, 3 Aug. 2005.

48    See 'The Jihadi Life Story of Commander 'the Slaughter' Abu Mus'ab al-

war on Iraq led to a refocusing of al-Qaida's operations, pushing the Iraqi and Kurdistani sectors to the forefront. Al-Suri later described the Coalition Forces in Iraq as 'the new Mongols' who were 'no less barbarian than their predecessors who came along with Hulegu'.[49] It is tempting to assume that al-Suri would travel there to offer his services; he had previously attempted to go to Algeria in 1994, and in 1997 he migrated to Afghanistan for the sake of jihad.

In the post-Taleban era, from late 2004, there have been many media reports that al-Suri teamed up with the new icon of international jihad, Abu Mus'ab al-Zarqawi, the Emir of al-Qaida's Iraqi branch, till his death in June 2006.[50] An article published in the conservative US magazine *The National Review*, portrayed al-Zarqawi and al-Suri as 'another "dynamic" duo', in which al-Suri exerted considerable influence over the uneducated and unsophisticated al-Zarqawi, in a way similar to al-Zawahiri's relationship with Osama bin Laden.[51]

Al-Suri knew al-Zarqawi well from Afghanistan, although they disagreed on many issues (see chapter 8). He reportedly gave the budding jihadi leader advice on guerrilla warfare strategies and the management of insurgency.[52] And al-Suri reportedly accompanied al-Zarqawi to Iran for some time and also briefly visited the Ansar al-

Zarqawi: Sayf al-Adl (the security official in the Global Army of Qa'idat al-Islam) writes down the history of Abu Mus'ab al-Zarqawi' (in Arabic), *muntadayat al-hikmah*, 25 May 2005, http://www.hkmah.net/showthread. php?t=8118, accessed June 2005.

49   *The Global Islamic Resistance Call*, p.63.

50   Steven Brooke, 'The Rise of Zarqawi: Is he the next bin Laden?', *The Weekly Standard*, 9 (377) (June 2004); Muhammad al-Shafi'i, 'Abu-Mus'ab al-Suri: "Bin Laden did not consult me on the Sept. attacks; I am now free to theorize",' (in Arabic), *Al-Sharq Al-Awsat*, 23 Jan. 2005, via FBIS; and Ahmad Rafat, 'Al-Qa'idah chief in Europe is Spanish' (in Spanish), *El Tiempo de Hoy*, 24 Aug. 2004, via FBIS.

51   Lorenzo Vidino, 'Suri State of Affairs', *National Review Online*, 21 May 2004, www.nationalreview.com/comment/vidino200405210939. asp, accessed July 2005.

52   Author's interview with European security official, Feb. 2006.

Islam enclave in Northern Iraq.[53] Due to his alleged meetings with al-Zarqawi, al-Suri was suspected of being 'the main intermediary' between al-Qaida's leadership and al-Zarqawi.[54] Furthermore, al-Suri's aide, Amir Azizi, was believed to be hiding in Iran where allegedly he had joined a group loyal to al-Zarqawi. There, at meetings in 2003, he had discussed the possibility of future attacks in Europe with al-Zarqawi.[55] Press sources also claim that al-Suri met with al-Zarqawi and other jihadi leaders in Iraq in mid-June 2004.[56]

There have also been reports that al-Suri became a kind of spiritual or ideological leader of al-Zarqawi's network. For example, the Italian daily *Corriere della Sera* described him as the 'ideologue behind the mujahidin [...] in Iraq', and 'the point of reference for the foreign militants', especially for those associated with the al-Zarqawi network.[57] This seems to be an incorrect assessment, not least because US officials have argued that their relationship was strained.[58] Both men were strong personalities, and al-Zarqawi would probably

---

53 Author's interviews with two European security officials, Feb. 2006 and Sept. 2006. Names and placewithheld on request.

54 Ahmad Rafat, 'Al-Qa'idah chief in Europe is Spanish' (in Spanish), *El Tiempo de Hoy*, 24 Aug. 2004, via FBIS. The source for much of this information appears to have been Arab intelligence/security officials.

55 Pedro Arnuero, 'Two Spanish terrorists control Al-Qa'idah's "Andalusian clan" in Europe', *La Razon*, 21 March 2005 via BBC Monitoring; Keith B. Richburg, 'Madrid Attacks May Have Targeted Election', *Washington Post*, 17 Oct. 2004, p.A16; and Ahmad Rafat, '3/11 mastermind's hideout' (in Spanish), *El Tiempo de Hoy* (Madrid), 9 Oct. 2004, via FBIS.

56 According to 'a very well-informed Arab source', cited in Ahmad Rafat, 'Al-Qa'idah chief in Europe is Spanish' (in Spanish), *El Tiempo de Hoy*, 24 Aug. 2004, via FBIS.

57 Guido Olimpio, 'A Syrian Ideologue for the Suicide Terrorist Network' (in Italian), *Corriere della Sera*, 28 Feb. 2004, via FBIS. See also Pedro Arnuero, 'Two Spanish terrorists control Al-Qa'idah's "Andalusian clan" in Europe', *La Razon*, 21 March 2005 via BBC Monitoring; and Ahmad Rafat, '3/11 mastermind's hideout' (in Spanish), *El Tiempo de Hoy*, 9 Oct. 2004, via FBIS.

58 Robert Windrem, 'U.S. hunts for "pen jihadi",' *MSNBC News*, 9 Dec. 2004 www.msnbc.msn.com/id/6685673/, accessed July 2005.

not have tolerated al-Suri's sharp tongue for very long. For his part, al-Suri has denied having any relationship with al-Zarqawi. In a statement in late 2004 he said that 'this is another honour in which I did not have the opportunity to take part', referring to the difficulties of travelling to Iraq.[59] Furthermore, the publications of al-Zarqawi's organization and especially its ally, the *Army of Ansar al-Sunna*, tend to be hard-line salafi, something which al-Suri is not. Nor should we be surprised therefore that they hardly ever mention his name or republish his works.

In mid-2005 press reports again suggested that al-Suri was in Iraq.[60] The CIA spotted al-Suri's Spanish wife and their children in Kuwait City in early 2005. This led to speculations that al-Suri 'may be hiding in Iraq'.[61] Elena Moreno and her children had reportedly entered Kuwait 'clandestinely' in July 2003, but the Kuwaiti authorities had learnt of their presence and expelled them.[62] The family was allowed to travel to Qatar, whose authorities were willing to host them, and from where Elena Moreno has given several media interviews.[63]

---

59  'Communiqué from the Office of Abu Mus'ab al-Suri' (in Arabic), 22 Dec. 2004, p.3.

60  David Williams, 'Wanted: The red-haired man of terror with links to Madrid', *Daily Mail*, London 11 July 2005, p.4; and 'Timeline of Mustafa Setmarian Nasar's activities', *Associated Press*, 3 Aug. 2005.

61  Edward Owen and Daniel McGrory, 'Madrid mastermind may plan UK attack', *The Times*, 5 March 2005, www.timesonline.co.uk/article/0,3-1511134,00.html, accessed July 2005. See also Daniel McGrory, 'Architect of mayhem is sure to have fled before the blasts', *The Times*, 11 July 2005; and David Paul and Mike Parker, 'Hunt For Terror Boss', *Sunday Express*, 10 July 2005, p.11.

62  José María Irujo, 'El hombre de Bin Laden en Madrid', *El País*, 2 March 2005, www.elPaís.es/comunes/2005/11m/08_comision/libro_electronico_red_islam/red_islamista_01%20doc.pdf, accessed July 2006, pp.14, 19.

63  See, for example, José Maria Irujo, 'Setmarian, en el limbo judicial', *El País*, 18 Nov. 2005, p.20; 'Abu Mus'ab al-Suri's wife confirms his detention in Pakistan: Spain pursues him and America has promised 5 million dollars in reward for his arrest' (in Arabic), *al-Sharq al-Awsat*, 27 Dec. 2005, www.asharqalawsat.com/details.asp?section=1&article=340381&issue=

If al-Suri spent time in Iran and Iraq, he did not remain there for long. In late 2004, US and Spanish authorities reported that he was most likely to be in Afghanistan or Pakistan, like many other veteran members of al-Qaida.[64] In January 2005, following the handover to the US authorities of the top al-Qaida operative, Ahmad Khalfan Ghaylani, the US Embassy in Pakistan posted a list of their fourteen most wanted al-Qaida suspects in a prominent Pakistani newspaper, reiterating their offer of a $5 million reward in return for Abu Mus'ab al-Suri's capture.[65] The advertisement indicated that the US authorities believed that al-Suri was hiding somewhere on Pakistani territory, an assessment that turned out to be correct when, in late 2005, al-Suri was allegedly arrested in the provincial city of Quetta, the capital of Baluchistan.[66]

## MASTERMINDING TERROR?

The extent of al-Suri's involvement in planning and directing terrorist operations is a contentious issue. In his writings al-Suri is careful to emphasize his role as a jihadi journalist, thinker, and ideologue who supports jihadi terrorism, but is not directly involved in its execution.

---

9891, accessed Dec. 2005; and Antonio Rubio, '"My husband has been abducted", says wife of Spaniard Setmariam', (in Spanish) *El Mundo*, 26 Dec. 2005, via WNC at http://search.epnet.com/login.aspx?direct=true &db=tsh&an=EUP20051227950019&site=isc, accessed July 2006. See also Emerson Vermaat, 'Mustafa Setmarian Nasar: A close friend of Bin Laden's and Al-Zarqawi's', *Militant Islam Monitor website*, 4 Dec. 2005, www.militantislammonitor.org/article/id/1355, accessed July 2006.

64 'WANTED: Mustafa Setmariam Nasar', *Reward for Justice website*, www. rewardsforjustice.net/english/wanted_captured/index.cfm?page=Nasar, accessed July 2005; and Carlos Fonseca, 'Setmariam Lived in Madrid for Three Years', (in Spanish) *El Tiempo*, 3 Sept. 2004, pp.14-15, via FBIS.

65 'Top al Qaeda suspect in US hands-Pakistan official', *Reuters*, 25 Jan. 2005.

66 'Officials: Al Qaeda operative captured: Syrian allegedly helped establish early al Qaeda cell in Spain', *CNN.com*, 4 Nov. 2005, www.cnn.com/2005/ WORLD/asiapcf/11/04/pakistan.terrorarrest/?section=cnn_topstories, accessed Nov. 2005.

Still, his name has been mentioned in the context of the 9/11 attacks, the Casablanca attacks on 16 May 2003, the Madrid train bombings (M-11) on 11 March 2004, and the bombings in London on 7 July 2005. However, no hard evidence has come to light to prove his involvement in any of these events. Al-Suri's alleged involvement in the Madrid train bombings has received the most attention. The Spanish press quickly dubbed him the 'autor intelectual' ('the intellectual author') of M-11,[67] while the *New York Times* reported that 'the authorities believe [al-Suri] is the mastermind of the Madrid bombings', citing the head of a European intelligence service.[68] Initially, Spanish authorities also acted on the hypothesis that al-Suri might have played a role in conceiving, preparing, and executing ('la ideación, preparación y ejecución') the attacks.[69] Hence, in a note to Juan del Olmo, the Judge presiding at the M-11 trial, the prosecutor requested in October 2004 all available information from the police investigation concerning al-Suri.[70] One of the lines of enquiry singled him out as 'a possible ideologue' of the Madrid attacks.[71]

---

67  Ibid.

68  Elaine Sciolino and Don Van Natta Jr., 'Bombings In London: Investigation; Searching for Footprints', *The New York Times*, 25 July 2005, p.A1.

69  'Los terroristas de Londres eran cuatro y su jefe es Mustafá Setmarian, un sirio-español', *periodistadigital.com*, 11 July 2005, www.periodistadigital. com/mundo/object.php?o=119923&print=1, accessed July 2006.

70  José María Irujo, *El Agujero*, p.375, fn 8; José Yoldi, 'La fiscal pide información de Setmarian, uno de los presuntos ideólogos del 11-M', *El País*, 12 Oct. 2004, www.elPaís.es/buscadores/articulo/20041012elpepinac_10/ Tes/elpepiesp/, accessed March 2006; and Al Goodman, 'Spain officials downplay bomb link', *CNN.com*, 11 July 2005.

71  In late 2005, the Spanish Ministry of Justice's website stated that 'Spanish investigators consider him a prominent al-Qaida leader and an ideologue of the March 2004 attacks'. The website even contained a disclaimer saying that this information 'has no official character'; but it nevertheless reflected the fact that the suggestion of al-Suri's involvement in M-11 was still current. See 'Pakistán/España.- Detenido uno de los presuntos organizadores de los atentados del 11-M', *Ministerio del Interior website*, 31 Oct. 2005, www.mir.es/DGRIS/Terrorismo_Internacional/Operaciones_

Various links were investigated, but the alleged evidence so far has been circumstantial. A Spanish police report from 13 January 2005, cited by the Spanish press, stated that the prosecution 'had not succeeded in obtaining "evidence" concerning his participation in these acts'.[72] Police sources interviewed in November 2005 stated that there were no 'objective elements' linking al-Suri to M-11.[73] In spring 2006, when the M-11 indictment was made public, his name was conspicuously absent from the list of defendants as well as on the flow-charts made available to journalists.[74] Only his pseudonym, spelled 'OMARABDULHAKIM' was mentioned in the indictment. The reason was that a study which he published on the Taleban in late 1998 had been found on a computer which was recovered at the Leganes apartment where several of the besieged M-11 conspirators killed themselves in early April 2004. The computer was used between 30 September 2003 and 24 February 2004, and al-Suri's piece was only one among hundreds of jihadi studies, articles and fatwas that the bombers had accessed.[75]

There were many reasons to suspect that al-Suri played a role in, or at least knew of in advance, the forthcoming terrorist massacre. Many of the M-11 bombers, beginning with its main organizer,

de_Lucha_Antiterrorista/2005/Colaboracion_Internacional/C103101. htm, accessed July 2006.

72  José María Irujo, 'El hombre de Bin Laden en Madrid', *El País*, 2 March 2005, www.elPaís.es/comunes/2005/11m/08_comision/libro_electronico_ red_islam/red_islamista_01%20doc.pdf, accessed July 2006, p.14.

73  'Spanish Want to Quiz Syrian-Spaniard Thought Captured in Quetta', *AFP*, 3 Nov. 2005, via WNC, http://search.epnet.com/login.aspx?direct=t rue&db=tsh&an=EUP20051103102015&site=isc, accessed July 2006.

74  For one of the M-11 flow-charts produced during the Spanish investigation, see 'La red criminal del 11-M' in Casimiro García-Abadillo, *11-M: La Venganza* (Madrid: Esfera Libros, 2004), within a collection of photographs and illustrations inserted between pp.224-5.

75  'Audiencia Nacional Madrid, Juzgado Central de Instrucción no.6, Sumario no.20/2004', (the M-11 Indictment), Madrid, 10 April 2006, available at www.fondodocumental.com/11M/documentos/Autos/auto1. doc and www.fondodocumental.com/11M/documentos/Autos/auto2.doc, accessed July 2006, pp.468, 490.

Sarhane Ben Abdelmajid Fakhet ('El Tunecino'), knew both al-Suri and Abu Dahdah very well.[76] Fakhet had belonged to Abu Dahdah's cell since 1996[77] and had assumed a leadership role in the Madrid bombings partly because of the capture of most of Abu Dahdah's cell members in November 2001 and in 2002.[78] Professor Javiér Jordán, an expert on Islamist terrorism in Spain, has noted that although the hypothesis of al-Suri's mastermind role 'has lost strength' the theory cannot be completely dismissed: 'The intellectual authorship of Madrid bombings is still unknown'.[79]

However, the links to a senior al-Qaida figure have proved elusive. In spring 2006, when the M-11 indictment was released, Spanish investigators concluded that al-Qaida had not directed or executed the Madrid bombings, but had only inspired the M-11 bombers. The Spanish judge drew particular attention to *Jihadi Iraq: Hopes and Expectations*, which was posted on a pro-al-Qaida Yahoo! message board, entitled 'Global Islamic Media,' in December 2003. The 48-page document, which was first brought to public attention by this author, recommended 'painful strikes' against Spanish forces in the run-up to the Spanish elections in March 2004, arguing that Spain was the weakest link in the US-led coalition in Iraq and therefore the most strategic point of attack because of the strong anti-war sentiments then prevailing in the country. The document's relatively sophisticated political analysis and clear policy recommendations contrasted sharply with much of the extremist rambling to be found

---

76  Author's interview with European counterterrorism adviser. Name withheld on request. See also Fernando Lazaro, 'At least 15 individuals investigated over 3/11 are linked to Abu Dahdah's cell' (in Spanish), *El Mundo*, 27 Oct. 2004 via FBIS.

77  For Fakhet's role in coordinating the attacks, see Jorge A. Rodriguez, '"The Tunisian" united four groups of Islamists after summer of 2003' (in Spanish), *El País*, 22 Jan. 2005 via FBIS.

78  'How the March 11 local cell was born' (in Spanish), *El País*, 12 Sept. 2004.

79  Email correspondence with Professor Javiér Jordán, University of Granada, 15 July 2006.

on jihadi websites. The M-11 bombers had reportedly read *Jihadi Iraq* on the Internet, or at least, they had visited regularly the Global Islamic Media site during the period it was posted.[80] Indeed *Jihadi Iraq* has become one of the single most important and well-known online al-Qaida documents, despite the fact that very little is known about its authors.[81] They portrayed themselves initially as disciples of Shaykh Yusuf al-Ayri, a leading al-Qaida figure in Saudi Arabia who was killed in May 2003. The document's semi-secular, rational, strategic study-type analysis is reminiscent of al-Suri's writings, but the phraseology appears to differ from his usual style. Moreover the intimate familiarity with Spanish politics that it displays suggests that someone from al-Suri's or Abu Dahdah's circle had written it or at least contributed to its drafting. Al-Suri himself devoted ample space to the Madrid operation in his later writings, hailing it as the first ever 'jihadi deterrence operation' and highlighting the far-reaching political outcome of the Madrid atrocity (see below, p.1392, for excerpts).[82]

The available sources do not allow us to draw any firm conclusions with regards to al-Suri's involvement. The Spanish and British media have occasionally carried detailed stories about his role, with one account alleging that al-Suri himself visited Madrid in December 2003 and ordered the M-11 attacks to be carried out. He was said to have travelled on a false passport provided by his contacts in Iran, and arrived on a flight from Tehran via Athens.[83] After the al-

---

80  Jorge A. Rodríguez, 'El juez culpa del 11-M a una célula local con dos jefes e inspirada en Al Qaeda: Los autores diseñaron el ataque tras estudiar un documento islamista de 2003 sobre España', *El País*, 10 April 2004, www.elPaís.es/articulo/elpporesp/20060410elpepinac_3/Tes/juez/culpa/11-M/célula/local/jefes/e/inspirada/Qaeda, accessed April 2006.

81  Brynjar Lia and Thomas Hegghammer, 'Jihadi Strategic Studies: The Alleged Al Qaida Policy Study Preceding the Madrid Bombings', *Studies in Conflict and Terrorism*, 27, 5 (Sept./Oct. 2004), pp.355-75.

82  *The Global Islamic Resistance Call*, p.1392.

83  Ahmad Rafat, 'Al-Qa'idah chief in Europe is Spanish' (in Spanish), *El Tiempo de Hoy*, 24 Aug. 2004, via FBIS; Juan C. Serrano, 'Mustafa Setmariam Nasar was "third man" linking 9/11 and 3/11 - Spanish daily',

leged visit to Spain in December 2003, al-Suri then returned to Iran shortly afterwards.[84] Another account suggests that it was one of his aides who came to Spain and gave the green light for the attacks.[85] It was alleged that Amir Azizi (Uthman al-Andalusi) and another Moroccan had passed on al-Suri's orders to the Spanish M-11 cell.[86] He and one of his associates reportedly arrived in Madrid around December 2003. Azizi left Spain in January 2004.[87] Another press story purported that al-Suri's envoy also travelled to London, 'bearing the order from Al-Qa'idah leader Abu Musab al-Suri to activate the "sleeper cells" in the UK and Italy'.[88]

The Spanish media has also alleged that the idea of attacking Spain in the run-up to the general elections, with a view to swinging the electorate against the incumbent government, was 'conceived' in Baramava in Iran where al-Suri and his cohort were based for some time.[89] For example, the Spanish paper *El Tiempo* wrote:

---

(FBIS-title) *La Razon* (Madrid), 11 Sept. 2004, via FBIS; and 'Nuevos agujeros negros: La vigilancia a El Tunecino y la casa de los terroristas en Morata de Tajuña', *libertaddigital.com*, 17 May 2004, www.libertaddigital. com/php3/noticia.php3?cpn=1276222932, accessed Dec. 2005.

84 Ahmad Rafat, '3/11 mastermind's hideout' (in Spanish), *El Tiempo de Hoy*, 9 Oct. 2004, via FBIS.

85 D. Martinez and P. Munoz, 'Man who activated 3/11 met Atta in Tarragona in 2001 to finalize 9/11', (in Spanish) *ABC* (Spanish newspaper, Madrid), 28 Nov. 2004, via BBC Monitoring.

86 Juan C. Serrano, 'Mustafa Setmariam Nasar was "third man" linking 9/11 and 3/11 - Spanish daily', (FBIS-title) *La Razon*, 11 Sept. 2004, via FBIS.

87 Ahmad Rafat, 'Al-Qa'idah chief in Europe is Spanish' (in Spanish), *El Tiempo de Hoy*, 24 Aug. 2004, via FBIS; and 'How the March 11 local cell was born' (in Spanish), *El País* 12 Sept. 2004.

88 D. Martinez and J. Pagola, 'Al-Qa'idah ordered 3/11 cell to prepare the massacre at end of 2003' (in Spanish), *ABC* (Spanish newspaper, Madrid, Internet Version-WWW), 17 May 04, via FBIS.

89 Ahmad Rafat, 'Al-Qa'idah chief in Europe is Spanish' (in Spanish), *El Tiempo de Hoy*, 24 Aug. 2004, via FBIS; and Ahmad Rafat, '3/11 mastermind's hideout' (in Spanish), *El Tiempo de Hoy*, 9 Oct. 2004, via FBIS.

According to documents signed by Setmariam [al-Suri], the jihadis considered Spain to be a politically important ally for the USA, but one which was extremely fragile insofar as Madrid's military adventure did not have the support of public opinion. A collaborator of the Iranian president, Mohammad Khatami, has had access to documents belonging to the terrorists and explained to *Tiempo* that 'there is no doubt that the Madrid attack, as well as the kidnapping of civilians, is a product of El Espanol's [i.e. al-Suri's] mind'.[90]

Al-Suri's role was said to be more conceptual than tactical and practical in nature, and the choice of targets and the training of the M-11 perpetrators probably did not occur 'outside Spain's borders'.[91]

The London *Times* newspaper has been frequently cited for an article it published on al-Suri's alleged involvement in the Madrid bombings. The article claims that documents uncovered in an apartment used by some of the Madrid bombers demonstrated that 'their leader, Mustafa Setmarian Nasar [i.e. al-Suri], ordered them to strike in the final days of the Spanish election campaign last March. The coded command was sent three months earlier; Nasar left it to his lieutenants in Spain to decide what the target should be.'[92] The seized documents with al-Suri's instructions allegedly revealed that the Madrid attacks were to be followed by a series of suicide attacks in Spain, but these were thwarted when the bombers were cornered in an apartment in Leganes where they blew themselves up. The newspaper cited Professor Fernando Reinares, one of Spain's leading counterterrorism experts, who has advised the government on these issues.[93] However, the *Times* article is misleading. As Fernando Reinares later explained to the author: 'the article you mentioned did

---

90    Cited in Ahmad Rafat, '3/11 mastermind's hideout' (in Spanish), *El Tiempo de Hoy*, 9 Oct. 2004, via FBIS.

91    Ibid.

92    Edward Owen and Daniel McGrory, 'Madrid mastermind may plan UK attack', *The Times* (London), 5 March 2005, www.timesonline.co.uk/article/0,3-1511134,00.html, accessed July 2005. See also David Paul and Mike Parker, 'Hunt For Terror Boss', *Sunday Express*, 10 July 2005, p.11.

93    Ibid.

not cite me correctly nor presented me correctly. Neither was I director of counterterrorism in Spain nor did I ever speak about any kind of document proving Setmarian's involvement in the Madrid bombings."[94]

The assertions about al-Suri's role in M-11 have been repeated so frequently that they have in many ways become a fact in most people's minds. Nowadays his name is hardly ever mentioned without referring to his presumed role in the Madrid train bombings. As stated above, however, his involvement remains unproven. Having studied al-Suri's life and writings in some detail, one should not be surprised to find that he had no hand in masterminding the Madrid events. In fact, by merely involving himself, even peripherally, in such operational activity, al-Suri would have contradicted his own doctrines upon which his entire body of strategic thinking since the early 1990s rested. For any jihadi organization to survive in the much harsher climate of the New World Order, propaganda, media, and incitement activities should never ever be mixed with operational ones, al-Suri argued. He never tired of reminding his audiences about this principle. In his ideal strategic model, there should be no traceable organizational links between an active operational cell and its leadership, apart from the common ideological and doctrinal basis. Hence, when Fakhet reportedly met with one of al-Suri's lieutenants, Amer Azizi, in Turkey and asked for assistance to carry out the attack, Azizi reportedly told him that he was free to act in al-Qaida's name, but he had to do the job all by himself.[95]

---

94    Email correspondence, 6 Oct. 2006.

95    See 'Spanish judge links Madrid attacks with 9/11 Al-Qa'idah cell' (FBIS-title), *El Mundo*, 29 April 2004, via FBIS. See also J. A. Rodriguez, 'Police put European Al-Qa'idah chief at pinnacle of 11 March network' (in Spanish), *El País*, 4 March 2005, via FBIS; Maria Jesus Prades, 'Spain Indicts Fugitive on 9/11 Charges', *Associated Press*, 28 April 2004, via http://groups.yahoo.com/group/unitedstatesaction/message/6229, accessed July 2006; and 'Madrid Bombers Met in Turkey to Plan Attack', *Financial Times*, 10 April 2004, via www.novinite.com/view_news.php?id=33265, accessed July 2006.

## A MESSAGE TO THE EUROPEANS, JULY 2005

In the wake of the Madrid bombings in March 2004, al-Suri largely maintained his silence, even though his name figured frequently as a mastermind figure in press reports and public assessments by antiterrorism officials. He claims to have sent emails to *Efe*, a Spanish news agency, and ten other Spanish media outlets, to deny any part in the attacks, but his messages were apparently ignored.[96] Having broken his silence in late 2004, following the US Department of State's announcement, al-Suri would issue only two more statements before his capture.

In the wake of the London bombings, the international media mentioned him as a possible mastermind of the attacks. *The Sunday Times* reported that al-Suri 'had identified Britain as a likely target', and that he 'had set up a "sleeper" cell of terrorists in Britain'.[97] This was information which Spanish authorities had transmitted to their British counterparts in March 2005, the newspaper claimed. Spanish investigators believed the attacks were timed to coincide with the general elections in May 2005, not with the G-8 summit in July, as was the case.[98] Later, Spanish authorities backtracked on this assessment, cautioning against speculation about whether al-Suri had had a role.[99] The theory has few supporters today.

In response to the media allegations, al-Suri wrote a 60-page communiqué entitled 'Message to the British and the Europeans – Its People and Governments – regarding the London Explosions, July

---

96  'Communiqué from the Office of Abu Mus'ab al-Suri' (in Arabic), 22 Dec. 2004, p.2. See also 'Biography of Shaykh Umar Abd al-Hakim (Abu Mus'ab al-Suri)' (in Arabic), p.3.

97  Nick Fielding and Gareth Walsh, 'Mastermind of Madrid is key figure', *The Sunday Times*, 10 July 2005, www.timesonline.co.uk/article/0,2087-1688244,00.html, accessed July 2005.

98  Ibid.

99  See, for example, statement by Foreign Minister Antonio Camacho, cited in Al Goodman, 'Spain officials downplay bomb link', *CNN.com*, 11 July 2005.

2005'.[100] It was dated August 2005, but it was released online only after his capture. The publication was accompanied by an audiofile, in which he reads, in his now familiar voice, an abbreviated version of the booklet, lasting 1 hour and nine minutes. The file also came with a 17-page transcript.[101]

Al-Suri had clearly read Western and Arab press coverage in the aftermath of the attacks and cited extensively from media reports that mentioned him by name. He strenuously denied any involvement with or foreknowledge of the tube bombings but nevertheless went on to issue his hitherto most specific call for attacks against Britain and other European countries. In justifying the violence, al-Suri outlined the 'imperialistic' history of European countries, and of France and Britain in particular, and their numerous crimes against the Islamic Nation. True to his predilection for satire, al-Suri seized on the oft-quoted assessment from the Spanish indictment against him that he had planted 'sleeper cells' in Europe: 'O' all sleeper cells, wake up now! The war is drawing closer and the enemy is near collapse, and the signposts are clear'.[102] Italy, Holland, Denmark, Germany, Japan, Australia, Russia and, in particular, France, were listed as priority objectives for the mujahidin, although he emphasized that

---

100 'Message to the British and the Europeans – Its People and Governments – Regarding the London Explosions, July 2005' (in Arabic), heading on all pages: 'The Global Islamic Resistance, no.2, 15/7/1426 [20 Aug. 2005]', dated Aug. 2005, *muntada minbar suria al-islami*, 30 Nov. 2005, www. islam-syria.com/vb/showthread.php?t=1804&highlight=%DA%C8%CF %C7%E1%CA%E6%C7%C8+%C7%E1%D4%C7%E3%ED, accessed 5 Dec. 2005.

101 'Text of Audio Communiqué by Shaykh Umar Abd al-Hakim (Abu Mus'ab al-Suri) Addressing the British and the Europeans regarding the London Explosions, and the Practices of the British Government' (in Arabic), Aug. 2005, *muntada minbar suria al-islami*, 30 Nov. 2005, www. islam-syria.com/vb/showthread.php?t=1804&highlight=%DA%C8%CF %C7%E1%CA%E6%C7%C8+%C7%E1%D4%C7%E3%ED, accessed 5 Dec. 2005.

102 Cited in 'Message to the British and the Europeans – Its People and Governments – Regarding the London Explosions, July 2005' (in Arabic), p.23.

any country with a military presence in Iraq and Afghanistan should be targetted.[103] The booklet was spiced up with a few details from his past history as a jihadi, such as his involvement in the Algerian struggle.[104] He also added his standard phrases on the need for the Islamic Nation to acquire weapons of mass destruction (see chapter 8), which he obviously knew would catch the attention of a Western audience.[105]

Although the communiqué was perhaps not one of his best-written pieces, it served its purpose. By releasing the communiqué and the audiotape precisely when his name was being featured in the global media, al-Suri managed to draw further attention to himself and his writings, even after his capture. Al-Suri understood that the more notorious he became in Western eyes, the more popular and famous he would become among the jihadis, and thus the more his books, articles, and lectures would be read and studied.

## AL-SURI'S TESTAMENT

His testament was published as an epilogue to *The Global Islamic Resistance Call* in January 2005 and also released separately on jihadi websites in early October 2005. Here, he again returns to the sufferings and tribulations he and his closest associates have undergone over the past few years:

> When I write this testament, we are enduring the tribulations which God has blessed us with in His way. We are still moving from one hideout to another, chased by God's infidel enemies and their hypocritical apostates, assisting them.[106]

Al-Suri was clearly worried about being captured by the enemy, and his testament was obviously meant to prepare his followers for that

---

103  Ibid.

104  Ibid., p.22.

105  Ibid.

106  Cited in 'The Testament of Shaykh Abu Mus'ab al-Suri', undated.

possibility. He warned that like several other imprisoned jihadis, he also might be forced to recant and retract publicly from his writings. He therefore stressed that if he should be captured and made statements that contradicted his previous writings, they should be ignored. His ideological thinking and program were fully explained in *The Global Islamic Resistance Call*, and this was the legacy he wished to impart to Muslim opinion in general and jihadi youths in particular.[107]

In his testament, al-Suri also expressed a desire that all his writings and lectures should be gathered together and published as 'the Complete Works' of al-Suri for the benefit of the Islamic Nation. His difficult circumstances had prevented him from doing this himself and he left it to others to do so. Al-Suri also touched upon mundane issues, such as outstanding debts he had incurred from some of the brothers.[108] However, his main concern was clearly to ensure that his legacy as a prolific and important jihadi intellectual survived and that his writings would be read by future generations of jihadis. By explicitly referring to Abdallah Azzam's complete works, his testament suggests that he hoped to occupy a place next to the founding father of the Arab-Afghan movement.

### THE CAPTURE OF AL-SURI

In early November 2005, Western media reported that Abu Mus'ab al-Suri had been arrested in Quetta, a well-known stronghold for militant Islamism.[109] One account has it that his whereabouts were detected 'after his wife had tried to reach him by phone from Qatar'.[110] On 31 October al-Suri reportedly had his *iftar* meal at seven

---

107  Ibid.

108  Ibid.

109  Lisa Myers, Jim Popkin and Robert Windrem, 'Key al-Qaida figure reportedly captured: Suspect is a leader of European terror network, officials tell NBC News', *MSNBC News*, 3 Nov. 2005, www.msnbc.msn.com/id/9909169/, accessed 5 Dec. 2005.

110  Paul Cruickshank, and Mohannad Hage Ali, 'Abu Musab Al Suri: Architect of the New Al Qaeda', *Studies in Conflict and Terrorism*, 30 (1)

o'clock in the evening with his Saudi bodyguard at al-Madina Utilities Store in the Goualmandi district of Quetta. They had been under surveillance by the Pakistani security services which had been ordered to capture him alive. During the ensuing police raid a terrorist suspect from the Pakistani militant group, Jaish-e-Mohammed, was arrested and a Saudi militant named Shaykh Ali Muhammad al-Salim, who had reportedly been in hiding with al-Suri, was killed. Al-Suri was captured alive.[111] Conflicting information later emerged about the initial reports of his arrest and cast doubt on its timing. Unnamed 'US counterterrorism officials' interviewed by NBC News maintained that al-Suri had been arrested prior to the Quetta raid.[112] This appears to dovetail with previous US arrests of top al-Qaida commanders whose capture was only announced well after they had been interrogated about the whereabouts of other wanted militants.

A further indication that al-Suri might have been arrested earlier came in a communiqué released on a salafi-jihadi web forum by an al-Suri aide who went by the alias Abd al-Tawab al-Shami, also known as 'the director of Abu Mus'ab al-Suri's library'. It refuted Western media reports that 'this was a new event' and went on to claim that in fact 'the Shaykh had been arrested three months ago'.[113] News

---

(Jan. 2007), p.1.

111  José María Irujo, 'El fundador de Al Qaeda en España está preso en una cárcel secreta de la CIA', *El País*, 15 Oct. 2006, pp.1, 18–19; and 'Pakistan kills al-Qaida suspect, arrests another: Man seized in Quetta may be Syrian suspected in Madrid, London attacks' (Associated Press), *MSNBC News*, 3 Nov. 2005, www.msnbc.msn.com/id/9905987/, accessed 5 Dec. 2005.

112  Lisa Myers, Jim Popkin and Robert Windrem, 'Key al-Qaida figure reportedly captured: Suspect is a leader of European terror network, officials tell NBC News', *MSNBC News*, 3 Nov. 2005, www.msnbc.msn.com/id/9909169/, accessed 5 Dec. 2005.

113  'Communiqué on the Arrest of Shaykh Abu Mus'ab al-Suri' (in Arabic), dated Shawwal 1426 (c. Nov. 2005) and signed by Abd al-Tawam al-Shami, [elsewhere presented as 'director of Abu Mus'ab al-Suri's library'], available on various jihadi web forums, including *muntada minbar suria al-islami*, 30 Nov. 2005, www.islam-syria.com/vb/showthread.php?t=180 4&highlight=%DA%C8%CF%C7%E1%CA%E6%C7%C8+%C7%E1% D4%C7%E3%ED, accessed 5 Dec. 2005. Also available at *muntadayat*

of al-Suri's arrest had not been announced because of unspecified 'security reasons', but the communiqué which al-Suri wrote in the aftermath of the London bombings (see above) was made available on the Internet. The posting provoked discussion on at least one web forum whose participants wished to know the source of the information, noting that the person who posted the communiqué had not participated in the forums before.[114] On the other hand, the posting of an audiofile containing the familiar voice of al-Suri appeared to confirm the authenticity of the communiqué. The communiqués left little doubt about al-Suri's role as an instigator of jihadi terrorism in Europe but they did little to clarify the circumstances of his arrest or his reported whereabouts prior to his capture.

The veracity of the press reports and the Internet discussions of al-Suri's alleged arrest have also been questioned. We know for sure that he remained on the run till at least August 2005, the date of his last audio recording. Following unconfirmed news reports of al-Suri's capture in Pakistan, the Spanish authorities made efforts to establish the facts and contacted their Pakistani counterparts for more information on the basis that al-Suri was a Spanish citizen who had been indicted for terrorism by a Spanish court. Spain and Pakistan have no extradition agreement, but Spanish judicial sources interviewed by AFP stated that 'Pakistan generally authorises extradition in these serious cases'.[115] The Spanish requests came to nought, however. Al-Suri's wife, Elena Moreno, gave an interview in December 2005, saying that her husband was being held and interrogated by

---

*shabakat al-hisbah* 1 Dec. 2005, www.alhesbah.com/v/showthread. php?t=29409, accessed 5 Dec. 2005.

114 See reactions on *muntada minbar suria al-Islami*, 30 Nov. 2005, www. islam-syria.com/vb/showthread.php?t=1804&highlight=%DA%C8%CF %C7%E1%CA%E6%C7%C8+%C7%E1%D4%C7%E3%ED, accessed 5 Dec. 2005.

115 'Spanish Want to Quiz Syrian-Spaniard Thought Captured in Quetta', *AFP*, 3 Nov. 2005, via WNC, http://search.epnet.com/login.aspx?direct=t rue&db=tsh&an=EUP20051103102015&site=isc, accessed July 2006.

'non-Pakistani forces'.[116] In several media interviews she accused the Spanish authorities of not doing enough to find out where al-Suri was being held.[117] Since he has not been officially imprisoned, Spain's high court has reportedly been unable to request his extradition. In May 2006, the international media reported that Pakistani authorities had officially confirmed that al-Suri had indeed been captured in Pakistan, but that he had been transferred from Pakistan to US custody. In June 2006, Judge Baltasar Garzón voiced his complaints about the US policy of withholding information about al-Suri and his whereabouts.[118] At the time of writing, media reports have alleged that he is being held at one of the CIA's secret detention facilities, and that he has been in CIA custody for nearly a year. His transfer to CIA custody came only a month after he was detained, which occurred as a result of the reward that the United States offered for the capture of al-Suri and his fellow al-Qaida fugitives.[119]

---

116  See 'Abu Mus'ab al-Suri's wife confirms his detention in Pakistan: Spain pursues him and America has promised 5 million dollars in reward for his arrest' (in Arabic), *al-Sharq al-Awsat*, 27 Dec. 2005, www.asharqalawsat. com/details.asp?section=1&article=340381&issue=9891, accessed Dec. 2005.

117  Antonio Rubio, "'My husband has been abducted", says wife of Spaniard Setmariam' (in Spanish), *El Mundo*, 26 Dec. 2005, via WNC at http://search.epnet.com/login.aspx?direct=true&db=tsh&an=EUP20051227950 019&site=isc, accessed July 2006.

118  'CIA holds an al Qaeda leader in secret jail: report', *Reuters*, 15 Oct. 2006.

119  José María Irujo, 'El fundador de Al Qaeda en España está preso en una cárcel secreta de la CIA', *El País*, 15 Oct. 2006, pp.1, 18-19.

# 10
# THE MILITARY THEORY OF THE GLOBAL ISLAMIC RESISTANCE CALL
## BY ABU MUS'AB AL-SURI

Ch. 8 / Sec. 4 [Page 1355-1404[1]]

This section is the heart of this two-volume book. The whole book was composed for the sake of this section, and all the prefaces and chapters were organized specifically for this part. It contains the essence and substance of our idea.

*This is the foremost idea of the Resistance Call. I wrote it for the first time in a communiqué at the end of 1990, and published it in the beginning of 1991. It was because of this idea that I returned to Afghanistan during the Taleban era, and made an heroic attempt to transform it into a project alive and moving on the ground. But by God's ordainment, the events that happened to us happened, and diverted us to where we are now, but our hope in God is great.*

In accordance with our method, our military theory was born through a study of our own experiences in the jihadi current, as well as through enduring and living in the field throughout the various stages. This is how I produce practical theories, as already defined. [2]

---

1    Pagination refers to the pdf-version of the document. The word-file document has a slightly different pagination.

2    [Translator's footnote:] The author uses the term 'practical theories' (*nazariyyat 'amaliyyah*) to describe theories induced from direct experiences in the field, as opposed to 'theoretical theories' (*nazariyyat nazariyyah*),

These kinds of theories can only be formulated by those involved actively, with the success granted by God the Almighty and Supreme. They are written for the battlefield. The details in their ideas have been accumulated in the field and during hours of reflection with the Mujahidun warriors when they rested. We ask God to make us one of them.

I turn my attention to an important matter, which is:

※

**Most of what I will mention here is a specific organizational and military interpretation *(ijtihad)*, based upon my own experiences, studies and comparisons, and conversations with experienced Mujahidun leaders and their cadre... most of these issues are not from the [religious] doctrines or the laws about what is forbidden (*haram*) and permitted (*halal*). Rather, they are individual judgments based on lessons drawn from experience with the issues of opinion, war and stratagem.**

※

In the summer of 1991, I already put down the first seed and essence of the idea, when the warning signs of [Operation] Desert Storm and its raging winds drifted towards us in Afghanistan. Thereafter, I developed it further with the earthquakes and tribulations of the latest jihadi experiences in Algeria. Then, it matured and took shape in my mind at the military camps and at the frontlines of the Islamic Emirate of Afghanistan. I attempted to implement it in cooperation with the Islamic Emirate. Then September came, and I could devote myself completely to formulating the idea in its final version after the tyrannical persecutions compelled us to a condition close to prison and house arrest. One of its advantages was that I could devote my-

---

which are hypothetic-deductive. See *The Global Islamic Resistance Call*, p. 877.

self to continuing to follow the events, thinking, revising and writing. Three years have passed since the fall of Afghanistan, and historical changes have taken place that have altered the face of civilization and the course of history... The American campaigns started, with their new military methods, and their full-scale attacks everywhere... It has assured me of the truthfulness of these ideas—God knows everything—and made me more confident in them, and helped me develop and adjust them, so that they fit to the new reality. The balance of material power between us and our enemies has been shattered. It went to their favour, and then it collapsed.

So between us and them there is no material or military balance. It cannot be compared... If we decided to confront [them], and we regard this a religious duty—which it truly is—I consider ideas like these, which I will set forth in detail in this section, with God's permission, to be the only workable method, from the perspective of a total confrontation theory. I ask Him for victory, facilitation, inspiration with the truth, blessing, guidance and devotion altogether, and that He will crown His generosity by accepting my prayers. Truly, He is all-hearing and responsive.

### REVIEW OF THE WAYS AND METHODS OF JIHAD DURING THE JIHADI CURRENT (1963-2001):

As I talked about in detail in the sixth and seventh chapters of part one, the jihadi experiences began at the beginning of the 1960s, and continued until September 2001, when a new world started...
The observer of these experiences is able to categorize them based on their method of confrontation, into three schools of jihad. Every jihad that was fought during this period can be subsumed under one of these categories.
The results are as follows:

**A. The school of secret military organizations³** (regional—secret—hierarchical). They are the kind of jihadi experiences and organizations I talked about earlier. They adopted the jihadi ideology and conducted organizational work on the regional level, through a secret system and hierarchical network. The main goal was to topple the existing governments and systems, and to establish the Islamic system through armed jihad.

**A summary of the result:**
1. **Military failure,** defeat in the field.
2. **Security failure,** disbandment of the secret organizations.
3. **Agitation failure (fashl da'wi),** inability to mobilize the Islamic Nation.
4. **Educational failure** due to the secrecy.
5. **Political** failure by not achieving the goal.

**Result: Complete failure on all levels.**

**B. The school of open fronts and overt confrontations.** They are the kind of experiences that took place in arenas of open confrontation. Most well-known are the recent experiences in Afghanistan, Bosnia and Chechnya. The method used in these confrontations was to confront [the enemy] from permanent bases, and semi-regular guerilla warfare.

**A summary of the result:**
1. Overwhelming **military success.**
2. **Security success** curtailing the role of the intelligence.
3. **Agitation success.** It mobilized the Islamic Nation behind those issues.

---

3    [Translator's footnote:] the term *tanzim* has been translated as 'secret organization' throughout the text. This is because the author uses this term consistently about militant Islamic groups such as EIJ, JI, LIFG, GIA, etc, not about organizations in general.

4. Partial **educational success** in the military camps and at the fronts.
5. **Political failure except in the case of Afghanistan,** where an Islamic state was established.

**Result: Generally a success, and a complete success in Afghanistan.**

C. **The school of individual jihad[4] and small cell terrorism.** They are the kind of single operations that were carried out by individuals or small groups. These are some of the operations:
– Sayyid Nosair al-Masri and his killing of the big Zionist Kahane
– Ramzi Yusuf al-Balochi and the first attempt to destroy the tower of New York.
– Al-Daqamsa, the Jordanian who killed the Zionist women on the border.
– Suleyman Khatir al-Masri, who killed guards on the Israeli border.
– The single operations during the Gulf War... and the list is long...

**And the summary:**
1. **Military success,** making the enemy tremble.
2. **Security success,** because these are operations that do not lead to the failure of establishing new cells [in the future].
3. **Agitation success (najah da'wi)** that mobilized the Islamic Nation.
4. **Educational failure** due to the absence of a program.
5. **Political failure due to the absence of a program that could transform it into a phenomenon.**

**Result: Success in confusing the enemy and activating the Islamic Nation.**

---

4    [Translator's footnote:] the Arabic term here is *al-jihad al-fardi.*

❦

So, we have arrived at the discussion of these three schools, in our search for the best method of resistance today. We find the following:

### FIRST: THE SCHOOL OF SECRET JIHADI ORGANIZATIONS (REGIONAL–SECRET–HIERARCHICAL):

As I summarized in the table above, this school led to complete failure on all levels. I do not say these words about this method as a critic from outside. Rather, I have been one of its leaders, agitators, and organizational theorists, God is gracious and I pray to Him for devotion and acceptance.

But I look upon the methods as means, and not as idols. We should use those methods that have given us a proven benefit, and leave behind those methods that have been surpassed by time. Otherwise, we will also be surpassed by time.

True, I have mentioned before that the September events put an end to the remnants of the secret organizations of the jihadi current—in particular the Arab ones—the repercussions of those events collectively destroyed what remained of those organizations, and left most of their soldiers killed or captured. But this is not the reason for the termination of this school. In practice, this school terminated ten years before that, with the onset of the New World Order in 1990.

Throughout the last decade of the 20th century, programs for fighting terrorism were able to disband those organizations security-wise, militarily defeat them, isolate them from their masses [of followers], damage their reputation, dry out their financial sources, make their elements homeless, and put them in a state of constant fear, starvation, and lack of funds and people. This was a reality that I knew, as other old jihadis like me knew as well.

Gradually, those secret organizations vanished and disbanded, and small groups of the remaining [jihadis] became refugees in the East and the West, persecuted, with their families, children, and individuals from their organizations. Fugitives of religion and thought, scorned upon here and there, they hardly produce anything...

The regime of the Dead Pharaoh Hassan II terminated, even before it started, the early attempt to form a jihadi organization by *The Moroccan Youth Organization* (tanzim al-shabibah al-maghribiyyah) in Morocco at the outset of the sixties.

This is also what the regime of Chadli Bendjedid in Algeria did in the middle of the seventies, when it destroyed *The Islamic State Movement* (harakat al-dawlah al-islamiyyah) without much difficulty.

The security regime of the heretic Nusayri Ba'th regime in Syria was able to destroy *The Fighting Vanguard of the Muslim Brotherhood* (al-tali'ah al-muqatilah lil-ikhwan il-muslimin), after an armed revolution that lasted about a decade, ten years before the emergence of the New World Order, and twenty years before September... and it completely annihilated it.

The criminal Pharaonic regime in Egypt under Hosni [Mubarak]'s leadership—may God never bless him or people of his kind—was able to put an end to all the jihadi organizations in Egypt, one after the other. The last of them were the secret organizations *Al-Jihad* and *The Islamic Group* (al-jama'ah al-islamiyyah), which were destroyed in the middle of the nineties. Egyptian intelligence disbanded their cells and the government captured most of their members and followers, and this happened years before the September events.

You can say the same thing about what happened in Libya, where Ghadaffi's regime terminated two major attempts, in the middle of the eighties and in the middle of the nineties.

This was repeated when the jihadi organizations in every Arab and Islamic country clashed with even the weakest security and intelligence regimes in Arab and Islamic countries! I briefly mention this here, as the details of this have been given in chapter 6-7 in Part One of the book. It culminated in the great cleansing and the most overwhelming success of the Arab security regime, which took place recently in Algeria between 1991 and 1997, in spite of all the propitious conditions for success that this experience offered. Then, the secret organizations' last jihadi pulsation in Yemen and in Lebanon faded away at the end of the 20th century.

The local security regimes in our countries were able to put an end to those attempts, due to the Arab and regional system of coordination. Their results came when the coordination reached the international level. Thus, as I said above in detail, this is a summary of the results of our method:

1. Our secret organizations were militarily defeated in all the confrontations. Yes, we won many of the battles, but we lost the war in all the [jihadi] experiences and confrontations. I do not spend time on discussions with the obstinate, for reality is the greatest witness.

2. Our secret organizations were defeated in terms of security, their cells were exposed and disbanded, and the attempts to build them were aborted. The security system of the enemy reached a level where even attempts to build cells were subjected to abortive strikes, before they were founded, or at their embryonic stage.

3. In those experiences we failed drastically with regards to the agitation for jihad. The jihadi organizations were not able to reach out to the masses, or to become popular, in spite of the truth they were holding. The number of their supporters did not exceed

the hundreds, or maybe tens, in countries with multi-million-size populations.

4. The jihadi organizations also failed on the level of educating, preparing, and training their members for confrontation in the field of ideology, doctrine, program, security, as well as in the domain of politics and military expertise... except in limited cases. This was especially true after the start of the confrontations, because none of these secret organizations were able to complete the programs of preparation and building under the slogan 'building through battle' (*al-bina' min khilal al-ma'rakah*), when the secrecy and the security conditions prevented that. In this way, the cadre and the supporters that had been formed through lengthy education were expended [i.e. killed or captured], and the level of education declined among the succeeding bases of cadre. This has happened in most of the experiences.

5. In the end, and due to the complete failure in the details, the complete failure manifested itself in the inability to realize the goals of the general project.

Let us now, on the basis of this summary, turn our attention to the result of these methods, in light of the current reality after the onset of the New World Order, and especially after September and the campaigns of fighting terrorism:

- If the methods of 'the hierarchical, regional, secret organizations' in confronting the local security regimes completely failed over the past decades, just imagine how much more we will fail in confronting the security apparatus of the New World Order, and the onset of the worldwide war to fight terrorism with all its security, military, ideological, political and economic means...?! This is no longer possible. Rather, if we insist on using these methods under the current circumstances, it is—in my opinion—like committing suicide and insisting on failure. It verges on the crime of deceiving the simple-minded Muslim youth who are dedicated to jihad. It means assuming responsibility for their destruction on roads that have proven to yield failure. We paid the price of precious blood for this discovery.

- The fault was not the methods of the secret organizations, nor the organizations in general, but it was the changes of time, and the premises of the new reality after 1990, which made those methods destructive. During some of the lectures in Afghanistan I gave an example to explain this, and I will repeat it here... Let us say you have a strong and excellent electric machine, but it only works with the old electric system, 110 volts. Then, as happened in our countries as well, all sources of electricity are transformed into 220 volts. What will happen if you insist on using it?! The machine will catch fire, and strike your electric system, and maybe give you an electric shock as well!! It is for certain that the weakness is not in the machine, because it is perfect and suitable for working in its time, but the new surrounding conditions have made it outdated, and its natural place has become the museum! In a corner of a closet, as a monument from the past. Your love for it, your memories with it, and the fact that it is your parents' heritage will not change a single bit of the reality. The machine was not any longer suitable for work. The time has changed and the machine has retired from service. This is what the New World Order did with our organizatory machine, the regional secret hierarchical model in spite of its splendor. As a result, significant phenomena occurred, a summary of which we will mention here:

- The battle between the governments and the jihadi organizations lasted throughout the sixties, seventies and eighties, for many years, until the governments were able to destroy the jihadi organizations. This happened after devastating battles and large losses for the governments. The jihad in Syria lasted for about ten years of confrontation (1973—1983), and in Egypt it was the same or longer. But look at Algeria, where in spite of the perfect premises for jihad and excellent conditions for the jihadi movement, the attempt was crushed during four years (1992-1995)! And the confrontations and the attempts that took place at the end of the nineties and at the beginning of the 21st century only took a few days to destroy! In Lebanon, the organization of Abu 'A'isha, God's mercy upon him, which was built over several years, was destroyed in five days! And in Yemen, the movement of Abu al-Hassan al-Mihdar, God's mercy upon him, was finished in three days, and so on.... This confirms that the old machine was no longer suitable, except for destroying itself and its owners, who insisted on working and continuing with it as it was. Here is another comment.

- The regional and international peripheries (lit. 'margins' *hawamish*) were closed to the operational activity of the regional and international secret organizations, even the non-Islamic ones, as a result of the emergence of the New World Order after 1990, and especially after September 2001. There were multiple poles in the old international political system. There were two camps; the Eastern and the Western, and inside the Western camp [sic] there were axes, the interests of states, and conflicts. This enabled insurgents in some of the regimes who were client states (lit. 'tails' *adhyal*) of a particular international axis, to flee to the territory of a state belonging to another axis, and resume operational activity. Here, the secret organizations received support and felt secure. They created safe havens, flourished and became wealthy. In this manner, the insurgents against Abdel Nasser in Egypt on the Eastern axis, fled to King Feisal in Saudi Arabia, which is on the Western axis. The opponents of Saddam operated against him from Syria, as the Muslim Brotherhood and the Fighting Vanguard operated against the Syrian regime from Iraq and Jordan. The jihadis, Islamists, and political dissidents traveled from all corners of the world and roamed through many countries, obtain-

ing political asylum and operating secretly across the borders...
etc.

However, with the downfall of Russia, and the emergence of a unipolar system (America) most states, and especially the small ones, became client states of one pole imposing a single policy, so the peripheries between the client states and axes disappeared. Hence, the states, the political parties and the small powers lost those peripheries, and were compelled to follow the orders of the politics of the dominant regime on Earth. The weaker the state, secret organization, or front, the greater was the damage inflicted by this New World Order. One of the biggest losers in this turnover was the secret resistance organizations and the opposition parties, as they were forced to cease their activities, dissolve, surrender, or repent and make compromises with their governments.

Otherwise, the other option is to be wiped out. One of the most awful examples is what happened to the Kurdistan Worker's Party [PKK] and its leader, Abdullah Öcalan. It is one of the strongest militant opposition parties in the world, and it has tens of thousands of fighters spread out in military camps and fronts in Turkey, Syria, Northern Iraq and Lebanon... and it has supporters in northwestern Iran. Hundreds of thousands of Kurds in Europe, especially in Germany, provide the PKK with a certain share of their monthly income, revenues amounting to hundreds of millions dollars. It even has a number of satellite TV stations... etc. It is an organizational empire when it comes to the Islamic jihadi organizations!

When the New World Order emerged, and Syria joined the American axis out of fear and greed, Syria wiped out the [PKK] camps in Syria and Lebanon against its will. The president [of PKK] was forced to emigrate to a number of countries, and then he was kidnapped in cooperation with the CIA, Mossad and the Turkish intelligence. Even Greece, Turkey's historical enemy, assisted in turning him over to Turkey. So the party was dissolved, and its camps were destroyed. America eliminated the remaining [camps] in Iraq, and at last, the ones who were left declared that they would refrain from the armed option, and form a political opposition party according to democratic standards and the New World Order!! While its imprisoned leader could only hope to not be executed..!

Now the last example: The Irish Republican Army (IRA). It is a militant organization whose history and roots go more than 100 years back in time. It is one of the huge organizations, and it has bonds with Irish communities in America, and receives billions in aid from them. It had excellent training camps in the United States, as well as connections in terms of training and support with Western [sic!][5] countries, like Algeria and Libya, and with a number of Arab leftist organizations... etc. When the New World Order emerged, and Great Britain joined the head of the axis of the American alliance, the Irish Republican Army was forced to accept a peaceful option. Its weapons were surrendered, it was dispersed, and the story ended!

**These are some of the glaring examples before us, and there are others. If we did not take a warning from these, we can blame nobody but ourselves when 80% of our forces were eliminated in the repercussions of September 11th during two years only! In order for us to realize that our 'Tora Bora-mentality' has to end.**

**The times have changed, and we must design a method of confrontation, which is in accordance with the standards of the present time.**
*So I repeat again... the main weakness is not in the structure of the secret organizations or their internal weaknesses, although they were underlying reasons. The main weakness is caused by the fundamental and revolutionary change of the times and the current premises, which has altered the course of history, the present, and consequently the future.*

---

5    [Translator's footnote:] The author probably meant to write 'Arab', not 'Western'. The two words are spelled almost the same.

## SECOND: THE SCHOOL OF OPEN FRONTS
### IN THE PRE-SEPTEMBER WORLD

The meaning of Open Fronts is that there are Mujahidun forces whose presence is overt and linked to permanent bases. They fight the enemy forces on open battle lines, or they fight a guerilla war from those fixed positions. I will illustrate this with some examples from our experience: 'The First Afghani Jihad', 'Bosnia', 'Chechnya' and then 'The Second Afghani Jihad in the Era of Taleban'. As I said, this method was proven, in contrast with previous methods. Some points are:

**1. Overwhelming military success:**
This in spite of the enormous difference [between the Mujahidun and] the enemy, in equipment, weapons, technology and all material balances. In the first experience the Afghani Mujahidun, and the Arab and Muslim Mujahidun who were with them—as previously explained—managed to, in spite of their shortcomings, defeat a great state and have folded its flags forever, God willing.

In Bosnia, a handful of Arab, Turkish and Muslim Mujahidun were able to alter the balance of power in the Serbian genocide war, and they performed miracles. It is enough to mention that 60,000 soldiers from the American forces were stationed at sea outside the coasts of Bosnia and Serbia, and they put as a condition for entering Bosnia after the Dayton agreement, that 600 Muslim Mujahidun should leave the country..! So every man planted terror in a hundred soldiers from the Great Empire and its allies..!

As for Chechnya, there is no objection that military miracles occurred that stunned the world, when a handful of men withstood the Soviet military apparatus..! From a people whose population is less than a million, in a country not bigger than 50,000 square kilometers!

In this way, the faithful Mujahidun proved that on the fields of overt confrontation, they are exceptional fighters. The imbalance [of power] between them and the enemy did not stand as an obstacle for them or for the victories.

**2. Structural security success:**
Considering that the confrontations were overt, the regimes' intelligence did not have any role worth mentioning, in that they had a role in the abortion of those fronts. Rather, the participation on the battle field was a [security] barrier by which many of the infiltrators and the intelligence agents were detected, so they had to repent or flee... their activity was limited to observing the movement of secret organizations who took refuge on those fronts, and not abortion of the fronts themselves.

**3. Agitation success:**
This is the third important matter, because those causes succeeded in mobilizing the Islamic Nation, with its hundreds of millions, behind them. This is in contrast to the experiences of the secret organizations, since the oldest jihadi organizations were unable to mobilize the people of the limited region where they were confronting the regimes. Most of the Islamic Nation's people had not even heard about their struggle, let alone supported them! However, in the case of the Open Fronts, the Islamic Nation with its hundreds of millions rose to support and advocate them, and her devoted sons joined the Fronts. The shaykhs and elders prayed to God for the Mujahidun's victory, and rich Muslims and poor Muslims alike donated their money and supported the jihad...
The mobilization for jihad that the Fronts generated was enormous... and the agitation to those causes was successful in a startling way.

**4. Educational success:**
The Islamic educational theory is based upon direct acquisition of knowledge, and on [role] models and examples of good behavior. This has been the case from the Prophet, may peace and blessings be upon him, to his Companions (*sahabah*), may God be pleased with them, and from them to the Followers (*tabi'in*), and from them to followers of the Followers. Then, to the senior clerics and the vener-

able forefathers of the Islamic Nation, and then to their students and followers, and in this way throughout history...

This cannot be done today, however, under the conditions of secret education. It is not possible to provide time or space for giving real doses of the education. Also, the secrecy does not provide any opportunity to become acquainted with the role model, the leader and the shaykh... and to be influenced by him and to take him as a model. By contrast, the jihad on the Fronts provided all of this... but unfortunately, the leaders who were in command in that period were largely incapable in terms of giving attention to education (*tarbiyyah*) in its various forms, and the troops gave attention to military and combat education only. However, this incapability cannot deny two points: First, that education was possible. And second, that it was conducted in a partial manner and by some people. It had a great impact, such as in the Afghani and Bosnian experiences, and much greater than in the experiences of the secret jihadi organizations.

### 5. Political success:

Political success is the realization of goals and slogans... And the goal of every jihad has been to defeat the enemy and to establish Islamic rule. In the first Afghani experience, the success was complete... After passing through trials and tribulations, the jihad resulted in the emergence of the Islamic Emirate. The dream came true. Although it was shattered after some time, it will return soon, God willing. In the case of Bosnia, the goal was to save the Muslims from genocide, and this was realized. However, the rise of an Islamic state in the heart of Europe, and in light of the New World Order, was an impossible matter. I think that whatever was realized, in view of the circumstances, was largely a success. In the case of Chechnya, the political project was not realized in spite of the military successes, because the strategic geographical factors for Chechnya as a country, and the given facts and numbers of its population, makes this a semi-impossible task. The persistence that was realized is regarded as an historical victory.

In general, political success is connected to factors, which are further away than those I teach in this paragraph, which are concerned with the military performance...

Thus, we are able to summarize by saying that the experience on the Fronts is regarded as a successful method of confrontation, when compared with the methods of the regional, hierarchical and secret organizations, which failed completely on all levels... this in spite of the devotion and sacrifice provided by the Mujahidun, and the achievements and victories that were realized, which in the end were futile, as a result of what we said above. And the command of Allah is a decree determined. [Quote from the Quranic verse Al-Ahzab, 33:38].

**However, the theory of resistance on Fronts has been subjected to decline in the post-September 2001 world. America has employed her stunning technological superiority, and used it for her strategy of decisive air strikes and complete control over space and the electronic world. We will discuss this later, God willing.**

### THIRD: THE SCHOOL OF INDIVIDUAL
### JIHAD AND SMALL CELLS

This jihadi school is very old... Maybe its first experience was the unit of the Prophet's great companion Abu Basir, and his well-known story when he formed the first guerilla group in Islam, and the great companion Abu Jandal subsequently joined him. A testimony to this method is what happened at the end of the life of God's Messenger, peace be upon him, when al-Aswad al-Ansi apostatized in Yemen, seized power and suppressed and humiliated the Muslims there. The man who put up resistance, was a blessed man from a blessed family, as God's Messenger, peace be upon him, described him. He carried out individual operational activity on his own initiative. He assassinated al-Aswad al-Ansi, altered the balance of power, and consolidated Islam in Yemen. Gabriel brought God's Messenger, peace be upon him, the good news of this decisive victory, which was won by a handful of enterprising men.

Throughout Islamic history, individual initiatives were repeated. During the Crusader wars, the corruption of the Emirs and the disintegration of the Islamic Nation, groups of Mujahidun fighters resisted the catastrophe, before the rise of the Zengid state, and then the Ayyubid state. Many isolated units and groups performed the religious duty of jihad. In contemporary Arab history, a well-known story is when a single Mujahid was able to alter the balance of power, and to influence the course of a large colonization campaign. This happened when the Mujahid Suleyman al-Halabi, God's mercy upon him, fled from Aleppo—my old city—in North-Western Syria to Jerusalem, where he asked one of the city's clerics to issue a fatwa on killing Kléber, the commander of the French campaign in Egypt, whom Napoleon Bonaparte had appointed as his successor. He then went to him and killed him, and this was one of the reasons for the departure of the French campaign from Egypt. The only price of this victory was the achievement of Suleyman al-Halabi and his shaykh, who issued a fatwa saying that al-Halabi would be a martyr in God's way, and the two of them were executed, God's mercy upon them.

Since the second Gulf War (Desert Storm) in 1990, and the emergence of the New World Order, this school has been revived. Since then, tens of individual operations have taken place here and there, in various spots in the Arab and Islamic world, and are still taking place... Sayyid Nusayr killed the fanatic Zionist rabbi Meir Kahane in the United States. He was one of the most hardline Jews towards the Muslims in Palestine. He had a program for expelling all Palestinians from Palestine. As a result of Kahane's assassination his group was dissolved and vanished. In 1993 Ramzy Yusuf, one of the Afghan Arabs (he is a Balochi Pakistani), and a group of Mujahidun tried to blow up the tower of the World Trade Centre in New York.

In Jordan, a Jordanian soldier from the Border Guards boldly opened fire at a number of female Jewish students who were making movements that were mocking the Muslim prayer, and killed a number of them. In Egypt, the heroic soldier Suleyman Khatir opened fire, by independent decision, at a number of Jews at the Egyptian-Israeli border. At the Jordanian border with Israel, tens of border-crossing operations were carried out by young Mujahidun, some of them were not carrying anything except a kitchen knife (!) for attacking the Jewish patrols on the Western banks of the Jordan river. In Beirut, a Mujahidun climbed to the roof of a building and fired a number of RPG rockets at the Russian Embassy during one of the Russian campaigns against Chechnya. During the days of the Gulf War, an old Moroccan stabbed ten French tourists in Morocco, and the body of an Italian was found in the Emirates. A youth stabbed a number of foreigners in Amman, Jordan, and fired upon them. In Palestine, many individual operations (*'amaliyyat fardiyyah*) are carried out by insurgent citizens against the settlers or the occupation soldiers. In Pakistan, Mujahidun have killed a number of Americans and Jews. In Egypt, a citizen delivered a letter to Hosni Mubarak, and then stabbed him with a knife. He was killed by the guards. In Jordan, an outstanding group consisting of four men created a cell to assassinate Freemasons in Amman, and succeeded in executing a number of them. They were subsequently arrested after clashing with the police, and some of them died as martyrs. And so on...

As for this spontaneous method, which started to spread with the intensification of the attacks of the American campaigns against Muslim countries, the adoption of the Zionistic project in Palestine, and the spread of news through satellites and communication networks, we may make the following observations:

## 1. Military success:
This is concluded from the amount of fear and the terror that was planted in the enemy, and its influence on his interests. Some opera-

tions in 1994 [sic] even summoned more than 34 presidents, headed by Bill Clinton, to the Sharm al-Shaykh conference for combating terrorism.

## 2. Security success:
Which means that these spontaneous operations performed by individuals and cells here and there over the whole world, without connection between them, have put the local and international intelligence apparatus in a state of confusion, as arresting the [members] of aborted cells does not influence the operational activities of others who are not connected to them. I have made use of this observation, to a large extent, when shaping the desired operational concept (*fikrat 'amal*) of the cells of the Global Islamic Resistance Call.

## 3. Agitation success:
The issue of individual jihad was a great agitation success. It had great influence on awakening the spirit of jihad and resistance within the Islamic Nation, and it transformed unknown individuals such as al-Diqamsa, Suleyman Khatir, Sayyid Nusayr and Ramzy Yusuf into becoming symbols of a nation. The crowds cheer their names, people's thirst for revenge is satisfied, and a generation of youth dedicated to the Resistance follow their example.

## 4. From a political perspective:
It has been observed that these events remained as responses and emotional reactions here and there, but number-wise they never became a phenomenon, in spite of their ferocity and their long history of existence. We will explain the reasons for this when we formulate the organizational and operational theories, God willing.

## 5. Educationally:
The absence of a common program for these resistance fighters led to a lack of an educational dimension for this phenomenon. This

is a shortcoming, which it is possible to avoid, as we will see, God willing.

It has also been observed that this method had a partial success, especially with regard to its impact on the enemy, and the fact that the method makes it harder for the security agencies to defeat the Resistance.

From the investigative study of these three schools of jihad over the past period, we deduct some very important principles:

1.  It is no longer possible to operate by the methods of the old model, through the 'secret—regional—hierarchical' organizations, especially after the September 11th events and the onset of the American campaigns, where the great majority of the existing secret organizations were destroyed, and the conditions made it impossible and futile to establish other secret organizations after this model.

2.  We need to concentrate the research on the methods of the open fronts, and the methods of individual jihadi operational activity, along with the methods of total resistance (al-muqawama al-shamila) in order to develop them, this in order to deduct a military and organizational theory which is suitable for the coming period. This by using methods whose benefit has been established. And those two are; operational activity at the open fronts, and secret resistance through individual jihad and small cells. Before we discuss these two methods, however, it is appropriate for us to turn our attention to an important matter, and that is the necessity of planting the idea of globalizing jihad in all fields. The enemy has forced us to do so, and the conditions help us to move in that direction, in accordance with our principles which are originally universal. This is one of the axioms of the doctrine.

Our new method for jihadi operations in the Global Islamic Resistance Call is a global method and call. Likewise, the present military theory is also dependent upon moving on a global horizon. This is a basic factor in the military movement, besides being a strategy, political, and religious doctrine.

### THE IDEA OF BELONGING TO THE WHOLE ISLAMIC NATION AND ITS NECESSITY FOR JIHAD:

This occurs on the level of religious belief, it is a personal sense of belonging, a geographical affiliation, etc. If we go to any Muslim now, and ask him: where are you from? Indeed, he will mention his country; from Egypt... from Syria... from Tunisia... from Saudi Arabia... etc...

He will not mention his city first, and tell you that he is from Damascus, Beirut, Cairo or Tashkent... because he is committed to the borders of Sykes-Picot, drawn in his mind by colonialism.

What we now need to establish in the minds of the Mujahidun who are determined to fight, is the true sense of belonging and commitment, which is according to the words of the Almighty: *Verily, this brotherhood of yours is a single brotherhood, and I am your Lord and Cherisher: therefore serve Me (and no other).* (The Prophets: 92)[6]

Praise God, the enemy's military attack now has put us within the borders of the same map, it is called 'The middle area of operations' *(mantiqat al-'amaliyyat al-wusta)* and in practice, it includes most of the states and countries of the Arab and Islamic world. It is the same in the political field, with the ideological, economic and civilizational

---

6    [Translator's footnote:] Unless stated otherwise, all translations of the Quran and Prophetic Traditions in this text are borrowed from Yusuf Ali or Shakir, via *Search Truth: Search in the Quran and Hadith* website, www.searchtruth.com, accessed August 2006.

attack... Bush has put us all on one map, which includes the same area, and its political name is 'the Greater Middle East'.

Hence, the enemy has globalized our cause by his attack on us, and God be praised. This helps those who are not supported by belief and understanding, to move towards this universal (*umami*)[7] thinking, which is among the fundamentals of our religion.

One must pay attention to the fact that this universal commitment has an important military dimension, which helps us to understand the military theory of the Global Islamic Resistance Call.

Strategically speaking, this theory emerges from the universal dimension of all parts of the larger Islamic homeland (*al-watan al-islami*), and it cannot succeed if we take away this global universal (*umami*) dimension.

If we should enter a jihad at Open Fronts, and decide to confront America at Open Fronts, we will find that in order for jihad to succeed on any front, it requires certain strategic conditions. These conditions are only present in limited areas in the Islamic world. When these fronts need a troop of Mujahidun from any Islamic country, reinforcements of different kinds of special expertise from any country, will fill important gaps on those fronts whenever they emerge.

In individual, secret jihad, the operational activity also takes place on a global and universal (*umami*) horizon. The horizons for this

---

7    [Translator's footnote:] Al-Suri uses the term *umami*, which may be translated as 'universal' or 'international'. It appears as if al-Suri uses the term in the sense that it addresses all Muslims, the whole Islamic Nation. See for example *The Global Islamic Resistance Call*, p. 936: 'The Global Islamic Resistance Call is a universal (*umamiyyah*) Call which does not consider any identity or affiliation to anything except to "There is no God except Allah, and Muhammed is His Messenger", regardless of race or tribe, color or nation, or language, or any difference.'.

operational activity open up regardless of borders and countries. The enemy occupies Iraq and we fight there, the same in Palestine now... It became a duty for a Mujahidun in Tunisia, or Morocco, or Indonesia... to go to Iraq to rush to his brothers' aid ... however, few are probably able to do that, and it will become harder with time, because the apostate regimes in the areas of confrontation cooperate with America against the Mujahidun. But any Muslim, who wants to participate in jihad and the Resistance, can participate in this battle against America in his country, or anywhere, which is perhaps hundreds of times more effective that what he is able to do if he arrived at the open area of confrontation.

It is absolutely necessary to have a sense of commitment to the Islamic Nation and its world, in the geographical, political and military dimensions and in every field.

Whoever looks at these established borders, curved and strangely twisted as they are when they draw the maps of our countries, see the drawings by the pens and rulers of the infidels in the colonial powers' ministries. It is strange, then, that these borders have been engraved in the minds and hearts of the majority of the sons of this Islamic Nation. It is astonishing that this catastrophe is not older than a few decades only. It happened after the downfall of the Islamic Nation's broad political entity in 1924, with the fall of the last of the symbolic Caliphs of this nation.

We must open the minds and hearts of the Islamic Nation's youth, so that they feel commitment to the Islamic Nation as a whole. This is a fundament in the religion and the faith, as well as in the politics and the strategic military concept.

Now, let us move on to our military theory.

## THE MILITARY THEORY OF THE GLOBAL
## ISLAMIC RESISTANCE CALL

۞

The military theory of the Resistance Call is based upon applying two forms of jihad:

1. The Individual Terrorism Jihad (jihad al-irhab al-fardi) and secret operational activity of small units totally separated from each other.
2. Participation in jihad at the Open Fronts wherever the necessary preconditions exist.

۞

*We turn our attention to these facts:*
*The jihad of individual or cell terrorism, using the methods of urban or rural guerilla warfare, is fundamental for exhausting the enemy and caus-ing him to collapse and withdraw, God willing.*
*The Open Front Jihad is fundamental for seizing control over land in order to liberate it, and establish Islamic law, with the help of God.*
*The Individual Terrorism Jihad and guerilla warfare conducted by small cells, paves the way for the other kind (Open Front Jihad), aids and supports it. Without confrontation in the field and seizure of land, however, a state will not emerge for us. And this is the strategic goal for the Resistance project.*
*This is a summary of the military theory which I already developed into its final forms and recorded in a lecture series in the summer of 2000.*
*However, the front confrontations happened after that, between us and the American forces in the battles of the downfall of the Emirate all over Afghanistan in December 2001, especially in the battles in North Afghan-istan and of Qala-I-Jangi in Mazar-e-Sharif, and the battles of Tora Bora and Kandahar... etc. In addition to some other battles after that,*

*like the battle of Shah-i-Kot, which has the American name 'Operation Anaconda', where hundreds were killed, as well as other confrontations...*
*And the high strategic price we paid in these confrontations, in spite of how the American forces and their allies suffered...*
*And then, through my continuous following and studying of the development of the method of military confrontation and the American performance during the invasion of Iraq in March and April 2003. And also [my studying] of some of the battles initiated by some of the armies working as agents for the administration of the American military and security command in the region, such as what happened when the Yemeni Army raided the positions and military bases of the Mujahidun in the Hatat mountains and other [places] there...*
*And what happened during the Pakistani Army's siege of and repeated storming of the areas of some of the Arab Mujahidun and those who supported them in the tribal areas in the Sarhad province in North-Western Pakistan...*
*And likewise, what happened when the Americans destroyed the positions of some of the Mujahidun in Iraqi Kurdistan in Khormal, by using the strategy of intense air and missile bombardment, followed by the advancement of agent forces, supported by American Special Forces, towards Mujahidun positions...*
*And what happened lately in the persistent battles of Fallujah, let God enlighten the faces of the city's Mujahidun sons and the faces of Mujahidun everywhere...*
*All of this has confirmed that confronting the campaigns of American and allied forces in an overt way, according to the methods of the Open Fronts, and through defending permanent positions, is still in its wrong time—time will come, God willing. At present, this is caused by the unimaginable technological superiority of the hostile forces, especially in the air, and in their control over space, and the enormous abilities of taking satellite photos and directing air and missile strikes. And also, the excellent and incomparable abilities of the hostile forces for air-borne strikes, reaching so far as to being able to bring down motorized and artillery units and*

*command forces in terms of strategic numbers anywhere they want, and at record speeds.*

*If we accompany these important and current lessons with the lessons from our many tragic jihadi experiences where we used the guerilla warfare method 'defense from permanent positions', such as what happened to us during the jihad in Syria in the 'Battles of Hama—February 1982', and the battles of Tripoli against the forces of the Syrian government, and during the defense of Tall al-Za'tar in Beirut, Lebanon, against the Syrian and Lebanese agent forces on the ground and Israeli forces at sea and in the air!!! And in Yemen, in the experience of al-Mihdar[8] in 1998, and second, in Nabatiyya in Lebanon in 2000, etc. We find that all these experiences confirm what we have studied and taught about 'the principles of guerilla warfare', and that 'defense from permanent positions' at the wrong time is one of the guerillas' most vulnerable spots. This is also elaborated upon in the books of the greatest theoreticians in military art, for example Mao Tse-Tung, Guevara, Giap and Castro... and others.*

### The conclusion which we have arrived at now, is:

**That the basic axis** (al-mihwar al-asasi) **of the Resistance's military activity against America and her allies now, must lie within the framework of 'light guerilla warfare', 'civilian terror' (al-irhab al-madani) and secret methods, especially on the level of individual operations and small Resistance Units completely and totally separated from each other.**

*However, along with this I say: Any alteration of the balance of power in favor of the Resistance and the jihad, which minimizes the effects of American control in areas which fulfills the requirements of the Open Fronts, which I will present, will again make the issue of open confrontation for the purpose of liberating land, settling on it, and establishing the starting points or seeds for a legal and political entity for the Islamic power, a goal that one must pursue whenever the opportunities arise.*

---

8    [Translator's footnote:] This probably refers to Abu al-Hasan Zayn al-Abidin al-Mihdhar, the leader of the Aden-Abyan Islamic Army (AAIA).

Now, let us examine the details of the military theory of the Global Islamic Resistance Call in the field of [Open] Fronts, and in the field of guerilla warfare of individual terrorism. I start with the Fronts, because it has few details, and because we do not need it so much now. I will only elaborate upon the basic method in the current situation, which I think will continue for a long time, unless God's mercy falls upon us so that the balance of power is altered.

## FIRST: OPEN FRONT JIHAD

While it is possible to perform individual jihad anywhere in the Arab and Islamic world, even all over the world, because this is not dependent on certain conditions where it takes place, the Open Front Jihad (*jihad al-jabahat al-maftuhah*) is dependent on strategic preconditions that are necessary in order to succeed, after success has been granted by God the Almighty and Supreme.

### *Necessary preconditions for success in Open Front Jihad*

**Geographical preconditions:**
These are the preconditions of the territory. It has to be:
1. Spacious in terms of area.
2. Varied, and with long borders.
3. Difficult to siege.
4. Contain partially rough mountainous terrain, forests or similar, which helps in concentrating enemy troops, and in confronting the forces advancing on the ground. It is best to have tree-covered mountains.
5. It is also a requirement of the territory that its food and water sources are sufficient in case of a siege.

**Population factors:**
They include the presence of a large number of inhabitants whose movements are not possible to register, especially if they are spread out in populated rural areas, and densely populated cities. In addition,

the youth of this area should be known for its military stubbornness, fighting ability and persistence, and the fact that sources of weapons are available to them in that area.

**Political factors:**
These factors include the presence of a cause in which the local inhabitants can believe, in a way that is sufficient for making them fight a jihad for its sake. Also, that cause must be able to mobilize the Islamic Nation behind it, so that the nation will help this people succeed, and fight a jihad with them, with their spirit and money... and other kinds of support. The most suitable cause among the causes that instigate resistance is foreign aggression, and an abundance of religious, political, economic and social reasons for revolution and jihad. This is called 'revolutionary climate' in books about guerilla warfare, and in our literature we will term it 'jihadi climate'.

According to these requirements, we may benefit from a study of these factors in the three main examples of Open Front Jihad that took place in the past:

In Afghanistan, in Chechnya, and in Bosnia. This is outlined in the following simple table:

&#9866;

### Afghanistan

*Geographical factors*
– 650,000 km²
– Roughness
– Many resources
– The borders are long, not subject to being shut, and other factors.
*Population*
– 24 million people, most of them youth
– Enduring warrior people

– Great abundance of weapons

*Political*

– Causes: Occupation and foreign invasion

– Religious motive

– Tribal motive

*Result*

Complete success

## Chechnya

*Geographical factors*

– Small area: 47,000 km$^2$

– A lot of roughness, partly open borders

– Abundance of resources

*Population*

– Limited number of people, some 850,000

– Stubborn fighter people

– Abundance of weapons

*Political*

– Causes: Occupation and foreign invasion

– Religious motive

– National motive

*Result*

– Military success

– Agitation success

– Political failure up until now.

## Bosnia

*Geographical factors*

– Small area, very closed and restricted borders

– A lot of roughness, abundance of resources

*Population*

Limited number of people: The Muslims are about 4 million. The people are not fighters, they are not stubborn and sources of weapons are limited.

*Political*

– Causes: Aggression and Crusader-Western genocide.

– Religious motive

– Fight for survival

*Result*

General failure, except in generating support from the Islamic Nation

✸

So, if we examine the countries of the Islamic world and its regions according to their political divisions, from the angle of these strategic preconditions, we will find that the regions and countries in which these preconditions are present, especially the geographical and population ones, are mostly weak, and are created artificially in the most cunning way.

Regarding the cause, if it does not provide a feeling of commitment to the Islamic Nation as a whole, the cause is weak. Regarding the revolutionary climate caused by religious, social, or economic motives for making revolution against the evilness of the rulers and their collaborators, this revolutionary fire was extinguished by the sultans' clerics and the leaders' propagandists. Everywhere, they inoculated the Islamic Nation's mind that 'the one who does not govern by what Allah sent down... those are the devoted ones!'[9] And that 'the one

---

9    [Translator's footnote:] He paraphrases a Quranic verse: 'the one who does not govern by what Allah sent down... those are the unbelievers'.

who befriends the enemies, he is one of us, our ruler, and crown of our head"[10]!!

Therefore, we must search for the keys to revolution, resistance, and jihad under the slogan that fighting today's American-Zionist invasion is for the entire Islamic Nation. One must take into consideration the fact that the sultans' clerics and the media will only fall in line with their rulers and their master, America, and oppose this Call. This is what is happening today.

Regarding the suitability of the Islamic world's regions for confrontation on Open Fronts: The most suitable, according to the abundance of factors, if we treat them as regions, and not political entities, are:

**1. Afghanistan:**
Its factors have already been pointed out.

**2. The Countries in Central Asia and vicinities that lie behind the river:**
It is a large area, close to 5 million km², and it contains close to 50 million Muslims. All the factors required for Open Fronts are present, especially with the continued Soviet occupation in some of the [area], and the semi-overt infiltration of American occupation in the remaining area, in form of a modern colonization the American way. I have already written a study with the title *The Muslims in Central Asia*, which dealt with this matter in detail.

**3. Yemen and the Arab Peninsula:**
It is a vast area, which in total exceeds 2.5 million km²... The total number of people is about 45 million. Its essential stronghold suitable for open confrontation is **Yemen**: It contains the religious and

---

Al-Ma'idah 32-33.

10   [Translator's footnote:] Apparently also a paraphrase of a Quranic verse or a well-known hadith.

economic strategic factors, and the location is well-known... I have previously also written a study on jihad in the Arab Peninsula, and its fundamental pillar is Yemen. It is not necessary to speak at length about this here.[11]

### 4. Morocco and North Africa:

It is also a huge area, with open land borders, long coasts, many mountains and natural fortresses, and an abundance of weapons and necessary resources. It is difficult to besiege because of its many and varied borders. The Arab and Berber inhabitants are historically known for their strength, courage, and fighting skills. There are large sources of arms in the region, provided from Central and Western Africa, and its sea connection to Europe provides the region with many favorable preconditions. Say nothing of that, in North Africa, and especially in Morocco, the situation means that most of the preconditions for a jihadi-revolutionary climate are present. Furthermore, the presence of economic occupation and Western and Jewish control provides a golden key for releasing the spark of jihad.

### 4. The Levant and Iraq:

They comprise a whole, continuous region with a total area of more than 700,000 km². It has all the preconditions for the Open Fronts, especially the mountainous regions in northern and western Iraq, northern and western Syria, and in most of Lebanon, and also in the mountains east and north of the Jordan River... The total number of people in the region also exceeds 60 million.

The now emerging American occupation has declared its determination to remain on a long-term basis. They also prepare to extend their aggression to Syria in order to control the whole Levant, after the Jews occupied Syria, the Christians took control over Lebanon, and America seized control over Jordan in all of its affairs.

---

11    See the letter *The Responsibility of the People of Yemen towards the Holy Places of Muslims and their Wealth* by the author.

There is an abundance of weapons and equipment in the region, and it also has varied borders, coasts, and passes. Israel creates a motive for a global Islamic cause, and the American occupation adds a revolutionary dimension, which is an excellent key to jihad...

There are other similar regions as well, in which there are many suitable preconditions for open confrontations, such as Turkey. It is one of the most suitable countries for jihadi guerilla warfare, because all the factors are present. Likewise, and even more so, with Pakistan,[12] and some regions on the African continent and other similar [regions]... However, the great majority of Islamic states and entities, which comprise more than 55 states, are not at all suitable for open confrontation, due to the absence of all or some of the suitable conditions.

Here, one must pay attention to the political cause, which will be the cause of struggle and mobilization for the confrontation. As explained, this cause should be driving the American occupation out of the region, fighting the Jews, removing the idolaters from the Arab Peninsula, oil and resources, the American hegemony, and the injustices and affliction caused by the occupation and its allies in the region.

## How to participate in the Resistance in Open Front Jihad:

In most Arab and Islamic countries, with their current political divisions and entities, the preconditions for Open Fronts are not present. In most cases, they are arenas suitable for Individual Terrorism Jihad, small units, and secret guerilla warfare, as a result of the dense presence of different American and allied interests, and of Western and Zionist hegemonic projects.

---

12   See *Musharraf's Pakistan—The Problem, the Solution and the Necessary Obligation*—by the author.

Those Mujahidun who want to contribute in open confrontations, must head for wherever the Fronts open up whenever they open. They must operate under the field leadership's command, as long as it fulfills the minimum criteria of being a legitimate banner *(al-rayah al-shar'iyyah)* and legitimate jihad under the slogan of universal Islam *(al-islam al-'amm)* and as long as it is in accordance with the principles of the Resistance, its ideology and jihadi doctrine.

When the jihad on one of those fronts leads to victory for the Muslims, that [front] will be the center of an Islamic Emirate, which should be ruled by God's *sharia*. It will be a center and a destination for those around it emigrating to fight jihad in the cause of God. The leadership and the Emirate will be for all people of that country. There will be certain inherited social traditions there, and it is of no use violating them or pretending to forget the traces of the past, until the Muslim society emerges which is built upon the universalness of Islam and the nationality of Islam. This requires a long time, only God knows.

This was a short and general description of Open Front Jihad. I will speak and instruct more about this later ...

Indeed, it is very important for those who refuse to carry the banner of jihad, that they understand their reality, the Muslims' reality, and the preconditions of the current American era, before God removes their country and disperses them...

There is American tyranny and despotism in every field; the economic, military, human and political. It is impossible and of no use to ignore this... Since the September 11th events we have examples that give clear indications... All of them point to the fact that one must consider the matter thoroughly before even thinking about confronting this tyrannical power on an Open Front. As long as the preconditions remain as they are, the most suitable method for the time being is to operate through secret resistance according to the principles of urban or rural guerilla warfare, suitable for the current conditions. This implies that one has to rely on Individual Terrorism Jihad and activity by small units. This is what we will explain in the remaining part of this section, God willing, which comprises the following paragraphs.

## SECOND: INDIVIDUAL TERRORISM JIHAD AND
## THE GLOBAL ISLAMIC RESISTANCE UNITS

### *Definition of Terrorism*

I think that one of the most important fields of success in the recent American Jewish Crusader campaigns is that on the media fields. They have succeeded in imposing terminologies and definitions of people, and in forcing upon humanity a meaning of these terminologies, corresponding with their view. Among the terms which they have imposed today, in a distorted way, in order to express the ugliest of activities, manners and practices... are the terms 'terrorism', 'terrorists' and 'combating terrorism'...

It has even become natural in the Arab and Islamic media, and even the media of the Islamic awakening *(al-sahwah)*, to reject this description, as if it was an accusation, a vice, and a disaster, which would cause those accused of it to be described by all the characteristics of depravity and everything derived from it in this world and the hereafter...

With all simplicity and courage we say:

We refuse to understand this term according to the American description. 'Terrorism' is an abstract word, and like many of the abstract words, it can carry a good or bad meaning according to the context, and what is added to it and what is attached to it. The word is an abstract term, which has neither positive nor negative meaning.

**Arhaba:** i.e. to terrify, and the masdar is **al-rahab**... i.e. excessive fear. The one performing the action is an 'irhabi'... The one whom the action falls upon is a **murhab** or **marhub**.

We have two types of terrorism...

**1. Blameworthy terrorism** (*irhab madhmum*):
It is the terrorism of falsehood (*irhab al-batil*) and force of falsehood (*quwwa al-batil*), it can be defined as every action, speech, or behavior which inflicts harm and fear among the innocent without a true cause.

This kind of terrorism includes the terrorism of thieves, highway robbers, invaders, and assailants, and the terrorism of oppressors and unrightful rulers of people, such as the Pharaohs and their servants... This is blameworthy terrorism, and its perpetrator is a 'criminal terrorist' who deserves to be punished for terrorism and its crime according to its damage and impact.

**2. Praiseworthy terrorism** (*irhab mahmud*):
This is the opposite of blameworthy terrorism. It is terrorism by the righteous that have been unjustly treated. It removes injustice from the oppressed. This is undertaken through terrorizing and repelling the oppressor.

The terrorism of the security men who fight against thieves and highway robbers is of this kind, the terrorism of those who resist occupation, the terrorism of people defending themselves against the servants of Satan. This is praiseworthy terrorism.

*Terrorizing the Enemies is a Religious Duty, and Assassinating their Leaders is a Prophetic Tradition:*

I remember that I was enrolled in a training course for cadres in the military wing of the Muslim Brotherhood organization during the days of the jihad and revolution against Hafiz al-Asad's regime. I was 22 years old. This was in the al-Rashid camp belonging to the Iraqi Army in Baghdad in 1980. When the trainer entered—and he was—God's mercy upon him—a distinguished man, an elderly shaykh from the first Muslim Brotherhood-generation, from those who pledged allegiance to shaykh Hasan al-Banna, God's mercy upon him, when he was 17 years old. He fought in Palestine in 1948, and was wounded in Jerusalem, and worked in the Muslim Brotherhood's Special Apparatus. He participated in the secret resistance against the British in the Suez Canal zone at the beginning of the fifties. He became friends with Sayyid Qutb, God's mercy upon him. He emigrated from Egypt and lived outside the country for the rest of his life. He was a trainer in the Shuyukh camps in Eastern Jordan with the Palestine Liberation Organisation in 1969, and devoted himself to helping several of the jihadi movements, which were backed by the Muslim Brotherhood. This was when the Muslim Brotherhood was still following the programme of al-Banna and Qutb, before the plague of democracy and parliaments began...

He was training us in military disciplines and he also ran with us when we had physical exercise—in spite of his old age. He held lectures for us. I remember when he first walked in on a troop of 30 young men, the elite of the military wing of the Syrian Brotherhood at that time. The first thing he said to us in his Egyptian dialect, was:

'Are you Muslim Brothers?' We said yes. He said: 'Are you sure, my sons?' We said we were sure. He said, pointing at his neck: 'You will all be slaughtered. Agree?" We all said, overflowing with happiness and joy: 'We agree, Bey..."

He turned to the blackboard, and wrote the title of the first lecture on it:

'Terrorism is a religious duty, and assassination is a Prophetic tradition'!

He drew a line under it and turned in order to start the lesson... and for us to start the work ... We paid attention to the lessons, the path was drawn out, and the good news continued... The hope in God's generosity is great for those who fulfilled their pledge from that troop, and for the ones who are waiting.

What the shaykh—God's mercy upon him—summarized for us is a part of this religion's doctrine. I begin the following part of my lesson with it.

God has given clear orders in His book to terrorize His enemies. Along with it came the Tradition of His prophet, the Chosen One, may peace and blessings be upon him, consisting of his deeds, sayings and approvals. The Book and the Tradition have established the rules of this praiseworthy terrorism against God's enemies in clear words. In the Quran, God the Almighty said:

'Against them make ready your strength to the utmost of your power, including steeds of war, to strike terror into (the hearts of) the enemies, of Allah and your enemies, and others besides, whom ye may not know, but whom Allah doth know. Whatever ye shall spend in the cause of Allah, shall be repaid unto you, and ye shall not be treated unjustly.' (Al-Anfal: 60)

The verse is clear in its text and unambiguous in its meaning... '**Make ready**' means train for combat. '**Against them**' means against your enemies. '**your strength to the utmost of your power, including steeds of war**' is the shooting, riding, and weapons. The Prophet Muhammed, peace and blessings upon him, said: '*Indeed, power is shooting*', repeating it three times.

Why this preparing and training for combat, the gathering of weapons, and making ready the steeds of war...? The verse itself has already explained it: 'to strike terror' means in order to strike terror, 'with it' means with what you have made ready for combat. 'The enemies of Allah and your enemies': They are the ones whom the terrorist act is intended for. 'And others besides': Means the ones who support and help them, or the ones who wait in ambush for you in order to attack you. When they witness your terror against the assailants, your resistance, and self-defense, they will 'be terrorized' and frightened, and deterred from attacking, without you even knowing about their determination to attack. But God knew it, and deterred the enemy through your preparation and through your terror against the assailant enemies of God. God the Almighty knows everything.

Thus, and in short:

*This generous verse has ordered preparation for the purpose of terrorizing the assailants' and God's enemies among the infidels and their servants.*

The fugitive has understood this verse better than many Muslim clerics of this time. America has demanded all the Islamic countries to omit it, and all of Al-Anfal, At-Tawbah and Al Umran ... from the educational curriculum!!

The one who terrorizes others is a 'terrorist' without any exception, and hence, there is:

1. An evil assailant terrorist.
2. A righteous terrorist defending himself or other oppressed people.

Thus, in the word **terrorist** we do not find any negative meaning when we use it to characterize the Resistance fighters or the Mujahidun... they are, in reality, terrorists towards their enemies, God's enemies, and His weak servants. So where are the ambiguity and the blame?!

**Yes, we are terrorists towards God's enemies.** We have already struck terror in them, and we have made them tremble in their holes, in spite of the hundreds of thousands of agents in their security agencies, praise God, and this happened after they terrorized the countries and mankind, and even put fear into the embryos in their mothers' bellies.

From this it follows that terrorism has been commanded in God's book, and in situations where the Mujahidun are repelling their enemy and the enemy's terror through a defensive jihad. This is one of the most important religious duties. In fact, there is no duty more obligatory than this, except believing that God is One, as has been established by Islamic jurists and clerics. [We must grasp this] before the enemy's media terror and ideological terror captures us and makes us disclaim our identity, our Lord's book and the duties of our religion...

God's enemies knew that the command to terrorize them is repeated in many of the passages in God's book, and in the tradition of His Prophet, may peace and blessings be upon him. Rumsfeld and others have stated this, and demanded from the Islamic countries that they omit many Quranic verses from the educational curriculum in the countries of the Arabs and the Muslims, even including the words of God the Almighty: *'Say: O unbelievers... You shall have your religion and I shall have my religion'*. [Al-Kafirun 109:1,6] They said that these verses instigate hatred and division among people of different religions, and must be omitted!! I do not know where the indifferent hypocrites should go [to escape] what God the Almighty said: 'Therefore, when ye meet the Unbelievers (in fight), smite at their necks; At length, when ye have thoroughly subdued them, bind a bond firmly (on them): thereafter (is the time for) either generosity or ransom:

Until the war lays down its burdens. Thus (are ye commanded): but if it had been Allah's Will, He could certainly have exacted retribution from them (Himself); but (He lets you fight) in order to test you, some with others. But those who are slain in the Way of Allah, - He will never let their deeds be lost.' (Muhammad: 4)

Muhammad, peace and blessings upon him, said: 'I was sent between the hands of the Hour with the sword until Allah will be worshipped alone with no partner, my sustenance was made under the shadow of my spear, and humiliation and lowliness were made for those who disobey my order, and those who imitate a crowd is with them'.[13] Muhammad, peace and blessings upon him, also said: 'O, people of Qureish, truly, I have come to slaughter you'...!

The rulers and the Ministries of Education responded to them, and adjusted the curricula several times. There are many examples, and the latest of them is the Pakistani Minister of Culture who went out publicly in front of the press to say that the two suras Al-Anfal and At-Taubah must be omitted from the curricula because they called for terrorism!!

Eventually, the matter brought America to a point where they gathered a number of the clerics residing in the West and the orientalists, in order to shorten the Koran and omit everything that, by their claim, incites hatred and fighting!! They came out with a new, shortened Koran named 'The True Koran' (*furqan al-haqq*)[14]. A number of media outlets talked about this, and afterwards I heard it in a press summary on the Saudi-Gulf Iqra' channel! And so on. God says the Truth, and we are warned by His words: 'They ask thee concerning fighting in the Prohibited Month. Say: 'Fighting therein is a grave

---

13    [Translator's footnote:] Translation from: http://www.iisna.com/articles/index.php?sid=tawheed&id=3.

14    [Translator's footnote:] Furqan means 'salvation' and is another name for the Quran.

(offence); but graver is it in the sight of Allah to prevent access to the path of Allah, to deny Him, to prevent access to the Sacred Mosque, and drive out its members." Tumult and oppression are worse than slaughter. Nor will they cease fighting you until they turn you back from your faith if they can. And if any of you Turn back from their faith and die in unbelief, their works will bear no fruit in this life and in the Hereafter; they will be companions of the Fire and will abide therein.' (Al-Baqara: 217). The command is clear and evident.

The most important terrorist actions against God's enemies, their leaders and the chiefs of Unfaith (*a'immat al-kufr*), are to combat the chiefs of Unfaith, as God the Almighty said: 'But if they violate their oaths after their covenant, and taunt you for your Faith,- fight ye the chiefs of Unfaith: for their oaths are nothing to them: that thus they may be restrained.' (At-Tawbah: 12)

So the most important of the jihadi actions is the liquidation of their leaders, by murder and assassination. This was confirmed in a number of separate events when Prophet Mohammad, peace and blessings upon him, sent Mujahidun units as teams and special units, 'commandoes' of elite Companions... to assassinate leaders of unbelief (*ru'us al-kufr*) of his, peace and blessings upon him, time. These events are firmly proven. Among them is when he sent [a unit] to assassinate a female poet who was harming God, His prophet and the Muslims by her poetry. So he ordered her assassination, and her tongue was silenced.

*This is what God's messenger, peace and blessings upon him, did. A Prophetic tradition which we are proud of, follow, and imitate, and we regard those who condemn it as unbelievers.*

At the end of his, peace and blessings upon him, life, Fayruz al-Day-lami assassinated the head of apostasy in Yemen, al-Aswad al-Ansi, who had seized power in Yemen. He wanted people to turn to apostasy, so Fayruz assassinated him. Gabriel informed God's messenger about the event while he [Muhammad] was on his deathbed, and delighted him by the good news. God's messenger, peace and blessings upon him, informed his Companions about it, and it is told that he said to them: 'al-Aswad al-Ansi has been killed. A blessed man from a blessed family has killed him.'

The assassination of leaders of Unfaith among civilians and military personnel, among men from politics, propaganda and media, among the ones who discredit God's religion, and among the supporters of God's enemies who invade the Muslims, is a confirmed tradition of God's messenger, peace and blessings upon him. It is one of the most important arts of terrorism and one of its most beneficial and deterring operations and methods.

These are methods, which are also implemented by God's enemies. The CIA has obtained a license from the American government to assassinate presidents, if that is in the American national interest, and they have used it time after time. In the CIA, there is a special department for that! So I do not know why they forbid us from doing this? Then, the riffraff and hypocrites among our clerics, may God fight them, agree with them on this falsehood?!

After this necessary introduction in which we have undressed the word 'terrorism' and its derivatives, in order to use it as a type of and one of the goals of jihad, we will now move on to the next point.

*Observations about past terrorist operations and individual jihad:*
We observe that those operations remained limited. They were performed by a few people here and there, as an expression of an emotional reaction following some hostile acts against Muslims. They increase in the places of aggression themselves, and this is because the minds and spirits are still naturally disposed towards a local or national awareness. If the colonialist invades a country, there would

be a lot of reactions there, but when the same colonialist, with his military and civilian power of different kinds, is present in neighboring countries, no one threatens their interest.

We also observe that the ones performing these operations are not programmed [i.e. part of an organized program], in order to become a phenomenon for the sake of setting an example, pushing the Islamic Nation's youth to follow it, and building upon it. They are merely emotional reactions.

They have not transformed into a phenomenon, because they are spontaneous, and nobody has occupied themselves with making them part of a program and presenting them as a strategic operational method. This is what we will adopt as a fundamental strategy at the base of our military theory in the Global Islamic Resistance Call.

*Conditions and needs which make it necessary for the Resistance to use the operational method of individual jihad:*

Among the things that impose this operational method as a strategic choice, are the conditions of imbalance of power between the Resistance and the grand aggressor alliance of infidels, apostates and hypocrites, and from this:

1. The failure of the operational methods of the secret, hierarchical organizations, in light of the international security campaign and the international and regional [counter-terrorism] co-ordination, which we have referred to above. Furthermore, the need for an operational method, which makes it impossible for those security agencies to abort the Resistance cells by arresting [some of] their members, based on [information extracted through] torture and interrogation [of other members].
2. Inability of the secret organizations to incorporate all of the Islamic Nation's youth who want to perform the duty of jihad and Resistance by contributing with some kind of activity, without

being required to commit themselves to membership responsibilities of a centralized organization.

3. The presence of the enemy over a wide area, the increased diversity of his goals, and his presence in many spots, makes it harder for battle-fronts to emerge, and it also makes it harder to establish centralized organizations.

4. Decline of the idea of the Open Fronts and confronting the enemy from permanent positions, as a result of the enemy's use of the strategy of decisive air attacks with devastating rocket bombardments and air strikes, directed by satellites which control the ground, they even see what is beneath the ground, with the help of advanced technology. This is a matter of fact, which must be recognized, and upon which the planning for confrontation must be made based.

### *The general principles for the theory of individual jihadi action in the Resistance Call from a practical perspective:*

1. Spreading the culture of the Resistance and transforming it into an organized strategic phenomenon, and not merely a collection of responses.

2. Spreading the ideology of the Resistance, its programme, its legal and political bases, and its operational theories, so that they are available for the Islamic Nation's youth who strongly wish to participate in the jihad and Resistance.

3. Directing the Resistance fighters to areas of operation suitable for the Individual Terrorism Jihad.

4. Directing the Resistance fighters to the most important targets which they must target in Resistance operations and jihad of small units.

5. Spreading the legal, political, military and other sciences and knowledge that the Mujahidun need in order to carry out Resistance operations, without this being in a direct way that leads to a series of arrests in the networks, as happened in the centralized organizations.

7. Instructing the youth in the armed operational method, in building the cells of the Resistance units as a 'system of action' (*nizam al-'amal*) and not as 'a secret organization for action' (*tanzim lil-'amal*), as we will explain later in this section, and in the section devoted to the theories on 'security, organization, training and preparation...'

8. Coordinating a method in which all efforts are joined, in order to combine their result in a mechanism which confuses the enemy, exhausts him and heightens the spirit of the Islamic Nation so that it joins the Resistance phenomenon.

## *Main arenas of operation for Individual Terrorism Jihad:*

*The Islamic Nation is vast and so are the arenas in which targets and interests of the invader enemy are present. It is furthermore impossible for all the youth who want to participate in the Resistance to travel to the arenas of [open] confrontation. It is even unlikely that such Fronts should emerge in the foreseeable future. Hence, our method should therefore be to guide the Muslim who wants to participate and resist, to operate where he is, or where he is able to be present in a natural way. We should advise him to pursue his everyday life in a natural way, and to pursue jihad and Resistance in secrecy and alone, or with a small cell of trustworthy people, who form an independent unit for Resistance and for the individual jihad.*

Regarding the priority of arenas in which we must strike the enemy, the list of priority arenas is as follows:

**1. Wherever you hurt the enemy the most and inflict upon him the heaviest losses.**

**2. Wherever you arouse Muslims the most and awaken the spirit of jihad and Resistance in them.**

Thus, the list of arenas, arranged according to their importance, is as follows:

*1. The countries on the Arab Peninsula, the Levant, Egypt, and Iraq:*
This area contains the holy places, the oil, Israel, the countries encircling her, and the American military and economic presence, and it is the fundamental and final site for the victorious sect *(al-ta'ifah al-mansurah)* for all time to come.

*2. The countries of North Africa from Libya to Mauritania:*
There are Western interests in this region, especially those of the main European countries allied with America in the NATO.

*3. Turkey, Pakistan, and the countries of Central Asia:*
They contain the second largest oil reserves in the world, and America's strategic interests, military bases, and main economic investments. They have large and historical Islamic movements, which are regarded as being a strategic depth for the Arab jihadi and Resistance movements.

*4. The rest of the Islamic world:*
The Americans and their allies have interests and a presence in this region. The Islamic world as a whole contains the main backbone of the Resistance, which is the Islamic Nation's youth sympathizing with its causes and wishing to participate in the jihad and the Resistance. It is a backbone consisting of hundreds of millions of Muslims.

*5. The American and Allied interests in third world countries:*
Especially in those countries participating in the Crusader campaign. This due to their weak security capabilities, compared with the security regulations that the Western countries implement in their own countries. Jihad in these countries rests fundamentally on the shoulders of the Mujahidun who basically reside in those countries, and

live a normal life there. This helps them in moving, hiding, gaining knowledge of the targets and dealing with them in an easy manner.

*6. In European countries allied with America and participating with her in the war:*
This is due to the presence of old and large Islamic communities in Europe. Their number exceeds 45 million, and there are communities of millions in Australia, Canada and South America as well.

Especially in Europe, because of its closeness to the Arab and Islamic world, and the inter-twining of interests between them, and because of all the movement and transportation between the two. The Muslims in those countries are like Muslims everywhere, the religious duty of jihad, of repelling the enemy and resisting him, rests on their shoulders in exactly the same way as for Muslims in their own countries [i.e. Muslims residing in the Arab and Islamic world].

Action in Europe and those countries must be subjected to the rules of political benefits versus political harms, judged against the positions of the European governments. At the same time, one has to adopt a strategy of winning the support of the people, and avoiding harming them. I will present this in detail in the political theory of the Resistance, God willing.

*7. In the heart of America herself, by targeting her with effective strategic operations, as will be explained in the following paragraphs*
God willing. She [America] is the viper's head, as shaykh Usama rightfully named her. And she is the origin of scourge and the head of the alliance. When defeated, this alliance will break up, and we will move to a new historical era, God willing.

*The most important enemy targets aimed at by the Individual Terrorism Jihad:*

The goal of the operations of the Resistance and the Individual Terrorism Jihad is to inflict as many human and material losses as possible upon the interests of America and her allies, and to make them feel that the Resistance has transformed into a phenomenon of popular uprising against them, because of their hostility that stretches from Central and South Asia, the Philippine Islands and Indonesia in the East, to the shores of the Atlantic in the West, and from the Caucasus, the countries of the Crimea, the Balkans and North Africa in the North, to India and Central Africa in the South, all along the Islamic world, in addition to places populated with Muslims.

The arena of the Islamic countries is the basic arena for the Resistance, as we explained in the political theory, and we will clarify this in the paragraph 'The Strategy of the Resistance' at the end of this important chapter.

The fundament for the operational activity is that the Mujahid, the member of the Resistance, practices individual jihad on his land, where he lives and resides, without the jihad costing him the hardship of traveling, migrating, and moving to where direct jihad is possible. The enemy today is one, and he is spread everywhere, praise God.

If we wanted to mention the most important targets according to their importance, we say that they are:

1. In our countries (The Arab and Islamic world)
2. In their countries (America and allied countries)
3. In other countries in the world.

*First: The targets in the basic arena (countries in the Arab and Islamic world):*

1. *Centers of missionary activity and Christianization, the cultural envoys, and the institutions in charge of the American-Western civilizational and ideological invasion of Muslim countries, without violating the houses of worship and the facilities of the Christians originally residing in our country.*

2. *All kinds of economic presence belonging to America or her Western allies: Companies, mines, experts, engineers, traders, representatives of foreign companies (except Muslims)... residences of the families of these colonialist thieves ... etc.*

3. *All kinds of diplomatic presence of America and her allies, including embassies, consulates, diplomatic envoys... etc.*

4. *All kinds of military presence of America and her allies... (Military bases—fleets—harbors—airports—transportation stations—military units...etc.)*

5. *All kinds of security presence of the intelligence organizations of America and her Western allies, such as the offices of the CIA and FBI and their likes, overt or concealed under presumed covers.*

6. *All kinds of Zionist or American delegations, responsible for normalization of relations with Israel, and who are invading our countries today through civilian, national, and governmental institutions: cultural, sports and arts [delegations]... and their likes.*

7. *All kinds of tourism presence: tourist companies and delegations of foreign tourists, their offices, their airline companies and so on. They are the ambassadors of depravity, corruption, [sexual] immorality and decadence, in addition to that they are the disgraceful representation of the occupation that took control over our countries and transformed them into a backyard for amusement and recreation for the adulterers and rich people among them.*

8. *The basic pillars of the apostate regimes cooperating with the aggressor campaigns.*

9. *The basic pillars of the collaborator forces and the different kinds of normalization with the aggressor campaigns in various fields.*

In short... Targeting all kinds of material and human presence of the Americans and their allies in our countries is the basic arena for the

**Resistance.**

*Important details:*
*The economic dimension of the American occupation:*
The economic dimension of the coming American occupation of our countries is one of the most important dimensions of this occupation and of the Crusader and Jewish invasion, after the religious and civilizational dimensions, which is driven by their Zionistic and Crusader motives, and by their belief in their myths and the fables of their spurious religious books.

The Muslim countries contain the principal oil lakes of the world; Saudi Arabia and the states of the Gulf Cooperation Council have the largest known reserves in the world, and Iraq has the largest unexplored reserve in the world, amounting to a minimum of 300 billion barrels. The Central Asian region and the Caspian Sea have the second largest known reserve in the world, and in Syria there are great reserves, which the modern colonization is keeping away from. In Sudan, and on the African continent there is a huge underground oil lake, and in Northern Africa, and especially in Algeria there is [one] like that too. Algeria's gas, which crosses over to Europe through Morocco and under the Gibraltar Straits, comprises about 65% of Europe's electricity consumption!!!

The Arab and Islamic world has large and various mineral resources as well, in addition to the agricultural and animal resources, and sources of fresh water...etc. So the first goal of colonization is the **plundering of those resources,** as an assistant of Bush the Father, declared during the Kuwait war in 1990, 'that they came to correct the Lord's mistake of creating oil in our countries'. God is supreme and his loftiness is far above what the offspring of monkeys and pigs say.

The second goal of the American and Western colonization is to transform the countries of the Islamic world, where the total population comprises one fifth of the population on the Earth, into a **market for selling products** from the West, the industrial and technological Western [products] which suffer from a great stagnation and competition from sources in East Asia and China. Thus, it is possible to summarize the economic goals of the colonization and the American and Western invasion with two points:

1—Plundering resources                     2—Selling products

These two goals must be a target for the Resistance and legitimate terrorism (*al-irhab al-mashru'*). We must hinder them from taking the resources. And we must prevent them from selling products. Not only through the jihad of the weak and crippled protagonists of peaceful boycott, and from the global verbal campaigns for repelling the aggression!—they are important [acts of] Resistance if combined with jihadi push (*daf jihadi*)—but through military resistance, an Individual Terrorism Jihad and operational activity of small Resistance Cells.

The jurists of Islam agree that selling the enemy anything that makes him superior to the Muslims is forbidden in Islam, how is it then with regard to fuel for the tanks and planes during the Crusader campaigns?!

*So, the most important enemy targets in detail:*
*First: The oil and sources of energy from the source until the drain:*
These are among the most important targets of the Resistance: 'Oil fields—oil pipelines—export harbors—sea navigation routes and oil tankers—import harbors in their countries—storage depositories in their countries'...

It is said that this oil is the source of income for the Muslims in those oil-exporting countries... and this is not true. Truly, it is a source for the enemy's plundering from this artery pouring out energy, industry and money onto them... It is the life-artery of our enemies, the killers, invaders and Crusaders. It is the blood of their military machine which has inflicted death and humiliation upon us, day and night, since the beginning of the twentieth century and up until today... In reality, only a tiny amount of this wealth returns to our countries, and most of it fills the pockets of a handful of the apostate ruling princes with their sinful, adulterous and boisterous offspring and sycophants who dispose of the oil wealth at will. Nothing falls onto the rest of their people except crumbs. On top of this, the poor among other Muslim people of the Islamic Nation are deprived of their share, in spite of the fact that everyone has a legal right to this blessing of God.

50% of the oil revenues go to foreign companies according to the colonialist contracts, and the remaining 50% is transformed into meaningless electronic numbers in the Jewish international banks! Their owners, the thieves among the shameless emirs, do not have the freedom or right to withdraw anything from them, except with the consent of the big thieves, their Jewish and Crusader masters.

The oil has become a curse, after being a blessing. The Muslim rulers replaced God's blessing with infidelity, and led their people to ruin!!

True, a disruption of oil exports will deprive those traitor governments of their budget balance. This will, in turn, be reflected in sectors of limited economic development, which will take place in those countries... But what is the weight of this partial damage in those limited sectors, measured against the damage of this oil not reaching the Zionistic and Crusader enemy?! The case is clear...!!

*In short, it is the life-artery of our enemies, it originates from our countries and we have to cut it off...*

When our resources have been passed into our hands and we own them, we will do true business with them, based on the rules of fairness and neighborliness.

*Second: Mines of mineral resources:*
Gold, copper, iron, aluminum, cobalt, phosphate...etc. The list of our mineral resources is long, and it is also necessary to prevent them from reaching the enemy and preventing the enemy from investing in them. This can also be done by preventing the export of these resources, by shutting down the mines and cutting off the export routes and means.

*Third: The straits and the main sea passages:*
On the Earth there are five (5) important straits, four of them are in the countries of the Arabs and the Muslims. The fifth one is in America, and it is the Panama Canal. These straits are:

1. The Strait of Hormuz, the oil gate in the Arab-Persian Gulf.
2. The Suez Canal in Egypt.
3. The Bab el Mandib between Yemen and the African continent.
4. The Gibraltar Strait in Morocco.

Most of the Western world's economy, in terms of trade and oil, passes through these sea passages. Also passing through them are the military fleets, aircraft carriers and the deadly missiles hitting our women and children... It is necessary to shut these passages until the invader campaigns have left our countries. This can be done by targeting American ships and ships of its allies, on the one hand by blocking the passages with mines and sinking the ships in them, or by threatening the movement there by piracy, martyrdom operations, and by the power of weapons wherever possible.

The enemy, and the people of the enemy's countries, must know that they have ignited a wicked world war because of the sudden moods of their Crusader and Zionist-friendly rulers. And that they have to depart from our countries and terminate their intervention there and their support of treacherous rulers. And that they, if they are not reasonable and behave in a fair and humanistic way, must take their share of the death that they gave our people and children to taste, and to take their lot of the poverty, economic collapse and the hardships of life which they caused us. We must persuade them with the power of weapons, the results of the Resistance, and the losses afflicted upon them... that it is best for them if they leave us and our affairs, so that we can topple our criminal rulers, and from there establish our own legitimate governments, and deal with them according to the rules of friendly dialogue and fair and just treatment.

It is necessary that we explain to our peoples, through communiqués, media and propaganda, that they must pay the costs of war side by side with the Mujahidun. We have to make it clear that we are at war. The enemy has imposed this war on us. We must carry its temporary economic losses, so that we do not lose our essence, resources, religion and all ingredients of our existence.

## *Striking strategic targets of the allies of the Jewish-Crusader campaigns in Arab and Islamic countries*

As explained in the second section, 'The Political Theory of the Resistance', the American campaigns in their offensive towards our countries, are generally dependent on enormous support they receive from the forces of apostasy and hypocrisy, as well as on a long and wide fifth column of Americanized people who welcome this invasion and tie their interests and efforts to it.

This enormous team of allies to the apostates and hypocrites are of all sorts and kinds. Some of them agree, some of them are rivals, and some of them are at war... We will choose the most important and prominent joints in this front of supporting pillars of colonialism, in order of priority. We will explain the importance of targeting them and how to target them in a way that suits the general strategy of the Resistance, which is to let the main focal point (*al-mihwar al-asasi*) of the Resistance be the confrontation with the invading forces, America and her allies, and to restrict the focal points on the secondary fronts in our countries, to [include only] the important and principal ones according to the theory of building and tearing down.

*As we are obliged to build up the Resistance forces and to spread its Units, we are also obliged to tear down, destroy and remove the important bases of the opponent's forces in our midst, as long as it does not divert our attention from our main focal point for strategic attack, namely resisting the occupation and the foreign enemies.*

*The most important military targets in resisting the forces of apostasy and hypocrisy in our countries are:*

*1. The Arab and Islamic governments*
*This should be done by targeting their kings, presidents, princes, important ministers and senior officials only, especially those upon whom the American invasion project is dependent, or those senior officials or men from the upper class who are indispensable to the security campaigns.*

This should not be transformed into a local revolution and a jihadi movement whose goal is jihad against the government and targeting its institutions and symbols, big and small, similar to what happened in previous jihadi revolutions in Egypt, Syria, Algeria and elsewhere, and which led to failure, as previously explained.
It is required only to liquidate the senior apostate leaders who are allied with the American invader campaigns, and to attack them directly.

*2. The security forces and political and military forces directly collaborating with the occupation:*
As with the case of the Iraqi police, and the Kashmirian police... And the army, if it operates under their [the occupation's] command. [We must] target them with attacks before these organizations expand, and their presence enables the occupation to dispense with their own forces. *This is only in the case of a direct and clear occupation.*

*3. Security forces, and the regimes' army and soldiers, who target the Mujahidun and the Islamists:*
*We will only fight with them defensively, and not target them offensively. However, they must be targeted with an Islamic, national and emotional rhetoric in order to make them join in the Resistance, and to guide their soldiers and officers to a role in defending their religion, country and Islamic Nation.*

But in case they oppose the Mujahidun and intend to kill, arrest and harm them, it is necessary to defy death while fighting them, and not surrender to them. The battle with them is a battle with the troops of apostasy and infidelity, without considering the infidelity of their leaders. (An explanation of this was given in the Theory of the Programme.)

**It is necessary to spread among the Resistance's youth a culture of non-surrendering, of refusing captivity, and of defense until martyrdom, as far as possible.**

*4. The advocates of colonization and its symbols:*
A new class of secularists and democratic dissidents has emerged in Arab and Islamic societies, who openly welcome the American project on every level; the military, political, ideological and cultural. [This class is made] of people like the well-known example, Doctor Sa'd al-Din Ibrahim. And these 'apostate and hypocrite role models' work openly today, taking advantage of the American cover under the pretext of civil society institutions and call for democracy, and they

have even gained immunity against the Tyrants' agencies of oppression. They have expanded and have institutions, action programmes and great finances which they openly receive from the Americans. These examples are among the most important military targets of the Global Islamic Resistance Units. [The Units] must seek to assassinate and liquidate their leaders, and blow up, burn and demolish their institutions, so that they join the mosques of harm (*masajid al-darar*), which God the Almighty and His messenger ordered to burn and eliminate.

### 5. *The American and Zionist normalization projects:*
The American strategic attack today relies on the spread of projects of an ideological, cultural, programmatic or academic character in Arab and Islamic countries. Their goal is to spread the colonial culture on one hand, and [on the other hand] to bring up generations of Americanized youth on a local level, or to send them to America and some of the allied states to obtain diplomas, gather experiences and to become qualified for becoming the rulers and men of the coming American[-dominated] era of the 'Greater Middle East.'

The American media are advertising these American-made gangs, holding them up as an example for imitation among religious or ethnic minorities, or among the financial, political and social elite in the Arab and Islamic societies. These projects are of the same kind as the 'Wadi Arabah Project' on the border between Israel and Jordan. These institutions and establishments are among the Resistance's primary targets to blow up, demolish and burn. Those educated by them, cooperating with them, and their main sponsors, are among the most important targets to liquidate and assassinate. They are apostates and hypocrites constituting the senior chiefs of Unfaith. They discredit God's religion, and betray the Muslims.

### 6. *Seniors among those who discredit God's religion, and representatives of media and colonialist thinking who are fighting the Mujahidun:*

This is a group that has started to expand greatly these days, and consists of literary men, poets, thinkers, writers or journalists... These are the ones who are launching the attack today on the doctrines of Islam and on those who defend them, publicly and in daylight without fear or shame. They have been arrogant towards God's religion and the Mujahidun's worship... They operate under the veil and cover of the 'International campaign against terror' as they call it, uncovering their hidden hatred for God's religion and its followers. The Islamic awakening, its men and institutions have been drawn into constant clashes with them through dialogues and on satellite channels, which is good.

However, this contest takes place under the title of respecting the other, and acknowledging the opinion of the other, and this is futile. Because these people are not merely ignorant or dissidents, even though they hold discussions in a friendly manner. Most of them are Muslims of origin, but apostates in reality. Or, they are not Muslims of origin, like the Christians and the atheist minorities in Muslim societies. They are not under protection (*dhimmah*), and if they were, it would be broken, because of the propagandist campaigns they launch on Islam and its people.

The Qur'an has called these people, in clear words, the 'chiefs of Unfaith' *(a'immat al-kufr)* and has ordered to combat and assassinate them. So it is necessary to kill them, responding to what God the Almighty has commanded in His great Book: *'But if they violate their oaths after their covenant, and taunt you for your Faith,- fight ye the chiefs of Unfaith: for their oaths are nothing to them: that thus they may be restrained'*. (Al-Tawbah:12).

*7. Advocates of dissoluteness, wickedness and depravity, and institutions spreading indecency among the believers:*
The American Jewish-Crusader invasions today are dependent on destroying the Muslims' religious, moral, cultural and ideological

basis. Among the methods of doing this is the spreading of a culture of decay, depravity, adultery and immorality, and of unveiling, nakedness and mingling [of genders]... and different types of social corruption. Many mass media and propaganda outlets have opened up for this, and they have employed many thinkers, artists, literary men, and their likes. One of the [American Jewish-Crusaders'] greatest tools today is the satellite TV channels which are financed by the millionaires of debauchery and corruption, some of the well-off Gulf Arabs and Saudis and their likes, like the Prince of immorality, al-Walid bin Talal bin Abd al-Aziz and his satellite network Rotana and others... and now...

※

Some of the respectable media, and some men from the Islamic awakening, are trying to resist this rotten torrent and sweeping epidemic of a culture of corruption, dissoluteness and depravity, through dialogue and [verbal] counter-attacks. They are trying to spread a culture of virtue and preserve the religious and moral identity of the Islamic Nation. This is good, but it is not enough.

When bacteria, epidemics and locusts spread:... dialogue is not enough!

Only insecticides, and medicines to kill bacteria [is enough], and this is self-evident for every rational person.

It is therefore necessary, legally, logically and rationally, that these institutions and their most important men, advocates, and leaders become targets for explosions, destruction and assassinations.

※

Among the ill-reputed examples are prince al-Walid bin Talal and his likes, the Rotana satellite channel... the programs 'Video Clip' and 'Star Academy' and other manifestations of the plague spreading through Lebanese satellite channels and other distributors of depravity and corruption...

The hole in the garment has become wider [i.e. the phenomenon has spread], but this does not make it necessary to start a war with every small and big one of them, but [only] with the leaders. The leaders of arts and literature *(adab)*, but first and foremost, the financial leaders who finance the gates of Satan into the Islamic Nation's religion and morals. God the Almighty said, *'Those who love (to see) scandal published broadcast among the Believers, will have a grievous Penalty in this life and in the Hereafter: Allah knows, and ye know not.'* (Al-Nur: 19)

### A VERY, VERY...VERY IMPORTANT NOTE:

*Some of the people affiliated with the flock of Muslim clerics, or with the agitators and leaders of the Islamic awakening, are people who broke away [from the Mujahidun], either because they were craving for worldly gains and government positions, or because they were afraid of being oppressed and accused of terrorism and violence. They started to hum the sound of 'moderate Islam', 'respect for the other' and 'the middle course' (al-wasatiyyah)... presenting a perverted and adjusted Islam in order to fit American standards. Some of them went so far that they attacked the duty of jihad and the principle of Resistance. They have started to fight against the Mujahidun [striving] in the cause of God, and have launched a merciless attack on the Resistance fighters, their leaders and their Mujahidun, the soldiers of God. They issue fatwas judging them as the doers of mischief (mufsidun) on Earth. They give fatwas to the rulers and the colonialist authorities saying that [the Mujahidun] are kharijites[15] and doers of mischief (mufsidun), and that it is lawful to kill, imprison and torture them. The matter has even reached a point where they misinterpret God's word[16] and say that this elite of the Mujahidun are not martyrs, and*

---

15　[Translator's footnote:] The term kharijites (*khawarij*) (lit. 'Those who Go Out') refers to the oldest sect in Islam. They were Islamic groups which rejected the caliphate of Ali, the fourth Caliph, and are distinct from the two main denominations in Islam, the Sunnis and Shiites.

16　[Translator's footnote:] *yata'ala 'ala allah*, literally means 'to swear on God', but is used when someone speaks on behalf of God without having

*will not enter paradise!!... They even started to call on common Muslims to cooperate with the security agencies of the apostate rulers and the colonialist authorities in order to reveal the secrets of the Mujahidun and inform on them under the pretext of cooperation against terrorism or protecting Muslims' interests.*

Here, I will point to a very important matter...

*In spite of the fact that many of them have carried this out under the command of the apostates and the hypocrites fighting against the faithful, with their loyalty to the Tyrant and the infidel invaders... and that it is deemed lawful under Islamic law to shed the blood of many of them, because of their apostasy, treachery and war against God and His Messenger and the faithful...*

🔯

However:
It is still among the strategic principles of the Global Islamic Resistance Call to use arguments, explanations and legal and political evidence, and logical realism, not weapons and swords to confront this heretic group of propagandists for Satan and the Sultan's clerics, who call people to the ports of Hell, and throw in [Hell] whoever responds to them.

Although many of them deserve it. This could have prevented great mischiefs which are well-known, such as placing the sword among the Muslims [i.e. sow discord among Muslims], their followers' fanatical support for them, their fight against the Mujahidun, and their turning against the Resistance to join the enemy camp... and so on until the last of their great mischiefs.

The confrontation with these... as we have repeated and emphasized, [must be] with sound arguments and explanations, from the people

---

the proper knowledge/authority to do so.

of knowledge, people of the pen and people of letters. And not with
weapons...

✺

*The weapons should be aimed offensively at the chests of the invaders and
their most important collaborators among the senior apostates and traitors,
as we explained. And defensively against the soldiers of the Tyrants whom
the Mujahidun intend to combat. This is a strategic principle of immense
importance in the Global Islamic Resistance Call's political and military
theories.*

SECOND: STRIKING THE INVADERS IN THEIR COUN-
TRY, IN THE HEART OF AMERICA AND ON THE TERRI-
TORY OF THE COUNTRIES ALLIED TO HER MILITARILY:

When it comes to striking America or any of her allies on their own
territory, and targeting a state or leaving another, or targeting it, and
then ceasing to target it, or turning away from it and then targeting it
a second time... This is not the place to research this, rather, [the place
is] in the first and second sections, which were devoted to the legal
and ideological dimension, and also to the political dimension, of
the principles of the Global Islamic Resistance Call. Here, however,
we study the matter from a military perspective, in a situation where
it actually is in the political interest [of the Resistance] to target a
state. Whenever the targeting of any state is legitimate according to
Islamic law, and in the political interest of the Resistance, then the
most important targets are as follows:

*The most important targets in America and in Western countries allied
to her militarily:*
1. *Main political figures who lead the campaign against the Muslims:
heads of states, ministers, military and security leaders.*

2. *Large strategic economic targets, such as: The stock exchange—power and oil installations—airports—harbors—railroad systems, bridges and highway intersections—tunnels on the highways—metro systems—tourist targets... and so on, [targeting] resources and sources for the economy.*

3. *Military bases and barracks where the armies are concentrated, especially the American military bases in Europe.*

4. *Media personalities and media centers that are leading the war against the Muslims and justifying the attacks on them, coming from the Zionist and Zionist-friendly Crusader media institutions.*

5. *Centralized information and computer centers that are in control of connecting the different institutions within the state, because this will completely paralyze the activity within that state.*

6. *Places where Jews are gathered, their leading personalities and institutions in Europe, avoiding places of worship and synagogues.*

7. *Official offices of the governmental institutions of those countries that are waging war, both on the state level and on the level of unions and political and military alliances, in the case where they participate in the aggression. Such as the offices of the NATO and the European Union..., this requires decisions that have been studied carefully from a political perspective.*

8. *Buildings of the security services and the central intelligence in the capitals of America and allied Western states.*

9. *Striking civilians in general, to deter them or for retaliation (avoiding women and children, when separated from men in places especially designed for them, like schools and the similar...).*

This for example... is when responding to a brutal practice carried out by America and her allied forces. The type of attack, which repels states and topples governments, is mass slaughter of the population. This is done by targeting human crowds in order to inflict maximum human losses. This is very easy since there are numerous such targets, such as crowded sports arenas, annual social events, large international exhibitions, crowded market-places, sky-scrapers, crowded buildings... etc.

Here, it is necessary to remind you of the comments we made about targeting civilians in the second section on the political theory, and also of the general legal rules presented in the third section, in the paragraph about the jihadi Islamic laws... In the case [where such an attack is legal and beneficial], there are a large number of easy targets. It is possible for ordinary Resistance fighters among the Muslims residing in America and the allied Western countries to target them, in order to participate in the jihad and the Resistance, and to stretch out a helping hand to the Mujahidun. This can be done as part of popular resistance action... such as destroying economic targets and burning forests during hot periods in the summer... and also as part of civilian resistance action. Here, we must turn our attention to the difference in the confrontation with America and with Europe, as I mentioned above when dealing with the political theory. The confrontation with America is fundamental, while the confrontation with Europe is secondary, [aimed at] making her leave the alliance by putting pressure on her.

### THIRD: AMERICAN AND ALLIED TARGETS IN THE ISLAMIC WORLD, THE REST OF THE THIRD WORLD AND IN OTHER COUNTRIES:

1. *American and Western economic targets in various countries of the world, because they are numerous and easy to target.*
2. *Diplomatic targets, such as embassies, consulates and envoys.*
3. *Economic interests of America and the allies in those countries.*
4. *Athletic, trade and tourist delegations and envoys from America and its Western allies.*
5. *Military bases and military missions—Army—Navy—Air Force.*

This is a wide area with many opportunities for participation, but one must pay attention to the rules of Islamic law, political benefits and security complexities.[17] We will return to the details later, God willing.

A final remark, related to the issue of targeting goals in the heart of the hostile countries, America and the Western allies, is that one should avoid targeting places of worship for any religion or faith, regardless whether they are Christian, Jewish, or other. One should also avoid harming civilians who are citizens of countries that have no relation with the conflict, even if they are non-Muslim. This must be done in order to maintain the reputation of the Resistance in the different spheres of public opinion.

### THE STRATEGY OF DETERRING WITH TERRORISM:

The theory of terrorism is based on deterring the enemy with fear, as God the Almighty said,
'Against them make ready your strength to the utmost of your power, including steeds of war, to strike terror into (the hearts of) the enemies, of Allah and your enemies, and others besides, whom ye may not know, but whom Allah doth know. Whatever ye shall spend in the cause of Allah, shall be repaid unto you, and ye shall not be treated unjustly'. (Al-Anfal 8:60) And God the Almighty said, 'If ye gain the mastery over them in war, disperse, with them, those who follow them, that they may remember'. (Al-Anfal 8:57)

The Resistance is basically at war with the invader campaigns, and it must deal with them by using the methods of terrorism and confrontation, as explained. However, there are essential enemy parties and there are secondary enemy parties. The latter ones enter the frontline

---

17    [Translator's footnote:] This sentence is grammatically incorrect, either due to spelling mistakes and/or because words are missing.

of this confrontation from time to time, either out of fear for America and her allies, or craving for what she [i.e. America] will give them in return. The Resistance must not neglect the importance of deterring these parties. It must also confirm that its arms are long and able to reach everyone who allows himself to be seduced into joining the aggression against the Muslims and the Islamic Resistance fighters, or to support their invader enemies.

Generally, most of our enemies, the supporters of the American invasion, and especially the apostates, the agents, the hypocrites, the corrupted, and those bragging about their so-called culture and development... are a group of cowardly rats, starting from the biggest of their kings, presidents and princes, and to the smallest of their writers, their media figures and their sycophants with all their fantasies... Most of them will be deterred if one sets an example by striking or severely punishing a few of them. Then, most of them will withdraw from the confrontation.

The basic idea is that every state, even the ones not allied with America... that arrests a Mujahid, a Resistance fighter, an agitator, or a cleric, and turns him over to America or to his own government, where he is killed, subjected to imprisonment or torture... should immediately receive a deterrence operation carried out by any Muslim or Resistance unit able to perform this religious duty. It is a duty to support the Muslims and to deter those who inflict harm upon them, especially those who capture them and turn them over to their enemies...

The basic idea is that any operation which kills civilians or harms faithful Muslims, or any action performed by troops of the country at war... should be met with an equally deterring action, as God the Almighty has said, 'If then any one transgresses the prohibition against you, Transgress ye likewise against him' (Al-Baqara 2:194). The basic idea is that every country which enters into alliance with the Americans with any kind of military, political or security support... will receive a deterring strike immediately... to break the joints of this criminal alliance, and so on...

However, what has taken place up until now is the opposite...

The Muslims, the Mujahidun, and the Resistance fighters accused of terrorism... they are in reality the ones who have been most terrorized... for several decades. They are terrorized by their rulers, by their security agencies, by America and her persecutions, by spies... and by all those who assist in this wicked chain.

All of these true terrorists, starting from America going down the chain of her allies and hypocrites, were able to turn the picture upside-down both politically and media-wise. They have been able to portray us to the public opinion as the phenomenon of repugnant terrorism. This is their real field of success...

The only solution to this must be to increase the efforts of the Call, media, and propaganda, as well as political activities based on knowledge, understanding and awareness of what is going on in the world today. In addition to real military deterrence...

Throughout history, 'armed terrorism' has proven its usefulness, as the best political method to persuade an opponent to surrender to one's will.

I draw these lines just a few days after a deterrence operation was carried out by a fighting Mujahidun unit in Spain on March 11th 2004. They carried out a series of explosions, which killed some 200 and injured 1700, according to Spanish statistics. The main results were as follows:

1. It changed public opinion in Spain. Statistics showed that three days before the parliamentary and governmental elections, support was in favour of the right-wing party and its leader Aznar, an ally of Bush, who sent about 2,000 Spanish troops to Iraq. It changed immediately in favor of the Socialist Party who opposed this alliance. The Socialist Party is headed by Zapatero, who promised to withdraw Spanish forces [from Iraq] if his party came to power. This led to his victory in the elections. Thus, the operation toppled the government. America lost a major ally by a single operation alone, at the cost of a small group of martyrs and captives, may God bless and accept them.

2. The new Prime Minister declared the withdrawal of Spanish forces from Iraq. They pulled out quickly shortly afterwards, followed by the troops from Honduras. Thus, a single deterrent operation led to the withdrawal of an army and an entire state from the war.

3. The entire European-American alliance was shaken, and a number of countries started to make statements that they were considering a withdrawal ... and this was the first real deterrence operation since these evil campaigns started against the Muslims more than fourteen years ago.

I deal with this operation as a case study of the political impact of military deterrence. However, there are some important observations and political considerations regarding such operations, which one must comply with before the decision is made. This includes careful politico-juridical considerations ... taking into consideration the benefits and drawbacks, the political power balances, and the welfare of the Muslims.

Unfortunately... since the outset of these evil campaigns in 1990 and up until now:

- In the first Iraqi War more than 300,000 people were killed, and during the blockade, more than one and a half million children died in the course of 13 years.
- In the last war to topple Saddam, around 10,000 civilians were killed, and tens of thousands are in prison today. God has disclosed America's deeds in those prisons.
- Thousands have been killed in Palestine, and the Israeli sword is still swinging...
- More than 200,000 Muslims were killed in Bosnia, and more than 60,000 cases of rape against Muslim women were registered there, which led to thousands of illegitimate births caused by rape. Their mothers threw them away so that they could gaze at the church vaults and be converted to Christianity!!
- In Chechnya, more than 300,000 Muslims were killed. Honors were violated, houses were destroyed, thousands of people were imprisoned, and hundreds of thousands were driven away.
- In Afghanistan, tens of thousands were killed in the civil war, which was sparked by America and administered by Pakistan. Then, more than ten thousand were killed during the latest attack in December 2001, and America has filled Guantanamo with hundreds of innocent captives!
- Thousands were killed in Indonesia. The Christians buried some of them alive, burned them, and photographed them while they were eating their flesh.
- There are many other [cases] as well, on the African continent, in Central Africa, in the Philippines, in Thailand and Kashmir...
- The number of prisoners among Muslim jihadis and Islamists who are held without charge or trial in all the Arab and Islamic countries has reached the tens of thousands. Clerics have been imprisoned, and agitators abducted... symbols killed... mosques and Islamic centers in Europe and America have been burnt down... Muslim immigrants in the Islamic diasporas have been unjustly and wrongfully assassinated ... etc.

*So where is the deterrence by these so-called Muslim terrorists?!.., The truth is that real terrorism, in the correct understanding of the word, has an embarrassingly low share on our part...! We are at the very bottom of the list, we are the most terrorized of all people, below all sorts of infidels, apostates and tyrants.*

Then came the September 11th events, in order to repel the Zionist-friendly West and the Americans, collecting a small amount of the enormous bill that they owe. The world rose, and has not lain down yet!!

The self-proclaimed philosophers will babble to us talking about the blood of the sinless, those who were promised protection, the civilians and the Muslims disloyal to the hypocrite clerics... until the last claim by evil jurists...

The reality is that the jihadi Resistance... only targets those who deserve to be deterred by terrorism, only those who should be liquidated, and only those who deserve punishment according to divine decrees and legal regulations on Earth. [The Resistance] even avoids many of those deserving this deterrence, in order to avoid negative effects [for Muslims] and promote their welfare.
The laws regarding human targets have already been discussed in detail in the passage on Islamic laws in the third section... it can be seen there.

***Let me add:***
*It is not possible for a few jihadi organizations, or for tens or hundreds of Mujahidun here and there, to deter this fierce international attack... It is absolutely necessary that the Resistance transforms into a strategic phenomenon... after the pattern of the Palestinian intifada against the occupation forces, the settlers and their collaborators... but on a broader scale, originally comprising the entire Islamic world. Its arms of deterrence*

*should reach into the homes of the American invaders and their allies of infidels from every nationality and in every place.*

*The Islamic Nation must start moving... with all its segments, towards Resistance and deterrence. In the next passage, we will explain the operational mechanism of the Resistance from a military and organizational perspective, in order to realize such deterrence with God's permission.*

## THE OPERATIVE MECHANISMS OF THE GLOBAL ISLAMIC RESISTANCE UNITS, ITS MILITARY THEORIES AND OPERATIONAL CONCEPT

The mechanisms of military activity in the Global Islamic Resistance Call were deducted by studying the three previous methods of jihad, and by a thorough and lengthy research of the old methods, which we have practiced in past jihadi experiences, and their results. And also, through a factual study of the military and security-wise power balance between us, the jihadis and the Resistance fighters in general, and the scope of American and allied forces outside and inside the Islamic world, especially after the latest attacks on Afghanistan and Iraq, in addition to their other pursuits.

Several years ago I started thinking about finding a method in which a minimum of the following requirements are met:

*1. It opens the possibility to participate for thousands, say hundreds of thousands or millions, of Muslims sympathizing with jihad and with their Islamic Nation's causes. The constricted jihadi secret organizations do not have room for all of them. Moreover, most of them do not want to be linked to this commitment with all its security-related and personal consequences... Also, they are not able to, or they do not want to get burned security-wise, by joining the Open Fronts which also have a limited capacity to absorb them.*

*2. Creating a method for secret action in which we are able to overcome the problem of security weakness inherent in the traditional secret organizations where the whole organization is destroyed when some of its members are arrested, are tortured, and are pursued by security services across international borders after security coordination moved from a national level up to the international level. In this way, the idea of secret urban guerilla warfare has finally and fundamentally failed.*

*3. Creating a method for transforming excellent individual initiatives, performed over the past decades, from emotional pulse beats and scattered reactions, into a phenomenon which is guided and utilized, and whereby the project of jihad is advanced so that it becomes the Islamic Nation's battle, and not a struggle of an elite.*

*4. The individual actions should be characterized by a general sense of unity around a jihadi Resistance current, which suits the era, so that the Islamic Nation's masses rally around this current, and create a form of centralism on the level of commitment, slogans, symbols and ideas on the one hand, while at the same time avoiding links to a centralized entity, so that it cannot be aborted security-wise, on the other.*

In short, I was searching for a method which the enemy has no way of aborting, even when he understands the method and its procedures, and arrests two thirds of its operators. A method, which is susceptible to self-renewal and to self-perpetuation as a phenomenon after all its conditions and causes are present and visible to the enemy himself. In practice, the idea was born in me when I was reflecting upon the meaning of the Quranic verse: *'Then fight in Allah's cause - Thou art held responsible only for thyself - and rouse the believers. It may be that Allah will restrain the fury of the Unbelievers; for Allah is the strongest in might and in punishment'* (An-Nisa 4:84). I was also inspired by the individual operations which some of the Mujahidun Fida'iyyun[18] undertook.

---

18    [Translator's footnote:] *fida'iyyun* is originally 'a devotee of a religious or national group willing to engage in self-immolation to attain a group goal'. Since the 1950s, the term has acquired a more specific meaning and has

I spread [this idea] secretly in a communiqué with the title: 'Communiqué in order to Establish a Global Islamic Resistance' at the end of 1990—beginning of 1991. Then the idea was developed, as I mentioned in the introduction, through various stages until it reached its final form in Kabul at the end of the year 2000. Following a study on the effects of the methods used in the confrontation between us and America and her allies in the post-September world and after the invasion of Iraq, it has now matured and has taken the form which I present here.

## CHARACTERISTICS OF THE OPERATIONAL METHOD OF THE GLOBAL ISLAMIC RESISTANCE UNITS:

### 1. A system, not a secret organization (nizam la tanzim)

It is a 'system of action, not a centralized, secret organization for action' (nizam 'amal la tanzim markazi lil-'amal). The idea is based on the concept that the bonds between the entire spectrum of Resistance fighters - individuals, cells, units and small groups - are limited to three centralized bonds only, and those are:

❧

### The central bonds of the Global Islamic Resistance Units:

1. A common name and a personal oath to God the Supreme on adhering to Him.
2. A politico-judicial programme, a common doctrine, and an oath to God on committing to it.
3. A common goal, which is to resist the invaders and their allies, and an oath to God on jihad in His way to defeat them, then to work on establishing His rule.

---

come to mean guerrilla fighters or commandos. The term was used about Palestinians operating against Israel from bases in neighboring countries. See *Encyclopaedia Britannica Online* http://secure.britannica.com/ebc/article-9105211, accessed October 2006.

෨

This is done in the following way:
1. Spreading the Resistance Call's ideology, its methods, its operational programme, its implementation method and its operational theories in the eight fields that we have mentioned: (The combat doctrine—the political theory—the method for comprehensive education of the Resistance fighters—the military theory—the media and instigation theory, and then the organizational theory, which contains methods on training, financing, organizing, and security.) This is done in order to mobilize the youth and men of the Islamic Nation who strongly wish to fight in the Resistance on any of its general axes, and especially on the military axis.
2. Directing the youth to strike enemy targets in our own countries in particular—which is the main arena of the Islamic Resistance—and in their countries, which is an arena for deterrence and retaliation, in accordance with the general rules of Islamic law and the programme as well as in consideration of the political benefits, in order to achieve political objectives and realize the goal of the Resistance.
3. Instruct the youth that every group should prepare themselves on their own regarding what the military operational activity requires, and they should execute operations in accordance with what they have managed to acquire in terms of training capabilities and preparedness, starting from the methods of popular resistance, and ending with complex strategic operations, passing through all kinds and levels of guerilla operations in cities, in the countryside, or other types of secret guerilla warfare.
4. There are no organizational bonds of any kind between the members of the Global Islamic Resistance Units, except the bonds of a **'program of beliefs, a system of action, a common name, and a common goal'**.
5. Every unit consisting of one person or more is regarded as an independent unit headed by its Emir, who is in charge of its affairs. It is oriented directly towards military operational activity,

and it is not oriented towards any kind of organization, agitation, incitement, or other such activities of the secret organizations. It forms itself, chooses its target, and attacks it. It notifies any media agency (in a secure way, which we will explain in the Media theory) that it is the Unit 'so-and-so', using the specific name it has chosen for itself, and stating that it is 'from the Global Islamic Resistance Units' which indicates the agenda of the operators, and adds the operation to the total production of the Resistance Units. We will give more organizational and operational details in the sections on operational and organizational theories, God willing.

6. *The idea is to unite the efforts of the Resistance fighters, the individual jihad fighters, the remaining elements of the jihadi current, its supporters, its new sympathizers, those angry at the American invasion, and those who wish to move forward among the various segments of the Islamic Nation at all its levels, and regulate and correct these efforts with a common method and a common programme, in order to achieve the result. Moreover, the idea is to transform the individual jihad into a phenomenon which embraces the efforts of everyone under a single name, for a single goal, with a single slogan, regulated by a single educational politico-judicial programme...*

## *The benefits and characteristics of this method:*

1. The method makes it possible for a single individual to act, whether he wants to operate completely alone, not trusting anyone else to participate, or in a very small unit of a few men and friends who have confidence in each other. They may form a unit consisting of two persons or more, pledging an oath to each other and to God on joining 'the Global Islamic Resistance Units', which consists of their fellow Muslims in every place, of every color and nationality. Thus, this method offers homogeneity, security precautions and possibilities for the group. It also opens up for broad, common operational activity without bonds with each other. The method instructs them to operate wherever they are and wherever they are

able to operate, thus avoiding the burdens of traveling to areas of confrontation, or of joining a collective organization with obligations, which they cannot accept due to their convictions. These comprise a very huge segment of the Muslim youth.

2. The method allows for a complete separation between those cells, so that if any action, whether emerging or under execution, is disclosed, it will not influence the others who operate or intend to operate, since there is no link between them of any kind. It is a type of 'idea organization', not 'an idea of a secret organization', and a 'system of action', not 'the action of a secret organization' *(tanzim al-fikra wa laysa fikrat al-tanzim, nizam ʿamal wa laysa ʿamal tanzim)*. This is the only method of survival in light of the fierce security attack we are witnessing today and which will confront everyone desiring to fight jihad.

3. The combination of efforts under a single name indicates to the Islamic Nation the presence of an organization, a common direction, and a centre which connects all by virtue of the common name, the common combat doctrine, and the detailed method of education. This increases the initiatives, and urges those who are indecisive to join a caravan, moving in a secret and controlled system of action... The common name, goal, and ideology also suggest to the enemy that there is a single organization behind those operations. An organization which: **is directed by the idea, trained by the instructions, united by the goal and the common name, and administered secretly from a distance.** However, when the enemy comes to seize it, or some of its parts, he will discover that he has not seized anything worth mentioning, when compared to the rest of [the movement's] body. This is because it is a nation who is fighting, not a group of fighters from an idle nation.

4. *Accumulating numbers and figures showing progression in the Mu-jhidun's operations: And this is very important...*
*We will set forth the idea and spread it in full, with whatever requires, if God the Supreme permits, and make it available in every way, directly or through correspondence, or through communication networks, the Internet, and the different means for spreading it, in written, audible and visual formats... We will attempt to distribute it in translations in the languages of the Muslim nations, and in the main languages of the world.If we assume, and this is what we ask from God, that at least a few will believe in this idea and that each of them will contribute to one operation every year once at least. This is easy if we present to him different types of goals, military jihadi thought, methods of popular resistance, and arrive at complex operations carried out by cells having obtained a certain level of training...Let us assume that all across the Islamic Nation with its hundreds of millions of humiliated and furious people, in the first year of spreading the Call, twelve groups were convinced, each comprised of an individual or a group of friends... and every group carried out one operation each year, in a non-centralized way, it would result in 12 operations per year, or one operation each month to begin with... If the number reached fifty-two Mujahidun or cells, each of them perpetrating one operation each year, the result would be one operation every week... and this is not in the capability of any secret organization or armed guerilla group...If we attributed the operations to a single, common name, 'The Global Islamic Resistance Units', and to a single ideology, slogan and goal, the result would presumably be, God willing, the agitation of hundreds if not thousands. Then, the operations and individual contributions will gradually become truly a phenomenon, as in the slogan of the Global Islamic Resistance Call:*

※

*Jihad and Resistance: The Islamic Nation's Battle, and not a Struggle of an Elite.*

*With the help of the other Resistance axes, namely, the civilian, media, ideological and political resistance... we will arrive at the pursued aim, with the help of God the Supreme. And that is the popular uprising of an entire nation, across the Islamic world and in places where Islamic diaspora communities of various nationalities are present, similar to the 'Palestinian Intifada', but primarily against America, and secondly against her foreign and local allies[19] in every place. This Uprising should be conducted within the framework of the general legal and political rules mentioned previously... At this stage, and with God's help, cells will emerge which will not just act once a year, but even more often than that...*

*If we calculate the arithmetic progression of operations, we find that it is possible to arrive at tens of operations or more daily, God willing. In this way, we have placed the duty of jihad on its right track, on par with the religious duties of prayer and almsgiving... This requires a joining of the efforts of the clerics, the agitators, the literary men, the mosque preachers, the theoreticians, and the writers, so that they pour all their efforts into the instigation, every one according to his abilities, and whatever his situation and methods permits him to do, in order to awaken feelings. In the end, this will make a visible impact in the form of a new desired unit among the Resistance units, with God's permission.*

5.  The idea of 'Global Islamic Resistance Units' allows every unit to have its specific name which it chooses for itself, regardless of whether the unit consists of one, two, five or more Mujahidun... This makes the unit aware of its production, and connects its name to its production. This is a feeling and a natural desire for the human being. It also opens the door of competition between the units and the commando units, everyone fighting according to his size... A competition and a race emerges on the path of martyrdom, obedience to God, and

---

19    'Foreign' refers to countries outside the Islamic world, while 'local' refers
      to countries within the Islamic world.

harming the enemy. Thus, it is possible to compare the idea of spreading the Resistance, where there is no organizational links between the members and units, with the idea of the 'Sufi orders' that are spread without connection to a leadership, and even without knowledge of the guide and the Sufi shaykh. **But with a main difference, and that is:**

✵

*The Method of the Global Islamic Resistance:*
**It is a comprehensive method which applies the Sunni doctrine** (*'aqidat ahl al-sunnah wa'l-jama'ah*), **the jurisprudence of its authorized schools and its leading imams, and is based on a comprehensive understanding. It is:**
*A comprehensive jihadi, political, behavioral, educational doctrinal method.*

✵

Some Sufi orders have spread to an extent where their followers amount to millions from every part of the world, without any connection between them except the name of the order, their doctrinal and educational programmes, and historical symbols... In the same way, we hope that this Global Resistance 'order' [same word as 'method'] will spread, and that the list of martyrs in the Resistance will provide... leading figures and symbols for this comprehensive jihadi method.

6. The idea of the Global Islamic Resistance Units is based on homogeneity of cells by selecting its members from the Sunni schools, and a common political, security-wise, military, and educational concept and understanding... suitable for their situation and area of operations. At the same time, this does not contradict the diversity present at the level of units as a whole, and in the Resistance Call with all its military, civilian, propaganda-

related, political, media and all other axes and fields.

7. The easiness of adherence to the Resistance Call and the direct nature of the operational activity, without any of the complications during stages of organizing, forming and education, which are well-known in traditional groups and organizations. As we explained in the theory of education, a slogan for performing the religious duty and the timing of it, is the words of the Prophet Muhammed, may peace and blessings be upon him: 'Embrace Islam, then fight':

❧

**The method of the Global Islamic Resistance considers fighting God's invader enemies and those who help them and fight Muslims along with them, to be an individual duty like prayer and almsgiving. The timing of performing this duty under the present conditions is regarded immediate. The only obligation is to embrace Islam. As said by the Prophet Muhammed, peace and blessings upon him: *'Embrace Islam, then fight'.***

❧

Thus:... Everyone who is a Muslim, even if he converted an hour after the occupation forces entered and made jihad an individual duty for every Muslim, has been assigned with this duty. As for the stages of education in the jihadi doctrine, the political understanding, and comprehending the Islamic laws... this will happen over time, but the Emir of every unit or group should seriously seek to train himself and those with him, through the programme of the Resistance Call, customized and facilitated in a simple and easy way.

*Thus, the only thing that those who want to fight jihad and adhere to the Call must do, is to make up their mind to do so, and pledge an oath to God to commit to its programme, name and slogans, and follow the way of direct action within his capabilities, especially those who previously received military training, either in a jihadi group, or in a official or unofficial military institution...*

The crux of the matter is, as we will explain in the theory of reality-based training, that the operational activity of the Mujahidun, especially in guerilla warfare, is based on the principle of 'desire to fight', providing it and heightening its level.

## THE TYPES OF GLOBAL ISLAMIC RESISTANCE UNITS AND THE LEVEL OF THEIR MILITARY OPERATIONS:

The level differs from one unit to the other, in terms of military, material and logistical preparation..., which also makes their capacity for executing operations vary, both inside and outside the Islamic Nation. We have already given some examples of targets of operations.

Here, we will distinguish between some types of units, according to their professional, military, technological, security and financial capabilities... They are listed as follows:

### First: Popular Resistance Units:
These units consist of individuals and small groups with limited opportunities with regards to financing, or the level of training. They are the overwhelming majority of Muslims.

They are able to carry out simple operations on a limited level from a military perspective, *however, their participation is of highest importance due to their large number in a situation where the Resistance has transformed into a phenomenon, because they will not give the invader the option of settling in our countries.* And they will cause enormous disturbance if the Resistance phenomenon spreads in

Muslim communities[20] residing in countries participating in the war on Muslims, especially Western countries.

### Second: The General Military Units:

These armed units have limited capabilities. They consist of individuals who previously had medium-level training in using light personal weapons and explosives. The majority of them are remaining elements from cells of the jihadi current and its secret organizations, or are Mujahidun who previously participated in some way in jihadi arenas, such as Afghanistan, Chechnya, Bosnia, Kashmir, the Philippines or elsewhere... or had previous training in other ways, or through serving in the security or military apparatus of their countries... The material and security obstacles would probably prevent these units from undertaking large-scale resounding quality operations. *However, their military contribution is the basis for the guerilla war fought by the Global Islamic Resistance Units, due to the large number of this kind of jihadi cadre in the Arab and Islamic world,* and even among the Muslim communities in the warring countries. The number is in the range of tens of thousands of jihadis and Resistance supporters, not to mention hundreds of thousands, say millions of men who have worked in a governmental security or military organizations at one point in their life, during their general (i.e. mandatory) service or as professionals, who have now left, or are still in the service. What moves them in a forceful manner is religious, patriotic, or national feelings, or a strongly felt conscientiousness.

### Third: Quality Resistance Units:

These units possess high security, organizational, military and material capabilities. They are comprised of individuals or groups that have received high-level training in the security field, in secret operational activity, civilian terrorism, and the management of cells in guerilla

---

20    [Translator's footnote:] The author has written 'armed communities', but he probably meant 'Muslim communities'. There is only one letter different in the spelling of the two words.

warfare, communications technology and its security aspects, and also high-level military training in the field of using weapons and explosives, and especially in combat tactics of guerilla warfare in various circumstances, especially the making and use of explosives, and mastering the use of various detonation methods, especially the electronic ones.

Another important factor for operational activity, which is available to them, is high financial capabilities, enabling these cells to operate at a high level inside the Resistance's first and main arena[21], or in the foreign arena within the enemy countries, America. First and foremost in America, and then in the countries allied to her.

*Fourth: Strategic Operation Units:*
**These units are special units. They can be formed by those fulfilling the following requirements:**
1. *Strategic understanding of the nature of the struggle and its political, military, and strategic aspects in general, and an ability to study the Islamic law aspects of large-scale operations and their political impact, in order to be able to lead and administer these kinds of units.*
2. *Very high financial capabilities, for training such units and financing their operations.*
3. *Very high security and organizational capabilities for mobile elements to operate and execute.*
4. *Mobile elements should have very high military skills in order to operate and execute.*
5. *Knowledge and operational abilities in acquiring and using weapons of mass destruction, in times when there is a need for retaliation, or for the strategic settlement of the conflict with America.*
   These units can be formed by an elite of wealthy Muslims believing in the method of the Resistance, in cooperation with

---

21  [Translator's footnote:] i.e. within the Arab and the Islamic world, as previously stated. 'Foreign' refer to countries outside the Arab and Islamic world.

prominent senior jihadis, and with some of the distinguished people who previously worked in the security apparatus, former members of governments in Muslim countries, as well as senior military personnel, experts on military strategy, and some sincere retired politicians, or even including people who still work in the agencies of Arab or Islamic governments. It must be possible to trust their loyalty to their religion, their nation and their country, and to trust their confidentiality and belief in the programme of the Global Islamic Resistance.

It is enough for them to execute operations once every year or every second year, provided that they have a decisive scope. God is the one who grants success, and to Allah belongs the Forces of the heavens and the earth... and none can know the forces of thy Lord, except He.

## TERRORIST CULTURE, TERRORIST TALENT, AND ACQUIRED SKILLS OF GUERILLA FIGHTERS

### Terrorist culture

is all the knowledge, information, and the general culture possessed by the ones fighting with 'terrorist' methods, especially in urban guerilla warfare... This includes in short headlines...

- Participation in daily life in a practical way, and knowing the aspects of people's activity.
- Knowledge and studies of books on intelligence, spying and secret warfare.
- Knowledge and studies of intelligence methods with regards to investigation, interrogation, inquiry, information-gathering, man-hunting, spying, and eavesdropping and its modern devices and equipment.
- Knowledge and studies in the forensic sciences, and the security

organizations' methods of following up security-related incidents, criminal events and similar.

- Knowledge and studies of the history of special operations and the details about their events, including military spec ops performed by a military elite of guerilla commandos, as well as operations by international armed groups. Furthermore, one should study the reasons of success and failure of those operations, especially with regards to the large ones...
- Knowledge of how the so-called 'anti-terrorism units' operate, their weapons, training, and operational methods. And study some of their successful and failed operations in various countries of the world, especially during the last ten years.
- Knowledge and studies of the books on different types of 'guerilla warfare'... guerilla warfare in cities, mountains, forests or rural areas, guerilla warfare in the desert, wars of attrition and others... Furthermore, one should study other types of such warfare, and the arts and weapons of each type of war, and its methods, the history of its experiences, its famous schools in modern history, especially during the large revolutions in the colonization period between the two world wars. And afterwards, the period of struggle against the American empire after the Second World War, especially in South America and Africa, and some other countries in Asia.
- General knowledge and information which will be helpful in the overall guerilla warfare activity, especially in urban guerilla warfare and in terrorist operations against civilians, for example:
- Computer science; it is today one of the most important sciences which contributes to all scientific and other cultural fields today, and also
- General knowledge of the science of electricity, the electronics and electrical devices. It is useful to have a general knowledge of the science of mechanics and machines, especially vehicles and weapons, and how to use, repair, and modify them whenever necessary...

- Some general information and studies in history, politics and economy... and in the geography, climate, economy, roads, and infrastructure of the country one operates in, and customs, traditions, and the general aspects of human life and activity in the area of operation for the guerilla fighter or the Mujahidun fighting with guerilla warfare techniques. And so on...

All of this knowledge and information forms, for the Mujahidun fighting in the field of urban guerilla warfare, or 'terrorism' as it is called, a culture for the terrorist and develops his talent. A talent for terrorism when it comes to selecting targets and the operations' nature, the ability to execute them, to meet their requirements, assess their impacts and consequences from political, security-related and other perspectives... etc. I really suggest to the supervisors who prepare the cells and the terrorist units that they add to their preparation program a subject entitled 'terrorist culture' which should include this, and add a library to assist the trainee in his studying and education.

### Terrorist talent

I remember that I held a lecture at a training course for some young cadres in the al-Qaida organization. They were selected from among the Arab Mujahidun in the days of the Afghani Jihad in 1989. It had the title:

'Terrorism is a talent'..

And really, after my lengthy contact with the jihadi current and the fields of training and operational activity, and close contact with hundreds of Mujahidun of different nationalities, types and levels... in addition to a lot of studying, facilitated by God the Supreme in these areas... I observed that the operational readiness in the field of terrorism is based on three elements:

1. Talent
2. A broad general culture
3. Acquired skills and preparation.

At times, it is possible to heighten the cultural level of the Mujahidun, and it is also possible to heighten the level of preparation and acquired skills, and this will contribute to refining the talent... but the talent is the fundament for producing a terrorist who is proficient in his work and performance.

*From this aspect, talent for terrorism is like talent for poetry, music, painting, and different aspects of the arts, literature and hobbies... The talents, intellectual, practical and others in general... are a gift. There are people who possess a disposition and personal qualities for becoming successful terrorists, who are proficient in selecting, planning and executing operations, and understanding their political considerations, how they are regulated by Islamic law and moral rules... etc.*

The trainers and those supervising the foundation of Resistance cells must discover those talents and refine them with culture and training so that they find their place in leading terrorist operations in this type of blessed jihad...

## Acquired skills of guerilla fighters

are all the skills, capabilities, perceptions, knowledge, and the physical and technical skills in which the guerilla fighter trains, in different direct military fields such as the use of different weapons, and so on, or other related skills... I will go into some of these details in the section on preparation and training, with the help of God the Supreme, and this is what is prayed for.

Finally, concluding the military theory, and after a review of the two fields of operational activity for the Resistance, on Open Fronts and through individual terrorism, it is worth pointing out the relationship between these two types of jihad before concluding this section.

## THE RELATIONSHIP BETWEEN OPEN FRONT JIHAD
## AND INDIVIDUAL TERRORISM JIHAD:

Some details about this point will be given in the section on organizational theory, but it is possible to summarize some thoughts about this point as follows:

1. Units operating in the field of individual terrorism may benefit from the Open Fronts in that they enable them to heighten their military skills and improve their training possibilities. It is necessary to apply rigorous security precautions if this is to be done.

2. Some elements working in the field of recruitment and the building of cells can benefit from the Open Fronts, by recruiting some of the elements coming to fight jihad, selecting them, and sending them to operate in their countries, or wherever they are able to operate in the field of individual or cell terrorism. It is very important to take into consideration that this should not take the shape of a secret organization or a centralized link.

3. The Open Fronts can provide a way out and a secure haven for those working in the field of individual jihad who are wanted fugitives on the run after having been exposed and are not able to resume their activities in an overt way, and are unable to hide.

4. It must be noted that the Resistance Units operating in the field of secret work, must stick to their secret methods in case they are transferred to operate on the Fronts, and not transform into overt operational activity and agitation. This is a fatal factor and dangerous slipping point, because of the secure and friendly environment.

5. Individuals of the secret Resistance Cells must, in case they go to the Open Fronts, work under the leadership of the Emirs of those fronts, especially the local ones, or under the general

administrations which are set up in case of such traffic... They must work under the [Front] administrations with devotion and self-sacrifice as long as they are present there. They should aspire to come to the first battle-line and to the training camps in order to perform their religious duty with devotion, and to have close contact with the Mujahidun, and spread the Call and its programme in a covert way when possible.

6. The Open Fronts also benefit from the units of individual and cell terrorism, because the activity of these units constitutes a long arm that is fighting jihad for the Open Fronts' causes. Through their operational activity they are able to provide the necessary deterrence to the enemy force; they are able to remove the opponents' leadership, operate behind enemy lines, and execute special operations in cooperation with the Emirs in those arenas and for those causes in a covert and programmatic way.

**Now, in conclusion we call upon those whom this appeal reaches...**

ॐ

O ye Mujahidun youth... ye noble men of this nation... O ye faithful determined to fight a jihad... Truly, the Islamic Nation today, most of her men have lost their firm will, and weakness has struck her out of love for the world and aversion of death, especially after the downfall of the Muslims' Caliphate and their political entity, and after their enemies colonized them.

We must revive the Islamic Nation and lead her from this wasteland...

At the time of the first American invasion of Iraq in 1991, some Mujahidun youth crossed the Jordan River carrying a knife or a revolver, or whatever was within reach for him, searching for a Zionist soldier to fight with, contributing to this Islamic Nation's jihad... Some Mujahidun traveled to the end of the world in order to conduct operational activity behind enemy lines, responding to his hostility towards this Islamic Nation... Some went to join an arena of jihad, which could only be reached with great effort.

Now, the matter has become easier... America has come to us with hundreds of thousands of soldiers and experts, and has spread them in our midst... in addition to the hundreds of thousands of civilians working in other fields of colonization; from the political, economic, and cultural to other fields... The cause to which we are calling does not require affiliation to a secret organization, and does not urge travel or migration, and does not alter the routines of daily life.

All the matter requires is:

– **A resolute, personal decision to perform the individual duty of jihad, and a strong determination to contribute to the jihad and the Resistance.**

– **An oath between you and God the Supreme, and then between you and those you will work with in joining the Resistance Call.**

– **Forming your unit... By this you become a member of this Call, and a unit within the Global Resistance Units.**

– **Expanding your understanding of the doctrinal program and implementing its educational program, and going by it according to the extent of your capabilities.**

– **Preparing yourself and those with you to the extent of your capabilities.**

– **Embarking upon your operations, because jihad is a personal duty, and selecting an enemy target commensurate with your material and military capabilities.**

– **Biding your time and thinking:... plan and ask God for guidance... then proceed..**

Be greeted on the path of the two blessings, either victory or martyrdom. This is a call for action and martyrdom... not a method for controversies or a programme of idle talk and endless questions. The Islamic Nation has had enough of this, and it has led us to where we are now...

This is what we ask from God when time has come for departing into battle...

*'Allah hath purchased of the believers their persons and their goods; for theirs (in return) is the garden (of Paradise): they fight in His cause, and slay and are slain: a promise binding on Him in truth, through the Law, the Gospel, and the Qur'an: and who is more faithful to his covenant than Allah. Then rejoice in the bargain which ye have concluded: that is the achievement supreme'.* (Al-Thawbah 9:111)[22]

🕉

---

22    [Translator's footnote:] Translation from Yusuf Ali, via *Search Truth: Search in the Quran and Hadith* website, www.searchtruth.com, accessed August 2006.

# THEORY ON THE ORGANIZATION AND SYSTEM OF ACTION IN THE GLOBAL ISLAMIC RESISTANCE UNITS

Ch. 8 / Sec. 5 [Page 1405-1413]

The operational theories and the organizational set-up are based on the basic rule and slogan in terms of the way they operate, which is 'a system of action: not a secret organization for action' (*nizam al-'amal, wa laysa tanzim lil-'amal*), in other words: '**a system, not a secret organization**' (*nizam la tanzim*). This means that the Islamic Resistance units develop their operational methods, as explained above with regards to the military theory, on the basis of a system or method for operations, and concentrate their efforts on its results, instead of relying on the centralized secret organization (*al-tanzim al-markazi*). In order to clarify this, we need to elaborate this further:

## THE BUILDING BLOCS AND ASSETS IN TRADITIONAL SECRET ORGANIZATIONS

I have summarized the assets and building blocs which the traditional secret organizations are based upon, in a lecture which I gave in Peshawar in 1990, and they are:

1. *Programme* (*al-manhaj*): which is the ideology and organizational doctrine, around which the secret organization's members gather.
2. *Leadership* (*al-qiyadah*): which comprises the Emir and the Shura Council and the Administration and the decision-making

process.

3. *Roadmap* (*mukhattat*): which is a program containing a strategy of practices to achieve the goals

4. *Financing* (*al-tamwil*): which is the material means which cover the expenditures related to the implementation of the roadmap.

5. *Oath of allegiance* (*al-bay'ah*): which is the system of bonds between the Emir and the subordinates in this organizational circle.

## THE BUILDING BLOCS AND ASSETS IN THE GLOBAL ISLAMIC RESISTANCE CALL AND ITS JIHADI UNITS

As referred to in the section on military theory and previous sections, the foundation of our Call relies on the following:

- *Belief in the ideology of the Call* [i.e. The Global Islamic Resistance Call], *its basic jihadi doctrine and its politico-juridical theory.*
- *Operational activity to achieve the common goal, which is to repel the invading and occupying assailants and combat those who collaborate with the invaders.*
- *Implementation of a comprehensive educational program for the members of each unit.*
- *Operational and organizational method including details defined in the various theories (military, organizational, preparation, training, financing and instigation).*
- *Carrying a general common name for all Units, in addition to a specific name for each Unit.*
- *Oath to God the Supreme on adhering to the program and the operational activity in order to achieve the aim.*

If we wish to make a comparison between the assets of the traditional clandestine organizations and the assets of the system of practices in the Global Islamic Resistance Units, we find, briefly speaking, the following:

❦

*A. Basis for operational activity: Assets of the traditional clandestine organizations*

- **Goal:** Topple the government and establish a legitimate government in a geographical area.
- **Program:** The jihadi clandestine organizations' ideology and program.
- **Leadership:** The central Emir and leadership.
- **Roadmap:** The clandestine organizations' operational program
- **Financing:** The financial sources of the clandestine organization, a program for spending these. The sources of incomes are donations.
- **Oath of Allegiance and Covenant:** A Central oath of allegiance to the Emir

*B. Basis for operational activity: Operational concept of the Resistance Units.*

- **Goal:** Resistance to repel the invading assailant and its collaborators.
- **Program:** The Global Islamic Resistance Call.
- **Leadership:** General guidance to the global Units and one Emir for each Unit.
- **Roadmap:** Resisting the occupation and striking against it in every place.
- **Financing:** Each unit has its own financing system. Its sources are war booty and donations.
- **Oath of Allegiance and Covenant:** Oath of allegiance to God on jihad and resistance and a covenant of obedience to the Unit's Emir.

❦

## THE GLOBAL ISLAMIC RESISTANCE CALL (KEY EXCERPTS)

The Resistance Call is founded on the decentralized cells. Its jihadi Units base themselves on individual action, action by small cells completely separated from each other and on complete decentralization, in the sense that nothing connects them apart from **the common aim, the common name, a program of beliefs and a method of education.**

*Building the cells and the units: 'A system of formation and practice'*
When I put forward the Resistance theories in their final form in 2000 in Kabul during the era of the Islamic Emirate in Afghanistan under the Taleban, I began the attempt to build their first nuclei on the soil of Afghanistan. The formula of the organizational setup, as I have explained in a series of lectures entitled 'Jihad is the Solution', and in video lectures entitled 'Resistance Units', was in a form which I will outline in this section, and I will subsequently mention the amendment [in this formula], which we were forced to make in the wake of the September events and the American campaigns, which forced us to amend the doctrine in order for it to fit the current reality.

### THREE ORGANIZATIONAL CIRCLES IN THE UNITS OF THE GLOBAL ISLAMIC RESISTANCE CALL

*First: the first circle is the centralized unit*
Its basic mission is guidance, counseling and calling to jihad. This is undertaken through spreading the literary production of the Call [for Global Islamic Resistance], its political-juridical, educational and organizational programs, among the various segments of the Islamic nation, the issuance of media, and programmatic communiqués in the name of the Call and its Units. These programs and communiqués should encompass the ideology, the implementation methods and viewpoints of the Call. In addition, its [the Centralized Unit's] mission is to build a militarily active centralized unit in the 'Open Front Areas'[1], which were in Afghanistan. It should also work through maintaining mutual contacts with whoever such contact is

---

1    See previous section on military theory.

possible in order to establish cooperative and coordinating relationships with non-centralized units which carry the Resistance Call and which, in terms of organization, operate completely separately.

*Secondly: the circle of coordination or 'the Decentralized Units':*
This consists of elements with whom mutual contacts are possible and who can be subjected to ideological, programmatic, and educational qualification courses. These courses should be comprehensive in terms of their ideological, behavioral, military and organizational content. Upon request, the program of these cadres will be to depart from the front, spread throughout the world, each one according to his circumstances and life situation, and operate completely freely and separately from the Centralized Unit in terms of organization, in the sense that nothing connects them except the name, the goal, the ideological and educational program, and the operational method. As for everything else, the bonds are completely separated. The advantage of these [Decentralized] Units over the following is that their leadership can oversee their education directly with regards to the Call, and this enables them to transmit the educational styles, the methods of ideas, thinking and operations in a correct manner. Furthermore, it enables the leadership to prepare the [Decentralized] Units thoroughly in military matters, and spread the necessary military skills.

*Thirdly: The third circle is 'the Da'wah circle' or the General Units of the Global Islamic Resistance Call*
These units are the basis for the Global Islamic Resistance Call whose slogan is:

**'The Resistance is the Islamic Nation's Battle and not a Struggle of the Elite'**

The Call is to convey the idea in succinct and detailed ways in order to enable the youth, who are determined to fight a jihad, to enter this

Call and form their own Units entirely independently. In this way, they will participate in the Resistance without any organizational links with the Center [i.e. Centralized Unit].

*The link, as we have shown above, is confined to the common aim, a common name, the common doctrinal jihadi program, and a comprehensive educational program, whereas the necessary programs and all the needed materials for the completion of their self-preparation are made available to them, so that they are informed of a clear and disciplined program for pursuing the [jihadi] activities.*

Hence, the individual, joining the Call's General Units, is not obliged to anything else, other than to believe in the idea, be absolutely certain in his intention, join the Call, and educate himself and those with him according to the Call's program, and in time, commence with activities in accordance with the methods and manners clarified in the Call's program and literature.

In the books and recordings in which I have explained the method (*tariqah*) [of the Global Islamic Resistance Call], I have emphasized that the foundation of the Call and its strategic area is the third circle, namely the Call's Units, 'the Units of the Global Islamic Resistance Call'. We have put forward details explaining to the disciples of this method[2], ways in which they can establish Units and their operational methods. I will clarify this below, but I will first discuss *the repercussions of the September events and the downfall of the Afghanistan Emirate and the final collapse of the theories of centralized confrontation, following the US military attack, which was overwhelming materially, technologically and in terms of human resources on every*

---

2    Al-Suri uses the expression *muridin li-hadhihi al-tariqah*, which also means 'disciples of this order'. The term *muridi al-tariqah* is also used about disciples of a Suri order. This is no coincidence. Elsewhere, al-Suri points to the Sufi orders as an organizational model for *The Global Islamic Resistance Call*, since they often combine a decentralized organizational structure with mass following.

*level. This was proven in limited confrontations that occurred between the centralized and overtly-operating Mujahidun forces, and the forces of the US campaign in Afghanistan, and subsequently in Pakistan, in Iraq and in other spots such as Yemen and elsewhere. This demonstrated to me the importance of the strategy of individual secret activity, and a concentration on the basic circle in the Global Islamic Resistance Call, namely the General Da'wah circle.*

I believe that it will perhaps be a long time, God knows, before we, or some other of the Mujahidun, *will be able to centralize once again and operate face-to-face [with the enemy] defending fixed positions and fighting along battle-fronts.* The premises of the current situation force us to operate through two circles: the first and the third:

*The First Circle: which is the Guidance Center:*
which supervises guidance, counseling, the distribution of the doctrinal program, educational programs, issuing of communiqués, and necessary research to follow up on this, and which operates clandestinely, in a manner suitable to the conditions.

*The Third Circle: 'The Resistance Call Units':*
These are the Units for which we have great hope and we expect that they will be established spontaneously by those who wish to act, and in accordance with this program and system. With God's help they will be formed through the spread of the Call among Muslims, who are experiencing conditions around themselves that drive them to join this Resistance. This will happen via secret propaganda activity to convince these segments of society of the necessity of a disciplined program for Resistance and the necessity to act from the vantage points of this Call and strive collectively in an attempt to reach the strategic goal, which is to defeat aggression and gain victory over the Nazi campaigns which are headed by American Zionism.

*If God permits me to live so long as to witness the emergence of the desired balance [of power between us and the Enemy], and the restoration of our capability for consolidation and defense from permanent positions, then, I will resume my efforts in forming three circles in practical terms. That beginning was promising and encouraging, and I am not opposed to reviewing that experience, which collapsed like the other jihadi attempts in the midst of the September repercussions and the downfall of the Islamic Emirate of Afghanistan.*

*I hope that if this balance of power recurs and the Mujahidun once again manage to consolidate their positions after I have met my Lord – I pray for mercy, forgiveness, and martyrdom in his way that pleases Him – and if God wishes, that some of the competent Mujahidun cadres will work on what I have dreamt of and strived towards, namely the formation of:*
***An Office for the Guidance of the Global Islamic Resistance Units', and a professional Centralized Unit** for this Call, in which I have summarized my organizational jihadi experiences and thoughts in the course of a quarter of a century, I pray to God for Salvation.*

*I wish that this idea matures and that it will be a serious and sincere contribution to drive out the aggressive raiding invader and their collaborators from this pious and oppressed Islamic Nation, whose time has come to rise up, with the help of God.*

As for now, I will provide further explanations in order to help those who are convinced about this Jihadi Call for Resistance to establish, in a comprehensive manner, their own independent secret units.

## TYPES OF GLOBAL ISLAMIC RESISTANCE CALL
## UNITS IN TERMS OF MISSIONS AND ACTIVITY

*A. The elements and Units, building the Operative Units [Building Units]:* These elements and Units specialize in spreading the idea of the Global Islamic Resistance Call, in convincing the jihadi cadres and the youth who strongly wish to fight (in the Resistance) about the ideas of the Call, in rushing them to form their independent Units, preparing them ideologically, militarily and in terms of security, supplying them with various juridical-theological, political, military, and security research, qualifying them so that they can train their own cadres to become effective Units. Among other possible missions for this type of Building Unit, is to furnish the Units with start-up money, wherever such funds are forthcoming.

*The necessary characteristics of the elements and Units whose mission is to build [new] Units, are:*
1. They should be undetected and capable of moving safely and freely in the surrounding society where they live.
2. They should have an understanding of the Call program and possess sufficient ideological qualifications to explain the Program to others and call others to join, and they should have significant theological-juridical, political, and organizational understanding.
3. High level of security awareness and security training in moving around in order to train others in traveling undetected.
4. A suitable level of proficiency in conducting secret training in light arms, explosives and other light guerrilla warfare weaponry.
5. Capability to stay in contact with some sources of financing for the Resistance in order to supply the Operative Units which they have established, with start-up money in order to get them going.

*B. The Operative Units:* consist of one element or more. It is preferable if the Operative Unit consists of between five to ten people at most. Wherever it forms spontaneously after having studied the idea [of the Global Islamic Resistance Call], and its literature and members share a belief in their adherence to the Call, it moves directly to operative action. Or the Operative Unit may be established through the assistance of an element from the Building Units, as mentioned above. The mission of these [Operative] Units is to commence with jihadi activity, join the combat immediately, educate themselves on the Call's program, and *not be dragged into expansion and transformation into building other cells. They should resist the instinctive feeling of a wish to expand in order to avoid a transformation into small hierarchical secret organizations. This is very dangerous* and might lead to their swift arrest, must God prevent that.

*C. The Secret Agitation Units:* These Units are formed by very small cells of one to three elements [persons] that have religious, political, ideological and media experience, organizational awareness, and experience in using the Internet and electronic communication equipment. The mission of these Units is to spread the Call and redistribute its literature, its research studies, and its various programs by clandestine means, especially over the Internet. They should work on translating the works and communiqués of the Resistance to the languages of the Muslims and to the world languages. With due regard to security precautions related to the distribution of material, these [Agitation] Units should innovate and find their own operational methods in accordance with the possibilities offered by the country and place within which they find themselves. There will be more explanation about the activity of these Units in the chapter on theories for media and incitement.

CLARIFICATIONS REGARDING METHODS OF BUILD-
ING AND OPERATING SECRET UNITS

*First: The method of building multiple Units by the building elements in the Operative Units*

We have previously discussed the method of building hierarchical secret organizations and its dangers due to the fact that the arrest of one element in the hierarchy leads to the arrest of those who are with him, above him and below him in the organization, and in this way the circles of arrest expand until they destroys the organizational hierarchy entirely. So if we have an organizational pyramid and one element is arrested, his arrest will lead to a confession by him about those who are on his [organizational] level, those who are above him, and those who have such responsibilities [sic!].. In this way the catastrophe repeats itself with the arrest of those below him. Everywhere during past experiences, the types of arrests, the brutal and immoral torture have led to the abortion of the strongest secret organizations. As we have shown previously some secret organizations have depended on the cluster model in which the leaders of the clusters have been placed in another country, in which the secret organization does not operate, so that the leadership can reside in a safe place and the elements are administered via secret organizational hierarchical clusters, operating inside the arena of the country in question, so that if the hierarchy linked to the central element is destroyed, it will not be arrested and the circle of collapse stops there. This method has been successful in providing some Arab and Islamic, and even international, secret organizations a certain margin of maneuver. The international cooperation today in fighting terrorism has destroyed this [margin], however, since the request for the wanted element by his government leads to his arrest by other governments and to his confession about whom [from his organization] resides in other countries. The arrests are carried out in terms of hours or days at the most. This happened after the slogan was adopted that one should eliminate safe havens when the leadership of the secret organizations sought refuge in certain safe havens outside the control of the New World Order, such as Afghanistan and Chechnya. The Enemy's program has been to topple these safe havens and subordinate them under the control of the [New] World Order. Hence, the cluster model with a leadership directing from a safe haven has failed, and with it, the time of the secret organizations is definitely over. It cannot be revived unless the New World Order is destroyed and only God the

Almighty knows. This is the aim and we strive towards creating a method to make it happen, with the grace of God.

*As for the method which we propose for the builders of Units, they are as follows:*
It must be undertaken by the operative element from among the Unit builders (*bunat al-saraya*). Their foremost distinctions should consist of acquired skills in security, religious and cultural affairs; they must have numerous acquaintances and an ability to influence a wider circle of people.

He selects some of his acquaintances from whom those he thinks may have the capability of leading Units. He broaches the subject for each of them alone and completely separated from the others. Gradually and after he has gained the trust of each and every of the candidates, he begins training them, either in a one-to-one fashion, or with the assistance of one or two aides at the most. He trains them during the preparatory period, using the printed and audio-filed programs of the Call, in particular this book and the series of my lectures entitled 'Jihad is the Solution: Why and How', as well as my video-taped lectures entitled 'The Global Islamic Resistance Units'. The most important of these studies have been included in this book with a view to expand it and make the information more accurate. Furthermore, I have a number of audio-recorded lectures on 'The Basis for Guerrilla Warfare', which is useful as an example of military culture on clandestine warfare and guerrilla activity. They consist of three collections of lectures: 'Abbreviated Lectures in Two Cassette Tapes' and 'Lessons in Six Cassette Tapes' and an extensive series of lectures, a course consisting of 32 cassette tapes, entitled 'Explanation on the Book War of the Oppressed'. This book is among the most important works explaining guerrilla warfare, and clarifying the reasons for its success and failures. The book is about 170 pages and is a translation of a work by an American expert on counter-guerrilla warfare.

In training and preparing [the candidates] it is also useful to benefit from what is easily available in terms of security-related and military studies on the market today and on the Internet in various languages. I have the intention, if God permits, to prepare some abbreviated summaries of these [studies], together with some completed ideological studies contained in this comprehensive book, in order to [make available] the most important [material] for ideological, political, religious, and organizational preparation [or training].

It is also incumbent upon those who build Units to subject them [the recruits] to the ideological, security and military training program for a period, which I believe, does not need to be longer that a month or two months, if he [the builder of the cell] follows up the recruits intensively. This is especially important with regards to the ideological training. We will demonstrate below ways of secret training preparation, if God permits.

Hence, if we presuppose that the element, the Unit builder has trained four or five separate Units, which are completely separate, and whose members do not know one another, and do not know anything about the others.

[A]   [B]   [C]   [D]   [E]   [F]

Now, each and everyone of them are given an assignment to build their own Unit, consisting of two or three elements, or only one element operating alone, if he wishes, and they are given a date, before which they cannot start operating in order to allow the builder to distance himself from their arena [of operation] because he is the only vulnerable spot for these groups.

*Prior to this date, the founding element from the Unit builders, [i.e. the person who founded the above-mentioned Units] must leave for a location which is unknown to the Units so that they cannot lead [the authorities] to him.*

He may leave either for one of the open fronts in areas outside [government] control or he may travel to another country using personal papers which nobody knows anything about, or he may go into complete hiding in a new arena.

*Or it may be in the program that the founding element should undertake a martyrdom mission after he has built a number of cells, because he represents the only fatal point [of weakness] from a security perspective for the Units which he has built. If one of the cells is arrested, its members cannot reveal information about anyone except him [i.e. the Unit builder] because they know nobody else.*

It is absolutely necessary that the founding element takes every precaution to avoid saying or revealing through his movements, or by hints or encouragement, anything that may suggest to some of the elements [i.e. Units] that he has recruited others. Some of them may be able to guess who these others are and inform on some of them. *It is possible that the Unit be formed spontaneously without the intervention of a founder from outside, and become active directly in the Resistance without acting upon invitation by others. This happens when a man becomes convinced of joining the Resistance Call, and forms his own small Unit and operates either only on his own or with a collaborating friend whom he persuades [to join the Unit]. They then prepare themselves based on these studies [i.e. apparently the book The Global Islamic Resistance Call], they find a name for their Unit and start operating immediately. They do not attempt to organize others, and they do not operate in the field of calling to Islam, instigation, but they devote themselves to direct action. These are the highest security precautions.*

*It is within the reach of those who have less experience and insight into the training and the basis for secret activity to undertake great deeds with a small Unit consisting of two or three elements with security and military qualifications and possessing 'the terrorist cultures'. It is possible for their Unit to transfer their activity inside their country and to*

453

*numerous cities. It is unimaginable for those who do not know this that in the country there are tens of operative groups, but I have numerous stories, live witness accounts, and terrific examples of this, but there is no space for retelling them here.*

## Secondly: Warning not to mix the Unit's military activity with media and recruitment activity

Those Mujahidun who undertake the building of Units must take all precautions not to mix media and recruitment activities with military activities. If they do, they will incur harm upon themselves and others.

*The basic idea is that the one who hears about the idea and becomes convinced about it, forms his own Unit, consisting of himself alone and operates within the limits of his capabilities, if he does not have anyone he can trust. Or he operates with two or three trusted [companions] at the maximum, and they form one Unit and operate in silence and in a calculated way in the military field. They select an enemy target which has been mentioned and referred to by some of them and they undertake an operation, not more often than once in several months, and they declare [responsibility for] it in an appropriate, secure and concise manner.*

❦

*You have to know:* The Call for organizing others, propaganda activity, media... collection of donations:... these are methods that contradict [the principles of] secrecy and the commencement of operations. They can never be combined. The combination between these contradictory methods has led to real catastrophes in our jihadi organizational history. These are the most important conclusions from our past painful experiences.

The principle 'the overtness of agitation and the secrecy of the secret organization' ('*alaniyyat al-da'wah wa al-sirriyyat al-tanzim*) is the most flawed of the organizational principles. Practicing this

principle has led to bloody catastrophes. Those who undertake propaganda and instigation activities, have to abandon secret combat
activities, and vice versa. You should know that during these times,
the Islamic Nation needs tens of thousands of fida'iyyun[3] fighters.
As for instigators, who call to Islam and jihad with words, only a few
are sufficient

Verily, the practice of combat, the infliction of harm on God's enemies, and the giving up of oneself in God's way, is the most effective agitative message which a nation, that has given up jihad, needs
in order to wake up from its slumber.

Verily, the practice of agitation does not relieve the Muslim from
the obligatory duty of combat today. Shrinking from this duty is
considered equal to abandoning prayer, almsgiving, fasting, and
pilgrimage, and even worse than that. This is because the Islamic
Nation is in need of this due to the harm of its enemies' oppression
and the vanishing of its religion and its worldly presence. So do
not mix one with the other. Beware of those who know the secret
and hide [from them]. *'Does he not know,- when [that] which is in
the graves is scattered abroad. And that which is (locked up) in (human)
breasts is made manifest.'*[4] [al-Adiyat, 100/9-11]. Verily, Our Lord is
knowledgeable and far-sighted about his worshippers.

§﷽§

*Thirdly: The Resistance Call is a call to serious activity*

The Mujahidun must be aware of the fact that a few Units are suf-
ficient for agitation, and that there is a pressing need for Operative
Units. The basis of the important obligation [of jihad] is combat,
*'Then fight in Allah's cause - Thou art held responsible only for thyself'*
[Surat al-Nisa', 4-84]. As for agitation, it is a community obligation
and for those who are able and qualified to undertake it.

---

3    [Translator's footnote:] for explanation of the term *fida'iyyun*, see above.

4    [Translator's footnote:] The Quranic verse is not correctly cited.

The activist does not let Satan turn him away from [jihadi] activity by convincing him that he [instead] instigates others or recruits others [to undertake jihad]. This is the delusion of Iblis [i.e. the Devil]. The mission of recruiting others is a huge responsibility because it requires [of the recruiter], as we have noted already, that he completely disappears from the arena in which he has recruited other activists. For this reason, the basic rule is that the person must recruit himself and operate with those with who he is in direct contact.

## Fourthly: Participate in the following mathematical assessment of the Resistance

I refer again to what I mentioned under the section on the military theories that the importance of the idea of Global Islamic Resistance Call Units stems from their proliferation and the concentration of efforts. As I said above, if twelve Units are formed throughout the Islamic world, and each unit carries out one operation a year, we will have one operation each month. If they carry out two operations annually, there will be one operation every fifteen days. This is something which not even the strongest secret organization is capable of doing. So let's say that during one year after the launching of the idea [of The Global Islamic Resistance Call], a hundred persons are convinced by our idea, and 50 of them are successful, and each of them carries out two or three operations a year, the result would be that with the passage of time, the efforts of the Resistance Units would be noticed several times every day. This will cause harm to the enemy and motivate the Muslims to become active [fighters]. We hope that God the Almighty and Supreme will bless this idea, prepare its men for it [this mission], bless the efforts of all of us, show us our enemies' defeat and bring us to martyrdom in his way.

# THE TRAINING THEORY IN THE GLOBAL ISLAMIC RESISTANCE CALL

Ch. 8/ Sec. 6 [Page 1414-1428]

### REVIEW OF OLD TRAINING METHODS UPON WHICH THE JIHADIS RELIED DURING PREVIOUS EXPERIENCES

In the same way as we have previously extracted appropriate theories and successful methods, with God's permission, we will now identify theories for training the Global Islamic Resistance Call Units by studying the training methods which were used during our jihadi experiences in the past. Over the years I have, by the grace of God, worked with most of these methods as a trainee, then as a trainer, then as a training supervisor in our special program during the days of the Taleban. In general, we find that the jihadi experiences have used one of the following methods:

1. Secret training in houses
2. Training in small secret camps in the area of operations itself
3. Overt training under the auspices of states providing safe havens
4. Overt training in the camps of the Open Fronts[5]
5. Training in areas of chaos and no [governmental] control

*Let us shed light briefly on the negative and positive aspects of each method, and examples of each of them in order to be able to select the most exemplary training method today under the conditions of the post–September world and the atmosphere of combating global terrorism.*

*Secret training in houses*

---

5     [For explanation of the term Open Fronts, see the previous Military Theories-section.]

The secret jihadi organizations have used this method in all their jihadi experiences. We may say that this method is the very foundation in preparing the secret organizations and bands in the world. Even if it only allows for training in the use of personal light weapons, some lessons in the use of explosives and weapons to be used in the first stage of guerrilla wars, its effectiveness has been firmly entrenched. However, the basis, [derived from] years of activity in armed formations, is the moral motivation and the desire to fight, not more knowledge about weaponry which the Mujahid would not use in practice.

In this method, the trainees learn how to disassemble and assemble the weapon, how to use it and how to aim with it in theory, and they undertake some practical rehearsals, as well as limited shooting practice in remote regions, caves or in sound-proof cellars inside the same houses. Often, the first shots which the trainees fire are the shots they fired during real-life confrontations.

The Mujahidun during the Syrian jihadi experience of 1975-1982 used this method, and it was successful and useful. It enabled the Mujahidun to kill some apostates and their collaborators by firing at them for the first time. They developed their skills through real-life activity. This was not an unique experience.[6] Similar experiences had happened in jihads in other countries.

*Training in small secret camps*

The jihadi organizations have used this method where it has been possible to use available remote regions in mountains, in forests, and in distant rural areas. The method consists of subjecting small groups in limited numbers, between 5-12 persons, to training, establishing mobile camps in remote and isolated areas and carrying out intensive training programs where [the cadres are trained in] some

---

6    It says 'This was an unique experience', but from the context, it seems likely that it should be: 'This was not an unique experience'

advanced military tactics in urban and rural guerrilla warfare, such as ambushes, executions and other practices. This is possible by using limited amounts of explosives in areas close to stone quarries and fishing places where explosives are used and the sound of explosions are heard, or even inside caves, using small amounts of explosives. This is a very effective and sufficient method in order to produce capable Mujahidun, who are able to enter the battles of the first stages of a guerrilla war, especially the urban guerrilla war.

*Overt training under the auspices of states providing safe havens*

This training method was used very much in the world before the onset of the New World Order. It enabled many jihadi organizations to benefit from free havens [lit. 'margins', *hawamish*] created by political contradictions and the axes of regional and international conflict, as we have shown in chapter six. Overt [training] camps were set up in states which opposed the same regimes against which the [jihadi] opposition had risen up... Among these experiences we find our jihadi experience in Syria. The Mujahidun from The Fighting Vanguard and the Muslim Brothers in Syria were able to establish developed training camps in Iraq, to which the Iraqi regime offered large-scale material military assistance. During the period 1980-1983 many batches of Mujahidun completed general and specialized courses, which included training in various types of infantry weapons, medium and heavy weapons, except aircraft. This also happened on a limited scale in Jordan through the assistance of King Husayn and under the supervision of his intelligence agencies. Something similar happened in Egypt where a specialized group of Mujahidun from Syria underwent high-level training on urban warfare operations and special operations under the supervision of the General Intelligence Agency in Egypt during the famous strife between Sadat on the one hand and Syria and some Arab states on the other, in mid-1981. I myself witnessed these experiences in Iraq and Egypt. It was most useful and we gained high-level skills [from these courses].

In practice, all Islamic and non-Islamic secret organizations have operated in this manner in the Arab and Islamic countries during the period lasting from the beginning of the 1960s until the mid-1990s, when this ended as I have previously stated, with the rise of the system of security cooperation between the Arab-Islamic countries under the supervision of America and from these practices...

The jihadi organizations in Syria operated with a number of neighboring countries, while the opposition groups to Saddam [Husayn], especially the Shiite groups, operated in Syria, Iran and Lebanon. Most, if not all, Palestinian organizations operated in Syria, Iran, Lebanon, Jordan, Sudan and elsewhere, and so did [various] Lebanese Islamic organizations as well as others... Some of the Egyptian organizations operated in Lebanon with Hizballah and the Palestinians and in Iran. So did some of the groups from North-Western Africa from Algeria, Libya and from some of the countries in mid-Africa [sic!] and vice versa... As for the topic of the margins, [one may refer to] the entry of international military organizations such as E.T.A. and the Irish Republican Army I.R.A. to receive training and material assistance from Arab and Middle Eastern countries. The Turkish Kurdish Workers Party benefited from Syria, Lebanon and Northern Iraq, while the Iranian Mujahidun e-Khalq movement and other groups grew in Iraq. And so forth. The examples are numerous, and this method is very important and useful where the conditions repeat themselves. If the secret organizations avoid the political and security drawbacks of such openings, then the military advantages are great.

## Overt training in the camps of the Open Fronts[7]

The last well-known experiences are so famous that one does not need to mention their details, such as what happened in Afghanistan during the time of the Afghan jihad 1986-1992, and in the second

---

7    [For explanation of the term Open Fronts, see the previous Military Theories-section.]

round of the Afghan-Arabs during the Taleban era 1996-2001. During these two phases, tens of thousands of Arab and Muslim Mujahidun were trained. Tens of jihadi organizations and many other Islamic and even non-Jihadi, organizations benefited from this great free haven (lit. margin *al-hamish*). This also happened on a smaller scale in Chechnya and Bosnia. Furthermore, in many camps of revolutions and Open Fronts in the Philippines, the Horn of Africa, Kashmir and elsewhere, there were similar benefits.

Training in such camps has been absolutely the best field of training since the means of military and educational training are comprehensive, and all aspects [of the training] are included in a completely free manner without being subjected to pressure and directions, which happens in training camps in safe haven countries. These countries mostly impose some political and ideological constraints.

*Semi-overt training in areas of chaos and no [governmental] control*

Prior to the rise of the New World Order there were many areas of chaos without governmental control in the world, especially in the Arab-Islamic world, and in particular in semi-autonomous tribal areas and remote areas lying far away from weak governments in some countries... Examples are the tribes in Yemen, Somalia, and the Horn of Africa, the tribes in the border areas of Pakistan, and the long arch of the Great Sahara countries in Africa, which stretches from Sudan to the shores of the Atlantic Ocean. The local and non-local jihadi organizations have been able to benefit from these areas, and they may still be doing so, in establishing semi-overt training camps where space, weapons, and ammunition are provided at low costs. However, after September [11th 2001], America has made it its first priority to control these uncontrolled holes. Despite this, there are still many holes from which [the jihadi organizations] can benefit, in particular the local groups or groups from nearby countries.

If we wish to record the observations on the operations of training and preparation, which the jihadi have undertaken over the past phase through these five perspectives, we may summarize these as follows:

### 1. Internal training: in houses and internal limited camps

During the practice of training in houses the level of military preparation is relatively low, but the security yield is high if it is carried out under conditions of secrecy and great security precautions. Similarly, the [level of] moral and ideological training is high. It is reflected in the level of jihadi doctrine, the level of ideological and political understanding, and the basis of jihadi guerrilla warfare theories, especially in the jihadi experiences in Syria, Egypt, Libya, Algeria, Morocco and elsewhere. I recall when I was a member of the training agency during our semi-secret stay in Jordan during the Jihadi Revolution against the Syrian regime in 1980-1982... We were teaching in secrecy in scattered houses of the Mujahidun in Amman and in other Jordanian cities. We taught fifteen military and educational subjects in theory... and we carried out exams for the various cells. After that, we sent those who had passed the tests, to the camps in Baghdad in Iraq where they were given intensive and abbreviated courses because they had already finished the theoretical training. Those who were to specialize in military activity were retained for specialized courses in various types of weapons, including tanks. We saw that the subjects which we were able to train in the houses [in Jordan] were not few and were very important, especially the doctrinal and the ideological courses. In a situation where the cells are able to teach in limited mobile camps, the practical part [of the training] accomplishes and occupies the best kind of preparation, even if it does not reach high military levels. This is in view of the absence of security and political drawbacks, such as when one travels to training camps abroad.

**2. *The experiences of external training camps in safe haven camps in other countries***
There are clear advantages and they are in the high military levels which some cadres have managed to attain through the possibilities of preparation, training and the high-level multiple material support which the countries [providing safe havens], their armies and security agencies have offered. However, there are serious disadvantages which our past experiences have revealed.

- *The revelation of many of the secrets of the [jihadi] organizations, their personal and informational secrets, to the states hosting the training camps. This information represents a vehicle of pressure and a bargaining chip. In the end, it colors the table of security and intelligence cooperation between the states which change their positions continuously in a Machiavellian manner. Experience has proven that this is strategically a mortal trap.*
- *This method enables the host states, with the passage of time, to penetrate the secret organizations, even the jihadi Islamic organizations, and win over some members of these organizations, and put them under their administration and intelligence work. This happens especially when the duration of the organizations' stay in the host states is protracted and they [i.e. the secret organizations] have political, military and media hierarchy, as was the case with the Syrian jihadi experience. During the presence of its leadership in Iraq, Jordan and elsewhere... these countries managed over time to intervene in the affairs of the [jihadi] groups and impose on them their will. [Hence, the jihadi groups] were forced to become regional political pawns in their hands, because these countries pursued a policy of financial closure and strangulation as we will see [below] in the section of financing.*
- *The process of departing for camps in neighboring safe havens represents often an Achilles heel in terms of security due to the movement of Mujahidun elements and their traveling to these places. The security traps set up by the intelligence agencies have been a wake-up call in such cases, because they have been able in many cases to plant their*

*agents in such camps and the open circles which usually drift into the overt movement, and abandon the necessary security alertness. This happens especially with the passage of time and when the departure and return of the jihadi elements is transformed into the scope of the opposition that emigrates for stability and empties the very scene of jihad itself.*

### 3. The camps of the Open Fronts[8]

The exemplary image of this situation is the Afghanistan training camps during the two Arab rounds, the first during the Russian era and the second during the Taleban era, and similarly, the Bosnia training camps, to a certain degree. While Chechnya has not represented an arena for training and for attracting the secret [jihadi] organizations and the elements wishing to take part [in jihad], it has been an arena for combat, jihad, and direct action where high-level field cadres have been formed.

The advantages of these experiences have been 'very great' from the perspective of training and preparation, especially with regards to the [high] military levels which they provided. As for the negative aspects, we may summarize them as follows:

* Loss of opportunity for doctrinal [programmatic] education, due to the multiplicity of jihadi organizations involved, the many arenas, and the rivalries and contentions which were not kept in check and within the boundaries of Islamic law, or rationality in many cases, as we have mentioned already.
* The problem of exorbitant costs of bringing trainees from the farthest point on earth to the scene of training (travel expenditures, accommodation...).
* The problem of security penetration during the process of obtaining visas from the embassies of neighboring countries, especially

---

8    [For explanation of the term Open Fronts, see the previous Military Theories-section.]

from Pakistan, during the crossing of borders and overt movement. The easy planting of spies and collaborators of all kinds of intelligence agencies with the overt movement of all of those present [in the camps]. The security complications caused by the [trainees'] return, relocation, and interaction with the world as a whole, in light of the campaigns combating terrorism which consider them potential terrorists. Great losses and much harm have been inflicted on many segments of them [the trainees of the Arab-Afghan camps] even if they have not carried out any jihadi responses justifying this hardship.

**4. The camps in areas of chaos**
There was generally no desire to use this method in the previous phase. Its advantages and disadvantages were closely related to the method of small secret camps, with the difference that it required high material costs to travel to them [i.e. the camps in areas of chaos].

**Summing up, we have briefly reviewed the most important types of training in the pre-September world and the current American campaigns against the Islamic world.**

Today, through the course of the campaigns [against Islam/the jihadi groups], it automatically becomes clear that most of these [training] methods have been made irrelevant due to the elimination of the margins [of the international system] which permitted them [the use of these training methods]. It is no longer possible and practical under the current conditions to establish Open Fronts. It will no longer be possible for countries to open safe havens or camps for the Islamists and the jihadis. The areas of chaos are on the verge of coming under American control and being closed, such as the tribal areas in Yemen and the tribal areas in Sarhad in North-Western Afghanistan... and the Saharan belt in the middle of Africa and elsewhere.

*In this way, it seems clear that the only [training] methods which remain possible for us now, in the world of American aggression and international coordination to combat terrorism, are the methods of secret training in houses and mobile training camps.*

The opportunities for training, when they are subjected to the methods of secrecy, and even strict secrecy, are under the current circumstances very harsh and tough. And we will attempt to give some perspectives and explanations [about this] in order to assist the Resistance Units and other Mujahidun everywhere in training themselves and preparing their forces to terrorize the American Zionist enemies of God, and their collaborators.

Before we move on to the crux of the matter, which is the key point of this section, namely, training methods of the Resistance Units, I will go through all the concepts and points which will help us to extract the basic meaning of this section, which are the necessary training methods for us today.

## THE CONCEPT OF PREPARATION, ITS CAUSE AND GOAL:

*Preparation:* which means familiarity with the collection of knowledge, sciences, learned and physical skills, in order to carry out the mission of jihad. It is combat in the way of God. Its concepts, means, and goals have been summarized in these two holy [Quranic] verses. On this [theme of preparation] there have been so many elaborations of Sunna texts, both words and deeds, that the theme warrants a whole book. Here, for the purpose of brevity, [we present] two Quranic verses: God the Almighty said in Verse 60 (Surat al-Anfal) *'Against them make ready your strength to the utmost of your power, including steeds of war, to strike terror into (the hearts of) the enemies, of Allah and your enemies, and others besides, whom ye may not know, but whom Allah doth know. Whatever ye shall spend in the cause of Allah, shall be repaid unto you, and ye shall not be treated unjustly.'*

466

And in the Quranic Verse 36 [sic!][9] in Surat al-Tawbah: *'And if they had wished to go forth they would assuredly have made ready some equipment, but Allah was averse to their being sent forth and held them back and it was said (unto them): Sit ye with the sedentary!'*[10]

Let us note some of the benefits which these Verses refer to:
As for the Al-Anfal Verse, it:
1. establishes that preparation to your best capability , but not beyond your capability is a legal commandment. Every Muslim must prepare his strength and weapons as best he can.
2. Strength and steeds of war: This comprehensive term refers to all kinds of weapons, instruments of war and means for moving and transportation. God's Prophet, may peace and blessings be upon him, has clarified this by saying 'Indeed, power is shooting', repeating it three times. The Quran has ordered all Muslims to possess weapons and not to be negligent of them: *'Taking all precaution, and bearing arms: the Unbelievers wish, if ye were negligent of your arms and your baggage, to assault you in a single rush. But there is no blame on you if ye put away your arms because of the inconvenience of rain or because ye are ill; but take (every) precaution for yourselves. For the Unbelievers Allah hath prepared a humiliating punishment.'* (al-Nisa: 102)
3. The verse clarifies that the duty of preparation is not merely to gain knowledge, to exercise, and other things like that. This is an idea which has spread recently, that preparation is like going on holiday without any intention to fight jihad. Preparation has a specific goal... *'make ready...' 'to strike terror into (the hearts of) the enemies, of Allah and your enemies, and others besides...'* This Verse has been explained previously.

---

9    [Translator's footnote:] The Quranic verse cited here is Surat al-Tawbah no. 46, not 36.

10   [Translator's footnote:] Translation from Pickthal, via *Search Truth: Search in the Quran and Hadith* website, www.searchtruth.com/, accessed April 2006. Pickthal's translation has been chosen here because it seems to be closest to al-Suri's understanding of the verse.

4. Then, after the command to prepare and possess weapons and instruments of war, the verse kindly points out that God knows the costs of what was spent in His cause, and that the wealth of most of those wishing to fight Jihad fails to reach this. Thus, as the verse closes with this command about spending, it promises a large recompense and grant from God.

**As for the Al-Tawbah Verse, it:**
Contains great instructions, and great jurisprudence regarding the relationship between preparation and faith, and its relationship with practical jihad, some of its subtleties are:

The verse talks about the hypocrites who claim to have a desire for jihad, after the previous verses have described the relationship of the faithful [to jihad]. The faithful fight with their money and souls, and do not excuse themselves from the fight in order to flee, as the hypocrites do, whose hearts feel doubt, and who excuse themselves in order to flee. (This is why the al-Tawbah verse has been called 'The Disgracer of the Hypocrites'). The verse we cited above establishes that it is a sign of the hypocrites' hypocrisy that they turn away from preparation to battle and jihad, and it says about them '**if they had wished to go forth**', or, if their resolution to fight and to go out [to do so] had been sincere, '**they would assuredly have made ready some equipment**', or, they would have made necessary preparations for the battle, in accordance with their capacities and to their best ability. It also establishes that God the Almighty and Supreme was averse to their being sent forth to fight, and held them back because He knew their condition, and made them sit down, being merciful to the Mujahidun, because their going forth would create disorder and harm.

Let us return to our subject, which is the relationship between jihad and preparation. The verse points to the fact that the stages of this can be found in His words: *'And if they had wished to go forth they would assuredly have made ready some equipment, but Allah was averse*

*to their being sent forth and held them back and it was said (unto them):*
*Sit ye with the sedentary!'* [Surat al-Tawbah 46][11]

From the instructions in this verse we understand that there are three stages:

'will' .. 'preparation' .. 'launch' ..

*This dynamic logical order summarizes the operational mechanism in the performance of jihad and Resistance.*

**Will: the will to fight is a prerequisite for preparation, and then jihad:**
All military schools agree that *a will to fight* and *moral strength of the fighter* is the basis for victory and good performance. Also, will is the basis for all actions and all aspects of human activity.

Whoever desires food, drink, marriage, business, travel or anything else, requires the possession of the sincere will to start with. The proof of the sincerity of this will is that he makes the necessary preparations for that decision...

In our situation, which is jihad... preparation is the fruit of sincere will. When the will is sincere and the determination is firm, one starts making preparations according to his capabilities, in order to terrorize the enemies of God and the Muslims... After the preparation, one is dispatched to the battle... Thus, if the desire is sincere and the preparation is undertaken according to one's ability, the individual moves to launch jihad unless [he paraphrases Surat al-Tawbah 46] God the Almighty and Supreme has not held him back due to the disorder and harm [he would cause] - we pray to God for his well-being and endurance - and unless he has not been taken control of by Satan or by his own inclinations due to cowardice and weakness, a motive which the Prophet Muhammed, peace and blessings upon him, described in short: Love for the world and aversion of death.

---

11   [Translator's footnote:] Translation from Pickthal, via *Search Truth: Search in the Quran and Hadith* website, www.searchtruth.com/, accessed October 2006.

This combat will is the incentive for preparation and activity. If it is very important and a basis for the regular soldier, then it is the fundament for the guerrilla fighter in general and the jihadi Resistance fighter in particular. Even more, it is his basic weapon, which moves him to do whatever he is capable of, even using civilian weapons, if there is nothing else available.

## A CURIOUS PHENOMENON IN THE CONTEMPORARY WORLD OF PREPARATION FOR JIHAD:

As long as I have referred to this strange phenomenon, I have liked to correct it, and to straighten it out because of its negative and dangerous impact on the Islamic Nation... It is well-known in the world of the idle and the hypocrites, and of those who flee from jihad, that they do not prepare, as the Quranic verse mentioned. If they had a will for jihad and for setting out to fight, they would have prepared themselves, but they do not have the will, so they do not prepare, and consequently they do not fight jihad...

However, I turned my attention especially to our great jihadi experience in Afghanistan, with its first and second rounds, where tens of thousands of youth came to train in the camps, without an intention to fight jihad!! They openly declared that they came for the sake of the religious duty of preparation!! These tens of thousands then returned to their countries, satiated with the military training lessons they had been through. They had learned how to use different kinds of weapons, and battle tactics... Since that time, the Islamic Nation has been struck by serious events, such as the arrival of American and Allied forces on the Arab Peninsula... then, the occupation of Afghanistan, and then the occupation of Iraq, and in between and before that, the bloodshed in Palestine... In addition to the apostate rulers who perpetuate a series of tragedies, treacheries, and tyranny through their agents. ... However, the overwhelming majority of those who had trained did not come forth to launch a jihad. They did not move, but dived instead into a curious tranquility...

Here, a new case appeared in the series of contradictions, and signs of downfall and collapse within the modern Islamic Nation. It is the **phenomenon of those who prepare for, but do not want, to launch jihad. They had the will to prepare, while at the same time intending to avoid jihad. They wanted to willfully and premeditatedly desist from jihad!**...

I do not intend to discuss the reasons for this here. Many of its causes have been discussed previously. But I mention this matter here, due to its relationship with preparation, because this is empty preparation which is of no use. It only creates an excuse for the individual in question to refrain from experience and be weak... There is no power or strength except with God the Exalted and Magnificent.

## *Weapons of the Resistance and the jihadi guerrillas:*

In my previous recordings and lectures, I have discussed the principles of guerrilla warfare, its stages, weapons, and its military and political methods. As for the topic of training, we will here concentrate on the weapons of the Resistance, and reliance on training methods that are in accordance with the needs and the requirements of the current conditions. Theoretically, guerrilla warfare can be broken down into three stages, according to the various experiences worldwide, and according to the writers on this topic. The weapons of each stage are different, and in general, the stages are:

*The first stage: It is called the stage of exhaustion.* It is the stage of small guerrillas and limited terrorist warfare, where the guerrillas, which are small in number, rely upon the methods of assassination, small raids and ambushes, and selective bomb attacks to confuse the enemy, regardless of whether the enemy is a colonial power or a despotic regime. The aim is to reach a state of security exhaustion, political confusion, and economic failure.

*The second stage: It is called the stage of equilibrium.* In this stage, the guerrillas move to a stage of large, strategic attacks, and the regular forces are compelled to enter decisive battles which might lead to the disbandment of some of their units, and that part of their cadre, officers and soldiers join the guerrilla forces. A state of open confrontation is not yet reached, however, and the raids and the ambushes are the basis for guerrilla operations, even if they expand. At this stage, the guerrillas will carry out operations in which they will temporarily control some areas, in order to achieve important military, media-related, or political goals. They do not consolidate their positions, however.

*The third stage: It is called the end stage or the liberation stage.* At this stage, the guerrillas enter operations that are semi-regular and others that are regular, and they control some areas from which they launch operations to liberate the rest of the country. This happens after units from the regular army may have joined the revolutionaries or the guerrilla fighters, and after they have attained the tactical capability and a sufficient level of armament to enter into open battles. Here, small guerrilla units play an important role in carrying out operations behind enemy lines, to confuse the enemy forces by using guerrilla tactics...

This very brief summary of the general stages of guerrilla operations gives us an idea about the weapons of each stage. The books on guerrilla warfare talk about this, and in short:

**Weapons of the first stage:** Are primitive weapons and personal one-man weapons, such as revolvers and light and medium machine guns at the most, light anti-tank weapons such as the R.P.G. and its equivalents, hand grenades, as well as home-made and military explosives.

**Weapons of the second stage:** Include the medium and heavy machine guns, which require more than one person [to operate them], or they are mounted on vehicles, some medium artillery, especially mortar, and also various kinds of mines. Also, some short-range ground-to-ground missiles which are easy to carry, in addition to explosives which, at this stage, are used by engineer units specialized in the use of explosives and mines.

**The third stage:** Includes the rest of the Army's weapons of all other categories, after the disbanded regular military troops enter the revolution and confrontation on the guerrillas' side.

Now, in view of this introduction, the present situation and according to the Global Islamic Resistance theory, its political and military goals, we find ourselves currently at the first stage. What we need now, and for a long time ahead, are weapons suitable for the Resistance and the jihadi guerrillas during the first stage. [This is true] especially for the popular and simple Global Islamic Resistance Units, which lead a war of attrition against American forces, her foreign allies and local agents, as explained in the second (political) and third (military) section. In areas where we are compelled to confront the enemy through semi-overt operations, as is happening now in Iraq and Afghanistan, and tribal areas in Sarhad, we are required to develop weapons of the second stage.

However, in light of the current strategy of the enemy, which is dominating the air, ground and sea, and in light of our strategy which follows from this, and the fact that we are compelled to enter what is called guerrilla war or the war of the oppressed, our training needs are summarized in two headings:

**1. Relying on the methods of secret training in houses and small mobile training camps**

**2. Limiting the training primarily to weapons of the first stage, and weapons of the second stage in some arenas suitable for this, such as Afghanistan, Iraq and similar arenas.**

The details on this are given in the following paragraph:

## Training of the Global Islamic Resistance Units: Methods and Weapons:

Our theory on training is based on the following building blocks:
1. Focusing on mental and ideological preparation, and developing the desire to fight and moral strength.
2. Focusing on understanding the theory of jihadi guerrilla warfare, or what is called the war of the oppressed.
3. Spreading the ideological, theoretical and military training programmes across the Islamic Nation by various means.
4. Relying on the methods of secret training in houses and in limited, mobile training camps.
5. Developing fighting competence through jihadi action and through participation in battle.

Let us shed some light upon the details of the aspects of this strategy on preparation and training.

As for the subject of doctrinal preparation, one has to establish firmly the principles of the Islamic doctrine in general, and the jihadi doctrine in particular, as a fundament for the Resistance's operations. The goal is to create the ideological Resistance fighter, and to increase the heat of the general climate in the Islamic Nation, to the level of jihad and revolution against the oppressors and their servants. This has been elaborated upon in many sections of this series.

Here, I will only point out that this must be done with a programmatic method. It must be done through efforts by every Unit, whether big or small, under the supervision of its Emir. The Unit's elements and cadre must be trained in a programmatic manner. For this, they must be provided with the necessary studies, books and readings, according to the level of their understanding and ability to comprehend.

In the present series of letters[12] on the Resistance Call a considerable number of programmatic principles were provided. In addition, I recommend most of the writings of our Martyr Imam Abdallah Azzam, God's mercy upon him, who has left a great heritage, the scope of which remains unknown until now. I also recommend utilizing the books of the Islamic library, both from the heritage as well as the contemporary ones. This will help to strengthen the will to fight and to instigate jihad. It also provides insight and knowledge, as I have previously referred to in the letter. Comprehensive Theory of Education.

It is also necessary to focus on understanding the theory of guerrilla warfare in general, and the basis for jihadi guerrilla warfare in particular. This can be done through the programmatic manuals (*mudhakkarat manhajiyyah*) (I will try to provide summaries of them) attached to this series of letters, God willing. Also, it can be done through the military office and reference works which talk about that. Previously, during the two periods of Afghani jihad, I recorded a series of my lectures on this art. It is a summary of numerous books and readings, granted by God, and I summarized them in those lectures. Due to their importance I will mention them here. They include:
- 'Lessons in Guerrilla Warfare', two cassette tapes of three hours.
- 'Management and Organization of Guerrilla Warfare', six cassette tapes, about nine hours.
- Then, a study and an extended highly important course, entitled: 'Explaining the Book 'War of the Oppressed',' and it is among

---

12    [Translator's footnote:] *The Global Islamic Resistance Call* has also been issued in many smaller publications, which al-Suri refers to as 'letters' (*rasa'il*).

the most important translated books on guerrilla warfare. I have explained it in 36 cassette tapes, lasting maybe about 25 hours... I will try, if God the Supreme grants me success, and I am still alive, to devote myself to transforming these audio-recordings into a book with the title 'The Basis for Jihadi Guerrilla Warfare in Light of the Contemporary American Campaigns'. If I am not able to do that, I wish that God grants success to whoever is capable, of transcribing the audiotapes with their formulation as they are, in written form. He who undertakes this task must be extremely accurate in order to preserve their content without any additions or attachments... I ask God that they [i.e. the audiotaped lectures] will be useful and that he will reward me for them. This art is very important among the military sciences, and overall in the Arabic library there are few who have written on this theme. In the jihadi and Islamic library I do not know of any important writings on this, or to be exact, I have not come across any such books even though I have searched for them... I hope that I have filled an important gap through these lectures and the books emanating from them, with God's help.

As for this section, we note that one of the most important fundaments for training in our jihadi Resistance Call is to spread the culture of preparation and training, its programmes and methods, with all their aspects, by all methods of distribution, especially the Internet, the distribution of electronic discs, direct correspondence, recordings, and every other method.

### Training methods of the Resistance Units in light of the American campaigns:

*I think that for a long time... it will not be possible, God knows, to establish overt camps similar to those we established in the last decade. The security conditions have profoundly changed. Moreover, the camps and the fronts, no matter how much they expand, will not be able to absorb the billion-sized Islamic Nation and her Mujahidun youth who will soon amount to millions, God willing. It is not possible to make room for them in camps. And it is necessary for Resistance Units to completely preserve*

*their secrecy and the secrecy of all their movements, including their train-
ing and preparation. Thus, this is the opposite of the training theory one
had in jihadi circles during the last two decades, which was based upon
calling the Islamic Nation to the camps.*
*In our Resistance Call, the training theory is based upon moving the camps
inside the Islamic Nation.*

§§

It is necessary to move the training to every house, every quarter,
and every village of the Muslim countries... This is done by spreading the programmes and their details, especially the military ones...
complete lessons on weapons use and on combat tactics in a military
operation, to the youth and men of the Islamic Nation, and even to
her women and children.
The matter is very logical; it is not possible to gather the Islamic
Nation in training camps, but it is possible to plant training camps
across the Islamic Nation, in all her houses and quarters.

§§

Thus, if we wanted to realize our slogan in the confrontation: 'The
Resistance is the Islamic Nation's Battle and not a Struggle by the
Elite',[13] then, *it is necessary to use the methods of training in houses and
in mobile, restricted camps as we have said above. During the stage of attrition, and of confusing the enemy with terror, the weapons of the popular
Resistance and urban jihadi guerrilla warfare are simple... revolver...
machine gun... hand grenade... rocket launcher... explosives... these are
simple weapons and the training on them is very simple. Whoever has
previous knowledge about these weapons and who received some training
on them must train those around him, and the programs that have been
published and simplified will contribute greatly to this [training].*

---

13    [Translator's footnote:] al-Suri is not entirely consistent with regards to
      the exact wording of the slogan. See, for example, p. 1393.

- \* However, one must be extremely cautious in the field of explosives. The training in houses on explosives must be limited to theory only. One must go outside populated areas when dealing with its components, even the simple ones, in order to avoid losses caused by accidents, and the security exposure that comes on top of it.
- As for shooting practices, this must be done by creating necessary areas and suitable conditions in caves... and uninhabited mountains... vast forests... deserts... etc., taking great security precautions and putting warning posts at large distances from the area.
- The reliance on this method has become very urgent in the post-September world. In reality, I became aware of this matter some time before that [i.e. 9/11], and I tried to spread these observations among the Arab Mujahidun in Afghanistan during the days of the Taleban, after cruise missiles had targeted Al Qaida's training camps in Afghanistan in the summer of 1998. I noticed the precise targeting, and the intensity of the shooting, when 75 cruise missiles hit the targets in a few minutes, when America was able to put one missile in every room in the camps... I talked to many of our brothers at that time, saying that after this event, the era of fixed camps had ended, and that we had to rely on the methods of training in houses and 'camps of nomadic Mujahidun' as I called them... Houses made of wood[14], two cars, a number of individuals, a camp in the desert and the wasteland. The training programme is implemented and they leave... Another group arrives at another place, and so on... However, the Arab circles were relying on the methods of propaganda, mobilization and calling upon the Islamic Nation to go to the camps, not paying any attention to the era of satellites and long-range targeting... The command of Allah is a decree determined [Al-Ahzab, 33:38]. Now, I see that the spread of knowledge of war experiences and its weapons is making everyone convinced

---

14   [Translator's footnote:] it says *sha'r* (hair), but it should probably be *shajar* (wood).

of the need to search for means to alternative means. I do not see any other alternatives than secret warfare in everything from study, training and execution... as long as the modern American technology controls the space and the skies... At the end of this letter[15] I will present an 'idea for a programme for this kind of training in sessions in secret houses and in the training camps of the nomadic Mujahidun.'

- As for the development of fighting skills through direct action and joining the battle, we have seen its benefits in practice, through the jihadi experiences that have taken place in some Arab and Islamic countries, among them the Syrian experience, and also the Afghan experience. The first Mujahidun units of The Fighting Vanguard of the Muslim Brotherhood in Syria relied on the following method for training in houses and implementation on the battlefield, as follows:

- The organization was divided into one group of secret, non-disclosed members that were not wanted fugitives, and another group of wanted personnel that were hiding in urban bases hidden in houses.

- The secret, non-disclosed division was carrying out surveillance, information-gathering, fundraising and recruitment, as well as some auxiliary operations.

- The exposed members were carrying out basic military operations, most of them were assassinations or limited ambushes on security patrols, or attacks on some government centers and the intelligence services.

- The training inside houses consisted of disassembling and assembling simple weapons, mostly revolvers, and light machine guns, especially Kalashnikovs, in addition to hand grenades. Some limited shooting practices were carried out, usually in gardens and isolated areas. The training was supervised by those who had

---

15   [Translator's footnote:] *The Global Islamic Resistance Call* has also been issued in many smaller publications, which al-Suri refers to as 'letters' (*rasa'il*).

previous experience which they had received during training with the Palestinian organizations, especially the camps of the Islamic groups, in 1969. Or, the supervisors had served in one of the governmental military agencies.

- Untrained members would participate in the first operation as an observer only, witnessing its execution among the public. During the second stage they would be armed and participate as an auxiliary element, not intervening unless necessary. During the third stage, they enter to execute the operation, supported by trained senior members. After this stage, they would perform both training and participation on the battle field.

- In this way, the expertise is developed through battle. After this, some of the members were sent to receive training in Iraq, starting in 1981, and they returned to introduce some medium weapons such as machine guns, anti-tank rockets, light mortars and explosives.

- Some of the training camps were active even shortly before the onset of jihad, through the scout camps, under cover of youth rover trips, where they were trained in physical skills and military tactics without weapons. There was training on the use of weapons in a few cases... This method educated excellent cadre which led to good performance. The basic factor for this was the very strong will to fight and the moral preparation. I have heard about experiences similar to this one. There was training in houses and shooting practices in local camps in isolated areas, in Egypt, Libya, Algeria, Morocco and other places...

- As for the Afghan experience, it was based upon subjecting the elements [i.e. trainees] to good training courses before they were transferred to the front. However, I saw many cases of training lessons during the battle, and the mixture of training and real fighting, and those were excellent experiences. Once, I witnessed a lesson on the use of mortars which took place directly on the front during the jihad against the Russians and the Communists... The trainer (Abu Hamam al-Misri) – God's mercy upon him – gave us theoretical lessons on artillery for two days. Then, it was implemented in practice, with live shooting at enemy targets, whereupon those targets responded by a similar bombardment... In the course of three or four days, the trainees were living in a live environment which was excellent for training and fighting at the same time.

Practical training in the field during battle is possible and effective. It has a particular fragrance and a whole different effectiveness, provided that experienced personnel are present to supervise the training... I repeat again that I have seen in practice through my work as a trainer during our presence in Iraq and Jordan at the time of the jihad against the tyrannical regime in Syria, during the first and second Afghan experiences, and also in some other limited experiences... that the basis when educating a fighter is the desire to fight and the moral training. As for the military training, it is fundamental and necessary, but it is possible to conduct it even by the simplest means and under the simplest conditions, and by joining operational activity, which compels the training to become effective. It is enough to [refer to] the words of God the Almighty: **'And those who strive in Our (cause),- We will certainly guide them to our Paths: For verily Allah is with those who do right.'** [Al-Ankaboot 29:69]. The basis for jihad is the support of God the Almighty and Supreme, and the success and help granted by Him in training and action likewise... And the fundament is the will. **'And if they had wished to go forth... they would assuredly have made ready some equipment'.**[Al-Tawbah 9:46]

### A BRIEF IDEA FOR TRAINING PROGRAMMES IN
### HOUSES AND SECRET MOBILE CAMPS:

With God's help, we will try to attach to the letters[16] of the Resistance a military attachment with programmes on detailed lessons in

---

16    [Translator's footnote:] *The Global Islamic Resistance Call* has also been

some of the military sciences necessary for guerrilla warfare, especially urban and secret, which is the basis for the operational activity of the Resistance Units in the current period. The programme covers training in light weapons, proficiency in shooting with these weapons, explosive sciences, and related [sciences] such as electricity and electronics... and some tactics of urban guerrilla warfare, God willing.

Here, however, I point to a light programme which can be implemented by the simplest cells that have the determination to [participate in] the Resistance, under the most difficult circumstances of security and secrecy. This programme includes the broad lines of training, and contains the following:

- Subjecting the individual himself and those with him to an intensive physical training programme, through joining a sports club in one of the following violent sports: Wrestling, karate, judo... boxing... etc... or through joining a personal daily training programme which includes long-distance and long-time running, and bodily movements which provide a high [level of] fitness.
- Lessons on how to disassemble and assemble revolvers and machine guns, available through numerous manuals which explain their properties, specialties, how to handle them and shoot with them.
- Starting to shoot with hunting weapons which use compressed air to hunt for sparrows and birds. These rifles and guns, which use small lead bullets, are widely available.
- A theoretical study on how to use hand grenades, through studying manuals, and training on how to throw them by throwing something similar, such as rocks of the same size and weight.
- A theoretical study on how to use explosives, their properties, how to store and handle them. Training the elements [i.e. the

---

issued in many smaller publications, which al-Suri refers to as 'letters' (*rasa'il*).

trainees] using materials similar to the original substances, such as wooden materials, ropes and plastic models, without employing the original substance, and using electrical cords to explain the ways to connect, and 'lamps' and small light bulbs instead of detonators. We have already tried this method in practice, and it was a complete success. The theoretical course on explosives is made up of about 40 hours of lessons on wooden and plastic models until [the trainee] is proficient in using explosives and the only thing that remains is the implementation in a proper place, with very small bombs.

- Proficiency in using wireless communication devices, and studying a manual on the security of their use, and avoiding using them in private houses, but only in open air, and for training periods of no more than half a minute so that they are not tapped, and having conversations similar to those of the government agencies.
- Theoretical studies which include the following military and tactical subjects, through the manuals that are available today on the Internet and similar, and the most important of these manuals are:
- Manuals on light and medium weapons.
- Manuals on the science of explosive engineering.
- Manuals on the science of military topography.
- Manuals on the science of wireless communications and on encoding.
- Manuals on security and movement, secret action, hiding and fleeing from security pursuits, and target reconnaissance
- Manuals on the science of electricity and electronics, and related sciences which support the science of explosive engineering.
- Manuals on assembling and manufacturing explosives *(provided that the implementation is supervised by a specialist in chemistry, and that it takes place in areas far from people, and with very small amounts).*

- Manuals on combat tactics, such as: − Tactics of urban warfare − Mountain warfare − Forest warfare − Guerrilla warfare − Tactics of the regular armies and ways to confront them... etc..
- Manuals on secret organizational conduct, setting appointments, sending and receiving messages secretly... etc...

*This military culture is very important and it is possible to provide it on computer discs, transfer it, to benefit from it and to educate the trainees in an intensive programme, and to run many useful practical exercises in houses or in sport and scout camps, and the similar. Hence, the only remaining need is to practice shooting and the use of explosives. This is done by searching for a proper place, and performing this at a specific time, either in mobile secret training camps, or through whatever is available... It is very important to pay attention to security of movement when carrying out this training. God is the provider of success.*

# BIBLIOGRAPHY AND SOURCES

JIHADI ONLINE SOURCES IN ARABIC

(All documents, videofiles, and audiofiles in this section are stored electronically with author).

ABU MUSʿAB PUBLICATIONS—COMPILATIONS[1]

'The Shaykh's Audiovisual Publications', (in Arabic), 683 MB.

'The Shaykh's Audio Publications' (in Arabic), 486 MB.

'The Shaykh's Written Publications' (in Arabic), 61 MB

ABU MUSʿAB'S LECTURES, SPEECHES AND INTERVIEWS

'The Management and Organisation of Guerrilla Warfare by Shaykh Umar Abd al-Hakim' (in Arabic), transcript of lectures given in Khowst, Afghanistan, 1998.[2]

'Explanation of the Book "War of the Oppressed"', (in Arabic), transcript of lectures given in Khowst, Afghanistan, 1998.[3]

---

1     Available from multiple websites, including www.mjotd.com/Library/books. rar; www.mjotd.com/Library/sounds.rar; and www.mjotd.com/Library/ video.rar, accessed via *minbar suria al-islami*, 30 Nov. 2005, www.islam-syria.com/vb/showthread.php?t=1804&highlight=%DA%C8%CF%C7%E 1%CA%E6%C7%C8+%C7%E1%D4%C7%E3%ED, accessed Dec. 2005.

2     Consists of six tapes, four of which are transcribed. Posted on *muntadayat al-firdaws al-jihadiyyah*, 21 Sept. 2006, www.alfirdaws.org/vb/showthread. php?t=16892&highlight=%E3%D5%DA%C8+%C7%E1%D3%E6%D1 %ED, accessed Oct. 2006.

3     Consists of thirty-two tapes, four of which are transcribed. Posted on *muntadayat al-firdaws al-jihadiyyah*, 21 Sept. 2006, www.alfirdaws.org/vb/ showthread.php?t=16892&highlight=%E3%D5%DA%C8+%C7%E1%D 3%E6%D1%ED, accessed Oct. 2006.

'Lessons in Guerrilla Warfare Theories' (in Arabic), transcript of lectures given in Jalalabad, Afghanistan, 1999.[4]

'Meeting with the Kuwaiti Newspaper (*al-Ra'y al-Amm*)' (in Arabic). An interview with the journalist Majid al-Ali in Kabul, Afghanistan, 18 March 1999. Transcripts.[5]

## ABU MUS'AB AL-SURI'S BOOKS AND BOOKLETS

Umar Abd al-Hakim, *The Islamic Jihadi Revolution in Syria: Part I. The Experience and Lessons (Hopes and Pains)* (in Arabic) (Peshawar: publisher unknown, May 1991).[6]

Umar Abd al-Hakim, *The Islamic Jihadi Revolution in Syria: Part II. Ideology and Program* (Studies and Basics in the Path of Armed Revolutionary Jihad) (in Arabic) (Peshawar: publisher unknown, May 1991).[7]

Umar Abd al-Hakim, *Observations on the Jihadi Experience in Syria* (in Arabic) (Peshawar (?), undated but probably May 1991).[8]

---

4   Consists of four tapes. Posted on *muntadayat al-firdaws al-jihadiyyah*, 21 Sept. 2006, www.alfirdaws.org/vb/showthread.php?t=16892&highlight= %E3%D5%DA%C8+%C7%E1%D3%E6%D1%ED, accessed Oct. 2006.

5   Transcripts made by Iman Lotfi at the request of this author. They consist of ten audiofiles and were posted on *muntadayat minbar suria al-islami*, 4 Nov. 2005, accessed 5 Nov. 2005 at www.islam-syria.com/vb/showthread. php?t=1601. Also published on other jihadi web forums, such as *multaqa al-mujahidin*, 3 Nov. 2005, www.mojahedon.com/vb/showthread.php?t =3214&highlight=%E3%D5%DA%C8+%C7%E1%D3%E6%D1%ED, accessed 22 Nov. 2005; and 'Meeting between the Kuwaiti newspaper al-Ra'y al-Amm and Abu Mus'ab al-Suri', (in Arabic), *muntadayat al-firdaws al-jihadiyyah*, 13 Nov. 2005, posted by 'muthabir' (in Arabic), http:// alfirdaws.org/forums/showthread.php?t=8079&highlight=%E3%D5%D A%C8+%C7%E1%D3%E6%D1%ED, accessed 22 Nov. 2005.

6   Accessed June 2006 at *muntada al-tajdid*, 31 May 2006, www.tajdeed.org. uk/forums/showthread.php?s=6548b36708e3c3eff8db8327623a51e8&thr eadid=41941.

7   Posted on *muntada al-tajdid*, 31 May 2006, accessed June 2006 at www. tajdeed.org.uk/forums/showthread.php?s=6548b36708e3c3eff8db832762 3a51e8&threadid=41941.

8   This publication appears to be an excerpt from Umar Abd al-Hakim, *The*

Umar Abd al-Hakim (Abu Mus'ab al-Suri), *Afghanistan, the Taleban and the Battle of Islam Today* (in Arabic), (Kabul: The al-Ghuraba Center for Islamic Studies, 11 October 1998, Issues for the Triumphant in Righteousness Series no.1).

Umar Abd al-Hakim (Abu Mus'ab al-Suri), *The Responsibility of the People of Yemen towards the Holy Places of Muslims and their Wealth* (in Arabic) (Kabul: The al-Ghuraba Center for Islamic Studies, October 1999, Issues for the Triumphant in Righteousness Series no.2).

Umar Abd al-Hakim (Abu Mus'ab al-Suri), *The Muslims in Central Asia and the Comming Battle of Islam* (in Arabic) (kabul: The al-Ghuraba Center for Islamic Studies, 5 November 1999, The Series Issues for the Triumphant in Righteousness Series no.3).

Umar Abd al-Hakim (Abu Mus'ab al-Suri), *The Sunni People in the Levant Confronting the Nusayris, the Crusaders and the Jews* (in Arabic) (Kabul: The al-Ghuraba Center for Islamic Studies, 22 June 2000, Issues for the Triumphant in Righteousness Series no.4).

Umar Abd al-Hakim (Abu Mus'ab al-Suri), *The Testimony of the Leaders of the Mujahidun and the Reform [Current] about the Sultan's Clerics in the Land of the Two Holy Places, Called Saudi Arabia: A Reading and Commentary of the Letters and Communiques by Shaykh Osama bin Laden and Doctor Saad al-Faqih to Shaykh bin Baz, Shaykh bin Uthaymin and the Clerics of the Land of the Two Holy Places* (in Arabic) (Kabul: al-Ghuraba Center for Islamic Studies and Media, 31 January 2001, Issues for the Triumphant in Righteousness Series, no.5).

Umar Abd al-Hakim (Abu Mus'ab al-Suri), *A Summary of My Testimony on the Jihad in Algeria, 1988-1996* (in Arabic) (Place and publisher unknown, 1 June 2004, Issues for the Triumphant in Righteousness Series no.6).

*Islamic Jihadi Revolution in Syria: Part I. The Experience and Lessons (Hopes and Pains)* (in Arabic) (Peshawar: publisher unknown, May 1991).

Al-Shaykh. Abu Mus'ab al-Suri Umar Abd al-Hakim, *Musharraf's Pakistan: The Problem and the Solution ..! A Necessary Obligation* (in Arabic) (Place and publisher unknown, October 2004).

Umar Abd al-Hakim (Abu Mus'ab al-Suri), *The Global Islamic Resistance Call. Part I: The Roots, History, and Experiences* (in Arabic) (Place and publisher unknown, December 2004).

Umar Abd al-Hakim (Abu Mus'ab al-Suri), *The Global Islamic Resistance Call. Part II: The Call, Program and Method* (in Arabic) (Place and publisher unknown, December 2004).

## SELECTED COMMUNIQUES AND ARTICLES

Abu Mus'ab al-Suri, 'The Ideological-Programmatic Gap in the Contemporary Jihadi Current: A Dangerous Fissure which has to be Mended', (in Arabic) *majallat qadaya zhahirin 'ala al-haqq* no.2 (Dhu'l-Hijja 1421 or late February/early March 2001), published in Kabul by the al-Ghuraba Center for Islamic Studies.[9]

'Communique from the Office of Abu Mus'ab al-Suri in Response to the US Department of State's Announcement' (in Arabic), 22 December 2004.[10]

'The Testament of Shaykh Abu Mus'ab al-Suri which He Requests be Fulfilled in Case of his Capture or Martyrdom' (in Arabic). Undated.[11]

---

9 The article was later posted on *minbar al-tawhid wa'l-jihad*, which has been the most important salafi-jihadi Internet library resource of the last few years: www.tawhed.ws/r?i=3702, accessed June 2006.

10 Published on Abu Mus'ab al-Suri's website, www.deluxesuperhost. com/~morshid/tophacker/index.php?subject=18rec=29, accessed Jan. 2005. It has also circulated on numberous jihadi web forums and has been published in the online jihad journal *majallat risalat al-mujahidin*, no.3, pp.4-13.

11 Posted on *muntada al-tajdid*, 5 Oct. 2005, www.tajdeed.org.uk/forums/showthread.php?s=240e1a4cc709589d5bc8bcd7a52d0c7d&threadid=38747, accessed Oct. 2005. Also published on other jihadi web forums. See, for example, *multaqa al-mujahidin*, 4 Nov. 2005, posting by "Ashiq al-Shahad' – the administrator of the section for latest news, new events and happenings', www.mojahedon.com/vb/showthread.php?t=3240&hig

Umar Abd al-Hakim (Abu Mus'ab al-Suri), 'Message to the British and the Europeans – Its People and Governments – regarding the London Explosions, July 2005' (in Arabic), August 2005.[12]
'Text of Audio Communique by Shaykh Umar Abd al-Hakim (Abu Mus'ab al-Suri) Addressing the British and the Europeans regarding the London Explosions, and the Practices of the British Government' (in Arabic), August 2005.[13]
Abu Mus'ab al-Suri, 'A Call to the Mujahidun Youth and the Jihadi Groups in the Islamic World' (in Arabic), undated article.[14]

hlight=%E3%D5%DA%C8+%C7%E1%D3%E6%D1%ED; *muntadayat bayt al-muqaddas al-islamiyyah*, 4 Nov. 2005, www.baytalmaqdes.com/vb/showthread.php?t=1349; *muntada al-safnet*, 4 Nov. 2005, www.al-saf.net/vb/showthread.php?t=18330&highlight=%E3%D5%DA%C8+%C7%E1%D3%E6%D1%ED; and *muntadayat shabakat al-hisbah*, 11 Aug. 2005, posted by 'Abu Asyad al-Faluji' on www.alhesbah.com/v/showthread.php?t=29409, all accessed Dec. 2005.

12 Published in a zipped pdf-file dated 21 Aug. 2005, headed on all pages: 'The Global Islamic Resistance no.2. 15/7/1426 [20 Aug. 2005]', signed, dated Aug. 2005, available on various jihadi web forums, including *muntada minbar suria al-islami*, 30 Nov. 2005, www.islam-syria.com/vb/showthread.php?t=1804&highlight=%DA%C8%CF%C7%E1%CA%E6%C7%C8+%C7%E1%D4%C7%E3%ED, accessed 5 Dec. 2005; and *muntadayat shabakat al-hisbah* 1 Dec. 2005, www.alhesbah.com/v/showthread.php?t=29409, accessed 5 Dec. 2005.

13 Published in a zipped pdf-file on 21 Aug. 2005, available on various jihadi web forums, including *muntada minbar suria al-islami*, 30 Nov. 2005, www.islam-syria.com/vb/showthread.php?t=1804&highlight=%DA%C8%CF%C7%E1%CA%E6%C7%C8+%C7%E1%D4%C7%E3%ED, accessed 5 Dec. 2005; and *muntadayat shabakat al-hisbah*, 1 Dec. 2005, www.alhesbah.com/v/showthread.php?t=29409, accessed 5 Dec. 2005.

14 The article appears to be an excerpt from his book *The Sunni People in the Levant Confronting the Nusayris, the Crusaders and the Jews* (2000). The article was also published in the online jihadi journal *majallat risalat al-mujahidin*, no.3, pp.18-19 and posted on many jihadi websites, including *muntadayat al-nusrah*, 14 Feb. 2006, at www.alnusra.net/vb/showthread.php?t=433&highlight=%C3%C8%E6+%E3%D5%DA%C8+%C7%E1%D3%E6%D1%ED, accessed Feb. 2006.

## MISCELLANEOUS

'Biography of Shaykh Umar Abd al-Hakim (Abu Mus'ab al-Suri)' (in Arabic), *Abu Mus'ab al-Suri's website*, undated.[15]

'The Abu Mus'ab al-Suri File: Broad Lines in the Life of Shaykh Abu Mus'ab al-Suri and his Jihadi History' (in Arabic), *minbar al-tawhid wa'l-jihad*, www.tawhed.ws/a?I=78, accessed 15 July 2005.

Abd al-Tawam al-Shami, 'Communique on the Arrest of Shaykh Abu Mus'ab al-Suri', (in Arabic), dated Shawwal 1426 (c. November 2005).[16]

*Journal of Issues for the Triumphant in Righteousness* [*majallat qadaya al-zahirin 'ala al-haqq*] (Ramadan 1421 / December 2000) no.1, jihadi journal published by The al-Ghuraba Center for Islamic Studies in Kabul).

*Journal of Issues for the Triumphant in Righteousness* [*majallat qadaya al-zahirin 'ala al-haqq*] (Dhu'l-hujja 1421 / March 2001) no.2, jihadi journal published by The al-Ghuraba Center for Islamic Studies in Kabul).

*The al-Ansar Newsletter* [*nashrat al-ansar*], nos1-164, selected issues. A jihadi journal published by GIA supporters in London between 1993 and 1998.

### ABU MUS'AB AL-SURI'S OFFICIAL AND UNOFFICIAL WEBSITES

The Website of the Library of Shaykh Umar Abd al-Hakim Abu Mus'ab al-Suri: *Your Guide to Jihad* (or abbreviated here as Abu Mus'ab al-Suri's website) has been located at various websites since January 2005, including:

---

15   Accessed 11 April 2005 at www.deluxesuperhost.com/~morshid/ tophacker/index.php?subject=4&rec=22&tit=tit&pa=0.

16   Communique is signed by Abd al-Tawam al-Shami, [elsewhere presented as 'director of Abu Mus'ab al-Suri's library'], available on various jihadi web forums, including *muntada minbar suria al-islami*, 30 Nov. 2005, www. islam-syria.com/vb/showthread.php?t=1804&highlight=%DA%C8%CF %C7%E1%CA%E6%C7%C8+%C7%E1%D4%C7%E3%ED, accessed 5 Dec. 2005. Also available at *muntadayat shabakat al-hisbah*, 1 Dec. 2005, www.alhesbah.com/v/showthread.php?t=29409, accessed 5 Dec. 2005.

http://abumusab.cjb.net/

http://www.deluxesuperhost.com/~morshid/tophacker

http://www.alerhaab.com

http://carriagehouseglass.com/peepingcam/peeping/

http://www.fsboa.com/vw/index.php

http://www.mjotd.com/Library/

http://www.so86a.jeeran.com, and http://so86a.jeeran.com/ (May 2006
- February 2007)[17]


SELECTED LIST OF RELEVANT JIHADI WEBSITES, 2005-7

*suria al-muslimah: mawqi' ahl al-sunna wa'l-jama'a fi bilad al-sham*,
http://syreah.1ksa.com/_.htm

*muntada al-ansar al-islami*, www.ansarnet.ws/vb/forumdisplay.php?f=3;
www.web4host.biz/vb/index.php?; www.inn4news.net/inn/; www.
ansary.info/forums/ etc.[18]

*muntadayat shabakat al-hisbah*, www.alhesbah.com/v/

*muntadayat al-firdaws al-jihadiyyah*, http://alfirdaws.org/forums/, www.
alfirdaws.org/vb/

*mawqi' al-qal'ah al-'arabi*, www.al-qal3ah.com/vb/, www.al-qal3ah.
net/vb/index.php,

*muntada minbar suria al-islami*, www.islam-syria.com/vb/index.php?

*muntada al-safinet*, www.al-saf.net/vb/index.php?

---

17    The website was entitled *The Library of al-Shaykh (Abu Mus'ab al-Suri)
      Umar Abd al-Hakim Sitt Maryam* (in Arabic), and contained most of al-
      Suri's written, audio- and audio-visual production, including his statements
      concerning the London attacks.

18    See, for example, posting by Abu Layli al-Bokhari, dated 24 July 2005, at
      www.ansary.info/forums/showthread.php?t=24&highlight=%E3%D5%D
      A%C8+%C7%E1%D3%E6%D1%ED, accessed 23 Aug. 2005.

*muntadayat bayt al-muqaddas al-islamiyyah,* www.baytalmaqdes.com/vb/index.php?

*TJN Yahoo! Group,* http://groups.yahoo.com/group/TJN.[19]

*Pegey Jihad website (in Kurdish),* http://www.pega7.com/kteb.htm

*multaqa al-mujahidun,* www.mojahedon.com/vb/

*minbar ahl al-hadith wa'l-jama'ah,* www.islam-minbar.net/

*muntadayat al-ummah al-jihadiyyah,* www.alommh.net/forums//index.php

*shabakat al-ikhlas al-islamiyyah,* www.alekhlaas.net/forum

ENGLISH TRANSLATIONS OF EXCERPTS OF AL-SURI'S WRITINGS

'Abu Musab al-Suri and his plan for the Destruction of America', *GlobalTerrorAlert.com* 11 July 2005, www.globalterroralert.com/pdf/0705/abumusabalsuri.pdf, accessed August 2005.

'Abu Musab al-Suri's Final "Message to the British and the Europeans",' *GlobalTerrorAlert.com* 31 December 2005, www.globalterroralert.com/pdf/1205/abumusabeurope.pdf#search='Abu%20Musab%20alSuri', accessed December 2005.

'Call to Jihad Against the Syrian Regime'. Document no.AFGP-2002-600966, *Combating Terrorism Center website* (West Point), www.ctc.usma.edu/aq/AFGP-2002-600966-trans1.pdf (1-6), and www.ctc.usma.edu/aq/AFGP-2002-600966-Original.pdf, accessed April 2006.[20]

---

19   See, for example, message no.497, dated 27 Jan. 2005, sent by an anonymous member with the nickname 'alfalujh'. Message entitled: 'New website for Shaykh Abu Mus'ab al-Suri – Umar Abd al-Hakim and a Communique where he responds to the American Administration' (in Arabic).

20   This is an English translation of a longer (82 page) version of Umar Abd al-Hakim (Abu Mus'ab al-Suri), *The Sunni People in the Levant Confronting the Nusayris, the Crusaders and the Jews* (in Arabic) (Kabul: al-Ghuraba Center for Islamic Studies, 22 June 2000, The Series Issues for the Triumphant in Righteousness no.4. The version published on al-Suri's website is shorter, only 68pp.

'Lessons Learned from the Jihad Ordeal in Syria'. Document no.AFGP-2002-600080. *Combating Terrorism Center website* (West Point), www.ctc.usma.edu/aq/AFGP-2002-600080-Trans.pdf and www.ctc.usma.edu/aq/AFGP-2002-600080-Orig.pdf, accessed April 2006.

## COURT AND POLICE DOCUMENTS

Ministracion de Justicia, 'Juzgado Central de Instruccion no.005, Madrid, Sumario (Proc.Ordinario) 0000035 /2001 E', dated 17 September 2003, [indictment against the Abu Dahdah network], available at http://news.lp.findlaw.com/hdocs/docs/terrorism/espbinldn91703cmp.pdf, accessed February 2004.

Audiencia Nacional, Sala de lo Penal, Sección Tercera, 'Sentencia Núm. 36/2005', Madrid, 26 september 2005, [verdict against the Abu Dahdah network], available at http://estaticos.elmundo.es/documentos/2005/09/26/sentencia.pdf, accessed July 2006.

Audiencia Nacional, Juzgado Central de Instrucción no.6, 'Sumario no.20/2004', [Indictment against the M-11 bombers], Madrid, 10 April 2006, available at www.fondodocumental.com/11M/documentos/Autos/auto1.doc and www.fondodocumental.com/11M/documentos/Autos/auto2.doc, accessed July 2006.

Comisaría General de Información/Dirección General de la Policía/Unidad Central de Inteligencia, *Operaciones de la C. G. I. contra el terrorismo integrista islámico entre 1996/2004* (Police report, Madrid, April 2004, 75pp.).

Testimony of Jamal Ahmed Mohammed Al-Fadl, United States of America v. Osama Bin Laden, et al. Defendants, transcript of trial, 6 February 2006, Day 2, http://cryptome.org/usa-v-ubl-02.htm, accessed July 2006

Testimony of Jamal Ahmed Mohammed Al-Fadl, United States of America v. Osama Bin Laden et al. Defendants, transcript of trial, 7 February 2001, Day 3, http://cryptome.org/usa-v-ubl-03.htm, accessed July 2006

Testimony of Jamal Ahmed Mohammed Al-Fadl, United States of America *v.* Osama Bin Laden *et al.* Defendants, transcript of trial, 13 February 2001, Day 4, http://cryptome.org/usa-v-ubl-04.htm, accessed July 2006.

Testimony by L'Houssaine Kherchtou, United States of America *v.* Osama Bin Laden, *et al.* Defendants, transcript of trial, 21 February 2006, Day 8, http://cryptome.org/usa-v-ubl-08.htm, accessed July 2006.

United States of America *v.* Osama bin Laden, Kenyan Embassy Bombing, United States District Court, Southern District of New York, Indictment S(9) 98 Cr. 1023 (LBS), www.terrorismcentral.com/Library/Incidents/USEmbassyKenyaBombing/Indictment/Count1.html, accessed July 2006.

United States of America *v.* Osama bin Laden, et al. Defendants (Kenyan Embassy Bombing), United States District Court, Southern District of New York, S(7) 98 Cr. 1023, transcript of Day 59 of the trial, 5 June 2001, http://cryptome.sabotage.org/usa-v-ubl-59.htm, accessed July 2006.

### AL-QAIDA DOCUMENTS REPORTEDLY UNCOVERED IN AFGHANISTAN

Emailed Letter from Abu Mus'ab al-Suri and Abu Khalid al-Suri to Osama bin Laden, Kabul, Afghanistan, dated 19 July 1998, and sent via Ayman al-Zawahiri. (A 7pp.English translation of a document recovered from a computer reportedly used by al-Zawahiri in Kabul. Courtesy: Andrew Higgins and Alan Cullison.)

Document no.AFGP-2002-002871, 'The Muslims in Central Asia and the Upcoming Battle of Islam: A Special Copy for al-Ghuraba Center'. (Arabic original and translation). Courtesy: Combating Terrorism Center at West Point.

Document no.AFGP-2002-000100, 'Synopsis: This document contains a flyer addressed to all Arab immigrants. The flyer lists the Islamic Emirate officials' names that would assist the Arab immigrants in entering the Emirate', *The Army's Foreign Military Studies Office (FMSO) website*, http://fmso.leavenworth.army. mil/documents-docex/Iraq/AFGP-2002-000100.pdf, accessed 17 March 2006.

Document no.AFGP-2002-602181, 'Political Speculation', *Combating Terrorism Center website* (West Point), www.ctc.usma.edu/aq/ AFGP-2002-602181-Trans.pdf and www.ctc.usma.edu/aq/ AFGP-2002-602181-Original.pdf, accessed April 2006.

Document no.AFGP-2002-601693, 'Status of Jihad', *Combating Terrorism Center website* (West Point), www.ctc.usma.edu/aq/AFGP-2002-601693-Trans.pdf and www.ctc.usma.edu/aq/AFGP-2002-601693-Orig.pdf, accessed April 2006.[21]

Document no.AFGP-2002-601402, 'Condolence Letter', *Combating Terrorism Center website* (West Point), www.ctc.usma.edu/aq/ AFGP-2002-601402-Trans.pdf and www.ctc.usma.edu/aq/ AFGP-2002-601402-Orig.pdf, accessed April 2006.

Document no.AFGP-2002-801138, 'Various Admin Documents and Questions', www.ctc.usma.edu/aq/AFGP-2002-801138-Trans. pdf, and www.ctc.usma.edu/aq/AFGP-2002-801138-Orig.pdf, accessed April 2006.

---

21  The authorship of this document has so far remained a mystery. The Arabic print is partly illegible and the available English translation of the letter is both inaccurate and misleading as to who speaks to whom. Finally, it does not cover the entire document. This author assumes that al-Suri may have been the letter's author, for several reasons. The style and phraseology are similar to his, and the themes discussed were all issues of intense interest for al-Suri. The most revealing detail, however, is the following passage about Abu Qutadah: 'I know this man well and want to expose him to everybody. At the time when everyone was fighting, he was the advisor to the devil. He came to Peshawar after everything was over and started to make fatwas in return for a few dollars from the Saudi Islamic Relief Center.' This is very similar in letter and tone to what al-Suri has written elsewhere about his rival. See especially Umar Abd al-Hakim, *Summary of My Testimony*, p.29.

SELECTED REPORTS BY THE COMISIÓN PARLAMENTARIA
DE INVESTIGACIÓN DEL 11-M

Cortes Generales, Diario de Sesiones del Congreso de Los Diputados, Comisiones de Investigación Sobre el 11 de Marzo de 2004, Sesión núm. 28, celebrada el lunes, 25 de octubre de 2004, http://www.congreso.es/public_oficiales/L8/CONG/DS/CI/CI_015. PDF, accessed August 2006.

'Proyecto de Dictamen de La Comisión de Investigación sobre el 11-M de 2004', 22 June 2005, via www.elpais.es/elpaismedia/ultimahora/media/200506/22/espana/20050622elpepunac_1_P_DOC. doc, accessed July 2006.

Grupo Parlamentario de Izquierda Verde (IU-ICV), 'Propuesta de Conclusiones y Recomendaciones Finales de la Comisión de Investigación del 11-M' (Madrid, 8 June 2005), via http://estaticos.elmundo.es/documentos/2005/06/08/iu_icv.pdf, accessed July 2006.

INTERVIEWS

*Islamists*
Abdallah Anas (Boudjemaa Bounoua), London, 16 September 2006
Abu Rached El Halabi, Aarhus, via telephone, 15 June 2006.
Noman Benotman, London, 15 September 2006.
Saad al-Faqih, head of Movement for Islamic Reform in Arabia, London, via telephone, 17 September 2006.

*Journalists and researchers*
Abdel Bari Atwan, editor-in-chief, *al-Quds al-Arabi*, London, 28 April 2006.
Peter Bergen, New America Foundation, Washington, 1 February 2007.
Paul Cruickshank, Center on Law and Security, New York University, Washington, 1 February 2007.
Rebecca Givner-Forbes, Terrorism Research Center, Arlington, USA, email correspondence, 26 July 2006.

Najib Ghadbian, University of Arkansas, USA, email correspondence, 3 October 2006.

Sajjan M Gohel, Asia Pacific Foundation, London, 15 September 2006.

Esad Heimović, journalist and researcher, email correspondence, 9 October 2006.

Andrew Higgins, *The Wall Street Journal*, email correspondence, 24 October 2006.

Mark Huband, former *Financial Times* reporter, London, 29 April 2006.

Javiér Jordán, professor at the University of Grenada, email correspondence, 18 July 2006.

Fernando Reinares, professor and former counterterrorism adviser to the Spanish government, email correspondence, 10 October 2006.

Michael Scheuer, former chief of the CIA's bin Laden unit in 1996-9, Washington, 14 March 2007. (Interview conducted by my research assistant Hanna Rogan).

Camille Tawil, *al-Hayat* reporter and author, London, 14 September 2006 and 3 January 2007.

Craig Whitlock, Berlin Bureau Chief, *Washington Post*, email correspondence, May 2006 and meeting in Oslo, 14 November 2006.

Aiman Zoubir, journalist, Denmark, 15 September 2006.

*Investigators and counterterrorism analysts*
Interviews with officials in five European countries, names and places withheld on request

### BOOKS AND ARTICLES

Abd-Allah, Dr Umar F., *The Islamic Struggle in Syria* (Berkeley: Mizan Press, 1983).

Al-Tawil, Camille, *The Armed Islamic Battle in Algeria: From "the Salvation Front" to the "Group"* (in Arabic) (Beirut: Dar al-Nahhar li al-Nashr, 1998).

Anonymous, *Through Our Enemies' Eyes: Osama bin Laden, Radical Islam, and the Future of America* (Washington: Brassey's, 2002).

Atwan, Abdel Bari, *The Secret History of al-Qa'ida* (London: Saqi Books, 2006).

Bergen, Peter, *Holy War Inc.: Inside the Secret World of Osama bin Laden* (London: Phoenix/Orion Books, 2002).

Bergen, Peter, *The Osama bin Laden I Know* (New York: Free Press, 2006).

Brisard, Jean-Charles with Damien Martinez, *Zarqawi: The New Face of al-Qaeda* (Cambridge: Polity Press, 2005).

Carré, Olivier and Gérard Michaud, *Les Frères musulmans: Egypte et Syrie 1928-1982* (Paris: Gallimard, 1983).

Cook, David, 'Paradigmatic Jihadi Movements', report (edited by Jarret Brachman and Chris Heffelfinger) published by The Combating Terrorism Center, United States Military Academy, West Point, New York, www.ctc.usma.edu/brachman/CTC-Paradigmatic_Jihadi_Movements-10_06.pdf, accessed October 2006.

Cozzens, Jeffrey, 'Dr Brynjar Lia's "The al-Qaida Strategist Abu Mus'ab al-Suri: A Profile",' *Counterterrorism Blog* 21 April 2006, http://counterterrorismblog.org/2006/04/post_1.php, accessed April 2006.

Cruickshank, Paul, and Mohannad Hage Ali, 'Abu Musab Al Suri: Architect of the New Al Qaeda', *Studies in Conflict and Terrorism* 30 (1) (January 2007), pp.1-14.

Hegghammer, Thomas, *Violent Islamism in Saudi Arabia 1979-2006* (Paris: Institut d'Etudes Politiques de Paris, PhD thesis, submitted July 2007).

Hegghammer, Thomas, 'Abdallah Azzam: L'imam du jihad', Gilles Kepel (ed.), *Al-Qaida dans le texte* (Paris: Presses Universitaires de France, 2005), pp.115-37.

Holtmann, Philipp, *The Jihad Concept of the Al-Qaeda Strategist Abu Mus'ab al-Suri: A Guideline to Global Terror* (Tel Aviv: Department of Middle East and African History, Tel Aviv University, Master of Arts-thesis, submitted October 2006).

Huband, Mark, *Warriors of the Prophet: The Struggle for Islam* (Oxford and Boulder, CO: Westview Press, 1998).

Irujo, José María, *El Agujero: España invadida por la yihad* (Madrid: Aguilar, 2005).

Lia, Brynjar, 'Abu Mus'ab al-Suri: Profile of a Jihadi Leader', Paper presented at *The Changing Faces of Jihadism: Profiles, Biographies, Motivations*, Joint FFI/King's College Conference, London, 27-28 April 2006, see www.mil.no/multimedia/archive/00080/Abu__Musab_al-Suri_-_80483a.pdf.

———, 'The al-Qaida Strategist Abu Mus'ab al-Suri: A Profile'. Paper presented at *Paths to Global Jihad: Radicalisation and Recruitment to Terror Networks*, an FFI-Seminar at Oslo Military Society, 15 March 2006, www.mil.no/multimedia/archive/00076/_The_Al-Qaida_strate_76568a.pdf.

———, 'Al-Suri's Doctrines for Decentralised Jihadi Training: Part 1', *Terrorism Monitor* (Jamestown Foundation) 5 (1) (18 January 2007), http://jamestown.org/terrorism/news/uploads/TM_005_001.pdf

———, 'Al-Suri's Doctrines for Decentralised Jihadi Training: Part 2', *Terrorism Monitor* (Jamestown Foundation) 5 (2) (1 February 2007).

———, 'Al-Qaeda Online: Understanding the jihadist internet infrastructure', *Jane's Intelligence Review* January 2006, www.mil.no/multimedia/archive/00075/Al-Qaeda_online__und_75416a.pdf.

———, *Globalisation and the Future of Terrorism: Patterns and Predictions* (London: Routledge, 2005)

———, *The Society of the Muslim Brothers in Egypt 1928-1942* (Reading: Ithaca Press, 1998).

———, and Thomas Hegghammer, 'Jihadi Strategic Studies: The Alleged Al Qaida Policy Study Preceding the Madrid Bombings, *Studies in Conflict and Terrorism*, 27, 5 (September/October 2004), pp.355-75.

Nasiri, Omar, *Inside the Global Jihad: How I Infiltrated Al Qaeda and Was Abandoned by Western Intelligence* (London: Hurst, 2006).

Nesser, Petter, *Jihad in Europe* (Kjeller: Norwegian Defense Research Est., 2004, FFI-Research Report no.2004/01146), http://rapporter.ffi.no/rapporter/2004/01146.pdf.

———, *The Slaying of the Dutch Filmmaker* (Kjeller: Norwegian Defense Research Est., 2005, FFI-Research Report no.2005/00376), http://rapporter.ffi.no/rapporter/2005/00376.pdf

Martinez, Luis, *The Algerian Civil War 1990-1998* (London: Hurst, 2000).

Mitchell, Ritchard, *The Society of the Muslim Brothers in Egypt* (New York: Oxford University Press, 1969).

Muhammad, Basil, *The Arab Helpers in Afghanistan* (in Arabic) (Riyadh, Jedda: The Islamic Benevolence Committe, Office of Studies and Documentation, 1991, second edn).

Paz, Reuven, 'Global Jihad and WMD: Between Martyrdom and Mass Destruction', in Hillel Fradkin *et al.* (eds) *Current Trends In Islamist Ideology* (Washington: The Hudson Institute, 2005, vol. 2), www.futureofmuslimworld.com/docLib/20060130_Current_Trends_v2.pdf, accessed October 2006, pp.74-86.

Vermaat, Emerson, 'Mustafa Setmarian Nasar: A close friend of Bin Laden's and Al-Zarqawi's', *Militant Islam Monitor website*, 4 December 2005, www.militantislammonitor.org/article/id/1355, accessed July 2006.

Vidino, Lorenzo, 'Suri State of Affairs', *National Review Online*, 21 May 2004, www.nationalreview.com/comment/vidino200405210939.asp, accessed July 2005.

'WANTED: Mustafa Setmariam Nasar', *Reward for Justice website*, www.rewardsforjustice.net/english/wanted_captured/index.cfm?page=Nasar, accessed July 2005.

Whitlock, Craig, 'Architect of New War on the West: Writings Lay Out Post-9/11 Strategy of Isolated Cells Joined in Jihad', *Washington Post*, 23 May 2006, p.A01.

Wiktorowicz, Quintan, 'The Centrifugal Tendencies in the Algerian Civil War', *Arab Studies Quarterly*, 23 (3) (Summer 2001), pp.65-82.

Wright, Lawrence, 'The Master Plan: For the New Theorists of Jihad, Al Qaeda is Just the Beginning', *The New Yorker* 11 September 2006, www.newyorker.com/fact/content/articles/060911fa_fact3

# INDEX